PENGUIN BOOKS

DONNE

'Not only a necessary new biography of John Donne, England's most important Metaphysical poet, but a roistering and critically acute synthesis of a life devoted to love' *The Times*, Books of the Year

'Magnificent, excellent, remarkable, sings with detail. Stubbs succeeds in placing Donne vividly within the tapestry of his world' *Daily Telegraph*

'Dashing as well as detailed . . . Stubbs manages to make Donne seem recognisable and sympathetic, and also the inhabitant of a world that has long since disappeared' Andrew Motion, *Guardian*

'A superb biography, a work of research that illuminates not only the poetry but the sermons and devotional writings, too . . . Goes into the history of the time in great and relevant detail' John F. Deane, *Irish Times*

'Extraordinarily accomplished' *Mail on Sunday*

'Superbly evoked, a commanding biography' *Daily Mail*

'Stubb's great gift is for visual evocation and physical narrative. He also writes marvellously about Donne's swashbuckling youth' Katherine Duncan-Jones, *The Times Literary Supplement*

'The best life of Donne which I for one have ever read . . . marvellous' Robert Nye, *Literary Review*

Donne

The Reformed Soul

JOHN STUBBS

PENGUIN BOOKS

PENGUIN BOOKS

Published by the Penguin Group
Penguin Books Ltd, 80 Strand, London WC2R ORL, England
Penguin Group (USA) Inc., 375 Hudson Street, New York, New York 10014, USA
Penguin Group (Canada), 90 Eglinton Avenue East, Suite 700, Toronto, Ontario, Canada M4P 2Y3
(a division of Pearson Penguin Canada Inc.)
Penguin Ireland, 25 St Stephen's Green, Dublin 2, Ireland
(a division of Penguin Books Ltd)
Penguin Group (Australia), 250 Camberwell Road, Camberwell, Victoria 3124, Australia
(a division of Pearson Australia Group Pty Ltd)
Penguin Books India Pvt Ltd, 11 Community Centre,
Panchsheel Park, New Delhi – 110 017, India
Penguin Group (NZ), 67 Apollo Road, Rosedale, North Shore 0632, New Zealand
(a division of Pearson New Zealand Ltd)
Penguin Books (South Africa) (Pty) Ltd, 24 Sturdee Avenue, Rosebank, Johannesburg 2196, South Africa

Penguin Books Ltd, Registered Offices: 80 Strand, London WC2R ORL, England

www.penguin.com

First published by Viking 2006
Published in Penguin Books 2007

3

Typeset by Rowland Phototypesetting Ltd, Bury St Edmunds, Suffolk
Printed in England by Clays Ltd, St Ives plc

ISBN: 978-0-141-01717-4

www.greenpenguin.co.uk

Penguin Books is committed to a sustainable future
for our business, our readers and our planet.
The book in your hands is made from paper
certified by the Forest Stewardship Council.

For Rob

Two Religions cannot be suffred in one kingdome: for diversities cause factions, garboiles and civill warres, which never end but with the subversion of the commonwealth . . .

Sir William Vaughan, *The Golden Grove* [1608]

This house thus batter'd downe, the Soule possest a new.

Donne, 'Metempsycosis'

We are all mere nuggets of incense on the one altar. Some burn down now, some later – there is no difference.

Marcus Aurelius, *Meditations*

Contents

III

1617–1631

A Note on Conventions

During the period in which this book is set, the year changed in March rather than in January. We know that Donne was born between January and June, but the year of his birth would depend on whether his birthday fell before or after 25 March. If before, he was born in 1571, according to the Old Style calendar. If after, he was born in 1572. This book adopts the now conventional New Style calendar, which dates the start of each year from 1 January. The year of Donne's birth is thus given as 1572 rather than 1571.

Quotations from early modern texts retain the original spelling and punctuation except for the long 's', and except in instances that would be unintelligible without much hard work on the part of the reader. Edward Alleyn's sputtering, outraged letter to Donne, for example, is fully modernized. The hope is that readers will get a feel for how very different early modern English looks and sounds to the contemporary language, but without having to stop in their tracks every twenty seconds. As a general guideline, however, it should be noted that 'i' at the beginning of a word frequently means 'j' ('Ianuarie', 'Iohn') and 'u' in the middle of a word frequently means 'v' ('couer', 'aduise'). 'Than' is also generally spelt as 'then'.

Superscribed numerals in the text refer to notes printed at the end of the book. These notes are purely bibliographical and evidential for the most part, and only very occasionally discursive; they should not be seen as interruptions to the flow of the text. Readers concerned with just following the story need only consult them if they wish to see exactly where a quotation comes from, or would like suggestions on further reading.

Introduction

One August day in 1532, a fight broke out between two priests in a parish church in London. The chronicles do not specify exactly why the brethren 'fell at variance'.[1] There is no mention of whether a brawl went on for some time, the men huffing and puffing in their heavy woollen robes; or whether a temper snapped suddenly and a single blow decided matters. But one of the clerics did draw blood, and those who heard the commotion and came running were appalled by what they found. The wriggling pair were split up and carted off to prison.

Christian rituals and practices at this time were part of the people's biological rhythms. The religious edifices that put men and women in touch with their maker were decorative, adornments of the earth, but also wholly functional, necessary fixtures of daily existence. Crosses stood on almost every corner, London's skyline bristled with steeples. In 1532, the main aerial of the Christian Church was still half a continent away, in the Vatican: England, officially, was a Roman Catholic nation. Yet its clergy in London were not universally revered. For those unhappy with the supremacy of Rome, the summer punch-up between two supposed men of God was one further small but distinct signal that radical change was necessary to the way the country worshipped. The Church authorities themselves took a serious view of the incident. When blood was spilt in a sacred building – by two priests, no less – grave measures were required to make the place fit for worship again.

All Hallows Church in Bread Street, where the scuffle took place, was closed for a month. No services were sung or said until it was re-sanctified, and in the middle of October the offending priests were brought to the grounds of St Paul's Cathedral, not far to the east, to perform an act of penance. Prayers were said, contrition expressed and forgiveness asked for. Then the two men trudged through the city 'before a generall procession, bare headed, bare footed, and bare legged, before the children, with beades and bookes in their handes'.[2] General satisfaction was expressed among the faithful: a wrong had been righted, and children had been able to jeer and throw mud. Yet such corrective ceremonies were not enough to appease or divert a multitude of protest against Catholic tradition. The two penitents were being marched against a Protestant movement that saw the clergy as inherently corrupt and spiritually inadequate; against an aspiring class that resented the power, wealth and influence of the old Church; and at the head of the crowd, a King who wanted a divorce which the Pope refused to grant. The following year, England split with Rome, Henry VIII married Anne Boleyn and crowned her Queen, and Roman Catholicism in England began to be dismantled.

Forty years later, Bread Street was a modestly affluent area, in which merchants were the most prominent residents. It had fine inns, good places for carriers and travellers to spend an evening or stop off for the night. It buzzed with trade and good living. Religion was still crucial to everyday life, of course, but much had changed since the scrap in All Hallows. Poor, often illiterate priests, such as the two pugilists, had either lost their livings, converted to the new doctrine or, if they clung to their vocations, been driven underground. Church property had been confiscated and redistributed, the great ancient abbeys of the Middle Ages had been dissolved and demolished. Heretics of both conflicting faiths had been burnt alive, as the balance of power swung either way. Those who stayed loyal to the old Church and the Pope, and were thus branded 'Papists', were fiercely suppressed during the later reign of King Henry, and that of his sickly young son Edward. After Edward's death in 1553 the old faith was violently restored by Mary Tudor, daughter of Henry's first wife, Katharine. The accession of Mary's half-sister, Elizabeth, however, marked the end of Roman Catholicism as the country's established religion. Papists continued to hope, but only a small space for compromise existed between the old creed and the spirit of protest and reform, the Protestantism that sought to erase it. To some extent, the same churches were still in use, but many had been pulled down, and most were spoiled of their old parochial treasures, their icons and ornaments, with their walls whitewashed over.

The sky was still sore with spires. In the autumn of 1559, the year after Queen Elizabeth's coronation – the year she made herself supreme head of the English Church – a midday tempest flared up, and the spire of All Hallows was struck by lightning. The chronicler John Stow noted long afterwards that the bolt dislodged a stone 'that slew a dogge, and ouerthrew a man that was playing with the dogge'.[3] The smallest of deaths, desecrations and over-throws merited an entry in the chronicles, and had its place in the urban memory. The greatest remembered absence in London's sky for the rest of the century was the steeple of St Paul's, which burnt down in a storm in June 1561, just as the Queen consolidated her regime in its initial phase. A sign, for many, that things were not as they should be.

For there were still substantial groups of people that could not accept things as they were. There were those who came to be known, somewhat indiscriminately, as Puritans – radical, impatient Protestants who felt that the doctrinal and institutional changes in the Church had to be taken much further. At more risk in 1572, however, when John Donne was born in Bread Street, were the Catholics who refused to let go of the old ways, and who still saw the Pope in Rome, rather than the Queen in London, as their spiritual leader. Donne by birth was one of them, the son of a Roman Catholic ironmonger, and his background put him at a disadvantage.

He became one of the great secular and spiritual writers of the late Renaissance, and of world literature. His poems, for which most people now remember him, are to be found in the spiky scripts of countless commonplace books dating from his lifetime and after his death, often supplemented with laudatory remarks. As a student, Donne's laconic, feisty, funny, barbed, demonically clever verse was admired and imitated by close coteries of readers, most of them friends or poetically minded young men. Later on, epigrams, verse letters and tributes by Donne were highly prized by influential figures in the royal Court. The limited but devoted following that collected and sought out his lyrics in manuscript multiplied exponentially after the first publication of his collected poems in 1633. By then it was generally accepted that a major new presence had entered the language. In 1619, the playwright Ben Jonson, the leader of his own tribe of acolytes, had declared Donne to be 'the first poet in the world, in some things'. Yet Jonson also said that Donne 'deserved hanging' for the liberties he took with the rhythmic conventions of the day. Later generations saw Donne as 'the late Copernicus in Poetrie', a decisive redrawer of the literary cosmos; and the master of

> All the softnesses,
> The Shadow, Light, the Air, and Life, of Love;
> The sharpness of all Wit . . .[4]

Donne never sought mass appeal, however: he saw himself as a literary gentleman, not a hack, and though he was occasionally tempted, he disdained to publish his verse in the common press. This attitude reflects the second great life problem that came to face the boy who spent his infancy in Bread Street. The first was his Roman Catholicism – a stigmatic inheritance for anyone born in England in the late sixteenth century. But the second, far from unrelated, was the problem of class. Donne's uneasy social status was embodied in his parentage. On his mother's side, he was descended from a family of Papist aristocrats. They had fallen on hard times, but could claim kinship with Sir Thomas More, the outstanding humanist, author of *Utopia*, Lord Chancellor of England and eventually martyr for the threatened faith. Donne's father's origins, however, are much less clear. Donne always claimed that his paternal ancestry went back to a noble family of Welsh extraction, but the fact of the matter was that his father was a Bread Street tradesman. Mr John Donne the elder was a successful and quite wealthy ironmonger, who tried staying true to his religion while still getting on in the world. He died when young

John was only four; and his own profession had no influence over the path his son took. Instead of being prepared to enter a trade and serve an apprenticeship, the boy was raised as a gentleman scholar.

Yet the money his father made from iron brought Donne a handsome education. He was taught scripture and the classics by private tutors, trained up in grammar and rhetoric: he thrived on languages, history, the severe yet versatile contortions of mathematics. As the life-crammed poetry of his early years bears witness, he was also sensitive to every scent and texture in the city. He could hardly have missed, for example, the public disorder created frequently by mobs of apprentices out on the town. Adolescents training as merchants and craftsmen had to endure seven years – longer, in some cases – of tedious labour and domestic confinement to grinding moralistic regimes. Very often, the strictures proved too much to bear. Hordes of apprentices regularly went out creating havoc, picking fights with fancy gentlemen and law students, looting and playing old-rules football – that is, *no-rules* football, with hundreds chasing and booting a bladder through the narrow thoroughfares, regardless of the young, the old and the neutral on their daily business. The black spots for the violence were the taverns and brothels to be found throughout the city, along with the theatres and districts where foreigners settled. The worst times were the public holidays. On May Day and Shrove Tuesday, foreign ambassadors advised their fellow country-people to lie as low as possible.

Although he was a merchant's son, rough apprentice boys were not companions for Donne. Soon after his father died, Mrs Donne married an affluent London physician, ensuring that her family remained comfortable. Although he posed as an outsider in the poetry he wrote in early adulthood, at no time would Donne ever accept that he was anything other than a gentleman, or that he could follow any profession unbefitting one; an attitude he was later willing to uphold at the cost of poverty and deep depression. He wanted to keep what he saw as his proper place in the world. Doing this, however, made it enormously difficult to obey his other great family imperative and remain a loyal Roman Catholic. The Protestant authorities made sure that perseverance as a Papist blocked the route to any promotion within the state. Recusancy meant accepting a life of diminished scope and liberty; taken to extremes, it entailed living as a fugitive. Such an existence proved insufferable to Donne. Despite his great idiosyncrasy as a writer and a man, he had no desire to dwell in shadows. It was crucial to him to remain involved in society and accept the obligations it conferred on all.

From Donne's earliest childhood, the fight over God was every-where. This was no argument over an abstraction: for the vast majority, the Creator and his morally ordered universe were mani-fest realities, assumed facts of life – of this one and the next. Religious controversy saturated public discourse. A short way from the Donnes' house in Bread Street was Paul's Cross, a great open space before the Cathedral, commanded by a high pulpit on a stone base with a timber crucifix above it. This was traditionally the land's foremost preaching venue. As Donne was growing up, in the 1570s and 80s, the dogma of the Reformed, Protestant Church would be broadcast to regular crowds of thousands here. Sermons could last hours. The sustained threat of the tortures of hell – and those of the Tower – raised waves of goosebumps in the flesh of the mass congregations. The sermon also became the most effective medium through which official policy and wisdom could be expressed and indeed contested, and public opinion moulded. Donne's family disapproved of such propaganda and did their best to shelter him from it, and combat it with their own dogma, from the moment he was born. No official record of Donne's baptism survives, and none may well have been made. His birth can therefore only be dated roughly, in the first half of 1572. He was probably christened privately and secretly, as a Cath-olic, by a family contact – perhaps even by his mother's uncle, Thomas Heywood, an old friar who was executed two years later for continuing to perform the abolished rituals. These were the beliefs that Donne himself was brought up to cherish and promote.

But his upbringing also endowed him with the intellectual

means to consider for himself the great doctrinal issues that preoccupied his age. As a young man, he came to see that every
thoughtful individual had an obligation of conscience to conduct
a personal search for God. The journey would not follow a straightforward path. It would involve many digressions and backtrackings,
but it had to be undertaken nonetheless:

> On a huge hill,
> Cragg'd, and steep, Truth stands, and he that will
> Reach her, about must, and about must goe,
> And what the hills suddenness resists, winne so;
> Yet strive so, that before age, deaths twilight,
> Thy Soule rest, for none can work in that night.[5]

These were not the thoughts of someone who was prepared to sit
back and coast through life on inherited creeds. They reflect instead
a commitment to thinking everything out anew, if necessary, the
radicalizing intellectual zeal that had possessed northern Europe
and England itself during the Reformation. But Donne also looked
for a period of calm later in life, an old age spent following the
Truth that his youth had fought so hard to reach. The one thing
he was wrong about was his notion that he would be unable to
continue working and thinking in 'deaths twilight'.

Nearly sixty years later, Dr John Donne, Dean of St Paul's, one
of the most revered Protestant preachers of the day, asked in his
will that his body might 'be buryed in the most private manner
possible' in the Cathedral. He had served there as the senior priest,
one step below the status of bishop, for ten years. It was 1631:
the nation was only a decade away from civil war and radical
transformation in the republican state that emerged from it; yet
in some respects, time had slipped backwards. Many complained
that under King Charles, and his father, James, the kingdom had
relapsed into the Papist customs rejected and banished almost a
century before. In response and provocation, Donne often argued
that the Church should be 'Catholic' in the literal sense of the
word: 'universal', with a place inside for everyone. Yet he also

realized that all people, certainly himself, become different people at almost every stage of their existence. Near death at the end of February, exhausted, emaciated, a living cadaver, Donne hauled himself into the chapel pulpit at Whitehall Palace to deliver his last sermon to the royal Court. It was received as his own funeral oration, and was published soon afterwards under the title of *Deaths Duell*. In it Donne envisaged life as a continuous dying, a reformation of the soul and a movement between lives: 'all our *periods* and *transitions* in this life,' he said, are so many 'passages from death to death'.[6]

Despite his request for a modest burial, Donne is commemorated by an imposing monument in St Paul's. A white marble statue depicts him rising in his graveclothes, presumably on Judgement Day. The image was taken while Donne was still alive, and he had designed it carefully himself. He orchestrated a masterly death. Throughout his many illnesses, his mind never tired: he could read and write from his sickbed. During his last days he felt strong enough to pose for one last portrait, and arranged a resurrection scene. He ordered charcoal fires to be lit in his official residence, a spacious house lying just to the south of the Cathedral itself. The braziers gave the scene a Purgatorial fog. With this stage set, the dying man stood facing east with his winding sheet about him, knotted at head and foot. The picture was drawn on a life-size wooden board, then copied for the coverpiece of *Deaths Duel*. Nicholas Stone, who carved the subsequent statue, used this illustration as his guide. But he was kinder on Donne than Donne himself had allowed the first, unknown artist to be. The mason gave slightly more flesh to the cheekbones, tidied the beard and moustache, eased the drawn smile; relaxed the closed eyes.

Many faces, many lives are hidden in the haggard but peaceful countenance of this final icon. One belonged to 'a great visitor of ladies' in the London of the 1590s, an aspiring swashbuckler who sailed for loot and glory on military expeditions against Spain. It was the face of the most tender, most scathing and most paranoid love poet in English letters, one who could claim total indifference to what his mistresses did, and crack a bald joke about his own infidelities; yet one who worried obsessively about betrayal, and the space that remained between lovers no matter how close they became. Donne the priest of St Paul's had fought hard to put this life behind him. Yet the expression of the statue, which Stone softened to resemble the face he had seen alive above the pulpit and about the town, is that of a man closing his eyes and remembering past pleasures calmly, not blanking them out.

Looking back, Donne admitted, 'I cannot plead innocency of life, especially of my youth.' He relied on God's mercy, claiming that he had 'nothing to present to Him but sins and misery'.[7] At the same time, he had many memories that were far from sinful and miserable, and he thought that his God would not regard them as such. One was the memory of lying with a woman at the side of a river, and just lying there, for hours, saying nothing. Their bodies, the younger poet imagined, were just casements their spirits had climbed out from, to mingle perfectly in the air between them. Below, stone-still, in the grass, amid the violets,

> Wee like sepulchral statues lay,
> All day, the same our postures were,
> And wee said nothing, all the day.

Donne's sepulchral statue could be smiling at the thought of this. The couple's souls coupled, were made more alive by being together. And the strengthened hybrid that emerged,

> That abler soule, which thence doth flow,
> Defects of lonelinesse controles.[8]

Donne probably wrote this great poem, 'The Extasie', for his wife, Ann. When she was sixteen, and he was nearly thirty, he mended the ways of his youth and ended the loneliness of promiscuity by marrying. As a lover and husband, then as a priest and widower, he searched strenuously for ways of controlling the 'defects' of solitude.

For Donne, we can never be completely on our own. During a

serious illness in 1623, two years after taking over at St Paul's, he became the great theorist of sympathy who declared that 'No man is an *Iland*, intire of it self; every man is a peece of the *Continent*, a part of the *maine*; if a *Clod* be washed away by the *Sea*, *Europe* is the lesse, as well as if a *Promontorie* were'. Humanity for Donne is a single living body of land. 'Any mans *death* diminishes *me*,' he wrote, 'because I am involved in *Mankind*.'[9]

As someone who often felt very alone, but who also needed his time in isolation, it was vital for him to figure out what it is that connects human beings, and what it is that keeps them apart. In 'The Extasie', the lovers on the riverbank are, briefly, not left by themselves. Donne required a momentary witness, an interpreter, someone refined enough by love to understand the 'soules language'. This kindred spirit, who would see the couple by accident, and then considerately depart, purified merely by passing them, is the figure of every reader who has used Donne's words to understand his or her own inner complications.

Almost all of these readers have a very personal sense of who he was. For some, the essential Donne is always the young seducer. For others, including Donne's first biographer, Isaak Walton, the very opposite man is the real one: one who shed the indiscretions of his youth to give his life its consummate meaning in the ministry of his later years. Others still see Donne's marriage to Ann, celebrated in a series of sublimely monogamous lyrics, as the centrepiece of the poet's life. But none of these, in fact, may be the actual John Donne: as we encounter them now, through the texts alone, they are all personae that Donne either produced himself or encouraged others to propagate. They are generated by his poems, his sermons, the imagery of his death, the panegyric rhetoric of Walton's *Life* – by texts and artefacts, in short, that cannot be read as empirical evidence of what Donne did or who he was. But neither can such texts be discounted. Without them, we have little more than the cold inscrutable stone of Donne's monument. The statue stops breathing and Donne ceases to be the poet whom we still read as 'we read the living'.[10] We lose too the evidence of how Donne saw life and how he saw those alive around him. The various Donnes that posterity has inherited represent stages in the life and growth of a singular individual, the different forms one soul took on, and reflect different aspects of that developing person. Part of the job of this biography is to trace the strands between these personae and point out the unity underlying them.

However, it also has to be accepted that inconsistencies and enigmas will remain insofar as Donne alone lies under scrutiny. We expect the words and actions of an individual to conform, overall, to something that is a logically coherent whole in itself. However irrational it might seem to others, everyone follows their own inner rationale. Yet lives do not always form neat stories. Aristotle warned all writers treating historical subjects that it was a bad idea to put a single person at the centre of an epic and expect the resulting narrative to be tidy and resolved. 'A plot is not unified, as some think,' he pointed out, 'if built round an individual' – as all biographies are. 'Any entity has innumerable features, not all of which cohere into a unity; likewise, an individual performs many actions which yield no unitary action.'[11]

Coherence in a biographical life often emerges by putting that life off-centre, placing the subject back in the crowd as well as picking him or her out from it. This is certainly the case with Donne. The plot of his life, to adapt Aristotle, becomes unified when it is built around the much larger social story of which it formed a small yet meaningful part, and of which it provides a revealing testimony. A singular portrait of Donne, from all the very different likenesses we have of him, becomes possible when the historical background swarms back into the foreground. This, it might be said, is nothing more than an expression of standard biographical practice; but it is worth restating here because Donne himself was immensely conscious of the principle. No man is an island, entire of itself. For Donne, this is because the bell tolls for everyone. All people die, and all know it, no matter how each one deals with that knowledge, and no matter how he or she meets their particular moment of extinction. Donne realized that this is possibly the one absolute that everyone has in common. Seeing this, as he did, was not so much a case of seeing the bigger picture

– he did not claim to be all knowing, all seeing – as realizing that a bigger picture was there. We can understand Donne not by treating him as an island, but by seeing his place on the volatile island he inhabited.

Looking back, he could position himself in the broader historical movements that had shaped his existence. In spite of all the suffering he experienced personally and recognized in his writing, he had truly positive thoughts on the social, political and religious upheavals of the sixteenth century:

God shin'd upon this Island early; early in the plantation of the Gospel, (for we had not our seed-corn from *Rome*, howsoever we may have had some waterings from thence) and early in the Reformation of the Church: for we had not the model of any other Forreign Church for our pattern; we stript not the Church into a nakedness, nor into rags; we divested her not of her possessions, nor of her Ceremonies, but received such a Reformation at home, by their hands whom God enlightned, as left her neither in a Dropsie [a swollenness] nor in a Consumption [a wasted state] . . . God continue to us the light of this Reformation, without re-admitting any old Clouds, any old Clouts, and we shall not need any such re-Reformation, or super-Reformation, as swimming brains will need cross the Seas for.[12]

Such a statement makes Donne one of the most sophisticated but also most genuine defenders of the English Reformation. It was its peculiar *Englishness*, in fact, that he most admired. In speaking of 'this Island', Donne blurs together the distinct religious and political histories of Scotland and England. Later in the seventeenth century, the Scots would show they took issue with that generalization. Britain was only just emerging as a political idea rather than a fully fledged nation under James I; but although Donne lends support to that idea by speaking of it here as something that was already a reality, his real point is directed at England's recent past. For Donne, the Reformation was not ultimately a betrayal of the English Catholic tradition. In his opinion the Church had been 'watered' by Rome, but had never eaten corn out of the Pope's hand. When the time came to reform, England had made the necessary changes to its ways of worshipping, but had not gone to the annihilative lengths seen in northern Europe. The Church was not stripped bare, he insisted, but had retained her ceremonies and possessions. The Church of Donne's ancestors was intact, but altered and enriched by what it had been through.

Paradoxically, the true Catholic Church for Donne was the one he served as Dean of St Paul's, the established Protestant Church with the English monarch at its head. Donne's interpretation of the English Reformation is simultaneously a defence of his personal Reformation, his ongoing conversion to Protestantism. By becoming a Protestant, he did not betray his Catholic origins but remained true to them. By the time Donne reached adulthood, the Roman Church in England was no longer catholic in the basic sense: it was not 'universal' any more, not a national Church that could include everyone, but a religious splinter group, a sect that in Donne's opinion wasted lives for a lost cause and threatened the security of the kingdom. The true Catholic Church of England had moved on, and Donne followed it; though not blithely, and not without misgivings.

He certainly did not become a Protestant for material gain or convenience. A few years after he had successfully built up a career in the Elizabethan government, he quite knowingly surrendered it for the sake of the woman he loved. As we shall see, marrying for love meant losing his job, his social standing and his prospects: all the tangible benefits, in short, that his conversion brought him. Converting, meanwhile, meant breaking with his family, going against the grain of youthful indoctrination, and appearing to disregard a tradition of fortitude and sacrifice. Throughout his life, Donne showed he was willing to take decisions that endangered everything he had; but at the end he was at peace with those decisions. His biography is worth studying not only because he was a splendid writer, but also because he was a brave and principled man.

At times he was somewhat embarrassed by the apparent contradictions his past presented. Yet despite moments of understandable

awkwardness, overall Donne was determined that the inconsistencies should be kept on record. Part of this magnanimity came
from looking at his earlier work and seeing how good it was. A
few years after he was ordained, Donne sent a book called *Biathanatos*, his treatise on suicide, to his influential friend Sir Robert Ker.
The work was never published in Donne's lifetime. It would have
been controversial had he released it at the time he wrote it, some
years before he took orders. Had it come out after his ordination
or appointment to St Paul's, it would have been cultural dynamite.
Writing to Ker, he insisted that this was 'a Book written by *Jack
Donne*, and not by *Dr Donne*'.[13] Jack and the Doctor were two
separate people, two different characters; and the latter, Donne
hoped, could decisively correct the one before it. Yet he still could
not resist preserving the book, nor indeed the rest of his earlier
writing, and with these works his previous incarnations also
survived.

As Dean of St Paul's, Donne spent the end of his life in some
prosperity, and was able to indulge a taste for fine art. The pictures
he left in his 'fayre old house' reveal him as a composite of all the
different images he left us with. They betray old loyalties and
lingering drives. His upbringing was reflected in a painting of
Mary, mother of Jesus, Queen of the Roman Catholic heaven,
which hung in 'the little Dynynge chamber'. In the hall was a
memento mori, a picture of a skeleton; yet pride of place in the
'Greate chamber' was taken by Adam and Eve, the first couple,
who tasted their forbidden fruit and bred mankind in spite of
'sin and misery'. Mary Magdalen, the fallen, loving woman
who washed Christ's feet with her tears, watched over Donne in
his bedchamber.[14] The collection's mixture of terror and faith,
deathliness and sensuality, is found in the last likeness of Dr Donne
himself, the shattered, aged man depicted on the cover of *Deaths
Duell*. But the same mixture was there from the beginning.

I

1572—1602

1. The Den

His mistress lived with her parents, and access was a problem. Donne had to devise a way of walking that kept his silk suit from 'whistling' as he skulked through the creaky mansion. The family's grim, eight-foot-high, iron-bound serving man was always on the lookout, and the lady of the house, who lay buried in her bed while the young couple shook the floor by night, looked carefully for signs of 'paleness, blushing, sighs and sweats' by day. The matron had her suspicions. She would take her daughter aside and try extracting a confession by revealing 'The sinnes of her owne youths rank lustinesse'.[1] She used her younger children as spies. The girl's little brothers, 'like Faiery Sprights / Oft skipt into our chamber', Donne complained, knowing the boys faced close inter-rogation the next day on their father's knee.[2] Yet still the lovers evaded their persecutors, and Donne kept his swishing 'silkes' quiet. These are events from a poem he wrote as a young man. It was classed as an 'elegy', and became known as 'The Perfume'. It might be a lusty account of an actual adventure; it might be all made up. The story, anyway, ends in frustration. After all their efforts, the girl's father smelt Donne out. He caught a whiff of the pungent fragrance the young man was wearing. 'Had it beene some bad smell,' Donne observed, the old man 'would have thought / That his own feet, or breath, that smell had wrought.'[3]

After the violent interview that ensued, Donne berated his mistress. He had been caught 'Once, and but once' in her com-pany, yet had received the blame for all the previous sexual esca-pades the anguished father now imagined her enjoying.[4] Yet the bitter, sardonic tone soon fades from the poem. The girl about whom 'The Perfume' was written may never have read it, may never have even existed, but Donne still reassured her that she and he were rare and special: it was merely their bad luck to be on an

'Isle emprisoned / Where cattle onely, and diverse dogs are bred'. They were tender, magical creatures, exceptions to the ruling ugliness. It wasn't their fault if the morons around them could only 'call the pretious Unicornes, strange monsters'.[5]

After a night out, Donne would pass back through the legal district in the heart of London and return to Lincoln's Inn, an exclusive college for legal studies. If entry via the main entrance, the imposing gothic gatehouse on Chancery Lane, proved impossible, a manoeuvre around the perimeter was required to sneak in through a side way to the serene, expansive precincts of the Inn of Court.

His college lodgings were tiny: he described his study as a 'standing woodden chest', a trunk turned on its side.[6] He would retire to it and shut the door-lid. Very often, however, he didn't get much sleep. Isaak Walton, Donne's first biographer and foremost apologist, some twenty years his junior, asserted that 'in the most unsetled days of his youth, his bed was not able to detain him beyond the hour of four in a morning: and it was no common business that drew him out of his chamber till past ten.'[7] All this time, Walton claimed, was spent in study. Walton's clockwork scholar cannot, of course, be taken at face value: he only knew (and deeply revered) the older, conservative and ascetic man of the 1620s, in Donne's days as Dean of St Paul's. Forty years earlier, before Walton had even been born, there were presumably many 'unsetled days' that fell out of routine for Donne; nights when he stumbled in during the small hours and knew no more until early afternoon. But it is obvious that frequently, when his head was clear, he wanted to do nothing but read and think. His 'worst voluptuousnes', Donne himself later said, was an 'immoderate desire of humane learning and languages'.[8] He came to feel that these interests were his worst excess because they distracted him from studies that might have brought him a steady job. But as the statement implies, he had other kinds of voluptuousness, each of which had to be allotted its own strict compartment of time. He liked structure, and demanded much of it. He moulded his experiences and imaginings into fabulously complex verse schemes, and also tried to give a regular shape to the varying activities of his days.

At Lincoln's Inn Donne was supposed, as he himself put it, to 'toughly chew, and sturdily digest / The immense vast volumes of our common law'.[9] But he had little taste for mere vocational concerns. 'Humane learning and languages', history and poetry were far more appealing; though in the summer of 1593, at the age of twenty-one, he was preoccupied with matters of divinity. He was concerned with Truth. He wanted to discover for himself which form of Christianity was the right one. He said later on that he refused to come to any decision which the fate of his immortal soul might rest upon, 'till I had, to the measure of my poore wit and iudgement, suruayed and digested the whole body of Diuinity'.[10] From the crack of dawn, he read solidly. By ten in the morning, according to Walton, the young scholar had completed over five hours of personal study.

However, 'he took great liberty after it.'[11] For, as though with a change in the light, something switched inside: his mind re-oriented itself. The 'wooden chest' suddenly seemed like a prison, a child's coffin of a room. Donne wanted out, and help was at hand to ensure his release. He had friends who knew his habits well, and one of them, some 'fondling motley humorist', would barge in, rub his shoulder and urge him to come out. Donne recorded the moment in the first of his satires. 'Shall I leave all this constant company,' he asked, probably with a gesture to the books heaped up around him, 'And follow headlong, wild, uncertain thee?'[12] Usually, after a show of reluctance, it seems that the answer was yes. As he later observed, 'it were not hard to assigne many examples of men that have stolne great measure of learning, and yet lived open and conversable lives.'[13]

Beyond the calm college enclosure lay Lincoln's Inn Fields: a large, open, rather dowdy space, yet an arena for a bit of everything in Elizabethan London. It was the rubbish-strewn site of public executions and discontinued building projects, a venue for all kinds of exercise, haggling, get-togethers and theatricals. Horses were taken there for a runabout, clopping perilously close at times to passers-by. Cripples and beggars assembled at their stations. Some of the city's pricier brothels and gambling dens were located in the lanes around the Fields, and prostitutes would come to take some air and loiter for early trade. The district grew livelier as the day wore on. Mountebanks would arrive with their cures and aphrodisiacs, set up their stalls, and crowds would assemble to heckle them. Puppet shows would open and throttled bears would dance on chains. By compressing his study into several airtight early hours, Donne could emerge into the jostling world beyond his mind, and his books, just as life was warming up again.

His scholarly habits were drummed into him early. Just under ten years before, in the autumn of 1584, he and his younger brother Henry were sent to study in Oxford. John was perhaps twelve, and Henry was only eleven, a good four or five years younger than the majority of the other students. Bright boys often went up to university early, however, and this might seem to demonstrate that the Donne brothers were precocious enough to cope with the work; but there was also an imperative working above and beyond their intellectual merit. It was necessary for them to complete their university education early if they were to avoid the persecution they would attract as Papists later on. As we shall see, a trap had been carefully set to test the loyalty of scholars when they turned sixteen.

Oxford was dominated by the colleges that together made up the university. Each one of these colleges, or 'halls' (as those without full collegiate status were called), provided for the teaching of undergraduates. A busy market town thrived in the gaps left by the academic cluster, but the students were distanced from it by physical and mental layers of separation. The teaching regime was tough and mind-numbing. Day upon day, the boys had maxims and exempla, and the elaborate means of expressing them eloquently, kneaded into their brains. This training served Donne's poetry well, of course: he learnt how to focus the whole universe on the smallest of subjects. Once a flea, for example, had bitten both him and his mistress, mixing and marrying their bloods in its gut, it could assume cosmic, sacramental significance. It became a temple, a marriage bed, an agent of communion. The flourishes of such poems as 'The Flea' owe a lot to the countless rhetorical exercises he performed as a boy at Oxford. Nevertheless a certain alienation from everyday life was integral to the curriculum.

John and Henry attended Hart Hall, one of the few university institutions to offer unofficial refuge for Catholics. The principal, Philip Rondell, ruled the Hall with an iron fist for half a century, instilling moral orthodoxy and the fear of God into generations of boys. But he too was an outsider: 'though in his heart,' said Antony à Wood, the Oxford antiquarian, Rondell 'was a Papist, he durst not show it.'[14] The Hall's master of divinity, a Spaniard called Antonio Corrano, was a Protestant, but had esoteric ideas of his own on the ways Christianity should develop. So besides putting up with xenophobic jokes against the Spanish, he faced continual rebukes for the heretical contents of his lectures from the Puritans who controlled Oxford in the 1580s and monitored its intellectual currents closely. The walls of Hart Hall provided a haven to serious, rather lonely characters, united by mutual oddity – and an understated tendency towards independent thinking.

John and Henry were lucky enough to have an alternative sanctuary. Their uncle Robert Dawson ran the Blue Boar Inn, a four-storey establishment just off St Aldates, one of Oxford's broad main thoroughfares. This place was awash with different registers. The Blue Boar was in the middle of the university district, and served its share of students; but was right beside the Guildhall, and so brought in craftsmen and traders, telling very different jokes, grumbling with concerns quite alien to most undergraduates. There were also those who fell between the factions of town and gown. One regular was Robert Dawson's cousin John, the butler of Christ Church College, with a reputation as a sharer and consumer of the institution's supplies. When he died in 1622, Donne's friend Richard Corbett, another senior cleric, wrote an elegy that cried 'Weepe, o ye barrells! Lett your drippings fall / In trickling streams!' Corbett envisaged the old servant being borne through Hades on rivers of beer, his ferry buoyed by 'wholesome waves'.[15]

   With this convivial backwash, the Donne boys also had company
closer to their own age. The Dawsons had two children, Edward
and Grace, and the brothers grew close to them. In the little
network of alleys running behind the Blue Boar, shady cobbled
passages on which it is still easy to turn an ankle after closing time,
in the big yard out the back, on the steep twisting staircases; or in
the tavern itself, one of those deep, deep pubs, stretching a long
way inwards, John and Henry had some of their relatively few
chances for play.[16] Tucked up in Hart Hall or a spare room at the
inn, they were relatively safe. But outside, they had to be careful
what they said and to whom. The establishment had a reputation
as a Catholic hideout: one of the Dawsons' lodgers was an academic
who had been thrown out of New College for his active 'Popery'.[17]

   The brothers' early enrolment at university was more a precaution than a sure sign of genius: as Roman Catholics, Papists,
the Donne brothers were members of Elizabethan England's ghetto
faction. The religious divide was inescapably political. In 1570, the
Pope had excommunicated Queen Elizabeth, officially excluding
her from the Catholic sacraments she rejected out of hand and thus
formalizing her damnation. More to the point, the Pope declared
in no uncertain terms that her reign was illegitimate: Catholics
could disobey, even murder her, with an easy conscience. The
Protestant authorities responded to this measure and the spirit of
insurrection it aroused with a series of aggressive crackdowns, often
inciting conspiracies in order to eliminate individuals they had
targeted. More generally, however, they pursued a ruthless policy
of disenfranchizing Papists from any part in the state system. The
universities were purged. After the age of sixteen, all those seeking
to take a degree at Oxford were obliged to make an oath of loyalty
to the Reformed, Protestant Church, and to the Queen as the
head of that Church. For the Donnes, this meant betraying the
faith. There was a race against time and puberty to get clever
Roman Catholic boys through college before the oath was
imposed.

   The Oath of Allegiance was one of many legal snares laid by the
Protestant authorities to catch out Papists who were trying to get

by without forsaking their religion. Donne's father, John senior, was one of these people, and practised caution. In 1563 or 1564 – no record of the ceremony has survived – Mr Donne married a woman with a highly literate, intellectual background, whose upbringing had exalted the sacrifices made by her ancestors. His own origins were obscure, but he brought practical acumen and a survival instinct to the match. He had made his way patiently as apprentice to a London ironmonger, and then stayed on to run the business with his master's widow, who remembered Mr Donne in her will. She left him the lease to a house in Bread Street, 'with a garden attached', next door to a tavern called The Mitre.[18] Trading in tools, utensils, horseshoes and doornails, Mr Donne prospered. In 1574 he was made a Warden of the Company of Ironmongers, a position that indicated wealth and brought added responsibility and prestige. Donne's father had much to lose in Protestant England; he was quiet and careful.

Caution was a perfectly understandable strategy, since the penalties for recusancy were severe, financially and often physically. As a student at Lincoln's Inn, Donne knew the odd joker 'which did goe / To a Masse in jest', just for the hell of it. Donne himself was more careful. If 'catch'd', the lark turned sour for the prankster: 'the Statutes curse', he knew, was a 'hundred markes'.[19] If you didn't have the cash, a trip to prison was required. On top of that, Catholics were still obliged to attend Protestant services, and faced increasingly heavy fines if they did not. Consistent absences were reported, and the consequences could be dire. Property would be confiscated, families left without homes, and unrepentant heretics imprisoned or executed horribly. It was not a case of putting all Catholics to the sword, but of making brutal, public examples of a few to deter the many. And recusants faced more than pressure from the authorities: the conflict split families and communities. When John Tippett, only eighteen years old, was arrested, condemned and mutilated as punishment for his Papism, his Protestant father wrote to him in shame and disgust as well as grief: 'Do you think it was not the greatest of sorrows to me to hear that my son had been whipped through the city tied to a cart, his ears pierced with hot irons like a criminal. Truly it made me wish I had never begotten you.'[20]

A bolt through the ear of a teenage boy: John and Henry had an imprecise but acute comprehension of the trade and manufacture behind such public tortures, which they could not avoid witnessing. Through family connections, they knew of the manacles and the rack; they heard too of clerics 'throwne into vnsauourie and darke dungeons, and brought soe neere starvinge, that some haue licked the very moisture of the walls'.[21] The word of such barbarities circulated freely and vividly among the Roman Catholic refugees at Hart Hall, many of whom were quite willing to brave it all for the salvation their religion would vouchsafe them. For Hart Hall's substantial quota of Papists, the virtually seminarian rhythms that still persisted in Oxford had extra meaning. The students were conditioned both to a religious life of the mind and the very physical suffering it could bring.

Despite the cautious pragmatism of his father, Donne was also brought up amid a spirit of resistance to this oppression. His mother came from an old and notorious line of Roman Catholic activists. There was Donne's uncle, Jasper Heywood, who was brought up and schooled with Queen Elizabeth, but was now an old Jesuit banished from England, living out his last years in Naples. There was John Heywood, Donne's grandfather, an effervescent, sunshiny man, a singer and comedian at the court of Henry VIII. In 1542, Heywood became involved in a plot to incriminate Thomas Cranmer, the Archbishop of Canterbury, and undermine the King's position as head of the Church of England. The conspirators were convicted of treason and condemned to die; Heywood alone was reprieved. Henry let him off, convinced that the funny man fostered no really 'harmfull conceit'. He did so, however, only after Heywood had been tied to a wicker carriage and had made the harrowing journey from the Tower of London to the place of execution at Tyburn.[22] Heywood later performed the conventional act of public penance, tramping through London holding a burning faggot and dressed only in a sheet, pelted with rubbish by the taunting crowds, and reading out a recantation of his beliefs at

St Paul's. The struggle went further back and further on through Donne's relations. At the root was Sir Thomas More, Donne's great-great-uncle, the writer, lawyer, Chancellor of England and martyr, executed in 1535. And budding at the tip were John and Henry Donne.

This legacy of resentment became the dominant force in the Donne brothers' upbringing. They lost their father when John was only four and Henry barely three, moved away from the house and workshop on Bread Street, and had to adjust to a replacement man in the house only months later. Mr Donne died in February 1576, when his wife was pregnant with their seventh child. He seems to have realized that his health was failing: he had his will, which provided amply for his family, drawn up the month before.[23] In July the same year, Elizabeth Donne married one Dr Symynges, a physician with connections in the royal Court. Like Donne's father, Symynges was a camouflaged Papist, with a similar knack of treading safely. Such hazards and harsh transitions were accepted as the facts of life: Elizabeth Donne wanted to keep going. At least one child had probably died before she lost her first husband; her eldest daughter and namesake, Elizabeth, died a year later, in 1577. In 1581, when Donne was nine, two other, younger sisters, Mary and Katherine, also died. By the time John and Henry went to Oxford they had one surviving sister, Anne, who was much older than they were, and already unhappily married.

There is a legend of seven Christian youths who in early times defied the persecution of the Roman emperor Decius. Sentenced to death for their faith, they escaped to the wilderness and took shelter in a cave. There they slept for two hundred years until the pagan world was converted to Christ, and it was safe to emerge. The tale was a Roman Catholic commonplace, widely disseminated through Gregory of Tours' *Lives of the Saints*, and commemorated every year at the end of July. Donne – one of six, perhaps seven or more children, if other baptisms and earlier deaths went unrecorded – dropped the story in casually at the start of one of his love poems, 'The Good Morrow'.

> I wonder, by my troth, what thou, and I
> Did, till we lov'd? Were we not wean'd till then?
> But suck'd on countrey pleasures, childishly?
> Or snorted we in the seven sleepers den?[24]

Childhood itself, for Donne here, is a strange suspension, an unconscious period before the real pleasure of life can begin. Without mature adult love, it is potentially endless, and endlessly stifling. Yet as a metaphor for the casual flings the young poet has been 'weaned' from, childhood is no longer childhood: it is made to grow up before fully grown. Donne's early years were characterized by the uncomfortable blend of insulation and accelerated maturity that lies behind those blissfully sexed lines. As the snorting little sleepers dropped off, one, sometimes two at a time, the young Donne was jealously sheltered from the religious storm. But he could still hear it beating outside the den, outside the safe house; and at some point he was expected to go out into it.

Precious, private legends and artefacts were vital charms against the intimidation and uncertainty in which he grew up. The most important treasures belonged to the body and ghost of his totemic kinsman, Sir Thomas More. His daughter Margaret Roper kept the bloodied shirt in which he had been executed, and also rescued his severed head from a pike on London Bridge, after 'bribing an executioner who would otherwise have thrown it into the Thames'.[25] Margaret asked to be buried with her father's head in her arms, but fragments from it were apparently passed down as heirlooms. Two of Donne's uncles came to possess one of More's teeth. An early biography of More records the tale that having 'the tooth between them, and either of them being desirous to haue it to himselfe, it suddenly, to the admiration of both, parted in two' – a minor miracle, or an indication that the Chancellor had tooth decay.[26]

The two pious brothers in this anecdote were John Heywood's sons, Ellis and Jasper. Both went to Oxford as boys, and both later settled there as academics; both, it goes without saying, were devout Roman Catholics, yet both also had a reputation as lively lads. As one epigrammist recorded,

> Old *Haywoods* sons did wax so wild and youthfull,
> It made their aged father sad and ruthful.[27]

Ellis, the elder and more retiring of the two, was brilliant enough to be made a Fellow of All Souls College at the age of only eighteen. Jasper, five years younger than Ellis, was another prodigious student, and one who never quite lost his wildness. After going to Oxford at the age of twelve, he too settled into a Fellowship when just nineteen. This allowed him to work on historically significant translations of Lucius Seneca's ancient Latin tragedies. But four years into Elizabeth's reign, Jasper found it impossible to stay. He became a Jesuit in Rome, and two years later was Professor of Moral Theology at the radical Bavarian college of Dillingen. There he annoyed his superiors by his unorthodox approach to scholasticism: he had little interest, for example, in what he 'regarded as superfluous or pretentious doctoral credentials'. Turning up at his viva voce examination after finally submitting his thesis, he crossed his arms and refused to say a word, dismissing the whole affair as a farce.[28] The college authorities soon tired of such behaviour, and turfed him out after a scandalous dispute over a loan. More time was spent roaming until Jasper met Edmund Campion, senior Jesuit and eventually a martyr, who recommended the maverick to the Pope for higher service. In the summer of 1581, when Donne was nine, Jasper returned to England, to help the growing Jesuit mission that was fighting to keep Roman Catholicism alive on the island.

This was a risky venture to say the least. Jesuits were members of the most militant branch of the Roman Catholic clergy: they were regarded as spies and agitators, and, if captured, could be hung, drawn and quartered. On his arrival, Jasper worked tirelessly, with only a few assistants, travelling the length and breadth of the country, teaching, training, encouraging hope and resilience in cells of faithful priests and recusants. Yet Jasper's upbringing and his long years abroad clouded his understanding of the way English Catholic clerics thought and organized themselves. He was a privileged academic, who had never actually served as a priest in his own country; brought up in the royal Court, he was also more accustomed to the company of aristocrats than the ordinary folk to which his colleagues and superiors felt their mission should appeal. The clerics who were now supposed to regard him as their superior had suffered and been hardened by almost twenty years of watching their backs in the service of the Lord. Jasper lacked their severity. He also took risks and lived lushly, aggravating fellow Jesuits. While his predecessors moved from house to house and province to province with excruciating stealth, Heywood defied detection by travelling with much display, 'in coach accompanied with many and in costly apparel'.[29] Donne's Victorian biographer stated that Jasper 'assumed the perilous airs of a Papal Legate, and was positively accused of a parade of wealth and pomp in his private life in London'.[30]

Late in 1583 Jasper was recalled by Rome. He had given the Protestant authorities the slip for more than two frenetic years, but was forced to leave the country by his own people. It was early winter, and as his ship sailed for Dieppe it encountered a storm which blew it back onto the Sussex coast; having thwarted the best spies in London, and narrowly escaped a drowning, Father Jasper Heywood was now arrested, transferred back to the capital, and locked up in the Clink prison in Southwark. At the trial that followed, in February 1584, 'Heywood and five other priests were brought to the Kings-bench barre, indited of high treason for conspiring at Rhemes [Rheims] and Rome . . . They all pleaded not guilty.' A contemporary who was present dispatched a report back to Robert Southwell, another senior Jesuit. Jasper 'was in Jesuit weed, so grave a man as ever I sett my eyes upon'. In a black cloak that almost brushed the floor, and a hat of black felt, leaning on his staff, Jasper heard the evidence against him and his companions. Three days later, 'The Jury found them out of hand Guilty, and the Judge gave sentence of death.' On hearing the sentence, the priests in the dock alarmed the court by suddenly lifting their voices and singing out '*Te Deum* and such like godly verses'.[31]

Jasper got off rather more lightly than his fellow prisoners. His five subordinates were executed while he, their leader, was spared, perhaps by special order of the Queen herself. Elizabeth must have remembered Jasper as her schoolmate, and could also, perhaps, recall his father, the musician and funny man from the Court of her earliest girlhood.

Imprisoned in the Tower, Jasper could still receive visitors. Amazingly, enemies of the state would pass in and out to see him. One of these was a newly qualified Jesuit priest, William Weston, who left an account of the interview with Heywood in his Latin autobiography; he also explained how such access was possible. Weston found Jasper 'suffering from a severe illness and in great pain'; in consideration of this, the old priest was allowed 'to receive visits from his sister, who was able in some measure to attend to his needs and nurse him'. Jasper's sister was Elizabeth, Donne's mother. Weston makes it clear that Elizabeth was a conduit between Jasper and members of the Catholic resistance on the outside: 'She was a Catholic, and it was through her that I got in touch with him.' Elizabeth reassured Weston that the meeting 'could be arranged without grave risk'. She was jeopardizing her own safety in the family cause, perhaps endangering her children. By late 1584, plans were afoot to make it high treason for a Jesuit merely to enter England. Jasper was about to be sent out of the country for the last time, and 'in view of his imminent exile he was granted greater liberty to deal with his friends': that is to say, Donne's mother had arranged other risky meetings, and was finding it easier to do so. She was much more confident by now than Weston, who entered the Tower 'with a feeling of great trepidation as I saw the vast battlements, and was led by the warder past the gates with their iron fastenings, which were closed behind me'.[32] Donne, who later recalled being present at 'a Consultation of Jesuites in the Tower, in the late Queenes time', seems to have been taken by the hand behind the same battlements.[33]

The condition of his uncle, surely one of those who Donne later said were responsible for the 'guiding, and rectifying of mine vnderstanding', was one of the heavier weights on the young scholar's mind during his first autumn in Oxford.[34] In the January

after the boys went to university, Jasper Heywood was shipped
away to Europe once more, never to return. The militant Catholic
died in Naples, far from his native London murk and Oxford fogs,
in 1598, within months of Donne gaining a promising job in the
Protestant government.

The university, meanwhile, was its own universe, created to
astound. The city was one great sheaf of spires and steeples; the
Divinity School, completed by 1504, was designed to aim every
outcrop from its grooved façade and every thought within it
towards heaven. Most of the institutional structures are made from
yellow sandstone: the quartz within it refracts the light, so on a
bright winter day the sunshine passes through the walls as much as
it bounces off them. If one approaches the city from the east,
Magdalen's tower, its base slightly askew to the rest of the college,
is a golden upright beam. But at night, or on the many dull midland
days, the walls are like grey bark. A tortuous, consciously awesome
building like the Church of St Mary leaves the people below like
ants on the floor of a rocky forest.

Donne was not out of his league. Isaak Walton asserts that the
boy went up to Oxford with 'a good command both of the French
and Latine Tongue'. Donne distinguished himself during his three
or four years there, impressing his tutors as one 'who was rather
born, than made wise by study' – as poets, of course, were traditionally supposed to be.[35] He also made friends with a group of
precocious youngsters like himself – many of whom would study
law with him down in London, and remain on good terms
throughout adult life. These were lively wits, poets, soldiers,
drinkers, who eventually became sensible religious men, like
Donne himself. The greatest friend in the group was Henry
Wotton, who delighted the university examiners with a learned
and elaborate disquisition on 'the *Form*, the *Motion*, the curious
composure of the eye'. Wotton's final flourish was to discuss the
moral function of sight as guardian of the soul and herald of the
creation, with attention to the problem of whether we see '*by
emission of the beams from within, or Reception of the Species from
without*'.[36]

The older boys at Oxford already had fluffy chins and uncomfortable voices; and though the drinking, gambling and chatting up of local maids was presumably closed off to young John and Henry Donne, they watched carefully. There were some serious scholars around, boys who wanted a priesthood, a teaching job or a secretarial post, and then there were 'roisterers'. Holinshed, the venerable chronicler, gravely regretted that most of the 'rich mens sonnes' turned to gambling, 'vice and trifles . . . they ruffle and roist it out, exceeding in apparel, and riotous companie (which draineth them from their bookes vnto another trade.)' And when they were asked to account for such behaviour, they merely 'thinketh it sufficient to saie, that they be gentlemen, which,' Holinshed sputtered, 'grieueth many not a little'.[37]

Donne, as he grew up, became a little torn. He was exceptionally bright, and deeply committed to his studies. He was not one of Holinshed's vilified 'gentlemen', but neither was he a bloodless bookworm. He had that 'hydroptique immoderate desire of humane learning and languages' which was its own form of 'voluptuousnes'.[38] As he ran with his various urges in the university, Donne might have felt a world away from the Catholic underground of London. But it was never far. Antonio Corrano, the eccentric teacher of theology, was replaced at Hart Hall by Richard Holtbie, and the new man was worryingly close to seditious elements. Antony à Wood observed of Holtbie that 'many persons who were afterwards noted in the Catholic Church, were educated under him'.[39] Holtbie had in fact trained a string of aspiring renegades, all very gifted young men, who met terrible ends in a series of what Donne later called 'seely [silly, futile] plots'.[40] Alexander Briant, a seminary priest, was executed for high treason in 1581; as in 1584 was Francis Throckmorton, another student of Holtbie's, for aiding and abetting a supposed plot to invade England. Donne may or may not have noticed that his own brother, Henry, was drawn by the desperate example of such people.

Jesuits and priests were hiding in safe houses throughout the city. Donne's mother, as a tested member of the resistance, on occasion probably made up a bed for one of the fugitives or offered him a meal; she is not known to have attracted particular attention from the authorities herself at this time. They were family friends, people Isaak Walton described as 'advisors', teachers and role models for the boys. All the time, they were observed with a mixture of scorn and glee by a team of spies led by Richard Topcliffe, the most innovative sadist in the land: the missionaries 'walk audaciously, disguised, in the streets of London', reads one dispatch. 'Their wonted fears and Timorousness is turned into Mirth and Solace among themselves.'[41] Such assurance – such as it was – ended in stoic agony. Priests faced the worst ordeal. From a life of extracting confessions and information, Topcliffe had perfected the science of incrimination through pain. Robert Southwell, who led a further wave of Jesuit agitation in the early 1590s, described the kind of treatment that the captives met with: 'Some are hanged by the hands, eight or nine or twelve hours together . . . Some are whipped naked . . . Some have been tortured in such parts as is almost torture to Christian ears to hear . . . Some with instruments have been rowled vp together like a ball, and soe Crushed, that the blood sprowted out at diuers parts of their bodies.'[42] Much later in life, Donne was one of the few men of his time to denounce torture as morally abhorrent, not just an inefficient means of obtaining evidence. Torture constituted a threefold offence against the dignity of God's greatest creation, the human form, against the Christian Messiah, Jesus Christ, who was incarnated in that form, and finally against the Holy Ghost, who also inhabits and inspires it: 'Transgressors of the first kinde, that put Gods organ out of tune, are those inhumane persecutors, who with racks, and tortures, and fires, and exquisite inquisitions, throw downe the bodies of Gods true servants.'[43] This was the historical nightmare from which he would try to awake.

But it never left him alone. In 1593, when Donne was in his first year at Lincoln's Inn, Henry was exposed and arrested as a religious subversive. By this time Henry had also moved back down to the capital to study law, and had taken lodgings of his own. It was discovered that he had been sheltering a Catholic priest. The government of Elizabeth I took no chances with such people: Henry was imprisoned. But that was not the end of it. Donne himself was suspected of holding seditious principles. Soon afterwards, the Dean of Gloucester, Antony Rudd, was appointed as Donne's spiritual adviser. Rudd's job was to find out if Donne was a heretic, and if he was, to convince him of the error of his ways before severer measures became necessary. He specialized in persuading obstinate young Catholics to avoid wasting their lives. He had broken Margaret Throckmorton, for example, a young woman of noble family with a secure future ahead of her, if she wanted it. Her brother Francis was a Jesuit and had been put to death. It was feared that she too would throw her life away on the lost cause of Catholicism. But Margaret saw sense, with Rudd's help, and he hoped that Donne would as well.[44]

The authorities knew all about Donne's family background. Many of the Queen's councillors had known old John Heywood, and had read his witty epigrams in their youth. They also read the imploring letters he wrote from exile some twenty years earlier, begging them to release some of his confiscated assets. For some time, Donne's father had been able to manage the old man's estates, and to send him some of the revenues; but this lifeline was presently cut off. Marooned in the sun of Malines, Heywood had pleaded for at least a portion of his old income, 'nowe in my poore old age, when my frendes are in a manner all dead, and manie of them utterlie forsaken me and my wholle lyvinge detained from me'.[45] Thomas Heywood, an Essex monk, and brother of John, had been executed for performing the forbidden rites when Donne was two years old. When John's son Jasper led his mission to convert England back to Catholicism in the 1580s, the authorities had dealt with him too. They were not going to allow anyone else from that brood to cause trouble.

When Donne reflected on this family history, he was by now more circumspect than Henry. He was researching the sectarian question personally, and had procured many books on the subject. Some had been shipped in illegally from the Continent. Among these was the *Disputationes* of Cardinal Bellarmine, a banned theological text. Bellarmine's treatise offered advice for young

Catholic priests who were working underground in Protestant countries such as Elizabethan England. Donne presented his copy of Bellarmine when he went to see Dean Rudd, who listened patiently, and even complimented Donne on his 'weighty observations' on the text.[46] Rudd was a shrewd man. He heard Donne's arguments and countered them learnedly. All that was needed, from time to time, was to remind Donne gently of the fate his brother had suffered.

2. Henry

At some point before he was sixteen, Donne was forced to leave Oxford without taking a degree. He could not stay on without taking the Oath of Allegiance to the Queen and the Reformed Church, and this was something his family simply would not allow. He and his brother Henry were removed from university for their own safety: by staying, and refusing to take the oath, they would immediately have betrayed themselves as recusants and thus dissidents. Dropping out before completing a degree, on the other hand, attracted no notice. To leave college without graduating was far from unusual at the time: many if not most students merely put in a few years at one of the universities, picked up the necessary elements of a gentleman's education – if they could be bothered – and moved on. All the same, this cannot have been so easy for a scholar as apt and talented as Donne, whose friend Henry Wotton passed both Bachelor and Master of Arts examinations with flying colours. Later on, Donne was glad to receive honorary degrees from both Oxford and Cambridge; he was also very happy for any opportunity to show off his learning. In early youth, he was denied this opportunity. Deprived of the chance to excel openly, and forced to creep out of the academy without receiving due honour, the teenager might have felt his first serious frustration with the world – and with the forces that were both protecting and constraining him.

Donne's adolescence is better described by a string of dots than a solid timeline. The early life splits into many possible lives. One recent theory has it that he spent hardly any time at Oxford at all. Dennis Flynn has argued that escape from England was absolutely imperative long before Donne turned sixteen: so the young Papist was smuggled out of the country as early as 1585, perhaps just days before his missionary uncle Jasper Heywood was deported. The

boy was then taken to Paris by the Earl of Derby, a Roman
Catholic sympathizer who had been sent as special ambassador to
present King Henri III of France with the Order of the Garter. As
a pageboy in the Earl's retinue, Donne was reunited briefly with
his uncle and was present at the fringes of anxious conferences
between Jesuit exiles and European nobles. These discussed the
future of the Roman Church and the empire it supported. Airy
plots were floated to invade England and assassinate Elizabeth, then
grew dense with reality and fell to the floor. Presently, Flynn
suggests, Donne was recruited into a crack team of thirty gentleman
volunteers, and transferred north to the Low Countries, where
religious war had been raging for decades. The Duke of Parma's
Roman Catholic forces were besieging the city of Antwerp. There
Donne witnessed one of the most advanced military operations of
the age, involving the construction of a twelve-mile canal to carry
supplies, and the conversion of little villages into strongholds.
According to Flynn Donne also wrote his earliest surviving poetry
there, five epigrams in Latin that describe the fortifications and the
mood in the camp, and voice earthy encouragement to the troops.

> A coy whore is with patience watched for, yet
> No honor's gain'd; glory with dangers met
> Here doth attend us; toyls are paid with praise.
> Let's weave us Crowns, then, of immortal Bayes.[1]

Through April 1585, the epigrammatist would have experienced
the all but unbearable tension amid the forces laying siege. The
citizens of Antwerp were supported by a large Dutch fleet poised
further up the river Scheldt; on 5 April, they sent a ship packed
with explosives downriver to destroy the incredible bridge that
Parma's army had constructed near Calloo. Almost a thousand
men were killed by the floating volcano, which blasted out lumps
of granite, 'cannon balls, chain shot, ploughshares and miscellaneous deadly projectiles'.[2] A nerve-racking standoff ensued
between the besieged city, the waiting fleet and the sleepless
garrison.

The evidence that involves Donne in this narrative is not, however, conclusive. Apart from the fact that neither he nor anyone connected with him ever made the slightest reference to him having such an experience, perhaps the strongest obstacle to Donne serving at Antwerp or writing the epigrams, with their casual references to coy whores and their impressive understanding of military engineering, is the fact that he was possibly not even thirteen at the time of the siege. It was quite usual for very young boys to see active combat, or serve officers in the field; but it is still hard to see Donne – still probably pre-pubescent – as the tobacco-smoking, womanizing trooper who comments expertly on fortifications or 'Upon a Navigable River cut through a Town built out of a Wood'.[3] It is also much more likely that those recruiting Catholic English exiles for the squadron that travelled to the Low Countries would have chosen someone fully grown, preferably with combat experience. A scholarly boy would have been more of a hindrance than a help on one of the most gruelling expeditions of the day.

There is also no mention anywhere of Henry Donne – who would also, surely, have been sent out along with his brother, if it was really so necessary to escape England immediately: he was only a year younger, after all, and the same conditions that made John's departure necessary would also have compelled his. Moreover, the Antwerp expedition was not the sort of escapade to which the Donne brothers' family were happy to expose them. The boys had to spend much of their early youth away from home, but were jealously protected: even at Oxford, they still had their aunt and uncle at the Blue Boar to keep an eye on them. Donne later noted in passing, but with great affection, that as a child 'My parents would not give mee over to a *Servants* correction.'[4] He and Henry were well looked after. Even if Mrs Donne did sneak her sons in to see their uncle in the Tower of London, the family went to considerable lengths to keep them safe. The traditional account of Donne's teenage years keeps him in England, and offers a much milder narrative, one that reflects a more tender upbringing. In this version, Donne moved across from Oxford to

Cambridge at the age of about fourteen. Isaak Walton, his first
biographer, reports that Donne 'staied there till his seventeenth
year; all which time he was a most laborious Student, often changing his studies'.[5]

Cambridge, further north and east than Oxford, surrounded by
fens and raked by Siberian winds from the North Sea that blow
across the flatlands, was a smaller, quieter place, with its architectural share of baroque gargantua, disproportionate to the little
market town in which they were raised, but with in general a
more parochial beauty. It was both drowsy and volatile: academic
clashes could be vitriolic and, where the translation of scripture
or points of Christian doctrine were concerned, could have profound political ramifications. Holinshed observed that those
who settled in the universities too long lived 'like drone bees on
the fat of colleges, withholding better wits from the possession of
their places':[6] the inmates were happy to sleep but could sting if
disturbed.

The Puritans had even stronger control in Cambridge of the
way the academy was run: there was no communal sanctuary for
Papists like Hart Hall. But there was also, as R. C. Bald observes,
'nothing at Cambridge corresponding to the requirements of the
Oxford Matriculation Statute' – the institutional rule that made it
easy to detect Roman Catholics who tried ducking out of the
Oath of Allegiance. 'Religious discipline was left to the colleges,
and for that very reason was the more strict';[7] yet since the place
was less centralized, that religious discipline might be avoided if
one studied there without matriculating or officially joining a
college. So although the Protestant zealotry of the place was if
anything greater than at Oxford, it was more localized, enforced
at ground level by individual colleges rather than from the top by
an overall governing body. As a result of the same lack of central
administration, the university records at Cambridge are less complete than those of its counterpart. It is not at all surprising that
Donne's presence should not have been documented: this was
precisely his family's hope and intention. As Bald also notes, the
honorary doctorate which we know for a fact Donne received

much later in life is also unrecorded in any official register.[8] Oxford was the ideal place to stow away two youngsters who needed a communal or family environment, at Hart Hall or the Blue Boar; but since it had no Oath of Allegiance, Cambridge was better for two older Papist boys who required still greater anonymity. A degree was still impossible without full membership of a college, but Donne could continue his studies while also living in greater peace. He and probably his brother too, as private scholars, would have had to lodge under the protection of an isolated sympathizer, someone like the Dr Legg, at Caius College, who had been 'Popishly affected; and bred up young Gentlemen, in Popish and disloyal principles'.[9]

Without college affiliation, or an official curriculum as such, Donne could begin to let his intellect find its own way, moving between subjects, 'often changing his studies', as Walton points out. And poetry, 'riddlingly', was beginning to catch him. Cambridge could be an exciting place for an adolescent just starting to realize the capacity of his mind, and for a writer making his first advances. A few years later, Donne encouraged a younger friend, still under the care of 'Cambridge thy old nurse', his 'braines rich hive / Fulfil'd with hony', to embrace his muse while he still had the time. He also advised Samuel Brooke, another Cambridge man 'Lately launched into the vast Sea of Arts', to 'take Fresh water at the Heliconian Spring' – the font of the muses – and to fan the first 'bright Sparkes of Poetry'. These verse letters seem to have been written with nostalgia and affection for the creative space that Donne had found for himself in the university town.[10] For some needs, however, the academy was probably stifling. Cambridge gave Donne room to begin writing, yet might have increasingly seemed a backwater. It is at this time, in his mid to late teens, that many scholars have seen him making his first excursions into the wider world.

He only emerges for definite in 1591, perhaps after a year or more of foreign travel, as a law student at Thavies Inn in London. An engraving survives of the nineteen-year-old: our first image of Donne. The portrait shows a skinny youngster, with long hair, brushed back; his forehead is high, his eyebrows arched, and a misty moustache is just appearing. He has dangly crucifix earrings and a big nose. The eyes are quite far apart, and not quite straight; but the expression is level, assured. The neck and jawline are fleshless, making his smart padded doublet, and perhaps his own shoulders, seem a little too big for him. A fragile, effeminate hand rests on the hilt of a rapier at his side. A crest is on display: azure a wolf salient, with a crest of snakes bound up in a sheath. This was the coat of arms of the Dwns of Kidwelly in Carmarthenshire, an ancient Welsh tribe with semi-mythological origins: the founding father, Meirick of Dyvet, is supposed to have been one of the guards of honour at King Arthur's wedding. Donne was obviously claiming lineage on his father's side, but no definite connection to the Dwns has ever been established.[11] It was quite customary, however, for ambitious families to assign themselves inventive genealogies. This was exactly what the Tudors did in linking themselves to another ancient Welsh family with Arthurian associations. The connection, they hoped, made them look as if they had an historic right to power. Donne's serpentine crest is just another example of the same tendency: this is a picture of someone trying not to look like a London ironmonger's lad. Donne chose a Spanish motto – suggesting Roman Catholic, perhaps even seditious affinities: '*Antes muerto que mudado*' – 'Sooner dead than changed'.[12] Like almost every other feature of the portrait, the phrase doesn't quite fit; it seems wrong for a changing, maturing boy, but also for the mutable man he would become.

The youngster in this picture was making his first excursions into the theatres and taverns on the Bankside, sneaking to his girlfriend's chamber in the dead of night, and trying not to creak the fixtures too loudly. Richard Baker, an old friend from Lincoln's Inn, later described him as 'very neat, not dissolute; a great visitor of ladies, a great frequenter of playes, a great writer of conceited verses'.[13] Donne was anxious for life to begin; he chafed at postponements. As a seasoned Lothario, waiting for a mistress to undress became an excruciating pleasure, but remained an agony nonetheless: 'Come, madam, come . . . Until I labour, I in labour

lie.' The disrobing was elaborate and prolonged, giving him time
to find an image for each discarded article: off went the girdle,
'like heavens Zone glittering', then the 'spangled breastplate'; next
the cruel corset, 'which I envie', had to be unlaced.[14] Her breasts
loose, and with the outermost layer of armour gone, the girl's skirt
still had to fall, a cloud's shadow leaving a meadow. Then a wire
headpiece let loose the crown of hair beneath. The lover himself
was 'naked first', ready and probably shivering a little on the bed.
His need was urgent:

> Licence my roaving hands, and let them go,
> Before, behind, between, above, below.[15]

And in the joyful tussle that ensued, he discovered a strange alliance
of constraint and liberty: 'To enter in these bonds,' he found, 'is
to be free'.[16]

The move to London was quite conventional and in all probability personally desirable for Donne: the capital was the place to
find a career or, as in Donne's case, finish off one's formal education
at the Inns of Court, and to step out in the world. Yet on returning
to his home city, Donne had to wait a while before gaining
complete licence to rove. His family thought he needed more than
his legal studies and extracurricular interests to keep him busy. He
was taught mathematics, and 'all the other liberal sciences', by
private tutors, and others who continued to supervise and secretly
'instil into him particular principles of the Romish church'.[17]
Donne's personal horizons finally opened in 1593, when he passed
the age of twenty-one and came of age. This allowed him to take
his share of the inheritance his father left him. Donne received
about £750 – serious money – and also, at last, became his own
man. The spiritual superintendents disappeared.

He wrote poems; but though he was perfectly familiar with the
classical adage that poets are born, not made, he never looked
upon verse as a mystical calling, a psychological privilege or an
existential burden. Words, Donne later said, are our 'subtillest and
delicatest outward creatures'.[18] He accumulated these little animals

and carried them around like parasites, complaining sometimes of
'this itch of writing'.[19] Poetry was a life-sign or a minor irritation.
He certainly didn't want to be defined by it, coveting in later life
'a graver course than of a Poet, into which (that I may also keep
my dignity) I would not seem to relapse'.[20] Significantly, he never
allowed his early poems – which were always best received, and
have been ever since – to be printed together. Writing was just
something he *did*: something he took seriously, and something he
knew he could do well. It wasn't going to be his profession. He
scoffed at London's playwrights with their 'labor'd sceanes', and at
those who wrote flattery in order to gain patronage. Contemporary
'Poore Suburbe wits' recognized, to their desperation, that his
verse was only a spare-time activity:

> For who hath read thee, and discernes thy worth,
> That will not say, thy carelesse houres brought forth
> Fancies beyond our studies, and thy play
> Was happier, then our serious time of day?[21]

He was neither a visionary, a hack, nor one of the multitudes of
young men who tried their hand at a sonnet or so. What he did
concede, though, was the unique intrigue of poetry: 'Though like
the Pestilence and old fashion'd love, / Ridlingly it catch men'.[22]
Barely noticed at an early stage, it *riddled* the whole body like
plague or desire; yet it also worked like an intellectual problem
that gave no rest until it was solved.

   Although he cordially saluted the literary efforts of his friends
and contemporaries, Donne set himself against the currents of
conventional poetic taste. He quite consciously ignored the preference of the 1590s for the metrical smoothness sought by everyone
from Philip Sidney to William Shakespeare. Donne's cadences are
those of someone thinking as they speak, making emphases that
go against the stipulations of prosody:

> I wonder, by my troth, what thou, and I
> Did, till we lov'd?

He does not set out to create an unrealistically even flow of speech that could sound artificial. In terms of the period's literature, there are virtually no contemporary poets who can be said to have influenced him. He admired the playwright Christopher Marlowe, author of *Doctor Faustus*, but was unaffected by Marlowe's metrical strictness and rhetorical expansiveness. Donne's models instead for his early poems were the Latin satirists and the Ovid of the erotic *Amores*; in English, one has to look further back for his influences, to the lyrics for example of Sir Thomas Wyatt, to whom Donne never openly referred, but whose rougher, snaggy rhythms are detectable in the texture of his writing.

Donne resisted too the loftier characterizations of the poet that were being advanced at the time. For Philip Sidney, held up by the Elizabethans as the exemplar, the poet was a kind of secondary or mini God, who, 'lifted up with the vigour of his own invention, doth grow in effect into another nature, in making things either better than nature bringeth forth or, quite anew, forms such as were never in nature'. For George Puttenham, a much less distinguished practitioner of verse but an influential apologist for poetry nonetheless, 'poets were the first priests, the first prophets, the first legislators and politicians in the world'.[23] Donne was rather more conscious of the actual circumstances of those who tried living by the pen, and scathing of them for even trying. Many poets wrote for the stage, which was hard work, poorly and inconstantly rewarded. Donne scorned the writer who 'gives ideot actors meanes / (Starving himselfe) to live'.[24] One could not make money by publishing verse; very often a writer had to cover the costs of publication himself. Instead remuneration came (or was supposed to come) by way of suing for the patronage of some wealthy person. In his thirties and forties, Donne was reduced to directing much of his poetry to this end: his elegies and complimentary epistles became much sought after. But as a younger, more independent man this custom disgusted him:

> And they who write to Lords, rewards to get,
> Are they not like singers at doores for meat?[25]

As it happened, Donne also intensely disliked another popular means of disseminating verse: setting it (or having it set) to be sung to an accompaniment by lute. The songs of John Dowland and Thomas Campion were immensely successful, but for Donne the sound 'a high stretcht lute string squeakt' had unfavourable associations.[26] In one poem, 'The Triple Foole', he expresses annoyance at some man for setting his 'whining Poetry' to music, and thus freeing once more the grief 'which verse did refraine'.[27] Donne had no desire, then, to be seen or to see himself as a minstrel; and he saw the other main channels of scratching a livelihood from writing as beneath him.

The successful poets of his time – successful in the worldly sense – combined their writing with another profession or had the means to indulge in it as a private occupation. Those who did not, or were not able to, led fairly miserable lives. Michael Drayton served the household of one of Donne's closest friends, the Goodyers, as a tutor, and fell in love with the younger daughter of the family; he published extensively, beginning with pastoral verse and moving on to long poems on English history. However, his means were always limited, and the girl he loved went on to marry one of his friends, Sir Henry Rainsford. The fate of Edmund Spenser, meanwhile, author of the epic *The Faerie Queene*, was a cautionary example against depending on one's literary output and reputation if money got tight. Spenser served as a fairly high official in the Elizabethan colonial administration in Ireland, sending his works back across the Irish Sea as offerings for her majesty. When his estate was burnt down and his family burnt to death by insurgents, Spenser's voluminous industry counted for naught: he returned to London and starved. For quite pragmatic as well as artistic reasons, Donne did not allow himself to be socially defined as a poet until he had no other choice.

His writing too was not 'poetic', in the schoolroom sense of that word as something airy and removed from actuality. In Donne's early poems, matters of the heart became matter. They could be touched, felt, lost, broken. He thought so much about a girl that her face became imprinted in him. Her face was minted on his heart like a monarch's profile on a penny: it brought value to a random, even base scrap of metal. He put it on a chain around his lover's neck. She carried his heart away like a trinket, and he became her medal.[28] He discovered the way that lovers end up belonging to one another, muddled together by being together: they leave their stuff, and bits of themselves, with each other. They possess each other's souls, but as everyday items, like keys, small change or cheap jewellery, things with functional or sentimental value: the things that go missing most easily, and stop life in its tracks until they are recovered.

In the lyrics he wrote as a young man, Donne eludes all classification. He is remembered for his *Songs and Sonets* and *Elegies* as a 'love poet', but this definition is far too narrow. His verse is tender, brutal, cocky, manically unsure, knowingly sad. He could express himself facetiously as a sexual gourmet, concerned only with his own nourishment:

> Chang'd loves are but chang'd sorts of meat,
> And when hee hath the kernel eate,
> Who doth not fling away the shell?[29]

He could, that is, give the misleading impression of being a lover with complete emotional contraception, someone wholly impermeable to the feelings of his partner – whichever partner. He could, at times, be nothing other than misogynous. In a prose 'paradox' that excited a great deal of protest – and which he indirectly recanted in a sermon given in the last year of his life – he suggested that women no more had souls than other creatures he deemed 'equall to them in all but speech' – oxen, goats, foxes or serpents. Or if they did, it was 'only to make them capable of damnation'.[30] 'Look not for minde in women', he advised elsewhere; 'at their best / Sweetnesse and wit, they'are but *Mummy* [preserved dead flesh, sometimes thought to have healing properties], possest'.[31] Still, he needed the women he later called his 'profane mistresses'.[32] 'I can love any,' he declared, so long as 'she be not true', and he did, or claimed that he did; the 'faire', the 'browne', the ones who trusted him and the ones who tested his patience – 'Her who still weepes with spungie eyes, / And her who is dry corke, and never cries.'[33]

But this was only one among innumerable attitudes he adopted and explored in his writing. He could be scathing about superficial, double-timing women; but also about men who were prone to 'discommend all they cannot obtain'. He evened out the playing field, granting the same moral liberties for a woman as he claimed for himself.

And what reason is there to clog any woman with one man, be he never so singular? Women had rather, and it is far better and more Judicial to enjoy all the vertues in several men, than but some of them in one, for otherwise they lose their taste, like divers sorts of meat minced together in one dish . . .[34]

He could articulate better than anyone, too, how fear of making a commitment might come from fear of being rejected or betrayed. The moment of climax, 'When my Soule was in her owne body sheath'd', was a complete transportation of the spirit which left every nerve in him open and vulnerable.[35] He also took on the conventional pose of the loyal lover slighted by the inconstant mistress, giving it his own unique twist. Most engaging, perhaps, is the voice of the wistful man tired of the upset and disillusionment, who discovers that love only leaves 'A kind of sorrowing dulnesse to the mind', and asks,

> Ah cannot wee,
> As well as Cocks and Lyons jocund be,
> After such pleasures?[36]

None of these perspectives can be said to define Donne or his conduct, or to form a journal of actual encounters. Rather, the *Songs and Sonets* show him testing out the different tones and registers suggested by a variety of situations. The relationship between Donne and the speakers of his poems is something like that which dramatists have with their characters. What this points to is the way he used his experiences for the sake of his poetry. They seem to have been sought out as fuel for the writing. The 'report' mattered more than 'the sport'.[37] Very self-consciously, Donne later repentantly criticized those who 'thought [it] wit, to make Sonnets of their own sinnes' – those who confessed, 'I sinn'd, not for the pleasure I had in the sin, but for the pride that I had to write feelingly of it.'[38]

Donne's friends at Lincoln's Inn received his material delightedly. Donne's earliest readers can be identified as the group of fellow students to whom his first surviving verse letters are addressed. These men were also, for the most part, trying their hand at sonnets and stanzas, and Donne encouraged them generously and expressed respect for their responses. There is no definite evidence that they got together for readings, no affectionate, even mildly embarrassed anecdotes. Yet a late poem by Michael Drayton strongly gives the impression that such evenings were common enough between friends with a passion for literature.

> My dearly lovèd friend, how oft have we
> In winter evenings (meaning to be free)
> To some well-chosen place used to retire,
> And there with moderate meat, and wine, and fire
> Have passed the hours contentedly with chat,
> Now talked of this, and then discoursed of that,
> Spoke our own verses 'twixt ourselves, if not
> Other men's lines which we by chance had got . . .

Drayton goes on to provide a personal survey of the writers he and his friends enjoyed, from the distant and the recent past, many of whom were known to him personally. He quite decidedly excludes Donne from his list; and noticeably so, given Donne's reputation at the time of writing, 1627, and the fact that Drayton certainly knew both Donne and his work. Yet towards the end of his poem, Drayton attacks what he takes as snobbery in those poets who do not share their writings openly through the press.

> For such whose poems, be they ne'er so rare,
> In private chambers that encloistered are,
> And by transcription daintily must go,
> As though the world unworthy were to know
> Their rich composures, let those men that keep
> These wondrous relics in their judgement deep
> And cry them up so [praise them so readily], let such pieces be
> Spoke of by those that shall come after me.[39]

Drayton's slight paradoxically offers the clearest contemporary view of how Donne's poems slowly found their way into their world, and the esteem with which they were progressively held. They emerged from their seclusion in 'private chambers' – shared, perhaps, in the kind of cosy yet animated discussions Drayton describes having with his own set – through delicate, limited transcription. In time these 'daintily' copied texts were passed on or exchanged until the author's name was established to the point at which such papers became collectable, even modestly prestigious items.

They became exactly what Drayton describes, 'wondrous relics'. The playwright Ben Jonson made a handsome gift of a presentation manuscript of Donne's Satires – long after they were written and first passed around – to the Countess of Bedford, their mutual patroness. Jonson's friend and acolyte William Drummond transcribed some rarer lyrics by Donne into a notebook he solemnly entitled 'Thirre [thirty] Poems belonginge to Jhon Don transcribed by William Drummond'.[40] *Belonging* here points up Donne's possessiveness: these relics remained his property. The word 'relic' is itself unmistakably Donnean, making it quite clear whose airs and graces Drayton is castigating here. The one thing that might really have upset Donne about the poem was Drayton's idea that his poems were 'encloistered': Donne hated the idea of living monkishly, locking oneself away from the world. But on this point Drayton was justified. Donne later did all he could to restrict the circulation of his verse. Drayton's objection was not so much to the work itself as to what he regards as the preciousness that went with it. The poems filtered outwards slowly: in consequence, it is only by the 1610s that we can say for sure Donne had a 'name afloate' with a wider public.[41]

Donne himself was far from being a cloistered person as a law student. At Lincoln's Inn he had more than wit enough 'to keepe the gallants of the towne'.[42] He also had a merciless eye for a 'silken painted foole', a 'many-coloured Peacock', and all the fashionable try-hards in their 'black feathers, or musk-coloured hose'.[43] His own dress at this time, the early portrait suggests, was meticulous and conservative, obeying the sombre dress code of his new academic home: no ruff, no flashy patterns. In 1592, he moved from Thavies Inn to Lincoln's Inn, another residential college in London where well-off young men purportedly studied to become barristers, but often worked harder at having a good time. He became popular but seems to have disliked too much public exposure. He was probably still a practising Roman Catholic; and was careful, reticent by nature. Early in 1593, his second year at the Inn, as the Plague ravaged the rest of the city, he was appointed a master of the revels. This gave him responsibility for organizing public entertainments and social events for the young lawyers in the communal hall, though the job was almost meaningless since the college had been largely abandoned due to fear of infection. At Christmas the following year, Donne was asked to organize and direct the Inn's festivities; a task he declined, and which he was willing to pay a large fine – of 26 shillings and eight pence – in order to avoid. All through this time, however, he was cherished as a friend and wit in more confined circles, and treasured for the private amusement his writing provided. He kept this work well away from the commonness of the printing press: it circulated instead in handwritten copies. Ten years after he left Lincoln's Inn, the 'Satyres, Elegies, Epigrams &c. by John Don' were appearing in hit lists of 'Manuscripts to Gett'.[44]

Since he had no desire to provide for himself by writing, he was much more interested in restricting infamy than pursuing fame. The poet's familiar concern with immortality and the durability of verse, so integral to Shakespeare's sonnets, was a matter Donne treated with faint irony. Donne was more grounded in the present than in distant ages; though in the present, he was not at all jealous, or insecure, about the attempts of others he knew who wrote. He paid tribute to the 'fatherly yet lusty Ryme' of his friend and patron the Earl of Dorset – an undistinguished poet – by saying that it worked upon him 'as the Suns hot Masculine flame' was thought to stimulate the slime of the banks of the Nile: breeding 'strange creatures' from the mud of his intellect.[45] As we shall see, by his late twenties, in distributing copies to friends, Donne expressed his anxiety in his letters at how far afield his works were going from those to whom he entrusted them – and his worry at the damage they were doing to the more sober reputation he was by then trying to cultivate. Instead of being established at one stroke his reputation leeched into being a little at a time, as individual pieces passed from acquaintance to acquaintance, initially in the Inns of Court. As these student readers and Donne himself graduated into further social and professional circles, such manuscripts journeyed further too.

The Inns of Court as they were at this time are difficult institutions to classify. Together they were frequently depicted as a third English university, in addition to Oxford and Cambridge, with each of the Inns comprising an autonomous 'house' or 'hall' equivalent to the university colleges. Ostensibly, the Inns provided only legal training, but they also accommodated a great range of literary, political and theological activity, and thus stood as a kind of finishing school for Oxbridge alumni. They were select communities, each Inn having only about two hundred active members. These came from all over the country – several of Donne's verse letters dating from this time are addressed to friends from the north, including two of his greatest and surest companions, the Brooke brothers from York. Only ten per cent of law students on average were Londoners; together, therefore, the Inns reflected a national elite. But like Oxford and Cambridge, they were also characterized by a mixture of those who were there because they belonged to a sufficiently affluent class, with those who were studying seriously in the hope of one day joining it. By rights, although enjoying a cash surge on the back of the inheritance his father had left for him, Donne belonged to the latter, needier and more diligent faction. But as he admitted himself, he behaved as though he was part of the former.

Recalling how he began 'the study of our laws', he would write years later that he was 'diverted' from this practical occupation by his 'immoderate desire of humane learning and languages'. Such subjects were 'beautifull ornaments to great fortunes; but mine needed an occupation', he accepted dolefully.[46] The curricular demands on his time at Lincoln's Inn were not overwhelming, however. Teaching was done through oral disputation, rather than written work, an apt preparation for courtroom debate. The daily focus was a 'case-putting' exercise, in which a senior member of the Inn – they were known as 'Benchers' – would outline a short case, and the students would split into small groups to discuss it. This was often conducted in the main hall of the Inn, the architectural heart of the society, after the midday meal. A more formal exercise was the 'moot', a mock-trial in which students took the part of attorneys while Benchers sat as judges. This could take weeks of preparation, or a glance at the relevant statute the evening before, depending on personal diligence. What record we have suggests that this all came rather easily to Donne: 'he gave great testimonies of his Wit, his Learning, and of his Improvement,' Isaak Walton assures us.[47] Showing one's ingenuity in the handling of a case, manipulating the material to an unexpected end, seems to have been more highly regarded than straightforward expression. A fashion grew up, in the occasional lectures or 'readings' on particular points of law, 'for presenting a great many intricate cases, often bearing only slight relation to the statute itself'.[48] The procedures such readings involved may well have had some influence on Donne's way of often expressing things in the most farfetched manner conceivable. He was certainly exposed to them for long enough; a reading could last for seven or eight hours. Donne's friend John Hoskins sent an apologetic note to his wife on being detained at a reading in 1619 that began at seven in the evening and lasted half the night: 'they say preachers are long,' he wrote, 'but sure the law is very tedious.'[49]

Completing one's law studies in order to enter into practice was a lengthy, arduous process that only a minority of Inns men bothered going through with. Besides teaching students, the Inns functioned rather like guilds for active legal professionals, who continued to meet, eat in the great hall and sometimes live and teach in their old stamping grounds. Practising and aspiring barristers, however, were generally looked down upon. The Inns contained a mass of gentlemen who had no plans at all for a legal career. Some, like Donne, were pursuing independent, idiosyncratic intellectual interests; others were just messing about. 'Those that are disposed, studdie lawes,' commented a contemporary; and those 'who so liketh, without checke, maye followe dalliance'.[50] Preaching to the congregation of the chapel at Lincoln's Inn many years later, Donne spoke fondly of the fair and frankly of the foul kinds of 'dalliance' that went on: 'A fair day shoots arrows of *visits* and *comedies*, and *conversation*, and so wee goe abroad: and a foul day shoots arrows of *gaming* or *chambering* [visiting brothels], and *wantonnesse*, and so we stay at home.'[51] Brawling and drunkenness were also rife. The ruling committees of the Inns were less than keen on licentious or over-youthful behaviour, but had traditionally taken a parochial view with disciplinary action. In the late 1480s, after a 'rash' of sexual offences, the bench at Lincoln's Inn introduced a fine of £5 for any student caught fornicating in his room or another college building. But the penalty for having sex in the grounds of the Inn or out in the street was only £1.[52]

The elders of the Inn were thus more concerned about propriety within the house. Women were in general forbidden to enter, and fads such as ruffs, white doublets, velvet caps, spurs and brightly coloured cloaks were also prohibited – hence Donne's plain, rather conservative attire in the portrait of 1591. The picture identifies him as an Inns of Court man. A sense of collective identity among members was clearly encouraged. Despite a shortage of space, Benchers disapproved, on the whole, of students living outside the walls of the Inn, 'as forraigners rather than fellowes associated together'. Admittedly, given the lack of interest that some inmates showed in their educational and professional activities, the Inns

operated 'like residential clubs or hotels' for itinerant gentlemen;[53]
but they also fostered an intermittently violent tribal loyalty. The
young population of the Inns lived together, ate together, organized in-house masques and entertainments, went to plays on
London's southside and danced at the revels that were held in
the dark winter months 'every Saturday between All Saints and
Candlemas'.[54] They shared extracurricular pursuits. Many took
dancing, fencing and music lessons together at specialist schools
around the city; the more literary-minded formed poetic coteries,
exchanging satirical and erotic verses. But most importantly, they
shared the solidarity that comes with mutual snobbery.

Members of the Inns of Court were gentlemen: they could look
down their noses and mock at those who belonged to London's
other main socially defined grouping of young men – the apprentices. These were perennially the most volatile faction of urban
society. Apprentices enjoyed absolutely none of the freedoms,
finery or dalliance that the law students flaunted. They were bound
to grindingly austere domestic regimes, living under the close
supervision of their masters. A typical indenture, which could
secure a young man's service for upward of twelve years, strictly
forbade all thought of 'cardes, dice, bowlis . . . unlawful games,
hores, harlots, alehowses' and all other 'unlawful and suspicious
places'.[55] An apprenticeship brought a life of dour working days
and evening prayers; in theory, at least. In practice, it was often
too much for testosterone-troubled youngsters to bear. Apprentices
were famous for whoring, gaming and ale-drinking like virtually no
other demographic banding; though also, paradoxically, for sweep-
ing through the streets in hordes on certain public holidays to attack
the very brothels and taverns they patronized so fervently under
normal circumstances. Their football matches made no-go zones
of entire districts of the city. At heart, apprentices were aggressively
conservative, with an historic dislike for foreigners and foreign
fashions – since both, to the apprentices, constituted a threat to
native goods and commerce. And as one might expect, they despised the airs, graces and fads exhibited by members of the Inns of
Court who regarded them as inferiors. Clashes occurred regularly.

The situation was virtually uncontainable for the authorities since both gangs, the gentlemen and the apprentices, liked to frequent exactly the same sorts of places. The theatres were notorious flashpoints. Returning to London one midsummer night, William Fletewood found 'all the wardes full of watches [guards, watchmen]'. All hell had broken loose earlier in the evening. 'Neere the theatre . . . at the tyme of the playes, there lay a prentice sleeping upon the grasse.' His boozy slumber was disturbed when another man, one Challes, came up and 'did turne the toe upon the belly of the same prentice'. Reeling from his kick in the guts, and incensed,

this apprentice started up, and after words they fell to playne blowes. The companie increased of both sides to the number of 500, at the least. This Challes exclaimed and said, that he was a gentleman, and that the apprentice was but a rascal, and some there were little better than roogs, that tooke upon them the name of gentlemen, and said the prentizes were but the skumme of the world. Upon these troubles, the prentizes began the next day, being Tuesday, to make mutinies and assemblies, and did conspire to have broken the prisones . . .[56]

A scuffle between two men could escalate into a battle involving five hundred, culminating the next day in riot and attempted jailbreak. Throughout the sixteenth century, the city's rulers had grown well used to such conflagrations. Fletewood's account of the fight that sparked off this one tells us a lot about the social insecurity that underlay the rivalry. Challes, the aggressor, condemns not only apprentice 'skumme', but also those who falsely labelled themselves 'gentlemen'. The competition had a lot to do with envy on the part of the apprentices; but also worry, on the part of the law-student gentlemen, that they weren't quite the genuine article.

Many of those attending the Inns of Court came from trade families; many had cousins and brothers currently serving apprenticeships, or had fathers who had served their time and prospered. Donne's own paternal background fell into this category. A contemporary at Lincoln's Inn made a swipe at those – perhaps even at Donne personally, with his ironmonger father – who 'Turn'd yron to sterling, drosse to land and fee' in order to give their children a push up the social ladder.[57] Snide references to 'sour prentices' are scattered here and there in Donne's poetry. He tends to bring them in whenever he expressly relishes his own ease and freedom – when, for example, he lies in late with his woman and tells the sun to leave them in peace.[58] But the frustrated aproned boys he passed at shop doors or on errands in the street merely embodied what he had left behind. Whatever evidence he had or had embellished about his forefathers' distinguished Arthurian lineage, Mr Donne had been an apprentice boy and then a shop-keeper. It is wholly unlikely that Donne would have followed in the ironmonger's footsteps, even if his father had lived; his mother's moderately aristocratic pedigree marked him out for a college education. Yet although John senior would no doubt have encouraged his son's efforts to cultivate an identity as a gentleman – which, in later years, through poverty and depression, Donne was quite unable and unwilling to give up – there was no disguising where the boy had started out. Donne's way of life at Lincoln's Inn, his 'voluptuousnes', his refusal to apply himself to the law as a profession, all indicate a discomfort with his lower middle-class origins; he had higher aspirations.

Donne's perception of his own gentility is every bit as important to understanding his life as the Roman Catholicism he was slowly leaving behind – even more so, in fact. Donne was in time prepared to stop being a Papist; but nothing could stop him from being a gentleman. His stepfather, Dr John Symynges, allowed both religious and social sensibilities to co-exist for a time. Symynges was a Catholic, but was also one of London's most successful physicians, a senior member of the Royal College. Symynges married Mrs Donne in 1576; and up to his death in 1588, when Donne was sixteen, oversaw a crucially formative period in his stepson's life. He moved the family into his more ample house in Trinity Lane, near Cheapside, and returned his wife to the level of society she had known in her youth. Symynges was wealthy, holding property in three counties; he was of gentle birth, and widely respected about town. Like Donne's father, he had a shrewd business sense, advising young doctors to settle the fee for treatment while the patient was unable to haggle: 'before you meddle with him make your bargaine wisely now he is in paine', was his mantra. He encouraged an appreciation of the value of money that Donne only learnt in later years; but possessed a status and lifestyle that may have blotted out any nostalgia Donne had for his earliest memories of the ironmongers' shop in Bread Lane. Symynges made it seem possible to be a gentleman and, providing one trod carefully, remain a Roman Catholic.[59]

Lincoln's Inn, however, offered plenty of warning on the latter score. The Inns of Court had for years been riddled with Papist cells, harbouring priests in order to receive the outlawed Roman sacraments. The Inns were ideal shelters, paradoxically, for illegal activity of all kinds, since no constable could enter without author-ization from the bench of the Inn itself. As Wilfrid Prest explains: 'Apart from the alluring prospect of a flood of well-born converts, the Inns lay conveniently beyond the jurisdiction of city and suburban justices, while the constant traffic of lawyers, clients, students and servants helped cloak a priest's movements, particu-larly if he happened to be a former student himself and knew the lie of the land.'[60] The government took care, however, to lace the Inns well with their own networks of informants, and after the first ten years of Elizabeth's reign, the legal societies were regularly purged. In March 1572, around the time Donne was born, the Bishop of London gleefully reported a raid on student digs in a house belonging to a Portuguese man: 'There was found the altar prepared, the chalisse and their bread god; and in the house, as I hear, a great number of Englishmen hyd, as ready to hear masse.' Among those apprehended, as so often, were 'four students at law, freshmen I suppose . . .'[61] The discovery and capture of rebel Catholics in the Inns of Court remained a frequent event in Donne's time.

His first years of independence in London, in the early 1590s, were years of plague: at such times, much of the city shut down. Lincoln's Inn seems to have been closed for almost half the year in both 1592 and 1593. Donne stayed in town, however, and reported that 'Our Theatres are filled with emptines.'[62] These venues of terrified quiet mirrored the state of his insides. In an early verse letter to his friend, Rowland Woodward, Donne says 'as Ayre doth fulfill the hollowness / Of rotten walls; so it myn emptines.'[63] Poetry, he told Woodward, was compensation: it had a 'cherishing fyre which dryes in mee / Griefe which did drowne mee'.[64] This 'Griefe' is mysterious and important. It was partly evidence of a young man's conventional melancholy. But it also went a long way back: it was older than the 'satirique fyres' he blasted it with, 'in skorne of all',[65] older than his dreams in the seven sleepers' den, and generations older than Donne himself.

In the spring of 1593, Topcliffe's Papist-hunters had turned their attention to Henry Donne, by now also a 'gentleman of the Inns of Court'. Agents raided Henry's lodgings, and there discovered William Harrington, a twenty-seven-year-old Yorkshireman who had trained as a seminarian priest in Europe. Both men were taken. Beaten, racked and questioned, Harrington denied being a priest; but Henry collapsed under similar treatment, and gave away his friend's identity. Not that the interrogators had any real doubts as to what their suspects were: both men were initially committed to the Clink in Southwark, and then, in the sebaceous heat of June, were taken back across the river Thames to Newgate. Harrington was then moved on to the Marshalsea, and suffered the standard fate of an heretical traitor.

Proceedings against him dragged on until February the following year. Harrington turned down a trial by jury, refusing to allow any more men than necessary to damn themselves by convicting him: he insisted on being tried by judge alone. Crucially, the authorities offered him a means of avoiding the death penalty. All he had to do was to stop practising as a priest and being a Papist. Harrington refused the deal, and retorted that his 'intent in coming into England was, and is, no other than St John Baptist's was in coming to Herod'.[66] On a bleak late winter day, he was brought to face the public at Tyburn. Shivering at the scaffold, he tried to address the crowd, saying he would pray for their souls. He protested his innocence of all treason, but was interrupted by the jibes of Richard Topcliffe, who was there to see his work finished. 'Thou liest,' cried Topcliffe, 'and so thou didst say the Queen was a tyrant.' Harrington insisted that he had never done a thing to offend the Queen: 'but I say *you* are a tyrant and a bloodsucker.' With the halter round his neck, he promised that others would continue his ministry.

The row was getting out of hand. Topcliffe ordered the cart supporting Harrington to pull away. The priest was hanged, then cut down before his spine could break. And then his strength returned. To the fury and consternation of the crowd, he fought back, and struggled with his executioner. The moment passed. Harrington was held down, straining. His genitals were thrown onto a brazier. The executioner slit open his victim's abdomen and methodically eviscerated him, burning his intestines before his eyes.[67]

Donne's younger brother was already months dead. Henry never made it to trial; in June 1593 imprisonment in Newgate was all but a death sentence. London was being devoured by one of the worst outbreaks of the plague for years, and the crowded, fetid conditions of Newgate made the place lethal. The transferral seems to have been a calculated move on the part of the civic authorities. A contemporary witness noted that Mr Donne had entrusted Henry's inheritance – a sum of about £500 – to the Chamber of London for safe keeping and to accrue interest. Henry, like his brother, was due to receive this portion of his father's estate at the age 'of Twentie and one yeres'.[68] The city had already just parted with John's endowment; the following year another payout had to be made. There was a whiff of foul play: Henry's removal from the relative safety of the Clink to almost certain fatality in Newgate was 'in all likelihood . . . contrived of purpose, to defeat him of his money'.[69] If this suspicion entered the mind of a bystander, it all but certainly tortured Henry's brother and his family. Any attempt to oppose the change of prison has passed unrecorded, but the decision was made so swiftly that there was probably no way of appealing against it. And once Henry had been taken into Newgate, it was suicide to visit him.

The prison stank and moaned. If you had the money, you could pay to be detained on 'the master's side', where some basic comforts were available. Most of the inmates, however, found themselves in the 'common side', packed together in chains, untried and convicted alike, regardless of the class of crime for which they had been arraigned. Grubby candles had to burn all day, and no fresh air got in. In the gaol's basement, 'swarming with vermin and creeping things', prisoners lay 'like swine upon the ground, one upon another'.[70] The spread of plague was unstoppable in such conditions. An infected prisoner would feel the sweat and ache, then discover the bubonic swellings and ulcerous blotches on the neck, under his arms and in his groin; and know it was all over. It was a matter of days.

Donne himself, that summer, was at large in London, footloose but listless. There was a ball of air inside him, a 'Griefe' he could detect but couldn't release. It filled him up, as though someone were forcing him to drink until his insides collapsed, and yet left him dry, thirsty, 'hydroptique'. Looking back more than twenty years later, and trying to console his mother, Donne saw the life of his family as an ongoing storm – 'a sea, under a continual tempest, where one wave hath ever overtaken another'.[71] At varying intervals, he watched his siblings swept under.

Though no precise allusion to Henry's death survives, it was an event that made Donne acknowledge a hollow space, 'myn emptines'; and we do have an account of how he felt and how he occupied himself around the time his brother died. In the plagued summer of 1593 he wandered the Bankside, around the stews, which were deserted; past the playhouses, which were all closed up. He found a ghost town:

> Now pleasures dirth our city doth posses,
> Our Theatres are filled with emptines.
> As lancke and thin is every street and way
> As a woman deliver'd yesterday.
> Nothing whereat to laugh my spleen espies
> But bearbaiting and Law Exercise.[72]

The city was an empty womb, lank and thin from a recent delivery. Remaining willingly in town required someone to have more than a slight death wish if there was any chance of escaping. Risking, almost inviting infection, the only recreation for the bilious young writer was either to join in half-hearted legal arguments, or go to the bear-pit. It wasn't far from his other haunts on the Bankside. But the show was predictable. Either the bear, chained to a post, was torn apart, or managed to dismember the hounds that were set upon it. There was no other outcome, and all the animals involved, except the roaring spectators, would be maimed by the performance. The sand in the pit went brown and sludged with tattered meat.

3. Cadiz

In 1595, Donne's mother Elizabeth told her surviving family that she was leaving for exile in Europe. She and her third husband were going to settle in Antwerp, the commercial capital of the Spanish Netherlands. Elizabeth had met Richard Rainsford, 'a gentleman, living in Southwark', also a Catholic, a while after moving south across the Thames. Her second husband, Dr John Symynges, physician of high standing and a Roman Catholic of carefully low profile, had died in July 1588, without leaving a will. Elizabeth took charge of his affairs herself and moved house again, hoping that she could live peacefully and practise her religion anonymously. But there was no end to the parochial hassle. Soon after she moved, the records of the church of St Saviour show that Elizabeth got into trouble 'for not komyng to chirche to receive the communyon'.[1]

The parishes south of the river were beyond the boundaries of the old city of London, and thus outside the direct control of the Puritan city fathers. Those who were liable to criticism and often persecution from the authorities tended to put down their roots in the outlying regions of the growing city. The southside was a sprawl of taverns where prostitution had been licensed for centuries, and where the theatres Shakespeare wrote for were just developing. Donne knew it well. He often caught a ferry across the Thames to sample the pleasures of Southwark. At Lincoln's Inn, he and his friends had standing arrangements to rescue one another from their cramped college rooms when the tedium of 'Law Exercise' proved too much. Donne was 'a great frequenter of plays',[2] no stranger to the dinning wooden circle of the theatre, though no partaker of the commonness associated with it. He was not one of the 'youths that thunder at a playhouse and fight for bitten apples'.[3]

His mother had moved across the river hoping for a little more breathing space, perhaps a fresh start; but when south London proved not far enough, a more drastic step became necessary. Spanish-controlled Antwerp was a traditional stopping-off point for Catholic refugees, among them many of Donne's relatives. His uncle Ellis, the elder brother of Jasper, fled England early in Queen Elizabeth's reign, becoming a Jesuit in Rome and wandering the Continent unhappily for many years. He led a life of unwelcome adventure, tormented by a 'demon' in his dreams, finally abandoning his library and his papers in Antwerp when a Protestant mob attacked the Jesuit college; he fled to Louvain, where he died a shattered man in 1578. Such poignant examples of sacrifice and hardship were causes for family pride, and Elizabeth probably noted with reproach the contrast between Ellis and her own agnostic brood. There was a great deal to weigh on her mind as she prepared to leave.

Anne, her one surviving daughter, had married a man whose profession was no less a sin than the observation and entrapment of Catholics. William Lyly, known about town as 'a witty and bold Atheist', had helped to ensnare agents and supporters of Mary, Queen of Scots, and had served as a spy in France in the 1580s during the civil wars. As elsewhere in Europe, the battle for power and territory in France fell along religious lines, between Protestants led by Henri of Navarre and a League of Catholics who followed the recognized king, Henri III. Lyly was based in the French court itself, where the King passed comment on the Englishman's 'manner of behaviour and readiness to answer all things marvellous well'.[4] Henri III was assassinated not long afterwards, and Lyly returned to England in 1590. This was a year before the death of Anne's first husband, a wastrel called Avery Copley. Having spent his way through Anne's whole inheritance, he then devoured a huge loan of £600 from her mother. It was good riddance to bad rubbish when he died in 1591. Yet then, in the eyes of Elizabeth, after marrying a gambler and a spendthrift, Anne went and hitched herself to an infidel. William Lyly was much worse, in fact, than your average heathen: an associate of the very men who left Henry Donne, Elizabeth's baby and the one true Catholic she had managed to rear, to rot of plague in Newgate.

Another worry was her remaining son John. He had no settled profession, no definite aim. Elizabeth might also have seen him wavering, contemplating conversion. In any case, when his mother left for Europe, there was no one to monitor the company Donne kept, no one to count the number of times he went to Mass in a year or make him take the sacrament at Easter. He was still dividing his time between intense personal study, writing and visiting ladies; spending the money his father left him while avoiding the prospect of having to earn some himself. The intricacies of canon law, the law of the ecclesiastical courts, interested Donne a great deal, since they knitted in with the tangled threads of theology, but he regarded common law as a hobby or a matter for hacks.

For most of the young men at Lincoln's Inn, becoming a lawyer was not the object at all. One might as well have been a leper, or one of the beggars hanging around and haranguing people in the Fields beyond the college. Walton says that Donne gave 'great testimonies of his Wit, his Learning, and his Improvement' at the Inn, but his legal studies 'never served him for other use than an Ornament and Self-satisfaction';[5] this is something of an exaggeration, since Donne would in a few years put his training to good use as a legal secretary, but is probably true of his feelings at the time he left the Inns of Court in the mid-1590s. He had acquired the necessary attributes of a gentleman, including a personal attendant. In July 1595, Donne graciously condescended to the 'speciall request and earnest intreatie' of one Christopher Danby 'to instructe and bring vpp one Thomas Danbye of the age of fifteene yeres or there aboutes'. Thomas was Christopher's younger 'naturall' brother – that is, an illegitimate sibling who was being pushed out of sight into service. Thomas was to be Donne's valet, and Donne was to be his guide and educator. Donne agreed to cover half the cost of the boy's keep, and gave him an additional allowance of 'fower shillings' a week to spend as he wished.[6]

Despite the increase in his expenses, Donne still shied away from committing himself to any profession. Though living just slightly beyond his means, he denounced those who studied for 'meere gaine' as being 'worse then imbrotheld strumpets prostitute'.[7]

One of Donne's best friends, Christopher Brooke, became one such 'strumpet'. He went on to practise law in York and seems not to have taken Donne's remark personally: Christopher and his brother Samuel, who became a priest (of the Reformed Church, not the Roman Catholic one), remained close to Donne, as did many of their set from the days at Lincoln's Inn. It might well have been the Brooke brothers who put Donne in touch with his servant, since the Danbys were also a Yorkshire family. The friendships Donne made as a law student had a strong literary dimension. Members of the set praised and consoled one another in poetry. There was Rowland Woodward, the son of a cockney vintner, and Everard Gilpin, a poetaster who turned shrewish when his career failed to develop. One friend, known only as Mr I. (or J.) L., was a gentleman from the north, already married: Donne wrote him verse letters, and cordially sent best wishes to his friend's 'lov'd wife'. Because I. L. lived in the country, Donne imagined a blissful pastoral existence for him. Each day, I. L. rose from his wife's 'embrace', and viewed his farm with its 'fat Beasts, stretched Barnes, and labour'd fields'; and then, Donne fancied, he would

> Eate, play, ryde, take all joyes which all day yeelds,
> And then againe to your embracements goe.[8]

There were times when Donne, fraught with or pursuing his affairs, envied this cyclical idyll: he could imagine an existence in which a man rose satiate from a woman's arms, surveyed his acres, took the air and then went back to where he had left off, in the same guaranteed clinch. But another male fantasy also had its attractions.

He was thinking of sailing away with Protestants. In 1595 Sir Walter Ralegh, the soldier, poet and favourite of the Queen, had led a colonial expedition to South America. Donne was entranced by the project. He was fascinated by the vast spaces that were still just appearing in partial outline in the European consciousness. He later met many of the men who went on the voyage, and followed closely the development of 'Guianaes rarities'.[9] Ralegh's account of the 'Bewtiful Empyre of Guiana' revealed a land with a wholly new spectrum, 'birds of all colours, some carnation, some crimson, orange tawny, purple, green . . . it was unto us a great good passing of the time to behold them.'[10] It had an unspoilt lushness: Ralegh claimed it was 'the most beautiful country that ever mine eyes beheld . . . plains of twenty miles in length, the grasses short and green, and in divers parts groves of trees by themselves, as if they had been by all the art and labour in the world so made of purpose.'[11] There was one other massive attraction: wealth. This was a country of gold as well as green. The emperor of Guiana, it was reported, possessed 'hollow statucs of gold which seemed giants, and the figures in proportion and bigness of all the beasts, birds, trees and herbs, that the earth bringeth forth.'[12]

On his way around London, Donne saw the evidence of an age of adventure. It had all the grubby sheen of a doubloon. You could not move far without encountering seadogs: men who boasted of a hundred voyages or more and a stash of booty, not to mention scars that could impress the lubbers in taverns and draw the sympathy of women. Donne saw them all the time, and they fleck his poetry here and there: 'Dunkirkers', pirates operating from just across the channel; a captain mopping up attention at Court, dressed in a gilded tunic, with the pay of forty dead men in his purse to blow on the pleasures of the town.[13] For all his sophistication, his library of unusual books and his own knowing poems, it is not difficult to imagine Donne as a young man looking around and feeling a certain lack in his urban, bookish pursuits. He had only to compare himself – however unwillingly – with his sister's husband, William Lyly, regarded with suspicious admiration by the Queen herself as one 'with a shrewd tongue and a shrewd head', a man used to danger in the courts of princes, to feel that there was more to be experienced beyond his law exercises.

Since the early days of Queen Elizabeth's reign, an unofficial trade war had been waged against the old enemy, Papist Spain, by individual loyalists and looters: these became known to historians as 'privateers'. The one difference between a privateer and a pirate captain was that the former carried an official 'letter of reprisal', issued by the English state. This authorized the captain to make good the losses he had suffered at Spanish hands by robbing any hostile merchant ship he might encounter on the high seas. There were a few notable incidents in which English ships had indeed been captured in Spanish ports and their crews imprisoned, but there were far more privateers than there could have been victims of such provocations. A 'letter of reprisal', if one came by it, was essentially a licence to plunder. For decades, English sailors had been capturing vessels bearing priceless loads to Spain from colonies in the Indies and South America. The privateers saw their efforts as being deeply patriotic: Spain cast 'Antichristian Papal Mists' across Europe and beyond, and its staunchly Roman Catholic King, Philip II, upheld an audacious claim to the English throne. He was the national foe. As such, missions of private but authorized piracy could blur with official military expeditions in defence of the realm. The most successful of these had been Sir Francis Drake's raids in 1587 on Spanish possessions at Cadiz, the Cape of St Vincent and Lisbon, a rampage that became known as 'The Singeing of the King of Spain's Beard', and from which Drake himself pocketed a cool £18,000.

It had been suspected for some time that King Philip was building another armada to invade England. Early in 1596, London buzzed with talk of a pre-emptive strike against the Spanish, a cruise for honour and fortune. The land forces would in all likelihood have as their Lord General Robert Devereux, the Earl of Essex, the apple of the Queen's eye and the favourite of all martially minded young men of quality. Like hundreds of others, Donne decided to join up. In terms of civic allegiance, this was decision time: signing up to the expeditionary force was a way of signalling just which side he was on, to himself as much as prospective employers and patrons, and any government agent who may have kept watch on him after his brother's treacherous association with the Roman Catholic ministry. It is likely, as Isaak Walton says, that Donne was at least introduced to Essex himself, since Henry Wotton, Donne's friend since Oxford, was one of the Earl's most valued secretaries.[14]

The Earl of Essex was a legend, the hero of flash young men 'with ladies' faces and with dragons' spleens'[15] – less for any tangible achievement than for his unfailing energy and panache. He had enjoyed his first full command in Normandy, at the age of just twenty-four, when English forces were sent to the aid of the French Protestant leader, Henri of Navarre. Essex began operations with a wild and quite unnecessary cavalry charge through enemy territory to clasp the hand of the dashing Navarre, who was something of a role model to him. He and Henri spent much of the remainder of his tour of duty in a personal competition of chivalry, athletics and inebriation. Essex never forgot the importance of victory, but was more concerned still that it be achieved with flair. A French eyewitness described Essex riding into Compiègne with six pages in attendance, 'mounted on chargers and dressed in orange velvet all embroidered with gold': the Earl himself 'had a cloak of orange velvet all covered with jewels' and his horses, needless to say, came with matching accessories.[16] Essex became associated with the Puritan faction in government, but this was a man who would not hold Donne's background against him. Anyone who embraced the cause and volunteered in the right spirit was welcome. Essex had nothing either against intellectuals: like Donne, he was also sent to university at a tender age, mainly because his father died when he was nine and Cambridge was a convenient orphanage. He graduated at the age of fourteen, then retired to a castle in Wales to bury himself in learning: later in life, he boasted of his bookishness.

On the surface, it is not difficult to see how Donne could have fallen into step with Essex's admirers. Although scathing about the excesses of fashion, the 'black feathers, or musk-coloured hose' sported by the city's young nitwits, he was far from dowdy: a dark suit of lace and satin, with a broad-rimmed feathered hat, was the costume he chose to be portrayed in around this time. He was also immensely graceful: 'He was of stature moderately tall, of a strait and equally-proportioned body, to which all his actions gave an unexpressible addition of Comeliness.'[17] He was just the kind of fellow that Essex liked to have around: Essex, a handsome man now in his late twenties, had both style and learning, and could recognize it in others. He does not, all the same, appear to have singled Donne out for any preference. From his first waking moment each day, Essex was pressed on all sides by business and appeals for favour, as Wotton shows in an account of the Earl's hectic morning routine:

His chamber being commonly stived with friends or suitors of one kind or other, when he was up, he gave his legs, arms and breast to his ordinary servants to button and dress him, with little heed; his head and face to the barber, his eyes to his letters, and ears to petitioners, and many times all at once; then the gentleman of his robes throwing a cloak over his shoulders, he would make a step into his closet, and after a short prayer he was gone.[18]

Such was the life of a Queen's favourite. Donne, like many others, was somewhat starstruck: he later referred to Essex as 'Our Earl'.[19]

After pledging himself as a voluntary for the voyage against the Spanish, Donne had time to work on his farewells. Much of Donne's writing is valedictory, recording, rehearsing, or perhaps making amends for separation. Because of the transfer of loyalties his action entailed, his enrolment in the mission was still more personally momentous than it may have been for most of his fellow volunteers. One early poem suggests that he was prepared to undergo a transformation. In his fifth elegy, which became known as 'His Picture', he upsets his lover by telling her what he will look like on returning from an expedition of the kind he was embarking on under Essex's command. He imagines himself returning as 'a sack of bones, broken within', weather-beaten, his soft hands tanned by a brutal sun, torn and hardened by oars, his skin burnt in places with the blue stains of gunpowder. To remind her of when he was 'faire and delicate', he thus gives her a picture of himself in the full flush of unspoilt youth. His partner worries, though, that his defects and injuries might contaminate *her*. 'Doe his hurts reach mee? doth my worth decay?' he imagines her wondering. Donne's conclusion and parting note is that growing up requires such change; they have to wean themselves from 'loves childish state'.[20] He was not only determined to grow, to refashion and reform himself, he accepted it as inevitable.

Events, meanwhile, were moving quickly. In March, the country was shaken by news that Sir Francis Drake's latest piratical cruise through the Indies was not going well. He and his lieutenant, John Hawkins, the great Plymouthian mariner and treasurer of the Admiralty, had lost a crucial battle at Puerto Rico. With this defeat, many Englishmen were captured, the much-loved Hawkins was dead, but most alarmingly of all, a clear route had opened up for huge Spanish frigates to bear thousands of tons of gold, silver and raw merchandise safely back to Spain, giving King Philip the capital he needed to raise and equip a massive military force. The shockwaves did not stop. At the end of the month, London was thrown into uproar and the English generals' plans into disarray when the Spanish sneaked a surprise attack on Calais, an English outpost for centuries, and took the port. Essex immediately felt that the planned expedition should be reoriented to take Calais back. He was dispatched post haste to Dover to make preparations. From across the English Channel, only a few miles away, he could hear the great guns booming as the Spanish forces sapped the last resistance of the garrison. The citadel in Calais was still holding out, but could only last days, even hours.

Back in London, gathering his kit, Donne saw a town going crazy with alarm and fury. Why, everyone asked, wasn't something being done, with Spanish Papists only a few miles off the coast? On 9 April, Good Friday, the men in the congregations emerged from church service to find themselves conscripted into an emergency army heading for Calais. They were mustered, but then, on Easter Sunday, the Queen changed her mind: the troops were dismissed. Wondering what was going on, Donne returned to his

lodgings with his armour on his back. Essex, furious with the
fireside generals who had persuaded the Queen to forsake Calais,
charged back to Court to bend her ear the other way. The hawks
prevailed, the mission was put back on, and Donne in all likelihood
joined more than three thousand gentlemen and commoners on
the march down to Dover. Across the water, explosions could still
be heard. Six new royal galleons sailed down the Thames and
along the coast to reinforce the English fleet. Then, on 15 April,
with everyone aboard, the cannons fell silent on the other side of
the channel.

Essex wailed with disappointment. The citadel had fallen, and
now the Spanish had unassailable control of the Channel port. It
would take a grinding siege of months or years to dislodge them
from Calais. This was unfeasible, partly because of the resources
such an operation would require, partly because a drastic counter-
strike was needed to reassure the English public with immediate
results, and partly because such a slow, painstaking campaign was
repulsive to Essex. The Earl had longed for a daring commando
landing: in an attack on Lisbon in 1589 he had plunged into the
chest-high surf, pike in hand, during a rush on the beaches, and
had, as his custom was, challenged the city governor to single
combat when the English troops were repelled. An adventure
like this at Calais was now impossible. So after more hesitation,
the Queen agreed to revert to the original plan. It was a rather
hazy one. In its most ambitious form, the idea was to knock out
the new Spanish armada at the island base of Cadiz; capture the
surrounding towns; if possible, push on to the Azores and sever
Spain's trade routes with its colonies in the New World. 'I know
God hath a great work to work by me,' wrote Essex solemnly.[21]
Preparations were still slow, however, and the Queen was not yet
entirely convinced that the mission was necessary. Week by week
in the spring of 1596, the fleet straggled down the coast to ready
itself at Plymouth, as the men rehearsed their manoeuvres on
the Hoe, the great headland overlooking the bay. On bad days,
obliterative drizzle swept through the ranks, out from the moors
beyond the town and in from the sea. On clear days they saw the

earth curve, as shoals of great hills stretched their backs towards the coast.

Eight years before, stationed off the Hoe in Plymouth Sound, Sir Francis Drake had received intelligence from a merchant vessel 'of a great Fleet of ships which came from Lishborne [Lisbon]'. The skipper and his crew could make out '150 or 200 sail' but 'so many as they could not nombre them . . . they could not see the Tail end.' Wall upon wall of giant Spanish galleons was being stacked against England. Writing to London from his swift light ship in the Sound, with Catwater Bay on one side and the forearm of Cornwall on the other, Drake was the serenest man in the country: 'I assure your good Lordshipe and protest it before God, that I find my Lord Admirall so well affected for all Honourable Services in this Action, as it doth Assure all His Followers of Good Success, and Hope of Victorie.'[22]

The armada, which was eventually scattered around Britain and Ireland by fierce storms, left the nation in profound shock. It also forced many English Roman Catholics to decide once and for all where their loyalties lay. Many, perhaps among them Donne's mother, would have welcomed the Spanish, because an invasion entailed the restoration of the old faith. Others, among them the ghost of Donne's pragmatic father, shrank from the loss of life and property that an occupation in the name of any religion would involve. Many Papists would desperately assert their patriotism. William Harrington, the priest and friend of Henry Donne, though convicted of treason, insisted that nothing could ever 'make me an enemy of my God, my prince, nor my country'.[23] These words were representative. But the threat from Spain only deepened the Protestant distrust of the Roman Catholic community: any Papist was regarded as an actual or potential collaborator. 1588 saw a new rash of illicit pro-Spanish literature circulating in London, works the authorities felt were 'forged with pestilent Calumniations'.[24]

Donne's second satire, written during the mid to late 1590s, declared that English Papists were 'poore, disarm'd' and 'not worth hate'.[25] Rather than saying Roman Catholics were despicable, Donne was saying there was no need to persecute them so vigorously. The satirical poetry he wrote in the 1590s reveals that he had grown ambivalent about all doctrinal claims to religious truth, whether Roman or Reformed, and suspicious of the political motives behind such claims. This ambivalence allowed him to consider his own political and moral position. Foreigners did perhaps need fighting, whatever their creed, when they mustered forces against a country he identified as his own. As we shall see, the poetry he wrote during his period of military service, while drawing out the comedy of boredom, disappointment and intermittent fright that life as a soldier involved, still identified firmly with the national mission against Spain. When Donne joined the expedition against the new armada in 1596, other motives besides patriotism no doubt played a part: his inheritance was running low, and his fortunes needed the boost that a share of the profits might bring; but such private gain, for one of Donne's rank, was uncertain to say the least, and subordinate to a public, political commitment to the national cause. By enlisting, he advertised himself to his peers and superiors as one who could be trusted to act on behalf of England rather than the Vatican.

For almost two months he spent much of the day training. It might well have come as a shock to his system: he was a skimpy young man, 'faire and delicate', unused to physical labour. Garrison life was also an eye-opener. The chronicler John Stow recorded that the generals 'gouerned their charge with very good Iustice and Martiall discipline'. Two English soldiers were hanged on the Hoe, with a note of each man's offence pinned to his chest. One had drawn his sword on his commanding officer. The other had tried to desert. In a Dutch regiment attached to the fleet, one soldier 'that had killed one of his companions, was by order of martiall law, tied to the party murthered, and thrown into the sea'.[26] Waiting for the Queen's final command, the camp grew tense.

In mid-April, the army and navy were hit by the news that Drake was dead. After the disaster at Puerto Rico and the loss of Hawkins, the piratical admiral had continued to scour the Caribbean for some scrap of success to bring home, insisting that they must find gold before they could see England once more. He saw no more of either; he died of dysentery, and was buried at sea. Back in Plymouth, Essex refused to be laid low, though he peppered for the order to leave. His officers were also getting tetchy. The senior staff consisted of a group of Elizabethan superstars – including Sir Walter Ralegh and the Lord Admiral, Charles Howard – each of whom felt he should be in sole command. Essex infuriated them all the more by heaping generous praise on their abilities in his reports back to London. He was so difficult to hate. The Earl was feeding his lieutenants and attendant gentlemen out of his own pocket, however, and this did grate a little. 'I have a little world,' he wrote to the Queen's secretary, 'eating upon me in my house.'[27]

Throughout May, the remnants of Drake's fleet made it back to England, shook off their tiredness and were incorporated into the new expeditionary force. At last the order came to leave. Essex was thrilled, and proud of his troops. One of his captains, Sir George Carew, boasted that they were strong enough 'to abide the proudest fleet that ever swam' and trounce 'a more puissant [powerful] enemy than we are like to find'. Moreover, they looked fantastic. At the head was Essex himself, in one of his amazing costumes. And his followers merited his approval: along with the experienced soldiers were 'three hundred green headed youths, covered with feathers, gold and silver lace'.[28] Among them was Donne: one of the boys. On 1 June, the fleet of over a hundred ships set sail.

And it returned, with some awkwardness, almost immediately. The wind blew the ships straight back to Plymouth. Some of the men, feeling the first lurch of seasickness and a pang of early nostalgia for the comforts they had left behind, thought that one last night in town might do them good; but Essex, annoyed by the cross weather, sent a message ordering the Lord Mayor's men to let no boats come ashore. On 2 June, the fleet tried setting out once more, to singe the King of Spain's beard.

How this was to happen was still not wholly clear. The captain of each ship had been given sealed secret orders on departure. A few weeks were spent picking up scraps of intelligence from friendly vessels the navy encountered on its way down to Cadiz, and picking fights with the occasional hostile ones. The English detained a flotilla of little Portuguese carvels, aboard one of which was a 'yong beggerly Fryer', a Catholic clergyman 'with a great packet of Letters for Lisbon'. He was brought aboard Essex's flagship, the *Due Repulse*, where the Earl was 'lying on a couch of brocade, dressed in white satin', with his officers in attendance. Essex scorned and humiliated the baffled young priest. The Earl promised to lay waste to the cleric's homeland, and reviled the ignorance and idolatry of the Catholic faith; the friar tried to respond that they were all Christians, but Essex shouted him down and called him a Papist dog.[29]

The raid itself on Cadiz was everything the green-headed youths involved could have wanted it to be. That autumn, when Donne resumed his place at the Mermaid tavern or in the humming chambers of the Court, he had a hoard of lurid and terrible new experiences to relate. He could tell of the horrific firefight in the broad bay of Cadiz, the Spanish galleons rigged with sails of flame. He could speak from first-hand knowledge of the famous characters who led the landing that followed. There was Essex himself, of course, the first to touch the shore, and Sir Francis Vere, the real tactician behind the operation; and then there was Sir John Wingfield, a desperate, depressive man, tormented by a rumour of past dishonour. During the voyage Wingfield told a friend that 'he had rather leave his life here than carry it into England'.[30] Donne could recount the story of how Essex and these lieutenants had led the men across the island of Cadiz over 'the dry deepe sliding sand' to take the main town on the isthmus, breaking its defences with a trick. A Spanish troop of five hundred was waiting for them outside the gates. But at Sir John Wingfield's bold suggestion, a plan was quickly worked out. An advance party led by Wingfield himself rushed forward, and then, after a brief clash, turned right around, pretending to retreat. The Spanish fell for it. They charged after Wingfield, who had stuck his pike through a Spanish colonel at the first encounter, and ran straight into the rest of the English force. Essex and his men then pursued the Spaniards back to the town, where the Earl himself led a small group that clambered up onto the decrepit battlements. A skirmish on the walls ensued, during which some of Essex's officers braved an eighteen-foot jump into the road below, and urged the Earl to follow. Yet Essex baulked at making the drop.

Donne, like every other volunteer who told the tale, might have had to explain why his commander held back. Essex's critics seized on this as a moment of indecision and lily-liveredness; but Donne was one of 'our Earl''s defenders. The general, he would explain, could not risk leaving the army leaderless. Anyway, there was much more of the story still to share. There was the chaotic streetfight for the Plaza when the town gates were finally breached, with the women of Cadiz hurling stones at the English from the roofs of their houses; and there was the suicidal valour of Sir John Wingfield. He took a bullet in the thigh outside the gates, but refused to let that stop him. Mounting a horse, he charged towards the Plaza, disdaining the calls to get down and take cover, until a Spanish musketeer blew his brains out and ended his 'mighty malcontent'. Donne penned an admiring epigram in the Quixotic knight's honour: many, he said, had travelled beyond the Pillars of Hercules, the Straits of Gibraltar, towards the very cradle of the sun, but 'Farther than Wingfield', he said, 'no man dares to goe'.[31]

Yet more stood out for telling. There was the sunken but dignified air of the governor of Cadiz, the gloomy Duke of Medina-Sidonia, as he surrendered the town and let Charles Howard, the sympathetic Lord Admiral, pay his ransom for him. The Duke had led the armada in 1588 and had been unfairly blamed for its loss ever since. He had suffered for years the taunts of children who twanged his nerves by shouting 'Viene el Draque!' – 'Drake's coming!' – under his windows; and now he was burdened with another national failure on home ground.

The citizens of Cadiz were allowed to keep nothing more than the clothes they stood up in; the streets were strewn with fruit and vegetables, slicked with wine and oil knocked over in the scramble for more durable loot. For 'the king had also much rich merchandice in his Duanias or Warehouses, and a great deale of treasure in the castle, all of which shoulde haue been preserued . . . for her maiesty by her right, if some had, or could have performed the trust committed to them.'[32] Instead, it was a case of finders keepers: too much private capital had been invested in the mission for the Queen's 'right' to be paramount. The raiders picked Cadiz clean and left it in flames; they spent the rest of the summer moving along the Portuguese coast, and took the town of Faro, where the men sunned themselves before firing the place, having seized the contents of the library in the bishop's residence. Donne must have itched to possess many of the rare and precious volumes, but Essex claimed the whole lot; he later donated the collection to the Bodleian library in Oxford. Elsewhere, his men took everything they could, even down to 'some fruits, some wines and a few hennes'. There were also 'some pieces of great Ordinance' to be requisitioned: the gun-lovers cooed over the chief prize in the cache, 'the fairest and largest Culuerin which the King of Spaine had, as it was esteemed'.[33]

4. The Islands

A portrait made when Donne was in his mid-twenties shows him as a handsome, affluent character. His suit and broad cavalier hat are black − or dun; the costume is expensive and exquisite, with an intricate lace collar and a gold-feathered motif on the sleeve of the mantle. Donne in this portrait has been interpreted as having the 'pose of a melancholy lover'. The picture, as Donne himself described it, is 'taken in Shaddowes'.[1] But his air is more haughty and thoughtful than morose. He has his arms folded, with one willow-fingered hand in view, supporting his elbow; and his head is turned sharply to the right of the looker, avoiding eye contact, gazing wryly at something or somewhere way in the distance.

The costume he wears in this painting is the uniform of a 'voluntary'. After the raid on Cadiz, Donne continued his old pursuits − there were long-needed friends, partners and books to renew acquaintance with. But he was also depressed. He found the tatty glamour of the Court increasingly repellent, and his satirical writing in the late 1590s became more and more appalled. Donne spoke of the Court as a vision of hell, a centre of vanity and corruption. He disembarked from the rankling male stench below decks into a city where conditions were an extension of those aboard ship. There was the same density of detritus and fodder but no ocean outside, no orange and magenta dusks. The poor lay on pallets of straw on the streets and died there like beasts; the houses tilted over open sewers. The sharp courtier in Donne's portrait was cushioned from such deprivation, but he still had to pick his way through it. He was scared of disease, and was stalked by it, in thoroughfares where 'Infections follow, overtake and meet.'[2]

His lifestyle came with risks. Syphilis, the 'pox', was rife, and there were no effective precautions. Some people experimented desperately with sheep's intestines, but no efficient prophylactic would appear in Donne's lifetime. He kept imagining himself dead, as a result of love. In 'The Apparition', he rebuked the promiscuous mistress who was killing him with her 'scorn', and promised that his ghost would come after her. 'Then thy sicke taper will begin to winke,' Donne warned; she was already ailing, 'sick', her lights low, and her new bedmate would be no use to her.[3] With Donne's ghost hovering above, she would try to wake his replacement by nudging and pinching; but the exhausted lover would shrink away, afraid that she was urging him 'for more'. Donne cruelly and comically enjoyed the prospect of her as a quivering 'poore Aspen wretch . . . Bathed in a cold quicksilver sweat', but he too was afraid.[4] His eye for venereal sickness was implicated in what it diagnosed. The woman's signs of fear (and sexual exertion) – her 'cold quicksilver sweat' – were symptoms of high fever: those with syphilis fought the disease by exposing their skin to the fumes of mercury in toxic sweatbaths.[5]

Donne frequently tried to set himself and his loves apart from the general mass of disease-ridden concupiscence. In some poems his affairs belonged not to stinking London, but to imaginary, distant locations. 'Come live with mee, and bee my love,' he beckoned, a little sardonically, in 'The Baite', offering a haven 'Of golden sands, and christall brookes'.[6] This was the bright setting of Cadiz or Faro, in contrast to the sludgy realities of English fishing along the Thames or at a Plymouth harbour.

> Let others freeze with angling reeds,
> And cut their legges, with shells and weeds . . .
> Let coarse bold hands, from slimy nest
> The bedded fish in banks out-wrest.[7]

He contemplated the slippery procedures on a real riverbank with the same vividness he brought to the 'silken lines, and silver hookes' that he and his lover were to use at their holiday retreat, but he wanted to get away from the mud of his native shores. Donne's drives were expansive: his lover undressed, and her body became the New World.

> O my America! My new-found-land,
> My kingdome, safeliest when with one man man'd,
> My myne of precious stones: My Emperie,
> How blest am I in this discovering thee![8]

Donne never went to the Americas. But when the chance came to join another expedition the year after the raid on Cadiz, this time targeting Ferrol and the Azores, Donne followed his conquering urges and joined up again. Explaining to his friend Christopher Brooke his reasons for going, Donne blamed 'a rotten state, and hope of gaine', along with 'the queasie paine / Of being belov'd'.[9] He was blotting out his home, and blotting out the real person – whoever she was – that he was sleeping with.

Donne's idea of the woman's body as a colony was arrogantly imperious – a deliberate, ribald provocation – but also openly neurotic. If this was a landscape possessed and exploited, it was also one that, as he knew very well, could confound, bewilder and bury the explorer alive. Elsewhere he made it a nervous archetype of female unruliness.

> The hair a forest is of ambushes,
> Of springes, snares, fetters and manacles . . .[10]

Donne imagined himself as a sexual explorer and colonist, but equally as a small stupid fowl in a masochistic forest of bondage, a rabbit caught in a 'springe' – a hunter's trap. Men could get lost in the woods or go missing at sea:

> The brow becalms us when 'tis smooth and plain,
> And when 'tis wrinckled shipwracks us again.[11]

Many rash young men found it easier to cope with seasickness than the complications of a relationship at home; and some underestimated the power of a frown on the real ocean's brow. As the troops assembled again at Plymouth in the early summer of 1597, the new fleet was joined by Sir Antony Sherley, returning 'alive but poor' from a disastrous excursion. His marriage was unhappy, and it was said by one fellow sailor that living with his wife made Sherley 'undertake any course that might occupy his mind from thinking on her vainest words'. A year before, Sherley had set out with a flotilla of five ships and a private army of over three hundred to see what was worth taking on the coast of Guinea. Two months into the voyage his crew-members started dropping like flies. Turning north to Cape Verdes, Sherley led an insane raid on Santiago that gave him nothing to show but more dead men. There followed a horrendous Atlantic crossing to Dominica, and a tour of Jamaica that still failed to provide any great bounty. Then, after an abortive attempt on Honduras, determined 'to doe some memorable thing', Sherley proceeded into the Golfo Dulce and decided to lead his remaining men on a tortuous march across the mountains of Guatemala. He was hoping to reach the South Sea, but for his beleaguered followers this was the last straw. When the mad trek failed, and Sherley suggested they get fresh supplies at Newfoundland, before proceeding 'by very good policie' to the Straits of Magellan, his fleet abandoned him. Sherley's battered ship was left to struggle on its own back to Plymouth, where he straightaway signed up for the Earl of Essex's new adventure against Spain.[12]

To the rookies gathering at the port, such catastrophic stories were glorious: it was the tale that mattered, not the failure. Enthused by what was seen as a triumph at Cadiz the year before, there were even more volunteers for the expedition in 1597. A force of over six thousand packed into Plymouth, along with five hundred gentleman 'voluntaries', again including Donne. A chronicler described them as 'very gallant persons . . . brauely furnished of all things necessary (besides superfluitie in gold lace, plumes of feathers and such like.)'[13] The plumes drooped and wilted a little, though, as the fleet's departure was delayed by continued bad weather. In 'The Storme', a verse letter to Christopher Brooke that became one of his most popular poems, Donne spoke of how everyone waited 'withering like prisoners' in the dock. On 9 July, the fleet set off, and enjoyed plain sailing for about two days. He observed the mainsail fatten like a stomach full of food, or a belly swelling with a miracle pregnancy, as his ship rushed for Spain;[14] the verse itself swelled up with new patriotism for 'England, to whom we owe, what we be, and have'.[15] In the other major poem he wrote on this voyage he took a swipe at the 'rotten state', but a distinction evidently existed in Donne's mind between government and country. On the surface at least, he believed in what he was doing.

The plan was to attack Ferrol, and then move on to the Azores, to hijack the annual fleet of cargo ships from the Indies. But on the third day of sailing, the fleet was caught up and scattered by one of the most frightening experiences of Donne's life. 'The South and West winds joyned,' he wrote, 'and, as they blew, / Waves like a rowling trench before them threw.'[16] Not being an active seaman himself, Donne could do little but observe the other gentle-man passengers fretting and bawling. His obsession with death was given new subject matter: the ships, he realized, were 'woodden Sepulchers'. He listened to the crying from private quarters.

> Some coffin'd in their cabbins lye, equally
> Griev'd that they are not dead, and yet must dye.
> And as sin-burden'd soules from graves will creepe,
> At the last day, some forth their cabbins peepe.[17]

It seemed like Judgement Day, the Apocalypse: the thirsty, 'hydrop-tic' sun had surely evaporated an entire sea, and it was now cascading back on top of them. There was no light except for the light-ning, and no sound but thunder.[18] Darkness was reigning, and the whole Creation had collapsed into a single gloop of 'uniforme de-formity'.[19] Yet certain things reminded Donne of home. The green-horns emerging from their cabin-coffins to ask for news were 'Like jealous husbands', asking to hear what they would rather not know. The tackle and rigging were snapped like lute strings. The ship itself suffered like a victim of the 'rotten state' Donne had left behind:

> And from our totterd sailes, ragges drop downe so,
> As from one hang'd in chaines, a yeare agoe.[20]

The ships tottered back into Plymouth with battered masts groaning like cruciform prisoners. Many of the volunteers were shaken and broken. The account of the voyage given by Sir Arthur Gorges, the captain of Ralegh's ship, says that 'many of our Gentlemen and Knights, with this boisterous and bitter entertainment on the Seas, returned extreame weake and lay dangerously sicke long after: Insomuch that some of them dyed thereof at Plimouth, and were there honourably buried of the Generall.' For a tough seadog like Gorges, such fragility was an embarrassment. He commented tartly that the 'boysterous winds and mercilesse Seas, had neither affinitie with London delicacie, nor Court bravery.' Many of the young gentlemen voluntaries, 'discharging their high plumes, and imbroydered Cassockes . . . secretly retired themselves home, forgetting either to bid their friends farewell, or to take leave of their generall.'

Donne, however, was one of those who stayed. He was becoming close to Thomas Egerton, a contemporary from Lincoln's Inn who was also the son of one of the most powerful men in the kingdom. Spirits in the fleet got an occasional lift: just when the 'unseasonable stinking Caske[s]' were running low, says Gorges, 'as God would . . . there came very happily into Plimouth for a supply, a tall prize laden with Spanish Canary Wines, which was distributed.'[21] Confiscated Spanish plonk could not, however, dispel the troops' impatience altogether. The addled ships were patched up soon enough, but the weather did not improve for weeks.

It would now be too late in the year to intercept the Spanish convoys bearing gold from South America and the West Indies; and the Queen turned down Ralegh and Essex's request to attack the Caribbean colonies. A rich crop had been lost, as Donne complained in verse to Rowland Woodward:

> Guyanaes harvest is nip'd in the spring,
> I feare; And with us (me thinkes) Fate deales so
> As with the Jewes guide God did; he did show
> Him the rich land, but bar'd his entry in:
> Oh, slowness is our punishment and sinne.[22]

They were like Moses; that is, tantalized with a glimpse of the Promised Land, but not allowed to enter. Donne found the daily reality of military life boring in the extreme. 'If, as mine is, thy life a slumber be,' he told Woodward, 'Seeme, when thou read'st these lines, to dreame of me.'

Stuck again at Plymouth, where the tavern- and brothel-keepers eagerly bled the young voluntaries dry of their spending money, Donne also wrote in a more jocose vein to a friend whose name is not preserved. In this his first surviving letter in prose, Donne wearily but playfully outlined conditions in the port. Even Jonah, he remarked, was not 'troubled with the stinke of 150 soldiers as I'. The troops were barracked aboard ship, and even if Donne had a cabin to himself there was no way of escaping the by-products of trapped men who probably never washed much at the best of times. It was pretty rank in there. The ovens and hearths were loose brick constructions installed above the bilge, the flat part of the ship's bottom that filled with filth and stale water; the food was unspeakable. The options on shore were not so wonderful either. Donne went on in his letter to complain about Plymouthian hospitality: 'I think when wee came in the burghers [townsfolk] tooke us for the spanish fleet.'

The harbour did indeed have a reputation for stripping vessels bare and leaving crews to fend for themselves. Plymouth pirates would head out of the Sound, capture frigates belonging to enemy – that is, Papist – states, and tow them back into Catwater or even right up the river Tamar to clean them out. This had been going on for decades: in March 1569, a Flemish vessel had been taken into the harbour and lovingly robbed of every last farthing it contained. The crew were turfed out onto the Barbican; none of the locals would help them. After begging at the doors of churches, the stranded Flemish men 'never got a penny', reads one contemporary account, 'and would have starved if it had not been for a countrywoman [of theirs] dwelling in the town.'[23]

Donne felt a bit like one of these fugitives. He was also intrigued to see how the community of hungry, penniless but expensively turned-out men was coalescing in the harbour. All the trappings

of Elizabethan society were becoming worthless. No one had been
paid, and 'he that hath 2 or 3 shillings is a king'. Lands, fine tunics
and knighthoods 'are reprobate pawnes,' Donne wrote, 'and but
for the much gay clothes (which yet are much melted) I should
thinke wee were in vtopia: all are so vtterly coyneles [coinless].'

Utopia was the distant island society imagined over eighty years
earlier by Sir Thomas More, Donne's great-great-uncle. It was
a moneyless state, the economy thriving instead by a mutual
exchange of goods and services. There was no pomp and ceremony
on Utopia, no 'gay clothes'. The Utopian marriage laws were
liberal, permitting divorce. There was no paranoia about invasion
from overseas, and no internal anxiety about religious or political
differences: the system worked so well that no one in Utopia felt
the need to be different. The island society crops up in the letter
from Plymouth as a casual reference; Donne knew that his correspondent would pick up on it and understand him perfectly.
Biographically, though it meant rather more to Donne than it
probably did to his reader.

There were good reasons for Sir Thomas More's status as the
prize heirloom of Donne's maternal family. More was an awesome
intellect, one of the most brilliant lawyers of his day and a prodigious writer, who rose to possess immense political power. He
was also a Roman Catholic of almost masochistic devoutness. He
often felt that he should have been a priest and for many years
wore a hair shirt beneath his fine garments and robes of state. As
he witnessed the early signs of dissatisfaction with the old Catholic
faith, the imaginative liberality of *Utopia* became increasingly alien
to More. At heart More was a conservative. He created his myth
about the island state fairly early in his career, before the growing
unrest at home and the frightening progress of Reformation abroad
entrenched his support for the old religious structures. Utopia was
the very country that its creator helped to prevent England from
ever becoming. He was instrumental in the first phase of a conflict
that would shape Donne's whole life. For More, the Roman
Church had served England well for hundreds of years, and there
was no need to change it. Indeed no one in his view had any

right to do so. The Church's sanctity put it beyond all human modification. But many felt the old rituals needed revising; many wanted to interpret the scriptures for themselves. Many had despised for years the stereotypic laziness, illiteracy and loose living of Catholic priests, like the two who brawled in All Hallows Church, near Donne's birthplace in Bread Street, in 1532.

More was prepared to oppose this new spirit of protest, this Protestantism, at all costs: for him, it was the work of the devil. As Henry VIII's Chancellor, he sent many people who believed in the Protestant heresy to die in flames. Yet his days were numbered as soon as King Henry decided that he wanted to divorce the Queen, Katharine of Aragon. The Pope would not allow this, so Henry broke with Rome, declared himself the spiritual leader of the English people, and initiated a Reformation of the national Church – unleashing a process that actually went much further than he desired. More scoffed at the idea of the syphilitic King as an English pontiff, then paid the price for his intransigence. He was beheaded in 1535.

More's martyrdom set a rather difficult example for his successors to follow. He haunted Donne for years, not as a genocidal zealot, but as 'a man of the most tender and delicate conscience, that the world saw, since *Aug*: [St Augustine]'.[24] Now, as a Protestant serviceman, the base at Plymouth seemed like a comic Utopia to Donne. As he wandered the Barbican and the steep streets of the town, his greatest ancestor was still with him; still with him, disapprovingly, as Donne tried chatting up local girls, offering valuable but useless trinkets in exchange for a drink or a bite to eat. Plymouth, in a province that would bear the brunt of any Spanish invasion, was fiercely Protestant: it had been the launching point for private vendettas against the Catholic enemy since the early days of the Reformation. One of the town's most popular drinking holes was called the Pope's Head, partly owned by one of Plymouth's greatest seadogs, the late lamented John Hawkins. Such taverns fostered a mythic camaraderie that was savoured for many years afterwards. One local historian of the nineteenth century imagined the Elizabethan adventurers as they 'drank the rare wines, and smoked in pipes of precious metals the newly-discovered tobacco. Richly appareled in silk, laces and velvets were these gentlemen, and armed with delicately tempered rapiers that bore the stain of many a confident and fatal thrust. They drank as heavily as devoutly they prayed, and swaggered as hilariously as fervently they toasted their maiden Queen.'[25]

That was all well and good if one got the jokes and felt the fervour; but Donne didn't, quite. He couldn't, not yet. The poems he wrote during the 1597 campaign preserve a fine but definite and calculated division between the homeland – 'England, to whom we owe, what we be, and have' – and the powers running it, 'a rotten state'.[26]

In mid-August, with repairs as complete as they were going to be and the weather more favourable at last, Essex, Ralegh and Howard took their squadrons out to sea again. It was a sluggish start. The ships had to be towed by long-boats out of the harbour, says Gorges, 'the wind being somewhat slacke and scant'.[27] The plan had grown almost impossibly fuzzy: the commanders were now authorized 'to range the coast of Spain and so do some service on some of the King of Spain's shipping'. By patrolling the area between the Cape of St Vincent and Lisbon, it was hoped that they 'might intercept some Indian fleet or carracks'.[28] The commanders took this order to 'service' Spanish shipping as a licence to chase and plunder whatever came their way, or wherever they got to. Essex especially had his eye on the crucial stations way beyond the coast of Spain, the Azores. But the fleet was hampered yet again by foul storms.

The worst casualty was the *Saint Matthew*, a galleon captured from the Spanish and now under the command of Sir George Carew. Four men were killed when the rigging snapped and the fore and main masts toppled and were swept overboard. Two anchors were broken and the third fell loose into the sea. The ship with its company of seven hundred now had no means of mooring itself safely or guiding itself on the wind. Other ships closed in to assist, but Carew refused to leave and would not let any of his men go either, 'having a more tender care of the losse of his Honour, then of the Hazard of his Life'.[29] The crippled galleon eventually made it back to Portsmouth where, 'not any thing dismayd with past perills', Carew requisitioned another bark, the *Adventure*. This too was presently blown off course, collided with a stray Spanish warship off south-east Ireland, was swept back and was eventually wrecked on the Sussex coast.[30]

Meanwhile, the others pushed on. This time Donne seems to have been aboard one of the ships in Sir Walter Ralegh's squadron, which became separated from the rest of the fleet because of damage suffered by Ralegh's flagship, the *Warspite*. Essex, whose own ship, the *Due Repulse*, had been troubled with an awkward leak, found its way to Finisterre. Ralegh's squadron, however, was diverted to 'The Rock' – Lisbon. Spotting the English ships on the horizon, mindful of the attack on Cadiz the year before, the Portuguese braced themselves.

It was busy aboard ship. The transport was packed with nearly two hundred men, and loud with the hauling and heaving of a working vessel. But Donne was not part of this activity. As an infantry volunteer he had no official fatigues: he was a passenger. Any books he had with him must have been long-finished after the delay at Plymouth, and conversation with other bedraggled beaux running dry. News of the mission's progress took days to arrive, and when it came it did so by a hoarse shout or a musket signal from vessel to vessel, passed about in a caterwauled game of Chinese whispers. There was, however, the excitement of the regular attempt to gather intelligence from the fleet of little Portuguese carvels that sailed past the squadron each day. These light ships, says Gorges, 'would daily come swarming about us like Butter-flyes, so neere, as that we might cast a stone into some of them, and yet could wee never catch any one of them, so yare and nimble as they are.'[31] Eventually, Ralegh got word that Essex had set off towards the Azores, having been informed that a Spanish fleet was being armed there and a convoy of frigates would stop off for supplies with the year's haul of wealth from the Indies. To the relief of the population of Lisbon, Ralegh's squadron headed after Essex, and raised the island of Tercera on 7 September.

The Azores is an archipelago of nine tropical islands in three groups, with two to the west, Flores and Corvo; two to the east, San Miguel and the smallest island, Santa Maria; and a central cluster of five – with Graciosa and Tercera to the north, Fayal and Pico to the south and one other, San Jorge, in the stretch between them. A great hive-shaped volcano overlooks Tercera, the principal island. Together they form a maze in which a whole fleet, Gorges said, 'could passe by unseene or unheard of'.[32] Following directions given by an English merchant vessel they had met on the way, the squadron began looking for the Spanish frigates and Essex's part of the fleet. As Ralegh's ships approached San Jorge, however, the wind dropped and the sea turned to glass. They were stuck.

Donne described the few days that followed in another verse letter for Christopher Brooke, 'The Calme', a poem which tells us for sure that Donne was among Ralegh's forces this time rather than Essex's. Along with its companion piece, 'The Storme', this was one of the poems by Donne that his contemporaries liked best. One admirer later wrote:

> The *Storme* describ'd, hath set thy name afloate,
> Thy *Calme*, a gale of famous winde hath got.[33]

The experience itself was gruelling. The ships, said Donne, were as rooted as the islands they sought; they were 'Venices', marooned cities. Instead of useless sails, the rigging was decked with 'seamens ragges' – the troops' laundry. Not a single mote stirred in the heavy air: 'in one place lay Feathers and dust, today and yesterday'.[34] A swim in the hot sea was no more refreshing than bathing in brimstone, so instead of diving Donne lifted his mind on a thermal, to a bird's eye view of the stranded squadron. From up high, where the air was cooler, the ships were like ants on the back of a dead reptile; then they were 'finny chips', scraps of dead fish or pieces of flotsam. Back down below, aboard the sea-prisons themselves, the men were going crazy, grilling themselves on deck or sweltering in their hammocks.[35] Young hotheads who had come along for a thrill and some money were close to despair. There were arguments, restrained only by the severe punishment that awaited brawlers. 'Deare friends', Donne jibed, were now drawn together only by 'calenture', delirium.[36] The pitch was melting and ungluing in the seams of the ship like molten lead pouring from the roof of a 'fir'd Church' – a memory of those stripped down and burnt during the Reformation.[37] The stagnation also afflicted Donne with a feeling of larger human futility: 'Wee have no power, no will, no sense,' he bleated, then changed his mind: he was not yet senseless. 'I lye – I should not then thus feele this miserie.'[38]

For the more experienced hands it was not so bad. Sir Arthur Gorges merely mentions that 'we were very much becalmed for a day or two'.[39] Donne could not shrug off the ordeal as easily as that: not only was he physically unprepared for the tropical heat, the dead calm was temperamentally abhorrent to him. He found it much harder to endure than the storm. He was a naturally energetic, unresting person, avoiding fatigue by moving efficiently between tasks and pastimes. In England, he swam from books to friend, from friend to lady, organizing his day by drastic switches in surroundings – from the study to the street, to the Court, or the theatre, or the tavern, to the bedroom. This was denied him now, and he was also deprived of the compensatory shift of the floor with the waves, the rhythm of timbers that changed with the pitch of the sea. Donne's poems make a continual appeal for 'variety', 'progress' – 'Waters stinck soon,' he warned, 'if in one place they bide, / And in the vast sea are more putrifi'd.' His days of scorching stillness off the Azores made such statements all the more trenchant. 'Change,' Donne insisted, 'is the nursery / Of musicke, joy, life and eternity.'[40] He wanted an unending power to mutate, to inhabit different forms and see things differently: 'The heavens,' after all, he said, 'rejoyce in motion'; so 'why should I / Abjure my so much lov'd variety . . . ?'[41]

Yet the heavens put on a display unlike anything the men had seen before. The ship was almost alongside the moon, which was so huge and low that it was 'then almost fallen with the Horison'. Gorges observed 'a large and perfect Rainbow by the

Moone light, in the bignesse and forme of all other Rainbowes, but in colour much differing, for it was more whitish, but chiefly inclining to the colour of flame of fire'. This miracle provoked much discussion among the well-read officers. They referred to their memory of the classics to explain it. Pliny, Gorges observed, 'denieth any Rainbow' except in sunlight; 'and yet Aristotle reporteth for a raritie, that in his time there *was* a Rainbow seene by night'. The learned men chatting in the cooler air, as the midnight sky glowed, could only agree that while Solomon said there was nothing new under the sun, 'yet all things have not bin knowne in all places, and to all men alike'.[42] The desire to know about 'rarities' was one of their main reasons for embarking in the first place: Donne was not without kindred inquisitive, thoughtful spirits aboard.

But they had also sailed in hope of booty, and most were grievously disappointed. When the wind rose again, Ralegh's squadron finally met with Essex, and began to hunt the archipelago for the Spanish treasure ships; but then got separated again in the labyrinth of islands. Ralegh travelled southward, waiting for Essex to rejoin him, and moored off the heavily fortified island of Fayal, where the Spanish troops hung out a red flag of defiance and shouted jeers across the bay. Ralegh's men, who had gone without fresh food for more than a month, had taken no fresh water aboard since leaving Plymouth, and had not a penny to show for their hardships, went berserk: they threatened to mutiny if Ralegh did not authorize an armed landing. Ralegh agreed, resolving either to 'win our landing, or gaine a beating'.[43] A hundred and sixty soldiers packed into long-boats and rowed ashore under heavy enemy fire. Their spirits failed, however, as the air exploded round their feathered plumes: 'the shot plaied so thicke . . . that in truth the Mariners would scarce come forwards, having the lesser liking to the businesse, the neerer they came to it.'[44] But there was no going back. The men clambered desperately onto the rocks and then surprised themselves with an unlikely victory in the skirmish that followed on the shore. His pride restored, Ralegh led the men on a four-mile march inland to capture Fayal's main town.

The men tramped slavering across a country of 'pretty little rising hils, and all the fields over full of Mellons, Potatoes, and other Fruites'.[45] The island town was protected, however, by two strong forts, and many of the men were mown down the following day when the troop attacked the first of these, which was positioned on a steep hill. Ralegh took an advance party of forty, 'Gentlemen of the best sort', to the bottom of the slope, expecting the rest to provide support from behind. They let him down. Peppered with musket and cannon fire, they instead 'fell to running flat in stragling manner' to the relative cover of the trenches at the base of the fort, almost overtaking Ralegh's platoon on the way there.[46] Many years later Donne alluded to an experience of this nature. 'We have all been in Wars,' he told his male listeners, 'and seen men fall at our right hand, and at our left, by the Bullet.'[47] As gunfire cracked about them, one shot ventilating the loose cloth of Ralegh's breeches but miraculously taking nothing with it, their commander called for volunteers to scout for a way past the fort and on to the town. The laced gallants deafened their leader with silence. If he was present, Donne kept his hands firmly over his ears and elbows on the ground: he was not mentioned in dispatches. Ralegh snorted indignantly, and undertook the reconnaissance himself, accompanied only by Gorges and a few others who felt suddenly guilty. A passage beyond the fort was found, and the troop slipped past it to the town, where they were bitterly disappointed. There was nothing to pilfer. The place was abandoned, 'bare of all things, but of such wares as could not suddenly be removed: which was Wine, Salt, and Corne.'[48] But the relief of being alive was some compensation. In camp the night before a rumour had gone around that the island held more than a thousand men ready to take arms. Yet the fort, it seemed, had been an isolated pocket of resistance.

They still had to get back past it to their ships, however, and while many of the voluntaries hoped they might nip quietly back by the way they had come, Ralegh's blood was up. He decided they would attack the fort. The suicidal mission was put off only when scouts reported that Essex's ships had appeared beyond the headland. Essex outranked Ralegh; he could not continue without further orders, and was in fact rebuked for proceeding so far without his superior's permission. Inexcusably for Essex, Ralegh had taken the lion's share of the mission's scarce glory.

There were no triumphant tales or trophies this time to carry back to London. Only stories of near misses and debates over who was at fault for the flop the mission turned out to be. Much acrimony, for example, surrounded an attack that never happened on the island of San Miguel. The English anchored outside Punta Delgada, the coastal garrison town, but Ralegh's memory of the chaotic landing at Fayal urged him against a direct attempt on the bay's treacherous rocky places. So while Ralegh kept the bulk of the fleet making threatening noises where it was, Essex took a few ships around to the eastern side of the island. At least, that was what he said he was going to do. The plan was that Essex would lead a force inland and attack Punta from behind. However, a westerly wind blew the detachment on around the coast to Villa Franca, a beautiful little village with a very convenient landing place. It was a paradise, 'being seated in a pleasant soyle, full of fruits, wines, and fresh victualls, and the Sellars stuffed so full of Oade and Wheat';[49] and Essex's men took full benefit of it. They enjoyed a six-day break in a pleasure resort, feasting together and bathing in the turquoise waters.

A few leagues around the coast, Ralegh's men festered. Donne was one of multitudes who had no idea what was happening. The ship had taken root again, it creaked in the choppy bay and yet went nowhere. There was a dead weight of mouldy biscuit in Donne's stomach. His guts were full of foul water and what even Gorges described as 'very vile and unsavoury' beer; his nerves were yanked at irregular intervals by the cannon blasts that ships let off occasionally to relieve tempers and keep the Spanish garrison on its toes. A life of supposed adventure, Donne was coming to realize, was little different to a life of containment in a home. 'To mew me in a Ship,' he complained, 'is to inthrall Mee in a prison'; it was like being confined

> in a Cloyster; save that there men dwell
> In a calme heaven, here in a swaggering hell.[50]

It had been months since Donne had peace and time among his books, or access to more. He could leave his cabin and gaze into a limitless heaven, lit up with the distortions of an alien atmosphere: there were light shows and shooting stars at night, moon-made rainbows, but no fresh currents of talk or books, no women. The swagger was under serious strain. The men were varnished with perspiration; frustrated in a carapace of dust and sweat, Donne could only miserably remember the fragrant oils of female skin, like 'the sweet sweat of Roses in a Still . . . the Almighty Balme of th'early east'; the drops on breast and throat 'like Pearl Coronets'.[51] It was all getting too much. And there was no hope or sign of the real perfumes, spices and pearls that the voluntaries had come out hoping to capture.

Meanwhile, Essex and his men were still missing. Writing up his account of the voyage, Gorges could barely contain himself: 'they never so much as sent word, to make us partakers,' he complained. Ralegh's contingent did, nonetheless, have one shot at a coup that would have wiped the grin off every well-fed face in Essex's party. A giant carrack from the East was bearing down on Delgada. This was one of the greatest and rarest prizes of all: it would be brimming with spices, drugs and perfumes, calicoes, carpets and silks, rubies, emeralds, diamonds. The English ships immediately lowered their flags to avoid being identified. 'They waited,' as J. S. Corbett put it, 'licking their lips.'[52] The carrack was theirs; it was almost within striking distance. Then an accidental cannon shot from somewhere in the fleet gave it a warning and the bay dinned with a thousand-fold cry of rage and disappointment. The captain of the carrack realized that there was a trap. On a lucky change of wind, the cumbersome giant was able to turn, and run itself aground on the headland. The English sobbed, spat and howled as the huge ship crunched into the rocks, where the Spaniards could salvage its cargo before they, three or four miles off, could get anywhere near it.

5. Captain Donne

After the frustrating expedition to the Azores, the bedraggled English fleet got back to Plymouth late in the autumn of 1597. The Earl of Essex came ashore to find the town and the country in a state of near hysteria. Spain had mustered another armada, which had given the English force the slip and gathered off the south coast just a few days before. Then, to the all too familiar dismay of the Spanish commander, another fit of stormy weather scattered the galleons, and Essex sailed in blithely a day or so later, completely oblivious to the threat that he had originally been dispatched to remove. He could not believe it, and was slightly embarrassed at the mix-up. He sent a defiant burst of bluster to the English Court, urging Elizabeth and her officials to keep calm. He vowed to set off again immediately, in pursuit of the blown-about armada. One can almost hear Donne and the other worn-out voluntaries groan across the centuries, but Essex was determined: 'Though we eat ropes' ends and drink nothing but rainwater, we will out.' He was thwarted, however, by the weather. The wind stubbornly refused to let the English ships put back out to sea. 'I will instantly out with as many ships as I can,' Essex wrote, but had to admit that at 'this hour the wind blows full up into the harbour.'[1] The fleet was back for the duration.

In any case, the diplomatic climate was changing. When King Philip realized that the armada was finished, and that there was no point mustering yet another one to furnish his English enemies with further relieved jokes, he tried threatening England by adopting a more conciliatory policy towards France. Henri IV was urged on by the hostile movement of Spanish troops along the French coast – Spain still, it must be remembered, held Calais. A pact between Spain and France, with Spain the dominant partner, was exactly what the English government didn't want. The Queen's

key adviser, Lord Burghley, was dispatched to prevent the reconciliation from taking place. A more covert attempt was also
made to protect the French region of Picardy from Spanish aggression, and so make the case for making peace less compelling. Yet
the Franco-Spanish alliance was formalized by treaty in April 1598,
and England was left isolated and vulnerable.

Early in the twentieth century, an intriguing document was
discovered by Sir Edmund Chambers, one of the greatest authorities on Renaissance England. He was scouring the accounts of Sir
John Stanhope, Treasurer of the Chamber, which show that in
1598 one 'Capten John Donne' was warranted to carry letters, and
assist in the transport of prisoners 'for her majesties seruice'. This
captain, Chambers concluded, was none other than the poet.[2]

Early in February 1598, Captain Donne carried letters to the
Queen from Sir Henry Poore, the commander of a small English
force stationed at the coastal town of St Valery in Picardy. He
delivered his dispatch, and was sent back to carry further information if the need arose. Poore, meanwhile, marched his troops
on to Dieppe, where the Captain joined them later in the month.
On 19 February, Captain Donne was given a more demanding
assignment. The records discovered by Chambers show that he
was commissioned by the Governor of Dieppe 'for bringing thence
to the [English] court two prisoners Spaniardes sent by the saide
Governor'. The identity of the two Spanish prisoners is not known,
but they must have been noteworthy soldiers or aristocrats required
in England for intelligence purposes or a ransom. Captain Donne
was entrusted with a delicate, dangerous task in getting them to
England. The French coast was volatile. On 16 February 1598, a
few days before the captain took his prisoners to England, twenty-
eight Spanish ships carrying four thousand men sailed brazenly up
the English Channel to reinforce the garrison at Calais: this was
Philip sending a warning to France, and advising England not to
interfere.

Stanhope's accounts show that the Captain was shortly sent back
to France yet again as a diplomatic messenger. On 19 March he
carried letters from the Queen to her ailing chief councillor, Lord

Burghley, who was by then with the French King in Nantes trying to scupper Franco-Spanish negotiations. The Captain's last dated mission was to carry dispatches from Nantes back to 'the courte at Grenwich' on 25 May, by which time France and Spain had signed the Peace of Vervin. From the point of view of the pragmatists in the Elizabethan Court, led by Burghley, the outcome of this treaty was not so bad at all. Spain gave up Calais and other, more minor snatches in Picardy, and the English Channel felt safe again. But to the followers of Essex – however jaded they might have been after the Azores – there was something much less favourable about the arrangement, something even more unsavoury, perhaps, than a defeat or a genuine crisis. It was inglorious.

Referring to Stanhope's logbook, Chambers argued that 'there is no reason to suppose that any other John Donne than the poet is referred to in these entries.' The assignment of carrying messages between the Court and English troop clusters in France is one for which Donne might have been suited: he spoke both French and Spanish well. So the chronology implied by Sir Edmund Chambers runs like this: Donne gets back, tired and disappointed, from the expedition to the Azores, and returns to London. There, in November or December 1597, he is recruited as a diplomatic messenger and promoted to captain – unusually, for such a young, and hitherto non-professional, soldier. Early in 1598, as the English delegation prepares to leave for France, Donne is dispatched on the first of his errands, 'sent with lettres for her maiesties speciall service'. In late spring, after the peace between France and Spain is concluded, Donne returns to England and gets on with the rest of his life. The sequence in itself is tight, given what we know came next, but just about feasible.

There was, however, at least one other John Donne present on the Azores expedition. A 'Note of the Fleete' on the 1597 expedition, written out by one of the commanders' clerks, gives a list of officers leading a contingent of Dutch troops which joined the English forces: among these names is a 'Captain Donne', sailing aboard a ship called the *Drake*. 'This man,' R. C. Bald concluded, 'is more likely to have been employed to carry letters and transport prisoners than the twenty-six year old poet.'[3] This document does not entirely dispel Chambers' theory, but does render it unlikely.

The best indicators of what Donne was really doing during the gaps before, between and after his trips to Cadiz and the Azores are his poems. One of these, the twentieth Elegie (known as 'Loves Warre'), was probably written sometime in 1598. It mentions the trouble that was deepening in Ireland at this time, which was 'with a strange warr possest / Like to an Ague'.[4] The Earl of Essex was presently dispatched with an army as the cure; and once again, the nation's feathery youth mustered to the cause. But this time Donne was not going with them. He had had enough of prison-like ships, bad food, rough company, and above all the sheer riskiness of it all. Instead, he was staying at home, and making love as energetically as though he was engaging the enemy: 'Here let mee warr,' he declared, 'Here lett mee parlee, batter, bleed, and dye.' He was interested in a much more amiable sort of tussle. 'Thy armes imprison me,' he wrote, 'and myne armes thee, / Thy hart thy ransom is: take mine for mee.'[5] These lines suggest that Donne was nowhere near St Valery or Dieppe in the early months of 1598; that it was not him chatting with the gloomy Spanish captives on their trip to England, nor carrying letters to and from Lord Burghley, the dry, cautious elder statesman. He had hung up his sword to stay at home; he ends 'Loves Warre' with a twinkle in his eye, asking, 'And shall I not do then / More glorious service, staying to make men?'[6]

The captain mentioned in Stanhope's account book may be one of history's lost namesakes, or he might just conceivably be our John Donne. The name was not uncommon in his time. A missing scrap of evidence – a letter, a register, a receipt – might exist somewhere, or might once have existed, that would rearrange the young Donne's circumstances yet again. The truth is that the remoteness in time of early modern people makes them vulnerable to fantastic or over-elaborate reconstructions of their lives. Donne himself was profoundly and comically aware of what can happen to what remains of us. In his love poem 'The Relique', Donne imagines his grave being dug up to accommodate another

occupant. Churchyard space was at a premium; and as the scene
with the gravediggers in *Hamlet* shows, old bones could be turfed
out to make room for a new corpse. But in 'The Relique' Donne
hopes that whoever comes to move him to the charnel house
might pause, on finding two skeletons linked by 'A bracelet of
bright hair about the bone':

> Will he not let'us alone,
> And thinke that there a loving couple lies,
> Who thought that this device might be some way
> To make their soules, at the last busie day,
> Meet at this grave, and make a little stay?[7]

Donne admits such clemency is unlikely. He envisages instead the
bones being sold off and taken 'to the Bishop, and the King' as
religious relics, deceitful shards that bear no relation whatsoever to
Donne or his partner. They would be marketed as the fragments
of saints, bits of holiness that could bring blessings to those who
bought them. 'Thou shalt be a Mary Magdalen,' he says ruefully,
'and I / A something else thereby'. Mary was the former prostitute
who washed Jesus' feet with her tears. Donne leaves the reader to
work out who the 'something else' might be. The charlatans will
thus promote the heresy that Christ and Mary Magdalen were
lovers. The idea, furthermore, of there being any physical remnant
of Christ – who was believed to have ascended bodily into heaven
– was a still more serious blasphemy. This could only happen, he
acknowledges, 'in a time, or land, / Where mis-devotion doth
command'. The 'mis-devotion' he refers to here may be the whole
Roman Catholic creed, or just one of its less reputable practices,
the relic industry. The hunger for miraculous cures and charms
was one of the original causes of protest against the old faith.[8]

Donne plays similar tricks with Roman Catholic ideas and customs in much of his secular poetry. He grew up in a family that
set some store by relics: his uncles Jasper and Ellis carried fragments
of one of Thomas More's teeth in their pockets. More's bloodied
last shirt, and even, it seems, the rest of his head, were also retained.

'The Relique' pokes fun at such behaviour. The poem itself is not irreligious: rather, it is satirical about practices that Donne considered irreligious. He was not taking such customs literally any more; they were material for invention rather than articles of faith.

It is not at all clear whether Donne saw himself as fighting actively against such 'mis-devotion' when he joined the two expeditions against Spain; or how strongly he identified with the Protestant rhetoric in which these military missions were couched. He suggested that he was driven away by 'a rotten state, and hope of gaine'.[9] Despite his satirical air, he was probably not immune to the urges that drove his fellow voluntaries – a desire for action and excitement, the hope of profit, promotion and an element of heroic glamour. But he also spoke of 'England, to whom we owe, what we be, and have': the context of this line is a little jokey, but the feeling it expresses is genuine.[10] If Donne had to give an idealistic reason for his service as a volunteer, he might simply have said he was defending his country. That he was willing to serve it against a Roman Catholic power suggests that a sense of national loyalty had taken precedence over his own original 'mis-devotion'. Strong ambivalences remained, yet by now Donne was moving away from the Roman Church to the one that was more truly 'Catholic', in a literal and practical sense, for all law-abiding English subjects. He could not have taken the next step in his career without acknowledging the legitimacy of the Reformed Church and Queen Elizabeth's reign. He had already done so by becoming a voluntary and joining the campaign against Spain.

6. The Secretary

When you get off the Underground at Charing Cross, and emerge like a bug from a plughole into Trafalgar Square, it is all but impossible to see past the overstatement of Victorian architecture, the neo-classical and baroque flourishes, the twentieth-century monoliths, the contemporary corporate glassware. The ravine of the Strand, via Fleet Street to St Paul's Cathedral, would be unfathomable to any time-travelling immigrants from the late sixteenth century. These would expect to see a rambling avenue of stately homes, with attendant wooden tenements, and a deep ditch running down the centre of the thoroughfare: a gulley known as 'the kennel' that could disable wagons and swallow horses whole. Elizabethan and early Stuart London belong to another era of civic geology.

Only fragments protrude. Down Villiers Street, in the Embankment Gardens, stands a chunky, elaborate stone gateway that nobody can pass through any more. Surrounded by railings on one side, cut off by a pond on the other, the squat structure bears the crest and family motto of George Villiers, Duke of Buckingham, and marks the original northern edge of the Thames at full tide. Buckingham had this watergate built in 1626, when Donne was Dean of St Paul's. It is made from stone initially meant for repair work on the Cathedral, which Donne allowed the Duke to 'borrow' for his private purposes, and the blunt-headed lions that rest their forearms upon it were carved by Nicholas Stone, the mason who eventually made the statue for Donne's sepulchre. But it is also the last remnant of a palace where Donne lived and worked, at a time when a career in the Church was the last thing he wanted or imagined for himself.

The streets leading back from the watergate were once the site of a grand if uneven mansion. For almost two centuries, York

House, or 'York Place' as it was sometimes called, was the London residence of the Archbishops of York. Thomas Wolsey, Archbishop and Lord Chancellor to Henry VIII, was its most extravagant owner. Wolsey put Midas in the shade. Cloth of gold and silver hung in all the rooms of state, the richest tapestries that could be acquired, the tables and cupboards groaning with precious plate. Wolsey also made sure that his train of servants, running to some eight hundred people, was decked out as luxuriously as the furnishings. Even the head cook wore a satin jerkin, with a gold chain round his neck. The palace was so lavish that the King decided it would do him nicely: after Wolsey became grist to Fortune's wheel – eventually disgraced, imprisoned, and dying on the road from Leicester – King Henry claimed York House as his own. He extended the precincts and 'builded there a sumptuous Gallery and a beautifull Gate house', where 'the Princes with their Nobility vse to stand or sit, and at Windowes to behold all triumphant Iustings, and other military exercises.' Adjacent to the gallery were gardens, orchards, 'faire Tennis courtes, bowling allies, and a Cocke Pit, al built by Henry VIII', in a complex that became known as Whitehall Palace, the monarch's central London home.[1] By the time Donne came to live there, York House was no longer run on the lines that Wolsey and Henry had allowed for themselves: it was now set aside for one of the Queen's busiest and most influential councillors, the Lord Keeper of the Great Seal – a post roughly equivalent, except in name, to that of Lord Chancellor. And Donne slipped into this sanctuary of power by knowing the right people.

As tans and sunburns faded and the dust settled after two years of macho high spirits, shifts of varying magnitude took place. Among London's ambitious, well-educated and well-preened gentlemen, spheres began to overlap, and old cliques altered. Donne's former friend and fellow poet Everard Gilpin, who went to neither Cadiz nor the Azores, wrote bitterly of companions who deserted him, 'Phantasmus butterflies', and others, their 'neere of kin',

> Which scorne to speake to one which hath not bin
> On these late voyages: or to one
> Which hauing beene there yet (though he haue none)
> Hath not a Cadiz-beard . . .

To be in with the in-crowd, Gilpin jibed, one not only needed to have gone to Cadiz, but also returned with the right kind of facial hair. Bearded or smooth, poor Everard found that his face didn't suit any more. But he took the chance to remind some people of where they had started out. He took another dig at a figure he calls Publius, whose 'dad', like Donne's, was an ironmonger. This old trader

> Turnd yron to sterling, drosse to land and fee,
> And got so by old horseshooes, that the foole
> Enterd himselfe into the dauncing schoole.[2]

To his credit, Gilpin doesn't turn this into an explicitly personal diatribe – the lines may not, as some have felt, or have wanted to feel, be about Donne at all. Gilpin is attacking a social type. But Donne is still recognizable by that type; and if this verse cut close enough for readers in the twentieth century to notice a similarity between Publius' father and Donne's, who also turned iron into hard cash, it might well have touched a nerve at the end of the 1590s.

One of Donne's comrades from the mission to the Azores was Sir Thomas Egerton, a former Lincoln's Inn man with a bright-looking future, expensive tastes and excellent contacts. He may not have had so bad a time of it on the islands. Whereas Donne seems to have been part of the contingent which got blasted on Fayal and parched off the coast of San Miguel, young Sir Thomas sailed in the Earl of Essex's portion of the fleet. He was, in other words, of that party which slipped around the island of San Miguel to surprise the garrison town, Punta Delgada, with an attack from behind; but which ended up instead right on the other side of the island, relaxing for a few days on the peachy shores of

Villa Franca. There Egerton became one of the very few on the expedition to receive a knighthood, which Essex conferred on him for reasons that aren't particularly clear – perhaps for services to beach sports. The Earl in any case recognized Egerton as one of his own, and the newly dubbed Sir Thomas returned to England as one of those prepared to follow Essex wherever he led.

Donne's ambitions were bent towards safer territory. Having won his spurs on the two voyages, he now felt entitled to follow a career that better suited his intellectual abilities and his fondness for urban living. He had not completed his studies at Lincoln's Inn, and apparently had little interest in pursuing a career as an attorney – which would take several further years before he qualified – but he had distinguished himself as being well able to handle legal complexities. So he looked for a career in the Elizabethan administration itself. On this score Egerton was ideally placed to help Donne out. His father, Sir Thomas Egerton the elder, was Lord Keeper of the Seal and the senior judge in the court of Chancery. He was made Lord Chancellor when King James succeeded Elizabeth, but this was a change in all but name alone: Egerton already held all the administrative power the position of Chancellor could bring. At some point in the first half of 1598, Donne was appointed as secretary to the Lord Keeper and moved into York House.

Sir Thomas the elder was born with two distinct disadvantages to someone of his time. The first was that his family was Roman Catholic, the other that he was an illegitimate child. These drawbacks were balanced out, however, by the lucky fact that his family was immensely wealthy, and by his father's tenderness towards him. Thomas was born in Doddlestone, a parish in the north-west county of Cheshire, the son of one Sir Richard Egerton, a rich squire with a wandering eye and a fond heart, and a local beauty whose surname was Sparks. Technically, Thomas might have been left with no legal rights or an education; but Sir Richard acknowledged him as his own, a 'natural' son. He took as much care of Thomas as he did of his legitimate children, and the boy responded precociously. A cloud of local folklore surrounds Thomas's early years. Reports had it that he glinted with intelligence and high ambitions. Thomas was apparently nursed and brought up by a local farmer's wife before being taken to Sir Richard's house. On the way to Doddlestone Hall he chuntered of the fineness of the world, and of his plans to rise in it and some day own it. The world was never quite his personal property, but whether or not their fondness came in retrospect, when Thomas became one of the most powerful figures in the realm, the locals remembered him proudly and affectionately. The leafy slope where his parents got together came to be known as 'Gallantry Banke'.[3]

Egerton blazed along the same educational trail that Donne would follow. He was taught first by private tutors, then proceeded to Oxford and on to Lincoln's Inn, where he was regarded in Donne's time as one of the greatest living alumni. It took him ten years, however, to get his career properly started, and to do that he had to stop being a Papist. A light brush with the authorities was enough to persuade him that conversion was a prudent move, and once the decision was taken he never looked back. He quickly made his name and fortune as a brilliant equity lawyer: once, after appearing against the crown in a case that Elizabeth had a stake in, the Queen declared that he would never do so again. By 1581, he had won his first official appointment and had fully appeased any qualms he might have had about converting to the Protestant cause: he was a lethal prosecutor of Mary, Queen of Scots, Elizabeth's rival to the throne. There was much worry that the trial – and execution – of a monarch would establish a precedent that could be used against Elizabeth herself, but Egerton bluntly asked the wealthy judges 'what would become of them, their honours, estates and posterity, if the kingdom were to be transferred from her present majesty to a Popish successor.'[4]

He was much more, too, than a prosecuting counsel or judge in the campaign of terror against leading Roman Catholics in the 1590s. Appointed Attorney General in 1592, Egerton became the operational head of the police system that ensnared, captured and tortured these enemies of the crown – many of whom were known to Donne personally. Topcliffe, Younge and other government agents reported back to Egerton, who was prepared to extract information and confessions at any cost. Thomas Campion, a friend of Henry Donne's room-mate William Harrington, was racked and manacled for so long, on Egerton's orders, 'that he could not hold up his arms to plead in court, and was kept in irons until his execution'.[5] Robert Southwell, another leading Jesuit, received similar treatment and published a chilling itinerary of the methods his interrogators used as a matter of course. There were many others. The campaign had subsided by the time Donne got his post with Egerton; yet his employment made him complicit in the administration's routine persecutions and propaganda. In February 1600, Egerton drafted a bill of information that declared recusant Catholics to be 'natural vipers, ready to eat out the belly of your mother'; and it could well have been Donne who transcribed and saw to the promulgation of the document.[6]

Considering his background, it is surprising to find Donne so close to such work. By now, there was no one really left in London to criticize him for what many of his family would surely have viewed as a betrayal. The year he got the lucrative job with Egerton, his mother was still in exile in Antwerp, and his brother Henry had been dead five years. His uncle, Jasper Heywood, the banished Jesuit leader, died in Naples. With such important figures gone, Donne was making his own way, defining himself against his family tradition. Hearing of his uncle's clandestine activities, living in hiding for much of his career at the universities, watching lives pass fruitlessly through stubborn non-conformity and losing his brother for the sake of a rebel priest had left no great positive impression on Donne. But it would be a mistake to see him as simply rebelling against his mother's influence, or, alternatively, forsaking his heritage out of fear. Rather he had come to see that the responsibility for the sectarian problem lay with the oppressed minority as well as the repressive regime. Those who accepted the spiritual supremacy of the Pope technically supported the removal, if not the actual assassination, of the ruling sovereign. Countless English Catholics protested their loyalty to the Queen, but such avowals were never actually put to the test.

  Ordinary 'Papists', for Donne, did not deserve or require the
persecution and torture they frequently received; they were weakened enough by the economic and social strictures put upon them.
As a government official, however, his quarrel was with those who
called themselves missionaries and whom the authorities defined
simply as agitators: the members of the militant Jesuit order, which
Donne actively despised, and individuals such as William Harrington, the priest who had incriminated his brother and had, in effect,
lured Henry to his death. In time, Donne would see the Roman
Catholic position as a denial of the historical moment, a failure to
adapt to an evolution in the Christian Church that was truly
'Catholic', universal. But when he left the army to take up his
job as a secretary in the Elizabethan government, his theological
position was not fully formed. He had taken a decision that was
personal and political, yet only intuitively religious, and it was only
over the following years and decades that he managed to explain
it to himself. His later writing on the issues of recusancy, in
Pseudo-martyr and throughout his sermons, suggests that he really
saw militant Roman Catholics as a threat to the peace and stability
of his country. By joining Egerton's staff, as by volunteering for
the expeditions against Spain, he was signalling his loyalty to the
governing order.

  It should not be thought that Donne lacked reservations about
the government's methods, however. He was not brutalized into
approving of the practices of Topcliffe and his men. An important
historical fact to bear in mind is that torture and physical violence
were generally accepted means of law enforcement; not so much
for any real efficiency in producing reliable evidence as in allowing the sovereign to show that the law had total power over the
bodies of all subjects in the realm. Even so, as a preacher during
the 1620s, when this assertion began to be questioned by legal
experts – among them an acquaintance of his, John Selden –
Donne was in the avant garde of those who attacked the use of
torture on both ethical and pragmatic grounds.[7] But already
thirty years before, in a poem possibly written during his time as
an apparatchik, he had subtly protested against the dreadful tools

of the state. In 'Loves Exchange', Love is depicted as both a devil and a tyrannical monarch, with whom Donne tries bargaining for leniency. At the end, however, he succumbs, and offers his body for Love to cut up as an example to others who might resist. Suddenly the clichéd 'pains of love' become actual bodily agonies, reminiscent of those exacted in the Tower and below the scaffold.

> If I must example bee
> To future Rebells; If th'unborne
> Must learne, by my being cut up, and torne:
> Kill, and dissect me, Love; for this
> Torture against thine owne end is,
> Rack't carcasses make ill Anatomies.[8]

'Anatomies' were cadavers used for dissection in medical lectures – a practice that was still (unlike torture, paradoxically) a subject of intense moral debate. The cutting and tearing going on here is vivisective; but Donne's point is that the carcass of someone who has been stretched on the rack does not offer up reliable or usable information. The line is as much about policing in general as it is about the metaphoric reign of love. Those who put their trust in torture to deter 'future Rebells' were in the long run defeating their own purposes.

To accept him as his secretary, a position of high trust and great potential in the Protestant regime, Egerton had to be satisfied that Donne could be relied on, and that he had also abandoned his Papism. He was expected to meet the most exacting standards of confidence and dependability. A contemporary instruction manual for aspiring secretaries described the job as follows:

The Secretorie, as hee is a *keeper* and conseruer of secrets, so is hee by his Lord or Maister, and by none other to bee directed. To a *Closet* there belongeth properlie, a doore, a locke, and a *key*: to a Secretorie, there appertaineth incidentlie, *Honestie*, *Care* and *Fidelity*.[9]

Living at York House, Donne had to show himself worthy of being a trustworthy 'closet' – making every necessary show of outward conformity. His political decision was made; yet his inner emotional and intellectual journey was still only beginning. Spiritually, by now he found it all but impossible to say just what he believed in any more. Blurts of anger against his first religion would occasionally escape him in his writing, but the channels of mind it had created still directed his thoughts. A few years earlier, railing against the literary and legal scene in his second satire, he dissociated himself from everyone and everything, including those he lived among and loved. 'I do hate / Perfectly all this town,' he spat, at the poem's opening. The deafening babble of the city and the Court was loud enough to 'teare / The tender labyrinth of a soft maids eare', louder 'Than when winds in our ruin'd Abbeyes rore'.[10] Donne's mind span beyond London, across a desecrated landscape. On his travels around the country, up to Oxford, perhaps up as far as the Brookes and his other friends in the north, Donne could not have missed the skeletal naves of medieval sanctuaries, pulled down some forty, fifty years before; and with the wind in their ribs, these were still *our* abbeys – part of a national heritage.

Yet when he could make the space, when he could make himself alone enough, Donne attempted in his mid-twenties to resist the stamp of both past Catholic and present Protestant affiliations. His important third satire – not satirical at all, more a desperately sincere cry for help from a mind lost in its own tender labyrinth – reasoned that it was perhaps futile to look for true religion in either the Vatican or the Protestant home city of Geneva. Donne tried instead to imagine a land of his own, an internal topography quite bare of abbeys, ruined or otherwise. Visible in a permanent distance,

> on a huge hill,
> Cragg'd, and steep, Truth stands, and hee that will
> Reach her, about must, and about must goe;
> And what the hills suddennes resists, winne so.[11]

Donne's private life consisted of nothing less than a search for the right eternity – which involved a search for the right earthly institution for worship. His concerns with divinity would not emerge in any public or professional form until he wrote *Pseudo-martyr* more than a decade later, but his life in and around the royal Court brought him into regular contact with leading churchmen, who were routinely invited to the occasional great dinners at York House. In the Reverend Thomas Morton, a leading theologian and religious polemicist, he made a friend with whom he could discuss his interests in doctrine and divinity. Some ten years later Morton was the first to suggest that he should become a priest. At present Donne's inquiries brought the risk of unorthodoxy, but so long as they were confined to the study these researches were much less noxious to the authorities than any lingering Papist sympathies might have been. The personal search for Truth, the priesthood of the individual soul, was a key Protestant tenet, one that Egerton could approve of. In any case, the most important seat of God-consolidated power on earth, so far as the Elizabethan regime was concerned, was neither at Rome nor Geneva, but London: the vital thing was that the Queen's religious, and thus political, supremacy was not questioned.

Egerton's position as Lord Keeper of the Seal put him at the top of both the English legal profession and the system of government. He was also one of the Queen's closest Privy Councillors. The Privy Council was something like a proto-cabinet, a group with particular responsibilities that gave the monarch advice on matters of policy. The Council consisted only of the most powerful aristocrats and officials, men who all had vested interests in the outcome of its proceedings. Elizabeth kept on average a Council of about nineteen members, which shrank to a more exclusive panel of eleven or twelve in the last years of her reign. Egerton was a member of this inner circle. His prominence increased when the Privy Council sat as a court of law, to try cases of high political import and public disorder, 'ryots, rowts and other misdemeanours', as John Stow put it;[12] in this form, the Privy Council was known as the Star Chamber. Its decisions provided the land with a barometric reading of official opinion at the highest level, and it was popular for the relative speed with which it processed and pronounced on petitions. Because most of the lords in the Council had no formal training, Egerton had to tell them where the law stood on any given matter, and at times rein in their punitive imaginations. Thus his duties on the Council, which sat almost daily, and on the Star Chamber, were a heavy workload in their own right. But Egerton's main base of operations lay in Chancery, a court with two major functions. It was both a court of equity and an administrative organ, a duct through which every major private and civic matter passed for determination or approval.

Egerton, it seems, was delighted with Donne's work. Although Donne was technically just one of his gentleman servants, the Lord Keeper insisted that his secretary sit with him and his family at dinner. According to Walton, Egerton saw Donne as a friend and declared he was '*Such a Secretary as was fitter to serve a King than a subject.*'[13] Donne was employed at his friend's recommendation, old Egerton 'taking notice of his Learning, Languages, and other Abilities, and much affecting his Person and Behaviour'.[14] He was well-read, well-spoken and his manners were impeccable. But what distinguished him from other bright young men was a phenomenal care for the finest particle of an idea or a concept. His mind could work comfortably at a nano-level of appreciation, in scrutinizing his own soul or analysing a mountain of paperwork. He hated blurry, lazy thinking, in any field. He later compared intellectual compromise to 'litigious men tyred with suits' who admit any ruling after a long case; and to princes so sick of war that they accept whatever conditions of peace they can get.[15] Donne was determined to see whatever matter he had at hand in the clearest possible light. The diligence he had brought to his early studies in law and divinity, the paranoid thoroughness with which he viewed a relationship from every angle, made him an excellent, assiduous secretary. The analysis of love, the search for Truth and success in a bureaucracy all require a mastery of detail.

As Egerton's aide, he gave his days to the back-and-forth rhythm of officialdom: Donne's duties, says Louis A. Knafla, 'would have included scheduling, meeting and greeting guests, legal research, and drafting memoranda'.[16] The Lord Keeper and his team roved from Whitehall to Westminster, often descending too upon the outlying royal palaces. Yet long stationary periods could be spent at any of these locations, particularly Westminster Hall, where most of the major courts actually held session. This was one of the major facilities that had not been very well maintained during the recent aristocratic fad for bigger, better and newer architectural triumphs. Richard II did the place up in 1397, Stow records, 'with a stately porch, and diuerse lodgings of maruellous worke, and with great costs'.[17] Yet by the time Donne scuttled through its corridors and antechambers, fetching and carrying, finding people and papers, the Hall had seen better days. A great fire ravaged it in 1512, and almost nothing had been done to restore it. Before, the Hall had been a palace, 'with dayly Joustings, and runnings at Tilt'; now it was a civic ant-farm. Going in through the main entrance, one had the court of common pleas on the right-hand side, 'where ciuill matters are to [be] pleaded, specially such as touch lands or contracts'; at the upper end of the Hall, on the same side, was the King's Bench court, 'where pleas of the Crowne haue their hearing'; and on the left-hand side was the Court of Chancery, where Sir Thomas Egerton presided. Business between the courts would often overlap, however, and the Lord Keeper and his team would frequently be wanted upstairs, where the Star Chamber held its sessions – in a room with a star-bedecked ceiling. The complex was a babel of squabbles over life and livelihoods, punctuated by a stentorian tower clock in the forecourt, 'which striketh euery houre on a great bell'.

Donne entered an environment in which it was very easy to make an enemy. A seeming trifle could have great impact on another bureaucrat's territory, since the frequently substantial livings made in Chancery were dependent on often minor, mind-numbing duties. Below the Lord Keeper and the Master of the Rolls were the other Masters of the Court, who handled the taxation of legal costs and processed oaths. Below these was the most influential faction of Chancery, at a practical level. This was a group known as the Six Clerks, which issued patents and vast quantities of writs and gave informal but costly advice to litigants. The Clerks felt they were the ones who ran the place, and frequently overstepped the mark: one of Egerton's predecessors, Sir Christopher Hatton, also distinguished as the Queen's Master of Dancing, had to order the Clerks to stop butting in when the court was in session.

Then there were Examiners who examined witnesses, Registrars who looked after the Registry, the Usher who provided ink and paper for the records, fetched old records from various storages, and occasionally had to take care of crowd control if the court grew restive. There were the Clerks of the Petty Bag – a bag of 'little matters' – the Clerks of the *Subpoena* office, who issued writs for Chancery, and the Cursitors, who wrote out writs for proceedings involving other courts. Snuggest of all were the Sealer and the Royal Chafewax, two individuals who spent a lot of time with the Lord Keeper of the Seal, because their business involved the seal. The job of the Chafewax was to provide the wax for the document that was to be sealed, and to heat it up; then it was the Sealer who did the actual sealing. All of these officers could make a charge for each item they dealt with, taking a cut from the overall costs. This was why they could get very annoyed if anyone – especially someone from outside the machine itself – tried to speed up the process, or just did so absent-mindedly, by doing part of their task for them.

When Donne took up his post on Egerton's staff in 1598, Chancery was undergoing a major review. A Commission on Fees had been set up to examine just how money in the court was being made, and who was making it. Evidence of widespread corruption was discovered – although less than was almost certainly present in the system, since many factions, such as the Masters, the Six Clerks and even the Cursitors had useful allies on the commission team. It was found to be all too easy for clerks to charge an extra few pence for a piece of paperwork that clients were often desperate to obtain; and when the charge was made per sheet it was all too tempting to put fewer lines, or larger letters, on the page than the hazy guidelines directed. Obviously, each department was eager to expose the others' shortcomings and dishonesty and underplay its own. But all court officials were neurotic about outsiders.

Because Queen Elizabeth's government was hard-pressed for funds, and because raising taxes often caused more trouble than it was worth, revenue was frequently raised by granting patents of monopoly to private individuals. For a price, an approved subject could buy the right to a hefty share of the profits from almost any conceivable venture. A patent could be issued for a product or a process, literally anything that made money. So, for example, the Earl of Essex had the royal grant for farming sweet wines; within Chancery, his former lieutenant and current rival Sir Walter Ralegh made a tidy amount from the clerkship for writing out licences for the sale of such wines. It did not take long for the Queen's advisers to realize that even official positions could be patented: people could buy the right to become bureaucrats, or sub-contract such posts in order to skim the fees that legal services demanded. The court's indigenous administrators, led by the Six Clerks, were furious at the very idea of their jobs being granted by the crown instead of the traditional way, by nod and handshake within the turbulent family of Chancery itself. Among Donne's daily tasks, one of the trickiest was to avoid treading on the toes of people who could make his life very difficult if they wanted to. This secretaryship, after all, if Walton is to be believed, was just the beginning – 'an Introduction to some more weighty Employment in the State; for which, his Lordship [Egerton] did often protest, he thought him very fit'.[18]

Despite his ruthlessness when legislating against Papists or pursuing a prosecution, Egerton was respected by his friends and those suing for his favour as a kind, wise and liberal-minded man. He was famous for his 'beauty of countenance', and ladies would apparently come to the court merely to gaze on him. His promotion to Lord Keeper was greeted, according to a contemporary, 'with a general applause, both of city, court and country, for the reputation he hath of integrity, law, knowledge, and courage'.[19] Controversially, when he became Lord Keeper he retained the position he had previously held, that of Master of the Rolls, which gave him control of the records of the court, along with a supplementary, very lucrative income. For many, this indicated a rather grasping nature – someone who 'would make friends with the meetest mammon', in John Chamberlain's unkind phrase.[20] He was famous too for being thin-skinned, and there were times when he lost all patience with the people around him.

At this point a distinct lack of mercy would rise to the surface. On taking offence, Egerton could respond not so much with temper as with a cold, wry implacability. A certain Richard Mylward caught the Lord Keeper on a bad day when he submitted a replication that was found to be too chunky, 'fraught with impertinent matter'. Egerton took the unconventional measure of ordering the warden to take Richard Mylward and 'cut a hole in the same engrossed [overlarge, fat] Replication . . . and put the said Richard's head through the same hole . . . and so let the same Replication hang about his shoulders . . .' The order against long-windedness rumbles on with a distinct lack of brevity on its own part. Egerton directed that the warder, having put 'the same [replication] so hanging [around Mylward's head], shall lead the same Richard, bareheaded and barefaced, round about Westminster Halls while the courts are sitting.'[21] After being paraded, Mylward was given a heavy fine. Over a longer period, Egerton could also pursue vendettas with calm efficiency and usually great success against those who threatened his position or the integrity, as he saw it, of the court. He was a good man to work for, and excellent to have on your side in a quarrel, but a dangerous one to cross.

Through much of 1598, Egerton was engaged in keeping his friend the Earl of Essex out of trouble. In July, a major spat broke out between the Earl and the Queen. Essex was upset about the lack of energy and direction being given to Ireland, which the English were trying to quell as a province of the realm. As the war against Spain had been put on hold indefinitely, the Earl had no other major cause to pursue. The Earl of Tyrone, Hugh O'Neill, had been mustering resistance to English rule for more than three years, and had successfully kept English forces out of his stronghold in the northern Irish kingdom of Ulster. What bothered Essex in particular, however, was that no one had been given overall command of the English presence in Ireland since the last incumbent, Lord Burgh, had died the previous October. Like other major English lords, Essex had a substantial land interest in Ireland; he felt that his own property and income were at stake. Of concern too was prestige, the possibility that someone else might be given the vacant command, an appointment that would necessarily diminish his own standing.

One day in a meeting of the Council, the pugnacious Earl pointed out to Elizabeth the facts of the case as he saw them; she promptly gave him a box on the ears for his impertinence. Thumped like a schoolboy, Essex reacted like one, stomping out of the chamber with his hand on the hilt of his sword. Elizabeth screeched at him to 'Begone, and be hanged.' Essex shouted back that even though the insult came from a woman, 'he would not bear such usage were it from Henry VIII himself.'[22] The moment to put in slow motion is that at which the Earl touches his sword. In some accounts he merely clasps it, in others it is half-drawn as he leaves the room. The question of how far out of the sheath the blade had to come before the gesture became treasonable was a delicate one.

Essex forestalled any action the Queen might have taken against him by leaving the Court in a huff, and taking his retinue with him into the country. Accompanying him were his secretaries, including Donne's friend, Henry Wotton. Writing from London, Donne regretted Wotton's absence, but assured him that he wasn't missing much. Taking in the gaudy trash that surrounded him in the halls of the great and good, Donne wrote to him, 'Here's no more news than vertue.' There was no need to go into great detail – he knew that Wotton would know what he was talking about:

> For here no one is from th'extremitie
> Of vice, by any other reason free,
> But that the next to him, still, is worse than hee.[23]

This was a world where all innocence was entirely relative, where there was no measure of absolute moral depravity only because everyone was equally bad.

Ever since he had written his first Satire, in which the 'motley fondling humorist' drags him from his study into town, Donne had voiced contempt for the Court and London society in general. His Satires and many of his verse letters condemn as vanity and lechery what he celebrates elsewhere, in his own experience, as natural urges. He felt it necessary to draw a distinction between his own lovemaking and the rough fornication of others, whose orgasms were 'harsh, and violent', like ploughshares breaking 'stony ground'.[24] His crueller poems goaded their listeners: he pointed out the 'ranke sweaty froth' that defiled '*thy* Mistresse's brows'. It reminded him of the 'spermatique issue of ripe menstruous boiles'. The early verse shoulders its way through a savage carnival, picking out the lecher's gouty hand that is 'like a bunch of ragged carrets'; looking into the chamber of a woman so unattractive that even dildos, bedstaves, mirror handles and other masturbatory equipment would shrink from touching her.[25] On his return from Cadiz, Donne described an encounter with one of the Court's most essential creatures, 'A thing more strange, than on Niles slime, the Sun E'r bred'.[26] This social leech, dressed in a balding velvet suit, sticks to Donne, rebukes him for his 'lonenesse', his aloofness, and tries to get him to say something slanderous: the hanger-on can 'Make men speake treason' and 'cosen subtlest whores'. It was a descent into the inferno. 'Such men' as Dante saw in hell, Donne said, 'I saw at court, and worse, and more.'[27]

As he settled into his new role as an establishment functionary, he became concerned that his writing had forged a permanent association between him and the disreputable social elements he described. He worried that he had wasted his talents on subjects that had contaminated him. Writing in verse to Rowland Woodward, Donne found his muse to be like a woman who 'in her third widowhood' had decided to become a nun, affecting 'a chaste fallownesse'. Donne regretted that this dowager had only enabled him to write scurrilous verse:

Since shee to few, yet to too many hath showne
How love-song weeds, and Satyrique thornes are growne
Where seeds of better Arts, were early sown.[28]

He was comparing himself to the stony and thorny ground on which the good seed was cast in Christ's parable, fearing that he had wasted his potential as a writer. 'There is no Vertue, but Religion,' he told Woodward; he suggested that they burn out the flaws in their souls under a magnifying glass of moral introspection.

Seek wee then our selves in our selves; for as
Men force the Sunne with much more force to passe,
By gathering his beames with a christall glasse;

So wee, If wee into our selves will turne,
Blowing our sparkes of vertue, may outburne
The straw, which doth about our hearts sojourne.

He wanted to reforge himself, to scorch his spirit clean. Yet the image of the merry widow–nun, accepting a life of chastity now that she was physically incapable of bearing more children, is equally characteristic of his eye for human nature. He never lost it: 'chastity is not chastity in an old man,' he declared, at a time when he was a chaste and ageing man himself, 'but a disability to be unchast'.[29] The great thing too about Donne's social observation is that he could always see his own part in the vice or little dishonesty of the heart that he pointed out. The nun discovering holiness after a life of marital and carnal enjoyment is his muse, his own poetic imagination; by association *he* is the nun, in fact. This ability to poke fun at his own position lends great self-awareness and also greater strength to the moral stringency in his poem to Woodward.

He remained a delightful and much–loved companion to his friends. William Cornwallis, poet, wit and essayist, struck a deal with his 'ever to be respeckted freand Mr John Done, Secretary to my Lorde Keeper':

> What tyme thou meanest to offir Idilnes
> Come to my den, for heer she allwayes stayes;
> If then for change, of howers you seem careless
> Agree with me to loose them at the playes.[30]

Idleness was always waiting for him to call, and there was always a den in which to curl up with her. The old ways were not lost completely; and although he had to be careful of the face he presented, there were still some smiles to be encountered at York House.

There was pleasant company. Sir Thomas junior was still living at home, along with his wife and three little daughters. His father's wife, Elizabeth, had a fifteen-year-old son from a previous marriage, Francis Wolley, who spent half the year in study at Oxford. She was also taking care of her brother's third daughter, a girl of about fourteen. Lady Egerton was the Lord Keeper's second partner; they had been married the year before Donne arrived, mainly for mutual social convenience, but had happily grown very fond of one another. Elizabeth's health was not strong, however, and she was also prone to melancholy – often, apparently, because of her spending habits. A letter from her to the Queen's secretary in October 1598, appealing for financial relief, complained that she was 'hoping to receive her final end, for her debts so overwhelm her that her life is most wearisome'.[31] A month later she came down with smallpox, and her husband's tenderness for her increased as he watched her face dissolve. Lady Egerton's ailments understandably made it difficult for her to keep her young niece, Ann, under constant observation. And Ann meanwhile saw Donne often, since Walton claims that Egerton always treated his secretary 'with much courtesie, appointing him a place at his own Table, to which he esteemed his Company and Discourse to be a great Ornament.'[32] Donne was dining with his master and family, and was entertaining them.

At home, life was pleasant enough so long as Donne took care. Yet the work began to eat at his patience. His anger was a complex disgust for a societal organism that he could not separate himself from, nor identify himself with. Only his writing provided a means of controlled release. Donne's fifth satire, his last, less poised, less zestful than any of the others, is a sustained tirade against the apparatus of Chancery. Part of Donne's frustration was directed at the system's victims. Every day, Donne watched widows, second sons, tenants and landlords, claimants of every hue, trying to secure a tiny decision that might bring them closer to a verdict in their favour. Westminster Hall was an arena of minute, meaningless victories. The wealthier a suitor or a defendant was, the more powerful they were; but ultimately there were too many wheels to be greased. Because there was so much to get through, each official department of Chancery took on private clerical staff to handle a great deal of the work. The bigger the department, the more hired hands they employed. This not only meant that many of those dealing with information of the highest personal confidence were not sworn to secrecy by the Court, and thus had no official trust to keep, but that litigants were ever more distanced from the parties with whom the crucial decisions finally rested. It took serious money to get a Master of Chancery or one of the Six Clerks to address one's cause personally.

Donne berated the plaintiffs for even trying. If court officers were like 'ravishing seas', suitors were like springs and rivulets, weedy little streams running towards the deep that would drown them. If the world was like a man, and lawyers and clerks were the 'devouring stomacke', then suitors were the 'excrement' they dumped. If Chancery officials prostituted the law, then suitors were 'wittols', limp men who acquiesced in their wives' adulteries. And as so often, Donne was implicated in the system he was criticizing. In May 1598, very early on in his time as Egerton's secretary, Donne sued Christopher Danby, the brother of his valet Thomas. According to his complaint, master and servant had stayed together for 'eighteen monthes' – from July 1595 until just after the mission to Cadiz. During this time, Donne had received no payment for Thomas's 'meate and drink' and 'apparell', which had come to the considerable sum of forty pounds. But Donne's real grievance lay with theft: Thomas had stolen from him a black cloak worth twenty shillings, a laced satin suit worth three pounds, a 'paire of blacke laced velvet hose' worth more than four pounds and some gold lace that came to the value of five pounds. The document is wonderful for the glimpse it gives us of Donne's finest attire. These stolen items were the requisite accessories of the voluntary following Essex, and their loss was too costly to overlook.

It seems that Donne was patient; he must have negotiated privately with Christopher Danby for several months before going to the law as a last resort. The suit passed quickly through court, and was resolved without contest by the end of the month. His place in Egerton's office probably helped get matters through. Yet though he was no doubt glad of the compensation he received, Donne was far from complacent about privilege. Just occasionally, he lost his reserve when he looked at the corruption around him. His last satire turned an appeal towards the Queen herself, asking if she knew just what was going on:

> Greatest and fairest empresse, know you this?
> Alas, no more then Thames faire head doth know
> Whose meades her arms drowne, or whose corne o'rflow . . . [33]

The great fair empress, Queen of England since 1558 and now a wigged old lady, scraggy-necked, black-toothed, had other things on her mind. Her death was both a personal and a national preoccupation. When Sir Thomas Egerton was sworn in as Lord Keeper of the Seal in 1596, Elizabeth had broken down with a sudden prescience that he would be the last she would ever appoint. She was childless, in a sense friendless. All people cared about was who would take her place, and the succession was disputed endlessly. They weren't sure how it might come about, but some talked of Robert Devereux, Earl of Essex.

In August 1598 Essex regained something of his former sway when the government was shaken by disastrous news from Ireland. In the north, a crucial garrison on the river Blackwater fell, with heavy losses, to Irish troops commanded by Hugh O'Neill, leaving the kingdom of Munster – more or less under the control of the

English, with Dublin and the Pale at its heart – almost hopelessly exposed. A rebellion across Ireland followed. Garrisons fell, castles were seized, colonizers fled for their lives. Reports reached London of babies plucked from mothers' breasts and dashed against walls, children dying in flames, noses cut off and tongues cut out by the marauders; whether truths or exaggerations, the accounts detailed atrocities to be logged with bitter care and paid back in kind. In England, the Court and the public cried out for reprisal. Essex, who had kept aloof from the Court for over a month, melodramatically offered his services to the Queen, putting a spin on the circumstances of their row: 'I had not gone into exile of myself if your Majesty had not chased me from you as you did . . .' Cometh the hour, however, and here was the man: 'Yet when the unhappy news came from yonder cursed country of Ireland, and that I apprehended how much your Majesty would be grieved . . . duty was strong enough to rouse me out of my deadest melancholy.'[34] As more tidings of bloodshed slopped across the Irish sea, a massive army in England was slowly raised to suppress the revolt.

Late in the year, it was decided that Essex would be given the command, and he was overjoyed at having overstepped his rivals: he was still, in his own eyes, the Queen's number one. He was to be Lord Lieutenant of Ireland, with an army of fifteen thousand or more. As soon as the appointment was officially announced, early in 1599, it immediately caught the imagination of the land's lace-attired feathery adventurers. Ireland might not have had the same allure as the coast of Spain or the Azores, but Essex's charisma was irresistible. Many of Donne's friends joined up. Henry Wotton was going, naturally, as Essex's secretary; but others obtained full military commissions, among them Sir Thomas Egerton the younger. The Lord Keeper wanted his son to go into the law, but young Egerton was one of those Lincoln's Inn men who saw life as an attorney as one fit for a 'strumpet'. Disappointedly, his father conceded that 'his mynde draweth hym an other course to folowe the warre, and to attende My Lord of Essex into Irelande, and in this he is so farre engaged that I can not staye him, but must leave hym to his wille.'[35] By mid-March, Sir Thomas junior had been garrisoned in his father's home county of Cheshire, waiting to sail. Apparently his division contained something of a wild bunch. A force of 2,600 embarked on 21 and 22 March, 'saving 23 of Sir Thomas Egerton's company,' wrote the mayor of Chester, 'who were returned back to this city by the master of their barque to avoid the danger of over pestering the company.'[36] These stragglers finally made the crossing from Holyhead in Wales a month later.

Committed anyway as Egerton's secretary, Donne felt he was past such exploits. He did not join the mission. Many friends left London, with mutual promises to write and keep in touch. And in York House, a teenage girl kept crossing his path.

7. Lost Words

In Dublin, the Earl of Essex received the sword as Lord Lieutenant on 15 April. Although the heart of the trouble lay in the north, in Ulster, the stronghold of Hugh O'Neill, Essex decided to 'shake and sway the branches', as he put it, instead of digging at the root straightaway.[1] He embarked with his troops and his personal staff on a tour of Ireland, receiving garlands and hearing orations in his honour. Wotton followed him, and as he and Donne tried to keep in touch, many of their letters were lost. The lines of communication were uncertain and unsafe: although a regular postal route between Dublin and London via the northern Welsh port of Holyhead had just been established, there were innumerable places and ways in which a letter or package could go missing. Many of the words Donne and his friend intended for one another went astray, and most of the letters that did get through complained about those which had disappeared: 'Sir,' moaned Wotton, 'It is worth my wondering that you can complain of my seldom writing, when your own letters come so fearfully, as if they tread all the way upon a bog.'[2] Donne had put a rebuke into verse, writing to 'Henrico Wottoni, in Hibernia belligeranti' ('at war in Ireland'):

> Went you to conquer? And have so much lost
> Your self, that what in you was best and most
> Respective, friendship, should so quickly dye?[3]

These are words of injured love, from someone who feels as though he has been stood up or forgotten. Donne sounds, in fact, like a spouse or lover asking a partner to spend a bit less energy on work, and channel some back home.

Letters were special for Donne. He came to see friendship as his second religion, and within that doctrine, letters were 'sacraments'.[4] Writing allowed an interfusion of selves. One verse letter to Henry Wotton opens with the declaration that 'Sir, more than kisses, letters mingle soules.'[5]

Here he was writing to possibly his oldest close friend, a man he had known since they were boys together at Oxford, addressing him at a special level of intimacy; yet the statement is still an assertion about letters in general. For Donne writing to a friend was not merely to exchange views or information, but to come closer than a joining of lips allows, letting divided spirits correspond. What mattered more than any information a letter might contain was the thought that went into it and the feeling it evoked, the act of penning a message and the event of receiving it. It was necessary, naturally, to have some material: but in one letter to Wotton, Donne wishes, 'I would some great princes or men were dead so [long as] I might chuse them, or some states or Countryes overthrowne so [long as] I were not in them, [so] that I might have some newes to ease this itch of writing . . .'[6] Satisfying this corporeal urge to write was well worth the death of someone high and mighty, or the fall of a kingdom. People long for something to report as an excuse to get in touch with those they love; but Donne was, in a way, more honest. He would write to a friend for friendship's sake, for the communion it brought, even when he had no news. A letter also provided him and his reader with a sanctuary from the world around them: 'If words seald vp in letteres be like words spoken in those frosty places where they are not herd till the next thaw, they haue yet this advantage that where they are herd they are herd only by one or such as in his iudgement they are fitt for.'[7] The glacial valley where this speech rings out is a controlled environment. The thaw is a directed event, experienced and witnessed privately. There are only two sets of footprints in the snow.

In the letter that begins 'Sir, more than kisses, letters mingle soules', Donne's advice, oddly enough, is for Wotton *not* to mingle, his soul or anything else, but to 'Be thou thine own home, and in thy selfe dwell'. He recommends that Wotton become a kind of human snail, or to move 'as Fishes glide, leaving no print where they passe, / Nor making sound'.[8] He tried to immunize himself and his friends from the hostile places they were forced to inhabit – and also from their own complicity in the wrongs that were committed in such places. Noble self-containment in Ireland was as rare among the English as humaneness towards the Irish. 'There is nothing in this country,' Wotton blustered to Donne, 'but it is either savage or wanton. They have hitherto wanted nothing more than to be kept in fear, which (by God's grace) they shall not want hereafter.'[9] The same letter went on to speak with pleasure at Wotton's party having ransacked a settlement where they had been 'guests' for the night. Donne, supporting the colonial effort from Whitehall, was by no means free from the same streak of nationalistic meanness. Banally, it comes through in connection with his 'ernest sorrow' for both 'the losse of many deare frends' and 'for the losse of a poore letter of mine . . . in wich though there were nothing to bee commended but that it was well suted for the place & barbarous enough to go thither.'[10]

To be fair to Donne, he also later complained about the 'barbarousness' of the Home Counties.[11] But Ireland was a special case. 'Savage', 'wanton', it *needed* to be tamed, reasoned Wotton, Donne and their contemporaries; it needed 'to be kept in fear'. Yet it is a commonplace now that the places that seem wild are often those that are incomprehensible, or simply fearful, to the traveller or invader. Much of Ireland was as dark to the English, geographically and culturally, as the unexplored New World. Often the edges of the place were all that was visible: John McGurk points out that although the English target was O'Neill's base in Ulster, 'the interior of the province remained uncharted until the Jacobean plantations'.[12] The English were unable to accept the nearby island as a neighbouring civilization and not a satellite. Although a colonial project had been going on since the Anglo–Norman invasion of the twelfth century, the English still had little idea what they were dealing with. Edmund Spenser's gigantic, hallucinogenic poem *The Faerie Queene*, perhaps the most unknowable work in English literature, was coloured in every line by the perplexing country. Spenser originally went to Ireland as a government official, a secretary like Wotton or Donne, and there acquired an estate in County Cork that was reclaimed and burnt in the 1598 uprising. In his eyes, the Irish were never quite human. At one point, his epic depicts a castle under attack from 'A thousand villeins', pouring

> Out of the rockes and caues adjoyning nye,
> Vile caytiue wretches, ragged, rude, deformd . . .[13]

These are clearly the 'savage and wanton' multitudes that Wotton felt needed the fear of God putting in them – despite Ireland having one of the most venerable and continuous of Europe's Christian cultures. Spenser goes on to compare these 'wretches' to a 'swarme of Gnats at euentide', rising from the fenlands in central Ireland, 'That as a cloud doth seeme to dim the skies.' The Irish had an insect hostility that required the imperial fly-swat of Elizabethan England.

'For our wars,' Wotton wrote to Donne, 'I can only say we have a good cause, and the worthiest gentleman of the world to lead it.'[14] Yet the campaign was not going well. Essex did a lap of honour around the country without any real triumph to celebrate. He won a few minor skirmishes, and managed to get supplies to a few stranded garrisons, but many men were being lost to sickness and desertion. Donne wrote frequently of his sadness at friends of his being 'gleaned' away. Essex's real commission, as everyone knew, had been to crush the Ulster rebels, and the Queen now pointed the finger. Reluctantly, warily, Essex took his troops northwards, and in early September his glittering career began to unravel completely. Meeting the Earl of Tyrone's army at Ardee, in County Louth, where it outnumbered his by at least two to one, Essex agreed to meet O'Neill alone, without witnesses. The Lord Lieutenant rode by himself to Bellaclinthe Ford, on the river Lagan, where O'Neill met him on the opposite bank. The water was too wide for them to hear each other properly so, courteously, O'Neill rode halfway across so they could speak. They talked awhile, and reached an agreement between themselves. The next day Wotton and the rest of Essex's staff ratified this chat as a formal truce.

In London, no clear word got through of what had happened; the worst interpretation of events was that Essex had concluded a private agreement with a traitor, overstepping his authority. The Queen gave him the benefit of the doubt, but absolutely ruled out any treaty with Tyrone. The Court hummed with rumour of just what Essex had done; many suspected he had cut a deal, acting not as a representative of the crown, but as someone with designs upon it. Factions within the Council itself became still more sharply defined and Donne's master, Sir Thomas Egerton, trying to keep the peace, came under great strain. This was personal as well as professional. His son and Donne's friend, the younger Sir Thomas, had been seriously wounded in a skirmish outside Dublin. In London, unable to go to his son, the Lord Keeper's administrative motor actions faltered, just occasionally, just momentarily. On 5 September, the Lord Keeper accidentally opened a sealed document for the eyes of Sir Robert Cecil, the Secretary of State: 'Bear with me,' he wrote, 'albeit grief hath made me unadvisedly to break open this packet, but I have seen no particular.'[15] News of the young Sir Thomas's condition dripped through sporadically, and the outlook was not good. Moreover, it now emerged that the dying young man was heavily in debt, as he confessed in a rambling, abject letter of apology to his father. Around London, the creditors were twitching, and Egerton senior began to hear 'that some are grounding a suit upon his poor son's head before he be buried'.[16] Soon the young man was past being able to care.

Sir Thomas junior left his young widow in trouble and also those friends who had stood surety for many of the tabs and loans he had notched up over the years. Revealingly, though Egerton senior made an effort to protect his daughter-in-law – and her three little daughters – he grew tight-lipped at the requests his son's former cronies now also made for help. It was their own fault, he reasoned, for helping his son get into so much trouble. They should never have put their names on the dotted lines. In this kind of situation, no matter how desperate or even deserving the pleas, Egerton did not waver.

Not all of young Egerton's friends, fortunately, found themselves in debtors' prison – for the moment, anyway. Those who were able gathered to attend the dead knight's funeral in the old family parish of Doddlestone, in Cheshire. With 'dromes and fife, Souldiers trayling pikes' and 'the Trumpet sounding dollfully', a military procession made its way through Chester to a requiem ceremony at the city cathedral. Various 'Esquires', former college-mates and comrades, including Donne's friend Christopher (or possibly his brother Samuel) from Lincoln's Inn, 'Mr Brooke', moved through the autumn sun in black cloaks. Others carried Egerton's accoutrements like things he had dropped or flung from himself in a last gallop. Captain Salisbury carried the dead soldier's spurs, Richard Brereton the gauntlets. Mr Marbury had the shield, Mr Hope the 'helme and crest', with 'the sword borne by Mr Jo[hn] done'.[17] Donne's prominence is testimony to how close the friendship had gone, and his importance to the family. Afterwards, the whole assembly celebrated Egerton's short, rash life in a grand dinner at the bishop's palace. His father, however, was simply too busy to be there.

In the following days the mourners all diverged again. A few of them, including one Robert Crockett, stopped for a pub supper at the Crown in Nampwich. The local postmaster, ducking in for a quick ale, asked them if they wouldn't mind taking the letters for him to his counterpart at the village of Stone, one Hugh Rathbone. They agreed: it was a common request, there being no such thing as a regular postman. Wobbling out into the autumn night, merry one moment, melancholy the next, Crockett with his friends rode to Stone, called on Rathbone, and left the mailbag on the counter for him. A month later a group of irritated postmasters descended on Crockett's house at Leighton, and asked what he'd done with the letters. There was stupefaction on all sides. Crockett was sure – pretty sure, anyway – that he had left them on the table, which Rathbone didn't deny, 'but said he delivered not the letters, nor did he know what was become of them'.[18] There was not much that could be done. This was how words and objects, dropped into the care of drunken soldiers and left lying around, could go missing in history, and how passionate correspondents such as Wotton and Donne could come to feel abandoned.

While some had leisure to tarry, Donne was needed back at work, as yet another crisis overtook the Court. A few days before, as the young Sir Thomas Egerton's friends rode towards Chester, the panic-stricken Earl of Essex was hurtling the other way, down from the north-west towards London. He was convinced that his enemies were infecting the Queen with lies about him. Disobeying a direct order that he should remain in Ireland until told otherwise, Essex sailed back on 24 September, and rode in a flap to Nonsuch Palace. What happened next was immediately logged in every newsletter leaving the Court: Essex charged through Nonsuch unannounced, in breach of all decorum,

And staied not [i.e. did not stop] till he came to the Queen's bedchamber, where he found the Queen newly up, the heare [hair] about her face; he kneeled unto her, kissed her handes, and her faire neck, and had some privat speech with her, which seemed to give him great contentment . . . Tis much wondred at here, that he went so boldly to her Maiesties presence, she not being ready and he soe full of dirt and mire, that his face was full of it.

Elizabeth had lived long enough to be undaunted – perhaps even gratified – by a young man storming into her bedroom, bespattered or not. But although she was pleased to see Essex at first, and happy to pet him, when he returned to her an hour later, he 'found her much chaunged in that small tyme, for she began to call hym to question for his return, and was not satisfied in the manner of his coming away and leauing all things [in Ireland] at soe great hazard.'[19] Essex found himself in deep trouble.

The consequences of Essex's fall from grace affected Donne's daily life considerably. For Elizabeth decided that the Earl should be detained in York House at her pleasure – and the Lord Keeper's expense – until she decided what to do with him. He was forbidden to come near the Court. Essex's rivals rubbed their hands, convinced that he was finished. Confounded, locked up in luxury confinement, Essex fell almost immediately into one of his spates of 'deadest melancholy'. He was also plagued with terrible diarrhoea. In October, Egerton apologized to members of the Council on the Earl's behalf: he had missed a hearing, and had been 'very ill for his health, did eat nothing, and this night hath rested little, being troubled with a great looseness which enforced him to rise often.' Essex's sickness touched the Queen's tenderness, and she paid him a visit in secret one night in November: she was used to his loosenesses. Despite such comforts, Essex was also troubled by the state of his finances. Egerton's letter asked if the Earl might have access to a couple of his servants, who 'could receive instructions to deal with his creditors (which be many and numerous)'.[20]

It might be expected that one of these servants should have been the Earl's private secretary, Henry Wotton. He and Donne now had ample opportunity to catch up with one another, and explain away all those lost, long-awaited letters. But around this time Wotton left Essex's staff and retired to the country; once again, the friends had to commit their relationship to the hazards of the post. Wotton may have simply been dismissed: Essex's household of followers was a potential small army, and the Queen herself disbanded it, allowing him to retain only a few. Yet this remnant seems to have consisted of Essex's administrative advisers: Henry Cuffe, his ill-fated but devoted chief secretary, stayed with him to the end. Wotton too might have remained if he had wished. In leaving Essex, Donne's friend appears to have been obeying an inherent family instinct for self-preservation. The Wottons boasted generations of pragmatic loyalists, unusual for their rank by their virtue of achieving influence but never desiring too much. Henry Wotton's grandfather, a Privy Councillor and governor of English-controlled Calais, turned down the top position of Lord Chancellor. His great uncle, Nicholas Wotton, refused to accept promotion to Archbishop of Canterbury. The Wottons were staunchly Protestant; but if a Papist monarch had returned to power, they might well have undergone a change of conscience and carried out the kind of adjustment that Donne's family, by complete contrast, had perennially failed or refused to make.

The tribal caution was congenital and even, it seemed, divinely inspired. Henry Wotton would never have been born without it. In 1554, at the time when the poet Thomas Wyatt was mustering men for an insurrection against the Catholic Queen Mary, old Nicholas was warned in a dream that his nephew Thomas, Wotton's father, was about to become involved in a conspiracy. To be on the safe side, Nicholas had the young hothead seized and imprisoned as Wyatt's men marched on London. Uncle and nephew thanked God together afterwards. Thomas confessed '*that he had more then an intimation of* Wyat's *intentions*; and thought he had not continued actually *innocent*, if his Uncle had not so happily dream'd him into a *Prison*.'[21]

This sixth sense came to Henry Wotton's aid now: he withdrew from Essex before the association became too dangerous, with serious concerns about the path his one-time master was embarking on, and retired to the country. Late in 1599, Donne kept him up to date with what he was missing. He wrote to Wotton from the Court, where he had to commit some kind of sin, so as 'not to be vtterly out of fashion and vnsociable', even though everyone else lived 'at a far greater rate & expence of wickednesse'. He chose Envy, telling his friend that he wished he too were in the country-side. The Court meanwhile was 'full of iollyty & revells & playes and as merry as if it were not sick'; in any case, it seems to have become preferable to York House, where the Earl was far from being a low-maintenance prisoner. 'He withers still . . .' Donne wrote, and 'the worst accidents of his sicknes are that he conspires with it, and yt is not here believed.' Essex was melancholy and making himself worse; yet he and his supporters were 'no more missed here [i.e. in Court, not at York House] than the Aungells which were cast downe from heaven nor (for anything I see) likelyer to retourne.' Essex, Donne concluded, was one of those men who 'want lockes for themselves and keyse for others'.[22]

Donne's letters to Wotton at this time do not survive in his own handwriting: we have them only because they were copied out and collected, out of personal, historical and stylistic interest – they served as both a good read and a model to others flexing their wits in correspondence. As a result, the authorship of many of the letters is less than certain; and given the circulation they received, the dejection they express at the corruption and depravity of the Court can be taken as fairly conventional – even from someone employed within the government. It isn't unusual, after all, for someone to share private gripes about working conditions. But although it might be permanently fashionable to complain about the degradation of the age, whatever age, Donne's disgust seems to have been almost pathological. He berated constantly, breathlessly, 'these tymes wich are ariued to that height of illeness that no man dares accuse them because everyone contributes much himself'.[23] His sense of revulsion arose predominantly from the sense that everyone, himself included, was part of the virulent 'illeness': everyone was implicated, passing on the contagion and receiving it again from those they encountered. He had no way of peeling himself free from the infected mass.

The Court was not a building; it was an entourage. It moved around like a weather system, and settled wherever the Queen took up her residence. For a government servant like Donne, it was always near, especially since she was based for much of the time at Whitehall Palace. But even without this physical proximity, it was essential to all those in the realm who sought promotion, protection or redress. Since its inevitable centre was the monarch, Elizabeth herself, the Court was the best place to press for title, property or a royal grant, or to plead for the release of an imprisoned relative. This lobbying was always mediated, for not everyone, naturally, had access to one of the great peers or the Queen herself. A suit could only be carried effectually by someone higher up the food chain than oneself, someone with contacts who had contacts they could call upon in turn; and no suit ever existed independently of other factors and other striving egos. The social stratifications, and the bartering at any given level, were reflected in the way that royal palaces were physically segmented. A petition had to pass, maybe in various hands, through a series of increasingly exclusive doorways, each supervised, formally or otherwise, by parties that would invariably require favours in return for access. Donne's writing records the pondlife in these outer chambers rather than the inner sanctums. As an important official awaiting decisions, rather than a governor making them himself, much of his time was spent milling about amid the hoi polloi, observing the dodges and the backhanders and no doubt being importuned; he mentions a 'great halle' hung with tapestries of 'the seaven deadly sinnes'.[24]

The world was sick and so, for some of 1600, was Donne. Run-down, he often caught fever, and rarely missed a chance to link his own ailments to those of the Court: recovering, he told Wotton, 'I am now free from an ague, though I am afraid the state bee not so . . .' He conceded that this was to be expected: moral decay was endemic, since 'all courts produce the same effects of envie & detraction of ielousy & other humane weakneses'. The daily round of backbiting was getting to him. He signed off gravely, without irony, '& so I wish vs a better world'.[25]

He found relief in friendship – or, at least, in writing of how much friendship meant to him: he assured one companion that if he had seen him, 'I would not haue beene sick or at least I would not haue beene well by so ill a meanes, as taking phisick [medicine].'[26] When it came actually to meeting a long-absent friend, instead of lamenting an absence, Donne's happiness could put him at a loss. When Sir Maurice Berkeley, a comrade from the expedition to Cadiz, rolled up in London, Donne sent his 'man' – apparently having replaced Tom Danby the suit-thief – to greet him 'cum salute plurima' – 'with multiple salutations'. The practical matter of suggesting where they might get together for a meal was almost beyond Donne. Instead of going round to see Berkeley directly, he wrote a letter to Wotton: 'I dare not wish him where we shall meet at supper,' he flustered, 'lest I commit some excess of gladness.'[27]

Berkeley may indirectly have brought Donne much anxiety as well as pleasure. Sir Maurice had a half-brother called Thomas Russell, a friend of William Shakespeare from a village just a little way along the river from Stratford-upon-Avon. He was eventually one of the executors of Shakespeare's will. Russell provides just one of several possible but tenuous connections between the two poets. Donne almost certainly knew Shakespeare by sight, since he was a great frequenter of plays and Shakespeare was a jobbing actor. Both belonged to very different scenes, though both enjoyed similar aristocratic connections: Shakespeare was close to the Earl of Southampton, an ally of Essex who also returned in disgrace from the escapade in Ireland. Both in all likelihood brushed shoulders in the bankside taverns. Yet the link between the two might have been historically closer. In January 1600, a book called *Amours by J.D. with certen other sonnetes by W.S.* was prepared for the press. The story behind this little volume of verse is a complete mystery: no copies are known to survive, and no one knows if this is because the *Amours* were suppressed, lost in a fire, or whether they failed to catch on and merely frittered away in time. Yet R. C. Bald, the twentieth century's leading scholar of Donne's biography, was willing to speculate that Thomas Russell, using manuscripts that Donne might have passed along to Maurice Berkeley, would have been ideally placed to cobble together a collection of both poets' work.[28]

If the 'J.D.' on the title page was John Donne, the publication must have flung him into a panic. As secretary to the Lord Keeper, it might not have been beyond him to pull a few strings and arrange for the book not to be issued – he might even have reached a private settlement with Eleazar Edgar, the printer who entered the book in the Stationers' Register. If these poems were Donne's, the title *Amours* suggests they included some of his 'elegies', or the lyrics that would become known as *Songs and Sonets*. By now Donne was doing his level best to control the circulation of such pieces: they did not sit well with the responsible image of himself he now tried projecting. These were the 'love-song weeds' that had sprung up 'Where seeds of better Arts, were early sown.' However, Donne could still not resist giving copies to a trusted few when they called for them: he was not mean enough to deny a request. More often than not, he urged acquaintances not to let anyone else see his early work, and to pay no great heed to it themselves, at precisely the moment he handed it over.

In a letter from this time accompanying one of his private anthologies, Donne insisted, 'Only in obedience I send you some of my paradoxes: I loue you and myself & them to well to send them willingly for they carry with them a confession of their lightnes.' In the next breath, however, he tried brushing off the harm these pieces might do: 'indeed they were made rather to deceave tyme then her daughter truth . . . if they make you to find better reasons against them they do there office: for they are but swaggerers.' Any jauntiness in Donne's own step disappeared a few lines later, as he sought earnest guarantees that these 'swaggerers' would go no further, demanding 'an assurance vpon the religion of your friendship that no copy shalbee taken'. A little later on, though, his mood softened again, promising his friend that 'I meane to acquaint you with all myne'. Even this thought, however, met with instant reservation, since 'to my satyrs there belongs some feare & to some elegies & these some shame'.[29]

The swaggering 'paradoxes' Donne spoke of here were prose exercises, written throughout the 1590s, that exhaustively pursued and bore out an apparently unreasonable assumption, for example, 'that all things kill themselves' – an idea that would preoccupy him much more deeply in future years – 'that women ought to paint themselves' or 'that only cowards dare dye'. This kind of writing was much in vogue at the time: Sir William Cornwallis, Donne's friend, who was knighted by Essex in Ireland, was also a keen maker of paradoxes. His included whimsical proofs 'That it is a happines to be in debt' and 'That a great redd nose is an ornament to the face'.[30] While Donne's paradoxes were out of keeping with his veneer as a government secretary, the body of verse that he described as bearing his 'Satyrique thornes' involved a different category of risk: to these, as he said, 'there belongs some feare'. The authorities occasionally made an example of writers who overstepped the mark in print; and as with all censorship, artistic merit was irrelevant. John Davies, another Lincoln's Inn scribbler well known to Donne, and another candidate, in fact, for being

the 'J.D.' who co-wrote the lost *Amours*, published work that set
his civil career back by several years. *Epigrammes and Elegies* (1599)
combined a hotch-potch of fart gags and jibes against Puritans
by Davies along with Christopher Marlowe's urbane, sensuous,
note-perfect versions of Ovid's *Amores*; the bishops, having read
the volume thoroughly and carefully enough, naturally, to qualify
their judgement, were disgusted, and the book was burnt in public.
Satirical and amorous verse could sometimes cut too close.

   There was another reason Donne now tried to keep his thorns
and weeds under wraps. He was close to a teenage girl that he
didn't want to upset. Her name was Ann More. She was staying
at York House under the protection of Sir Thomas Egerton and
the supervision of his wife, her aunt and guardian: Ann's mother,
who had given birth to nine other children, died in 1590. Ann
came from a family of very wealthy and well-landed country
people, the Mores of Loseley, and had been sent to learn the ways
of London society. Though he was technically just a senior servant,
Donne dined with the Lord Keeper's family, so he saw Ann at
supper each evening. The old house abounded with nooks and
crannies, and Donne was well practised at finding space and opportunity to confer. Ann and John could meet and walk together in
the gardens and courtyards of the surrounding Whitehall Palace,
and talk amid the din in the crowded assembly chambers of the
Court. Whitehall afforded long galleries with large bay windows
one could stand and speak privately in, along with a warren of
much smaller reception rooms and private lodgings. Ann was very
young, perhaps too young to have been tainted by the 'sickly
dotage of the world' that Donne complained of to everyone within
his confidence.[31] Yet she was never far away from the centre of
affliction: like Donne, she was an inmate, a fellow sufferer, someone with whom he could find mutual refuge. She was also unob-
tainable. Ann was his master's ward, carefully surveilled by her
aunt, Lady Egerton. A wrong move could be disastrous.

   'I wonder,' Donne would one day ask, 'what thou, and I /Did,
till we lov'd?' He of course knew perfectly well what he had been
doing, and the memory of his 'many profane mistresses' was to be

less than comfortable for the rest of his life. The 'elegies' detailing and embellishing Donne's earlier affairs, with their hard sexual bargains and bedside stripteases, were likely to distress Ann if she knew they were getting around. It is impossible to know if she was aware that these poems existed or, if she did, how she viewed the past they recorded. In 1600, having known her perhaps two years, Donne himself seems to have been unsure of where he stood. He was anxious to take precautions. 'I be tough enough,' he said, in the letter that accompanied his 'Paradoxes', 'yet I have a ridling disposition to be ashamed of feare & afrayd of shame.'[32] It was an anxious wait.

The build-up before love was difficult to bear. 'The Flea', one of Donne's most famous poems, describes the frustration he could feel. He picks a bug off a woman's neck and tries to prove that its life is no more important than her virginity; and since it has bitten and 'sucked' both of them, their bloods have already been 'mingled' anyway. She shows him what she thinks of his argument by squishing its subject. The speaker responds,

> Cruell and sodain, hast thou since
> Purpled thy naile, in blood of innocence?

Donne's annoyance is pretend, though the purple aftermark is real enough. The flea's death may not take very much life from either Donne or Ann, if the poem is written with her in mind, but that isn't to say that it is a meaningless amount. If innocence matters, then so does innocent blood, and the innocent union it represents. The poem seems all in favour of casual sex but in fact realizes there is no such thing – no lovemaking can be casual in the moral universe which Donne creates through his performing flea; nothing is without consequence, no matter how tiny the detail.

'I wonder, by my troth, what thou, and I / Did, till we lov'd?' The conditions at York House put Donne's question in another light. They probably 'Did' other things besides make love. They had no choice. Almost every aspect of his and Ann's circumstances enforced a deferral of desire, down to the way their bodies were encased and regulated. Each day began in a separate chamber, with the assembly of an elaborate costume: Donne pulling on his clinging breeches, fastening himself in his doublet, clamping his neck in a ruff; Ann undergoing a still more rigorous ordeal, being combed, bodiced, kirtled and gowned, probably in chaste white, with her neck covered. They could not stay together, expose themselves, talk openly or touch for long. Their respective supervisors deprived the couple of many chances to inspect each other's fleas thoroughly.

The relationship was difficult from the start, but its first great trial began early in 1600. Lady Egerton, never strong, died on 20 January. Egerton was devastated. He had lost his elder son just four months before; with the sordid account-settling that followed Thomas's death, not to mention the national emergency in Ireland, the Lord Keeper had had no chance to mourn. Now he broke down. 'My Lady Egerton died on Monday Mórning,' wrote Rowland Whyte to his master, Sir Robert Sidney, on Thursday: 'the Lord Keeper doth sorrow more, then the wisdom of soe great a Man ought to doe. He keapes privat . . . And it is thought he will not come Abroade this Terme.' The private luxury of grief was a matter of public concern. Life in York House was frozen; Egerton refused to see anyone. His importance to the state was such that the metabolism of government grew dangerously slow. Egerton had missed only a week's work, but a critical clogging soon built up in the courts and in council. Whyte reported, 'Vpon Friday, there was no Starr Chamber kept, and a great Miss of hym in Chancery.' By now he was under pressure to shrug off his sorrow. 'Her Majestie sent comfort to hym,' wrote Whyte, 'and, as I heare, to tell hym that the publiq Service must be preffered before priuat passions.'[33]

Egerton was soon back in Chancery and Star Chamber; but the strain had told. He was sick of having no personal space. When Lady Egerton died, he demanded that something be done about his irregular domestic arrangements: 'he is greatly discontented,' Whyte heard, 'that his House is made a Prison of soe long Continuance, for the Earl of *Essex* hath remained there, these 17 Weekes.'

The Queen, no doubt relieved, accepted this complaint, and also realized she had kept Essex, now in better health, on ice for long enough. By mid-February, after an elaborately staged process of deliberation, it was widely expected that the Earl would soon 'goe to his owne Home, and soe by Degrees haue more Liberty'.[34]

The pressure put on Egerton during his fraught week of re-clusion indicates the difficulty of relieving any 'priuat passions' in a manically watchful social environment. Yet for John and Ann the period was a decisive interlude. Perhaps really grieved by the death of her aunt, perhaps guiltily pleased to have her out of the way, and with her family caught up in mourning and making funeral arrangements, for a short time Ann had nobody keeping track of her movements. Donne too, with Egerton's office in paralysis, may have had more time on his hands. The house was far from still, but John and Ann lay in a vortex, neither of them quite important enough to attract much attention or play leading parts in the surrounding commotion. Egerton's prisoner also found himself at the eye of the storm. On clear days in the late winter, the lovers might sometimes have run into the Earl of Essex, doing his best to look meditative, wrapped up against the cold: 'The Earl hath recovered his Health, and I heare walks in the Garden at Yorke House, in a Cloth Gown, Cloth Jerken, Cloth Hose, Cloth Stokins, Cloth Mittins.'[35]

There has been no thaw in the frosty places where the words of John and Ann are still sealed up. Yet they plighted their troth while living under the same roof: Donne would write, 'So long since as her being at York House this had foundacion, and so much then of promise and contract built upon yt as withowt violence to conscience might not be shaken.'[36] In their own eyes, they were all but married already. His master might have had his suspicions; he might have been beyond noticing such things. Isaak Walton believed that Ann's father had 'some intimation' of her romance with Donne.[37] But in any case, while Egerton was unable to acceler-ate Essex's removal, there were at least a few people in his home he could get rid of. With her guardian dead, there was no reason why Ann should remain in Whitehall: soon she was sent away.

8. The Rebels

February, a year later, and friends spent hours in the company of paper, supplying news and recommending books, lamenting one another's absence. Celebrity life continued in the vicinity of Whitehall. On the Strand, Lord Grey fought on horseback with Essex's closest ally, the Earl of Southampton. Just up the road, Essex himself was back in his own house, and had opened his doors to the city's desperados. The Court was anxious about his conduct. But then, the Court was always anxious. Pranks and wagers kept the city diverted. A man bound in a sack hopped all the way from Charing Cross, past the Lord Keeper's door, along the Strand and up Fleet Street to St Paul's Cathedral. Another joker found a way of riding his horse up the bell-tower stairs and out onto the top of the Cathedral's steeple, which was blunt and flat from a lightning strike some forty years before. Below and beyond, legal business proceeded interminably, and Donne as ever followed at Egerton's heels through Westminster Hall.

But there was a new regime at the Lord Keeper's house. The previous autumn Egerton had married Alice Stanley, the Countess Dowager of Derby, a woman twenty years his younger. He had grown tired during two grieving seasons. The loss of his second wife was still recent and no doubt raw, but he was not a man who could bear to be locked in himself for long. Every ounce of his life was directed outwards. In whatever spare time he had, Egerton was a great reader, but even study was for public application as much as private solace. His vast book collection, thick with works on history, geography, law, science and philosophy, was a social commodity, not just a solitary resource. He was an eager patron of writers and students who paid the right kind of respect to the state and held the right kind of contempt for the Roman Church. The new lady of York House complemented his extroversion perfectly.

The Countess Dowager enjoyed a wide circle of dependent poets. Edmund Spenser had dedicated 'The Teares of the Muses', one of his shorter poems, to her in 1591, marking out 'excellent beautie' and 'vertuous behaviour' as her chief characteristics.[1] Had a strict historical record been Spenser's priority, he might also have mentioned her immense practical knowledge of the legal system. Since the death of her husband Lord Ferdinando Stanley, Earl of Derby, in 1594, the Countess had been caught up in a series of protracted suits over allowances and property. Appearing as 'Amaryllis' in another work of Spenser's, she was said to have been 'freed from *Cupids* yoke by fate' – the death of husband number one – and living since then in chaste 'dread' of the bands of matrimony.[2] Or, just waiting for the right man to become available. The Lord Keeper of the Seal, the head of the legal profession, offered cover and influence. For her part, Alice guaranteed the bastard son of a Cheshire squire a place in one of the wealthiest and most influential families in the country. It was a match that neither could turn down.

The Countess lost no time in taking over York House and fleshing out the skeleton staff that her smallpox-stricken predecessor had left. Moving in, she brought with her a retinue of over forty servants, along with her three daughters. Egerton's own people now had to make room. It was Donne's turn to be asked to leave, and he moved just a little way up the Strand to digs in the Savoy. This was another sprawling complex, originally the site of a medieval palace, but for some time now a hospital with private lodgings in its precincts. Though with mixed feelings, Donne was probably glad of the move. The Countess, her daughters and their train of hangers-on brought a flush of life to the Lord Keeper's home, but they also enervated the place. A fraught atmosphere surrounded the marriage from the beginning. The wedding took place in Russell House, which Alice and her sisters had inherited from their father, Lord Russell, but which had also been the home of the Dowager Lady Russell, their stepmother and the mother of Egerton's second wife (family connections at the Court were somewhat intertangled). A struggle had been going on for some time over the control of the property, particularly over Alice and her sister's desire to rename the place: Lady Russell, then Egerton's mother-in-law, had complained that 'whensoever they weeded out their father's name out of Russell House they should root out my heart from them.'[3] The Lord Keeper had experienced such family arguments from a relative distance in the course of his profession; now they moved in a procession to take up permanent residence with him. 'God send him good lucke' was the only blessing one contemporary could offer.[4]

The move to the Savoy gave Donne some breathing space. Whitehall remained an important centre of his working day – and he probably still ate at Egerton's table – but at least now he had a place of his own again. The company the Lord Keeper brought into York House could often be onerous to say the least. There Donne mingled with theological partisans such as George Downame, at this time composing his equanimous deliberation on the Roman Catholic position, *A Treatise Concerning Anti-Christ*. In theory at least, Donne had more opportunity now to mingle with a sprightlier crowd. Seeing even just a little less of the Lord Keeper was no bad thing either, since Egerton could be very touchy. During his previous marriage, Egerton's mother-in-law had spared few pains to let him know that he was thought of about town as a greedy, sanctimonious hypocrite, and the ambitious nature of his third match did little to change that opinion. Such comments aggravated Egerton's nerves; yet, undaunted, he presented a yet sterner moralistic front to the world, and demanded still higher standards from his entourage. Coming home of an evening to his own lodgings, secretary Donne was able to undo a few buttons and slip off his straight face.

Sleeping away from York House also gave Donne a break from the constant physical memory of happier times. Almost a year had passed since Ann More had been packed off to the country. Occasionally she might pay a visit to the capital with her father, Sir George More, who had lodgings at Charing Cross and was already scouting around for a suitable bachelor for her. Donne saw her very seldom, if at all. Down at the Lord Keeper's, meanwhile, the Countess Dowager was busy matchmaking. Apparently without Egerton's knowledge, she arranged a marriage between her middle daughter, Frances, and his second son, John; but first, in January 1601, she married off her youngest girl, Elizabeth, only thirteen, to the fifteen-year-old Lord Hastings, who was let out for the morning to attend the ceremony and then sent straight back to his tutors. Donne evidently felt the occasion called for a poem: Elizabeth, who became the Countess of Huntingdon when her husband was made an Earl in 1604, grew to be one of Donne's closest female friends. What Donne came up with after her wedding, though, was neither epistle nor epithalamion, but a monologue on love, longing and the techniques of seduction. The poem would have been better addressed to someone heading out into the singles jungle than a child bride whose whole sexual life had just been predetermined.

He expressed impatience with the messing about that came with courtship, insisting that he was not one to beat about the bush or pine away. He was no

> white-liver'd dotard that would part
> From his slipperie soule with a faint groan . . .

You wouldn't catch Donne sighing and folding his arms, talking to trees and whispering himself away. Yet the poem is preoccupied too with first love, with Eden, and what breaks through intermittently is a sense of paradise lost, a primal, innocent attraction, 'an unripe willingnesse' that was disrupted before it could be explored or understood. The sexual veteran in his late twenties betrays a novitiate Donne, uncertain of feeling, uncertain of how to express desire, or translate it into touch; suddenly awkward, despite all his experience, moping along at Ann's side during their days together at York House:

> What pretty innocence in those dayes mov'd!
> Man ignorantly walked by her he lov'd;
> Both sigh'd and enterchanged a speaking eye,
> Both trembled and were sick, both knew not why.[5]

On the map, she was not so far away. Ann was living at the More family home at Loseley Park, near Guildford in Surrey – not a long ride from London. Yet within the walled gardens or the cavernous mansion, she might as well have been at the other end of the kingdom. Loseley managed to be both lavish and austere. The house itself, built in the early 1560s, partly of stone plundered from a nearby abbey in the Reformation, was of a rather plain design, dignified but gloomy. Yet Ann's dictatorial father, Sir George, an ambitious squire with an apoplectic temperament, ran an extravagant household, with at least fifty servants, and his family and guests devouring 'an ox and twelve sheep' every week.[6] Sir George tried very hard to impress his guests, though his hospitality was often compromised by a tendency to explode into anger when things didn't go according to plan. He was extremely wealthy, yet very frustrated. Part of his problem was that he suspected the very suaveness and sophistication he tried cultivating in his own manner. He never quite got it right and, realizing this, became yet more maddened with himself and the world. For Ann, who had grown up away from him, he must have been almost insufferable. What made it worse was that he had very definite plans for her.

For years, the Mores had laboriously forged connections with the royal household, which they exploited in choosing their interior decorations. The great hall at Loseley is still adorned with *grottesche* painting, interweaving humans and animals with dense fantastic plant-life and royal mottos. These fittings were taken across Surrey from Nonsuch – the royal home built by Henry VIII – sometime before the palace was destroyed in the late seventeenth century, and might well have been installed by Ann's day. There were other exquisite imports, including a *trompe l'oeil* panel carving of 'elongated arches and passageways'.[7] Ann was surrounded by a thick montage of space-fillers and status symbols, some fraught with meaning, some not so deep as they seemed, down to the family emblems, moorhens and cockatoos, that were sculpted and painted on various fixtures. Amid the costly things about her, some beautiful, some tacky, there was no escaping who she was, the class to which she belonged, or what was expected of her.

In many ways, Ann's life mirrored Donne's: it was colourful, crowded, rich; yet bleak. Visitors infested the house continually, feasted by Ann's father to stock up favours and boost, though with little long-term success, his standing at the Court. Ann, one of nine children, was the third of five daughters – all of whom married dependably wealthy country gentlemen. Sir John Oglander of the Isle of Wight, who married Ann's youngest sister Frances, is perhaps the defining example of a fitting partner for a More girl: rich, well-landed, educated but not esoteric, and of good loyal stock. Oglander, by his own admission 'one of the Revelers' in his early days at Oxford, was an amiable traditionalist who kept the same beliefs and allegiances throughout his life. He was made Deputy-Lieutenant of the Isle of Wight, and supported the crown through the Civil War right to the end. Charles I, on the run from the Parliamentarians, sought refuge with him long after both men had little but shreds of their former authority.

The man Ann loved, if her family considered him for a second, was a very different proposition. Donne was invalid for reasons that had little to do with his personal qualities. He was thirteen or fourteen years older than Ann, who was only fifteen, but this difference in age was not remarkable for the time, and no objection could be based on that alone. Neither was Donne's Roman Catholic background an obstacle in itself, so long as it remained renounced. Had any of Donne's poems reached Sir George, as they conceivably might, since he made a point of keeping up with new writing, whatever opinion he drew of their literary merit he was unlikely to have welcomed their author as a son-in-law. This at least was the reaction Donne feared when he expressed concern at the copying and increased circulation of his work: 'to my satyrs there belongs some feare & to some elegies & these some shame,' he worried.[8] It was poetry that ridiculed conceit, pomposity and small-mindedness, and celebrated free love: the very kind of writing men love to read except when it may have some bearing on their own wives, daughters and sisters. In Egerton's household, Donne was well placed to do great things, but also to progress no further or fall back should his fortunes decline. His position brought him influential friends; but he also had former shipmates that now seemed shady, disreputable – the kind of potentially desperate characters who had been congregating at the Earl of Essex's house since the autumn before, toasting their fallen commander, enjoying free meals, wishing for better times. This was how Donne's past and his connections made him appear; yet as Sir George More scanned English society for a good match for Ann, it is most unlikely that he went so far as profiling Donne as a possible suitor. There was nothing personal involved, in fact, it was strictly business: the secretary was poor, technically nothing more than a servant, and had nothing to offer.

Both Ann and John had to cope with long silences. A year went by in which both wondered if they were in the other's thoughts, and what the lack of news might mean. There was no guaranteed way of getting letters through. Up to his neck in drab legal paper-work, Donne had to torture himself with the thought of infinitely more eligible bachelors encamping Ann's palatial family home. Cooped up in the rustic stronghold, meanwhile, Ann could only wonder which flirt from Donne's past might have caught his eye at some glamorous soirée. Both were stuck with the nauseous romance of living with an absence, feeding the heart on thin air. Most people know what this is like, if only for a few days or weeks. The only nourishment is speculation, sometimes affectionate, some-times jealous, maybe wildly anxious with imagined disasters. But in the second week of February 1601, Ann had just cause to craze herself quietly with worry. Reports pulsed to the country of a pitched battle on the Strand – a man run through the face – a gunfight lasting hours. The Lord Keeper and other senior councillors had been taken hostage. The city was blockaded and the Queen herself was under armed guard. And somewhere in the middle of all this was Donne, lying dead on a corner or, hopefully, trying to get a note through to Ann reassuring her that he was all right.

On Sunday the eighth, a while before ten in the morning, all was as it should have been. London's churches donged and boomed, calling the faithful and rebuking anybody trying to lie in or recover from the night before. The destitute shifted in their straw, dogs and tame hawks picked up scraps in the streets. On the Strand, people moved to worship; others, perhaps hobbling down from the red-light district of Holywell and Wych Streets to the north, moved home to scrape off their infections. Yet at either end of the main thoroughfare, there were unusual comings and goings. Men were mustered, muskets loaded; key positions around Whitehall were guarded and fortified. And a posse of dignitaries with their aides, led by the Lord Keeper, left the palace and headed up the Strand towards Essex House. Like York House, this was an impressive aristocratic property, and it followed the basic outline of other mansions on the Strand. Its grounds spread down to the Thames, and on the Strand side it had a large courtyard, bordered by stables and domestic offices, and fronted by a gateway through which a horsedrawn carriage could pass. Five or so years earlier, Donne had probably called on Essex here to pay his respects and offer his services as a gentleman soldier. As the secretary now went along the street with his master, the familiar stretch might have been strangely allied with an incongruent feeling from years back; the feeling, perhaps, that he got as a voluntary, when waiting off-shore from Cadiz, or marching towards a fort on the island of Fayal.

Egerton had been sent to get an explanation. The previous evening, the Earl of Essex had ignored a summons to appear before the Privy Council. A specially commissioned performance of Shakespeare's *Richard II* – in which a king is seen to be 'justly' deposed – had been put on at the Globe. Peers and gentlemen, and rowdy, disappointed, ex-military types, followers of the Earl through the Low Countries, the Spanish raids and lastly in Ireland, had banqueted at Essex House but had not left afterwards. Elizabeth and her officials knew the place was full of munitions. So she sent her top lawyer, Egerton, to tell Essex to stop before he started. When the party reached the gateway, beyond which was a courtyard crowded with a private militia, Donne must have experienced some embarrassment as well as anxiety; many of those inside, perhaps even the heavies on show at the entrance, had formerly been his comrades. It seemed as though he always had to feel like a turncoat.

Egerton's group was not well received. These were the bureaucrats and grey fellows, the cost-counters who had undone the
flamboyant Earl. These were the ministry men on whom Essex's
entourage blamed all their frustrations. Acting calm, Egerton
demanded to speak to the Earl. Inside, Essex, high on paranoia,
was all but cracking up. Materially and politically he had lost
everything with the ruling order; and he had given the rein to a
pack of desperate men who had little to lose in the first place. He
sent out a message that he would see the Lord Keeper and the
other councillors who were present, but that their attendants –
younger men, like Donne, armed, and with some experience of a
fight – could not cross the threshold. Donne could be excused if
he gave a sigh of relief; Egerton could be excused for looking at
him askance. But the Lord Keeper bravely agreed to the terms,
and took Chief Justice Popham, the Earl of Worcester and Sir
William Knollys – controller of the Royal Household – inside
with him. His secretary heard cries of 'Kill them! Kill them!' as the
little group of very powerful, yet suddenly very vulnerable, men
passed into the courtyard.

More than the men had gone in there, however. The only
subordinate taken inside was the Bearer of the Great Seal – or
rather, whichever clerk to whom the holder of the patent on the
office had delegated the daily job. Now the Great Seal was no mere
rubber stamp, even though its sole purpose *was* to rubber-stamp all
legal and governmental documents of any real importance. Bearing
the wax impression of the seal, these papers carried by visual proxy
the presence of the monarch herself, giving a clear message to
anyone, even those who couldn't read, that the words they held
were authentic and authoritative. The seal itself was a large disc
with a picture of Elizabeth on each side: on one, she is a woman
of action, defender of the realm and the faith, wearing a breastplate,
riding a horse without holding the reins as she carries an orb and
sceptre. On the other, she is the archetype of regality, surrounded
by sunbeams from heaven, with deferential, disembodied hands
holding her cape aloft. And now she had been taken hostage.

In a desperate interview, Essex told Egerton what he had made himself believe – that a plot had been laid against his life, and that he had summoned his forces to defend it to the last, 'since my enemies cannot be satisfied unless they suck my blood'.[9] Egerton tried to persuade him to come quietly. Instead Essex locked the Lord Keeper along with the others in a back room under armed guard. An irresolute morning passed. Left outside, leaderless, Donne can have had little idea what to do next. It was in fact almost safer to be inside Essex House than a potential target in the middle of the Strand. For presently a squadron of rebels on horseback, with Essex at its head, clattered from the courtyard. Dodging unfriendly glances, indifferent hooves, perhaps even an occasional swipe, Donne could have only scampered for cover in a back street, or tried to get back to Whitehall. But this was no safe port of call either: it would most likely be Essex's first target after raising the mob. Donne would have been a very loyal subject indeed if he did not experience a moment of split allegiance in the torn-up mud and confusion of the Strand. A herald rode through town, proclaiming Essex a traitor. If the rising failed, Donne could not afford to be anywhere near renegades who might claim him as an acquaintance or an ally. Yet as the Earl, fantastically arrayed, hurtled out with his elite bodyguard, it must have seemed quite possible that Donne's former general would not fail, would in fact seize power, and that all the steady paper-shuffling of the previous three years might count for nothing.

For the coup to have succeeded, however, Essex should have taken a left on his way out, and led his forces down the Strand towards Whitehall while their spirits were still high. Instead, the rebels cantered the other way, in the direction of St Paul's, hoping to meet with popular support in the old City of London. There was no reason for Donne, a mere spectator, to have followed them. St Paul's was now the epicentre of a danger zone. Donne's options, if he had sense, were to stay where he was, anxiously watching for developments at Essex House, or to withdraw to Whitehall, where there was safety in numbers. But if curiosity or concern proved too much, he could still have skulked up to Ludgate Hill, where the huge, blockheaded cathedral stood; where Essex and his men

had reached the crowd of thousands that stood listening to the
sermon at Paul's Cross. This was a wide, open space where the
populace gathered on Sundays and religious feast-days to have
their consciences flayed and their politics righted. This was where
Donne's grandfather, John Heywood, had carried a faggot in
repentance for his heretical views. If Donne as a toddler ever sat
on the old comic's lap, he would have seen the scar on the old
man's hand and wrist that the smouldering twigs had left; the
burn-marks were the characteristic stigmata of the penitent, and
were recognized about town, frequently attracting further scorn.
The Cathedral had overlooked more burnings, gnashings and
weepings than it had years on its back: Essex was just one more in
an ongoing procession trailing through the decades.

Essex's pack sent up the cry that there was a plot to murder him,
and that his present show of arms 'sought nothing but a sudden
defence till her Majesty might be better informed of it'.[10] Essex
tried rallying the city to his cause, but did not meet the surge of
spontaneous backing he had counted on. This is not to say that he
was not well treated. People waved and cheered as he and the
other nobles pranced about. The Lord Sheriff welcomed the Earl
to his house and sent beer out for his men to drink. An armourer,
they were promised, was going to bring the rebels extra equipment
– most of the aristocrats were only wearing their Sunday best. But
there was little in the way of solid reinforcements. The Sabbath
was, after all, a funny day for an uprising. The February sun began
to slump. Amid the speechifying, some of Essex's men slipped
away. One lieutenant, Sir Ferdinando Gorges, was acutely aware
that the hostages were still in the custody of cohorts who would
be getting anxious about the delay, and possibly trigger-happy. He
asked the Earl if he might nip back to Essex House to release
Egerton and the others, and try persuading them to urge the Queen
for a pardon. By now events had overtaken the conspirators.
Earlier, a warrant had been issued urging all loyal subjects 'forth-
with to arm yourselves, as many as you can with horse and armour,
and the rest as foot with pike and shot . . . to march to the Court
for the defence of her Majesty's person.' With the Court secure,

measures were then taken to hem in the rebels. When Essex, realizing that he might as well head home to make the best of a bad lot, led his men past St Paul's once more, he found a heavy company of soldiers barring his way back to Ludgate.

At this point the former hero of the realm found himself stranded with only a few fellow dreamers. Disdaining to speak in person with the commander at the barricade, Sir John Leveson, Essex sent a reluctant lackey called John Barger 'to tell Sir John that the sheriff of the city willed him [Essex] to go to Ludgate, that he [the sheriff] would send him arms thither'. Essex was crazily asking the Queen's man to let him through so he could pick up more weapons and armour; but his motives were pure. He only wanted these supplies because so many of those present, 'his kinsmen, earls, barons and gents', had no protection but their rapiers, and 'must enter upon armed pikes and shot'.[11] All the Earl wanted was a fair fight.

Leveson neither blinked nor budged from his post. Gorges was sent with the same message, but had no joy either. In need of a bargaining card, Essex now accepted Sir Ferdinando's advice about the hostages. He told him to return to Essex House and set Chief Justice Popham free, but that the others, including Egerton, had to stay. Gorges slipped off, cutting round the blockade by the back streets. Other representatives were sent to cadge a way through for the shrinking band of men. Then the standoff broke. Someone on Essex's side shouted 'Shoot, shoot!' – forgetting, presumably, that only a few had anything to shoot with – and the Queen's troops immediately opened fire. There was a flurry of feathers and spangles in an all-or-nothing rush that failed to breach the line. A skirmish at the barricade ensued in which Essex took two bullets through the hat, and saw his pageboy killed. Other friends were wounded and taken. The government soldiers also took losses, but held firm, and the rebels retreated, their party shrinking like a meteorite falling through the atmosphere. Scrambling down to the Thames, Essex was able to load his singed and crestfallen supporters onto a barge, and get home by water to the back entrance of his house. Disembarking, he discovered that he had just missed the Lord Keeper and the other prisoners leaving from the same wharf. Sir

Ferdinando Gorges had disobeyed his master's orders and set all the hostages free in the hope of saving his own neck. He had begged them to be lenient, and unlocked and escorted them to the river, down which they were rowed back to Whitehall. The Earl, arriving from the other direction, found himself standing less on a riverbank than an atoll. Soon gunfire began battering Essex House from the street and surrounding rooftops: artillery had been brought from the Tower of London; and he could do nothing but sit out the bombardment for long enough to salvage a little dignity.

After surrendering, Essex was imprisoned in the Tower. His supporters were rounded up, and many began fighting to exculpate themselves, spooning out the water from cover stories that kept springing leaks. Everyone, it seemed, was merely in the wrong place at the wrong time. Pleas and disavowals inundated the Queen's Council. Part of Donne's job, in the following days and weeks, was no doubt to help interview prisoners, to transcribe and circulate their dissonant testimonies. Some denied the charge of conspiracy flatly, others promised to be different men from that day forth. Some tried plucking at heartstrings and appealing to religion: 'I had no hand in the contrivance of any plots,' implored one. 'Let the doleful cry of my poor wife and children move your heart to a Christian commiseration of me; let them not be exposed to beggary and misery.' Others tried blaming dire coincidences, frightful mix-ups that had trammelled them in the moment: Francis Manners claiming 'that my brother was gone to Essex House, I went to him' – *why?* – 'from whence, not knowing, I was carried with this sway . . .'[12] Essex had staged a rebellion with somnambulant traitors: none could say what they were doing. The truth may be that Essex himself wasn't sure quite what would have happened if the coup had succeeded. He plucked excuses from the shadows on his cell walls. He blamed his advisers, his secretaries, claimed variously that all he had wanted was to speak with the Queen, not to harm her, and that he actually wanted to protect her from the *real* traitors – men like his old lieutenant and rival, Sir Walter Ralegh – scholars of night who had a plan to kill him in his bed. He was past knowing quite what he meant any more.

'I must confess that I loved my lord of Essex. I had reason to do so. I served her majesty as a voluntary in four actions under him, which had cost me well near a brace of a thousand pounds. His smiles only promised me recompense.'[13] These words of John Bargar could easily have come from any of the gentlemen voluntaries whose imaginations and ambitions were seized by Essex. And the feeling of resentment, of disappointment, that underlies this confession could also be attributed to the Earl himself. He felt let down by his own reputation. He had high martial hopes of a great imperial, and Protestant, adventure, and these had been betrayed. To him the national loss and his personal losses were all but indistinguishable. The previous autumn, the Queen had refused to renew the royal grant Essex held for the sale of sweet wines, crippling his estate. He began to recruit the disenchanted and pay heed to desperate counsel. He was convinced to the last, however, that Elizabeth herself meant him no wrong; she was merely misled by other councillors and courtiers who were implacably opposed to him. Donne, knowingly or not, was one of those small yet significant political beings who had slipped into this other faction, from the adventurers to the administrators. His experience with Essex in fact set a pattern of good fortune with doomed patrons that would continue for the rest of his life. Usually more by luck than judgement, he would always get away from them before they were quite minced by Fortune's wheel. Meanwhile his friend Henry Wotton, who had quite possibly seen it all coming, arranged his affairs and took a crossing to France before he too was brought in for questioning.

Essex's trial in Westminster Hall was swift and brutal, the prosecution conducted viciously by Sir Edward Coke and Francis Bacon, and the sentence was death. They took the loquacious Earl to pieces in court, and also in print, in a *Declaration of the Practises and Treasons committed by Robert late Earle of Essex*. This was drafted by Bacon – then approved by senior councillors and the Queen herself – in order to make it clear to the public just why their fallen hero was in the wrong. Donne owned a copy. A caustic note on the title page indicates that he found Bacon's behaviour difficult to stomach. Only a few years before, Bacon had been an earnest supporter of the Earl, and a great depender on his favour; his brother Antony, another senior figure in Westminster, was deeply involved in the conspiracy, but was spared trial because he was already dying. Donne gave his opinion of Francis with a curt quotation in Latin from the second book of Samuel: 'Sinite eum Maledicere nam Dominus iussit' (16:10).[14] The Old Testament line has a complex resonance here, satirical and sympathetic. It comes from a moment when King David – slayer of Goliath, man of the people – is cursed and spat at by a lone provincial critic. One of David's attendants offers to go and disembowel the churl, but his master is magnanimous: 'So let him curse,' says David, since the bystander is only doing what God has judged to be right. The man then follows the royal party along the roadway, reviling David and throwing stones at him. The analogy between the unruffled Biblical king and the dishevelled Earl of Essex is perhaps less important than the identity of the abuser. The main barb may be directed at Bacon's spitefulness, but the little excerpt Donne put on the title page cuts at the general moral compromise. Bacon may have been the first to throw, but Mr Secretary Donne also had a stone in his hand; he merely acknowledged the fact that he was standing in a glasshouse.

'If he have not a friend, he may quit the stage': the last period of Bacon's essay 'Of Friendship' is perhaps the best epitaph for Essex.[15] There is, however, a story that the Queen was willing to grant him a reprieve. Some time before, she had given him an exquisite ring, and now expected him to return it as a sign of repentance. Understanding this, Essex is said to have asked Lady Nottingham to pass the ring back to Elizabeth. It was a typical miscalculation: he entrusted his last hope of avoiding the axe to the wife of one of his sternest opponents in the Council. He went to the block, the Queen learning only afterwards that he had indeed shown the necessary contrition. She was upset.

Donne may have been compelled to watch at the event. Years later he described a beheading in an elegy for a girl he never saw, and gave full flow to a baroque morbidity. The dank chill, the crowd baying or weeping outside, the prosecutors with their arms folded, the prayers and the speeches had no part in Donne's sense of the execution. His focus was on the cut itself, and the parting of soul and body. When the blow came, head and torso became the vents of 'two Red seas'; the dead man's last nervous twitches made him clown about in the shambles:

> His eyes will twinckle, and his tongue will roll,
> As though he beckned, and cal'd back his Soul,
> He graspes his hands, and he puls up his feet,
> And seems to reach, and to step forth to meet
> His soule; when all these motions which we saw,
> Are but as Ice, which crackles at a thaw.

Sometimes the world lost its reality for Donne the more he gazed at it. It melted away like the last frosts of winter. As did everything: the great Essex was gone. Wotton was gone. Ann was gone.

Yet the motions of government kept going, egesting people half broken-down. In December the previous year, Donne used his position to help out a friend who had been thrown into gaol – probably for debt. Writing to him with the required documentation, he apologized for the delay and tried putting a jolly spin on the procedure involved – but a note of unmistakable weariness came through: 'if it [his friend's business] have hung longer then you thought, it might serve for just excuse, that these small things make as many steps to their end, and need as many motions for the warrant, as much writing of the Clerks, as long expectation of a Seal, as greater. It now comes to you sealed, and with it as strong and assured seals of my service and love to you.'[16] Once, Donne had insisted that service in love should not be hopeless or slavish. In one of his 'shameful' elegies, he aspired to be free of all patronage and the need to fawn:

> Oh, let mee not serve so, as those men serve
> Whom honours smoakes at once fatten and sterve;
> Poorely enrich with great mens words or lookes . . .[17]

Now, in 1601, his daily existence involved a round of humouring powerful whimsies, his hopes for promotion fattening and withering on 'great mens words or lookes'.

He had restrained his satirical urges, but Whitehall still provided an abundance of material. At York House the Countess Dowager was ruling the roost. During her first year as Egerton's wife she consolidated her influence in the Court, pursuing personal suits and securing positions for her favourites. She knew everyone, every flicker of change almost anywhere gossip might travel. One night in 1601 – the exact date is unknown – the chaplain of the Savoy hospital died. The next morning, as Donne left his nearby lodgings to go to work, he might have noticed a little stir at the death of the priest: the odd murmured conversation, perhaps, at a corner of a cloister. A few hundred yards away, the Countess already had all the details, and was already moving to install her own man before the deceased was even cold. She asked her friend and relative Sir Robert Cecil, the Queen's secretary, to give the now vacant post to her household chaplain, Mr Philips, 'a man', she could assure, who was 'both godly and learned'.[18] Like her husband, she was a wholly political being, accruing power from the accumulation of small favours and little persuasions, but lacked his strict bureaucratic reserve, and had an explosive temper when her will was crossed. Egerton poured still more of his energies into his work, demanding that his staff did the same.

In the autumn of 1601, the Lord Keeper had to concentrate on one massive political occasion. The Queen summoned Parliament for what would turn out to be her last time. Unlike today, the Houses of the Lords and Commons only sat for a spell once every few years, when new taxes had to be levied and a budget determined. Obeying the call, peers dusted off their ermine robes and headed to their London homes; and across the realm, in the boroughs and shires, the great landowners recruited trustworthy knights and gentlemen who would vote the right way as Members of Parliament. Among these was Donne, selected as one of the Lord Keeper's men on the inside, to see things ran smoothly for the government. The secretary was now a man of modest property.

His position had enabled him to obtain a lease for confiscated lands in Lincolnshire belonging to one John Heywood – not Donne's grandfather, who had died years before, but a distant cousin. This Heywood had clung on stubbornly to the family faith, and like many other recusants was forced to relinquish two-thirds of his estate as a penalty. The crown commonly leased such confiscations to a more compliant subject, and made a killing from the rents. So now Donne took control of the property. His position can be viewed in many ways. In one sense, he was taking advantage of a blood relation; in another he was at least preventing the land from falling out of the family altogether – and may even have been able to channel some of the revenue back to Heywood. When Heywood died in 1605, the possessions reverted to his eldest son, who, like Donne, kept his beliefs in step with the ruling conviction.

As a man with a lease of land from the crown, Donne could now sign himself 'esquire' when he took his place in the House of Commons. But it was still not enough to impress another Member of Parliament, Sir George More of Loseley, who came to town in October – and brought with him his daughter Ann.

9. The Member

For the opening of Parliament, if the weather held and the town was clear of plague, a grand, golden procession would go the short distance from Whitehall to Westminster, a slow treacling stream of nobles and courtiers in their heaviest regalia: the Earl Marshal and the Lord Steward, the Serjeants-at-arms, the Chief Gentleman Usher, the Queen herself in an open carriage, with a guard of honour, the Master of the Horse, the Lord Chamberlain and Vice-Chamberlain, the Captain of the Guard; with the company bulked out by many noblewomen and almost all the Members of the House of Lords. Those sitting in the Commons, however, were not part of the parade. They had to assemble independently, after a service at Westminster Abbey, to await the speeches that would open the session.

In 1601, unfortunately, the ceremony did not run smoothly. The Lords gathered in the Parliament chamber, where Elizabeth took her throne for the occasion; in their own hall, the Commons got together more rowdily, waiting to be called in for the opening. Old cliques reformed, squires and gents from far-flung boroughs and shires, some of whom had maybe not met since the last Parliament, some four years earlier. The new boys, Donne included, mulled among themselves or edged their way into the more influential packs. Then there was a glitch in the ritual. When the time came for the Commons to move to the Upper House, they found that the doors to the chamber had been shut and that proceedings already begun. The Lord Keeper, presiding, made his opening address to the peers, stressing the need for both Houses to be efficient with time and respectful of the Royal Prerogative. He soon had to speak up. Outside, less than deferential, the locked-out Commons banged the doors, thudded and stamped and demanded to be let in. Donne could not hear his master's lengthy solemnities on the Queen's virtue and authority, but had been well briefed beforehand on the policy detail. The noise did not abate. Eventually the Usher came and threatened to have them all thrown in the stocks if they did not shut up.

One of the more obsequious members of the Commons was Sir George More. Ann's father was a loyalist by inclination, and was also eager to be considered for a position at Court. He felt he had been overlooked; he was one of life's backbenchers. In his youth, Sir George had waited on the Earl of Leicester – the Queen's great love – but Leicester had died and no promotion had come. Every year, the knight would build his hopes towards some little honour; these would always be disappointed, and there would always be someone to blame. He had trouble with his temper. A deep need to look down on others also made it hard for him to accept that he was a very short man. Sir John Oglander, his even-tempered son-in-law, was fond of him nonetheless: 'He was but little of stature, but of great abilities. By nature very passionate, yet in his wisdom he conquered that passion so much that you would think him to be of a mild disposition.'[1] Unless, that is to say, you knew better; in which case you knew that a straw might snap, a servant might drop something or arrive a moment too late, and the squire would go wild. He could be generous nonetheless. Oglander said he was 'little, and good'. He had 'a wondrous free disposition, many making use of his good nature': while his money lasted, Sir George held great feasts at Loseley that enabled him to make a show of his wealth. He was also an educated man, who thought a lot of his own intellectual gifts. In 1597, he published a modest little tract that set out to prove unequivocally the existence of God – a monarchist, Protestant God, moreover. The work is conventional but also demonstrates an inability to understand doubt or misgivings, or deal with ambivalence: agnostics and atheists were 'as pictures or images, of wood or stone', carrying 'the resemblance but not the substance, of those bodies which they represent'.[2] Such people were nothing more than the icons of the old Roman Church that the true religion had thankfully reformed.

More's seat in Parliament brought him into some proximity

with Donne, the Lord Keeper's urbane, good-humoured secretary, with a Papist background and a reputation about town as being too clever for his own good. Sir George was a keen reader, and it was possible that he had come across some of Donne's work in manuscript. R. C. Bald wondered if More ever read the poem that became known as 'The Perfume', in which Donne's persona creeps to his young beloved's bed and is discovered when her father smells the scent he is wearing. The bourgeois patriarch stirs in his bed and sniffs with sudden suspicion:

> Had it beene some bad smell, he would have thought
> That his owne feet, or breath, that smell had wrought.

Such lines would not have gone down well with Sir George. However, the knight probably did nothing but look up and nod at the young reformed secretary: reprehensible, but with no money and little influence; beneath attention. According to Isaak Walton, More received 'some intimation' of Donne's relationship with his daughter before she left York House;[3] but if he had indeed heard of the affair he was satisfied it was over. Otherwise he might have thought twice before bringing Ann to London with him.

But Sir George had other things to concentrate on. The parliamentary session was an important chance for him to impress. He spoke on almost every issue that was considered. One of the first questions that came up for debate was that of monopolies – the granting by the crown of patents for specific commodities and services. It was of pressing concern: the grudges the system created lay near the heart of the Essex rising earlier in the year. Almost every Member in the chamber had an interest at stake: many wished to defend patents which they or their patrons already held, while others resented their exclusion from the market. On the government side, there was a great pressure to keep things as they were, since monopolies generated vital revenue for the exchequer. Donne must have started with surprise when Geoffrey Downall, his colleague on the Lord Keeper's staff and fellow plant, spoke up to support the reading of a reform bill. Government men were supposed to toe the line. But something else had taken over in the crowded hall of chiding and perspiring whiskered gentlemen, squashed together and crouching on benches, some forced to stand, many rising to their feet and hurling abuse: a centuries-old Commons tradition that every Member had a right to his say. The debate proceeded stormily, and Sir George More saw his chance to offer a voice of prolix moderation. He tried to make the point that the House should simply petition the Queen to revoke some patents, since if a bill was passed she had the power to ignore it anyway. In doing so though he got rather knotted in a metaphor of impossible physical contortions. He likened the Queen to the head, the patent-holder to the hand and the ordinary subject to the foot of the body politic: 'the head gives power to the hand,' Sir George declaimed, 'the hand oppresseth the foot, the foot riseth to the head.'[4]

A thoughtful pause may have greeted this image of the realm kicking itself, but as the arguments continued, Donne kept quiet. He was one of the few in the chamber who had at present nothing of his own to lose from the debate on patents – except his standing in the Lord Keeper's regard should he say or do anything imprudent. The cautious secretary made no speeches or interjections, in either the main House or any of the subordinate committees. He may not in fact have entered very wholeheartedly into the proceedings at all; and when he did pay close attention his satirical antennae must have twitched almost uncontrollably. There was a widespread, humorous public suspicion of the pontificating and hair-splitting that went on in Parliament. A few honourable Members were well aware of this and were far from happy about it. One day, an MP called Henry Doyley rose to his feet to tell the House 'of an Infamous Libel that is Printed, and Spread abroad, since the Beginning of this Parliament'. Ears pricked up. Gravely, Doyley continued, 'saving your presence, Mr Speaker, it is titled the Assembly of Fools'. A debate ensued over Doyley's motion that the offending printer be brought to the House and forced to grovel before them for publishing such an 'Infamous Libel'.[5]

No 'parliamentary' satire, sadly, took its place among Donne's
send-ups of the Inns of Court, the literary scene, the religious
debate and the court of equity. His mind was elsewhere: while her
father listened and opined in Parliament, Ann sat in their lodgings
at Charing Cross, a stone's throw from York House, or visited
friends around the city. Donne must have followed her in mind at
every moment. It was socially all but impossible for them not to
see each other in the normal course of things. Sir George and his
daughter were still welcome to visit the Lord Keeper's home. They
probably reminded Egerton of more restful domestic times with
his previous wife. It is also easy to see Sir George's verbose civility
going down well with the word-loving Countess Dowager – and
being sniggered at in private. For a little while, John and Ann
went back to seeing each other at dinner, filtering personal signals
through constrained public conversation. But on just a few precious occasions, they managed to be alone together. 'At her lying
in town this last Parliament,' Donne soon admitted, 'I found
meanes to see her twice or thrice.' They had surely been able to
write, however infrequently, during the past eighteen months or
more. Donne held up their faithful correspondence as a guide to
all lovers who lived after them:

> Study our manuscripts, those Myriades
> Of letters, which have past twixt thee and mee,
> Thence write our Annals, and in them will bee
> To all whom loves subliming fire invades,
>   Rule and example found . . .[6]

The love-notes on which these unwritten chronicles were based
may simply have been too dangerous to keep; but no doubt they
were a means of achieving the extraordinary communion Donne
spoke of in other letters. This was now intensified by the renewed
compulsion of touch. And it proved too much to lose.

He realized that the relationship with Ann was the awakening
he had been waiting years for.

> I wonder, by my troth, what thou, and I
> Did, till we lov'd? were we not wean'd till then?
> But suck'd on countrey pleasures, childishly?
> Or snorted we in the seaven sleepers den?

He could leave the sleepers' den at last; he was able to roll the boulder away from the cave and step out into maturity. When they came together late in 1601, Ann might have been nearly sixteen; Donne was twenty-nine. The age difference, in itself, was not exceptional at a time in which childhood was both compressed and extended depending on personal circumstances. One became an adult on marrying, not at any given age; those who remained single were confined to an eternal infancy. A girl might find herself a married woman at thirteen; a man's boyhood might not end until he married in his thirties. But more importantly, the difference in John's and Ann's ages did not necessarily mean they had nothing in common except their attraction. These were two people who talked, and who needed each other.

Dating Donne's poems with any precision is an unsafe venture. But what sets apart those which seem to have been written for Ann is a new tone of companionship. His very earliest poetry talks about women, rather than with them, and when it does address a lover – real or purely dramatic – it scolds, goads or coaxes; it never just chats. This isn't to say that Donne never used his writing to cajole Ann, far from it. Yet 'The Good Morrow' has a wholly different air of confidence. She was in on the jokes, not their victim. We only have brief, tantalizing ideas of what she was actually like, but enough to see why she and Donne were suited. Writing forty years later, Isaak Walton, who viewed Donne's affair with Ann as the great mistake of his hero's life, and who probably never knew her personally, curtly described her as being 'curiously and plentifully educated'.[7] By that he meant that she had a 'curious' education for a woman of the time: she had a plentiful knowledge of the texts and abstruse moral issues that formed the basis of a male-dominated liberal education – from which women were generally excluded. The relationship was a strict secret, but Donne evidently took a select few friends into his confidence about it. One of these was of course Henry Wotton, who admired Ann for her intelligence as well as her looks. In 1599, by which time it is likely that she and Donne were already in love, Wotton wrote asking if he might 'kiss the fair and learned hand of your mistress, than whom the world doth possess nothing more virtuous'.[8] These might seem like pat compliments from anyone who did not weigh his words so exactly as secretary Wotton; from him, they tell us something about why Donne was so taken with Ann. She was 'fair and learned'.

'Both their natures,' said Walton, were 'generous, and accustomed to confer.'[9] Donne himself commemorated her in Latin as being 'Faeminae lectissimae dilectissimaeque': she was a woman 'most choice and most beloved' but also, through a pun in 'lectissimae', as M. Thomas Hester comments, a woman who read a lot and was herself 'well-read' by Donne. She was 'learned', and her husband learned her by heart: they knew every line in each other, back to front, cover to cover.[10] The verses by Donne that seem to be about her were not written to the wall, but were an extension of their love; a reading of it. It is infuriating and scandalous that no portrait of her, no letter by her survives. This loss of a person is partly circumstantial, a sign of the way women disappear from patriarchal history; and partly, it seems, due to the way Donne deliberately shielded her. But from the oblique notes towards a sense of who Ann was that do exist, we can at least infer why she was attracted to Donne. This was a girl who lost her mother in infancy, was sent down to London and saw the wider world at an early age. She discovered books. Her past consisted of grotesque ostentation in a rural backwater; while her future might have comprised an arranged marriage to some dull squire who would handle her like a cow. Instead she met Donne: funny, good-looking, almost embarrassed by sexual experience; intelligent, urbane; and also rather lonely.

The couple met 'twice or thrice' as Parliament was held. In the meantime history was passing, and passing away. Late in November, the Queen agreed to meet the Commons' demands and rescind a number of monopolies: salt, aqua vitae, starch – vital for keeping those ruffs sufficiently stiff and white and painful – blubber-oil and woad were among the substances it was now possible to buy, make and supply at a free rate. The whole Commons was permitted to come to the Council Chamber in Whitehall Palace to express thanks and pay respects to Elizabeth. The solitary old woman stood and surprised them with one of the greatest speeches of her reign, addressing her realm as the lover her life had never allowed her to keep. 'I do assure you there is no prince that loves his subjects better, or whose love can countervail our love. There is no jewel, be it of never so rich a price, which I set before this jewel: I mean, your love.' No one present was immune to her: she held them all. Even Donne could be completely seduced by majesty. His last satire, which spluttered with ire and contempt for the whole institutional set-up, had nonetheless invoked the Queen as 'Greatest and fairest Empresse', exempting her entirely from the mire of political life, even though she lay at its centre.[11] Listening to her on this bleak November afternoon, the men were all kneeling. She allowed them to stand at more ease so they could follow her words without physical discomfort. Her words kept coming and coming. She was fully conscious that she was placed where others had been before her, where yet more would follow. But she asserted her own moment: 'And though you have had and may have many princes more mighty and wise sitting in this seat, yet you never had nor shall have any that will be more careful and loving.'[12] Within the space of hours or days at most, Donne was touched by two extremities of affection – in the small white arms of a teenage girl, holding his own life together, and at a distance, in the rhetoric of an aged lady trying to cohere a nation.

Once, the old woman was a girl. All being well, the girl would one day be an old – but happier – woman. Things would be different yet the same. Like many of his contemporaries, Donne was fascinated by the superficial constancy of form amid the constant flux of matter, the disappearing lives that just about held the world in shape. Around this time he was at work on one of his longest poems, an unfinished mock-epic called 'Metempsycosis'.

The idea behind it was the ancient theory of the transmigration of souls – that a spirit might be reincarnated in many different lives. Donne later dismissed the doctrine of reincarnation as 'a Pythagorean bubble', but it offered rich potential for a satirical poetic fiction.[13] He imagined a soul originating in the forbidden apple that Eve and Adam ate in the garden of Eden, and the same essence then passing through a multitude of fallen beings. 'Metempsycosis' is a politically directed piece of writing: one theory has it that, if the poem had ever been finished, the itinerant spirit would have ended up as Queen Elizabeth's most senior councillor, Robert Cecil – the Earl of Essex's greatest enemy at Court.[14] As Donne wrote, he was acutely aware of his own point in time. Invoking Destiny, 'the knot of all causes', he asked to be kept free

> Of steepe ambition, sleepie povertie,
> Spirit-quenching sicknesse, dull captivitie,
> Distracting businesse, and from beauties nets.[15]

His 'six lustres' – a lustrum is a period of five years – were 'almost now outwore'. So he was nearly thirty at the time when he wrote the poem; which, seeing that his birthday fell between the end of January and the middle of June, was probably between late 1601 and the summer of 1602. He asked Destiny to give him the same number of 'lustres' again.

Destiny had selective hearing. Donne would get not quite another thirty years, but would fall into every trap on the list of those he wished to avoid. Ambition, poverty and sickness would be especially painful; 'beauties nets' perhaps the one consolation.

Parliamentary business continued. A Spanish force had landed in Ireland, and money for arms and men was needed urgently. Strident voices rumbled around Donne as he sat with Ann on his mind. On the home agenda, an attempt was made to reinforce the fine of a shilling for anyone who failed to go to church on a Sunday: atheists and Papists were no more popular than ever, but many of the gents in the Commons were less than enthusiastic about the bill. They saw no reason why a man should have to pay if his wife or servants failed to go and pray to the Lord. Tempers rose high, the tactics got dirty. One member, Matthew Dale, complained that he was held down by the britches when he tried to cross the hall to vote in favour of the bill. Sir Walter Ralegh caused an uproar by saying there was no harm in that – it was a time-honoured practice, he had often prevented a fellow member from voting the wrong way. Many in the chamber found the speeches tedious. A contemporary diarist noted how 'an old Doctor of the Civil-Law spake; but because he spake too Long, and too Low, the House hawked and spit, to make him make an end.'[16] Sir George More followed all that was said in 'the Assembly of Fools' as avidly as he could, and spoke whenever he got the opportunity.

10. The Undoing

Parliament was dissolved on 19 December 1601. It was deep winter, and endurance levels were waning; a day or so before, one member of the Commons had passed out in the debating chamber. By this time, Donne was a married man – albeit one living alone and feeling rather faint. The ceremony itself, 'about three weeks before Christmas', was kept deadly secret. Donne got his old friend from Lincoln's Inn, Christopher Brooke, now a practising attorney in York, to make the long hard journey from the north to give away the bride. The rites were performed by Christopher's brother Samuel, who had preferred holy orders to a career in the law. A few other close friends – no more than five, Donne later said – were also present. R. C. Bald speculated shrewdly on the circumstances and location of the wedding. Donne was still living in lodgings near the Savoy, and the hospital chapel was an ideal venue since it lay within what was termed 'a "liberty", free from the ordinary civil and ecclesiastical jurisdiction . . . notorious later in the century for its clandestine marriages'.[1] The service was probably followed by a very private little party. The pleasantly dazed, hollow-kneed sensation of having committed his life to another was complicated for Donne by panic about the trouble he and Ann had now brought upon themselves. Decades later, a joke about the furtive couple's situation was still in circulation. According to one version, it began with Donne himself, at a moment of high exertion or anxiety:

Doctor *Donne* after he was married to a Maid, whose name was *Anne*, in a frolick (on his Wedding day) chalkt this on the back-side of his Kitchin-door, *John Donne, Anne Donne, Undone.*[2]

Perhaps after spending the afternoon at Donne's place, Ann had little choice but to find her way back to her father's apartment at

Charing Cross. Donne would soon reassure her father that they did not 'use any suche person' in the enterprise 'who by furtheringe of yt might violate any trust or duty towards yow'.[3] But it is hard to see how they could have brought 'yt' off without at least one ally among Sir George's family, friends or servants. Even if Ann met Donne without an escort, someone at home or somewhere in the city – a maid, a relative, a girl friend – had to provide her with an alibi. And even with this cover, she could not stay long. There was little time for much more than a brief 'frolick'. Donne had often lived through the necessary sunderance in his writing.

> So, so, breake off this last lamenting kisse,
> Which sucks two soules, and vapors Both away . . .[4]

Ghosts formed and dissolved from her breath, in the cold December air. Then she was out of sight again.

Undone perhaps, but the lovers had defined themselves against almost every social and marital convention in the land. They had taken a massive risk, but had at least declared themselves free to each other. In the past forty or so years, a rich historical literature has explored the sociology of marriage in Renaissance England. Custom and law dictated that marriages had to be licensed and publicized by banns, and to be conducted by a priest; they were also supposed only to take place at certain times of the year, avoiding the periods of Lent, Rogationtide – the three days before the feast of the Ascension in early summer – and Advent, in the Christian calendar. John and Ann's wedding was obviously not a public occasion, and took place well within Advent, the month before Christmas. Their marriage falls under the complex category which R. B. Outhwaite designated 'Clandestine'. Breaches of procedure were pardonable in some instances: the Lord Keeper, for example, had married the Countess Dowager of Derby with no announcement of banns beforehand, in a private ceremony at Russell House. But then, both Egerton and the Countess were powerful figures with independent means, in late and early middle age respectively. The Lord Keeper was also the most senior lawyer

in the land. The rules were different for some people. John and
Ann, however, had no such autonomy; they were well within the
marriageable age bracket – fourteen for boys, twelve for girls – but
crucially Ann was still a minor: she could not marry without
parental consent. And this was where the transgression really lay.

The newly-weds had completely bypassed the open principle
that fathers and mothers had a decisive say in the marital choices
of their offspring; especially among the gentry, since there was
more materially at stake. In the case of the arranged teenage marriage of the Countess Dowager's youngest daughter, for whom
Donne wrote his Eden-fixated verse letter, the manacling together
of the young couple was conducted with at least some care for
their immaturity, since both boy and girl were kept apart until
they were old enough to have their conjugal wrangles for themselves. Ann grew up among similarly pre-contracted partners. Lady
Egerton, Ann's guardian aunt, had a son by her first marriage called
Francis Wolley. At the age of about fifteen, Francis was married
to Mary, the daughter of one Sir William Hawtrey. Hawtrey had
been close friends with Sir John Wolley, the boy's father, and the
two knights had struck a nuptial agreement between them. By Sir
William's will, Mary inherited the splendid family estate at
Chequers in Buckinghamshire, and presently, when the young girl
was orphaned, she became the ward of her mother-in-law: by this
Lady Egerton held the rights over the young girl's person and a
third of her property. Legal and social practice bolted valuable
young people into family designs.

Donne's background was a mixture of the petit bourgeois and
the minor aristocratic, but he was completely out of his social
league in even thinking of marrying Ann. And it must be stressed
that when one says 'social' in this context, the term 'financial'
should also be inferred. Even on the happy occasions when there
was some love to begin with, or when some came as a result of a
couple living together, marriage was a transaction, and nuptial
arrangements more often than not involved hard bargaining. Sons
and daughters presented their parents with different opportunities
and obligations in the marital contract. The father of the groom

had to provide an annual allowance – known as a jointure – to support the bride in the event that she was widowed. He also had to make sure the young couple had somewhere to live, and funds to live on; they usually lived with the groom's family, in fact, for the first year or two of their married life. The father of the bride, meanwhile, had to come up with a cash sum known as a portion, which varied according to many factors, the most important of which was probably social rank. The portion required to marry into a Duke's family was generally higher than the asking price of a lord or well-off baron's son. So depending on his wealth first of all, but also the value he set on his daughter, the portion enabled an aspiring father to buy his way into a higher set of family prospects – higher, that is, in terms of title, political influence and property. The daughters involved in this exchange were expected to do their parents' bidding, and to go wherever the highest bid lay. Lawrence Stone, the magisterial historian of the family, sums up the emotional prospects bleakly: 'Given parents with these rigid views of filial obedience, the best hope of freedom of choice for a girl was either that her father should die young, leaving her a portion without strings, or that her parents should quarrel over the choice of the bridegroom.'[5]

Ann's mother was dead, but both of her parents could easily have agreed that someone like Donne was no match for her. By marrying Ann, Donne knew that he was preventing Sir George from cashing in on a lucrative property in the society market. He knew that Sir George, for whom money was no obstacle and for whom social advancement was an evident priority, was unlikely to take such a loss kindly or be impressed by any tales of star-crossed love. And he was well aware that this short man with a short fuse was more than capable of finishing the secretary's career, which was still, despite almost four years' service, at a tentative stage. Donne had robbed his father-in-law of a valuable chattel, and had no immediate prospect of providing a return on the investment Sir George had made by bringing Ann up as his daughter in the first place. Donne's position with the Lord Keeper gave him an income, but according to Walton his finances were not in good condition: 'Mr *Donnes* estate was the greatest part spent in many and chargeable Travels, Books and dear-bought Experience.'[6] The poet had expensive tastes, living well, and was probably still counting the cost of earlier affairs and his jaunt as a voluntary with the Earl of Essex. Which places his marriage in another, potentially less savoury light. Donne needed money, was also ambitious; and his wife was the daughter of a very rich man. Whether he and Ann snatched an hour or two alone together on their wedding day, or only had time for a quick rendezvous at 'the back-side of his Kitchin-door', Donne might have looked at her and seen a woman who could either ruin him or set him up for life.

Isaak Walton called Donne's marriage 'the remarkable error of his life; an error which though he had a wit able and very apt to maintain Paradoxes, yet he was very far from justifying it.'[7] Donne may have always been at a loss to explain quite how he and Ann came together. At times he saw their love as beginning with a gradual coalescence of feeling; at others it stemmed from one decisive moment, their 'first strange and fatall interview'. Either way, it was undoable.[8] There is a carnal version of events, in which two people who wanted each other like mad could stop at nothing; or a Platonic one, in which the marriage was the necessary union of a couple who were simply meant to be together, whatever the cost. There was social pressure to account for, but also pressure from within the relationship. Ann had been Donne's mistress for some years; and he had, as he soon averred, plighted his troth to her. 'In conscience', they were already married, and she surely urged him to honour his commitment. Then, in the least edifying interpretation, Donne might have taken a calculated gamble. He was well aware that his father-in-law would take it badly; but also hoped – perhaps timidly expected – that More would see sense and help his new son out for the sake of his daughter.

All these inflections of the story, and doubtless many of the others that began fluttering around London society in February 1602, bear some scrutiny; though none of them work independently. The romantic version ignores Donne's blatantly ambitious streak; the cynical one is blind to the tenderness for Ann that pervades the poetry he wrote for her and would soon emerge in the letters Donne wrote to Sir George. None of these readings can be exclusive; and no one is better than Donne at showing how very different thoughts and drives can conglomerate in one mental and emotional space under a single name. Love for Donne the poet is composite, a swirl of different motives: it has undercurrents and crosscurrents that confuse any singularity of feeling. What is more, it keeps changing:

> I scarce beleeve my love to be so pure
> As I had thought it was,
> Because it doth endure
> Vicissitude . . .

Love is 'no quintessence, / But mixt of all stuffes'. It can be rough or gentle, soulful or materialistic. This variety keeps love accumulating, 'as in water stir'd more circles bee / Produc'd by one'. One moment it uses the music of the spheres, the next it needs the language of the exchequer:

> As princes doe in times of action get
> New taxes, and remit them not in peace,
> No winter shall abate the springs encrease.[9]

Donne might have been criticized by his contemporaries as an upstart with designs on a young girl's fortune, or, equally, as a foolish young romantic. For Donne himself, when he had space to contemplate, the complex mixture of forces behind 'loves deedes' was precisely what stopped the coffers from running empty. It made life richer.

After the wedding, Ann had to go back to her father. When the parliamentary session ended, she and Sir George returned to Loseley for Christmas. Donne was left behind, a single husband, with his paperwork, the dour clerical staff at Chancery, the increasingly testy conversations between Egerton and the Countess at

York House; the streets muddy lagoons, the snow going brown, the choppy river. Donne might have thought that a change would be registered as soon as he got married; that even though the service was held in secret, the fact that it had taken place would make something happen, impel a crisis and change life forever. Instead, precisely because he and Ann had been so careful, there was no definite response from any quarter. The holidays passed as usual. Donne spent the New Year and the following weeks dreading the moment when Sir George would find out, yet also needing it to arrive. The secretary grew nervous and queasy. There is no saying whether Sir George was attentive enough to notice any difference in his daughter, or whether Ann was self-possessed enough to let nothing show.

By late January, however, tongues began to wag; or Donne was hypersensitive enough to believe that they had. He decided it was best that he break the news to Sir George himself, instead of leaving it to distorted, embellished reports. He was sure that the knight had heard something. Whether or not he seriously contemplated riding to Loseley in person, however, he found that it was physically impossible. The worry proved too much, Donne's nerve broke, and he fell ill. On 2 February 1602, he sat down – or sat up on his sickbed – to write a letter explaining everything. Bracing himself, he began his confession by admitting to Sir George that he had not come to see him because he was scared:

Sir,
If a very respective feare of yowr displeasure . . . did not so much increase my sicknes as that I cannot stir, I had taken the boldnes to have done the office of this letter by wayting upon yow myself to have given yow truthe and clearnes of this matter between yowr daughter and me . . .

He was gulping at his words before getting to the point. He knew, he wrote, a little defiantly, 'the limits of owr fault', but hoped that 'yowr wisdome wyll proportion the punishment'. He decided to cut a long story short:

So long since as her being at York House this [their love] had foundacion, and so much then of promise and contract built upon yt as withowt violence to conscience might not be shaken. At her lying in town this last Parliament, I found meanes to see her twice or thrice. We both knew the obligacions that lay upon us, and adventurd equally, and about three weeks before Christmas we married.

Donne was careful to point out that the marriage was an equal venture: Ann knew what she was doing – he had not misled or taken advantage of her. The new husband was also at pains to say that they had done the morally right thing; he and Ann had made promises to one another that could not be violated without a kind of sacrilege. As Diana O'Hara and R. B. Outhwaite have shown, marriage in the sixteenth and early seventeenth centuries was not 'defined by a single event' – a morning service in a church, for instance – 'but was rather a process which involved a complex series of formalities'.[10] A couple might hold private rituals of their own, with or without witnesses or a priest, 'handfastings' in which the lovers plighted their troths. These domestic promise sessions could precede or even supersede a public church ceremony, and were felt by the participants to be just as binding as a legally authorized marriage. The point at which a couple went to bed together was indeterminate; what mattered more than the marriage licence was the repeated promise to be faithful. It was a very old English tradition, 'the dominant form of clandestine marriage in the middle ages';[11] and Donne invoked it. Even before the secret wedding, he and Ann already felt they were married, through a clandestine 'promise and contract', 'obligacions' that had been forged since their early days together at York House.

Having presented the facts, Donne then began to brazen out his motives. The letter's argument turned suicidal. He did not 'foreacquaint' Sir George with his matrimonial plans for the following reasons:

I knew my present estate lesse then fitte for her, I knew (though I knew not why) that I stood not right in yowr opinion. I knew that to have given any intimacion of yt had been to impossibilitate the whole matter.

He addressed his reader as a confidant, rather than the party he needed to convince, who would in fact have done almost anything to 'impossibilitate' the event at issue. Having freely acknowledged his and Ann's deception, Donne however begged More to believe they had nothing but 'honest purposes in our hartes', and that he personally had 'neyther had dishonest end nor meanes'. Then he remembered that the woman he loved was still in the custody of a man who was renowned at times for his raving furies:

But for her whom I tender much more then my fortunes or lyfe (els woould I might neyther joy in this lyfe, nor enjoy the next), I humbly beg of yow that she may not to her danger feele the terror of yowr sudden anger.

Donne kept wrong-footing himself. Having made a humble plea, and allayed for a moment terrible visions of Sir George beating his daughter or locking her up, Donne went on to provoke the rage he had just tried to mollify. 'I know this letter shall find yow full of passion,' he said, and a little too hopefully, 'but I know no passion can alter yowr reason and wisdome.' In any case, he continued, with a dreadful and probably most unwelcome quip on his name, there was no point getting worked up about the marriage, since 'yt is irremediably donne'.

Yf yow incense my Lord [i.e. the Lord Keeper, Sir Thomas Egerton] yow destroy her and me; that yt is easye to give us happines, and that my endevors and industrie, if it please yow to prosper them, may soone make me somewhat worthyer of her.[12]

By encouraging his father-in-law to give a helping hand – and perhaps some capital – to 'prosper' his labours, Donne hardly managed to dispel the view that he had no 'dishonest end' in mind. And by urging him not to go in a rage to the Lord Keeper, Donne may well have put the 'passionate' Sir George in mind of the form his revenge had to take.

There are vital letters that can probably never be made perfect, no matter how many times they are rewritten and agonized over. But this one had self-destruction built into it; many passages are simply primed for detonation. Unable to carry it himself, Donne then made a mistake in his choice of a messenger – or was perhaps unable to turn down an open-hearted offer of help from a friend. It was Harry Percy, ninth Earl of Northumberland, who took the letter to Sir George. On paper Northumberland might appear a very useful emissary, since not every earl would have acted as a note-carrier for a secretary. A few surviving letters among the Loseley manuscripts indicate that in the normal course of things More and Northumberland – who had neighbouring property – had a cordial relationship. This was not, though, the ideal time for that accord to be tested. However well intentioned he was, Percy brought with him historical associations that did not stand to Donne's advantage in Sir George's eyes. Northumberland belonged to ancient noble Catholic stock; his ancestor, the seventh Earl, had led a rebellion from the north against the Queen in 1569. He was an enemy of the state by descent, and he was Sir George's social superior: at Loseley the 'little, and good' knight not only had to cope with a shocking revelation about his daughter, but had to do so while looking up at someone with renegade connections.

The Earl's personal image was also less than orthodox. Northumberland was known as 'the Wizard Earl' for his avid interests in anatomy, alchemy, cosmography and distillation – 'the fourth designed,' Lawrence Stone points out, 'more to provide choicer and more potent alcoholic spirits for his lordship's table than to advance the cause of pure science.'[13] In a few years' time, the wizard would be confined to the Tower of London for alleged complicity in the plot to blow up Parliament. This fate was not so bad as it might sound. There he had the means and received permission to build a bowling green for recreation, and was reunited with his friend Sir Walter Ralegh, also confined on a charge of treason. In the Tower Northumberland surrounded himself with a group of macabre experimenters to explore the new sciences and distil his days out of their aimlessness. Donne probably went to visit them. They were an odd bunch. It was said of one of Northumberland's assistants, William Warner, that his 'mother was frighted, which caused this deformity so that instead of a left hand he had only a stump with five warts upon it.'[14] The wizard, like Donne, was at home amid the odd, the out of the ordinary: he saw the beauty – or at least the fascination – of the unusual. Sir George, by complete contrast, was someone who used all his reading and experience to regularize his view of the world and cancel out the bizarre. Donne was worried about the rumours Sir George might have heard of him, but the wizard's embassy alone was enough for the squire to decide that his 'curiously educated' daughter had got herself mixed up with a no-good crowd.

A fly on the ceiling of More's study would have been able to offer no report of the interview with Northumberland: it would have been blinded by spittle. Sir George went wild at the disclosure. He seems to have been incoherent with rage. He then hastened to do exactly what Donne had begged him not to: to 'incense' the Lord Keeper, insist upon the secretary's dismissal, and generally wreck his son-in-law's life. 'This request,' says Isaak Walton, 'was followed with violence.'[15] Now Egerton was not only fond of Donne, he also valued his services. He had weathered many a temper tantrum before this from irate plaintiffs, and was not going to yield easily to his former brother-in-law's demands. But he was also a stern moralist, and could not deny that a deception had taken place in his household. Moreover, Donne had betrayed any trust that Lady Egerton, Sir George's sister and Ann's guardian in London, may have placed in him. It was easy for Sir George to ply Egerton's tender memory of his second wife, especially during his presently stressful marital circumstances, and he managed to open one of the deep pockets of coldness in the Lord Keeper's character. Egerton sacked Donne, and also withdrew any protection he might have offered against the legal consequences of the clandestine affair. Whether or not the marriage would stand was a matter for lengthy litigation in the months ahead, but the circumstances in which it had taken place were in specific breach of canon law. Within a few days Donne not only found himself without a job; he was arrested, taken up the Strand and thrown into the Fleet prison. His friend and confederate Christopher Brooke was also imprisoned, in the Marshalsea.

Donne felt his life flaking apart. All that he had spent almost ten years trying to avoid had suddenly come to pass. His struggle to convert outwardly – and inwardly – to the prevailing religious orthodoxy, his ordeals at Cadiz and in the Azores, his day-to-day t-crossing and i-dotting for the Lord Keeper, might all be traced to the simple fear of being confined and hurt, even dying, merely for the sake of who and what he was. The death in prison of Henry Donne nearly a decade before provided the catalytic terror behind a monumental effort to conform. Now Donne had ended up in exactly the same position as his younger brother, albeit for quite another offence. On being imprisoned, he became acutely ill. The Fleet, London's oldest prison, a wet-walled medieval building, took its name from the ancient, fetid rivulet running by it – and was, like almost all of London's gaols, notorious as a deathtrap. Surrounded by an especially plague-prone district of tanneries, the prison stood 'on a muddy island made by ditches carrying the waters of the Fleet . . . befouled by the refuse flung into the stream by the butchers of the Shambles, by furriers' waste, sewage and the like.'[16] The conditions inside varied according to the means of the prisoner, who was charged for his or her stay. Donne is likely to have been able to avoid detention in the basement, from which only the most brutal and resilient could emerge alive or intact; but he had little means to provide much comfort for himself. Whether given his own little cell to rot away in, or packed into a room with other inmates in tattering finery, despair and malady completely overwhelmed him.

Yet after six or seven days inside he realized that he had to do something to save himself. Visitors informed him, or else he simply intuited, that London society was rife with stories about him – his Roman Catholic past, his 'many profane mistresses', his scornful, lurid writing, his debts – and that Sir George was susceptible to all of them. On 11 February, pulling himself together as best he could, he wrote appealing to More for clemency, this time with no attempt to justify his actions, speaking only against the rumours he claimed were distorting his motives:

Of nothinge in this one fault that hear sayd to me, can I disculpe [exculpate] myselfe, but of the contemptuous and despightfull purpose towards yow, which I hear ys surmised against me. But for my dutifull regard to my late lady [i.e. Lady Egerton], for my religion, and for my lyfe, I refer myself to them that have observed them.

The whole place smelt of death. The stench of detritus and effluent drifted from the river. Donne pleaded and pleaded. He wrote that he knew, or hoped, that Sir George could see 'how litle and short the comfort and pleasure of destroyeing ys'; he begged him to let reason take over from rage, out of pity if nothing else, for he was plummeting through fever:

And though perchance yow intend not utter destruction, yet the way through which I fall towards yt is so headlong, that being thus push'd, I shall soone be at bottome, for yt pleaseth God, from whom I acknowledge the punishment to be just, to accompany my other ylls with so much sicknes as I have no refuge but that of mercy . . .

He promised that 'all my endeavors, and the whole course of my lyfe shal be bent, to make my self worthy of yowr favor and her love, whose peace of conscience and quiet I know must be much wounded if yowr displeasure sever us.'[17] In spite of everything, Donne was still insisting that he and Ann should be together. No doubt she also steadily protested to her father, perhaps with more effect, and together their determination slowly began to work on Sir George.

The next day, Donne wrote to Egerton, having received terse word that 'Sir George More, whom I leave no humble way unsought to regaine, leaves all to yowr Lordship': the ex-secretary's immediate fate lay at the mercy of the Lord Keeper. Donne begged

Egerton to 'admit into yowr favorable consideracion how farr my intentions were from doing dishonor to yowr Lordships house'. He had 'much profited' from his sufferings – had deserved all he got – but asked if 'yow would be pleasd to lessen that correction which yowr just wisdome hath destind for me'.[18] On receiving this, Egerton evidently felt that a dunking in the sink of iniquity had done his former servant enough good for the time being; for he allowed Donne to be confined in his lodgings instead.

Donne was escorted from the walled nausea of the Fleet and back down the Strand, through moderately fresher air, past the Middle Temple, past Somerset House, and back to his rooms near the Savoy. There he regained a measure of calm, considering his next move. Among his possessions was the stylish portrait of him from a few years before, dressed in lace and satin with a broad-rimmed feathered hat, a picture 'taken in Shaddowes' that he kept until he died. The motto on the dun-toned canvass reads, *Illumina tenebras nostras domina*: 'Lighten our darkness, lady', a prayer for aid. Quite another Donne should be imagined in the late winter of 1601–2, much changed even by the experience of the previous couple of months: his dress more conservative, and more be-draggled, his beard heavier, his face shorn of its old serenity. As Egerton's secretary, he had become a more directed, single-minded person than the dreamer in his earlier portrait, changing from melancholy lover and gallant to desperate husband and endangered professional.[19] And now he had a wife to reclaim and a future to salvage.

> Who ever loves, if he do not propose
> The right true end of love, he's one that goes
> To sea for nothing but to make him sick . . .[20]

On 13 February, he renewed his letter-writing campaign. Something of a twinkle returned to his words. Rich 'onely in that coyne . . . which ys thankefulnes', he expressed his gratitude to Egerton for 'this vertu of mercy'.[21] He also thanked Sir George – 'to whom next to God I shall owe my health' for 'this mild change of imprisonment' – thus managing to praise More's clemency while at the same time implying that the change of situation wasn't all that significant. He hoped that his name was now clear, 'as that fault which was layd to me of having deceivd some gentlewomen before, and that of loving a corrupt religion, are vanishd and smoakd away'. Perhaps he faltered just slightly here: if he had 'smoakd away' the allegation that he had tricked gentlewomen into bed *before*, was he inadvertently admitting that he had in fact deceived a gentlewoman now? But he continued pleading his innocence: 'How many of the imputacions layd upon me would fall off, if I might shake and purge myself in yowr presence.'

This was more like it. This was the kind of abjection and repentance that would go down well with Sir George. But there were practical matters to address. Donne was a prisoner in his own home and had no job. He therefore hoped, 'when yt shall please God to soften yowr hart so much towards us [i.e. he and Ann], as to pardon us, I beseech yow also to undertake that charitable office of being my mediator to my Lord [Egerton], whom as upon yowr just complaint yow found full of justice, I doubt not but yow shall also find full of mercy.' This may have been wishful thinking, and now he began pushing his luck a bit far: his clear conscience, he said, 'emboldneth me to make one request more'. He asked for Sir George to pass 'some kind and comfortable message' on to Ann, 'to give some ease of the afflictions which I know yowr daughter in her mind suffers'. He also asked permission to write to her himself, 'for withowt yowr leave I will never do any thing concerning her'. Yet he then declared, 'I am unchangeably resolved to bend all my courses to make me fitt for her' – which could easily be achieved if More and Egerton would only help him out.

Weeks had passed since he had received any word of or from Ann, and he could only think the worst of how she had suffered from the 'terror' of her father's sudden anger. Assuming she was not beaten or sealed up at home for her disobedience, she was left in a strange and extremely frightening state of social non-being. There was still every possibility that her father would not recognize the marriage; that he might even disown her. And while a man in her position at that time might conceivably rebuild a life by his own industry, a woman of her status could only look forward to a future of taint and ostracism, with no means of providing for herself. Even if he was allowed to write or speak to her, Donne was the wrong person to offer her comfort unless Sir George acknowledged their marriage.

On his side Donne was lucky enough to have at least two genuinely selfless friends. By the end of February Christopher Brooke, who had taken Sir George's place as father of the bride and given Ann away, was still stuck in the Marshalsea prison, along with his brother Samuel, the priest. The law had not yet finished with these two: they were waiting for a nod from the Lord Keeper. Shut up in his room, Donne could do little to help them. Christopher Brooke therefore wrote to Egerton himself, apologizing for his 'offence against the canon lawes'. The northerner had a blunt way of putting things: 'What other satisfaccion I (but such an offender as I am) should make, I knowe not, but I allwayes submit my selfe.' He asked to be released; he had a legal practice in York that was losing business because the court session had already started. Yet very lovingly he also insisted that in spite of his misdemeanour, 'I would have chosen rather to have undergone for Mr Donne some other more apparent daunger' – that is, an enterprise that seemed more risky than just turning up to walk down the nave of a church. He knew that Donne had been sacked, and that Egerton had left him dangling. There had been no news of a reprieve. So Brooke now stuck his neck out further by asking whether this nonsense had not gone on long enough:

And pardon me a word for him, my Lord; were it not now best that every one whom he [i.e. Donne] any way concerns [i.e. Egerton, his employer, and Sir George, his father-in-law] should become his favourer or his frind, whoe wants (my good Lord) but fortune's hands and tonge to reare him upp, and sett him out?[22]

February passed with no breakthrough. Though Donne understood that Sir George had expressed no objection to the idea of
him writing to Ann, he wrote to More insisting that 'I have not,
nor wyll not without yowr knowledge do it.' Sir George was
apparently taking time to cool off. Donne's spirits improved a
little, but he was still confined and festering. He borrowed books
from his friends, and wrote letters to various authorities appealing
for the release of the Brooke brothers.

Sir George meanwhile was still determined to extricate his
daughter from Donne if it was humanly and legally possible. He
had instigated proceedings, and a hearing was due at the High
Commission to assess the legality of the marriage. The procedure
was common enough with 'clandestine' (or even seemingly orthodox) weddings where an interested party disapproved of the match.
More had a strong case, since John and Ann had broken canon
and civil law on at least two counts: firstly by marrying in Advent
and secondly by marrying without parental consent, which Ann as
a minor required. Sam Brooke's right to consecrate and license the
marriage was also contestable. But, equally, if Sir George's suit
failed, then his protest would lose its impetus in law, and the
advantage would swing to the other side. For by now Donne had
launched a suit of his own in the ecclesiastical courts – one that he
could ill afford – to prove that he was lawfully married. Before the
matter got out of hand, and the expenses became utterly ruinous,
he again tried to get his father-in-law's support. 'Yf these waights
opprest onely my shoulders and my fortunes, and not my conscience and hers whose good is dearer to me by much [more] then
my lyfe, I should not thus trouble yow with my letters.' But he
saw 'that this storme hath shakd me at roote in my Lord's favor,
wher I was well planted', and he needed 'to beg both yowr pardon
and assistance in my suit to my Lord' – to regain his secretaryship.
He also needed help with money: his imprisonment and that of
the Brookes – whom he felt honour-bound to reimburse – had
cost him the hefty sum of £40. He also complained that many of
his friends had gone quiet on him.[23]

This letter was probably written on 1 March – it is dated simply

'Mar.' Perhaps later the very same day, Donne met Sir George in person, at the Commission hearing. As it turned out, the outcome was favourable to Donne; and more importantly, he at last had a chance to speak to Sir George and mollify him in person. This was the first encounter of many in which Donne progressively melted his father-in-law's dislike for him: his manner had 'a strange kind of irresistible elegant art', said Isaak Walton, and time presently 'so dispassionated Sir *George*, that as the world had approved his Daughters choice, so he also could not but see a more then ordinary merit in his son.'[24] Angry men, Walton felt, were often like that. For the time being, however, the crucial development was that Sir George agreed to support Donne in the attempt to retrieve his old job. Donne went and wrote to Sir Thomas Egerton immediately, telling him that God's mercy had assured his conscience that his offence had been pardoned, since the Commission was also inclined 'to remitt yt'. He could also now tell the Lord Keeper that Sir George 'hath sayd before his last goinge, that he was so far from being any cawse or mover of my punishment or disgrace, that if yt fitted his reputacion he would be a suter [suitor] to your Lordship for my restoring.' With a deep breath, Donne tried setting the record straight with the short-short version of his biography.

How soone my history is dispatched! I was carefully and honestly bred; enjoyd an indifferent fortune; I had (and I had understandinge enough to valew yt) the sweetnes and security of a freedome and independency . . . I had a desire to be yowr Lordships servant, by the favor which yowr good sonn's love to me obtein'd. I was 4 years yowr Lordships secretary, not dishonest nor greedy. The sicknes of which I dyed is, that I begonne in yowr Lordships house this love. Wher I shal be buried I know not.

Egerton initially had no wish to inter the 'carefully and honestly bred' young man in a social grave. And he now had every rational cause to re-accept Donne. Any magnanimity involved was not his, in fact, Donne reasoned, since the Lord Keeper had not dismissed the secretary on his own account, but at Sir George More's request. Moreover, Donne was an excellent secretary – 'fitter to serve a

King', as Egerton is supposed to have said, 'then a subject'. Donne was 'a Friend'.[25] Yet something in Egerton froze, and froze Donne out, when he read this letter. Donne's mention of his friendship with the Lord Keeper's son, for example, the younger Sir Thomas, killed in action in some Irish marshland, touched a very raw nerve. Suddenly Donne may have appeared less the family friend than another self-seeking crony – like those who had helped young Egerton to wind up in debt, and like those he went off to fight with; like the good-for-nothings the Lord Keeper saw every day, wheedling through Chancery and falling into the debtors' gaol.

The whole affair with Ann also tainted a period in Egerton's life that he increasingly needed to see as precious and pure. It involved a nasty trick on his dead wife, a lady with a loving nature; quite unlike his present partner, the Countess Dowager, whom he had married without really thinking, and without getting properly over his grief. He would eventually present his surviving son John with 'An vnpleasant declaration of thinges passed betwene the Countesse of Derby and me since our mariage', venting years of trapped spleen. He damned her for her 'cursed railing and bytter tongue', and declared, 'I thanke God I neuer desired long lyfe nor neuer had lesse cause to desire it then synce this my last mariage.'[26] He might be said to have developed, from personal experience, a deep distrust of impulsive matches.

When Egerton finally broke his silence he gave Donne word that he would not take him back, no matter what Sir George felt. Walton recorded the public reason Egerton gave for his decision: 'his Answer was, *that though he was unfeignedly sorry for what he had done, yet it was inconsistent with his place and credit, to discharge and readmit servants at the respect of passionate petitioners.*'[27] In this disdainful declaration, Donne was relegated in his master's eye from a friend and secretary worthy of a king to one of the 'servants', the case involving merely one of innumerable petitions his daily business presented. The grounds for Egerton's official response can be deduced from Donne's own words. Begging the Lord Keeper to re-employ him, he argued,

To seek preferment here with any but yowr Lordship were a madnes. Every great man to whom I shall address any such suite, wyll silently dispute the case, and say, would my Lord Keeper so disgraciously have imprisond him, and flung him away, if he had not donne some other great fault, of which we hear not.[28]

Donne had expressed the view, albeit indirectly, that Egerton had acted 'disgraciously' in throwing him into gaol. This was unlikely to please the Lord Keeper, who could easily turn Donne's reasoning against him. If he did readmit him, having 'imprisond him' before, 'every great man' with whom Donne might have sought employment would think that the Lord Keeper was becoming weak or morally lax, welcoming corruption back into his house. No, a judgement of this kind had to be irrevocable. Thomas Egerton, the illegitimate son of a woman called Sparks, and originally a Roman Catholic, had spent his whole professional life striving to be a model of orthodoxy: he was not going to blemish his record now.

So Donne was left with neither prospects nor an income. By the end of spring in 1602, however, he could at least declare himself a married man. He had maintained his ecclesiastical lawsuit, and tradition has it that his poem 'The Canonization' was written during the tense weeks of awaiting judgement. Here Donne adopts the unworldly yet world-weary tone of one who cannot believe the fuss and opposition that he and his lover have met with.

> Alas, alas, who's injured by my love?
> What merchants ships have my sighs drown'd?
> Who says my tears have overflow'd his ground?
> When did my colds a forward spring remove?
> When did the heats which my veines fill
> Add one more to the plaguie Bill?

This bill was the document pasted up weekly during times of pestilence to update the numbers of the dead. But if his love had caused no death, he was sure that the spite they had encountered would bring about both his and Ann's. In one of his most famous and justly admired stanzas, he drew characteristically mordant solace from the prospect of being buried with her, both sainted for mutual devotion. It formed also one of the comparatively rare moments at which he found strength in poetry itself, and credited it with a power to last.

> Wee can dye by it, if not live by love,
> And if unfit for tombes and hearse
> Our legend bee, it will be fit for verse;
> And if no peece of Chronicle wee prove,
> We'll build in sonnets pretty roomes;
> As well a well wrought urne becomes
> The greatest ashes, as halfe-acre tombes,
> And by these hymnes, all shall approve
> Us *Canoniz'd* for Love.[29]

Late in April the court that spoke with the authority of the Archbishop of Canterbury himself finally ruled that the marriage was valid in the eyes of the established Church.[30] This was not enough, of course, to make amends for the essential contravention it involved. John and Ann had cut loose from the constraints that held them apart, but in doing so had set themselves adrift from the social mainland. They were now outsiders, with nowhere to live and nothing to live on. Sir George presently let his daughter join her lover – he now had no legal right to detain her – but if she and Donne had ignored certain conventions, then so, More reasoned, could he. He refused to provide them with any financial support. In the lines quoted above from 'The Canonization', Donne satirically accepted that even after being worn to death, he and Ann would have to cut their cloth according to their means. Yet if they could not afford a half-acre tomb, their remains would at least settle down nicely in a well-wrought urn.

II

1603–1616

11. Sunrise

For three years the dawn found John and Ann lazing together in a country home where they lived free of rent and largely of troubles. Ann's nineteen-year-old cousin, Francis Wolley, had come to their rescue when they were left homeless and penniless. Wolley, coupled at the age of fifteen to a girl he didn't love, had little sympathy for the marital conventions which Ann and John had broken so notably. He gave his young cousin and her husband a place to stay at his house at Pyrford in Surrey. The mansion has long gone, but according to the diarist John Evelyn, who visited the place eighty years later, the house was made of timber, 'commodious, & with one ample dining roome, & the hale adorned with paintings of fowle, & huntings &c'.[1] It lay on flat ground, with plush pastures all around. Pyrford itself was a modestly comfortable village, though scarred in familiar ways by the previous sixty years: Newark Priory had been blasted to pieces during the Reformation by cannon positioned especially for the purpose on an overlooking slope. At leisure on the estate, though, John and Ann were able to lose themselves in each other. Donne came to describe a complete fulfilment that made wishes lag behind what was real. 'My Dreame thou brok'st not, but continued'st it,' says the waking-up voice of one poem:

> Enter these armes, for since thou thought'st it best,
> Not to dreame all my dreame, let's act the rest.[2]

Wolley was an easy host, splitting his time between sport on his estate and a spendthrift existence in the city, and probably expecting little more of Donne than occasional help with ordering his legal and financial affairs. A regular stream of guests came up from London to keep the young household company; and meanwhile, John and Ann could work tentatively on building bridges with Sir George More, whose home at Loseley was only a little way off. They probably saw him quite often, and it would be reasonable to assume that he missed few opportunities to encourage Donne to go and find himself a job, but for the fact that Sir George himself had created his son-in-law's present need of one. But he may have taken secret pride in having such a man of letters in the family. Sir George, the author of *A Demonstration of God in His Workes*, thought of himself as a good amateur scholar, and may well have taken the opportunity of foisting ideas on Donne. But he was also the kind of man who would urge the couple lying in on summer mornings to get up and pray, then get out in God's fresh air: 'Who seeth not the glorious arysing of the Sunne,' he boomed,

his coming forth as a Bride-Groome out of his chamber, and his reioycing like a mighty man to runne his race . . . ? The course of the Sunne, goeth round the earth, and his light will have entrance, wheresouer the body of man can have passage.[3]

If Donne ever paid much attention to Sir George's little tract on the existence of God – he was probably obliged to read and comment on it for courtesy's sake – the passage above seems to have stuck in his mind. He retorted snappily.

> Busie old foole, unruly Sunne,
>   Why dost thou thus,
> Through windowes, and through curtaines call on us?

There were some places where the sun certainly couldn't follow the body of man, at least if Donne had anything to do with it; and with Ann curled beside him, he put the old fool firmly in check:

> Thy beames, so reverend and strong
>   Why shouldst thou thinke?
> I could eclipse and cloud them with a winke,
> But that I would not lose her sight so long . . .[4]

Outside the bed curtains, beyond the timbered mansion and the placid Surrey estate, the sun had fallen and risen on two different eras. Early in 1603, the old Queen spent weeks passing away, 'in obstinat silence', knowing death was coming near but refusing to lie down in case it did. It did, and she died, with nothing on her lips but the murmur of an old lover's name. Apocryphal versions of her end soon multiplied, 'some whispering that her brain was somewhat distempered'. Gossipy John Chamberlain complained that 'the papists do tell strange stories, as vtterly devoyde of truth, as of all civill honestie or humanitie'. Anxiety about the succession had mounted as Elizabeth's terminal illness set in; her chief councillor and secretary, Sir Robert Cecil, conducted delicate negotiations with her wily cousin and heir, James VI of Scotland. Both men were determined to ensure a smooth takeover. Especial heed was taken of any factions that might have caused trouble: 'During the Quenes sicknes some principall papists were made sure [i.e. watched, detained, or worse] and some dangerous companions clapt up.'[5] The mood in London was anxious, as Donne later reminded the citizens, teasingly, with vivid wit: 'every one of you in the City were running up and down like Ants with their eggs bigger than themselves, every man with his bags, to seek where to hide them safely.'[6]

The new ruler was something of an unknown quantity. Having fought hard for political survival among the Scottish clans, he had a reputation as an absolutist that troubled many in England. Thirty-seven when he became King of England, James was an opaque, ambiguous character, with wide-ranging intellectual interests, and was predisposed to give an opinion on any matter that absorbed his mind. He was a prolific political writer, and offered personal contributions to the debates on witchcraft, heresy and demonology. Deeply appreciative of letters, well read and sensitive, he was also a good craftsman as a poet – his translation of the Psalms of David was published after his death – though his language lacked personal inspiration. He had a great and sincere concern for Christian doctrine, and genuinely enjoyed skilful preaching; his appreciation for learning and eloquence would eventually be the basis of a strong respect for Donne. As a King, he had no martial prowess whatsoever – soldiers scared him – but he loved hunting, and devoted his huge estate at Royston, on the border of Cambridgeshire and Hertfordshire, entirely to the sport.

King James made a long, circuitous progress from his Scots throne in Edinburgh down through England to take possession of his new realm at Westminster. His first concern was to get everyone who mattered on his side: his first official communication to Cecil promised the whole existing Privy Council all 'offices and dignities in the same quality and condition you did possess them heretofore'.[7] It soon became apparent that great handfuls of dignities and benefits were now on offer. Queen Elizabeth had always been very mean when it came to bestowing titles, thinking it better policy to keep her courtiers hungry, but James had no such reservations. He inspired hope in all quarters, even in those accustomed to neglect or downright persecution: 'not only protestants, but papists and puritans, and the very poets with theyre idle pamflets promise themselves great part in his favour.'[8] Many English Papists indeed began to hope that a new period of religious tolerance might have come south of the border with the King: his wife, Anne of Denmark, was reported to be Roman Catholic, and the Vatican opened up a hopeful dialogue with the new regime. In response, James professed himself to be an unconvertible Protestant, but offered words of measured, rather prolix conciliation:

Yet should our constancy to that religion [i.e. Protestantism] beget no such severity toward those who are otherwise persuaded [i.e. Catholics], but that they may enjoy under us the same fruits of justice, comfort, and safety, which others of our people do, till we shall find that disloyalty is covered with the mask of conscience.[9]

Many Catholics greeted James's assurances enthusiastically; others decided to wait and see what the 'fruits of justice, comfort, and safety' might turn out to be.

The King was delighted by the popular response on his entry into England:

the people of all sorts rode and ran, nay rather flew to meet me, their eyes flaming nothing but sparkles of affection . . . their hands, feet and all the rest of their members in their gesture discovering [i.e. displaying] a passionate longing and earnestness to meet and embrace their new sovereign . . .[10]

Greeting him with all members or not, this reception was caused as much by relief that the accession had gone – or was going – peacefully, as by a particular delight in James himself. Not only the commoners, but the local authorities of any given district also made their presence felt to make sure that their patch was not forgotten in the coming reign. In general, James lacked Elizabeth's common touch with 'the people of all sorts', but also her terrifying *hauteur* with the gentry and peers: he was more willing to buy praise and support with privilege.

James made it clear that the rewards for loyal service would be plentiful. In the year of his accession, nonetheless, the full formation of the Court was impeded by a violent outbreak of the plague. Throughout 1603 councillors had to prepare the ground for their new monarch in a city that was restive at the best of times, but was now a positive deathtrap. A sense of imminent extinction made much of the populace skittish, randy and careless: one bowling alley in Westminster became notorious as a place 'where all kind of common people without respect of contagion promiscually resort, not sparing the Sabbath day'. Citizens let their domestic animals wander freely as in ordinary times, to the despair of local officers: 'The swine,' one complained, 'run without order in every unclean place about the street day and night, dispersing the offals of every house heaped in the street.'[11] London was feverish, overrun by plague and pigs. Many thought it worth the risk of going to the capital to seek an office in the new regime, but then succumbed to infection: one of these was William Lyly, Donne's 'shrewd' brother-in-law, who had worked as a government agent and courier in Picardy for much of the 1590s. In 1598 he entered the service of Sir Robert Drury, who was later crucial to Donne's own fortunes. Joseph Hall, another of Drury's servants, described Lyly

as 'a witty and bold Atheist' and gleefully reported that 'this malici-
ous man going hastily up to *London* . . . was then and there swept
away by the Pestilence, and never returned to do any farther
Mischief.'[12]

Tucked up at Pyrford, Donne therefore had plenty to deter him
from going down to London in search of employment. Moreover,
he was burnt out from the goings-on at Court after his long years
as an insider on Egerton's staff, and the months of struggling to
establish that his marriage was legal. The sun rapped at the windows
and squinted through the curtains, but Donne lifted his head and
shooed it away:

> Sawcy pedantique wretch, go chide
> Late school boyes and sowre prentices,
> Goe tell Court-huntsmen, that the King will ride,
> Call countrey Ants to harvest offices;
> Love, all alike, no season knowes, nor clyme,
> Nor hours, days, months, which are the rags of time.

It is unlikely, anyway, that he and Ann had money spare to buy
the finery they needed to step out at Court. But they were happy;
all the kingdoms beyond the casement were nothing, for a
moment, in comparison:

> She is all States, and all Princes, I,
> Nothing else is.[13]

Just for a while, Donne demanded some exemption from the
world, at least for his inner life with Ann.

Yet in high summer, as the numbers of the dead mounted up
in the city's mass graves, Donne found the hub of the political
world shifting into the country to meet him. On 10 August 1603,
around the time that Donne's brother-in-law William Lyly must
have been 'swept away by the Pestilence', King James set out
with his retinue on his first royal progress. His first stop was
Pyrford, where he was entertained for a night in the mansion's

'one ample dining roome';[14] the party then moved on to Sir George More's home at Loseley. Donne was presumably present, and on both occasions it would have been very difficult for him not to have felt very left out. Sir George finally received what he hoped was the leg-up he had waited years for: he was made Treasurer of the Household to the Prince of Wales. More also had the satisfaction of seeing his son, Robert, knighted, along indeed with his nephew Francis Wolley. Donne also saw similar honours handed out to friends and acquaintances. In the aftermath of the coronation, Francis Bacon and Richard Baker – the friend from Lincoln's Inn who described Donne as 'a great visitor of ladies' – also received knighthoods. Sir Thomas Egerton's surviving son John, and Donne's fellow member for Brackley in the 1601 Parliament, Edward Montagu, were made Knights of the Bath. After four years of dedicated and distinguished service to the state, it is almost certain that Donne's name would have been among those receiving honours, if his career had not been cut dead the previous year. 'Wee can dye by it, if not live by love', he had asserted in 'The Canonization'; but now social rigor mortis was setting in.

Donne's closest male confidant in the years ahead, an easy-going, outgoing knight called Sir Henry Goodyer, was made a Gentleman of the King's Privy Chamber – one of James's personal attendants. Donne had known Goodyer for quite some time, since his early secretarial days at least, and slowly the two men picked each other out for deeper friendship from the general amiability of the cliques they shared. Donne's introspective, meditative tendencies satisfied a seriously intellectual aspect of Goodyer's character; while his pleasure-loving, extrovert nature gave air to the sociable part of Donne's temperament. Goodyer became Donne's main lifeline to the Court, and he flung himself with relish into all its recreations. His duties as a Privy Chamber man also gave him time to serve one of the new Queen's ladies-in-waiting, the poetically minded Lucy, Countess of Bedford. Goodyer and the Countess were both keen participants in the royal Court's latest fad – the masque. This was theatre in which the aristocrats themselves took part – and the parts they took were often means of playing out rivalries, making appeals for royal favour or taking social revenge: masques could be indications of who was in and who was out, on the way up or on the way down. They required a team of special artists and crafts-men, of whom the greatest was the architect Inigo Jones. Unlike the sparser staging of popular theatre, they were strong on heavy-duty scenery and special effects – contraptions to drift clouds and undulate waves were devised, machinery to change locations. 'The Vision of the Twelve Goddesses', in which Goodyer played a minor role in January 1604, packed the royal banqueting hall with a mountain, cave and temple; shimmering seas and forests would be created and refined in later productions, the technology growing ever more elaborate as years went by. The space 'was so much lessened by the workes that were in it,' noted Dudley Carleton at the time, 'so as none could be admitted but men of appearance.'[15] Donne was not a man of appearance, however; he was not even one who could put in an appearance.

He could get frustrated; but his resentment was directed at the conditions and conventions he had flouted, not his wife. A handful of poems among those finally collected as Donne's *Songs and Sonets* celebrate a single, life-changing relationship: if these were written for or about Ann, Donne evidently recognized the change she brought about in him. His lyrics include many that extol free love, a sexual 'Communitie' in which 'Chang'd loves are but chang'd sorts of meat'.[16] Yet the emotional correlative of being proudly promiscuous was for Donne, at least in his verse, a fear of making a commitment, the sense that fidelity only invites betrayal. One of his elegies ends by declaring that 'Change is the nursery / Of musicke, joy, life, and eternity', arguing that a change of sexual partner was actually a way of freshening up a love affair. Yet this conclusion is as much a retreat from insecurity as it is a challenge to monogamy. The same poem opens mottled with a jealous and desperately possessive man's comic anxiety that his woman would inevitably betray him. Despite all her shows and avowals of love – 'much, much I feare thee', he murmurs.[17]

Liaisons required pre-emptive escape strategies. 'Womans

Constancy', for example, addresses a lover, real or fictitious, with the caustic question

> Now thou hast lov'd me one whole day,
> Tomorrow when thou leav'st, what wilt thou say?[18]

Donne goes on to furnish the companion of his one-night-stand with many elaborate reasons for ditching him. He airily concludes that he could, naturally, dispute with her 'and conquer', if he chose, but then abstains from doing so, since by tomorrow he might need to use the same arguments against her himself.

But in other places a strain of poetry comes through that belongs to a wholly different kind of human connection. Apprehension gives way to a balance of free and equal interchange between two people who become 'One, and one anothers All'.[19] In just a few pieces Donne was able to record or imagine a love without nervousness. The moment of seeing it and feeling it was one of waking up, a moment of sunrise:

> And now good morrow to our waking soules,
> Which watch not one another out of feare;
> For love, all love of other sights controules,
> And makes one little room, an every where.[20]

He could envisage a point of trust at which he found that if one loved and was loved enough, it was actually impossible to cheat or be cheated on; all 'sights' that might have once seemed attractive were instantly disabled, eclipsed by a wink like the morning sun through the bedroom curtains. When John and Ann's first child was born at Pyrford in 1603, they christened her 'Constance'.

In Donne's imagination, souls awakening every day to such secure intimacy got mixed together, refined, concocted, so that one could 'Forget the Hee and Shee'.[21] In 'The Extasie', he holds his lover fast on a 'Pregnant banke'; as the day and the river run by, their souls 'negotiate' in the air above.[22] They stay like this so

long, in fact, that Donne has to remind his partner of their bodies
and suggest that they go back to them. For about three years he
and Ann lived out a 'dialogue of one'.[23] This was interrupted,
naturally, and frequently, at times, by the squawling of their little
daughter, and in the spring of 1604 by the arrival of a son, John.
But Donne seems to have avoided all other disturbances.

   He stayed away from the city whenever possible during these
years; the emotional bubble was only perforated by the guests and
letters that arrived at Pyrford. One of his correspondents at this
time was Tobie Mathew, an acquaintance from the legal circles at
the Inns of Court. Mathew, a close friend of Sir Francis Bacon,
was the son of the arch-Protestant Bishop of Durham. He gave his
father grief by living debauchedly through his early independent
years, and then converting to Roman Catholicism during a long
trip abroad in 1605–6. If Donne had not met him beforehand, the
two men probably got to know one another during the 1601
Parliament, at which Mathew was also a Member of the House of
Commons; his attendance record was patchy, however, because
of repeated illness – 'probably the result of the dissipated life which
he led,' his biographer notes, 'in common with other young men
in his station, who gave free rein to their grosser animal instincts,
unrestrained by the elevating influence of the Christian religion.'[24]
Donne might not have spoken quite so sternly of him – he wasn't
really in a position to – but he always kept a certain distance
between himself and Mathew. He read and answered his letters,
but maintained a precautionary reserve.

   The post from Mathew and many others was one way of keeping
up with events. One letter to Donne, dating from late autumn
1603, contains a long account of the proceedings against Sir Walter
Ralegh for treason, in which Mathew gives excessive weight to
his own judgements and opinions on the matter. The grand style
halts, however, when Mathew drops in the odd bit of tittle-tattle:
'I hear that *F.B.* is gotten with Child either by *Fra. C.* or by her
brother George Brooke, which is rather thought [i.e. 'thought
more likely'].' The letter also gives more personal news and at one
point places Donne in a slightly awkward position. Mathew's

room-mate was trying to acquire land in which Donne's host Francis Wolley had also taken an interest:

My Bedfellow, Mr *John's* [probably Johnstone] bids me say this much to you, he hath been long in hand, with Sir Eskins, for Oaking Parke, wherein he finds it a great impediment, that S. F. W. [i.e. Sir Francis Wolley] is about it [i.e. making a rival bid], whereby the price is already grown much higher.[25]

Men at this time who shared lodgings often shared a bed together, talking over their finances, or what they were reading, like married couples of many years standing. 'To be someone's "bedfellow",' writes Alan Bray, 'suggested that one had influence, and could be the making of a fortune.'[26] Homosexual or not, they felt physically comfortable with close male company, and had no problem expressing affection in the warmest terms. Sir William Cornwallis, the friend who urged Donne to 'come to my den' whenever he had a spare hour, wrote telling Donne that they would have to stop saying they love each other. 'Often haue I tolde thee I loue thee,' he said, but 'our loue is now of some Continuance': those words were no longer even necessary.[27] Donne and most of his male friends would have been horrified by the suggestion that they were gay in the modern sense. Whatever subconscious drives one reads into their behaviour, sodomy was regarded as one of the deepest offences against law and nature, as the seamy libels against Sir Francis Bacon, who was accused of sleeping with boys, later bore witness. Elizabethan and Jacobean male society was sweetly oblivious to the contradiction between men publicly embracing and kissing and yet sustaining an air of intensely homophobic machismo. Yet in their avowals of love and loyalty for each other, most heterosexual men were expressing their regard through an expressive convention of the day. The classical moralists on which such men were reared and trained placed great value in the civic virtue of *amicitia*, amity, 'the unique excellence of which was held to lie in the feelings of loyalty to which it gives rise'.[28] *Amicitia* was encouraged for its civilizing properties. In his correspondence with his friends, Donne was adapting and intensifying a rhetorical custom to his own deeper emotional requirements. The same need for spiritual proximity – thought alone was strong enough to bring two friends together – can be seen from his earliest verse epistles to his friends at Lincoln's Inn, through to his last letters as a dying man:

Sir,
When we thinke of a friend, we do not count that thought a lost thought, though that friend never knew of it. If we write to a friend, we must not call it a lost Letter, though it never finde him to whom it was addressed: for we owe our selves that office, to be mindefull of our friends.[29]

Whether Tobie Mathew and his 'Bedfellow' had such a profound relationship is not known, but it meant enough for him to urge Donne, on his friend Mr Johnstone's behalf, to discourage Wolley from pursuing the bid for Oakley Park too far if he wasn't really interested.

Mathew seems to have been quite a regular visitor to Pyrford – 'When I see you next, you cannot shake me off in a senight ['seven-night', a week]' – and always sent his regards to Wolley, but there were significant gaps between his meetings with Donne. In March 1604, when the handout of royal honours, favours and benefits was passing its peak, Mathew wrote to reproach Donne for neglecting his cronies and to warn him of what he was missing.

Your friends are sorry, that you make yourself so great a stranger; but, you best know your own occasions. Howbeit, if you have any designe towards the Court, it were good you did prevent the losse of any more time . . . the King's hand is neither so full, nor so open, as it hath been.

The letter gave extensive coverage of the pickings. At the very top of the aristocratic ecosystem there was a rumour that Donne's old boss Sir Thomas Egerton would at last receive the much-cherished title of Lord Chancellor; lower down, 'There will be good plenty of knights at an easie rate.'[30] Mathew was not among those who received a knighthood, but he evidently held out strong hopes for himself and was enthusiastic about the Court and its workings. He had just come into fleeting contact with King James himself, when Francis Bacon asked him to carry a letter to the Court; he wrote enthusiastically, eager to be in the very thick of things.

Another letter written in May chides Donne for not taking an opportunity to catch up with friends and secure an income for himself.

It is long since you were in *London*, and long since I was at *Purford*; but not so long. I did once adventure to persuade, that we might see you, though you had begun with good fellowship, you might, perhaps, have proceeded with businesse . . .

But Mathew also suggests, noting from hearsay or perhaps a letter, that Donne was getting rather down:

In the meantime, I trust, it shall be no offence to interrupt your melancholy, in which so ever of the fair walks it shall possesse you, with this remembrance, of my good wishes . . .[31]

The letter is by a young man who hasn't yet felt anything very deeply. For Mathew melancholy is almost entirely decorative and recreational, a despondent garden with 'fair walks' that any self-respecting, thinking literary gentleman should wander through and tend. If he has picked up on a genuine mood in Donne, he does little to help it, especially if the cause of the dejection was indeed what he takes it to be, estrangement from the palaces of London. Mathew bursts with news of the Court. He describes at length the gifts and honours flooding in to the new King and, by association, his clingers- and hangers-on: the Duke of Florence had presented James with 'two Horses, with Furniture, four mules, two Litters, fourteen Tun of Wine. And the Dutchess to the Queen, great store of Sweet-meats for the next Christning.' Earlier in the spring,

Donne's first son John had been born; indelicately, Mathew remarked that 'If your wife had been delivered a little sooner, you might here have been provided at an easie rate.'[32]

The joke is that Donne might have been spared the cost of providing refreshments at the little christening feast he and Ann must have held; but it is made at the expense of the couple's straitened circumstances. Enclosed in the little jibe is the faint implication that Ann was holding Donne back from his rightful share of the pickings at Court: he had gone soft and was letting her keep him at home. And conversely, of course, he might have inferred that he was failing to look after her properly. Tiny little hints about his responsibilities, even ones that were probably quite unintentional, like those in Tobie Mathew's gleeful correspondence, might well have begun to chafe.

In 1604, Mathew was a Member of King James's first Parliament. Writing to Donne, he complained about the 'vild speakers', including one that Donne knew only too well at close quarters: 'surely, saving that Sir *George Moor* is your father in law, and not in conscience, he speaks as ill as ever he did, saving that he speaks not so much.' Mathew also dealt with matters of national moment, offering 'Considerations upon the Union'.

England and Scotland now had one monarch, but were still very separate countries. 'Touching the Union, divers projects have been sent to the House . . . The name of Brittaine [for a united England, Scotland and Wales] was absolutely refused.' Mathew sides with this opposition to the union, and assumes that the body of sane opinion is in agreement with him. The parliamentary debate ended with the compromise that English and Scots commissioners would meet to discuss 'matters concerning both kingdoms'. Mathew accepts, however, that the rot has set in and change is inevitable: 'the meaning is, whatsoever the pretence be, that the points of differences may be accommodated for an Union to follow after.' He mentions that Donne's old friend Cornwallis, also a Member of the Commons, 'lamely' attempted 'to answer the objections against the Union', but Mathew addresses Donne himself as someone whom he takes to share his views. Donne, however, came to accept this union and the Protestant state it created as a working reality: he would speak of 'the Kings of *Britaine* . . . and the other Monarkes of the first sort, which have utterly cast off *Rome*'.[33] For the coming century and long afterwards, British history would be deeply marked by the repeated failure to 'accommodate' those 'points of differences' between the two states; not to mention the political fracture lines that riddled each of them separately.[34] Yet James made it clear to Parliament that he now regarded both kingdoms as a single possession: 'What God hath conjoined then let no man separate, I am the husband and the whole isle is my wife.'[35]

Various factions had their own reasons for wanting to hijack the wedding of the states. Some were keen to murder the bridegroom. In the November after James took power, there were two plots against the King's life. One involved an unlikely alliance of fundamentalist Catholics and ultra-Protestants – including George Brooke, the man whom Tobie Mathew snickeringly accused of incest. The other was a more serious affair in which the senior royal councillor, Lord Cobham, and Sir Walter Ralegh were judged to be the main culprits. Brooke, a minnow at Court, went to the scaffold and surrendered his intestines; Ralegh, a man who proved difficult to execute, was sent to the Tower of London for the time being. Even before the accession to the English throne, however, 'there were many indeavours, first to excommunicate, and then to shorten the life of King *James*';[36] and Henry Wotton, Donne's close friend since their spell together at Oxford, was instrumental in thwarting one of these conspiracies.

Wotton, it may be remembered, had fled the country after the fall of his old patron, the Earl of Essex, and shrewdly decided to stay away until the Queen was dead. He spent a period of leisurely exile exploring Italy, settling first in Florence and then Rome. On returning to Tuscany, he found a mission awaiting him. This was early spring 1602: the Duke of Florence had come to possess letters containing a plan to assassinate King James of Scotland. The Duke decided it was necessary to send a warning through a totally secure channel of communication; and his secretary, Vietta, said he knew the very man for the job. Wotton was recruited to deliver the message. He felt, however, that he could not attract attention or suspicion from any would-be conspirators by going to Scotland as an Englishman. Instead he disguised himself as an aristocratic Italian tourist, under the name of Octavio Baldi: he spoke the language fluently, and he had undoubtedly been in the country long enough to work up a convincing tan. Carrying papers from Florence, and an emergency kit of antidotes against special-grade Italian poisons, he took the added precaution of going all the way up to Norway, and travelling to Scotland across the North Sea. He probably had to, in fact, since he still faced arrest if he was recognized in England.

Reaching the Scots Court at Stirling, Wotton used a connection with one Bernard Lindsey, a gentleman of the King's bedchamber, to gain an audience with James, merely saying that the Duke of Florence had sent him on important business. Entering the presence chamber in sharp Florentine garb and with a long '*Italian*-like' rapier, Wotton found King James; and in shadows at the corners of the hall, three or four tough Scots lords. Wotton was asked for his name. 'Octavio Baldi,' he replied, but then asked if the bodyguards could leave, since he had been promised a private meeting. The attendants closed in to fling Baldi out, but James coolly told everyone to stand down, assuring his guest that he had perfect confidence in all who were present. Wotton's disguise had in any case been an elaborate safeguard against such a situation. He delivered his warning in Italian, confident that no one else in the room but he and the King could understand. Then, having gained James's trust, he drew closer, whispering 'That he was an *English* man, beseeching Him for a more private conference with His Majesty, and that he might be concealed during his stay in that Nation.'[37] His mission completed, he remained in Scotland for a while, with only one reported breach of cover. Years later, the story went around that Henry *alias* Octavio was 'interrupted' with a woman one Sunday morning 'by another wench who came in at the door'. Forgetting his Italian accent completely, he cried out, 'Pox on thee, thou hast hindered the procreation of a child' – thus compromising his disguise.[38] But in any case, Henry 'Baldi' Wotton went back to Florence three months later with letters of special commendation.

Elizabeth's death made it safe for him to return to England. After becoming King, James recognized Wotton at Court, and greeted him by his Italian pseudonym, '*saying, he was the most honest, and therefore the best Dissembler that ever he met with*'.[39] Wotton from this point on seemed destined for great things, and his reward was not long coming. In July 1604 he left Dover as Sir Henry Wotton, English ambassador to Venice. With him as an assistant was a mutual friend of his and Donne's, Rowland Woodward. Donne was happy for Wotton, though sorry to lose him again so soon. They were of a mind on so many things: by now Wotton was probably the author of his polemic *The State of Christendom*, a book written largely on the road, mapping out the schisms of the times. Although not published until 1657, it is more than likely that Donne read the work in manuscript, and approved of the unusually tolerant views it expressed on religious matters.[40] Privately, the two men had much in common; in public, they seemed to be on very different tracks.

Wotton's appointment made Donne take stock of his achievements and his disappointments; he felt the contrast keenly. He wrote Sir Henry a modest but dignified verse letter to tuck in with the 'reverend' papers of State he was carrying for the King, the 'learned' papers containing his personal notes, and the many other 'loving' papers which other 'friends send / With glad griefe, to your Sea-ward steps, farewel'. In a self-effacing postscript to the poem Donne asked if Sir Henry had already been given his last dispatches, or whether he had time enough so that 'such a one as I may yett kisse *your* hand'.[41] For Wotton, this was the next stage of an illustrious career; for his assistant, incidentally, the future was not so bright. Carrying dispatches home from France a couple of years later, Rowland Woodward was badly beaten up by robbers and left for dead. He later fell out with Wotton, accusing the ambassador of abandoning him.[42]

Still beached at Pyrford, Donne continued his studies in civil and canon law, and tried reconciling himself to his dependent situation. Two hungry little mouths now bawled and gurgled at his back when he tried to read. He was happy yet frustrated. In his poem for Wotton he declared that Fortune 'Spies that I beare so well her tyranny / That she thinks nothing else so fit for me', insisting that he was managing perfectly, but accepting at the same time that he had hardship to cope with, and expected more. He promised Wotton frequent prayers, and looked for solace in the thought that 'God is as neere mee here' as he was to the ambassador in Venice: the stairs to heaven 'In length and ease are alike everywhere'.[43]

This did not mean that Donne felt he could stay in the same place indefinitely. Restlessness eventually set in. No position at Court or any hope of other employment that Donne considered suitable was forthcoming, so in February 1605 a passport licence was granted to 'Sir Walter Chute knight and John Donne gent to travaile for three yeares with two servntes four nagges & iiij[xx] [£400]'.[44] Shortly afterwards, Donne followed Wotton across the Channel.

Donne left neither an account of his journey nor any comment on his reasons for travelling. He may have hoped that a spell abroad, during which he could refresh his modern languages and get up to date with foreign events and trends, might have made him more eligible for another secretarial post. Privately, he may have wished for a break from the confines of domestic life and the awkwardness of living on another man's charity. His companion, Sir Walter Chute, a little younger than Donne, had also served on the Islands expedition, but nothing suggests that the two were especially close friends. It is likely that Chute, knowing Donne to be a cultured man and gifted linguist, simply picked him out and offered to cover the expenses. It looks a little as though Donne took the first chance that came his way. Whatever his motives, though, there were excuses to be given and a wife and two children to mollify. Donne's canon contains many valedictions. Some offer grave and heartstruck farewells; in others the speaker edges away rather uncomfortably:

> Sweetest love, I do not goe,
> For wearinesse of thee,
> Nor in hope the world can show
> A fitter Love for mee . . .[45]

But one poem, Donne's sixteenth elegy, 'On His Mistris', seems
to belong specifically to the time just before he set out from Ann
for the first extended separation of their married life. It begins with
Donne trying to sound authoritative while also pleading with her
to be calm. He recounts the whole story of his and Ann's lovelife
up to that point; their 'first strange and fatall interview', their 'long
starving hopes', 'the memory / Of hurts' which spies and rivals
had threatened to inflict on him – and most tellingly of all, perhaps,
'thy fathers wrath'. And then it becomes clear what the row is
about: Ann is not only upset that he is leaving, she wants to go
with him. She has offered to dress up as a boy if needs be: Donne
turns this Shakespearean strategy aside, telling her, 'Be my true
Mistris still, not my faigned Page'. With cheerfully certain xeno-
phobia, he was anxious to protect her from lascivious foreign eyes.
The disguise would never be good enough to fool 'Men of France,
changeable Camelions, / Spittles' – they would all come after her.
And as for the homosexuals one found in Italy, they wouldn't care
if she was a boy anyway. 'Th'indifferent Italian,' he warned,

> as we passe
> Through his warme land, well content to think thee Page,
> Will hunt thee with such lust, and hideous rage
> As *Lots* fair guests were vext . . .[46]

So the answer was no, she couldn't come. The trip to Sodom was
strictly a boys-only affair. Wives couldn't join the great male tour
of Europe: that simply wasn't the point. There was in fact another
pressing reason for Ann not to accompany her husband – and a
good one, even considering the standards of the age, for him not
to leave her. She was already pregnant with their third child,
George, who was born in late April or early May.

It was customary for men to spend time abroad to complete or complement their liberal education. France was particularly popular for study and the refinement of manners; Italy was the top destination for sightseeing, despite fears about the influence of the Papist Antichrist's heartland on good but young and impressionable English Protestants. From the poem quoted above, both these countries seem to have been on Donne's itinerary. Like many English tourists before, Donne and Chute, with their two servants and four nags, set out amiably convinced both of the benefits of travel and the endemic vices of foreigners. For a sense of the nature and extent of their travels we are indebted, as so often, to the detective work of R. C. Bald, and his informed speculation can be fleshed out with the perceptions recorded by contemporary travellers – some of them known personally to Donne.

Paris was of course the premier location for the gentleman flâneur moving through France, and it was probably one of the ports of call at which Donne stayed longest. The journey from London could take many days, especially if the Channel winds were playing up. Perhaps travelling up the Somme to Amiens and so on to the capital, in 1605 Donne encountered the city undergoing one of its many architectural transformations, alive with the hope that the long religious wars were in permanent abeyance. In 1605 Tobie Mathew was also in Paris – noting regretfully that 'there will be this year little good fruite or wine' because of the bad weather – and taking in the building work admiringly. The Louvre was being splendidly extended with the Grande Galerie, which by now nearly adjoined the palace of the Tuileries, where 'the Kinge hath given order for a very great Pavillion to be erected'. The Place Royale was being constructed on the site of an old marketplace near the Bastille. The complex was intended for the sale of superior merchandise, 'stuffes of silke and golde' from Italy and the Netherlands. It was only half-built, but one could already see it was a 'wonder of a building . . . with galleries to walk dry, round about a goodly fountaine, in the midst, and a Pavillion on one side of the square to lodge the Kinge.' Donne was able to wander across the Pont Neuf, opened just two years before, the first bridge in Paris from which citizens could actually get a proper view of the river: all the others, as in London, were lined with houses and other buildings. On the west bank of the Seine, he saw the fabulous new palace, 'a yonge Towne', on which the divorced Queen Margaret was spending the ample pension King Henri IV provided for her.[47]

The young Englishman came to Paris to soak up the culture, polish his manners, learn or refine his French, and to acquire other skills befitting a gentleman with aspirations. Academies grew up for foreign students of this very kind, and after years of strict academic regulation at grammar school and probably university, these men found it easy to regiment their days. Set periods of time might be devoted to languages and worthy Latin authors, horse-riding and fencing – arts in which the French masters were thought to preside – and to dancing classes. There were notable outbreaks of disorder among the residents and visitors, but even these followed predictable patterns. Swordsmanship was a vital attribute: keen to do as they thought the sophisticated French were doing, English émigrés frequently challenged one another to duels over the faintest hints of a slur or dishonour. 'I am still much troubled here about the quarrels of the young gentlemen of our Nation,' wrote Sir George Carew, the English ambassador, in a dispatch at the end of a weary day. Sir Thomas Lucy – a friend of Donne's – had laid down the gauntlet to another Englishman, 'one Mr Helmes'. Carew had promptly sent servants chasing all over the city to find the two combatants and stop the contest from happening. When found, Lucy was packed off out of the city with orders to go home to England, but sent word to his opponent that he would wait for him at Rouen. There they would settle the matter. On discovering this, Carew reported that he had 'forcibly taken Mr Helme into mine howse' – and planned to keep him there until Lucy 'may be past the seas'.[48] Donne's companion, Sir Walter Chute, was far from passive company when affairs of honour were at stake: he had his chance to fight a duel on another trip to Paris some six or so years later.

Donne's habitual sense of caution kept him well away from such scraps, though he mixed freely among the English community: many within it were good friends of his, and some might have been able to put in a word for him at home. It is likely that he gravitated towards influential circles. Both he and Chute would have presented themselves to the then newly appointed ambassador, since they probably both knew him in person. Sir George Carew had been a senior officer on the mission to the Azores a few years earlier, though he did not make it beyond the early stages of the voyage, wrecked in his first ship and blown all around the British coast in the next. He also came from the same professional stable as Donne: he too had begun as one of Sir Thomas Egerton's secretaries. His career was an example of how advantageous a start this could be in the right circumstances. Carew knew Donne, knew of his abilities, and probably received him at his big house in the Faubourg St Germain, but was also aware of all the facts concerning the former secretary's current situation; and probably regretted them. Here lay the discomfort of Donne's position: he had to keep meeting those who liked him, respected his talents, perhaps even enjoyed his poetry – but found him too socially untouchable to help. Yet Donne had no choice but to keep moving among such people, reminding them of his existence, bestowing his courtesies where they would be received, and trying not to flinch at chilly responses or unkind remarks. He followed the English contingent into the French Court, where King Henri's four-year-old son was already receiving state visitors. Carew found the boy 'to be of a very strong, and vigorous Constitution, and of a hardy, and ready spirite'.[49] Donne, who saw him again in January 1612, by which time the prince had become Louis XIII, eventually decided that the child's 'inclinations are cruel, and tyrannous'.[50]

If Carew and Donne paid their respects to the infant Louis at the same time, Donne would have been on the return leg of his journey: this was January 1606, the date of Carew's first dispatch. By then, Donne and Chute appear to have visited Italy. To explain how this can be surmised, and their journey reconstructed, we need to go forward in time some twenty-five years.

By then few mentioned or cared about the widower's rebel

marriage or his wild youth. In his official residence as Dean of St Paul's, a spacious house a few streets away from the Cathedral, and not so far from the place where he was born, Donne exhibited all the artworks and souvenirs that were in keeping with his image as an established man of the Church. His will often specifies exactly where in the Deanery they were hung or placed; those for which no fixture is given, in fact, may well be those he put away from view. The portrait 'taken in Shaddowes', for example, of Donne in his prime, dressed in black satin and lace, seems to have been *kept* in the shadows, as a threat to his hard-achieved respectability. His will states merely that it 'was made many years before I was of this profession'. Among those from his past that were on display, however, were portraits of two Italian Servite friars, Fulgentio Micanzio and Paolo Sarpi.[51] The latter in particular was renowned as one of the finest theological minds in Europe; though his researches roved far beyond canon law and his religious duties. He was a keen medical scientist, whose work on anatomy contributed to the discovery of blood circulation. Galileo, a friend and devotee, thanked 'Padre Paolo' for helping him construct his telescope. Sarpi's counsel was also much in demand on affairs of state, and he developed a close working relationship with Sir Henry Wotton during his time as English ambassador. According to Isaak Walton, Donne's Italian travels also gave him an opportunity to meet Sarpi.[52] The friar certainly possessed the kind of wide-ranging, deep-searching intellect that Donne loved to encounter.

Donne might have met Sarpi on an earlier trip to the Continent, perhaps just before he enrolled at Lincoln's Inn. But in 1590, as Bald points out, Sarpi was (though undoubtedly brilliant) 'comparatively young and obscure'.[53] At the end of 1605, he was fifty-three, thoroughly established and moving towards his finest hour, at the centre of one of the tensest political standoffs of the day. In the autumn of that year, two Venetian priests were charged with gross misdemeanours. One was accused of trying to have sex with his niece, the other of 'murders, frauds, rapes and every kind of violence against his dependants'.[54] Naturally enough, the civil authorities arrested them. But this infuriated Rome: as priests, the papacy insisted, the two clerics could only be tried in an ecclesiastical court, and thus demanded that the prisoners be handed over. The Venetian authorities refused. This brought to a head other disputes, most of which concerned contested Church property. By May the following year, the Pope had excommunicated the whole Republic of Venice. Yet by then Padre Paolo Sarpi had been appointed as the Republic's chief theological councillor, and had begun an exhaustive publicity campaign that wholly undermined the Vatican's position in canon law. The priests in Venice were told to ignore the Papal sentence and continue serving Mass as normal. While rallying the citizens, Sarpi also worked hard to assemble international support. Spain naturally threw its weight behind the Vatican, but England and the Low Countries sided with Venice; France, Roman Catholic but with the former Protestant, Henri IV, as its ruler, tacitly backed the Italian republic. With this stack of alliances, the conflict was evenly poised; if it came to outright war, nothing was guaranteed for either side but massive losses. Sarpi urged the Vatican to consider what might happen if other Roman Catholic nations found they could disobey its dictates, and worship independently. After a year, the Pope backed down.

Though Donne later expressed firm support for the Venetian stance against Rome, he witnessed only the earliest stages of the crisis at firsthand. He can only have spent a few months at most in Venice. But this would have been long enough for him to catch up with Wotton, long enough to get to know the strange glistening city of islands, channels and inlets, and long enough to sample the odd autonomy the floating Republic created for itself: overtly Roman Catholic, but not dominated by Rome; a place where one might reach one's own ideas on questions of eternity.

The place was miraculous. Donne's friend Thomas Coryat, a comic travel writer, was stupefied by the palaces along the Grand Canal: the Rialto Bridge, 'so curiously compacted of only one arch'; the Piazza, 'the greatest magnificence of architecture to be seene, that any place under the sunne doth yeelde'. He stared and stared at the Ducal Palace and the Church of St Mark's, unable to stop looking and move on, 'because I knew it was uncertaine whether I should ever see them againe.' Venice was incapable of leaving the traveller without heartache; but English tourists saw it all through neither Canaletto's pure, frank sunshine nor the teary light that Turner found there on the stone and water. They were conscious of the swamp and the stench of garbage from the canals. With regard to Venetian culture, they were mesmerized but also suspicious. It was a place to savour wide varieties of the human, 'Polonians, Slavonians, Persians, Grecians, Turks, Jewes, Christians of all the famousest regions of Christendome, and each distinguished from another by their proper and peculiar habits'. It was rough too, and dangerous for the uninitiated; the gondoliers might glide the tourist away to who knew where, in order to rob them or worse. Coryat warned that the ferrymen at the Rialto Bridge were 'the most vicious and licentious varlets in all the city'. And it had a reputation throughout Europe for concupiscence – 'the name of a Cortezan of Venice is famoused all over Christendome'.[55] For Donne, of course, many of the city's recreations were off limits.

During a sojourn in Florence in 1606, Tobie Mathew seems to have written complaining at Donne (as ever) for not coming to visit him.[56] But it is unlikely that Donne confined himself to Venice during his stay in Italy. The route from France lay over the Alps, and the journey down to see Wotton would have taken Donne through Turin. Years later, in a sermon, he spoke of the famous shroud held in the cathedral there, noting how the sheet 'does still retaine the dimensions of his [Christ's] body, and the impressions and signatures of every wound that he had received in his body'. He read the practical implications of such adhesion with a pathologist's attention to detail: 'it would have beene no easie matter for those women to have pulled off that sheet, if it had had no other glue, no other gumme, but his own precious blood.'[57] Donne was familiar with a treatise on the shroud, and may simply have embellished his description from imagination. Yet there is every reason to suppose that he did actually see the relic in the cathedral and stored up his impressions for future meditation,

wondering if the 'signatures of every wound' were real signs of
Christ, or features of an idol, an image of the kind that the
Reformed Church refuted and condemned.

He and Chute must have tried to get back across the Alps into
France before the end of autumn 1605. A decent guess can be
taken of the way they took: one expert declares, 'if a traveller does
not name the route he took across the Alps it is almost certain that
it will turn out to have been the Mont Cenis pass.'[58] This can be
reached directly from Geneva, Lyons or Grenoble. After a steep
climb, most of the journey consisted of a trek or ride by mule
across a great plateau, with the chance of a toboggan slide when
the snows lay thick enough. Teams of incredibly hardy 'marons'
made their living guiding the many tourists up, across and down
to Lanslebourg. These men were equipped with crampons, cus-
tomized iron gauntlets, and for extra warmth often wrapped themselves in thick paper or parchment underneath their furs. The
marons could also be generous with their survival gear, especially
if their wards dared go with them on a climb up one of the peaks.
One traveller related how they 'gave him wine to drink, tied
crampons and iron claws to his feet and hands' – and gave him a
lift at difficult points with their arms under his shoulders. We will
never know if Donne received such assistance, or attempted any
of the summits. Climbing directly was certainly not his preferred
mode of ascent, even metaphorically: Truth, he had written, stands
'on a huge hill, / Cragg'd and steep', but to reach her one 'about
must, and about must goe'.[59] Perhaps he had his wife's worries still
ringing at the back of his mind. He had warned her not to halluci-
nate, nor to frighten her maid

> With midnight startings, crying out, oh, oh,
> Nurse, ô my love is slaine, I saw him goe
> O'r the white Alpes alone . . .[60]

He was almost certainly not alone, but yomping across the snow
with an old army comrade and a team of goat-footed minders.
All the same, he might have felt a more elemental loneliness in

the Alps. For all he had seen, and for all the weight and scale of snow and rock about him, landscape was not enough for him. He felt that the essential human borders could only be mapped out in ways beyond sheer line and physical dimension: 'mankinde hath very strong bounds to cohabit and concurre in other than mountains and hills during this life,' he later wrote.[61]

12. The Close Prison at Mitcham

Donne returned from the Continent in time for a familiar English spectacle – the execution of a Roman Catholic priest. In November 1605 the famous attempt was made to blow up Parliament, and with it King James, his sons and most of the governing order. Donne's caustic assessment was that 'All the Isle of Britaine had flowne to the Moone' if the explosives had gone off; and even though they didn't, the result was still 'noise and horror'.[1] King James himself had deep reflexive fears of gunpowder, reaching far back into his childhood. His father had been blown up by a bomb placed in his bedchamber, in the course of bitter dynastic wrangling for the Scottish throne. Opinion is still divided, and probably always will be, as to whether the terrorist threat in 1605 was genuine, or whether the real plot was laid by Robert Cecil, by now Lord Salisbury, to entrap a cell of extremists. But in any case, national hysteria resulted – the echo of the tremor is still felt every bonfire night – and at the end of January the following year, eight of the Papist conspirators were publicly hanged and dismembered in the churchyard of St Paul's. The government then turned their attention to Father Henry Garnet, head of the Jesuit order in England, and charged him with involvement in the treason.

No one could directly implicate Garnet in the planning of the operation, nor in the procurement or planting of the thirty-six barrels of gunpowder in the basement where Guy Fawkes was discovered; but he knew of the conspiracy and, as the land's senior Jesuit, was thus for his vitriolic prosecutors a prime agent of the rebellious drives that lay behind it. Garnet, a mild, myopic, corpulent man with thinning hair, had lived on the run for years, performing the rites of the covert Church, hiding in secret compartments in sympathetic homes, and fostering a chaste, mute romance with his female minder and devotee, Anne Vaux. He was possibly among the priests Donne encountered at 'the Consultation of Jesuites in the Tower, in the late Queenes time' that he witnessed as a boy.[2] Immediately after Garnet's inevitable conviction late in March, a vast storm blew from the west across England, the fiercest for twenty-five years, gusting way off course any ship that tried crossing the Channel. By this time, however, Donne was back, or made the journey soon afterwards.

Father Garnet went meekly to his death on 3 May. The execution capped two or more years of disillusionment for English Papists. The tolerant gestures of the opening days of James's reign had long disappeared; the King had found that he didn't need the Papists' allegiance to make his position secure. In 1604, the banishment of all Roman Catholic priests had been proclaimed, the legal penalties for recusants were enforced with new vigour; then, after decades of intermittent war, Spain signed a peace treaty with England that made no mention at all of freedom of worship. The defence of the English Roman Catholic communion had been one of Spain's main justifications for belligerence against England, but this holy cause was now quietly forgotten. Persecuted by their state, English Papists felt abandoned from outside. Their own community was also divided. Some, with the Gunpowder plotters as their exemplars, insisted that active resistance was essential; others, by far the majority, were determined to show they could be loyal English subjects *and* good Roman Catholics. Most were appalled by the conspiracy, and saw that such acts would only make their lives all the more difficult. A few years later, Donne referred to them as 'over-obedient Papists' – deriding their timidity, but also suggesting they had conceded too much.[3]

On returning from Europe, Donne was more eager than ever to steer himself away from the threatened faction in which his life had started out. Certain connections had to be played down, though some could not be ignored entirely. In 1606, Donne's mother Elizabeth and stepfather Richard Rainsford returned from exile in Antwerp, where they had lived since 1595. By 'his Maiesties free gift and favor', they were granted a sum of £2,000 that had been left by John Symynges, Elizabeth's previous husband, but was then confiscated by the crown when the couple 'wente beyond Seas and remayned there without licence'.[4] Re-entering English society after almost a decade away, they soon found that times were hard.

Another of Donne's more illustrious Roman Catholic contacts was also in trouble. Harry Percy, his friend and one-time emissary, the 'Wizard' Earl of Northumberland, who broke the bad news of Donne's marriage to Sir George More, was found guilty of involvement in the November plot. It was a cousin of Northumberland's who rented the basement where the explosives were installed; and this was enough to send the Earl to the Tower of London, where he played bowls with Sir Walter Ralegh and conducted his esoteric experiments. Much as he might have enjoyed it, such a life of free intellectual speculation was not open to Donne if his prospects failed: his circumstances, not to mention a very keen and frustrated sense of ambition, made it essential that he regain a place and an income in the Protestant regime. Before setting out on his travels, he had left Ann pregnant: another son, George, shrieked him a greeting when he came back to Pyrford in the spring of 1606. He needed more room for his multiplying family, and a base nearer London from which he could search for the opening that had so far eluded him.

John and Ann had gone to Pyrford at the invitation of Ann's cousin Sir Francis Wolley; where, says Isaak Walton, 'they remained with much freedom to themselves, and equal content to him for some years; and, as their charge encreased (she had yearly a child) so did his love and bounty.'[5] But the domestic situation became rather more difficult and delicate than Walton lets on. Wolley's own marriage was unhappy and childless; and he was having an affair with a woman called Joan Harris, who bore him a daughter. He named the girl after his wife, Mary, then made her stand as godmother. The house became fraught with crying, chuntering children and adult complications. Though no doubt glad of the company his cousin and her husband brought, Wolley evidently decided that it was time they moved on; for their part,

John and Ann were probably keen to get clear of the triangular arguments their host had brought on himself. This did not, however, mean any sharp cessation of Sir Francis's 'love and bounty': Wolley got his uncle and neighbour Sir George More to accede at last to a marriage settlement for his daughter. Perhaps mollified a little further by the naming of John and Ann's second boy, George, the previous summer, More agreed to give the couple an income of £80 a year – enough for them finally to set up a home of their own. The payment of the allowance was John and Ann's first step towards respectability. If anyone recalled their young rebel wedding, Donne could now show that his ultra-orthodox father-in-law had given the marriage his financial blessing, and thus social legitimacy. This had come very late, however, and did little to ease the qualms of potential employers and patrons.

The couple moved with their children – three-year-old Constance, two-year-old John and baby George – to a cottage at Mitcham, nearer London. The village was a flat parish with a reputation at the time for its fresh air and clean water from the river Wandle. The Donnes' house was roomy though draughty, with good-sized gardens, two projecting gables at the front and a wing built on at the left. A row of yews lurched over the path from the front door to the lane that led to the village. It was large enough – certainly by modern standards – to accommodate a growing family, but proved difficult (or just expensive) to keep warm, offering little protection from the colds and bugs that soon began to assail the new residents. Donne set aside a ground-floor room as a study, his 'poor Library', where he spent long candlelit hours continuing his research on law and divinity, and where 'raw vapors' crept up from the cellar below, slowly breaking his health. He came to refer to the house variously as his 'prison', 'dungeon' and 'hospital', though it put him only an hour's ride from the city and the Court, and within easy reach of the main outlying royal palaces. Even this proved to be too far away from the centre: he felt that he needed to be closer to where the daily business of running the nation took place, a feeling that coincided with the advanced stages of Ann's fourth pregnancy. By early 1607, Donne had two homes: his family house at Mitcham, and lodgings for himself on his old stamping ground, near the Savoy in the Strand, in a house belonging to one Mister Tincomb.

Here Donne was able to keep in regular contact with his friends. By now these included the playwright Ben Jonson, a gruff admirer of Donne's writing, though even more so of his own; George Garrard, a successful barrister and fellow-lodger at Tincomb's; Sir Thomas Roe, later to travel as ambassador to India and Constantinople; and a constellation of other wits and men 'of affairs'. His quarters gave him a venue from which it seems that he developed a practice offering informal legal advice: Walton says that Donne was 'often visited by many of the Nobility and others of this Nation, who used him in their Counsels of greatest consideration'. He obviously worked hard at gaining contacts and strengthening connections, but while his wealthy casual clients were happy to consult him occasionally, giving him 'some rewards for his better subsistence', they were slow to help him to what he desired most – a secure secretarial position like the one he had had with Sir Thomas Egerton – now further ennobled as Lord Ellesmere.[6] Part of the problem was that Donne had much more to offer than high and mighty men of state were looking for in an ideal secretary. Put bluntly, lords and councillors wanted bureaucrats who were doctrinally sound, socially approved, meticulous about procedure and good at writing letters. Donne had fought pitifully to make his credentials presentable, and certainly possessed the right practical qualities, but was made of stuff that would not quite fit the mould.

While clearly signalling his public allegiances, Donne still felt most comfortable in moderate, tolerant company. He was starting to see that everyone involved in the religious strife of the time – that is, more or less everybody in the land – had their own point of view, their own concerns of conscience; and he liked being with people who could see more than one side to the question. The most important friend with whom Donne could enjoy this rare confidence and sympathy was Sir Henry Goodyer. A well-read Warwickshire squire, knighted by Essex during the terrible Irish campaign, Goodyer was about the same age as Donne, with similar sensitivities but a more extrovert, hale and hearty cast of mind. He still took part in masques at Court when he got the chance.

The big New Year production of 1606, for which Donne, as ever, was of too little standing to attend, was Ben Jonson's *Hymenaei*, staged in honour of the ill-fated marriage between the new Earl of Essex and Frances Howard, the Earl of Suffolk's daughter. The centrepiece was a giant globe, with gilded landlines and a silver sea, turning softly. Stationed below stage, it is said, was Ben Jonson himself, a heavily built man who had started out in life as a bricklayer, now turning the winch that made the world revolve. His domineering ego was thus ideally placed in the proceedings, making the earth move. Goodyer by contrast was perfectly content to be an extra. Besides his minor theatrical activities, out in the open he was devoted to hunting and hawking: 'God send you Hawks and fortunes of a high pitch' was Donne's characteristic blessing for his friend, and he accepted that 'if I transgress into a longer and busier letter than your Countrey sports admit . . . you may read it in winter.'[7] Portly Ben Jonson also seems to have been a guest at Polesworth, Goodyer's slightly dilapidated country estate, as 'witness of thy few days' sport'; and he roundly praised Goodyer's learnedness and amiability:

> When I would know thee Goodyere, my thought looks
> Upon thy well-made choice of friends, and books;
> Then I do love thee, and behold thy ends
> In making thy friends books, and thy books friends . . .[8]

In fact Goodyer did use his friend as a kind of sourcebook at times, when he needed material for his own laudatory and tributary writings. Donne was more than happy to oblige: 'I am always glad, when I have any way to expresse my love,' he wrote, a little blearily, one 'Friday [at] 8 in the morning', after a late night of writing letters for Goodyer to use – 'for in these commandments you feed my desires, and you give me means to pay some of my debts to you.'[9] Goodyer, though troubled by increasing debts and expensive legal problems, was well set up in life: as a Gentleman of the Privy Chamber to the King, he was an insider at the Court, ideally placed to put in a word for Donne with the people who counted – something he never, apparently, failed to do. He also smoothed the way for Donne with his patroness, the Countess of Bedford.

But Goodyer's greatest gift to Donne was sympathy and confidence. Donne wrote to Goodyer as one who was 'not easily scandalized' by expressions of religious tolerance and even-mindedness, or by Donne's growing belief that in the disputes of the time 'both sides' in the conflict 'may be in justice, and inno-cence'.[10] These were, nonetheless, sentiments Donne uttered in secret, and he worried at times about his friend's discretion. He was in fact afraid that Goodyer went around broadcasting too freely 'that sound true opinion, that in all [note: *all*] Christian professions there is way to salvation (which I think you think)'. The opinion itself was sound and true, but one had to be careful who heard one expressing it; note the nervous little probe at the end with which Donne checks that Goodyer thinks as Donne thinks he does. In public it was necessary to avoid the dangerous charge of religious 'flexibility', or being associated with 'inobedient Puritans' and 'over-obedient Papists'.[11] At heart Donne's feeling was that religion was simply 'Christianity', in whichever institutional creed one happened to profess, but he was careful to profess himself as a loyal Protestant. He often, paradoxically, revealed his own libertari-anism towards 'those friends which are religious in other clothes then we' by urging Goodyer not to be so openly tolerant of such 'friends'. Goodyer was close to Tobie Mathew, who converted suddenly and scandalously to Roman Catholicism around this time, and Donne was watchful of his friend's generous inclusive spirit.

In time, Goodyer became closer to Donne than anyone except Ann. Donne lived emotionally, as before, largely through his letter-writing, which 'when it is with any seriousness, is a kind of extasie, and a departure and secession and suspension of the soul, which doth then communicate it self to two bodies'.[12] Donne also applied the term 'extasie' to the most intense form of communion with his love, in the poem that took the word as its title. This 'dialogue of one', this communication of the soul 'to two bodies' is one that Donne had prescribed in his most intense forms of correspondence; but it seems to have applied especially to Goodyer. He could begin a letter to his friend as though just emerging from a long daydream about him alone: 'It should be no interruption to your pleasures, to hear me often say that I love you, and that you are as much in my meditations as my self.'[13]

This freedom of exchange and the fact that he thought of Goodyer as much as he thought of himself meant that Donne did not have to pretend to qualities he did not actually possess. The relationship was strong enough for him to show his weaker traits without embarrassment – even without consciousness. Goodyer was a friend who was well used to giving his shoulder for leaning and weeping on, even when his own problems and sadnesses were much greater than those he was listening to. They were both in Europe during 1605 – Goodyer had gone to Brussels as part of the embassy to ratify the peace with Spain – and renewed their friendship on a still more intimate footing when they returned. Not long after Donne came back, Goodyer's wife, Frances, died. The couple were cousins, and had shared the troubled inheritance of her father's estate at Polesworth. On her death, friends sent in elegiac verses. Donne was still living at Pyrford, and it was some time before he heard of his friend's grief. He responded as soon he did. 'I live so farre removed,' he wrote to Goodyer, 'that even the ill news of your great losse (which is ever swiftest and loudest) found me not till now.' He wrote quickly while the messenger stood waiting, and without bothering to filter out the sense of his own troubles from his condolences. 'I am almost glad that I knew her so little,' Donne said bluntly, 'for I would have no more additions to sorrow.' Rather than sympathy, he offered comradeship in emotional beggary, saying that for him to comfort Goodyer would be like 'when poor give to poor; for I am more needy of it then you'. It is as though Donne forgot that his whole purpose in writing was to commiserate: the letter would be unbearably self-obsessed were it not for a rush of warm, active generosity at the end. Donne wrote in hasty and unthinking confidence, empathizing with Goodyer's grief by sighing out his own melancholy. But he then promised to 'make best haste after your messenger' in order to console Goodyer in person at Polesworth – just as soon as he found a way of getting there: 'if my self and the place had not been ill provided of horses,' he complained, '*I* had been the messenger, for you have taught me by granting more to deny no request.' He signed off as '*Your honest unprofitable friend*, J Donne'.[14]

Donne's letters to Goodyer also show his long struggle to make himself a more profitable friend, husband and father, as honestly as he could. He made a habit of writing to Goodyer on a Tuesday, from his little library, 'where to cast mine eye upon good Authors kindles or refreshes sometimes meditations not unfit to communicate to near friends'. He also prepared messages in his head as he daydreamed on horseback along the highway to London, 'where I am contracted, and inverted into myself'.[15] Usually he avoided giving explicit news or personal information; more often his letters were more like essays, 'meditations', written for Donne's own relief or pleasure and his reader's diversion. Domestic matters, Donne implied, were 'unfit to communicate to near friends'.

Very often, nonetheless, they slipped through. In January 1607, Goodyer received a letter written in the afterburn of high distress. Ann had just given birth to their fourth child, Francis – named affectionately after the cousin who for so long had put a roof over their heads – and it had been a difficult delivery. Obstetrics and midwifery were still primitive sciences, and the fee paid was not necessarily proportionate to the level of care. The forceps – brutal enough, but at least somewhat efficient – were not invented till later in the century, and a complication might be tackled only with a damaging and agonizing tug of war, with the infant as rope. Men were conventionally (and voluntarily) banished from the bedroom during the birth. Having sat with his books through the small hours, Donne told his friend, with weak conceitedness, that it was 'the saddest lucubration [nocturnal study] and nights passage that ever I had'. One wonders, then, what it must have been like for Ann, since it 'exercised those hours . . . with extreme danger of her'. The night thankfully 'encreased my poor family with a son', Donne reported, but he was faint and rattled, stemming his anxiety in a clot of verbiage: if Ann had died, he said that 'I should hardly have abstained from recompensing for her company in this world, with accompanying her out of it.' But since it had turned out all right, 'I thought it time not unfit for this dispatch.'

Already such meditations seemed 'unfit' for communication even to a friend as near as Goodyer. Donne was apparently helping him out with one of his protracted legal disputes. A disinherited relative kept challenging Goodyer's entitlement to his estate, which sank into further and further disrepair as the suit went on. Donne apologized that Ann's 'anguish, and my fears, and hopes, seem divers and wild distractions from this small businesse of your papers'. But he was evidently grateful for the diversion minor paperwork provided from matters of life and death, and from the sound of his wife shrieking and gnashing upstairs as he lucubrated below in his study. Although the only way of 'recompensing' for the loss of her company would have been to follow her out of the world, he had had to slip away from her – and from the busy house of women and children – for a while the next day. The letter was not written from Mitcham, but from Donne's lodgings in the Strand, at ten in the morning 'whilest my fire was lighting'.[16]

Months passed with few developments; Donne made his regular social rounds and meditated on the journey from the noisy house at Mitcham to his shelter on the Strand. In June, though, he stirred to act when a position at Court on the Queen's staff became vacant. Donne had met Queen Anne's Scots secretary, William Fowler, during the royal visit to Pyrford and Loseley in the summer of 1603; Fowler had written an appalling sonnet in which he compared the whole Court to the working of an ornate timepiece in Sir George More's home: 'Court hath me now transformed into a clock,' he intoned, 'And in my braynes her restles wheeles doth pace.'[17] This was the expansive, flagrantly inefficient machinery that was working quite well, nonetheless, without having Donne reinstalled. He was a spare cog, and felt like one.

Still, he hoped that the royal secretary might recall meeting him.

As so often, Goodyer had made the crucial introduction, and Donne now pressed him to repeat the favour. 'You may remember that long since,' he wrote, 'you delivered Mr *Fowler* possession of me': Donne was a 'gift' for Fowler to do with as he pleased, though the official might have forgotten the 'right and power' he still held over his human property. Donne asked that the secretary be reminded in the strongest terms, especially if there was any chance of a place in the Queen's household: 'if my means may make me acceptable to the Queen and him, I should be very sorry . . . that I fail in it.' Which he did: neither the Queen nor her secretary were interested in appointing him. Donne admitted at the beginning of his letter that 'the wide distance in which I have lived from Court' made it likely that Fowler had forgotten him, but if anything the opposite may have been true: he had *not* been all that far from the Court – he had been back in England, and socially active, for well over a year – and Fowler like everyone else probably remembered him and his past all too well. Donne might describe himself as the secretary's 'possession', but nobody was interested in a free gift.[18]

The arts of self-demeaning ingratiation were perfectly conventional, but Donne was forced to practise them more than most. This was a depressing comedown for the independent-minded young poet who had snarled at the mere idea of living by slavish flattery, 'Poorely enricht with great mens words or lookes';[19] but Donne was still delighted when one of his finely turned (though sometimes heavily loaded) compliments was accepted and valued. He had no problem with giving praise – he liked being kind and courteous, applauding and embellishing positive qualities – but what he sought was a response, recognition: he enjoyed social venues in which he could apply his charms, the 'elegant irresistible art' in his manner of which Isaak Walton wrote.[20] But while the people he most wanted to impress and be accepted by, the William Fowlers of the world, gave him the cold shoulder, his manners were still very well received in other quarters. Much as he needed Ann's 'company', his personal graces and ease of articulation may have had little exercise amid the domestic routine at Mitcham, except in the letters he wrote from his cold little study. He was

growing close to the Countess of Bedford, Goodyer's other main
source of patronage, who received his choice, courtly admirations
delightedly; and he had been on warm terms for a long time
with another highly cultured, highly lettered woman, Magdalen
Herbert.

It isn't clear whether Magdalen re-entered Donne's life during
the summer months of 1607, or whether a few letters from this
time are the surviving relics of a relationship that had continued
and grown without a break since his days as Egerton's secretary.
She was five years his elder, a widow and the mother of ten
children; and they met first at Oxford, where Magdalen was over-
seeing the studies of her son Edward, keeping the boy 'in a moderate awe of herself'. This she managed to do, at least according to
Walton, 'without any such rigid sourness, as might make her
company a torment to her Child'.[21] Edward, perhaps unsurprisingly, became a writer of sombre, tortuously complex poems, but
also an aggressively self-dependent man who shook off all maternal
care from the many women he grew to fascinate. He was a keen
admirer of Donne, who wrote to him on his travels:

> Man is a lumpe, where all beasts kneaded bee,
> Wisdome makes him an Arke where all agree.[22]

While Edward was being kneaded into shape at Oxford, Magdalen
got to know 'most of any worth or learning, that were at that
time in or near that University'. Donne, 'who then came accidentally to that place', met her by chance: this was probably in
1599, when Lady Egerton's green-eared son, Francis Wolley, was
just completing his final year of study. Donne may have been
on some errand to him from London when he encountered the
commanding, intelligent older woman, and was much taken with
'the Beauties of her body, and mind'.[23]

One of the poems that has often been attributed to Donne's
relationship with Magdalen is 'The Autumnall', a piece supposedly
in praise of female maturity:

> No *Spring*, nor *Summer* Beauty hath such grace
> As I have seen in one *Autumnall* face.

The poem, though, has many lines that were unlikely to have been taken kindly by Magdalen if it was really for her, or about her:

> I hate extreames; yet I had rather stay
> With *Tombs*, then *Cradles*, to weare out a day.[24]

Although he had married a woman more than ten years younger than he was, Donne seems to have found it funny that he should be attracted to one a few years older than him. 'The Autumnall' is actually a rather hurtful bit of work; though he and Magdalen were certainly close. In July 1607, Donne mentioned his 'resolution of writing almost daily' to her;[25] and Walton possessed many more letters for her than the four he cared to print. The friendship that grew up between them, Walton protested a little too earnestly, 'was not an *Amity* that polluted their souls'; which is to say, Donne and Magdalen were never lovers. Nonetheless, they both may have thought about it. In 'The Relique' Donne imagined his grave, where he would be lying with his love, linked to her by 'A bracelet of bright hair about the bone', being dug up. Their skeletons would be scattered and sold off as fake religious artefacts:

> Thou shalt be a Mary Magdalen, and I
> A something else thereby.

The pseudo-Christ who speaks the poem goes on to suggest that they had miraculously fought the temptation to break their physical 'seales': they were 'harmlesse lovers'.[26] The identity of the Mary Magdalen in this poem, 'The Relique', is not one that could ever be made explicit; but whether it is about Ann or someone else, then as now, Magdalen Herbert's memory is present in the name.

The 1607 letters show that he and Magdalen shared a language of coquettish, excessive compliment: he spoke of her as 'not only a World alone, but the Monarchy of the World your self'.[27] In one letter, however, the tone is a little different. Donne had noticed that Magdalen was paying him serious attention. A message from her awaited him wherever he went: 'Your favours to me are every where . . . I enjoy them at *London*, and leave them there; and yet find them at *Micham*.' It was Sunday morning. He had returned to the family house and found one of Magdalen's servants waiting for him since the evening before. He said that he was almost sorry to encounter the messenger, 'because I was loth to have any witness of my not coming home last Night, and indeed of my coming this Morning.' Donne, in other words, had sloped in after a Saturday night away, and had perhaps managed to annoy two women: most importantly Ann, by his absence *and* by the urgent messaging of another woman. 'But my not coming was excusable,' he justified himself to Magdalen, 'because earnest business detein'd me.' He then described his return home in terms that seem to set a limit on his relationship with her, possibly as the result of a row with Ann.

And my coming this day, is by the example of your St. *Mary Magdalen*, who rose early upon *Sunday*, to seek that which she lov'd most; and so did I. And from her and my self, I return such thanks as are due to one to whom we owe all the good opinion, that they whom we need most, have of us.[28]

A very complicated signal is being given here. At one level, Donne is merely paying thanks and making a little joke on the name of his lady friend. He had reached Mitcham, stabled his horse and wandered through the dewy grounds to his house, as Mary Magdalen, the woman who bathed Christ's feet in her tears, had gone to the tomb on Easter Sunday, discovered it empty, and encountered the Messiah in the awakening garden. 'That which she lov'd most' was Jesus; 'that' which Donne loved most, he was now spelling out, was Ann, and he was using Mrs Herbert's name to drive the point home. The romance with Magdalen, if there ever was one, was laid to rest: she remarried in 1609. They remained

on familiar terms nonetheless. Donne wrote her a verse letter
expressing the hope that he could be friends with both her and
her new husband, Sir John Danvers – who was less than half
her age, and a strikingly handsome man: 'his complexion was so
exceeding beautifull that the people would come after him in the
street to admire him.'[29] He eventually rolled the stone across the
tomb of his relationship with Magdalen by preaching her funeral
sermon twenty years later.

   Exactly what Ann's feelings were about Donne's friends and
connections can only be surmised; she is a woman stifled by history,
and the extent of her own social life is unknown. The images in
negative that the poems retain of her – if they are of her – suggest
that it was Donne who was very often the jealous party:

> To make the doubt cleare, that no woman's true,
> Was it my fate to prove it strong in you?

'The Expostulation' froths and champs at the betrayal of early
pledges and kisses 'stolne' at great risk:

> Who could have thought so many accents sweet
> Form'd into words, so many sighs should meete
> As from our hearts, so many oaths, and teares
> Sprinkled among, (all sweeter by our feares
> And the divine impression of stolne kisses
> That seal'd the rest) should now prove empty blisses?[30]

The trouble the poem speaks of started, it turns out, when Ann
(if she is the 'weake you' being shouted at) shared some confiden-
tial matter of their relationship with some 'treacherous beast' who
'betray'd each simple word / Wee spake'.[31] The poem reads as
though it might date from when John and Ann's romance was
strictly secret; but internal evidence shows it was clearly written
sometime during the reign of King James. Donne proceeds to rant
a thorough curse upon the 'black wretch' Ann has shared their
secrets with:

> May wolves teare out his heart, Vultures his eyes,
> Swine eate his bowels, and his falser tongue
> That utter'd all, be to some Raven flung,
> And let his carrion coarse [corpse], be a longer feast
> To the Kings dogges, then any other beast . . .

According to Walton, Donne was 'by nature highly passionate, but more apt to reluct at the excesses of it' − that is, only really lost his temper when he encountered stroppiness in others ('reluct', from Latin *reluctari*, means to 'struggle against').[32] In other words, he was quick to regain control if people let him be. Normal relations could be restored by rekindling old passions and returning to the copycatting and the cautious politeness of early love:

> Now I have curst, let us our love revive;
> In me the flame was never more alive;
> I could beginne againe to court and praise,
> And in that pleasure lengthen the short dayes
> Of my lifes lease . . .
> I could renew those times, when first I saw
> Love in your eyes, that gave my tongue the law
> To like what you lik'd; and at maskes and playes
> Commend the selfe same Actors, the same wayes . . .
> All which were such soft pastimes, as in these
> Love was as subtilly catch'd, as a disease . . .

Donne's poetry not only records the ecstasies of soulmates, but also the work that had to go into a relationship. Love was much harder to keep going than it was to begin, he said:

> And ought not be prophan'd on either part,
> For though 'tis got by *chance*, 'tis kept by art.[33]

The months passed by in rather aimless social circulation. In autumn 1607, Tobie Mathew returned as a Roman Catholic convert from travelling in Italy. His staunchly Protestant parents, especially his father, Tobie senior, the Bishop of Durham, were dismayed. But Mathew claimed that his change of heart was about much more than delayed teenage rebellion (he was thirty years old, five years younger than Donne). 'For I had resolved to do the best I could to save my soul,' he later pleaded; 'yet I was extremely desirous to carry myself so, in this change, as that no manner of unnecessary offence might be taken at it.'[34] If this really was his intention, he failed miserably. A major scandal blew up about his desertion of the established faith, and Mathew found himself a prisoner in the Fleet, facing deportation, indefinite incarceration or worse. Donne went to visit him in his own old place of detention, no doubt with a shudder as the smell of dead things in the streams surrounding the gaol brought back unwanted memories. But he went as part of a cheerful crowd: Mathew's visitors included Sir Maurice Berkeley, an old campaigner from the days of Cadiz and the Azores; Richard Martin, a lawyer famed for getting hit over the head by the poetaster Sir John Davies at an Inns of Court dinner; Sir Edward Sandys, a founding colonizer of Virginia; and Sir Henry Goodyer.

The whole group always avoided the reason for their being there with great tact: 'ordinarily there was no set discourse of religion,' Mathew reported huffily. We can imagine the uncomfortable silences. 'Both Dunne and Martin were very full of kindness to me at that time, though it continued not to be hearty afterward.' Donne, certainly, grew less and less impressed with Mathew. He had seen too much real suffering as a result of the religious divide to have much sympathy with a rich boy's contrived crisis of conscience. Donne was beginning to feel that those who persisted in the outlawed Roman Catholic creed were causing unnecessary harm to themselves and their children. Mathew, for his part, perhaps out of frustration at not being taken quite seriously, denounced Donne and the other refugee Protestants as 'mere libertines'.[35] But Richard Martin, a fearless and outspoken opponent of royal totalitarianism, was said to have 'a sweet and fair disposition to every man that kept his distance'.[36] He was not one to care about getting on the wrong side of Mathew.

The image of himself as a 'mere libertine' was nonetheless exactly that which Donne sought to diminish in much of the company he kept: he assiduously cultivated relations with the Countess of Bedford, one of the Queen's ladies-in-waiting. He had visited her home at Twickenham some time before: 'Twickenham Garden', one of the weaker poems in his early style of a weary but willing lover, describes him bringing the serpent love into the earthly paradise of the grounds. Sir Henry Goodyer was close to her partly through family connections: her father was a good friend of Goodyer's uncle and benefactor, an elder Sir Henry. Born Lucy Harrington in 1581, she was married off at the age of thirteen to Edward Russell, Earl of Bedford, who threw his lot in with Essex during the abortive rising of 1601. He then found himself in the Tower of London. But as soon as King James's succession was proclaimed, and his long ride down from Scotland began, the young Countess journeyed north to meet the royals. Her plan was to rehabilitate her husband's status and restore her own fortunes; and she succeeded, becoming one of Queen Anne's most trusted intimates and one of the most influential women at Court into the bargain. She was bright and vivacious, with a great love of both poetry and the attention of poets. Ben Jonson hailed her on first-name terms as

> Lucy, you brightnesse of our spheare, who are
> Life of the *Muses* day, their morning-starre![37]

Donne was one among many writers, professional and otherwise, who sought Lucy's patronage and approval. He could not, however, win her favour with the same variety of arch witticism that an old friend like Magdalen Herbert enjoyed, but addressed her in careful, formal and elaborate complimentary notes that he usually passed on through Goodyer. Late in December 1607, she and Goodyer were deep in rehearsal for the royal masque. This year's major offering was another piece by Jonson, 'The Masque of Beauty'. The theatrical machinery, to Jonson's increasing but for now suppressed annoyance, was becoming so elaborate as to completely upstage his hard-turned poetry. The set design featured 'an *Island* floating on a calme water', that drifted forward on a concealed wagon during the course of the performance; it meanwhile had 'a circular motion of it owne, imitating that which we call *Motum mundi* [movement of the world], from the *East* to the *West* side'.[38] Cut off as ever from this high social scene, stranded at Mitcham on New Year's Eve, Donne wrote to Goodyer, asking him to 'deliver this Letter to your Lady, now, or when the rage of the Mask is past'. His short message ends on a lonely note: 'If you make any haste into the Country' – that is, back to Polesworth, and beyond regular visiting distance – 'pray let me know it. I would kiss your hands before you goe, which I doe now.'[39]

By March Donne could write to Goodyer as one in regular contact with Lady Bedford. She had been trying to get Sir Henry to come to town from the country, and Donne jabbed him gently for non-attendance: 'When I saw your good Countesse last, she let me think that her message by her foot-man would hasten you up.' News concerning another social scene was in the air, however: Tobie Mathew, it had been decided, was to be sent out of the country; and Donne was sure that Goodyer, Mathew's good friend, would indeed hasten up since 'I knew how near M. *Mathews* day of departing this kingdome was.'[40] Donne himself was largely indifferent to the departure; but Mathew had entrusted Goodyer with the care of his financial affairs and estates, and the connection would prove a troublesome one for Goodyer when officials began to ask awkward questions about the exile's money. Donne himself was acutely conscious of the undefined but palpable danger that went with over-proximity to certain people.

The group of friends and acquaintances that visited Mathew in gaol had also included one Captain Whitlock, formerly in the pay of the 'Wizard' Earl of Northumberland, who was still in the Tower for his alleged part in the November 1605 Gunpowder Plot. Whitlock was a boozy, disappointed adventurer who fought as a mercenary in the French civil wars, and was made a captain by the Governor of Provence. He was coarse and garrulous, and was suspected for some time of knowing more about the Wizard

Earl's involvement in the conspiracy than he ever let on. Whitlock often went to see Mathew, 'and would be talking to me like a madman . . . drolling, and fooling, and blaspheming'. He did at least offer Mathew some 'discourse of religion', though it did not go far beyond saying 'that, for his part, he maliced nobody, but loved them lustily that loved him'.[41] He died a startled death in September 1608, and with him went whatever secrets he held about his former master.

Donne knew the captain; he observed that 'without doubt want broke him'. Whitlock had stumbled in a fever from one house to another of non-committal patrons and suddenly cold companions. Applying for aid firstly at the home of one Mrs Jones, 'who in her husbands absence declining it, he went in the night, his boy carrying his cloakbag, on foot to the Lord of *Sussex*.' Sussex set out the next day to hunt, and told Whitlock 'he would see him no more'. The captain wandered destitute for a while, and died in the brief care of a chaplain. Donne hoped piously that the dead man had had the chance or inclination to make his peace with God: 'Perchance his life needed a longer sicknesse,' he told Goodyer, in order to ready his soul, but he hoped that Whitlock's sudden end jarred him into a state of terminal sanctity. 'And the grace of Almighty God doth every thing suddenly and hastily,' Donne solaced, 'but depart from us.'[42] His own sense of religion was becoming ever more vital to his morale. The fate of Whitlock was a frightening example of what might happen if patronage and friendship failed to break one's fall.

Whitlock died with a smear on his name that spread to others who called on Tobie Mathew in his cell at the Fleet. Many were vaguely implicated in sedition by association with Whitlock and, by extension, the Wizard; Donne's own close connection with the Earl was also far from forgotten. These men were suspected in certain quarters of possessing some knowledge of the Gunpowder Plot; all were men of Court; and some, like Mathew and Donne, were former parliamentarians. It may be too farfetched to suggest that Donne's absence from England in 1605 was prolonged when he heard some rumour from an old Catholic contact about the likelihood of an attack; but he still had to tread with moderate care.

The stately homes of the Countess of Bedford were much safer territory. In August, she stood as godmother to John and Ann's fifth baby, Lucy; and November saw him as a confident man about town, 'going to sup with my Lady *Bedford*'.[43] But it had been another year of crushing disappointment so far as his career was concerned. The Donnes were living on the money Sir George More paid as Ann's settlement, and whatever handouts Donne himself could wheedle out of various aristocratic contacts at Court: too often the largesse consisted of little more than the odd invitation to supper. Donne continued sending melancholy dispatches to Goodyer from his 'prison' at Mitcham. Sometimes he lapsed from the intellectual subjects 'not unfit to communicate to near friends', and described life at home. One evening he felt guiltily obliged to emerge from his 'poor Library', and sit for a while with his family:

I write to you from the fire side in my Parler, and in the noise of three gamesome children; and by the side of her, whom because I have transplanted into a wretched fortune, I must labour to disguise that from her by all such honest devices, [such] as giving her my company, and discourse . . .

He felt bad about himself, though here he does salvage some pride from having made the special effort to spend some time with his loved ones. While he couldn't quite admit it, the situation was creating silent spaces in his marriage, covered over with 'honest devices': merely keeping Ann company could now require the labour of a disguise. He strained every nerve to conceal from her a sense of confinement and a complete loss of physical lustiness: 'As I have much quenched my senses, and disused my body from pleasure, and so tried how I can be mine own grave, so I try now how I can suffer a prison.' He did not, though, see or mention the possibility that she too was putting on a stoical mask to spare his feelings, in the same way he claimed to be protecting hers: 'But if

I melt into a melancholy as I write,' he sighed on paper – having already dissolved quite thoroughly into dejection – 'I shall be taken in the manner: and I sit by one [i.e. Ann] too tender towards these impressions.'[44] The picture is of two hypersensitive people thoroughly aware of the other's 'wretched fortune', each made to feel even worse by the sense of being the cause of it, and surrounded all the time by the steady 'gamesome' cacophony of five little Donnes.

In November, another campaign for employment ended fruit-lessly. 'Sir *Geoffrey Fenton* one of his Majesties Secretaries in *Ireland* is dead,' Donne told Goodyer, 'and I have made some offer for the place.' This was always going to be a long shot: Fenton, though he had a reputation as 'a notorious bribe-taker', had been one of the senior officials in Ireland since the early 1580s, with a long queue of deputies and insiders waiting to take his place.[45] But Donne felt obliged to have a go, and managed to muster a few nervous hopes. Goodyer as ever had put him in touch with some-one who could help. Besides the support of Lady Bedford, Donne also felt that he could count on another rising star at Court, Lord James Hay. 'I owe you what ever Court friends do for me, yea, whatsoever I do for my self,' Donne thanked Goodyer earnestly. Hay was a raffish but good-hearted Scot, one of the beautiful young men with whom King James liked to surround himself. He and Donne got on well from their first meeting, and Hay was eager to help him to the vacant secretaryship. Donne initially suspected the younger man of making empty pledges, but was pleasantly surprised: Hay carried out his word 'so readily and truly, that his complements became obligations, and having spoke like a courtier [he] did like a friend.' With one of the King's favourites on his side, Donne felt entitled to think he was in with a chance. At any rate, 'I am content to go forward a little more in the madnesse of missing rather then not to pretend [aspire],' he declared in his letter to Goodyer, 'and rather wear out, than rust.'[46]

But he was still inescapably tarnished. Hay did his best, but could not prevail with the King, and cruel rumours made Donne only too sure of what had disqualified him from being considered for the post. He wrote thanking Hay for his good efforts: 'I have been told,' he continued awkwardly, that 'his Majestie remembred me, by the worst part of my historie, which was my disorderlie proceedings, seaven years hence, in my nonage.' By this, of course, he was referring to his clandestine marriage. He was still stigmatized, even though he could now insist that Egerton and 'Sir G. M.' had forgiven him. The letter painfully reverses the sense of escaping childhood that Donne had celebrated in his poem 'The Good Morrow'. Whereas before, meeting Ann had felt like growing up at last – 'Were we not wean'd till then?' – now the fugitive romance itself seemed like something carried out in his 'nonage', during infancy. He went on to express his hope that Hay would not see any 'dishonourable staine' in his character, nor hold anything against him for 'that hastie intemperate act of mine' seven years before. Ann would never have seen such 'businesse' correspondence; but as one all 'too tender towards these impressions', she surely felt the letter's contents in other ways.[47]

Another application for a secretarial post, this time with the Virginia Company, failed in February the next year, even though Donne had many friends and connections on the syndicate's council. This turned out to be a stroke of luck, since the colonists who set out in June were shipwrecked in the Bermudas; but it was a hard knock to bear in a cold month. It all started to get too much for Donne. Stuck in his draughty study with the raw vapours rising from the cellar underneath, he would complain of 'a sicknese which I cannot name or describe. For it hath so much of a continuall Cramp, that it wrests the sinews, so much of a Tetane, that it withdraws and puls the mouth . . . .'[48] On occasion he was hit by 'such storms of a stomach colick as kept me in a continuall vomiting'.[49] His wife and children, meanwhile, offered continual testimony to their 'wretched fortune', and at times he could only freefall through depression, resenting more and more his 'close prison at Micham'.

At least those servants of the Virginia Company whom the great tempest washed up on the Bermuda islands in 1609 were employed in some endeavour, useful to some purpose and active in the world.

Donne almost envied them: 'When I must shipwrack,' he said, 'I would do it in a Sea, where mine impotencie might have some excuse; not in a sullen weedy lake, where I could not have so much as exercise for my swimming.'[50] In the outskirts of London, Donne was more truly marooned: 'all retirings into a shadowy life are alike from all causes, and alike subject to the barbarousnesse and insipid dulnesse of the Country,' he lamented. He tried hard to fight his misery down: 'But truly wheresoever we are, if we can but tell our selves truly what and where we would be, we may make any state and place such,' he declared, with weak defiance. Place and time were irrelevant: much more important was the mental condition. We can control our lives, he tried arguing, if we keep our state of mind in check: 'for we are so composèd, that if abundance, or glory, scorch and melt us, we have an earthly cave, our bodies, to go into . . . and cool ourselves: and if we be frozen . . . we have within us a torch, a soul, lighter and warmer then any without.' Donne then tried laughing off his own solemnities, describing the thoughts he set down on paper for Goodyer as 'the salads and onions of *Micham*, sent to you with as wholesome affections as your other friends send Melons and Quelque-choses from Court and *London*.'[51]

He was all too aware, though, of the mechanisms that stalled his resistance of melancholy. For without any change of fortune to improve it from outside, he could only fight the 'disease' in his mind with the very powers of mental fortitude it was eating away. 'If I knew that I were ill, I were well,' he cried. Ailments of body and soul could be treated with medicine and religion, but with those of the mind, diagnosis and cure were desperately hard – because, he said, 'there is no *Criterium*, no Canon, no rule; for, our own taste and apprehension and interpretation should be the Judge, and that is the disease itself.'[52] It was occurring to him that the real 'close prison' at Mitcham was not his poor library, his little parlour full of gamesome children, or even the rickety house itself – but his own being; its ceiling was the roof of his own mind, and its bonds the veins and sinews that roped him to life.

He gave expression to thoughts of killing himself in a strictly secret treatise on suicide, *Biathanatos*. Suicide had always been classified in religion and law as an ultimately sinful deed, since it was an act of despair, a deed that rejected God's gifts outright. But Donne sought to show 'that Self-homicide is not so Naturally Sinne, that it may never be otherwise', suggesting that even Christ had taken his own life by going willingly to a death he had the power to prevent. Donne saw different causes in his personal history and in his character for the state of despondency he had reached. It might, he said, have been

because I had my first breeding and conversation with men of a suppressed and afflicted Religion, accustomed to the despite of death, and
hungry of [for] an imagined martyrdome . . .

It might have been that he was susceptible to the 'Common Enemie', the devil; or because he really felt at heart that he *didn't* bear 'any rebellious grudging at Gods gifts'. In any case, he won-dered if he didn't have 'the keyes of my prison in mine own hand'.

Biathanatos was as much a way of containing and shaping such feelings as of letting them loose: technically, it has a lot in common with the 'Paradoxes' and 'Problems' in which Donne defended extreme and seemingly unreasonable positions. It also took him down deeply heterodox passages of thought – it occurred to him, for example, that the God-made universe was not, perhaps, innately moral: 'to mee there appears no other interpretation safe but this, that there is no externall act naturally evill; and that circumstances condition them, and give them their nature.' If it had got around, such a relativistic sentiment would have been the death knell of any hope Donne held of a public career; but at this time, there seemed no hope of one anyway, so he set it down. Presenting a copy of the book to the lugubrious Edward Herbert nearly ten years later, he defended the tract's esoteric argument, saying 'that though this doctrine hath not been taught nor defended by writers, yet they, most of any sort of men in the world, have practised it.'[53]

The hidden book was an exercise in the theory of 'Self-homicide' that kept Donne from getting too close to the practice. He was not permanently suicidal; rather, he hungered to be more alive. He hated above all the sense of being cut off from the human mainland. He needed to be needed – involved, employed, absorbed but also distinguished – in what was going on. He could not bear to live as a mere spectator. The country was nothing but 'barbarousnesse and insipid dulnesse' if there was nobody there or nothing to do: 'onely the employments, and that upon which you cast and bestow your pleasure, businesse or books, gives it the tincture, and beauty'.[54] Donne could take no pleasure in a landscape as a landscape – it was inert, lifeless, detached from the world, if devoid of activity.

At least once a week during these years, Donne sat among his books and shared his meditations with Henry Goodyer. In September 1608, in the same letter which concludes with his account of Captain Whitlock, he reflected on his own redundancy. Whitlock's shabby death had disturbed him. While he would end by musing on the state of the Captain's soul, he considered his own first:

Every Tuesday I make account that I turn a great hour-glass, and consider that a weeks life is run out since I writ. But if I aske my self what I have done in the last watch, or would do in the next, I can say nothing; if I say that I have passed it without hurting any, so may the Spider in my window . . .

He had an idea of the world and of humanity as an organic entirety, something in which every fibre and feature had to be present for a reason, linked to all others and doing something for them: 'to be no part of any body, is to be nothing,' he complained.

At most, the greatest persons, are but great wens, and excrescences; men of wit and delightfull conversation, but as moales for ornament, except they be so incorporated into the body of the world, that they contribute something to the sustentation [sustenance, sustainment] of the whole.

He was ambitious; he wanted to be among those 'great men'; and he probably considered himself a man 'of wit and delightfull conversation' (for he was) – but these were nothings unless they were incorporated together and supported one another. He hated being an outsider, a hanger-on. And all the time, his personal 'historie' reproached him for squandering his potential and going awry. He had begun usefully, he felt, by studying law; but had been diverted by 'an hydroptique immoderate desire of humane learning and languages'. Then he had recovered, during his years of service with Egerton: 'And there I stumbled too', he wrote – a little guiltily, perhaps checking that Ann wasn't close enough to overhear his thoughts – 'yet I would try again'.[55]

'My fortune hath made me such as I am,' Donne griped, 'rather a sicknesse and disease of the world then any part of it.'[1] Yet by now, despite his sustained attempts to gain Court employment, he knew that there was another way of re-establishing himself in society and easing his financial worries. Late in June 1607, the Reverend Dr Thomas Morton, newly appointed as the Dean of Gloucester, asked Donne to pay him a visit. The meeting probably took place in the 'Deanery house of St *Paul's*', where Morton stayed whenever he needed to be in London, and where he housed an extensive private library.[2] Morton could speak to Donne as a friend and ally of some standing; they may have met at Cambridge, or through mutual acquaintance with the family of Christopher and Samuel Brooke. The fine house to the south of the Cathedral would be Donne's home for the last decade of his life, and it seems that he had been invited there before by Dr Morton. As this particular conversation progressed, Donne might well have wondered whether history was repeating itself. Over fifteen years before, at around the time of his brother Henry's death, Donne had been summoned to give an account of himself by a previous Dean of Gloucester, Antony Rudd, who had urged him to give up his Roman Catholicism. Now the new Dean, in friendlier circumstances, was attempting to take the reformation a stage further. 'I know your expectation of a State-employment,' Morton said, 'and I know your fitness for it; and I know too, the many delays and contingencies that attend Court-promises.' Donne listened patiently to a long account of both his talents and frustrations.

What Morton was offering was this: he had just been made Dean of Gloucester, but he still held his previous church benefice, and he proposed to give this up for Donne to take over, if he would enter the priesthood. Morton was a single man, was resolved to remain so, and his Deanery would be more than sufficient for his needs. 'You know I have formerly perswaded you to wave your Court-hopes, and enter into holy Orders,' said Morton. This was the first time, however, that Donne had been tempted by a guaranteed living in the Church. He was startled: 'Mr *Donne's* faint breath and perplext countenance gave a visible testimony of an inward conflict.' Morton told him to say nothing yet, but to return with an answer in three days' time. He warned Donne not to think that he, or any man, was 'too good for this employment, *which is to be an Ambassadour for the God of Glory*'.

To most who knew or knew of him, the idea of Donne taking orders would have come as a complete shock – as something almost blasphemous. Beyond the prison of his mind, body and house at Mitcham, by this time Donne had several social identities. The way he appeared to a contemporary among London's gentry depended greatly on how much of his past that person knew about or shared, and the particular walk of life to which the same person belonged. Those who knew him through his work dating from the 1590s knew him as the erotic and critical poet of the elegies and satires. In some quarters it was beginning to be seen just what a treasure of a poet he was. For Ben Jonson, Donne was 'the delight of Phoebus'.[3] This was the start of the literary reputation that has recovered steadily in the past two centuries; but at the time Donne found it something of a constraint. It prevented others from taking him seriously enough to offer him what he would term 'a graver course'.[4] To those who knew of his more recent fortunes, he was still put down as 'John Donne undone', the man who had messed up a promising career in government by marrying for love, or the hope of a girl's fortune, depending on how one viewed the affair. This was how Donne was sure King James himself saw him, so far as he noticed him at all: 'his Majestie remembred me, by the worst part of my historie' – his clandestine marriage.[5]

Some with a better knowledge of the former secretary were aware that the state had lost a considerable legal and administrative brain through his dismissal, and a few continued to make use of it

on an informal basis. In 1603 or the year after, the eminent antiquarian Sir Robert Cotton asked Donne for a report on a vexed
question of diplomacy. English, Spanish and French ambassadors
frequently argued over which of them had due precedence in the
various foreign royal Courts, and Cotton asked to know how the
matter stood in law. Donne consulted a polemic on the debate by
a Spaniard, Diego Valdes, and sent a lengthy and detailed written
response back to Cotton with a copy of the text he had used.[6] This
was probably one of many more such consultations. Cotton and
others still, however, knew that Donne's main use for his legalistic
turn of mind lay in theological questions. For these few acquaintances, among them Dr Thomas Morton, he was a talented amateur
scholar of canon law and divinity. These subjects had been integral
to his personal reading since at the latest the death of his brother
Henry, when he had impressed his counsellor Rudd with 'weighty
observations'.[7] His third satire, on 'religion', had shown an unspar-
ing awareness of the doctrinal controversies of the Reformation.
Although it had never surfaced in any professional form, this was
the knowledge and talent that Morton was hoping to channel. Yet
even those who knew of his interest in this field would have been
surprised to see Donne as a priest.

He turned Morton's offer down. Not, he insisted, because 'I
think myself too good for that calling, for which Kings, if they
think so, are not good enough'. The reasons he gave instead
for declining were concerns about his social reputation: 'some
irregularities of my life,' he said, 'have been so visible to some
men, that though I have, I thank God, made my peace with him
by penitential resolutions . . . yet this, which God knows to be so,
is not so visible to man.' He did not, he protested, wish to bring
'that sacred calling' into dishonour. 'To these I might add other
reasons that disswade me,' he concluded, 'but I crave your favour
that I may forebear to express them.'[8]

These were Donne's words as remembered by Morton over
fifty years later, at the age of ninety-four, and at the very end
of a career as one of England's most noted Protestant scholars
and polemicists. Just a few months before his death, he sent his

reminiscences for Isaak Walton to include in the second edition of
The Life of Dr John Donne in 1658. Morton had risen to be Bishop
of Durham, a position that was threatened during the Civil War,
when he openly expressed support for the Royalist cause and paid
for it with a spell in prison, and which he eventually lost under
Cromwell's reforms. The Republican Commonwealth carried
much further the stripping of the altars that began with the
Reformation well over a century before. Morton, as his zealous
apologist Dr Joseph Naylor reported in 1669, lamented at 'all those
Illiads of *evills*, and mountains of miseries, which have fallen upon
these fate-blasted and star-stricken kingdoms' – England, Scotland
and Wales – since the Civil War; and of them all, Naylor complained, 'the extirpation or suppression of the true Religion' was
the worst.[9] Naylor was well entitled to think so. Morton had
bestowed on him 'the rich Rectory of Sedgefield' under the system
of ecclesiastical patronage that was then swept away and replaced
under Parliamentary rule.[10] Morton himself, though he 'bewailed
the bold Crimson sins', was more even-tempered. He was in
London, at his episcopal palace on the Strand, when he was told
that both Houses of Parliament had resolved to displace all bishops,
deans and chapters from their lands and mansions – in effect ruining
him. 'Did he bewray any discomposure or passionate perturbation?'
asked Naylor rhetorically. Hearing the news, Morton merely 'three
times repeated that Seraphicall ejaculation of holy *Job*; *The Lord
hath given, and the Lord hath taken away* . . . and so returned in quiet
(from whence he came) to his Study and Devotions.'[11]

   In 1607 things were very different. Morton was offering Donne
a secure place with potentially lucrative prospects. The social function and political powers of the Church were vital elements of its
spiritual authority. In a religious society where every subject owed
allegiance to the monarch not only as sovereign but also as the
head of the established Church, King James, like Elizabeth before
him, was completely aware that the status of the Church's hier-
archies greatly supported his own. Three years earlier, at a carefully
stage-managed conference in Hampton Court, James announced
that 'it is my aphorism, "No Bishop, No King".'[12] This had

gratified senior churchmen but deeply offended the Puritan faction – of whom only the most moderate representatives were allowed to attend the conference. These much more radical Protestants resented the lingering fixtures and rituals of the old Papist culture, and the supposedly Reformed Church's retention of power, wealth, land and patronage. Puritans had theological and material grievances with the elaborate class-system of priests, chapters, deans, bishops and archbishops of which King James approved; the system in which Morton had set aside an opening for Donne.

Morton was not asking Donne to renounce the world, and with it wife and family. Morton's secretary noted how it was widely felt that 'Mr *John Donne* had cast himself into a Sea of Misery, by the marriage of the Daughter of Sir *George Moore*.'[13] Whereas the Roman Catholic Church required celibacy of its priests, at least in theory, Reformed ministers were free to marry, though many found it better suited their temperament and their calling to remain single. Some in fact vaunted their chastity. The Reverend Naylor was willing to clear Morton of 'any carnall knowledge of that Female Sex, or act of uncleanness with any woman living, or dead'. No man except Jesus, Naylor conceded, could be exempt from 'those *Primi Motus*' – the primary physiological stirrings – but he could vouch that Morton 'went as pure a Virgin to the wombe of the Earth, as erst he came from the wombe of his Mother'.[14]

Morton was one of the leading participants in a war of words that had been raging long before the Gunpowder Plot but which entered a phase of especial intensity shortly afterwards. There had been just a slight lull in hostilities early on in James's reign: convening the bishops at Hampton Court in 1604, the King had said that in the Church of England's creed 'there should not be so general a departure from the Papists, that every thing should be accounted an error wherein we agree with them.'[15] Yet the conciliatory mood had broken with the conspiracy of November 1605. The Protestant and Roman Catholic divines of England and Europe continued to crush one another at the printing presses. These arguments, frequently over small doctrinal details, invariably called on lawyerly skills, with scripture and the works of the

Church Fathers taking the place of statutes and cases. Casuistry, a vigorous branch of legal and ethical debate, was developed for precisely this region of inquiry, testing the dictates of laws against the principles enshrined in the Bible and divinity in cases of individual conscience.

Frequently in theological controversy, however, struggles degenerated into personal vendettas. A particular opponent of Thomas Morton's, for example, was a Catholic priest writing under the name of 'John Brerely', who in 1604 published an *Apologie of the Romane Church* ('apology' meaning a 'reasoned defence', rather than any retraction or acceptance of having done wrong). The tract hit out at the authenticity of Protestantism and questioned the assumption that all English Roman Catholics were necessarily traitors. Morton responded at punitive length with a massive two-part work entitled *Apologia Catholica*, which came out in 1605 and 1606. Even then he had not finished with Brerely's *Apologie*. Responding in 1608 to a vicious pamphlet written against him by the veteran Jesuit campaigner Robert Persons, Morton warned that he was working on a further voluminous refutation that would annihilate the Roman priests' claims to legitimacy by using their own arguments against them.

All through this time, Donne was one of the informed, interested observers whose opinion Morton sought about his work. As one who had been brought up and had for some time persisted as a Roman Catholic, Donne was especially well qualified to comment on both the intellectual and emotive effectiveness of Morton's writing. Although Donne turned down Morton's offer of assistance, the two remained in regular contact. In March 1608, Donne nagged Goodyer to return a lent copy of John Brerely's *Apologie*: 'of the book, by occasion of reading the Deans answer to it, I have sometimes some want.'[16] He was trawling his way avidly through a draft of Morton's *A Catholike Appeale for Protestants*, which finally appeared in October 1609, in a folio volume running to almost seven hundred pages. To Morton's dismay, Brerely released an expanded version of his *Apologie* at almost exactly the same time, weighing in at just under eight hundred pages. Morton received a copy the day after presenting his own book to the King. His enemy sent it with jibing good wishes to the 'Worshipfull Maister Doctor', in the event that 'you should haue committed some ouersights'.[17]

The reading and note-taking required for the arid thrill such propaganda campaigns brought took up most of the Dean's existence. 'Whether he passed by Water or rid on Horseback (as he used in his private estate) or traveling in his Coach . . . he had always some choice and usefull book,' enthused his biographer and former secretary, Richard Baddeley. Morton slept very little, for

he either continued reading himself, or others reading unto him, till late at night, and after some few houres repose, he was alwayes ready to fall on his study afresh with early *Aurora* . . .[18]

This was the life to which Morton tried enticing Donne. Yet despite all the hours Donne certainly devoted to reading, and the serious thinking he did about religion, he was not prepared to dedicate himself to the 'sacred calling' – at least not yet. Along with the 'irregularities' in his life that he gave as his main impediment, there were 'other reasons' that he preferred not to make plain.

These may well have been reasons of conscience. Donne probably still had doubts about his conversion from the Roman to the Reformed Church, lingering resentment for Henry's death and his mother's exile, and this may have made him more reluctant to serve as a Protestant priest. As a soldier fighting for England and a secretary serving the Lord Keeper he had shown that he accepted the Protestant order and its Reformed Church politically. But this was different to embracing Reformed theology with his full soul. His writing and his collaboration with Morton over the next few years show him testing out this next demand upon his conscience. It would grow on his mind as an exigency and a duty, and contribute to the crisis of spirituality recorded in his Holy Sonnets. For the time being, it made him assess how far he had already gone as a convert. As for the suffering of his family and others like them, he would put the blame for such misery squarely upon the Roman Catholic Church and its militant agitators, rather than the Protestant establishment.

Ever since his early years as Egerton's secretary, a note of religious solemnity had been strengthening in his poetry: 'There is no Vertue, but religion', he had written to Rowland Woodward, in a verse letter complaining of his muse's 'chaste fallownesse'.[19] This was not a mood that many of those with bootlegged copies of his elegies and satires would have recognized in him. Yet his more recent poems continued to offer sober reflections on faith and spirituality, and began seeing that a capacity to change and adapt was essential in the religious as in all other parts of life. In 1608 Donne wrote a birthday poem for Sir Henry Goodyer, a piece that was unique in its noble openness but typical of the kind of verse that would dominate Donne's output for the next decade: a poem offered as both gift and tribute, dedicated, addressed and presented to a particular person. Although the form was private, manuscript collections show that such poems, frequently written as epigrams to other works, were copied and disseminated for a wider audience to enjoy and use for their own purposes. In this one, Donne offered Goodyer advice for future happiness and better fortune. The secret, he said, lay with the ability to reform one's habits and oneself. And importantly, he identified a characteristically Roman Catholic habit of devotion with a failure to do this:

> Who makes the Past, a patterne for next yeare,
> Turnes no new leafe, but still the same thing reads,
> Seene things, he sees againe, heard things doth heare,
> And makes his life but like a paire of beads.[20]

On such beads Roman Catholics would count off their decades of the rosary (and still do), each Ave Maria marked by a movement of finger and thumb from one to the next. The rosary puts the believer in an incrementing cycle of prayer, trance-like and self-sustaining. Yet for Donne here the 'paire of beads' symbolizes a mentality locked in the past, going through moribund actions over and over again; and this was an image in miniature of how the Roman Church and its customs now appeared to him. He was fighting their hold on his imagination.

In another poem of 1608, this time given over entirely to a religious theme, 'The Annunciation and Passion' (which in that year fell upon the same day), he talked about the way the dates of the sacred calendar varied from year to year. In doing so he developed a more positive idea of a temporal Church, and how it should guide Christians on earth:

> As by the selfe-fix'd Pole wee never doe
> Direct our course, but the next starre thereto,
> Which shows where the other is, and which we say
> (Because it strayes not farre) doth never stray;
> So God by his Church, neerest to him, wee know,
> And stand firme, if wee by her motion goe . . .[21]

God himself was like the northern celestial Pole, definite and immoveable, the ultimate reference point for all those navigating their way through his Creation. But on earth, people had to take their bearings by the sign that showed where the Pole was, the Northern Star, which, although its position did change minutely over the centuries, still appeared constant 'Because it strayes not farre'. The crucial argument Donne develops from this metaphor is that the Church, although to all intents and purposes unchanging, was nonetheless subject to its own 'motion'. Like all other things visible to humanity, the Church existed in space and time, and although its shifts were minimal, it still moved. Donne was suggesting here that Christians could only stay close to God if they kept in step with his Church – 'if wee by her motion goe' – which could not be motionless, but could certainly prevent believers from veering off track.

The question was, which Church was the true Northern Star? Papists defended the authority of Rome and the Pope on the basis that the Church and the Papacy were divinely instituted, and thus to alter them was to try tampering with God's work. The lines above show that Donne was resisting that stance. For him the Church had to change, slowly, barely noticeably to the naked eye – not so as to move with the times, but to ensure that it could still direct the way the times were moving. This was how he came to accept the English Reformed Church. Unlike the continental Protestant Reformations of northern Europe, the English Reformation had not swept away the old religious edifices altogether. Many of the old customs, rites and rhythms persisted in translated form; as, importantly, did the Church's institutional hierarchy. Extremists, Puritans and Papists, those who wished to transform the old structures entirely or leave them wholly untouched, were doing themselves out of their own national religious inheritance: the true 'Catholic', universal Church, so far as England was concerned, was the Reformed one governed by the King and his bishops. Donne could side instinctively with a 'high' churchman such as Morton, who in 1609 issued his *Catholike Appeale for Protestants*.

Donne was coming to accept the principles Morton was actively defending, and in fact helped his friend set them forward more coherently by reading and commenting on his work. If he was to go about the job in earnest, though – and he never considered doing otherwise – becoming a priest would have involved a spiritual change he was not prepared for yet. Despite his passionate interest in questions of the soul, nothing suggests he had yet felt any personal sense of vocation. It was too great a jump to consider himself a Protestant minister; or, as he seems to have been aware, for others to accept him as such. At the time Morton made his proposal Donne was doggedly and assiduously courting the high opinion of a number of influential aristocrats. Whatever his learning, these figures understood him as something other than a man of the cloth. He particularly valued the regard of Lucy, Countess of Bedford. If Donne had become a priest when Morton advised, no social convention would have barred him from visiting or writing to her. But it is possible that Lucy might have wanted nothing more to do with him. Several years later, when he was eventually ordained, he was hurt and mortified by her sceptical reaction.

The more he got to know her, the more often he wrote to her, usually passing on his missives through his best friend and her regular attendant, Goodyer: 'in stead of a Letter to you,' he told him in August 1609, having complained that he had no news, 'I send you one to another, to the best Lady . . .' He was a regular visitor at the Countess's town house and at her country estate, Twickenham Park. He composed epistolary poems in her honour, declaring that 'only [she] hath the power to cast the fetters of verse upon my free meditations'. He came to see himself as a kind of laureate for Lady Bedford, even though she held court to many other poets, including Ben Jonson, who was a master of writing epigrams for patrons and influential friends.

The ornate poetry of compliment was a distinct genre of Renaissance literature. In the grammar schools and universities, students were taught about three fields of rhetoric: the judicial, for use in the law courts; the deliberative, which covered debates on policy and future action in councils and assemblies; and the epideictic, oratory that conferred blame or praise. Of all three, the last was the most important for educated people to be skilled in, especially in written expression. Epideictic encompassed the art of panegyric, honouring and paying respect, in eulogy for the living or elegy for the dead. Because so many careers and livelihoods depended on patronage and good opinion, the ability to come up with a good compliment was a vital civil gesture. It was a talent that poets and writers in particular had to possess. Donne himself was a master: his panegyric did more than just enumerate virtues, real or fictitious, and this had a great deal to do with why these compositions became so collectable, as models and sources for others to use. With due decorum, his verse letters laid claim to a certain freedom of speech with those he praised; and paid the greater genuine compliment of addressing them as people with whom he could share his often demanding conceits.

'I am but mine own secretary,' he told Goodyer, 'and what's that?'[22] He still felt the lack of official status, and his writing helped

fill the void. He needed to address, and be appreciated. Lucy for
her part was delighted with his attentions and greatly admired his
writing. She loved the company of witty, literary men and the
conversation that her husband, a failed desperado of the Essex
rebellion to whom she had been married when just a girl, could
not supply. Despite a moralistic streak, she had a soft spot too for
the early, bawdy, scathing Donne. She asked Jonson to procure
her a copy of Donne's satires – and she may have gone to some
lengths to obtain his elegies too. To his credit Jonson suppressed
any jealousy he might have felt at the request. 'Rare poems ask
rare friends,' he wrote, in the dedicatory poem he presented with
the manuscript he gave her.[23] Donne himself was a little worried
by the interest Lucy took in work he had tried putting behind him
nearly ten years before. 'In me you have hallowed a Pagan muse,'
he thanked her – a remark that again suggests he felt unfit for life
as a priest.[24] 'Madam, You have refin'd mee,' he told her in another
poem.

When she descended from her coach at Twickenham, he
described her arrival as a spring in deep winter, a nocturnal dawn:
'Out from your chariot, morning breaks at night'.[25] He was a
possessive admirer, scrutinizing Lucy's habits and the company she
kept, 'your deeds, accesses, and restraints, / And what you read,
and what your selfe devize'.[26] The last in the list of activities is
significant: Lucy herself was a shy poet, a 'deviser' of language.
One summer day when they were walking in her country garden,
she nervously showed Donne some of her own writing. He was
thrilled by the confidence, and happily told Goodyer of 'the verses
she shewed in the garden'.[27] He wrote to Lucy, asking her for
copies he might keep, assuring her that their contents would
remain secret. 'I humbly beg them of your Ladiship, with two
such promises . . . that I will not shew them, and I will not beleeve
them.'[28]

He continued to interest himself in all of the goings-on at the
Countess's residences, and all the passings-away too. In late July
1609, he returned from a visit to Twickenham shaken by the
worsening condition of Cecilia Bulstrode, one of Lady Bedford's

closest friends and, like Lucy herself, a lady-in-waiting to the Queen. Cecilia was a young beauty who wrote poetry in private and fell for a series of glamorous young men, the latest of whom was Donne's friend Sir Thomas Roe. Now at the age of twenty-five she was dying. 'I fear earnestly that Mistresse *Bulstrod* will not escape that sicknesse in which she labours at this time,' Donne wrote. He sent for word of how she had passed the night, and learnt that she was just as he had found her the day before: fevered, intermittently hysterical and suffering from 'an extream ill spleen'. Yet he suspected too that there was more to her illness than physical malady. 'By the strength of her understanding, and voyce, (proportionally to her fashion, which was ever remisse)' – Donne seems to be implying that Cecilia was a bit scatterbrained – 'by the eavennesse and life of her pulse, and by her temper, I could impute her long life, and impute all her sicknesse to her minde.'[29]

She was sick both from the way she had lived and from the ways her life had been perceived, mistreated and slandered. She was one of those women whose every word was in danger of being taken as a public utterance, and some time before she made the mistake of criticizing the royal masque-maker Ben Jonson. The exact offence is not recorded, but she seems not to have realized that she was picking a scrap: 'Does the court pucell then so censure me, / And thinks I dare not her? Let the world see,' he retorted. Jonson was a convicted killer and a satirical bruiser well formed and adapted for a literary bearfight. He mauled Cecilia, 'the court pucell' – the Court trollop, as he branded her in one of the nastiest epigrams of the day. He gave a horribly layered image of her bedchamber as 'the very pit / Where fight the prime cocks of the game' – a public venue where she fucked till she bled and was torn to pieces. She was vain, licentious, had betrayed at least two engagements; she wrote bad verse and had a face which 'none can like by candle-light'.[30] The rabid lines may only have been written for private relief by a notoriously vitriolic man: Jonson claimed that the manuscript was 'stolen out of his pocket by a gentleman who drank him drowsy, and given [to] Mistress Bulstrode'.[31] This hardly made the sentiments the paper held any more creditable;

and the carelessness with which they slipped out seems rather
deliberate.

Shortly after Cecilia's death on the fourth day of August, George
Garrard, Donne's housemate at Tincomb's in the Strand, sent out
for commemorative verses from around literary London. While
Garrard's servant stood waiting at the door, Ben Jonson sat and
coolly composed a quick-fit elegy for the woman he now described
as one 'fit to have increased the harmony / Of spheres, as light of
stars; she was earth's eye'.[32] He then scribbled a note expressing
his hope that Garrard could 'See what the obedience of friendship
is, and the hazard it runnes.' The hazard for Jonson, presumably,
lay in contradicting his earlier character assassination; but he was
very upset, he insisted, that the young 'virgin', as he called her
now, was dead. Had she lived, or if he had seen her before the
end, she might have spoken up against those who now harangued
him for hounding her; so that 'some that live might have corrected
some prejudices they have had injuriously of mee.'[33]

It took Donne longer to come up with a memorial poem. Some
time after receiving Garrard's request, he made the routine journey
back to Mitcham, having left Cecilia's lover, Thomas Roe, 'so
indulgent to his sorrow, as it had been an injury to have interrupted
it with my unusefull company'. He sat in his study wondering
what to write; he may even have unconsciously avoided the task.
'I have done nothing of that kinde as your Letter intimates,'
he apologized to Garrard, 'in the memory of that good gentlewoman.'[34] Only a few months before, in May, he had had to
produce an elegy for another of Lady Bedford's friends, Lady
Bridget Markham. Bending his mind to a similar exercise, he had
trouble engaging with the actual subject of the required piece, the
young woman he had seen thrashing in fever and hysteria, now
buried at Twickenham.

When he lost someone really close to him he found it difficult
to say anything in writing. In 1609 his wild-living friend and
rescuer, Sir Francis Wolley, also died, of unknown causes, aged
just twenty-six. Donne's only response was silence. There is no
doubt that he and Wolley had been on excellent terms: the fact

that the Donnes named their third son Francis can be taken as just one sign of their gratitude. But there was no one, really, to whom Donne could address his condolences. At Pyrford, Wolley left only his wife and the little girl he had had with another woman; his friends could only quietly agree how much they missed him and their visits to his country estate. The person who grieved for him most was probably Donne's wife. Sir Francis had saved Ann from being cast out when her father shunned her, had negotiated a marriage allowance for her and supported her children till it came through.

Private grief could go unspoken; but the elegy for Cecilia Bulstrode was a social requirement, almost a commission, written to please Lady Bedford by commemorating her friend. The poem would not have been read aloud at the graveside. The piece was a written, material token, to be passed among friends and relatives and copied for those who desired it. It was high summer; the streaks of damp in his 'poor Library' at Mitcham may just about have dried. But there was still a shiver at his back. The person called Cecilia he had known – known slightly, at any rate – was blotted out. He addressed death directly. And death merely slavered:

> Th'earths face is but thy Table; there are set
> Plants, cattell, men, dishes for Death to eate.
> In a rude hunger now hee millions drawes
> Into his bloody, or plaguy, or sterv'd jawes.[35]

The world was a farm: and its inhabitants, from the 'monastique silence' of the ocean floor to the great houses of society, were just so much livestock. And it was occurring to Donne with increasing urgency that he too was destined to supply the same indiscriminate appetite.

His health had been far from strong. He spent much of the first half of the year recovering from a bout of neuritis, and for a while during the winter he was afraid he might spend the rest of his life as an invalid – shuffling near the exit of the world 'like a porter in

a great house, ever nearest the door but seldomest abroad'. Locked
with pain and inflammation in his limbs, chest and abdomen, face
and neck, he still found it necessary to turn his thought into
writing: 'Since my imprisonment in bed,' he informed Goodyer,
'I have made a meditation in verse, which I call a Litany.' The
term carried Papist associations that Donne was anxious to cancel,
stating to Goodyer that 'the word you know imports no more
then supplication'.[36] He meant it literally: his 'Litanie', running to
over 250 lines, is a sustained appeal to God for clemency, so that
'I may rise up from death, before I'm dead.' From his sickbed he
reviewed his spiritual condition endlessly, and with increasing
anguish:

> My heart is by dejection, clay,
> And by selfe-murder, red.

Nearing middle-age, looking back 'Halfe wasted with youths fires,
of pride and lust', he begged for his soul to be purged.[37] The sheer
manual labour of transcribing the poem for Goodyer, and penning
the long letter that went with it, was a kind of penitential exercise:
'pardon me if I write no more,' he apologized. 'My pain hath
drawn my head so much awry, and holds it so that mine eye cannot
follow mine hand.'[38]

   A few months later, after the illness had abated, Donne sat
writing the poem for Cecilia Bulstrode. She had cheated death, he
wrote: the monster could only devour her used-up body, which
her soul cast aside as a willing sacrifice. But it was hard to be sure.
She was a victim of 'youths fires', a fatality of the passionate,
corporeal existence that Donne had just about survived till now.
The signs in his own soul were not good.

   The elegy for Cecilia was dispatched, and received appreciatively
by the Bedford circle. Another influential woman, meanwhile,
expressed an interest in renewing ties with him. In 1609, Henry
Goodyer visited the Countess of Huntingdon, daughter of the
formidable Countess Dowager of Derby, and returned to London
with her. Lady Huntingdon had been married – at a very tender

age – while Donne was still in regular attendance at York House. He had probably not seen her since her days as a girl-bride, but she remembered him fondly, and Goodyer advised his friend to write something for her, since she too was well placed to help him. Donne was reluctant. Lady Huntingdon had known him as Egerton's secretary, an established man, and he was embarrassed at the impression he might make on her now: 'that knowledge which she hath of me, was in the beginning of a graver course, then of a Poet,' he said. But the idea of being an unfaithful praiser also troubled him: his 'integrity to the other Countesse', Lucy, weighed him down, since he had reserved for her 'not only all the verses, but all the thoughts of womens worthinesse'. He was at pains not to betray the intimacy that grew up between him and Lady Bedford; or at least he was anxious that she should not think badly of him when he did – and if possible not know about it at all. (The question of where his wife might have fitted in this conflict of superlatives is one Donne does not openly consider. His existence allowed for wholly separate categories of faithfulness – each of which presented sufficient difficulties on its own, without muddling them together.)

As so often, nonetheless, he found himself unable to turn down a request for his words, and flatly contradicted himself by slipping a poem for Lady Huntingdon in with the very same letter in which he refused to send her anything. The letter ends with a series of nervous security checks: he sought Goodyer's assurance 'that by this occasion of versifying, I be not traduced, nor esteemed light in that Tribe, and that house where I have lived' – that is, Twickenham, and Lady Bedford's circle. Goodyer may have wondered quite how he was to ensure this didn't happen, since Lady Huntingdon was sure to speak out about her new courtier; that was the whole point of accepting the literary services of a poet like Donne. They heightened the receiver's prestige. Turning his attention to Lady Huntingdon, Donne instructed the redoubtable Goodyer to keep the verses for his own amusement – 'as a companion and supplement of this Letter to you' – if he found them unsuitable, 'too bad, or too good, over or under her understanding'.[39]

Donne was ever sensitive about the kinds of writing it was appropriate for him to practise. He had religiously kept his poetry away from the press for years, considering that medium beneath him. His models among the ancients were those poets who left it to posterity to take care of their transmission, and thus survived in tantalizing fragments: Pindar and Lucan, Sappho and the 'mysticall bookes' of Sibyl, the Cumaean prophetess. His poem for Ann, 'A Valediction: of the Book', asserts jokily that his manuscripts will be as 'long-liv'd as the elements, / Or as the worlds forme'.[40] He affected not to care about the practicalities of preservation. His poems went into the world as handwritten letters or gifts for people he cared about or respected, not impersonal publications that just anyone could pick up from one of the bookshops clustered around the churchyard of St Paul's. He also had the contempt of a classicist for the contemporary: 'For with how much desire we read the papers of the living now, (especially friends),' he teased his father-in-law, the proud published author of *A Demonstration of God in His Workes*, 'which we would scarce allow a boxe in our cabinet, or shelf in our Library, if they were dead?'[41] Saying this he not only slighted Sir George More, but also infinitely more eminent published contemporaries such as Shakespeare, Jonson, Marlowe and Chapman, the translator of Homer.

The press was not fit for poetry; his, at any rate. But it did have other purposes. Donne's correspondence in 1609 reveals him hard at work on the first book that he would see into print. Remembering that Goodyer 'purposed a journey to fetch, or meet the Lady *Huntington*,' Donne asked him urgently 'to send to my lodging my written Books' and to return a letter containing 'certain heads which I purposed to enlarge'.[42] These papers contained his earliest draftings of *Pseudo-martyr*, Donne's most explicit statement on the plight and obligations of English Roman Catholics.

As he continued his routine friendships, mounted frustrated campaigns for employment and balanced his relations with various female admirers, Donne kept up with the doctrinal and political debate that went on across the land and continent. The main bone of contention was a new Oath of Allegiance, introduced as a security measure after the Gunpowder Plot. This obliged Roman Catholics to acknowledge that the King could not be deposed by Papal decree; to swear, in fact, to 'abhor, detest, abjure, as impious and heretical, this damnable doctrine and position, that princes which be excommunicated or deprived by the Pope may be deposed or murdered by their subjects'. Although the oath was clearly couched in objectionable terms, many Roman Catholics in England accepted it, deferring their offended sense of religion for the sake of a quiet life. Those who took the oath included the archpriest George Blackwell; those who condemned it outright included the leaders of the Jesuit order, who maintained that the Pope had every right to intervene in temporal matters where a greater spiritual question was at stake. The Vatican issued two breves – the second when the first was actually suppressed by leading English clerics – denouncing the oath as yet more heresy.

In the bitter debate that ensued, Donne's ecclesiastical patron and mentor, Thomas Morton, was one of the leading voices for the monarchist, Protestant establishment. His *Exact Discoverie of Romish Doctrine in the case of Conspiracie and Rebellion*, hurriedly prepared in the immediate wake of the Gunpowder Plot, provoked *A Iust and Moderate Answer to a Most Iniurious and Seditious Pamphlet* by an anonymous Catholic; to which Morton retaliated in turn with nothing less than *A Full Satisfaction concerning a Double Romish Iniquitie: Hainous Rebellion, and more then Heathenish Equivocation*. At this, in 1607, the veteran Jesuit campaigner Robert Persons threw his weight into the fight, with a vitriolic *Treatise to Mitigation* that made a personal attack on Morton. The same year, King James himself also entered the ring, albeit as a masked combatant, by publishing *Triplici Nodo Triplex Cuneus or an Apologie for the Oath of Allegiance*. Many aspects of his windily delivered argument were vulnerable, and his opponents seized gleefully on the tactical opportunity this presented.

Cardinal Bellarmine, one of the Vatican's doughtiest controversialists, unkindly pointed out that James had been happy and eager to accept Catholic assistance back in the days when he was anxious that his succession to the English throne might not come through. And while everyone knew that the King had written *Triplici Nodo Triplex*, Robert Persons pretended to take the anonymous title page at face value, expressing his bewilderment that James had ever let such rubbish reach the press. Persons ticked off the author for both his learning and his manners: 'I most certainly do persuade myself that his Ma*jes*tie never read aduisedly all that in this *Booke* is conteyned: For that I take him to be of such judgement and honour, as he would never have let passe sundry thinges, that heere are published, contrary to them both.'[43] Persons scoffed at the idea that Catholics in England enjoyed 'liberty of conscience' and that the oath was to be taken freely – this was 'the very same freedome . . . that a merchant hath in a tempest, eyther to cast out his goodes into the sea, for lightening his shippe, or to be drowned himselfe.'[44]

Poor James got mauled, more by superior wit than deeper political theory. Disdaining to reply personally, he entrusted his revenge to the Bishop of London, William Barlow. R. C. Bald, normally the most even-tempered of historical writers, remarked that Barlow owed his status to 'his florid rhetoric, his wide and pleasing command of literary allusion, and his assiduous bootlicking'.[45] In April 1609, Barlow's unctuous *Answer to a Catholike English-man* was brought out – to little effect and much cackling from the Papist opposition. At this point Donne became irritated. He remarked that 'the Divines of these times, are become meer Advocates'. He expressed his complete dissatisfaction with the *Answer*. 'I looked for more prudence, and humane wisdome in him, in avoiding all miscitings, or mis-interpretings, because at this time, the watch is set, and every bodies hammer is upon that anvill.' In confidence to Goodyer, he offered his own fair-minded view of the situation:

I think truly there is a perplexity (as farre as I see yet) and both sides may be in justice, and innocence . . . for clearly, our State cannot be safe without the Oath; since they professe, that Clergie-men, though Traitors, are no Subjects, and that all the rest may be none to morrow.

And, as clearly, the Supremacy which the Ro. Church pretend, were diminished, if it were limited . . .[46]

He saw quite clearly that there was too much at stake for either side to back down; but he also made it quite clear which side he was on. He was a dutiful subject, loyal to 'our state' and the King at its head.

Yet Donne still had contacts with many Roman Catholics, and heard their grievances with sympathetic reserve. The outcome of Donne's reading and conversations was *Pseudo-martyr*, dedicated to the King and written to consolidate the royal position on the oath, but also urging radical English Papists to stop wasting their lives. He understood their anguish, acknowledging in his preface that he was 'deriued from such a stocke and race, as, I beleeue, no family . . . hath endured more in their persons and fortunes, for obeying the Teachers of Romane Doctrine, than it hath done.' This made his struggle of conscience all the more difficult. In thinking out his religion for himself, Donne 'had a harder work to doe then many other men,' having 'first to blot out, certaine impressions of the Romane religion'.[47] But rebelling against 'our state' on behalf of that religion was not only treacherous, it was also sinful, and he was scathing of those factions within the Roman Catholic Church – in particular the Jesuits – who said otherwise. For Donne, those who insisted on conspiring against a legitimate ruler were not real but false martyrs, fake religious heroes. They were not honouring God but merely harming themselves – committing suicide, in fact – and others. Among such people Donne must have privately numbered William Harrington, the priest whose zealotry led to the imprisonment and death of his younger brother Henry. He poured scorn on those who were duped by such people and who venerated them as saints. 'I haue seene at some Executions of Trayterous *Priests*, some bystanders, pray to him whose body lay there dead,' he snorted. This is the only hint that Donne may have gone in person to see Harrington hung, drawn and quartered; seen him struggle with the executioner under the knife, and witnessed the clamour that followed.

Pseudo-martyr reveals that Donne did not hold the Protestant English Church or state responsible for his family's unhappiness. He instead blamed the militants of the Roman Church for inciting people such as his brother to commit criminal acts. In effect, he accused Papist elders such as his own uncle, Jasper Heywood, the leader of the Jesuit mission in the early 1580s, of holding impressionable consciences to ransom. He accepted neither the holiness of the Papist cause nor the sanctity of its supposed recent martyrs.

True martyrdom was only possible, he contended, as a last resort, when those who suffered death for their faith had absolutely no other option; Papists in England, for Donne, still had other courses open to them, and one was the simple pragmatic measure of swearing not to murder the King. As for the position of the monarch, Donne did not, though he was keen to please, say exactly what his ruler wanted to hear. He didn't quite corroborate James's view that 'Kings are not only God's lieutenants upon earth and sit upon God's throne . . . even by God himself they are called Gods.'[48] In Donne's opinion, God inspires us to obey and accept being ruled when power has taken such a form 'as may be aptest to doe those things, for which that *Power* was infus'd'. God, that is, bestowed power on governors in order for it to achieve specific ends; and these ends, Donne went on hopefully, 'are, to conserve us in *Peace* and *Religion*'.[49] On paper at least, this coincided with James's feelings on the matter: he regarded himself as a peacemaker and defender of the faith. He would also have approved of Donne's declaration that the powers of the sovereign in any state were absolute. But these powers were not granted unconditionally:

God inanimates euery State with one power, as euery man with one soule: when therefore people concurre in the desire of such a *King*, they cannot contract, nor limitte his power.[50]

The most crucial word here is 'when'. A Stuart King might justly claim to possess full sovereignty – might even claim he had a divine right to it – only when people agreed that they wanted 'such a

King'. Donne is not being democratic here so much as pragmatic. Historically, peoples have tended to get rid of rulers they don't want. He anticipates the hard lesson it would take a civil war and revolution for English monarchs and monarchists to learn. His wholehearted support for James's authority comes with a quiet warning.

Donne travelled to the royal estate at Royston to present his book in person, hoping to catch James in the evening, when he came back from hunting. Further complimentary copies were also dispatched to high-placed nobles, but friends were not forgotten either. Rowland Woodward's *Pseudo-martyr* bore the punning Spanish inscription 'De juegos el major es con la hoja', at once scholarly and cavalier: 'the best of diversions is to turn the page (or the blade)', Donne wrote.[51] He was anxious about the response the book would receive. His preface sought to direct those who were about to read his work, and those who had already seen portions of it in draft. Something like the sheaf of early notes that Donne had left with Goodyer − and asked him then to return − had circulated, with or without his approval, among potential critics and supporters alike: in the preface, he complained that 'Some of the Romane profession, having only seen the Heads and Grounds handled in this Book have traduced me, as an impious and profane under-valewer of Martyrdome.'[52] He suggested that they now try reading the whole thing properly.

Donne braced himself for a savage onslaught from the Roman Catholic side, but it never really came. His book brought neither fame nor reprobation. Robert Persons did him a favour by dying later in 1610, before he could mount an attack. Another Jesuit, Thomas Fitzherbert, made a bitchy dig at Donne's earlier life and writing by condemning him for going 'beyond his old occupation of making Satyres (wherein he hath some talent, and may play the fool without control)'; but no blood was drawn.[53] After flicking through Fitzherbert's book several years later, Donne told George Garrard airily, 'I held it but half an hour.'[54] R. C. Bald remarks that 'Donne can be taken as having had the last word in this phase of the controversy.'[55] Even so, the treatise had little impact on the views of some who were close to Donne – by blood and marriage, anyway. His stepfather, Richard Rainsford, refused to take the Oath of Allegiance: in 1611 he was flung into Newgate prison, where he spent the best part of the next two years.[56] As a letter to his mother written five years later tacitly acknowledged, Donne had little to do with her – or Rainsford – at this time. Among the specialist readership of the Protestant clergy, *Pseudo-martyr* won great respect for dispelling the 'fooleries' of the Papist opposition.[57] As for Donne's wider social image at Court and in the city, however, *Pseudo-martyr* changed little in the short term. To those who knew his other work, the drily analytical treatise was battling the vibrant aura of the satires and elegies.

The reader who concerned him most, however, was King James, for his opinion would make or break Donne's career. Interestingly, the preface takes considerable pains to squash the idea that the author should be thought of as a professional controversialist or clerical heavyweight. Donne insisted modestly on his 'natural impatience not to digge painefully in deepe, and stony, and sullen learnings'. He took self-deprecation to the point of emphatic dis-avowal. Researching and writing *Pseudo-martyr*, he said, had gone against the grain of his personality, upsetting

my Indulgence to freedom and libertie, as in all indifferent things, so in my studies also, not to betroth or enthral myself to any one science, which should possess or denominate me.[58]

As a young man Donne had clung hard to his 'so much lov'd variety':[59] he had always been reluctant to surrender other options, close off other ways of living. It was the same in-built curiosity and desire for variation that made his life at this time so diverse, so irregular. But here Donne is strenuously fighting the idea that he be enslaved, possessed or denominated – named, tagged, pigeon-holed – by one 'science' in particular: that of a theologian. For the inevitable course of one bearing such a label was towards the priesthood.

Pseudo-martyr is predominantly a work of scholastic theology, but Donne insists throughout that the question he discusses – whether Catholics should or should not take the Oath of Allegiance – is above all a matter for civil law, a purely civic affair. As such, it was none of the Pope's business: 'the differences between vs are brought to this; Whether a Subject may or may not obey his Prince, if the Turk or any other man forbid it?'[60] He was trying to show the King and other influential readers how well suited he was to a secular appointment. He refuted the idea that he was professionally inclined towards 'writing of Diuinity and spirituall points, hauing no ordinary calling to that function'.[61] His drift was clear enough too from the dedication in the copy he gave to James's son, the Prince of Wales: 'since as well as the whole body of this state I also felt the benefitt and sweetnes we enjoy in this government, it became mee to contribute some thing in testimony of my thankfulnes.'[62] Writing *Pseudo-martyr* helped Donne work through many of the issues he had with his own and his family's past, and publishing it enabled him to declare his loyalties. But he was also trying to get noticed, to put his talents on display in the hope that someone might employ them, preferably in the service of the state.

But King James, leafing through the tract after a day's hunting, had other ideas. Donne's statements on kingship may have left the King ambivalent; but the doctrinal point-scoring greatly impressed him. *Pseudo-martyr* was far more effective at making the crown's case than mere toadying by the likes of William Barlow. To the King, it was clear where he really needed Donne's talents, and where they truly belonged: 'when he had read and considered that Book,' says Walton, he urged the reluctant sectarian 'to enter into the Ministry'.[63]

This was the constant suggestion now hanging over and redirecting Donne's aspirations. The only secular recognition Donne got for his political services was an honorary Master of Arts degree from Oxford – where he had been unable to take his BA, as a boy, because of his Papism. The degree was bestowed in April 1610. Yet despite the apparent blockade that had been put on all his attempts to gain almost any other kind of preferment, he still resisted the pressure to enter the priesthood. Three years after Thomas Morton suggested the Church to him, Donne's answer might have been much the same as it was then: he was still conscious of 'irregularities' in his past, though was now more willing to admit that those in his present had a lot to do with his 'indulgence to freedom and liberty'. His lodgings in London were more precious to him than ever, an essential escape from draughts and depression at Mitcham. He had also not given up his convivial instincts. He was part of a loosely organized club of literary-minded gentlemen, most of whom were connected with the Inns of Court, which met regularly in taverns near Donne's birthplace in Bread Street.

In his dispatches from India, the comic travel writer Thomas Coryat fondly remembered 'the Right Worshipfull Fraternitie of Sirenaical Gentlemen, that meet the first Fridaie euery Moneth, at the signe of the Mere-Maide in Bread-streete in London'.[64] Donne's name appears on the list of dignitaries to whom Coryat asked to be remembered. Some of these were clearly not 'Sirenaical Gentlemen', but Donne certainly can be counted among the fraternity that met at the Mermaid, a tavern famed for its fish suppers. No mention is made of the family man's existence at Mitcham; for Coryat Donne was a city-liver, to be found at 'his abode either in the Strand, or elsewhere in London'.[65] Others in the group included Richard Martin, Christopher Brooke, John Hoskins, Ben Jonson and Inigo Jones. The 'Right Generous, Ioviall, and Mercurial Sirenaicks' were witty, bookish men of the world, all with ambitions or interests at Court, luring one another to evenings of jocular destruction. Thomas Coryat was the set's entertainer, an openly ludicrous character, more than happy to laugh at his own silliness, but with a fine sense of ease at merely being in the world. Donne among others may have been honest enough to envy him. Coryat was 'contented with what was present', and thought those 'who had more suits and shirts than bodies' were troubling themselves over superfluous things. Coryat himself, it was noted, rarely changed his clothes 'till they were ready to go away from him'.[66]

Donne was respected above all in these circles as a poet, rather than the nascent controversialist of *Pseudo-martyr*. Although he scrupulously preserved his status as an exceptional amateur, and his best poems could only be found in manuscript, he was well known among the discerning. In 1607, he had applauded Ben Jonson's hit comedy *Volpone* with a Latin commendation, and Jonson returned his admiration warmly. For him, Donne was 'the first poet in the world, in some things', setting the standard that all others still had to match:

> Whose every work, of thy most early wit,
> Came forth example, and remains so, yet . . .[67]

One of the most revealing tributes came from the poet John Davies of Hereford, with whom Donne was on friendly terms. Making a familiar play on his subject's name, Davies compares the dun ('dark-featured') man to a little black mouse:

> Dunne is the mouse (they say) and thou art Dunne;
> But no dunne mouse thou art; yet art thou one
> That (like a mouse) in steepe high-waies dost runne
> To find food for thy muse to prey vpon . . .[68]

Not great verse by any means, and it must be said that Davies had something of a rodent fixation – one of his love poems took the mating habits of weasels as its inspiration – but the scurrying mouse-image this piece leaves us with is of Donne as a demure, cautious character, treading precarious pathways while keeping his head low. For this reason he is not one of the period's outspoken and caricatured literary characters. He was an irregular Sirenaic, enjoying the fun at the Mermaid but reluctant to be defined by the association.

The tradition of meeting went back several years, with the personnel changing slightly and the venue shifting from meeting to meeting. One gathering of a 'convivium philosophicum' took place just up the road from the Mermaid, at the Mitre, adjacent to the house where Donne was born.[69] Later, most of those who

attended wrote comic eulogies of Coryat and his forthcoming
collection of travel writing, wishing him well on his oriental trip.
The heir to the throne, Prince Henry, enjoyed these so much that
he insisted they be published; the poems were brought out in a
volume called *The Odcombian Banquet*, and then included as pre-
fatory material to Coryat's collected adventures, the *Crudities*.
Donne's contribution and tribute to this suitcase-sized book was
made up of a series of joshing, backhanded put-downs:

> Infinit worke, which doth so farre extend
> That none can study it to any end.[70]

Coryat was something like Prince Henry's court jester, a figure
of fun: 'Indeed he was the courtiers' anvil to try their wits upon.'
This particular clown, however, was no fool: 'sometimes this anvil
returned the hammers as hard knocks as it received.'[71]

When he set out again in 1612, the bon voyage proved to be
adieu; Coryat never returned from his journey to the East, and his
salutation of the 'sirenaical gentlemen' passed into the mythology
of London's literary pub-life. The Mermaid in particular was at
the centre of a long anachronistic tradition in which great writers
were imagined rubbing shoulders, cracking jokes and sometimes
falling out in the city's alehouses. Thomas Fuller told of the 'wit-
combates' between Ben Jonson and Shakespeare, in which the
former was 'like a *Spanish great Gallion* . . . Solid, but slow in his
performance', and the latter more akin to an '*English man of War*,
lesser in *bulk*, but lighter in *sailing*'.[72] While such accounts were
generally given by people who weren't actually present at the
parties being described, but wished they had been, Donne certainly
enjoyed an evening in the company of funny, clever men. A
letter to Goodyer in the summer of 1609 shows him relishing
the prospect of a get-together at 'my Temple, the Rose in
Smithfield'.[73]

A contemporary description of the archetypal London tavern
shows a murky place where 'the rooms are ill-breath'd, like the
drinkers that have been washt well [i.e. dowsed well in booze]

overnight . . . not furnisht with beds to be defiled but more necessary implements, Stooles, Table, and a Chamber pot.' A pub might
be open all day and night, and after a long session it could become
'like a streete in a dashing showre, where the spouts are flushing
above, and the Conduits [gutters] running belowe'. The place was
a 'Theater of natures . . . the busie mans recreation, the idle mans
businesse, the melancholy mans Sanctuary.'[74] For Donne, the
tavern fulfilled a little of all these purposes: it allowed him to relax,
make contacts, and also find some refuge from his cares. Yet on
occasions it seemed just one more spectacle of an irredeemable
world. Few of those who read the products of his 'early wit',
copying his satires and erotic verse into private commonplace
books, could have imagined the turn his most personal poetry
was taking. Few of those who knew him, even those who read
Pseudo-martyr, and marked him as a man destined for the Church,
could have known that there were frequent times when absolutely
nothing at all made sense to him.

In the city streets, some out of bounds when the plague returned
in 1610, or on the highways between London and the 'country'
at Mitcham, he saw beasts of burden ridden and beaten, and 'prodi-
gall elements' exploited for the benefit of a corrupt civilization.
He couldn't understand it. 'Why brook'st thou, ignorant horse, sub-
jection?' These animals and plants were much purer than men
and women. 'Why are wee by all creatures waited on?' he asked;
they didn't sin, make war, slander, get drunk, or write abusive
pamphlets.[75] The order of creation was absurd enough, but still
harder to accept was the idea of a world breaking into life only to
feed death. 'Thou hast made me,' he bargained privately with God,
'And shall thy work decay?' He couldn't believe it. Yet he was
steeped in death. A wry, unwavering mordancy filtered through
even in his compliments to the young ladies he still admired so
much: 'Your going away hath made *London* a dead carkasse,' he
told young Bridget White in June 1610. 'I think the onely reason
why the plague is somewhat slackned, is, because the place is dead
already, and no body left worth the killing.'[76] But his levity was
fleeting. When he looked at dying individuals, even ones he only

knew slightly – Captain Whitlock, Cecilia Bulstrode – or at his own 'ruinous Anatomie', he saw that Death, and what followed, was to be taken personally.

> I runne to death, and death meets me as fast,
> And all my pleasures are like yesterday,
> I dare not move my dimme eyes any way,
> Despaire behind, and death before doth cast
> Such terrour, and my feeble flesh doth waste
> By sinne in it, which it t'wards hell doth weigh . . .[77]

When he looked at himself, he saw a creature that would die. And when he looked within himself, he saw a 'black soule' that was already being dragged to the inferno. Donne had many reasons for refusing to become a priest. Not least among them were his love of freedom, his irregular lifestyle, his worldly ambitions; but important too was a reluctance to compound his earlier sins by preaching salvation as one of the damned.

14. The Apparition

In January 1611, almost exactly a year after *Pseudo-martyr* appeared, Donne set a satirical trance-vision of hell before the public. 'I was in an *Extasie*,' begins the narrator of *Ignatius His Conclave*, whose soul was turned forth into the heavens 'to comprehend the situation, the dimensions, the nature, the people, and the policy, both of the swimming *Ilands*, the *Planets*, and of all those which are fixed in the firmament.' Presently he passes beyond the physical universe: 'In the twinckling of an eye, I saw all the roomes in Hell open to my sight.'[1] Down there, an argument is going on. Lucifer is trying to decide which souls among the damned he might permit to take a place of note within his kingdom. The devil hears applications from various illustrious Renaissance figures, including Copernicus, Machiavelli and Columbus.

But every rival bid is turned on its head by one of Lucifer's most jealous courtiers – St Ignatius de Loyola, theologian and founder of the Jesuit order. More devilish than the devil, he speaks out successfully against anyone who would challenge his own niche. So successfully, in fact, that Lucifer fears for his own position, and decides to offer Ignatius a kingdom all of his own for him and his troublesome Jesuits. Lucifer decides to commission Galileo, astronomer and upsetter of the cosmic order, to build a special telescope with attractive properties. With this 'he may draw the Moone, like a boat floating upon the water, as neere the earth as he will. And thither,' the devil enthuses, 'shall all the Jesuites bee transferred, and easily unite and reconcile the *Lunatique Church* to the *Romane Church*.' Satan could guarantee that his good servant the Pope would give the lunar venture his blessing. 'Without doubt,' Donne makes him add, rubbing it in, 'there will soone grow naturally a *Hell* in that world also.'[2]

Read as propaganda, *Ignatius* might seem like Papist-bashing, with special attention to Jesuits, a comic follow-up to the reserved, lawyerly case set out in *Pseudo-martyr* the year before. But Donne also uses the savage little book to signal his disillusionment with the religious disputes of the day; to ridicule, in fact, the whole business of controversy. The division between the Church of Rome and that of Lunacy is a satire on the very idea of a schism in the Christian faith. In his published works, Donne was just as committed a partisan as any other polemicist, and could exhibit most of the engrained prejudices and atmospheric bigotries of the time in support of his cause. *Pseudo-martyr* falls heavily on the side of the Reformed Church because unlike its Roman opposite, he says, it was not 'deformed with the leprosies and vlcers of admitting Jewes and Stewes [brothels]'.³ When it came to anti-Semitism, anti-Islamic thinking, homophobia or sexual discrimination, Donne was in public no more enlightened than most other mid-Renaissance gentiles. But with regard to Christian Europeans, his private opinions show a remarkable intolerance of intolerance. If they conspired against the peace it was another matter, but he intensely disliked the idea of condemning people simply because they believed in something different to the institutional view of things. Two years before, he approved to Goodyer of 'that sound true opinion, that in all Christian professions there is way to Salvation', and observed that the two main Churches were in different ways '*both* diseased and infected'.⁴ In 1611 he defended his record on the issue:

You know I never fettered nor imprisoned the word Religion . . . nor immuring it in a *Rome*, or a *Wittemberg*, or a *Geneva*; they are all virtuall beams of one Sun, and wheresoever they finde clay harts, they harden them, and moulder them into dust; and they entender and mollifie waxen.

'Religion is Christianity', he said, and if on occasions its ministers had to berate and pulverize, its overall purpose was to mollify and 'entender' human cruelty and pride.⁵

Religion also had to help those who, like Donne, were often

nauseous with the fear of what lay after life. He began to carry the potential imminence of death around with him like a second shadow. It might all end so suddenly: 'What if this present were the worlds last night?' begins Holy Sonnet XIII. And if it *were* the night before Judgement Day, he felt that he had only a sinful account to make of himself. In an appendix to *Pseudo-martyr* he denied that he was 'a carnall or over-indulgent favourer of this life';[6] but the memory of his flesh-fuelled, 'idolotrous' youth was torture. Lining up in mind accusingly, salaciously, were 'all my profane mistresses'.[7] Yet before he could be judged, he had to sicken and die; and the struggle, he realized, even in a house teeming with children, would be a lonely one:

> Oh my black Soule! Now thou art summoned
> By sicknesse, deaths herald, and champion . . .

He found himself going one-on-one with an unbeatable adversary:

> And gluttonous death, will instantly unjoynt
> My body, and soule, and I shall sleepe a space . . .[8]

But then came Hell; and Donne had vivid ideas, from both his reading and his experience, of what its torments might be like. He had read Dante, and the Church Fathers' elaborate disquisitions on unending suffering, but from his own daily life he had a stock of terrible images that he could multiply by an eternity – the routine flagellation of felons in the streets, the diabolically inventive executions he had attended, the bubonic agonies in times of plague. Imagining the apocalypse, he saw 'numberlesse infinities / Of soules' going to retrieve their 'scattred bodies', some to be swept into the inferno, others rising to the citadels of heaven.[9] Yet he had perhaps one definitive memory of what the anguish of multitudes could mean. It came, like so many of those that troubled his nights, from his youth: the assault on the bay of Cadiz in 1596.

One contemporary observer noted that 'the Bay it selfe is very large and exceeding beautifull . . . some six or seven miles over or there abouts, yet be there many rockes, shelves, sands and shallowes in it.' The English fleet encroached; and from first light on, the Spanish ships that had sailed out to defend the port were driven back under savage bombardment. These were vessels of massive burden, cumbersome, hard to manoeuvre. The target was the flagship, the *San Felipe*, and its cargo of fabulous treasure. The anger of the guns was unceasing, and by noon the *San Felipe* could retreat no further. As the English closed in to board, the Spanish crew were ordered to gut their ship on the rocks, and set it alight. Little thought had been given to how the Spaniards were to escape. The fire spread too fast for them to save themselves. Ralegh saw 'tumbling into the sea heaps of soldiers, so thick as if coals had been poured out of a sack in many ports at once . . . some sticking in the mud' around the rocks. As the English ships mobilized their landing parties, the men saw that 'many drowned themselves and many half burnt leapt into the water, very many hanging by the rope ends by the ship's side . . . many swimming with grievous wounds strucken under the water.'

What struck Donne himself as particularly terrible was that the Spaniards' options consisted only of a variety of pain. They could only choose whether to be burnt alive, raked by gunfire, or to drown in burning water. There was no way out:

> Out of a fired ship, which, by no way
> But drowning, could be rescued from the flame
> Some men leap'd forth, and ever as they came
> Neere the foes ships, did by their shot decay.

Pity was redundant. Donne's epigram 'On a Burnt Ship' ends with a businesslike acceptance of the outcome: 'They in the sea being burnt, they in the burnt ship drowned.' Ralegh wrote that it was 'so huge a fire . . . as if any man had a desire to see Hell itself, it was there most lively figured'.[10]

Donne had no trouble envisaging the incinerated masses of the inferno; nor, by his religious belief, any difficulty in recognizing hell as an almost geographical reality, an actual place to which he might be consigned – 'damn'd and hal'd to execution' – with sackfuls of numberless souls.[11] He could bargain with, chide, even taunt the reaper:

> Death be not proud, though some have called thee
> Mighty and dreadfull, for, thou art not soe,
> For, those, whom thou think'st, thou dost overthrow,
> Die not, poore death . . .[12]

But the downside of this argument, of course, was that the souls who 'die not' might be forced to live in everlasting pain. When terror-sweats broke out, Donne felt he could only run to God; and yet to earn refuge he had to be purged. He pleaded for his coal-black soul to be turned red with the blood of Christ rather than the fire of hell; he took Jesus' sufferings on himself, urging, 'Spit in my face you Jewes, and pierce my side, / Buffet, and scoffe, scourge, and crucifie me.'[13] He needed to be seized, beaten – 'Batter my heart, three person'd God; for you / As yet but knocke' – even raped into obedience and sanctity:

> Take mee to you, imprison mee, for I
> Except you' enthrall mee, never shall be free,
> Nor ever chast, except you ravish mee.[14]

He is cowed by the full force of what the universe might inflict on him, a broken hostage willing to endure anything to save himself. And in places he resents having to feel this way. Just occasionally the Creator of all things emerges and is blamed as the causer of sorrow. Turn to God, Donne urges his 'pensive soule': 'he knowes best / Thy griefe, for he put it in my breast.'[15]

The Holy Sonnets, most of which were composed between 1609 and 1614, are the journal of a soul that finds itself alone, even among 'numberlesse infinities'; a Protestant soul, in other words, stripped of the support of the old Roman Church. The letter of 1611 in which Donne protested that he had never 'fettered . . . the word Religion' also stressed the responsibility of the individual conscience in the choice and pursuit of faith: 'To do things by example, and upon confidence of anothers judgement may be some kinde of a seconde wisdome, but it is but writing by a copy.'[16] Donne insisted, by contrast, that he did not make up his mind until 'I had, to the measure of my poore wit and iudgement, suruay'd and digested the whole body of Diuinity.'[17]

There has been much argument as to whether Donne really ever left his Roman Catholicism behind. There has been much argument as to whether *anyone* did, or could. Many Papist practices were carried over by the Reformed religion. Yet in the old Roman Church, the Church on which Donne turned his back, the afterlife was a different prospect: all the trusting believer needed to do, to reach heaven, was to attend services, receive the sacraments, observe the holy days, feast days and times of abstinence. The rituals were lengthy, exacting and elaborate; but a continent of monks and nuns was busy praying on behalf of the rest of humanity. The Church offered a complete package. For parishioners merely to witness the priest blessing the communion bread and wine was enough to infuse them with the real presence of Christ's body and blood. You were close to God, and you could ask your favourite saint – one of literally hundreds – to put in a good word for you. Catholicism before the Reformation was, as Eamon Duffy has shown, a community religion, with 'a shared repertoire of symbols, prayers, and beliefs which crossed and bridged even the gulf between the literate and the illiterate'.[18]

Donne's longing to be absorbed, his deep repeated wish to be an active 'part' of the world, suggests that he found such a community of faith deeply attractive. The very word 'Catholic' had a nostalgic power. Ten years later, in the teeth of ecclesiastical disunity, he declared that 'The *Church* is Catholike, Vniuersall, so are all her Actions; All that she does belongs to all.'[19] Here he was speaking of the Reformed Church, but in a manner that quite openly tries giving it the breadth and reach of the old institution. The crisis of spiritual loneliness recorded in his Holy Sonnets records the sensations of one extracted from that supportive culture; a culture that had, in fact, been largely erased by the

Reformation and which, to most, seemed like 'another country, another world'.[20] For those born as Protestants, there was no Mass, no benevolent saints. There was no sense of Christ being really present in the bread and wine; no strangely comforting notion of Purgatory, where souls might only have to endure punishment for a limited period, aided by the prayers of the faithful on earth. These were 'superstitions'. And Donne supported the movement that stripped away such solaces; he ridiculed the Roman Church's 'vnwholesome and putrifying Traditions, and Postscripts', the paraphernalia that cluttered up the Word of God.[21] What mattered was scripture, and the sense a Christian could make of it. Donne manifested a classically Protestant belief, in both his words and actions, that the individual soul had to act as its own priest, and find its own way to heaven. But it was a long, lonely run, in many cases futile. Following the teachings of Calvin, many Protestants believed that the fate of all souls was predestined, and that only an elect could ever be saved. Donne's Holy Sonnets are racked by that thought.

Intellectually and politically, Donne was committed to the Reformed Church; but he could not bear to think that ordinary Papists were damnable by default. He had barely known his father, but in the Holy Sonnets he is quite sure that the soul of John Donne senior, ironmonger of Bread Street, is among those in paradise. His one sad doubt is whether Mr Donne could watch over him from heaven.[22] He was, in other words, mixed up; and also in great need of emotional care. He was a living concoction of differing, frightened spiritualities, the one in which he had been brought up and for which his family had suffered, and which he had cast off, and the one he was slowly forging for himself within a different creed. But as so often, he was quite capable of defining his own condition, even if only when describing it in others. He told Goodyer,

You will seldome see a Coyne, upon which the stamp were removed, though to imprint it better, but it looks awry, and squint. And so, for the most part, do mindes which have received divers impressions.[23]

These words probably refer to Tobie Mathew, Goodyer's friend, now in exile in France; but it is unlikely that Donne would have denied that he too was one of the diversely influenced minds he describes here. One of the reasons Donne might seem 'awry' to us is that his expression, and the mood behind it, changed constantly. He should not be thought of as brooding uninterruptedly on eternities of anguish. All through this time he was still kissing ladies' (and gentlemen's) hands and relaxing with his pub cronies. Rather, these fears came in fits and starts, bursts of great anxiety that found a way out in bursts of poetry. The factor of surprise made the attacks all the more frightening; and the guerilla war of emotions that had to be waged as a result made them all the more tiring.

Ignatius His Conclave, Donne's second work as a civilian controversialist, was also his last. He sought to keep his options open. By way of contrast with his theological activity, through 1611, the year the book appeared, he began to think seriously about publishing some of his earlier poetry. His resistance to doing so had gone undiminished up until now, to the annoyance of some contemporaries who felt he was being precious, and to the frustration of a growing readership who found his verse hard to obtain, and wanted more from him. A laudatory epigram published a few years later gives an idea of how his literary reputation was taking shape with a wider audience, and also how that public image differed from the very private poet of the Holy Sonnets. He was hailed for his wit.

> The *Storme* describ'd, hath set thy name afloate,
> Thy *Calme*, a gale of famous winde hath got:
> Thy *Satires* short, too soone we them o'erlooke,
> I prethee *Persius* write a bigger booke.[24]

Donne, that is, was best known still for the poems written at sea on the voyage to the Azores in 1597, originally as verse letters for Christopher Brooke, and the series of just five satires he had completed by 1601. In addressing him as Persius, the writer was identifying Donne with an ancient aristocratic Roman poet who wrote only six dazzling satires, in a very obscure style, all of which he left in an unfinished state. Donne would probably have been pleased by the comparison: Persius Flaccus never got the chance to take care of posterity, since he died in his late twenties, but Donne regarded himself as a similar poetic noble, who wrote in a manner only fellow members of an intellectual elite could really follow, and who disdained the drudgery of propagating his writing. The epigram is one among many indications that Donne might not have had to bear the printing costs himself had he chosen to publish: there was a public ready and waiting to snatch up whatever he offered, making the volume a sound commercial proposition. When the epigram above by Thomas Freeman appeared in 1614, it was of course testimony to the fact that Donne's 'bigger booke' had not by then appeared. Back in 1611, however, he did briefly consider putting one together.

He set about establishing his own personal canon, and explained the process of winnowing to Goodyer in grim, witty, habitually infernal terms. His poems, he reported, were 'about to undergo the last Judgement'. Although this would exclude all possibility of heaven, he had nonetheless arranged them into three piles, according to the old Roman Catholic model of the afterlife. As so often in his previous writing, he uses a Papist concept as a metaphor when he is not talking seriously about an actual religious question. Some poems would suffer the pains of Purgatory and eventually emerge into the light. Some, which had slipped out into the world in unauthorized copies, would go straight into the fire, 'condemned by me to Hell'. And there were others that no one had ever transcribed from his original manuscripts, 'virgins (save that they have been handled by many)', which would be sent to 'utter annihilation (a fate with which God does not threaten even the wickedest of sinners)'.[25] He had created a special category of damnation harsher than God himself allowed. Behind the joke, he seems to have been rather insecure about the work itself. Part of his reluctance to print his poems may, at heart, have lain with reservations about the writing as much as disdain for the medium.

When he gave out manuscripts, he knew who would receive them: even the texts that were copied without his say-so went to friends of friends, and so forth. It was a gradual, cushioned release. But a printed collection would fling his poor poems straight into the world; and he could not relish the idea, at least not for his old material. A 'bigger booke' of Donne's poetry would not appear in his lifetime. But still he was tempted, and his aversion to the printing of poems *per se* was weakening. He would have much less of a problem with impersonal verse designed and armoured specifically for the press; and this willingness would be important to his relationship with a new patron who distracted him from his never-to-be-finalized collection in 1611. The same letter in which Donne condemns his well-handled virgins to nothingness speaks much more excitedly of an offer he had received from a wealthy courtier.

Sir Robert Drury, a Gentleman of the King's Chamber, had asked Donne to accompany him on an extended trip to the continent as his companion and amanuensis. Drury was a plain-speaking military man in his mid-thirties, three years younger than Donne. At the age of sixteen, he had been knighted for bravery by the Earl of Essex at the siege of Rouen, and had served with some distinction in every major theatre of operations throughout the 1590s – France, Cadiz, the Azores, the Low Countries and Ireland. He was passionately loyal to Essex, and would probably have lost his life or at least his fortune in the rising of 1601 had he not been already under house arrest for speaking 'certain buggwords' against Elizabeth and the government.[26] He had a heedless tongue and a hot temper, but what he lacked in discretion he was prepared to make up for with pugnacity. Having fallen out with a comrade, Sir William Woodhouse, over a nebulous matter of honour in 1599, he survived an ambush on the road in which his servant was killed, and he was left to fend for himself against Woodhouse and a team of four 'cutters'.[27] But as soon as his wounds would allow, a few weeks later he sped to join up with Essex in Ireland. He was a man whose reactions could have fatal consequences, but he was willing to let bygones be bygones when they did not:

he and Woodhouse, for example, later became firm friends again.

Drury's choleric nature, aggressive physicality and intolerance of verbal elaboration did not make him an ideal patron for the nervous, intermittently ailing and frequently convoluted Donne. On mercenary grounds alone, the relationship was not an especially promising one from Donne's point of view. Although he was one of the King's attendants, Drury had spent most of James's reign rather aimlessly: he was someone who needed a war to wage, and the peace with Spain left him somewhat redundant. He had married Anne Bacon, a niece of Sir Francis Bacon, but was rarely at home with her. He travelled extensively in France, Italy and Spain, hoping that such journeys, when considered along with his combat experience, might put him in line for a diplomatic posting – one from which his reputation as a hothead pretty much disqualified him. He coveted an ambassadorship, and not being the most politic or intellectual of men, he needed someone with a good command of modern languages and the art of letter writing.

Lady Drury also welcomed Donne. Long spells alone while Sir Robert was off fighting or touring had made her devoutly religious, and she welcomed the company of softer-spoken, milder-mannered men. She had personally overseen the appointment of a young Cambridge academic, Joseph Hall, as the family chaplain. Hall was an occasional poet with an evangelic character, convinced that God directed his every action. He later went on to great things in the Reformed Church; in terms of his training and aptitudes, he was of a mind with Donne, if not sharing his humour, though he too had written satires. With *Pseudo-martyr* behind him Donne would have been more than acceptable in the rather airless clerical company that Lady Drury kept around her at the family estate of Hawstead in Suffolk.

Donne probably got to know the Drurys through his older sister Anne. She had married William Lyly, the resourceful Machiavellian who served as a soldier and spy in France and who, on his last mission, was attached to an embassy led by Sir Robert Drury's uncle, Sir Edward Stafford. When this ended in 1598, Sir Robert took the out-of-work agent on as an attendant, messenger and

general helper, and let him and his wife, Donne's sister, settle at
the Drury residence – to the discomfort of Joseph Hall. Lyly was
by no means a religious man, and took every opportunity of
winding up the earnest young priest. 'Having then fixed my foot
at *Halsted*,' Hall recollected decades later, 'I found there a dangerous
Opposite to the Success of my Ministry, a witty and bold Atheist,
one Mr *Lilley*.' Lyly had 'deeply insinuated himself' into Sir Robert
Drury's favour, and continually undercut Hall's efforts 'to work
any good upon that Noble Patron of mine'. Hall felt neglected,
and presently left Drury's service when he received a better offer.
Drury urged him to stay, but Hall turned him down. An extra ten
pounds a year, he complained, would have made all the difference;
but he did not give up his place until William Lyly 'was swept
away by the Pestilence' on a trip to curry favour with the King
'and never returned to do any farther Mischief'.[28] Hall later rose
to be a bishop, and was never afraid to revel in the fall of the
unrighteous.

Sir Robert and Lady Anne had only two children – both daughters. This was an unusually small family by the standards of the
time, certainly by those of Donne's warren of a home at Mitcham,
but unsurprising. The marriage had ample opportunity to go cold,
if it had ever been very warm to begin with. It was another union
grounded on a socially viable contract, made between two people
with little in common who became content to see very little of
each other. Sir Robert and Anne Drury lost their first daughter,
Dorothy, in 1597, aged just four; but then in December 1610 their
second daughter, Elizabeth, died, a few weeks before she turned
fifteen. Some local stories said she died from a clip round the ear;
according to others, she died of a broken heart. She had a crush
on one of the grooms who worked on the Drury estate. One day,
the lad she adored accidentally shot himself instead of the dog he
had been ordered to put down. On hearing of this, Elizabeth was
said to have dropped dead, and fallen into a corn-bin.[29] In real life,
she probably succumbed to one of the innumerable killer diseases
that are routinely cured in modern times. But in any case, her
parents were devastated by grief for her, and for themselves. The

last bond between them had been plucked away. They were left childless, and there was no real prospect, emotionally or physically, of any more children. Even if they had somehow rebuilt their relationship, Anne was thirty-eight when their daughter died – almost exactly the same age as Donne. There had been no new birth at Hawstead for fifteen years; and it would never happen now.

Donne wrote 'A Funerall Elegie' for Elizabeth Drury, probably at a suggestion or request from one of his and Sir Robert's mutual Court acquaintances. It was just another memorial poem written to order – Donne never actually set eyes on the child he was elegizing. But the bereaved couple seized on the comfort it provided. Joseph Hall suggested that he write something more. Eager to please, Donne composed a much longer piece, entitled *An Anatomy of the World*. 'Anatomy' meant 'dissection': this was literally a post-mortem of the earth. It was a torrential work, almost five hundred lines long, a sustained cataract of overstatement: 'By occasion of the untimely death of Mistris Elizabeth Drury,' ran its preface, 'the frailty and decay of this whole world is represented.' Everything for this poem, every miracle of earth, was rotten. Mountains and volcanoes, rising so high 'that one might thinke / The floating Moone would shipwrecke there', were for Donne just blemishes: 'warts, and pock-holes in the face / Of th'earth'.[30] Not very much in the huge baroque poem may have been to Sir Robert's blunt taste: he might even have felt that the reality of his loss was diminished by the idea that his daughter's death left 'the world itselfe . . . dead'.[31] But he must have seen that such words did reach and speak to his more devout, pietistic wife; and as such, this was something he should be seen to encourage. Donne's poetry may actually have helped the couple grieve together. It was the new *Anatomy*, an autopsy of the creation, rather than the collection of old poems Donne had initially planned that was published in 1611. Sir Robert and his wife joined the list of those he could rely on for occasional patronage.

In July that year Drury became keen to enlist Donne's services for a long trip abroad, lasting years rather than months; on which, most unusually, Lady Drury was also going to come along. Sir Robert was doing his best to bridge the divide he had let grow and grow within their marriage for more than twenty years; and Donne, notwithstanding his great secretarial skills, was evidently essential to this process. Yet going abroad with the Drurys raised the problem of Donne's own wife and children. Bringing his family of eight (nine including himself) was obviously not an option. Donne accepted Drury's invitation nonetheless; but he actually broke the news to Goodyer before Ann. When he did, she was utterly distraught. She was expecting another baby, 'and otherways under so dangerous a habit of body', says Walton, that she could not bear to let him go. The prospect of being left alone for what might have been a period of several years was sickening enough; but she also, according to Walton, protested that '*her divining soul boded her some ill in his absence*' – she was vulnerable, and very scared of something terrible happening. So Donne decided not to go after all.

But Sir Robert Drury 'became restless in his perswasions': he was determined that Donne would accompany them. It is unlikely that Drury had much sympathy with Donne for backing out of an agreement at the request of his wife, or for letting her cling to him. Sir Robert himself had left his own wife alone for long periods on many occasions. Now the only thing he and Lady Drury could still try and nurture together was his career; so they were going together, and Donne was coming with them. By this stage Donne had accepted so much material support from the couple that he simply felt unable to refuse. He felt that 'he had sold his liberty . . . and told his wife so.' Ann, 'with an unwilling-willingness', eventually consented to the journey, on the condition that it would only last two months – leaving just enough time for Donne to be back for when the baby was due.[32] But when the Drury party set out for France in early November, with a coach and twelve horses, a pack of hounds and a couple of hawks for hunting with, it carried a permit granting travel 'for three yeares'.[33]

In a letter to Goodyer shortly before the departure, Donne admitted he was keen to be off. The arrangement with Drury was rather less of an opening than he had once hoped for, but he had learnt to lower his expectations: 'if it do but keep me awake, it recompenses me well.' At least it gave him an occupation of some kind: 'I am now in the afternoon of my life,' he wrote, 'and it is unwholesome to sleep.'[34] It also finally released him from his 'thin little house' at Mitcham.[35] The place had been a draughty germ-trap, a den of depression, illness and stressful times with Ann, who was just as 'tender towards these impressions' as Donne himself.[36] While he prepared to leave for France, she was packed off south with the children, to stay with her younger sister, Frances, and brother-in-law, John Oglander, on the Isle of Wight. Oglander was a decent, upright, amiable, yeomanly islander in his late twenties, Justice of the Peace and pillar of the community, blissfully happy with his wife and content, on the whole, with his existence. He took pleasure in watching the saplings he planted turn into trees. He had none of Donne's urbanity, and Donne had none of his peace of mind. He was just the sort of person Ann needed to be near.

After the coach journey to the south coast, and the short but often turbulent sailing across the Solent, she and the children settled in at Nunwell, the Oglanders' ancestral home on the eastern side of the island. Conditions were as comfortable as they might be; the original medieval building had burnt down a generation before, but Oglander, in his own words, had built 'a convenient house and fitted all things up handsomely'.[37] Wight itself is an island of trim, low hills with a sprinkling of little towns. It has the shape, on the map, of a slightly squashed heart; and quiet, then as now, was its principal virtue. Despite the place's sickly sounding name, there were worse places than Nunwell. The children were kept busy; in the grounds where they could play, they had gardens and meadows and ruins. Oglander could point out the young ash he was nurturing, growing where the parlour chimney in the old lost house once stood. Ann herself had space, fresh air and the supportive presence of a sister.

But it was also winter, closing in on an outpost where Ann knew no one and was beyond any regular contact with her husband in France or her friends on the mainland. She had little company amid the bustle of a working farm. However close Ann's sister was to her, Frances was a busy woman. Oglander noted with pride that his wife always got up in the morning before he did, to supervise work in the outhouses, and was unafraid to wet her shoes to see that it was done properly.

Ann's only consolation from Donne was one of the greatest poems he ever wrote. Tradition has it that on leaving Ann to go to France, he wrote 'A Valediction: Forbidding Mourning'. In the lyric, he tells her not to be sad, because separation is merely an illusion for two people who love each other as they do. As so often, he uses the idea of an unbreakable bond between two souls made of the same stuff. When their bodies moved away to different points on the earth, their spirits weren't really parted, just stretched, 'Like gold to ayery thinnesse beate'. There was no need to cry: 'So let us melt, and make no noise,' he shushed, 'No teare-floods, nor sigh-tempests move.'[38] The piece is a sustained, masterful denial of the reality of the loneliness that might follow death or desertion. On his side of that reality, Donne himself was careworn, disappointed, and eager simply to get on with the trip, glad of the break it afforded if nothing else: 'It is ill to look back, or give over in a course,' he told Goodyer, 'but worse never to set out.'[39]

Not long after his arrival in France, however, Donne began suffering from precisely the symptoms of loneliness and edginess that 'A Valediction: Forbidding Mourning' attempted to dispel. He continued writing his weekly letter to Goodyer, and also wrote regularly to his former house-mate George Garrard. Disturbingly, he received no replies. The party was wintering in Amiens, where Sir Robert spent much of his time hunting with a nobleman friend, the Comte de St Paul. While Drury enjoyed the sports of the field, his wife had little to do. Donne meanwhile was kept busy with the composition of yet another memorial poem for Elizabeth Drury. This one, 'Of the Progres of the Soule', imagined how she must have been enjoying the afterlife. He was being drawn into a strange three-way symbiosis with Elizabeth's bereaved parents. Drury, eager to be thought of back home as an attaché without portfolio, sent informal dispatches to influential quarters – mostly delivering little but compliments and apologies for the lack of definite news. These missives would be drafted by Donne, and presented for Sir Robert to sign. By February, it seems that Lady Drury was keen to be involved in the business: one letter survives that was clearly composed by Donne, copied out by Anne Drury, and then signed by Sir Robert. Presumably there were others like it.[40] Donne, providing words for the husband to approve and the wife to transcribe, acted as both a bond and a safety cordon between them. He helped them be together, gave them a common focus, but spared them having to speak to each other when they couldn't communicate.

The poetry he produced also gave the couple something that was still commonly theirs, something they could share in. But they in turn helped Donne in more than the material sense. They gave him an outlet for the manic despondency that had been festering for years with only occasional, private release. They let him wail at length. 'Of the Progres of the Soule' is another masterpiece of active, aggressive, suffocating darkness, premised once again on the idea that nothing worthwhile remained now that 'Shee, shee is gone; shee is gone'. And when one realized that fact, Donne claimed, one saw 'What fragmentary rubbidge this world is'. He could express the full disgust he felt at being an incarnated being, a 'small lump of flesh' like 'curded milk'. 'The World is but a Carkas,' he told the world; and 'thou art fed / By it, but as a worme, that carcas bred.'[41] The manuscript was sent back to London and the poem was published in early 1612 with a reprint of the previous one, as *The First and Second Anniversaries*.

This was not all the poetry Donne wrote to commission during his sojourn. Towards the end of January the Drurys were visited by Sir Robert Rich, who persuaded Donne to write some laudatory verses for his sisters. Donne always found it hard to turn down a request. So he dashed off a letter in which he invoked the two girls, Essex and Lettice, as 'saints'. He felt entitled to do so, having never laid eyes on them in person: he saw them instead by an 'extasye / And Revelation of yow both'. Sir Robert Rich left

Amiens happy with what, for Donne, was a perfectly routine, rather bored piece of flattery, but which by the standards of the time was quirky, prizeable writing: a collector's item for all those who knew his name and work. And this made it a risky thing to do: for he not only endangered his own integrity but also risked making his other patrons jealous, especially Lady Bedford. His association with Drury alone was enough to bring him disapproval from respected quarters. Before setting off, Donne's main anxiety with regard to his affairs in England was that Lady Bedford should not feel slighted by the priority he was giving his new patron: he begged Goodyer, 'I must intreat you to continue . . . to maintain me in the same room in my Lady *Bedfords* opinion, in the which you placed me.'[42] Praising Drury's daughter as the only good thing left in the world was already pushing it quite far; describing Essex and Lettice Rich as 'saints' was exceeding the bounds of a countess's ability to share devotion. The girls' mother, Penelope Rich, was notorious as a man-thief and serial mistress. In flattering them, he made his compliments to Lady Bedford seem cheap. In time he would learn that she was not amused.

As the winter passed, he became increasingly twitchy. He kept writing letters to England, and none came back. Partly this seems to have been because of unreliable postal links; but it was also partly due to a slight frostiness in his friends. Stuck in a place he found increasingly hateful, with only the dreary Drurys for company, he was greatly in need of a letter. One from Goodyer, written in mid-December, did finally reach him a month later. Donne was by turns reproachful and insecure: in one letter, he asked Garrard 'if there be a Proclamation in *England* against writing to me'. In another, he begged him to send even the briefest of notes, since 'I do not know how short you will be with an absent friend. If you will but write that you give me leave to keep that name still [i.e. of 'friend'], it shall be the gold of your Letter.' He repeatedly gave information of how he might be reached, citing a pub-acquaintance who would carry a message: 'At the Queens armes in *Cheapside*, you may hear of one M. *John Brewer*, who will convay any Letter directed to me at Sir *Rob. Druries* at *Amiens*.'[43]

Donne for his part kept writing, largely because his letters were his main way of understanding himself.

Much of the day passed staring at a blank horizon; and most of his anxiety lay with Ann. He had received no word from her or about her for months. Early in February Donne wrote sheepishly to his brother-in-law, Sir Robert More, at Loseley, asking him to forward a letter to her, since direct communication had failed. The problem was that one could only get to the Isle of Wight 'by the north-west discovery' – that is, by landing somewhere on the long topside of the island, nearest the English mainland. No ship sailing directly from France would drop anchor on the fortified eastern side, where John Oglander's house stood, in case its intentions were misinterpreted as hostile. The only way of getting a message through was to send it first to Portsmouth or Southampton; and as repeated attempts failed, Donne grew haggard with worry: 'this silence,' he told his brother-in-law, 'especially at this time when I make account that your sister is near her painful and dangerous passage, doth somewhat more affect me than I had thought anything of this world could have done.'[44] This is one of the few times when Ann's historical 'silence' might be interpreted: it was reproachful, and unfathomably sad. Donne knew that the baby was long due, and clearly suspected something was wrong. But through commitment to his post, fear of upsetting Drury, or just inertia, he did not go to her.

In March, Drury and his entourage moved on to Paris, where Donne was seized upon by Tobie Mathew, the Papist convert, who had been aimlessly wandering in exile for years. Mathew still had most of his capital tied up in England, and had left Sir Henry Goodyer in charge of his affairs. This was a bad choice: Goodyer could barely take care of his own. Mathew was, Donne told Goodyer, 'diligent to finde a means to write to you' – naturally keen to contact his executor. Donne, however, coldly assumed that Mathew 'provides for himselfe'. He did not offer to send a message on to Goodyer with his own packet, and made no invitation for Mathew to call again.[45] Donne may have been thinking of Mathew, or one of his associates, when he warned Goodyer not against 'those friends which are religious in other clothes than we', but those 'which are not onely naked, without any fashion of such garments, but have neither the body of Religion . . . nor the soul'.[46]

Mathew chose the wrong time and the wrong man to ask for help. Soon after arriving in Paris, Donne's health had collapsed. He came down with 'such storms of a stomach cȯlick as kept me in a continuall vomiting'. This gastric disorder was only relieved when overtaken by an 'honest fever' that kept him confined to his bed while the Drurys began moving through the French Court. Donne had, however, brought an extensive collection of books with him, and having entered the vicinity of the great college of the Sorbonne, pursued his interest in the theological debates of the time.

The previous year Edmond Richer, a leading ecclesiast and academic, had published a short, deadly treatise arguing that the Pope had in truth only limited power over temporal matters. Donne had of course attempted to demonstrate much the same thing in *Pseudo-martyr*, and was keen to lend Richer whatever support he could – he flattered himself 'that there was no proposition in his Book, which I could not shew in Catholique authors [over a period] of 300 years.' But for the first meeting the two men arranged, Richer stood Donne up: he had a more pressing engagement with a number of aristocrats and European ambassadors. For the next, Richer had a more urgent excuse: 'the Jesuits had offered corrupt men with rewards to kill him'. Donne's messenger found the poor theologian cowering indoors 'in an extreme trembling, and irresolutions'. The only response Richer would offer was to ask Donne 'to withdraw comming to his house, or drawing him out of it, till it might be without danger or observation'.[47] Richer was soon removed from his post at the Sorbonne – France was Catholic, and owed allegiance to Rome – and little more was heard of him in his lifetime.

Donne continued sending his letters, using them to talk to himself. 'I am not weary of writing,' he said, in a circular letter addressed '*To all my friends*' through Goodyer; 'it is the coarse but durable garment of my love; but I am weary of wanting you.'[48] It was springtime in Paris; but his intestines hurt at either end. Convalescing from the 'distemper' that had struck him down, along with the 'Fever, and dysentery' that followed, he looked on the social whirl with an eye even more jaundiced than usual. A double royal wedding took place, with public celebrations on a massive scale. The French boy-king, Louis XIII – whose inclinations Donne found to be 'cruel, and tyrannous'[49] – was married to an Infanta, and his sister to the heir of the Spanish throne. Donne was not the only Englishman to feel uncomfortable at the friendship developing between France and Spain, but even the spectacle of cavalcade and carnival left him cold. Almost two hundred thousand people packed into the Place Royale to watch the pageant's fabulous mobiles: chevaliers taking on the role of knights of old, 'a chariot drawn by lions, five giants and a great rockery all covered with nymphs, which made its way to soft notes from the lyre'.[50] But Donne didn't think much of all that. He was unimpressed too by the tourneying of the French knights: instead of clashing, all they did was gallop at targets; 'for their Gendarmery, there was no other trial then I told you,' he sniffed; '& for their bravery, no true stuffe.'[51]

To make things worse, almost the only news that did filter through was word that the *Anniversaries* had provoked widespread embarrassment and ridicule. 'I hear from *England* of many censures of my book,' he told Goodyer.[52] The idolization of the dead teenager was felt to be in very poor taste. For Ben Jonson, the work was 'profane and full of blasphemies', and he later made a pointing of telling Donne as much: 'if it had been written of the Virgin Mary, it had been something,' he said.[53] When letters finally trickled through from home, instead of humour and support Donne found criticism. 'The fault which I acknowledge in myself,' he admitted cagily to Garrard, 'is to have descended to print any thing in verse.' But his defence was equivocal. On the one hand, he declared that 'my purpose was to say as well as I could: for since I never saw the Gentlewoman [i.e. Elizabeth Drury], I cannot be understood to have bound my selfe to have spoken just Truth.'

He assumed that everyone would understand that he had just been overstating things; being brutally honest, he said that that was the whole point. Elegies *exaggerated*. But on the other hand, he still asserted, 'I would not be thought to have gone about to praise any body in rime, exept I tooke such a Person, as might be capable of all that I could say.'[54] He was both shielding and disavowing his elegiac overstatement all at once; and avoiding what was probably the real 'just Truth' – that he had been currying favour and indulging his own melancholy.

The Countess of Bedford was put out by his vagrant praising. The *Anniversaries* had been published, and word no doubt got around of his verses for the two 'saintly' Rich sisters. It looked as though he was willing to talk up the truth about anyone. To make matters worse, the Countess was in a more than usually delicate way: 1612 was a bad year for her. Her husband was lamed in a riding accident. He had been something of a social recluse since being pardoned for his involvement in the Essex rising, and was never an intellectually engaged character. Now he could no longer even speak well; and his partial paralysis left a cold marriage insensate. Lady Bedford herself drifted increasingly towards Puritanism, renouncing the vanity of outward beauty, but she had more than enough self-concern to feel jilted at Donne hiring out his compliments on request. Trying to make amends, he began a verse letter to her which humbly admitted to his indiscretions: 'First I confesse I have to others lent / Your stock,' he confessed, 'and over prodigally spent / Your treasure.'[55] That is, his highest regards were still hers to command; they were her riches, and she could cancel the cheques he was writing for others. Yet he never found the will to complete the piece. Its title explains that it was 'begun in France but never completed'.

He simply had too much on his mind. It was now mid-April, and still no word had reached him of Ann – or from her, for that matter. 'I am yet in the same perplexity, which I mentioned before,' he wrote: he still had no idea 'whether I be increased by a childe, or diminished by the losse of a wife'.[56] The possibility that Ann was dead is expressed swiftly and sharply, as a matter of gain or deficit; and the letter moves on to address at more length the charges about Elizabeth Drury. But according to Walton, Donne was soon shaken into real terror for Ann's life.

He and the Drurys were still in Paris, perhaps residing somewhere in the Faubourg St Germain, popular with English visitors, and where the ambassador himself traditionally had his home. After supper with Drury and a few other friends, Donne was left alone in the room where they had eaten. When Drury returned, he found the poet in a state of extreme shock – 'in such an Extasie, and so alter'd as to his looks, as amaz'd Sir *Robert* to behold him.' It was some time before Donne could speak; but after a 'long and perplext pause' he tried to explain what had happened. 'I have seen a dreadful Vision since I saw you,' he stammered – as though days, not minutes had passed since Drury left the room, presumably to see out his guests. 'I have seen my dear wife pass twice by me through this room, with her hair hanging about her shoulders, and a dead child in her arms.'

Drury tried to snap Donne out of it by taking the rational approach. The ghost had shattered the companionable atmosphere of the gentlemen's soirée, and brought with her something still more discomforting than the supernatural into the cosy dining room: an accusation of neglect in which Drury, the bereaved father who persuaded Donne to leave Ann behind, was also implicated. 'Sure Sir, you have slept since I saw you,' said Sir Robert, 'and, this is the result of some melancholy dream.' It is easy to imagine Donne nodding off, and the spectre walking out from the back of his mind. Yet Donne refused to accept that he might have been dreaming: 'I cannot be surer that I now live, than that I have not slept since I saw you: and am as sure, that at her second appearing, she stopt, and look'd me in the face, and vanisht.'

It was easier, perhaps, to believe that it really was a ghost, and not something his own head was doing to him. Walton's account, given him by 'a person of honour', may of course be a tall tale; but there is no reason to suspect it did not originate with Donne. It reads almost like a deliberate reversal of one of his earlier fictions. In a poem called 'The Apparition', probably written many years before, he imagined his spirit returning to disturb his mistress when she has killed him by her 'scorne'. She is suitably terrified. But the spirit finds her in bed with a new lover, who shrinks away exhaustedly when she tries waking him, thinking that she wants more sex. The story in Walton turns all that upside down: Donne is the haunted one, and the visitation is no laughing matter – it is proof, in fact, that his soul and Ann's really were inextricably bonded. Walton says that first thing the next morning a messenger was dispatched. He returned twelve days later with news that Ann was alive, but 'very sad, and sick in her bed'. After a long period of labour she had given birth to a stillborn child, delivered on 'the same day, and about the very hour that Mr *Donne* affirm'd he saw her pass by him'.[57]

Many of the details in Walton's story are wrong, but none is more important than his mistaken chronology. By the middle of April, when Donne was still ignorant as to whether Ann and their child were dead or alive, two months had gone by since the baby was lost and the mother left 'very sad, and sick' on the Isle of Wight. On 22 January the family at Nunwell made the short trip across the downs to the port of Brading, to bury 'the abortive of M*i*stris Dunne'. In the parish record there, John Oglander left a brief note to mark the occasion. It was a bleak midwinter setting, exposed to everything the coastal elements could throw down on the mourners. The low surrounding land has been engulfed many times; an ancient sea wall stands just beyond the twelfth-century church. About ten years later, Oglander expanded his terse little record after he was knighted and Donne was made Dean of St Paul's, when the stillborn child became associated with two worthy names. He seems to have treated the 'abortive' as a fact of life, but Oglander remembered his sister-in-law tenderly: 'At S*i*r John's she was brought a bedde,' he wrote, 'the best of women.'[58]

Donne was oblivious to the whole ordeal. Here and there, his letters from the Continent imply that he resented the burden family life placed upon him. He found strength in his friendship with Goodyer, from whom 'I learn that there is truth and firmnesse and an earnestness of doing good alive in the world', enough to make him wish to remain alive; but he complained sardonically that 'I dyed ten years ago' – that is, early in 1602, when his clandestine marriage was revealed: it had killed his career. Around the time of Ann's miscarriage in January 1612, Donne was not seeing visions of her, but reflecting that 'I dyed at a blow [i.e. 'at one strike'] then when my courses were diverted'.[59] He hoped that Goodyer and others could see that he had done his best to get back on track; but he was buckling under repeated failure. With a shoddy image of himself, the responsibility of being the head and provider of a household was proving too much. For Donne, humans have 'common, and mutuall necessity of one another': he freely admitted that 'no man is lesse of himselfe [i.e. 'on his own'] than I'. But he found that having a family made him feel lonely rather than connected, because of the great pressure his wife and children put on him: 'in so strict obligation of Parent, or Husband, or Master . . . where all are made one, I am not the lesse alone, for being in the midst of them.' Without a fitting place in the world, he was an unhappy patriarch.

However traumatized he may have been by news of the stillbirth – and through whatever medium he received that news – he did not hurry to return to Ann's side. There is no record either of what he wrote to her in response. Through late spring and summer, the Drurys toured Germany and the Low Countries, visiting Frankfurt, Heidelberg, Spa, Maastricht, Louvain and Brussels. Donne wrote expressing his hope to 'sneake into *London*, about the end of *August*'.[60] At Nunwell, Oglander watched his orchards blossom and bear fruit, and read in the evenings when he could. 'Above all things,' he wrote in his commonplace book, 'love thy wife and children. Otherwise thou canst never love thy home, and then all things will be distasteful unto thee.'[61]

15. A Valediction to the World

Donne liked to compose on horseback. On the road, he said, 'I am contracted, and inverted into myself'.[1] On Good Friday, 1613, having spent the early spring with Goodyer, he set out from his friend's estate at Polesworth and found the creative vacancy his mind needed to talk to itself. Poems for his own needs were becoming rarer events; when he wrote lyrics now, they were generally client-based, required by occasion or personage and written to order. The previous year the ultra-Protestant heir to the throne, Prince Henry, died of typhoid, to the country's dismay; and Donne had made his contribution to the fistfuls of elegies that were brought out in response. It was a dry, overwrought piece of work. Yet poetry was still, sometimes, a recreation; once at Polesworth, though perhaps not this time, he and Goodyer sat down and composed alternate verses of a poem in honour of two unnamed gentlewomen. Goodyer wrote of trees coming into blossom, 'Perfuming and enamelling each bough', and the 'calme face' of the river Anker which ran through his lands; Donne wrote of the 'poore old sunn', nightingales, and 'the feare of Autumns stinge'.[2]

Leaving Polesworth behind, instead of turning to the east and heading back from Warwickshire, Shakespeare's county, towards London, Donne continued west towards Wales. Behind him lay his wife and still-increasing family – Ann was pregnant again – and the capital, where he had kept up his efforts to lift his fortunes. While he was inverted in himself, a poem took shape. Although on this Good Friday he was being carried 'towards the West . . . my Soules forme bends towards the East'. His mind was on neither dusk nor dawn but on a sun rising in one place as it appeared to sink in another. Behind him to the east, he imagined Christ's Passion on the cross developing like a thundercloud. He could not look; it was

> A spectacle of too much weight for mee.
> Who sees Gods face, that is selfe life, must dye;
> What a death were it then to see God dye?

The priesthood was still open for Donne, though these were lines that few orthodox churchmen could openly approve of. However theologically apt it might be, the idea of God actually dying was a risky one to propagate: this was a poem for the appreciation of Goodyer, and one or two friends such as the fellow poet Donne was riding to see. Donne in any case was keeping his back to the ministry; and he could only bear to look Christ in the face if an abrasive purification were possible first:

> O thinke mee worth thine anger, punish mee,
> Burne off my rusts, and my deformity,
> Restore thine Image, so much, by thy grace,
> That thou mayst know mee; and I'll turn my face.[3]

With the eyes of his saviour boring through his shoulder blades, he was travelling to visit Sir Edward Herbert at Montgomery Castle in Wales.[4] The castle was torn down by parliamentarians during the Civil War, but in its day was described as 'a most romancy seate', commanding beautiful views in all directions.[5] Sir Edward was the son of Donne's close friend Magdalen Herbert. Once a sickly boy-scholar, tutored at Oxford under close maternal surveillance, Herbert had grown into the complete Renaissance man – swordsman, scholar, poet and courtier, the last a role he sniffed at with the right kind of elegant disdain. He was also an all-round hard-case. He won considerable fame as a soldier and was well known for his feather-sensitive code of honour. The faintest slur to a nearby gentlewoman by any male would automatically incite the fiercest response: he once chased a French cavalier across the countryside for playfully running off with a lady's ribbon, then took it as a personal affront when the rattled Frenchman tried returning the trifle without admitting first that he had been *made* to give it back. Herbert married young, then spent his travels meeting the European aristocracy, hunting wild boar on their endless estates, and looking for opportunities to prove himself in rash displays of martial bravado.

Herbert's closest scrape to date had come when a group of swordsmen attacked him in London. The band of cut-throats had been gathered and was led by Sir John Ayres, who accused Sir Edward of 'whoring' his wife. Lady Ayres had certainly fallen in love with him but Herbert insisted that nothing improper ever took place; he knew no surer defence than to say that '[I] my selfe was not ingaged in any affection towards her.' Wandering into her bedchamber one day – with perfectly innocent intentions – Herbert 'sawe her through the Courtaines lying vpon her bed', gazing with touching desperation at a portrait of him in miniature. Herbert was perfectly willing to fight her husband; he would in fact have been disgusted had this not been required of him. But while Ayres had the sense not to issue a formal challenge to single combat he still made the mistake of thinking that four hired assassins would be enough to take down his enemy. Ayres and his team were instantly repelled and quickly appalled. Herbert broke his sword with the first stroke, but still fought all of them off with just the stump of the blade. A friendly passer-by, Sir Henry Carew, decently pulled a dagger from Herbert's ribs so that he could go and knock Ayres down for a third time. With the hirelings vanquished and the jealous husband on the ground, Herbert straddled him, hacking furiously: 'when kneeling on the Ground and bestriding him I struck at him in fowre seurall places and did almost cut off his left hand,' he reported. It took Herbert just ten days to get over his injuries, whereupon he offered to meet Ayres at a time of his choosing to finish the affair like gentlemen. Incredulous, the Privy Council asked to see 'that little fragment of weapon' Herbert had done so much damage with.[6] The buckled shard was accordingly presented and passed around. Herbert, it was agreed, was to be treated with care and deployed only when absolutely necessary.

This was no worry to Donne, whom Herbert greatly admired. Herbert too had written an elaborate lament for the dead Prince Henry; according to Ben Jonson, Donne's own elegy for Henry was written in a morbid duel of wits, 'to match Sir Ed: Herbert in obscureness'.[7] Edward had some of Donne's stylistic complexity, but none of his humour, and he did not allow his metaphysical poetry to compromise his reputation as a serious man of action. A short way from Montgomery Castle, a servant of Herbert's had watered his horse in the river Usk, and been swept downstream. Hearing the cry that 'Dick Griffiths was Drowning', Herbert immediately galloped to the rescue – forgetting that his mother had forbidden him, as a boy, from learning to swim. He had, however, refined his own technique for falling into water on horseback. Once riding over an unwalled little bridge in his demesnes, his horse had almost stumbled headfirst into the river. With split-second reflexes, Herbert readjusted himself and his steed so he fell 'vpon all fowre into the Ryver whence after some three or fowre plunges he brought mee to Land'.[8]

Herbert was rougher, tougher, richer and nobler – in the ignoble, purely material sense of the word – than Donne: he was born into a venerable, massively wealthy and powerful family, and was created a Knight of the Order of the Bath in King James's first major distribution of honours. His outlook was also, in many respects, much more confined to that of his time than Donne's, since he never had cause to look beyond conventional perspectives. He was exactly the sort of man that Sir George More would have been quite happy for his daughter Ann to marry instead of Donne. Herbert had married another Ann, the only surviving child of another Welsh Herbert, Sir William of St Julian's in Monmouthshire, who insisted in his will that his daughter could only inherit his possessions if she married someone with the same family name, so that his line would not be discontinued.[9] Edward was happy to oblige. In 1608, when he felt it necessary to consider the future of their children, he pointed out bluntly that they were both still young, and that if God 'pleased to call either of vs away That Party which remained might marry againe and haue Children by some other to which our Estates might bee disposed.' To prevent this, Edward offered to guarantee their sons any quantity of lands with revenues of between £300 and £1,000 a year. He was upset when his wife did not see the wisdom of his proposal, but knowing that she had always been afraid of losing him overseas, offered to stay at home with her always if she agreed to his deal. She hated the idea of Herbert going off, but still refused. So he left her to go travelling.

Donne never had to consider such transactions, however much by now he might have liked the luxury of juggling the numbers. By marrying, he and Ann opted out of the regular marketplace, and had faced the consequences. The severity of his ruination no doubt came as a shock, but Donne had been well aware, over ten years before, of the risk he was taking at his secret wedding. He married for emotional reasons and thus set different standards for his relationship with Ann to be seen against. Like Herbert, like many husbands, though, he spent a considerable amount of time away from her: as he was now, in spring 1613, idling at country estates, talking religion, politics and poetry with likeminded friends. Still 'A Valediction: Forbidding Mourning', the poem he gave Ann on his departure for France a year and a half before, urged that she should never feel lonely because their united souls were never really apart. He was the roving, circumscribing leg of a pair of compasses, she the 'fixt foot' which

> When the other far doth rome,
> It leanes, and hearkens after it,
> And growes erect, as that comes home.[10]

He was now forty, she was not yet thirty. While clearly written to soothe, the 'Valediction' also suggests that he had, in actual fact, never really considered what it might be like to be without her permanently. He found it a relief to have periods away from her so long as he knew she was still there for him: the tour of his friends' homes in the spring of 1613 was not a family trip. After the birth in August of another son, Nicholas, he made the odd remark to Goodyer that 'I have now two of the best happinesses which could befall me, upon me; which are, to be a widower and my wife alive.'[11] By this he seems to have meant that Ann was simply away, perhaps in the country with friends or relatives, recovering from her labours, but the personal sense is clear. He often needed space from her, periods as a temporary widower, but always needed her still to be there.

At least his time was no longer split between two homes. On returning from Europe in early autumn the previous year, Donne moved his family to a town house in Drury Lane, which was named after his patron. There the Drurys had a fine winged mansion, set back from the street by a large but densely packed courtyard, and with gardens at the back. The courtyard was fronted by a central gatehouse with a row of terraces and other entries on either side of it. Behind these, jumbled around the courtyard, were other buildings, among which was the house where the Donnes now settled. This was connected to Drury Lane by a separate passage and gateway, giving the house its own private entrance. Direct access to the main courtyard and the Drurys' big house was apparently via another, back gate. The Drury accounts show that twopence was given to a smith 'for mendine the Laches and sneches [snitches] of the same dore'. This caused R. C. Bald to muse, 'One cannot help wondering if Donne's children had broken it.' The Donnes' house was roomier and warmer than the dismal country cottage at Mitcham, though city living and maintaining a courtier's abode may have forced Donne to keep up appearances in a manner he could not really afford. The rent Sir Robert charged was subsidized, but not so very generously, and Lady Drury could give John and Ann a hand with only a few personal furnishings, lending them among other things 'one fether bedd . . . and twoe ould Redd Chayres'.[12]

Living in the fashionable and affluent area of Drury Lane meant that Donne had to work harder than ever at fostering connections at Court and drumming up every odd bit of income he could come by, but it also meant that he was in a better position to do so. He had easier access too now to his city friends, as did Ann; one of their oldest mutual allies, Christopher Brooke, who had given Ann away at their wedding, soon moved into a house on the other side of the street. They were also better placed to make provision for the education of the children. The girls were, of course, kept at home; but John, the eldest boy, was sent as day-pupil to Westminster School, the best in the country. George, seemingly brighter, followed in his father's footsteps by going up to Oxford as a mite, entering Broadgates Hall there in 1615, aged only ten. The move to London made it easier for Donne to keep an eye on his formidable mother, who persisted in her faith, but who was now left for extended spells with only her daughter, Anne, since her husband, Richard Rainsford, spent much of his time in Newgate Prison as punishment for his own refusal to conform. However, Donne does not seem to have visited his mother frequently, and later regretted his negligence.

Donne's chief focus remained the Court of King James, where by now he was a well-practised (though perennially frustrated) operator. The King was fickle and temperamental, living in con-stant fear of attempts on his life by political enemies, and attempts on his soul by the devil. He possessed a strange blend of extreme personal sensitivity and frequent unflinching coarseness in speech and manner. This mixture is best shown by his attitude to personal contact with his subjects. Common people approaching him 'in troops' was an intrusion not to be borne. One of the best contem-porary descriptions of the King was made by John Oglander, in the private commonplace book he compiled for the benefit of his descendants. Like every other provincial gentleman, Oglander was expected to visit the Court from time to time; this was the mon-arch's traditional means of keeping tabs on subjects. But James, Oglander noticed, would ask why the hell all these people were coming to see him. Even if they said they came purely out of love for him, 'Then he would cry out in Scottish, "God's wounds! I shall pull down my breeches and they shall also see my arse."' The best way to get to the King was through one of his favourites. Some years before, it might be remembered, Donne had tried for employment through one of James's less aggressive beaux, the easygoing, good-looking Lord James Hay. In a time of great and open shows of affection between men, the King's tendencies were clearly more than homosocial: 'I never yet saw any fond husband make so much or so great dalliance over his beautiful spouse as I have seen King James over his favourites,' observed Oglander, who also noticed on one of the King's visits to the Isle of Wight that 'he was much taken with seeing the little boys skirmish'.[13]

The dominant favourite in 1613 was Robert Ker, Viscount of Rochester, a young blond Scot, namesake of one of Donne's longstanding allies at Court, Sir Robert Ker, later Earl of Ancram. Donne asked Lord Hay, from whose household Rochester had originally been introduced to the English Court, to pass on a letter offering his services. In this he informed Rochester that he had resolved to go into the Church, but would also leave himself open to any more lucrative secular task that the Viscount might care to bestow on him. As it happened, Rochester was in need at this time of someone with a quick wit and a ready pen. Until recently, he had relied for secretarial work on his general fixer and panderer, Sir Thomas Overbury. Overbury had proved particularly useful in arranging for Rochester to begin an affair with the young Countess of Essex, but it had been necessary to sacrifice him. Rochester had some powerful backers at Court who were willing to help him nullify the Countess's marriage and make her his own, but these had no time for Overbury, who was generally seen as being too sharp for his own good. Realizing that the Countess would undermine his position, Overbury for his part was not prepared to help Rochester marry her. And so in late April 1613, around the time, perhaps, when Donne left Sir Edward Herbert and rode eastward back to the capital, Overbury was clapped in the Tower on fabricated charges. Donne's application to serve was quickly and readily accepted: 'ever since I had the happinesse to be in your Lordship's sight, I have lived upon your bread.' In another letter he thanked Rochester for 'buying me'.[14]

These were murky waters. Some of Donne's other friends at Court, notably Lady Bedford, who despised Rochester, were concerned and offended. In return for Rochester's financial support – which does not, in fact, seem to have been worth the price Donne paid for it, in terms of work and the strain on his conscience – Donne was expected to act as a kind of propagandist if the need arose. In September the Countess of Essex's marriage was declared invalid, though only after the Countess was physically inspected for proof that she was still a virgin. The verdict was of course decided beforehand, but the examination was still felt to be necessary for the sake of appearances. Shortly afterwards Rochester was created Earl of Somerset so that he would be equal in rank with his bride. Donne provided an epithalamion for the socially awkward wedding, though he delivered it much too late for the occasion itself at the end of 1613. A rumour in the meantime got about that in some quarters the nullification of the Countess's original marriage was held to be illegal; and that a personal attack on Rochester, now Somerset, would be published soon. Writing in the new year, Donne made it clear that he would be expected to use his talents as a controversialist, and refute the tract: 'My poor study having lyen that way, it may prove possible, that my weak assistance may be of use in this matter.' He insisted, 'I deprehend [seize upon, surprise] in myself more then an alacrity, a vehemency to do service to that company [Somerset and co.].'[15]

There was no escaping such company now that he had started keeping it. In the same letter he mentions that he is going to dine with Sir Arthur Ingram, a relative outsider at Court but a massively wealthy merchant who was part of the Somerset faction. Donne was probably grateful that no pamphlet was eventually required. Mixed feelings about the affair are actually hinted at in the epithalamion he wrote for Somerset and his bride. The poem is a rustic dialogue in which *Idios* ('the self', i.e. Donne) is pestered by *Allophanes* ('One who seems like another'), who asks why the 'Unseasonable man, statue of ice' has not bothered going to the great wedding.[16]

Idios replies that he knows how great it is anyway so he has no reason to witness it personally. It is unlikely in any case that there would have been a place for Donne at the wedding; yet one important reason for his absence was that he could hardly see. In September, he told Garrard that 'if I doe mine eyes a little more injurie, I shall lose the honour of seeing you at Michaelmas; for by my troth I am almost blinde.'[17] As the Court got ready for the big day, Donne's eyesight worsened; this both prevented him from attending and physically blotted out the whole spectacle for him – an occasion that his younger anti-sycophantic self would have found too hypocritical even for a satire. Without quite willing his condition to afflict those around him, he found himself wondering what would happen if his semi-blindness proved catching: 'It is one of my blinde Meditations to think what a miserable defeat it would be to all these preparations of braverie, if my infirmitie should overtake others.'[18] Whether his complaint was the result of an infection, or a stress-related reaction to events, he still seems to have been disturbed by the selective blindness of the Court – the choice people made not to see what was going on. He was close enough to Somerset to know why Sir Thomas Overbury had been locked up in the Tower; and perhaps to suspect why Overbury had died there in September, after days of convulsive vomiting.

As the new year progressed, Donne recovered, but his family all fell terribly ill. His new son Nicholas died while just a baby, probably in this burst of sickness. On top of this Ann, already pregnant again – though she had given birth only five months before – suffered a miscarriage, and fell into a depression broken only by anxiety for her other children. In February, Donne wrote from amid his fevered little ones: 'I have already lost half a child, and with that mischance of hers, my wife hath fallen into an indisposition, which would afflict her much, but that the sicknesse of her children stupefies her: of one of which, in good faith, I have not much hope.' While Ann, seemingly catatonic with grief and tiredness, did her best to nurse the ailing babies, Donne's mind was clearly twitching with worry about feeding and housing them. A bemused postscript to this letter notes that he has heard nothing from the Earl of Somerset since dispatching the epithalamion. Conceivably, Somerset was put out by the lateness of the poem; despite lavish expense, his December wedding had been socially a rather lonely affair. He and his bride had received few gifts and fewer tributes. In any case, the supply of tips from this patron had evidently dried up, for the moment at least, and Donne was unsure how he was to meet the medical costs that his children were building up for him. He was driven to admit that 'if God should ease us with burials, I know not well how to perform even that.' He was saying here that he couldn't afford the funerals, but admitting that he was incapable of 'performing' them personally – digging graves for his children himself.[19]

For in mid-March, he and Ann also succumbed: 'Sir,' he wrote to Goodyer, 'it hath pleased God to adde thus to my affliction, that my wife hath now confessed herself extremely sick.' She had struggled on nobly, then collapsed: 'She hath held out thus long to assist me, but is now overturn'd, & here we be in two beds, our graves.' Donne, it seems, had 'confessed' to being very ill some time previously, when he had become unable to keep his food down: 'I have passed ten daies without taking any thing . . . I have purged and vexed my body much since I writ to you, and this day I have missed my fit: and this the first time, that I could discern any intermission.'[20]

As he often did, Donne had resumed his correspondence as soon as his malady made it physically possible, and as usual he was unwilling to speak for long about mere domestic concerns. It took him the rest of the spring to be able to report that he had 'relapsed into good degrees of health'. But in mid-May, when he wrote to his Court sponsor Sir Robert Ker, 'desiring to be maintained in your memorie', he explained that his own recovery brought him no relief: 'I have paid death one of my Children for my Ransome.' The letter is ostensibly just a courtesy note, one of hundreds Donne dispatched to influential and well-disposed parties; but it stands out as a stifled sob. He apologized for even mentioning his bereavement, yet explained 'Because I loved it well, I make account that I dignifie the memorie of it, by mentioning of it to you, else I should not be so homely.'[21] The *it* in that sentence was his three-year-old daughter Mary, who was buried on 18 May at a cost of five shillings and sixpence:[22] Donne no doubt respects the grammatical fact that 'child' is a genderless noun, and so best represented by the impersonal pronoun. But the *it* his daughter becomes in this apologetic note makes her very dead indeed; and indicates a growing numbness in Donne himself.

He worried a great deal that he was not taking proper care of his family. Yet although to some extent he led a fairly leisurely life, he worked tirelessly to improve his prospects. In a way, he was damned by his upbringing. His father had made an excellent living as an ironmonger, and if Donne had gone into the trade himself he would almost certainly have been materially much better off. But that would have meant surrendering not only an intellectual life, but also the class aspirations that his background had fostered in him. Donne was educated and nurtured as a gentleman, and his early poetry shows that he clearly regarded 'prentises' as social inferiors.[23] For Donne to go into reverse was unthinkable, and practically impossible: even had he been so inclined, there was no trade he could pick up. Instead he had to compete for one of the very few lucrative offices that were granted by royal or aristocratic favour from time to time. And for twelve years he had been passed over every single time one had come up.

He may have felt intermittently that he was regaining some ground. The spring and summer of 1614 found him back in the House of Commons. He represented the south-west borough of Taunton, a constituency in the gift of Sir Edward Phelips, the Master of the Rolls, a senior official in Chancery, whom he knew through mutual connections with Egerton's office, the Inns of Court and the literary lawyers of the Mermaid group. Several people, in fact, were prepared to offer Donne a seat: he was based in London, was needy and diligent, and thus could be counted on to attend sessions regularly. Sir Edward Herbert, who was going to the Low Countries on a tour of duty, asked him to represent his family borough of Montgomery in his absence. Goodyer too, who also entered the Commons, offered to procure him a place.[24] Yet Phelips's offer, coming from outside his fixed set of friends, evidently appeared the most advantageous. Donne thus became a Member of the 'Addled' Parliament of 1614, which in the course of its lengthy wrangling managed to pass absolutely no legislation whatsoever. Donne was appointed to several committees and was well placed to make something more of a name for himself as a political figure; but as it turned out, he once again found it more prudent to keep his mouth firmly shut. The old question of confining the royal prerogative came up in debates over monopolies and customs duties levied by authority of the crown; and while Donne belonged to a faction in the Commons that was determined to assert the will of Parliament, led by his old friend John Hoskins, he owed too much to the King's personal circle – men like Somerset and Lord Hay – to do or say anything controversial.

Several of Donne's friends, however, directly criticized royal policy and practice. John Hoskins and Sir Walter Chute, Donne's travelling companion from ten years before, were sent to the Tower for speaking their minds too plainly on the King's Scots favourites' – with Somerset the target – financial abuses in Court, and the repression of parliamentary rights. Sir Henry Wotton, who was also a Member, had little sympathy. For him these backbenchers had illusions of grandeur, acting as if they were in the Senate of Venice, 'Perpetual Princes' rather than humble subjects who would go back to ordinary life as commoners when the Parliament closed.[25] It would be interesting to know where Donne stood on the matter; but his dependent position denied him the luxury of expressing an opinion.

As parliamentary business fumbled on, he kept up his attempts to gain employment that would bring in some real money and a little more self-respect. He kept doing the best he could to milk his connection with Somerset. In March, the ambassadorship to Venice was vacated by Sir Dudley Carleton. Donne felt entitled to put himself forward for the post, which Somerset was still in a position to secure for him. 'I humbly beseech your Lordship to pardon me the boldness of asking you, Whether I may not be sent hither,' he wrote.[26] It was an extremely speculative effort, which sure enough failed, as did another campaign for office, Donne's last in state affairs, that came to a head just after Parliament closed in the summer.

Donne wrote to remind Somerset that he had informed him over a year ago of his intention of entering the Church, which the favourite had persuaded him to defer for the time being.

Remarkably, Donne managed to be both firm *and* obsequious: since, he argued, 'I am now a year older, broken with some sicknesse, and in the same degrees of honestie as I was, your Lordship will afford me one commandement, and bid me either hope for this businesse in your Lordship's hand, or else pursue my first purpose [i.e. of becoming a priest].'[27] Donne still seems to have regarded going through with this 'first purpose', and actually taking orders, as a last resort – little short of a desperate measure. The exact nature of the 'businesse' in hand, an office or patent to be conferred by royal authority, has not been recorded, but Donne seems to have felt that his chances were good. King James was apparently considering his application. On 17 July, the Court set out on its annual progress through the shires, and Donne prepared himself to follow wherever it went. Straitened circumstances had obliged him to sell his horse, so he borrowed one from his brother-in-law and fellow MP, Sir Robert More. Five days later his hopes were dashed: the King of Denmark arrived on a surprise visit, obliging James to rush back to London, pushing all other business, including Donne's suit, out of the way. Donne was flattened: 'Our predecessors were never so conquered by the Danes as I am this time,' he told More dejectedly. The sudden arrival had 'dispossessed me of so near hopes as lacked little of possession'. He had almost been there; he could all but taste success. Now he was back at the bottom of the heap. 'Therefore, Sir, I send back your horse.'[28]

As the Danish ships moved back down the Thames, the smoke of several great banquets rising behind them, and King James renewed his tour of the country, Donne refused to allow his hopes to be drawn out again: 'I forebear to make any further tryall in that businesse till the King come into these quarters.' He had, however, been greatly encouraged by an interview with his old master Thomas Egerton, now Lord Ellesmere, the Lord Chancellor. Egerton's co-operation at Chancery would be vital in completing the paperwork and putting the Seal on whatever grant Donne was hoping to receive; he may also have been able to help Donne with securing it in the first place.

The former secretary, visiting his old precinct at York House, was delighted by his reception. Egerton was still enduring his hellish marriage to the Countess Dowager of Derby, with her 'cursed railing and bitter tongue'. But he was stoical: 'I thank God I neuer desired longe life nor neuer had lesse cause to desire it.'[29] The old man was grateful for whatever friendly company he could come by, especially that of a former servant who reminded him of happier days. Donne told Goodyer that Egerton 'gave me so noble and so ready a dispatch; accompanied with so fatherly advise, and remorse for my fortunes, that I am now, like an Alchymist, delighted with discoveries by the way, though I attain not mine end.' The pleasure here is tinged with a sad admission. Donne was relieved and thrilled to make peace with his past, and recover the respect and goodwill of the man who had dismissed him: he felt a 'voluptuous loathnesse' to let the taste of reconciliation 'go out of my mouth'.[30] Yet despite such passing fortuitous 'discoveries', comparing himself to an alchemist, he seems to have lost all real hope of his end – finding the 'philosopher's stone' that would turn the lead of his life into gold.

The venture of course fell through. According to Walton, King James's opinion was now set: '*Mr* Donne *is a learned man, has the abilities of a learned Divine; and will prove a powerful Preacher,*' he is reported to have told the Earl of Somerset, '*and my desire is to prefer him that way, and in that way I will deny you nothing for him.*'[31] Donne had hit the same wall again and again so far as his secular ambitions were concerned. He was deeply in debt, with no hope of any improvement in his circumstances. There were plenty of potential patrons and patronesses, all happy to receive the gift of an authentic Donne tribute in verse; but few that he could really look to for steady support. The Countess of Bedford, for example, had grown very distant during the past two years. She loathed the Earl of Somerset, disapproved of many others Donne had publicly praised and benefited from, and had long ceased to be the one for whom Donne reserved 'not only all the verses, which I should make, but all the thoughts of womens worthinesse'.[32] He supplied poems pretty much on demand, especially when encouraged by alms. In

August, having been urged to pay his respects to Lady Salisbury in verse, he explained the difficulty of his position as follows: 'I should be loath that in any thing of mine, composed of her, should not appear much better then some of those of whom I have written. And yet I cannot hope for better expressings . . .'[33] The dilemma may be taken as typical: besides the danger of going stale, there was the risk of repetition. If different ladies received too similar compliments, and then compared notes, he would be ruined.

Earlier in the year, however, he had made one last supreme effort to win back Lady Bedford's favour. In February her twenty-one-year-old brother, Lord Harrington, died of smallpox, and Donne composed long, dark 'Obsequies' in his memory. Delivery of the work was delayed by his poor health, but it was presently dispatched, along with a letter to Lady Bedford pleading for assistance. She may not quite have gathered the depth of his need: a serious illness two years before, just after he returned from his trip abroad with the Drurys, had left her a changed and shaken woman. She had since become attracted towards Puritanism, had abandoned make-up and finery, and relied for guidance on an extremist preacher called John Burgess, whom many of her former dependants learnt to despise. And although she was, it seems, really touched by the poem for her brother, her own financial difficulties made it impossible for her to alter Donne's. Increasingly, it seemed that he had nowhere to turn for help. Except, perhaps, to the crucified figure that had loomed behind him on the road on Good Friday the year before.

On his way between leisurely sojourns at the homes of Goodyer and Sir Edward Herbert, he had kept his back to Christ – not from any lack of religious feeling, but from a surfeit of fear and humility. How could he look upon the precious blood, 'The seat of all our Soules . . . Made durt of dust'?[34] For years, every time that he had considered becoming a priest, the spiritual load had seemed too much; and also, more secretly perhaps, the material benefits had simply seemed too little. If he took orders, that would be it: there could be no further applications for lucrative positions within the state. And if the Church failed to provide him with a reasonable

benefice – one worth at least a little more than the living he scraped
together from fawning and favour-mongering around Court –
then his family situation would only be worse than ever. The older
his children grew, the more money he would have to spend on
them if they were to stand any chance in their own struggle to
sustain themselves as tattered gentry.

Yet by November, it must have seemed impossible for things
ever to get any worse. Donne's seven-year-old son Francis died,
either still suffering or no doubt weakened from the bout of
sickness that hit the entire family the previous winter. The move
from Mitcham may have given Donne drier walls, but it brought
no luck in terms of welfare: the noxious city air, the greater
risk of infection from the denser populace, made Drury Lane an
unwholesome place for bringing up young children. Francis was
the third child the Donnes had lost in a year. The usual payment
of five and a half shillings was made for a little grave and for the
bell to be tolled at the family's parish church of St Clement Danes.
Donne made no open reference to this loss in any letter, but a
two-line epigram, 'Niobe', may date from this time. Niobe was
the bereaved mother who, in myth, wept for her children even
after she was turned to stone:

> By childrens births, and deaths, I am become
> So dry, that I am now mine owne sad tombe.

Donne still clung to his wife. However much he was away from
her, there was no question in his mind of their marriage ever being
shaken. The impulsive initial passion, and the complacent later
sense of being spiritually at one, had merely given way to an
assumed union, maintained with gruff tenderness: as he told Ann's
brother in August, 'we had not one another at so cheap a rate, as
that we should ever be weary of one another.'[35]

Not long after Francis died, Donne gave in: he decided once
and for all on becoming a priest – mainly because it seemed the
only way left to him of taking care of his family. When he made
the decision public, however, it did not seem an abrupt one to

those who knew him well. He had maintained both his studies of divinity and his connections within the Church. He was on good terms not only with Thomas Morton, Dean of Gloucester, the controversialist who first urged him to consider the priesthood, but also with, among others, Morton's friend John Overall, recently promoted from Dean of St Paul's to Bishop of Coventry and Lichfield, and John King, Bishop of London. Isaak Walton reports that Donne had been working hard on his knowledge of Greek and Hebrew, and he seems to have been studying with one of the most noted experts of his day: while still convalescing from his illness in spring 1614, Donne mentioned that 'Dr *Layfield*' – one of the senior churchmen who worked on the Authorized Version of the Bible – was coming around to spend the day with him.[36] He had also been trying his hand at the kind of composition that sermon-writing would involve, and produced a series of learned, technical commentaries on the opening verses of the first two books of the Bible. These were the *Essayes in Divinity*, which his son John – who edited and published them – claimed were written while Donne was still 'obliged in Civill business, and had no ingagement in that of the Church',[37] They were, in the literal sense of 'essays', 'attempts', trials, test-pieces. A note of personal prayer comes through at the end: 'Thou hast set up many candlesticks, and kindled many lamps in mee,' Donne said to God, 'but I have either blown them out, or carried them to guide me in and by forbidden ways.'[38]

Many who knew him by name and reputation, however, might well have been shocked by his decision. For most of his admirers and enviers alike, Donne remained the erotic poet and satirist who had made a scandalous marriage. But his friends were generally supportive. On impulse, now that he had opted definitively for the religious life, Lady Bedford offered to pay off all his debts for him. These had evidently increased drastically since he had taken on the expense of a sizeable city house, and he needed to get rid of them if he was to have the right public image as a minister. Taking the offer at face value, almost weeping with gratitude towards the 'good Lady', Donne told Goodyer in December that

he had gone about 'fixing times [i.e. for repayment] to my creditors; for by the end of next terme, I will make an end with the
world, by Gods grace.'[39]

About a week later, Donne explained that he was going to say
goodbye to his old life in one other special way. He begged his
friend that Lady Bedford must not hear a word about this, however,
until the last possible moment: 'One thing I must tell you; but so
softly, that I am loath to hear my self: and so softly, that if that
good Lady were in the room, with you and this Letter, she might
not hear.' He was afraid his words would cry aloud like Abel's
wounds. 'It is,' he went on, 'that I am brought to a necessity of
printing my Poems, and addressing them to my Lord Chamberlain.'
This was the desperate measure he had contemplated back in 1611,
and then put aside when Drury required his services abroad. By
1614, Donne was a 'name afloate' in literary London and beyond.
But publishing the *Songs and Sonets*, the elegies and satires, at this
juncture was much more impolitic on two strong counts. Firstly,
these poems sent an ambivalent signal, to put it mildly, from one
intending to enter the ministry. As handwritten mementos of his
youth, they were perhaps acceptable. Hot off the press for an
audience of new corruptible minds, they were probably outrage-
ous. Secondly, and more importantly, Donne's choice of dedicatee
was imprudent, and suggests he was out of step with developments
at Court. The Lord Chamberlain was the Earl of Somerset; and
the days of his pre-eminence were numbered.

A move was afoot to replace him in James's favour with another
beautiful boy, George Villiers. Somerset had grown increasingly
isolated, and increasingly insecure about the King's disposition
towards him. But he had given Donne sufficient aid to keep him
just far enough from the breadline to get by, and still apparently
regarded the candidate priest as his own property. Until recently,
Donne had encouraged this attitude in his patron. The dedication
to an edition of his poems – 'not for much publique view,' he
muttered to Goodyer, 'but at mine own cost, a few Copies' – was
perhaps all that lay within Donne's gift to pay Somerset off; while
possibly wringing out a further contribution for the alleviation of

his debts, and gaining some extra help in finding a good living within the Church. But the prospect made him wretched. He had always kept his early, and more recent personal, work away from the press: now he had the added indignity of the attachment the edition would announce to the world. 'I know what I shall suffer from many interpretations: but I am at an end, of much considering that.' Reduced to being a 'Rhapsoder of mine own rags', Donne even had to call on Goodyer to help him gather his material, since he had not kept copies of many of the poems he wished to include. This had to be done now, he said, because it would be impossible for him to print such poems as a priest – in terms of purchasing power, they would soon be valueless: 'I must do this, as a valediction to the world, before I take Orders.'[40]

At this time Donne comes across as dead-witted, heavy, dark beneath the eyes, pursuing social tactics that only the mixture of exhaustion, bereavement, disappointment and sheer worry in his heart could make seem like sense. He had considered publishing his earlier verse before, but as it happened, once again no volume of the poems appeared. He may just have been unable to go through with it; he may have dropped the scheme in a desperate attempt to appease Lady Bedford. If this was so, his retraction came too late. The Countess went back on her earlier offer of paying off his debts, donating only £30 instead. As so often, Donne wrote to Goodyer for emotional release; who, as so often, actually had his own money troubles to think about. Goodyer had recently refused to obey a summons from Chancery, leaving Egerton, the Lord Chancellor, 'moved, and incensed'. The good-natured knight had also continued to look after Tobie Mathew's affairs for him, damaging his own reputation by doing so.[41] But he seems to have been one of those rare friends who could simply absorb the shockwaves from the lives of those close to him without losing his own balance.

Donne's letter howled: the Countess had gone back on her word and betrayed him. He was not at all impressed that the elegy he wrote for her brother should have moved 'her to so much compassion heretofore', when his real need now, now he wanted to be made a man of God, left her cold enough to insult him with a meagre gift. 'I would you could burn this letter, before you read it,' he said, having let off some steam, 'at least do when you have read it.' He was broke, broken, and in need of help; but underneath this sense of practical emergency was the fear that Lady Bedford merely thought he was a hypocrite, grabbing at his last possible chance. And if she did, having known him so well, then so might everyone: 'she had more suspicion of my calling, a better memory of my past life,' he complained, 'then I had thought her nobility could have admitted.'[42]

Donne took holy orders on 23 January 1615. He was ordained by John King, Bishop of London, in a ceremony at the bishop's palace on the north side of St Paul's.[43] He was at a riper age than most ordinands, but in casting away his worldly nets no great changes in lifestyle were initially required of him. He received a gift of clerical vestments from his friend and supporter Lord Hay, who rejoiced in the title of Master of the Great Wardrobe. Hay sent him a congratulatory note with the present, in which he congratulated himself for coming up with the idea of Donne's career move in the first place: 'I think my perswasion first begat in you the purpose to employ your extraordinarie excellent parts in the affairs of another world,' he purred.

There were others who might have claimed the credit, including the King himself and Donne's friend Thomas Morton, but the issue was beside the point. The day was a watershed; and one small, significant, personal thing Donne did to mark it was to change his letter seal. Since early manhood, he had used the faintly demonic emblem of a crest of snakes bound up in a sheaf. This device was taken from the coat of arms of the 'antient family of *Wales*', the Dwns of Kidwelly in Carmarthenshire, from which Walton said Donne claimed descent.[44] He now replaced this crest with one of Christ crucified upon an anchor, and used his new seal on a letter to Sir Edward Herbert, who was then travelling in Italy after a period spent fighting the Spaniards in the Low Countries the year before. Writing on the 'very day wherein I took orders', Donne signed himself 'Your very humble chapleyn'.[45] He also wrote a poem about the seal to Herbert's brother George, another priest and poet. The Latin original was Englished by a contemporary:

> A sheaf of Snakes used heretofore to be
> My Seal, the Crest of our poore Family.
> Adopted in Gods Family, and so
> Our old Coat lost, unto new armes I go.
> The Crosse (my seal at Baptism) spred below,
> Does, by that form, into an Anchor grow.[46]

Donne had shed his old coat snake-fashion, and had the robes for his new life ready in the closet. He was still faintly uncomfortable, though, about the discrepancy between his former colours and those he had now taken on, and welcomed the best wishes of old friends. He wrote to thank Wotton for a letter of support: 'though better then any other you know my infirmity yet you are not scandalized with my chang of habitt.'[47] An edgy month may have passed, however, until Donne began to see the first sign of any improvement from the change. He had hoped to see the King at Newmarket a few days after his ordination, but had dropped the idea of going up to Cambridgeshire in foul January weather when he heard that James had already left.[48] Then in late February he learnt that the King had decided to have a doctorate of divinity from Cambridge conferred on him; and he was also appointed as a royal chaplain to the King. He was on his way.

On a wretched day in early March, King James and his Court struggled up to the university town. The retinue was to banquet, tour the different colleges, hear learned disputations, watch plays and generally celebrate the institution. The weather was terrible, the highways were mires, and it was hard work maintaining an air of splendour and regality. A certain diplomacy was also required: this royal pampering of Cambridge was seen as a slur to the sister-city, Oxford, whose senior dons were in grudging attendance. James ignored their feelings, however, by saying straight out that he thought Cambridge was the much more beautiful of the two cities. To the delight of the Oxford men, then, the entertainments on offer fell rather flat. The fare on the first night of the trip was a lamentable comedy called *Aemilia*. The second night's play admittedly went down a little better: this was a satire on the legal profession by George Ruggle, called *Ignoramus*, but still required sterling displays of endurance because of its length. The King's public dislike of lawyers was well known, and so too was his intolerance of long plays, but a long play berating one of his pet hates evidently satisfied him a great deal, since he returned a couple of months later to see a repeat performance. Sensitive egos, nonetheless, had been upset. The play was seen as being typical of the intellectual snobbery of university men towards practising lawyers. The society gossip John Chamberlain reported that *Ignoramus* 'hath so netled the Lawiers that they are almost out of all patience'. The Inns of Court were volatile communities, and the play caused an uproar among them. Egerton, the Lord Chancellor, did his best to calm the tumult down, but his colleague Edward Coke, the belligerent Lord Chief Justice, had no qualms whatsoever about pitching in – he 'galled and glaunced at schollers with much bitterness'.[49] King James serenely allowed the row to intensify around him.

Donne, as usual, kept his active part in the festivities to a minimum. He was there to be made a doctor of divinity, not to upset anyone. With the Cambridge dons' self-esteem carefully brought to glowing point, the real Court business of the visit could begin. James had arranged for a mass conferral of honorary degrees: 'almost all the courtiers went foorth masters of art at the Kings beeing there,' noted Chamberlain. The senior officers of the university accepted this block-booking, grudgingly, as necessary payback for their few days in the limelight, but would on no account hear of doctorates being granted as royal gifts. 'The vice chancellor and university were exceeding strict on this point,' wrote Chamberlain. Among other requests, they turned down 'the Kings intreatie for John Dun . . . yet they are threatned with a mandat'.[50] The King left Cambridge in something of a huff, and a miserably awkward few days followed for Donne, who remained behind, as the spat continued. Presently the vice-chancellor and the other intransigents were levered into obliging the King's request, and Donne was invested with his degree. This would be a vital sign of prestige if he was to reach high places in the Church. But the academics' recalcitrance reflected a wider feeling that Donne in becoming a minister was getting something for nothing: Chamberlain recorded a rumour that the fledgling priest would be immediately appointed Dean of Canterbury Cathedral, a position that was as yet beyond Donne's wildest hopes. The letter-writer begrudged it 'that a man of his sort should seeke *per saltem* [at a bound] to intercept such a place from so many more worthie and auncient divines.'[51]

Donne resisted such suspicions by quietly adapting himself to his new profession. The most important skill he had to learn was public speaking. In Donne's heyday as a preacher, Walton enthused, he spoke 'with a most particular grace and an unexpressible addition of comeliness'.[52] But it took him a good while to perfect his delivery. Up until now, Donne had consistently avoided all kinds of public performance: he had kept scrupulously silent in both the Parliaments he attended, and even as a student at Lincoln's Inn had willingly paid a fine to be excused from his duties as master of the revels. After taking orders, he began with modest venues, speaking as a guest. Walton says that his first ever sermon was preached at a church in Paddington, then a village outside the city proper. He gave his earliest surviving sermon at Greenwich in April 1615 – probably, again, in a little parish church rather than the Queen's palace.[53] In June, he was invited by his in-laws, Sir Thomas and Lady Grymes (Ann's sister), to preach before them at Camberwell, near Southwark, apparently speaking from the pulpit in both 'forenoon and afternoon'.[54] Then on Midsummer's Day, he delivered his first sermon before a congregation of lawyers. Richard Prythergh, of the Inner Temple, informed Sir Edward Herbert (by now sojourning in Paris) that 'this day Mr donn preached att our temple; he had to much learninge in his sermon for ignoramus.'[55] The remark shows that the Inns of Court were still smarting from the Cambridge play that had lampooned them earlier in the year; but also admits that Donne had pitched his argument a little too high for his audience. Meanwhile, and more demandingly, he had also taken up his duties as one of the King's forty-eight 'chaplains-in-ordinary'. Each chaplain was required to preach every year on one Sunday of a given month; and those who pleased the King were sometimes asked to preach a second time. Donne's usual month was April, but on top of this he was also frequently asked to give additional sermons in Lent.[56] He set about learning his new craft with all the diligence he had once given his duties as a legal secretary and Court insider.

Thus began his reincarnation as 'Doctor Donne'. His former life was dying behind him – literally, in some ways. Sir Robert Drury, his demanding patron, passed away suddenly only a short time after Donne got back from Cambridge. Drury's death made little personal and material difference to Donne: they had never been close. He remained on equable terms with Sir Robert's widow, though, and it suited him to keep his family in the house on Drury Lane. London was still the place to be if he was to move up in his new profession. He was still a long way from affluence, but at least now he had a course to work and concentrate on. Besides his intellectual qualifications for a Church career, years of scrimping and scratching for alms had also equipped him with the courtier's art of self-promotion – an art he had regarded as beneath him in his youth.

One poem from around this time, however, suggests that it took him a while to come to terms with his new life. He was sensitive to the way the priesthood perhaps compromised his social status. He protested that it shouldn't be like that:

> Why doth the foolish world scorne that profession,
> Whose joyes passe speech? Why do they think unfit
> That Gentry should joyne families with it?
> As if their dayes were onely to be spent
> In dressing, mistressing and complement;
> Alas, poore joyes, but poorer men . . .[57]

He had indeed been a poorer man before taking orders: he could barely make ends meet. And no matter what lingering doubts he may still have had, in September a scandal broke that left Donne with every reason to be glad of his conversion, his ordination and the cover his new life provided. The Earl of Somerset was completely engulfed when it emerged that his former helper Sir Thomas Overbury had been poisoned in the Tower two years before. Somerset's beloved, the Countess of Essex, was terribly insecure about her new lover; she asked the notorious physician Dr Simon Forman to prepare an elixir that would help her retain Somerset's desire for her. She was also afraid of the power that Overbury still might hold over Somerset's judgement, since the two men went a long way back together. She despised Overbury; she never knew that it was he who wrote most of the love letters Somerset presented to her.

He also knew too much: he could easily have scuppered the delicate process of nullifying Lady Essex's first marriage if he revealed his role as panderer in her affair with Somerset. Sometime after he was imprisoned, it was therefore decided that Overbury should be done away with. An absurdly wide circle of assassins became involved in the murder. It took two years for the story of the crime to leak out, when the young assistant of Overbury's doctor in the Tower admitted on his deathbed that he had given the prisoner poison. A wide variety of lethal substances, in fact, had been slipped into Overbury's food by a reprehensible pair of old gaolers, a Richard Weston and one 'Mrs' Turner, whose advice the young Countess cherished. The story reached Sir Ralph Winwood, Secretary of State, who promptly accosted Sir Gervase Elwes, the Lieutenant of the Tower, for neglecting his duty. Elwes had known what was afoot. Overbury had been given poisoned tarts and jellies, which the Lieutenant had seen change colour and palpitate suspiciously with the furious chemicals inside them. Having decided to make a clean breast of what he knew to the King, in order to clear himself, Elwes was rewarded for his honesty (or guile) by being put on trial and convicted as part of the conspiracy.

At the top of the chain were the Earl and Countess of Somerset. By March 1616, they were both prisoners in the Tower, where the King now needed as governor someone in whom he could place an absolute trust; someone with neither the talent nor imagination for intrigue. He chose Donne's father-in-law, Sir George More. The Countess broke down in prison and confessed her guilt, but Somerset refused to admit to anything. He decided to fight. When the King insisted on a full trial, the fallen favourite threatened to reveal all the dirty secrets he had possessed and traded in during his years as James's favourite. The couple were eventually tried and convicted, but a deal was done: their sentence was remitted to life imprisonment, and after just five years in the Tower they were merely asked to confine themselves to a pleasant estate in the country. During his incarceration in the Tower, Somerset became the bane of Sir George More's life. More's hopes of high office had never materialized, and Somerset delighted in telling him why. His taunt was that he had often heard King James nominate More 'for great places when they fell vacant, and that he [Somerset] had still crossed him and moved the King for others'. Sir George, still 'by nature very passionate', must have wondered just what he had done to deserve such a tormentor. But the lieutenancy was an honour in its own way, and he did his duty loyally.[58]

Donne of course had nothing to do with the murder or the cover-up, but he was more than close enough to Somerset to be seriously tainted by association. It might have been impossible to gather the backing to enter the Church had he left his decision a year more. Seeking preferment through powerful figures at Court was still unavoidable, nonetheless: insider dealing was just as integral to ecclesiastical promotion as it was to state appointment. Donne, like many others, now turned his attention to a young man whom Lady Bedford had helped establish at Court with the aim of displacing Somerset. Within a few years George Villiers, soon Duke of Buckingham, would be running the country.

Donne's home life remained quietly eventful, though it settled down somewhat after the traumas of the previous year. In April he and Ann celebrated the birth of another daughter, Margaret. He surveyed the clamour of his animated household and wrote, 'I see that I stand like a tree, which once a year beares, though no fruit, yet this Mast of children.'[59] In some parts of the house there was only gurgling, squawling and hush-a-bying to be heard; more vocal playing and squabbling in some; and in others the scratchy sound of study. His elder surviving son and future editor John went through the city every day to Westminster School; the younger, George, also the brighter, would go up to Oxford in the autumn. And Ann was still coping. There is no way of knowing how hard she found her life, but the accounts we have – all male, of course, none knowing from experience what it was like to bear a child every year – insist that they remained solid as a couple. They might only have repented of their marriage, says Walton, 'if God had not blest them with so mutual and cordial affections, as in the midst of their sufferings made their bread of sorrow taste more pleasantly then the banquets of dull and low-spirited people'.[60]

There were still losses to be borne. Donne's sister, Anne Lyly, died, leaving him as the very last of the seven sleepers. He wrote sorrowfully to his mother that he was now alone 'to do the office of a child; though the poornesse of my fortune, and the greatnesse of my charge, hath not suffered me to expresse my duty towards you, as became me.' When he looked at the life of their family, it seemed like 'a continuall Tempest, where one wave hath ever overtaken another'. But now he would put things right. While meaning no disrespect to his stepfather – who spent much of his time these days in and out of gaol – he was determined to look after his mother properly, along with the rest of his great 'charge', his ever-growing 'Mast of children': 'for God's sake,' he begged her, 'pardon those negligences, which I have heretofore used towards you.'[61] They had evidently fallen out of touch in recent times: Donne could only have alienated her by branding the Papist missionaries as *Pseudo-martyrs*, by attacking the Jesuits in *Ignatius His Conclave*, and after the final reversal of his upbringing, his ordination as a Protestant priest, a conciliatory gesture of some kind was obviously necessary. He swore he would do better by

her from now on. In a miniature portrait made of him by Isaac
Oliver in 1616, he is a handsome, thoughtful-looking, self-
possessed man in early middle age, showing none of the harass-
ments of the past few years, his hair still dark, set off by a crisp
white medium ruff. Revealingly, he is in civilian, not clerical attire.
Rather than forcing him to make a valediction to the world, taking
orders had finally enabled him to recover a place within it.

III

1617–1631

16. Stone

By the time he was thirty, Nicholas Stone had already established himself as one of the kingdom's leading sculptors. He lived in a fine town house near the London church of St Martin-in-the-Fields, which he took in 1613, at the age of twenty-six, on his return from serving Henrik de Keyser, master mason of Amsterdam, as journeyman. A pair of thickset lions and a frightening gateway, made by Stone for the city's Zuider Kerk, had so impressed de Keyser that he was happy for the apprentice to marry his daughter, blessing the match by including a great quantity of Portland stone in the young girl's dowry. Stone has been accused of lacking lightness of touch in his statuary, but his stylistic excesses were exactly in key with the taste of his age for emblematic emphasis. Among his trademarks were meaty skulls and cumbersome cherubs, and they were soon in demand all over the country. Huge monuments were commissioned for among others the first Earl of Northampton, which was installed in the chapel at Dover Castle, and the tenth Earl of Ormond, in St Canice Cathedral, Kilkenny. Both of these works in time bore witness to the principle of oblivion their sculpture both expressed and resisted, in accordance with a thousand commonplaces: all on earth falls back into dust and comes to nothing. Northampton's great shrine lay among rubble by the end of the century; Ormond's was destroyed by rebellion.

But Stone by temperament and profession was not one to allow the lessons of ruins to lower his output. He worked hard, travelling as far as Scotland in 1616 to perform a relatively menial job for King James on the chapel at Holyrood Palace, showing willing in the hope of securing future royal contracts. Despite his growing prestige, Stone did not put himself above accepting smaller orders. His account books for the summer of the following year were typical: in July, he prepared a small memorial for Martha Palmer, née Garrard, the sister of Donne's former room-mate, with two winged female figures on either side of a modest cartouche. A month or so later, he carved a similar, though probably simpler piece, 'a letell tombe in a wall', for Donne's wife Ann. The Latin inscription, written by her husband, recorded her descent from the male line of the Mores of Loseley. She had died of a raging fever in her thirty-third year, it reported, after giving birth.

> At this the widower himself, infant with grief,
> Commanded that this stone speak.

Donne's handwriting, as it happened, outlasted Stone's chiselled letters. A copy of the epitaph survived in the papers of Ann's father, who presumably received it for his comments or just for his records. As if to reinforce the fact that nothing concrete would remain of her, Ann's monument itself was broken up, probably in 1680, when Christopher Wren rebuilt the Donnes' parish church of St Clement Danes, where it was placed, according to Stow, 'in the Chancel, on the North side, at the upper end'.[1]

The word Donne used to describe himself, in his Latin original, was *Infans*: literally, 'without voice', incapable of speaking, but also, as in the modern sense, infantile. The loss of Ann plunged him back into the childhood from which she had freed him. Yet his professional duties required him to suppress the needs of this infancy. As a preacher he had to keep writing and speaking tirelessly, and had to offer guidance to the children of God.

He still had something to live for; something to live on, at least. His career in the Church was making moderate progress. For any aspiring cleric to get by comfortably, without gaining a really big appointment – to a deanery or a bishopric – it was essential for him to gain livings in as many churches as possible. Although they were ecclesiastical appointments, however large or small, benefices generally lay in the control of whichever rich and powerful land-holder within whose political or geographical demesne a church might happen to be; in some cases, this would be a bishop, in others a wealthy member of the Court, in others the crown itself. A successful priest living in one parish might be simultaneously responsible for several other parishes, collecting the revenues that all brought, while living and preaching in only one or even none of them. This practice, known historically as pluralism, was an accepted aspect of the ministry. To critics, it was innately corrupt, leaving parish flocks without a shepherd. The Church responded by saying that if priests were better paid there would be no need for them to seek extra livings, but in practice most of those who gained from having more than one benefice were already quite comfortable clerics. Pluralism was technically illegal except for senior members of the clergy – bishops, deans, the heads of Oxbridge colleges, and royal chaplains. As one of the last, for Donne there was no legal limit to the number of livings he might hold along with his position at Court. As the historian Christopher Hill has said, pluralism was quite simply 'a social privilege'.[2]

To many Protestants, in particular the more Puritanically minded, Donne now belonged to a parasitical careerist clique that brought the Reformed English Church into disrepute. He was part of the 'Court clergy'. Though he appears to have had some scruples about how far pluralism should be carried, Donne by no means disqualified himself from the advantages his position brought. According to Walton, he was offered as many as fourteen benefices 'within the first year of his entering into sacred Orders', but he turned them down because 'they were in the Countrey, and he could not leave his beloved *London*'.[3] In the second year of his priesthood, though, he did accept two positions. The first was the rectory of Keyston in Huntingdon, a gift from King James in January 1616, and the other was the rectory of Sevenoaks in Kent, in June the same year. This was arranged for him by his old master Thomas Egerton, the Lord Chancellor. The paperwork for the grant of Sevenoaks contains a note that 'This was graunted by my Lord without anie petition in writing.'[4] In other words, Donne was given the benefice without the expense and trouble of having to apply for it. The rectory was ideal for a priest not planning to spend much time in the parish. In recognition that the rector

would be largely absent from his flock at the church of St Nicholas
– that he might never set foot inside the door, in fact – a vicar was
employed to do the actual work. This was habitually a minister
from quite another class of clergyman to that which Donne hoped
to join. During Donne's time, the vicar of St Nicholas in Sevenoaks
was one William Turner, appointed in 1614. Turner stayed and
served the parish for thirty years.[5] For Donne, the position involved
an easy (if insubstantial) £13 per annum without pastoral obligations, though he did on occasion come to Sevenoaks to preach.
His patrons the Earl and Countess of Dorset had their residence
nearby at Knole, and entertained him as their guest. The Countess
in particular was an admirer of Donne and his work – one of
the well-read aristocratic females he found so easy to enchant,
she could, he is supposed to have said, 'discourse of all things,
from Predestination to Slea-silk'. The Earl, her husband Richard
Sackville, was also a 'great lover of scholars and soldiers', and indeed ruined himself through 'an excessive bounty towards them'.
Among other indulgences, 'His life is an empty record of gambling,
cock-fighting, tilting; of balls and masques, women and fine
clothes,' according to one of Sackville's descendants, who found
that he was a trial to his genuinely subtle and thoughtful wife.[6]

The sinecure at Sevenoaks was the last favour that Thomas
Egerton, now Lord Ellesmere and Viscount Brackley, had chance
to bestow on Donne. He too died in the summer of 1617, provok-
ing the customary hail of elegies that followed the demise of a state
figure, along with the odd sour remark. He was remembered by
some as 'severe and implacable, a great enemie to parlements and
common law, only to maintain his own greatness, and the exorbi-
tant jurisdiction of his court of chancerie.' He was also reputed to
have been stingy. 'One thing is much noted in his will that he
gave nothing to the poore or to his grandchildren but lefte all to
his sonne.'[7] He had been promised an earldom by the King before
his death, but time ran out before he could be presented with it.
The gigantic fortune Egerton amassed during his lifetime, however, easily enabled his heir to afford the bribe that the ruling
favourite at Court required to secure the title. Having paid the

Marquis of Buckingham the astronomic sum of £20,000 to inter-
cede with the King on his behalf, Egerton's gout-ridden son John
became Earl of Bridgewater.

Presently, though, Egerton's wealth and property became a
subject of dispute in the legal labyrinth over which he had presided
for decades. The strife Egerton had arbitrated for so long now
became part of his family's inheritance. The widow of his elder
son, Thomas, stepped up to fight for the portion of capital that she
and her children had been promised in her marriage settlement.
Thomas Egerton the younger had been the friend who recommended Donne to his father for a secretarial job. He was killed in
the Earl of Essex's terrible Irish campaign, leaving his wife in
severe trouble with his debts; and now she wanted her dues. Her
experience of meeting the demands of her spendthrift husband's
creditors had given her the strength and instinct to claw for every
shilling, though it was eventually found, in the new Earl of
Bridgewater's favour, that her prenuptial agreement became invalid
when her husband died before his father. At around the same time
that Bridgewater was being sued by his sister-in-law, he was also
taken to court by her daughter, the wife of one Sir Thomas
Leigh. This foully convoluted case was fought over the rights to a
parsonage at Gresford in Denbigh. It heightened old Egerton's
reputation for tight-fistedness, and in the course of the proceedings
Donne himself was asked to testify in writing to Chancery. Donne
gave his general opinion on such matters from the pulpit. The
Church Fathers, he commented, 'scarse excuse any suite at lawe
from sinne, or occasion of sinne . . .' His own legal advice was: 'yf
any man will sue thee at lawe for thy coate, Let him have thy
cloake too, for if thine adversary have it not, thine advocate will.'[8]

The jibe at the expense of the legal profession surely raised a
quiet laugh at its original venue, in the dilapidated and over-
crowded old chapel of Lincoln's Inn. Donne was returned to his
old haunt in October 1616, when the Benchers of the Inn voted
him their Reader in Divinity. The Benchers constituted 'the self-
perpetuating oligarchy of senior members who ruled the house',
and they were glad to have Donne among their number.[9] The

appointment reunited him on a daily basis with many friends of his youth, including Christopher Brooke. Brooke had been a Bencher since 1610, and was probably instrumental in having the necessary quiet words that secured the position for Donne. He was nonetheless an ideal candidate for the Readership. The Benchers were young blades, former wenchers, who had become old codgers without quite seeing the change in themselves. The Inn provided a mixture of institutional comforts: it was part scholastic college, part guildhall, part gentleman's club for professionals of similar intelligence and social standing. The Benchers paid Donne £60 a year – not a fabulous amount, but a sound income – gave him lodgings and bestowed other little courtesies. 'The love of that noble society was expressed to him in many ways,' wrote Walton.[10] Donne's sermons address the 'dearly beloved' of Lincoln's Inn as friends. It was like coming home or, put less kindly, being admitted into a home, and it may well have been the supportive community the Inn held that stopped Donne breaking down completely in his first years as a widower.

The terms of his employment required him to preach in the morning and the evening of every Sunday in term-time, amounting to about fifty sermons a year. This was a heavy writing task that certainly called for a great deal of time in seclusion, but which still directed his studies and his solitude to a public end. Subordinate to the Reader was a chaplain who took care of most of the pastoral duties: this man, Edward May, was awarded a pay rise at the same meeting of the Bench which confirmed Donne's appointment as preacher. The Benchers recognized and rewarded May's 'good carrage and paynes in his place', perhaps in expectation that he take on further duties.[11] But Donne himself still seems to have been active in the collegiate society, in particular in encouraging a long-delayed and cash-starved project to construct a new chapel for the Inn. The Black Books containing the minutes of the Benchers' council pay eloquent tribute to 'the kind and loving respectes of the said Mr Doctor Donne towards them'.[12] Furthermore, his sermons frequently reiterated his feeling that a life of self-inflicted isolation was practically and morally impossible.

Earlier in 1617, before Ann died, he had restated his commitment to fulfilling his share of humanity.

Gripping the lectern in the yard outside St Paul's Cathedral, 'In a word, he that will be *nothing* in this world, shall be nothing in the next,' he declaimed. 'Nor shall he have the *Communion of Saints* there, that will not have the Communion of good men here.' The pulpit was a sculpted cabin of stone and wood, offering the preacher moderate shelter from the intermittent skiffs of March rain. He scanned the vast crowd about him, a coughing, murmuring mixture of the high and low. It was immensely arguable how many good men there were standing among the multitude, and hard to say, quite often, what a good man actually was. The most important thing for Donne was that everyone took their place, involved themselves in society. He had no patience, despite the gratitude he felt for the peace of his study and silent communication with his books, for those who 'retire themselves into *Cloysters* and *Monasteries*'. Instead, he insisted,

Every man hath a *Politick life*, as well as a *naturall life*; and he may no more take himself away from the world, then he may make himself away out of the world. For he that dies so, by withdrawing himself from his calling, from the labours of mutual society in this life, that man *kills himself*, and God calls him not.[13]

The specimens of higher political life on display on this early spring morning were some of the Court's most senior administrators, among them the Archbishop of Canterbury, the King's Secretary of State, and 'divers other great men'.[14] The new Lord Keeper of the Seal, Francis Bacon, was also present. King James had confirmed his friendship to Bacon by appointing him Lord Keeper immediately after the Lord Chancellor, Egerton, had resigned the Great Seal. A week later, Bacon was one of the last to see Egerton alive. He brought his predecessor news that the King intended to make him an Earl. Egerton, barely able to breathe, gasped out thanks, but confessed that such things were to him by now 'all but vanities'.[15] For Bacon, such sentiments were entirely fitting as

commonplaces for a great man on his deathbed, but not a feasible
attitude to honour for one with years ahead of him. His promotion
fulfilled his greatest wish. His father, Nicholas, had served as Lord
Keeper for twenty-one years, and he had grown up determined to
match this example.

This was Donne's first sermon at Paul's Cross, the most important preaching venue in the land, and the occasion was the anniversary of King James's accession. The King himself was not in town.
He was in Scotland, visiting his first kingdom for the first time
since inheriting the more lavish lifestyle that came with the English
crown. Donne's text was Proverbs 22:11, 'He that loveth pureness
of heart, for the grace of his lips, the king shall be his friend.' It
might have to be admitted that pureness of heart was scanty in
'*Politick life*': but impurity was a reality of 'mutual society', no
excuse for a man to 'take himself away from the world'. For his
part, Donne met the requirements of the occasion. He thanked
God for the stability of the realm, and for the (still largely theoreti-
cal) union of Scotland and England, remarking how 'it is a pleasant
sight to look upon a *Map of this Island*, when it is all one.' He
elegized and eulogized Queen Elizabeth, and praised James.
Though not present physically, the King was still with them,
Donne averred, through the reach of his authority and his oneness
with his subjects: 'He is not gone from us; for a *Noble* part of this
Body, (our Nation) is gone with him, and a *Royal* part of his Body
stays with us.'[16] Donne used his old idea that absence, if one
thought deeply enough of the missing party, was only an illusion.

The political reality was somewhat different. While James was
gone, Bacon and his faction 'effectively controlled the government
of Britain'.[17] The Lord Keeper set about enjoying himself. 'There
was much ado, and a great deal of world,' he would airily inform
his patron Buckingham, after a long inaugural day of processions
and ceremonies, culminating in a feast costing an astronomical
£700. 'But this matter of pomp, which is heaven to some men, is
hell to me, or purgatory at least.'[18] In the following weeks he
developed gout, skimped on his legal duties, and ignored a couple
of the King's specific orders.

The Paul's Cross sermon touched on themes that preoccupied Donne greatly over the years. Time and again elsewhere he reiterated his commitment to the 'Politick' as well as the 'natural' life. Living might well, he accepted, be a matter of endurance, but 'There cannot be a greater unthankfulnesse to God then to desire to be *Nothing* at all . . . To desire to be out of the world, rather then to glorifie him, by thy patience in it,' he told the faithful at Lincoln's Inn, echoing his own words to Henry Goodyer, in depression and frustration at his career a decade earlier.[19] 'It is not enough to shut our selves in a cloister, in a Monastery, to sleep out the tentations of the world.'[20] One had to come out, to work, to fail, to sin, to enter into things. Donne realized that for his part it was preaching that had called him into the open. He worked hard at mastering the craft it required. He quickly saw that there was more to it than coming up with good ideas and expressing them ingeniously. There was the much greater obligation of making a moral lesson understood. Different venues came with differing licence and expectations; but it was equally important that his words reached all his listeners at the level of comprehension he desired. 'No man profits by a Sermon that he heares with paine, if he doe not stand easily,' he said, adapting St Augustine; the same was true 'if he doe not *understand* easily'.[21] This principle did not deter Donne from developing elaborate and imaginative conceits to illustrate his arguments, as he had in his poetry, but it was clear to him that preaching involved getting a point across.

The sermon was for many worshippers now the most important and interesting part of the religious service. King James himself often only arrived at chapel when the preaching was to begin, and there was a high level of discrimination in the audiences Donne faced. Public speaking itself was still a relatively new ordeal. Before being ordained Donne had always avoided all kinds of performance, at college, at Lincoln's Inn, and during two stints as a Member of Parliament. Now his regular work involved speaking for hours on end under popular scrutiny; and the stadium conditions of a Paul's Cross sermon called for especial stamina. Coming back to Drury Lane, hoarse in the throat after this his first attempt, he returned to Ann, then midway through her last pregnancy. During his sermon, he had warned of the dangerous slumber a woman could induce in a man when 'she possesses him, fills him, transports him'. But he had also spoken more softly of the companionship of marriage. Passion and physical love, he said, 'must necessarily have intermissions'. But, 'if a woman think to hold a man long, she provides herself with some other capacity, some other title, then meerly as she is a woman: Her wit, and her conversation, must continue this love; and she must be a *wife*, a *helper*.'[22] What might seem now the rather condescending patriarchal notion of a partner as a helpmate, an assistant, was for Donne an elevating idea. For a marriage to work, a husband had to be able to converse with his wife. As a preacher, Donne had to be able to test out on Ann the clarity of an expression in a sermon, much as he had been able to share a poem with her. The highest compliment Donne could have paid the depth of their relationship was that he and Ann did not love each other merely as man and woman.

His first public engagement after she died was to preach in the church where she was buried, St Clement Danes. He had no official connection with the parish, but since the rector had died back in March and now, in the dog-days of summer, a successor had yet to be appointed, Donne could easily fill in for a few Sundays until the legal term began and his obligations at Lincoln's Inn resumed.[23] That he took on extra work points to a need to keep himself busy and his mind moving, but the occasion itself was specifically cathartic. With Ann's monument newly installed in the chancel, the enclosed space near the Communion table, usually reserved for members of the clergy and segregated from the rest of the church, it was both an intimate and a public venue for him to grieve in. He addressed both his neighbours and the cool stone bearing Ann's name. In the service that Isaak Walton describes, Donne relieved private feelings by calling on the support of those present: breaking down intermittently, 'his sighs and tears, exprest in his Sermon, did so work upon the affection of his hearers, as melted and moulded them into a companionable sadness'. Donne was developing a sense of common humanity and religious community that saw pain and suffering, indeed all individual experience, as concerning, even involving, everyone. But the question remained of what was left of this solidarity when the gathering dispersed. Walton points out that as the congregation left St Clement Danes, 'their houses presented them with objects of diversion'. They went back to the separate complications of their own lives. Donne's, meanwhile, 'presented him with nothing but fresh objects of sorrow, in beholding many helpless children, a narrow fortune, and a consideration of the many cares and casualties that attend their education'.[24]

Donne's fortune was not so 'narrow' by now as Walton says – his pay from Lincoln's Inn made him reasonably secure – but he was left with the question of how to arrange his life. What he did suggests that he decided neither to withdraw and nurture his sense of loss nor to try covering it up. After a struggle to dislodge a former tenant, one debt-ridden Mr Skinner, the Benchers of Lincoln's Inn made a very comfortable set of rooms available to Donne.[25] It would have been quite possible for him to disperse his children among his wife's relations – as he certainly did, from time to time, when he went away – and closet himself in the masculine sanctuary of his workplace. But '*Cloysters* and *Monasteries*' were not for him. He chose to keep his family at their house in the busy little courtyard off Drury Lane. He also resisted another pragmatic life-move that may in time have recommended itself: a swift second marriage, in the next year or so, to a woman who could look after the family and keep the home ticking over. For many of his contemporaries, such alliances constituted a betrayal that only heaped further woes upon the widower: 'Stepdames seeldome wish and worke any good to their husbands children,' warned one social critic. 'They think they must not suffer so much a let and blocke in their way to their husbands wealth.'[26] Donne vowed to his children that he would never remarry; 'which promise he kept most faithfully'.[27]

The words carved for Ann in the little tomb in St Clement Danes suggested he could neither let go, nor accept that he and she might not one day be together again.

> Her husband – now the most abject of titles –
> Once dear to this dear one
> Vows that his ashes will join with hers here
> In New Marriage, God willing.

This hope for a 'Novo matrimonio', however, skirted close to heresy, since Christ had warned couples not to expect mortal love either to begin or resume in heaven: 'For when they shall rise from the dead, they neither marry, nor are given in marriage; but are as the angels in heaven.'[28] In one sense, Donne resisted the word of scripture and the sexless afterlife it set in store. He wanted his wife back. Another meaning, though, strives to come through or overcome the irrevocable separation death involves: an idea that instead of a bond between partners, heaven creates a union of everyone to everyone. In the first surviving sermon after the loss of his wife and 'helper', preached at Whitehall in November 1617, Donne said that 'this death . . . this Divorce is a New Marriage.'[29]

In the writing he did in the first months without her, grief emerges here and there as something more than just one feeling. It comes across as a process in which many quite contrary emotions spill out and clash. There were times, his sermons suggest, when he felt the loss as a profound relief: an opportunity to renounce once and for all his enslavement to flesh. Echoing St Augustine, 'I tooke no joy in this world, but in loving, and in being beloved,' he told the congregation at Whitehall Palace, in December: 'in sensual love it is so, but in sensual love, when we are come so far, there is no satisfaction in that . . .' This love is 'nothing but to be scourg'd with burning iron rods, rods of jealousie, of suspition, and of quarrels'.[30] His skin was branded, but at least he was free now. There were no more arguments, or excuses to be made, or comfort to be given, no more lust to relish or suppress. A deepening suspicion of 'sensual love' and all sexuality began to set in, and seeps through Donne's work for many years afterwards. We should observe, Donne said, 'that God would shewe us in the losse of our children, the sinnefull wantonness in which they were begotten and conceived'.[31] Ann and he had had twelve children, her epitaph recorded, and lost five of them; but what could anyone expect? Bereavement was a necessary punishment. Ann's death, he tried telling himself, in the most painful of his Holy Sonnets, was a lucky escape for them both.

> Since she whom I lov'd hath payd her last debt
> To Nature, and to hers, and my good is dead,
> And her Soule early into heaven ravished,
> Wholly on heavenly things my mind is sett.[32]

The first two of these lines have been described by one of Donne's editors as 'almost intolerably harsh'.[33] Read one way, they say 'She has paid her debt to Nature and is dead, to her good and my own.' He was glad, he tried telling himself, that she was gone. But the poem's opening is ambiguous. It discloses too the very opposite feeling, of irredeemable loss. For the lines also say, 'She has paid her debt to Nature, and to her own nature, and my good has died with her.' She was, as he told Goodyer years before, his 'golden one'.[34] His mind may have been wholly set on heavenly things, but years would be necessary to put it at rest with them.

'Helas, Monsieur, my tone must change,' wrote a French neighbour on Saturday, 15 August 1617, having sent his man round to Drury Lane to inquire after Dr Donne and his wife. The servant returned while he was still writing, with the news that Ann had gone into labour on the Sunday morning before, and had been delivered of a baby girl who lived barely minutes.

The ordeal behind Jean l'Oiseau's brief sympathetic note is one from which men were conventionally excluded, for their own sake as much as the mother's.[35] The darkened, candlelit bedroom where the birth took place became a female province. The mother was surrounded by her women friends, her 'gossips', there to lend help and moral support, to bring her a drink of caudle – warm sweetened ale or wine, mixed with spices – and on occasion to hold her down.[36] The ruling authority in the room was the midwife. Herbal remedies to some complications were based on subtle medicinal lore, but the physical interventions were excruciating.

If the woman's breasts were slack, devoid of milk, this was a sure sign that the baby was either dead or ailing, and swift action was required to save the mother: 'but if she travel [travail, go into labour] when she is sick of a sharp Feaver, or some such dangerous disease,' as Ann soon was, heatsick from August, 'seldom doth either Mother or the child escape death.' If the child was dead or dying, 'There must be no delay at such times especially to drive the dead Child forth before it be corrupted.' The woman had to be held down; and the midwife, having anointed her hands 'with Oyl of white Lillies, Butter, or Ducks grease . . . let her shut her hand and thrust it up into the womb to feel how the Child lyeth.' If the head was coming down foremost, the child was to be drawn out on a hook attached 'to one eye of it, or under the chin, or to the roof of the mouth', with another fastened to a parallel point. If the feet came first, each hook needed to tug 'upon the bone above the privy parts, called *os pubis*, or by some rib or back bones, or breast bones'. It was to be expected that 'by the violent drawing forth of the child, the Privy parts and Genitals of the mother [will] be so torn that her Urine and excrements come out against her will'; in which case a concoction containing bay-leaves, sage, 'Rupture-wort' and camomile, among other leaves and herbs, would help make her continent again.[37]

The science of midwifery was far from standardized: every practitioner had her own techniques, her own variations on a body of accepted wisdom. But whatever was done for Ann, her baby was dead on delivery, or died almost immediately afterwards. Donne wrote on her tomb that she in turn was taken away by a remorseless fever seven days later.

He always felt guilty towards her, the wife he 'transplanted into a wretched fortune'.[38] She had given him a child almost every year of their marriage, and the last one killed her. After watching her die, he developed an almost ferocious attitude to sexual love. The harsh task he faced, week after week, was to tell the faces looking up at him how to love and lose, and cope with sorrow when it came; how to invite it, even, and take it as God's will. 'God hath beaten downe thy greene fruite from thy beloved tree, God hath hewen downe the beloved tree it selfe, the young children and the mother of those children he hath taken from thee,' he told the students and Benchers of Lincoln's Inn, speaking also to himself, a year after Ann died.[39]

17. The Torn Ship

The true Church, Donne insisted, 'loves the name Catholique'. If one followed 'Those universall, and fundamentall doctrines, which in all Christian ages, and in all Christian Churches, have been agreed by all to be necessary to salvation . . . then thou art a true Catholique.'[1] Yet as he knew only too well, the rifts between Protestants and Papists showed little more sign of closing than they had when he published his defence of King James, *Pseudo-martyr*, in 1610; and those within the Reformed Church, between religious conservatives and radical Puritans, were worsening steadily. Sectarianism remained Donne's most heartfelt political grievance. His view of the issues involved had not changed substantially in the years since he published *Pseudo-martyr*. He still had no sympathy for the suicidal Jesuits and fugitive priests – covert missionaries such as William Harrington, for whom his brother Henry had died in Newgate – who put themselves and their loved ones at risk without proper cause. From the pulpit Donne castigated fake heroes 'suffering for schisme in pretence of Zeal, suffering for Treason in pretence of Religion'.[2] He had no patience for those 'who colouring and appareling treason in martyrdome, expose their lives to the danger of the Law, and embrace death'.[3]

Yet, as in *Psuedo-martyr*, on occasion he also quietly urged moderation on the part of the authorities, curtailing in particular the right of the King to persecute and torture. 'In intestine Conspiracies,' he would warn a few years later, '*voluntary Confessions* doe more good, than Confessions upon the *Rack*.'[4] Commenting on draconian penal laws in one of his earliest sermons, given at Whitehall, Donne urged that a King should have the right to use extreme brutal measures only as a deterrent, 'as a Bridle, the better to govern that great charge committed to him, in emergent necessities, though not in an ordinary execution [i.e. everyday punishments]'. The making and enforcing of laws required, Donne said, 'besides the authority of that Prince, the counsel and the consent of the Subject'.[5] For their time, these are actually rather brave words against tyranny. The only ruler with the power and right to proceed by martial law, striking his minions down at will, was God himself; and he, Donne warned, 'can hang thee upon the next tree; he can choak thee with a crum'.[6] This power to kill anyone, to do anything, at any time, set limits on the rights and powers of those beneath the Lord on high.

What pained Donne above all about religious schism was that God was supposed to be the glue between humans, not their greatest point of contention. Everyone, for one thing, had equal cause to be terrified of God – or, alternatively, equal cause to love and feel grateful to him. Instead, differences of faith were used to cover up political and personal differences, dicing humanity. Everyone's life, Donne was sure, was implicated in everyone else's, the common denominator being that everyone suffers, dies, comes from and returns to their maker. If someone does wrong, everyone else is implicated, since we are all fruit from the same tree:

If a man of my blood, or alliance, doe a shamefull act, I am affected with it; If a man of my calling, or *profession*, doe a scandalous act, I feel my self concerned in his fault; God hath made all *mankinde of one blood*, and all *Christians of one calling*, and the sins of every man concern every man . . .[7]

Addressing the familiar worshippers in the relaxed atmosphere of Lincoln's Inn, one early summer evening in 1618, he told them that the 'dissention in Christian churches' put him in mind of a riven community of Protestants he had encountered on his travels in Europe. While accompanying Sir Robert Drury on his tour in 1612, Donne had stayed for some time in the German cathedral city of Aix-la-Chapelle (Aachen), to take the restorative waters there. He had resided in a large but crowded house that was annexed into apartments for separate families. Inquiring who lived in the rooms above him, he was told, 'Anabaptists'; and on asking who lived above and to either side of these, he received the same answer. Assuming there was some room put aside for so many members of the same sect to meet and practise their religion, Donne was informed that, although crammed together, they could never abide to meet: 'for, though they were all *Anabaptists*, yet for some collaterall differences, they detested one another.'[8]

Standing on the frontier where modern-day Germany, Belgium and the Netherlands meet, Aix-la-Chapelle was a convergence point for almost all of Christianity's clashing denominations. It was also the city of Charlemagne, the first of the German Emperors, his capital and birthplace, and still held his almost unrivalled collection of holy artefacts. Every seven years, in one of the time-honoured rituals that so infuriated members of the Reformed confession, a crowd of pilgrims massing in the square outside the Cathedral would be shown the tunic of the blessed virgin herself, the swaddling clothes of the infant Jesus, the loincloth worn by Christ on the cross, and a bloody shroud that was said to have blanketed the severed head of John the Baptist. In Roman Catholics, such objects commanded great reverence; in Protestants, they produced only ridicule or disgust. The followers of these faiths were still irreconcilable. Donne's memory of his stay amid the feuding Anabaptists was possibly jogged by the ominous course events were taking in central Europe as a result of sectarian strife.

In Prague, on the evening of 23 May 1618, a band of irate Protestant nobles had burst into the Hradschin Castle, demanding the rights and freedoms which their Roman Catholic ruler had promised them. The two senior councillors who met them turned down these requests with the authority invested in them by their emperor; but then found themselves the sacrificial victims of a symbolic protest. Cornered in a small room beyond the assembly chamber, they were seized by many hands and bundled through a window eighty feet above the ground.

Despite all the conflict that had followed the Reformation, the Roman Catholic monarchs of the Habsburg dynasty, who saw themselves as the heirs of Charlemagne, had never quite grasped the reality of the fractured, multi-confessional territory they ruled.

The Holy Roman Empire, a loose federation of smaller loose federations, stretched across the continent from the plains of Hungary to Flanders' fields, from Holstein down to the lake of Geneva. By this time, the centre of power had long drifted eastwards from Aix. The provincial rulers of the Germanic lands all owed their allegiance to the Habsburg base of Vienna. Austria ruled; but geographically, financially and martially, the Empire's backbone was Bohemia. This was a kingdom that covered, roughly, the present Czech Republic and the south-eastern corner of Poland, up to just beyond where the river Oder crosses from Germany. With Prague as its capital, Bohemia encompassed the historical regions of Lusatia, Silesia and Moravia. The make-up of its population was complex in the extreme, a difficult mixture of different Protestant sects, who together made up the majority. But the country was run by an elite of Habsburg-appointed Catholic aristocrats, and the Protestants were sick of them. When the two leading members of the puppet government were flung from the casement at Hradschin in May 1618, a defiant signal went south to Vienna.

Unlike in England, where the monarch named a close blood relative as his heir, the Bohemian and Holy Roman rulers had to be elected. Whoever was voted King of Bohemia then got a vote, one of only seven, in the election of the Holy Roman Emperor. There were no rules against an Elector voting for himself, so the more German titles a noble possessed or controlled, the greater his chances of ultimate power. In practice, the current monarch nominated a successor and a diet made up of subordinate princes and bishops confirmed his choice − providing, that is, the Habsburgs got their way. But in 1618, the Protestants of Bohemia upset this arrangement. The then King of Bohemia was the Holy Roman Emperor, Maximilian. Now it had already been agreed that the ailing Maximilian's younger cousin, Ferdinand of Styria, a vehement defender of the Roman faith, would succeed him to both his titles. Once he was King of Bohemia, Ferdinand was also expected to proceed to the Empery. However, the Bohemians had only accepted Ferdinand as their future King on the condition that he preserve their religious and political liberties. To Ferdinand, this was too great a demand; but he gave his word, following advice from senior Jesuits that lying to heretics was no sin worth mentioning. With the agreement sealed, Ferdinand's Habsburg government did not wait long before starting to close down the Protestants' churches. The Bohemians were outraged by the betrayal. They quickly made their displeasure known by defen-estrating the two councillors in Prague. Remarkably, both men survived their fall by hitting a 'pile of mouldering filth' in the castle courtyard below, but the point was made.[9] Riding the momentum, the rebel leaders then declared that Ferdinand had acted illegally by reneging on the deal. This meant, they argued, that they no longer had to accept him as their King, but could choose one of their own. Ferdinand was unimpressed. In the summer of 1618, the rebels faced a massive Imperial offensive that would have taken Prague were it not for mercenary troops sent by another of the German princes, Count Frederick of the neighbour-ing Palatinate, a staunch Protestant who by the end of the year had emerged as the leading rebel candidate to take Ferdinand's place in Bohemia.

As soon as this became clear, Britain was brought deep into the crisis. Frederick was the son-in-law of King James, whose daughter Elizabeth he married with great pomp and national jubilation in 1612. English Protestants thus felt they had a vested national interest in the region: Frederick was their man. With the inheritance of his grandchildren at stake, James received appeals from home and abroad to plunge into the fray and aid England's Protestant brethren in Bohemia. The dispute had long since become an international affair. Spain was seriously alarmed by the idea that the rebels might make Frederick their King. 'The broiles in Bohemia are here much taken to heart,' wrote the English envoy from Madrid in October 1618, 'and this Kinge professeth that he will understand that business as his owne quarell.'[10] The Spanish concerns were under-standable. With his Palatine dominion in southern Germany, Frederick already had one precious vote in the Imperial election; with Bohemia as well, he would have yet another, raising the un-thinkable prospect of a Protestant Holy Roman Emperor. Furthermore, if King James's only surviving (and rather sickly) son Prince Charles should die, Frederick would control England too. The future balance of European power rested on Bohemia.

King James blanched at the thought of getting sucked into a religious war. This was exactly what he didn't want, by strategy and temperament. His motto was *Beati Pacifici*, 'blessed are the peacemakers'. He had a personal horror of human violence, induced by a brutal childhood spent as a pawn to rival Scottish kingmakers, including his own mother. Understandably, he never seems to have shaken off a fear of assassination, commemorating the Gunpowder Plot of 1605 with religious strictness every year, and protecting his own person with 'great quilted doublets, pistol proof'.[11] But his aversion to conflict came from more than mere fearfulness. His early experiences in Scotland had sickened him to the wider permutations of the politics of warfare. His first major act of foreign policy, on becoming King of England, had been to reach a peace with Spain. As the troubles in central Europe deepened, he was the one head of state to have a real sense of how far they would spread and how long they would last if external powers waded in with force. Adopting a studiously neutral position, he voiced the hope that he might act as an arbitrator rather than an antagonist, and advised his son-in-law Frederick to tread carefully. James was also keen to avoid annoying Spain: for the sake of future harmony, in fact, he hoped that his son Charles might take a Spanish bride. So he shooed the calls for aid from fellow Protestants in central Europe by offering to send a peace delegation instead, to get the jarring sides talking.

During his years of social frustration, one of Donne's pet hopes had been that he might win a state appointment overseas. He clearly saw himself as being good diplomatic material. He had travelled extensively to perfect his modern languages and gain first-hand experience of foreign affairs. Of the formal attempts that we know about, he bid for positions in Ireland, in Virginia and even the ambassadorship of Venice. Cruelly, though, it was not until the Bohemian crisis deepened that his old wish was granted, at the wrong time and – from the perspective of his earlier self –

in the wrong capacity. King James chose Donne as the chaplain for the peace mission to Bohemia. The ambassador, meanwhile, was to be a man who had done his best to help Donne's stunted earlier career: it was Lord James Hay, now Viscount Doncaster, the friendly patron who promoted Donne's effort to become secretary to the governor of Ireland in 1608. At that time Donne's scandalous marriage, 'the worst part of my historie', as he termed it, still counted against him, and he was overlooked.[12] Now that past was buried – quite literally, since Ann was dead – and his qualifications were needed.

Hay was one of the Court's beautiful people. Donne remained fond of him from their first meeting. He was an easy-going, agreeable, good-looking man, who never struggled as others did to worm his way to the top of the Court, but merely relaxed in the King's steady favour. There had been difficult times for him too, nonetheless. His first wife, Honora, was attacked and robbed in her carriage one night in summer 1614. Pregnant, she was so traumatized that she miscarried her child, and quickly slipped away herself, never recovering from the shock. Donne grimly informed Goodyer, another friend of the couple, that 'to her end she was anguished with the memory of the execution [i.e. the conduct, actions] of that fellow which attempted her in her carriage'.[13] Two years later, however, Hay fell in love again. The lady was Lucy Percy, daughter of the Earl of Northumberland. More than fifteen years before, Northumberland had broken the news of Donne and Ann's clandestine marriage to Sir George More, and had been greeted explosively. Now the Earl experienced some fatherly alarm himself. Hay was beneath him in rank and also no friend of the northern set of Roman Catholic aristocrats to which Northumberland belonged. Northumberland was still incarcerated in the Tower of London, for his supposed part in the Gunpowder Plot. There he had passed the time in a bizarre range of scientific researches with two oddball assistants, exploring the mysteries of nature and refining a number of idiosyncratic liqueurs. On hearing of Lucy's courtship, he decided that the only sure way of protecting her was to have her detained along with him. High among the reasons for his objections was the inherent prejudice with which one tribe regards another on the far side of a shared frontier. Hay was a Scot, Northumberland was the head of one of the oldest northern English families. He made it clear 'that he was a Percie and could not indure that his daughter shold daunce any Scottish giggs'.[14]

Like More years earlier, Northumberland evidently felt that his daughter's choice of husband was too important for anyone but himself to make. He did not, however, reckon on Lord Hay's persistence. Hay used his contacts inside and outside the Tower, including the murderess Lady Somerset, still a prisoner, to maintain his relationship with Lucy. He and Lucy were married in November 1617, and Lord Hay was created Viscount Doncaster, to bring him closer in rank to Northumberland. Like Donne, it took Hay some time to win his father-in-law over; but it helped that he was soon enough able to charm the King into granting Northumberland a pardon. Some years later Donne preached a sermon at a lavish entertainment put on by Doncaster for Northumberland to mark their reconciliation.[15]

Doncaster had established his diplomatic credentials by leading a flamboyant embassy to Paris in 1616. And although Donne's knowledge of foreign affairs – especially the international intrigues of the Church – had not been officially recognized with a posting, neither had it been let go to waste. In 1615, he was given a cipher for use in diplomatic correspondence. The document, still in the Public Record Office, details the codes by which Donne was to refer to a wide variety of rulers, factions, officials, countries and contingencies, including 'Owre King', 'the King of Bohemia', 'The Jesuites', 'Warr' and 'Marriadge'.[16] As Bald points out, Donne's field of expertise was likely to have been in matters of religious controversy, a further sign that his skill in doctrinal argument, established by *Pseudo-martyr*, had not gone unnoticed. Though none of his secret correspondence has survived, by early 1619, as preparations for the trip to Germany gathered pace, Donne had probably been in occasional contact with religious leaders and English agents across Europe for four years. This was one further reason for his reluctance to go. He was convinced that he had enemies abroad: 'I goe into the mouth of such adversaries, as I cannot blame for hating me, the Jesuits, and yet I go,' he complained.[17] He was exaggerating the personal danger he faced, and aggrandizing his own status on the expedition by doing so – he ran the same risk as the others in the diplomatic party entering a war zone – but he felt threatened on all sides, from real and imaginary hazards. The mission would involve negotiations in Roman Catholic territories, notably Ferdinand's, but the international atmosphere was far too tense for any violence – any offence, even – to be offered against the diplomatic privilege of a visiting English chaplain. He recoiled, rather, from the unpleasantness of conflict itself. His place in the embassy marked the greatest test of his commitment to the 'Politick life', to leaving the cloister behind and taking up the task the world outside required of him.

The appointment was a preferment. It put Donne a little further into the limelight, and into the running for a higher post within the Church, if he performed his duties well. Yet he was appalled by the prospect of going. It was clear to his friends, too, that he was in no fit state for the long journey. Noting his continued 'sadness for his wives death', his colleagues at Lincoln's Inn had feared for some time that 'his troubled mind, with the help of his unintermitted studies, hastened the decays of his weak body'.[18] Though only forty-seven, Donne himself felt that he was succumbing to consumption. He was distraught by the state of his health, and also of his motherless household, as he distributed his seven children among relatives: 'I leave a scattered flock of wretched children, and I carry an infirme and valetudinary body,' he told Goodyer.[19] Slowly, morbidly, the thought dawned on him that in sailing for Germany he would not be going off into the wide world, but passing out of it forever. Having sent away his children, he also dispersed manuscript copies of his work among his friends, with letters that read like bequeathals. To Robert Ker, Earl of Ancram, he sent his poems and *Biathanatos*, his 'misinterpretable' treatise on suicide, famously stressing that 'it is a Book written by *Jack Donne*, and not by *Dr Donne*'. He asked Ker to keep it safe 'if I live, and if I die, I only forbid it the Presse, and the Fire: publish it not, but yet burn it not; and between those do what you will with it.'[20] The thoughts voiced in *Biathanatos* did not accord well with the public view Donne had given on suicide: he had told the crowds at Paul's Cross that a man 'may no more take himself away from the world, then he may make himself away out of the world'.[21] But the fixation with his own mortality had deepened with bereavement, and the prospect of leaving the fragile supports he had made for himself frightened him.

He was preparing for his death, willing it, even, with his mind on posterity. 'I am going out of the Kingdom, and perchance out of the world,' he wrote in the dedication to a sermon he presented to the Countess of Montgomery. 'If I never meet you again till we have all passed the gate of death, yet in the gates of heaven I may meet you all,' he told the congregation that heard his valedictory sermon at Lincoln's Inn.[22] He developed and concentrated his thoughts on the impending voyage out of existence in one of his very greatest poems. Again, as in the Holy Sonnet about Ann, he tried setting his mind on heavenly things, addressing Christ directly:

> In what torne ship soever I embarke,
> That ship shall be my embleme of thy Arke;
> What sea soever swallow mee, that flood
> Shall be to mee an embleme of thy blood . . .[23]

The ship is torn by the mere suggestion of Donne setting sail in it: the storm in his head is enough to split the timbers. He tried fixing his thoughts on God, but God offered accusing scrutiny rather than refuge. The Lord saw all, in Donne's mind, and forgot nothing. From the earliest days of mankind, the soul faced constant surveillance: God had 'hovered like a Falcon over Paradise', as Eve and Adam shared the forbidden fruit.[24] During his early years as a preacher, Donne was still plagued by thoughts of damnation, by the knowledge of his own sin and that which he, and all humankind, had inherited. His imagination went septic from dwelling on the consequences: 'Miserable man! a Toad is a bag of Poyson, and

a Spider is a blister of Poyson, and yet a Toad and a Spider cannot
poyson themselves; Man hath a dram of poyson, originall-Sin, in
an invisible corner, we know not where, and he cannot choose
but poyson himselfe and all his actions with that.'[25] Yet on top of
that was the thoughtless, inescapable sinfulness of those actions
themselves. Donne was stricken by just how easy it was to do
wrong, through 'the dangerous slipperiness, the concurrence, the
coincidence of sins'.[26] Even if one shook off the old sinful ways,
one could relapse merely by remembering them with even a hint
of pleasure, or by thinking that their taint had still not gone,
through 'a suspicion and jealousie in God, that he hath not forgiven
them'.[27] There seemed to be no way out.

Despite his reluctance, even dread, Donne saw his departure for
Germany as a symbolic opportunity to cut himself loose, and put
clear water between himself and his former failings. He offered
God a deal:

> I sacrifice this Iland unto thee,
> And all whom I lov'd there, and who lov'd mee;
> When I have put our seas twixt them and mee,
> Put thou thy sea betwixt my sinnes and thee.[28]

Much personal contact with his loved ones would be difficult in
any case, given the discretion that would be required of him as a
diplomatic envoy. On a morning spent 'surveying and emptying
my Cabinet of Letters', Donne wrote Goodyer an apology, 'If I
write no letters into *England*', adding: 'I foresee some reasons,
which may make me forebeare; but no slacknesse of mine own,
shall.'[29]

Donne's 'Hymne to Christ' suggests that he came or at least
tried to see the embassy as a cleansing exercise. The letters before
leaving England show a weary desire to be off. On hearing that he
had been appointed chaplain in early March 1619, Donne supposed
that 'we are within fourteen days of our time for going';[30] but
Hay's departure was repeatedly postponed. The greatest delay was
caused by the death of Queen Anne a week earlier. It became

impossible to leave since James, on hearing the news, fell profoundly ill. As the nation feared for the King's life, domestic concerns took priority. In the meantime Donne continued his ordinary preaching duties at Lincoln's Inn and the Court. On Easter Day, he preached to the House of Lords, 'The King being then dangerously sick at New-Market'. His theme (Psalms 89:48: 'What man is he that liveth, and shall not see death?') and his words were more sombre than ever: 'We are all conceived in close Prison; in our Mothers wombs, we are close Prisoners all; when we are borne, we are borne but to the liberty of the house; Prisoners still, though within larger walls; and then all our life is but a going out to the place of Execution, to death.'[31]

Yet the King eventually pulled through, and the peace trip to Europe was reconfirmed. When Donne took his place in the embassy that finally set out in early May, he was still in high mourning, wearing black like the others for the dead Queen.

The mission started inauspiciously. To the King's great annoyance, before setting out Doncaster misplaced a letter containing important information from Brussels. Although the document was discovered soon enough – while pouring a drink for Prince Charles, Doncaster remembered, he had absent-mindedly left the paper on a window seat in the Prince's palace chamber, where it was then hidden beneath a plumped-up cushion – the absent-mindedness did not end there. Having got as far as Gravesend, where he planned to embark, Doncaster realized that he had forgotten the cipher he was to use in relaying his secret correspondence, and had to ask for it to be sent on.[32] The state of British intelligence, then, with sensitive paperwork floating almost freely, gave James's covert adversaries little cause for concern. For in many respects the King's peace initiative was entirely seeded and nurtured by a Spanish subterfuge. Spain's great aim in the Bohemian crisis was to keep England from sending military and financial aid to the Protestant rebels: the neutrality desired by the Spanish was ensured by massaging King James's diplomatic ego. The great Machiavellian Spanish ambassador, the Count of Gondomar, reassured his masters that 'the vanity of the present King of England is so great that he will always think it of great importance that peace should be obtained by his means, so that his authority may be increased.'[33] So long as this illusion was encouraged, Gondomar advised, England would be of no trouble to the continued Imperial and Catholic domination of Bohemia. Viscount Doncaster was being sent on an expensive wild-goose chase.

The embassy, comprising almost thirty coach-loads of assorted knights and gentlemen, was treated with the utmost courtesy wherever it called: firstly, after much delay, at Calais in May, where the visitors were allowed a tour of the citadel; then, via Antwerp, at Brussels, where a great reception awaited them ('I must admit the cheare was royall, and I am even now also risen from a sumptious dinner of the Marquis of Spinola,' Doncaster reported).[34] But Doncaster's priorities, it turned out, were to be repeatedly frustrated. He was concerned above all to speak to the main players in the dispute, Ferdinand and Frederick, but was hampered by problems with transport and by the two princes' peripatetic movements at this time, as they travelled round about their territories mustering and consolidating support. In early June, having travelled to Cologne and then along the Rhine to Frankfurt, Doncaster expected to find Frederick at his symbolic stronghold, Heidelberg, but discovered that he was meeting Protestant allies in Heilbronn for a final deliberation on how they could defend their 'desperately embroyled' lands against the Imperial aggressors.[35] Frederick nonetheless was mindful of the respect he needed to show the English ambassador, especially if he was to persuade his father-in-law to lend arms to his cause. He rode back to Heidelberg through the heat of mid-June to grant Doncaster an audience.

He received the ambassador early the following day – a Sunday – before Donne gave his regular sermon to the English party. Doncaster found Frederick to be 'muche beyond his yeirs, religious, wise, active, and valiant'; he was particularly impressed that the young Prince esteemed the English King so highly that he met him, James's mere 'shadow', in person, at the entrance to the apartments where the interview took place.[36] Frederick wasted no time in availing Doncaster of the desperate situation, news of which 'dayly beates my eares from all partes', Doncaster confirmed, and asked him to pass on immediately an appeal for money and men. For his part, Doncaster had to urge Frederick to be cautious about accepting the crown of Bohemia – an action which would be the final provocation to Ferdinand and which might be legally indefensible. Yet by now it was all but impossible for Frederick to disentangle himself, even had he wished to do so. He had come under irresistible pressure, not least from his own wife. In weighing up the political factors, James had not given sufficient weight to the persistence of his daughter. Elizabeth was a bubbly, spoilt but lovable girl, who let her pet monkeys play with her in bed and addressed the Viscount Doncaster as 'camel face', but she took her Protestant politics in earnest. She also liked power. She is said to have remarked tartly to her husband one night at dinner that she would rather eat crumbs at the table of the King of Bohemia than a banquet with the Count of the Palatinate.[37] The common judgement of the wise, Doncaster informed King James, was that the English effort to placate and mediate was a waste of time and energy; especially since, while England remained sanctimoniously neutral, Spain was quite obviously readying itself to arm Ferdinand.[38]

A meeting with Ferdinand was Doncaster's next goal; an even more urgent one, since by July the Catholic ruler's forces seemed to be gaining the ascendancy. Skirmishes in Bohemia sent distressing ripples across the surface of the whole region. The diplomatic party that made its way – as comfortably as possible – by coach and boat from one German fiefdom to another saw the early signs of war: troop movements on the roads and rivers, and, against the flow towards battle, the first of the dispossessed taking what they could of their lives to safety. There was constant news of the conflict itself. In July, the Bohemians suffered their first substantial defeat in a major engagement. Hours of bitter fighting at the village of Sablat, near Budweis, well within the Bohemian frontier, forced a withdrawal to Prague. The Imperial army took the opportunity to lay waste to the surrounding countryside, burning 'above fifty townes and villages, putting the people, without regard of sexe or age, to the sword'. The Protestant ministers captured in this advance were singled out for 'more then barbarous cruelty'.[39]

When Doncaster finally got access to Ferdinand, at Salzburg, after travelling through Stuttgart, Augsburg, Munich and Wasserburg, he found the Prince calm and confident. But then, Ferdinand was rarely anything but self-assured. Earlier in the year, with Bohemian rebels pressing on Vienna itself, the very heart of Habsburg power, it had been unsafe for him to sit in his own study for risk of a shot through the window. As morale in the city collapsed into fear and trembling, Ferdinand lay flat in front of the crucifix in his chapel, with serene conviction of the divine rightness of his cause. Ferdinand was no less a zealot than his Protestant adversary, but with a degree of fanaticism that gave him virtual immunity from doubt. Nothing stood in the way of his faith, for it was the guarantor of his power. 'I have known,' Donne remarked later of Ferdinand, 'the greatest Christian prince, (in Style and Title) even at the audience of an Ambassador, at the sound of a Bell, kneele downe in our presence and pray.'[40] Vienna was saved, at the last moment, by a cavalry detachment sent by Ferdinand's brother, Leopold of Tyrol. Now, he was all but certain of election as the next Holy Roman Emperor. If Frederick were then to be elected King of Bohemia, his relation to Ferdinand would be morally and legally clear: that of a traitor to his monarch.

Ferdinand politely but firmly blocked all of Doncaster's attempts to persuade him to make peace, and there discussion ended. The English embassy summered impotently, as events unfolded regardless. In August, Frederick was confirmed King of Bohemia, and Ferdinand was elected Emperor. Complete implosion into war seemed inevitable.

Donne, amid all this, was in attendance on Doncaster, performing religious services for the party, offering advice on points of doctrine and no doubt conferring, when there was opportunity, with the senior Protestant clerics they encountered on the journey. He preached at least twice for Frederick and Princess Elizabeth at Heidelberg.[41] He was also forced into correspondence with a largely unwelcome figure from the past. Tobie Mathew, the invet-

erate continental stray, saw Donne's presence in Europe as a means
of applying for leniency in his ongoing campaign to get his banishment from England lifted. As ever, though, Mathew had done
little to aid his own cause. At present he was involving himself
with a community of English Jesuits based in Louvain, a move that
in some quarters disqualified him from having anything more to
do with loyal countrymen. Mathew was outraged. He called upon
'*th*e ingenuity and prudence of Doctour Dunne' to bear him out
in saying that the sodality of English Jesuits offered no political
threat at all – a request that was wholly at odds with the professed
general aims of the Jesuit order, the Roman Church's most militant
contingent.[42] For Donne, the call upon his friendship was strange
to say the least, since he had treated Mathew very coldly when
they last met, in Paris; and he was quite aware that Mathew
had berated him, much earlier, behind his back. However, with
Doncaster's permission, he replied to Mathew that he was happy
to resume correspondence, offering cagey forgiveness for past slan-
ders. 'When I have been told,' he wrote, 'that you have not been
so carefull of me abroad, I have not been easie in believing it' –
although, 'at some times, the authoritie of reporter, hath brought
me to a half-belief of it.' He then offered an ironic pardon for
Mathew's rebellious Papism. 'We are fallen into so slack and negligent times, that I have been sometimes glad to hear, that some of
my friends have differed from me in Religion.' At least, he said,
'It is some degree of an union to be united in a serious mediation
of God.' This was the best he could hope for from the slack and
negligent, from those who could not meditate seriously enough to
avoid seeking out confrontation as Mathew had.[43]

    Doncaster's party had regular evidence, meanwhile, that differ-
ence in religion resulted in madness. By the autumn, the advantage
appeared to have left Ferdinand, despite his supreme position now
as Emperor. The Prince of Transylvania, Bethlen Gabor, a staunch
Protestant, overran Hungary – which also belonged to Ferdinand
– and pushed on, quickly laying siege to Vienna. This was elating
news for the rebels in Bohemia. Prague was decked out in blue
and silver to receive its new King, Frederick, and the city's

fountains were set aflow with red and white wine. Those looking at the long term, however, were not deceived: Ferdinand's resources – especially with Spain ready to lend support – heavily outstretched Frederick's. Behind the festivities, there was considerable anger in Prague at the futile English delegation wending through Germany. Doncaster put the now apparent truth bluntly to James's secretary: 'I feare the King of Spaine never intended to make other use of our master's interposition then by that meanes to diverte his royall intentions to assist the Bohemians.'[44] Frederick had insufficient men, arms and money; taking whatever advantage he could of the difficulty presented to Ferdinand by the Transylvanian incursion, Doncaster decided on a last-ditch bid for peace by again making an offer of mediation on behalf of his King.

In October, he took the senior members of his embassy into the Emperor's Austrian heartlands, sailing from Ratisbon down the Danube to Vienna. Moving downriver, the party saw a land laid to waste, covered in crosscurrents of refugees, deserters and retreaters. There were still the broken remains of the Catholic forces driven back over the Danube by the Transylvanian army's advance. Villages and estates smouldered. Straggling on the roads were people with nowhere to go – peasants on the run from Hungary, Bohemia and Upper Austria, along with nuns and monks who had escaped the retribution exacted by Bethlen Gabor for the Protestant clerics murdered in preceding months. The Transylvanian siege of Vienna, though, was cut short by another example of fickleness and tactical opportunism. While Bethlen Gabor had pressed his advantage against Ferdinand, his neighbour Sigismund, King of Poland, had launched an attack of his own on Transylvania. Gabor hurried his army back to defend his own lands. Strangely detached, officially impartial, Doncaster and his group could only observe the military surges and backwashes of men, going to their graves like beds, as they sailed towards Vienna.

Ferdinand regained the upper hand, this time decisively.[45] Doncaster's embassy was an abject failure, as he was quite aware. A Spanish invasion of the Palatinate would take place in August the following year, the Bohemian rebels would be routed at White

Mountain near Prague in November; Frederick would take his wife into ignominious exile in the Dutch Republic, and a systematic suppression of the Protestants of Bohemia would begin. In England, public opinion would be outraged, all the more by the annihilation of a force of English volunteers defending Frederick's – and, by marriage, Britain's – Palatine interests at Heidelberg. It would be years, however, before James would be willing to take a more belligerent stance towards the Roman Catholic faction in what would become the Thirty Years War. For now, the delegation slunk quietly home. On the way, Donne preached a sermon at The Hague, and was presented with a gold medal depicting the Synod of Dort, an ecclesiastical conference that had been called to prevent war breaking out in the Low Countries. Private concerns slowly regained the attention of the embassy members. Donne's obligations at Lincoln's Inn were on his mind: he had missed the autumn term completely, and was expected 'with some impatience'. Back in the autumn, Doncaster had requested that a letter be written to the masters of the Bench, explaining that his chaplain was absent by royal command and that 'he cannot returne till I do, which they may justly beleeve will be shortly'.[46] It was, however, New Year's Day before Doncaster and his train finally got back to London. None in the company could be more exasperated with international affairs than the ambassador himself; but few too could have been more weary than Donne, who had been the most reluctant to set out in the first place.

In the months that followed, however, he offered a sympathetic assessment of the English peace policy. Around the country, a lobby was gathering strength in favour of sending military aid to the Protestants in Bohemia. Donne, though, spoke against war-mongering, and against the mass panic that followed 'as soon as a *Catholique army* hath given a blow, and got a victory of any of our forces, or friends'. He advised people not to assume the worst; and not to presume, either, that they knew better than their sovereign and his advisers. God and the King moved in mysterious ways: 'In civill affairs, that are above us, matters of State, there is exercise of our hope,' he urged; 'He is a good Christian that can ride out, or board out, or hull out a storme ... and does not forsake his ship for it, that is not scandalized with that State, nor that Church, of which he is a member, for those abuses that are in it.'[47] Such statements increasingly recommended Donne to King James as a preacher he could trust with higher office.

Donne kept in touch with fellow members of the embassy. One of them was soon virtually a family member. In February 1620, one of Doncaster's secretaries was married to the eldest daughter of Donne's best friend. It was natural that Sir Francis Nethersole and Lucy Goodyer, named after her godmother, Lucy, Countess of Bedford, should ask Doctor Donne to preach at their wedding. For the lovers it had been a long year waiting. Their engagement had been prolonged by the unexpectedly drawn-out mission abroad. Upsettingly, however, Donne was unable to encourage them to nuptial bliss, or even give them a lyrical paragraph or two to soften their hearts when they recalled the ceremony in years to come. It is hard to imagine those gathered for the service listening without wincing as he declaimed, 'Mariage is but a continuall fornication sealed with an oath.'[48] The sacrament they had just witnessed, he argued at length, had gone into terminal decline. Marriage was now about sex, and nothing more. The spiritual benefits of celibacy had been forgotten: 'Few strive, few *fast*, few *pray* for the gift of continency; few are content with that incontinency which they have,' he cried, 'but are sorry they can expresse no more incontinency.' People no longer fought their libido, they regretted that they could not live up to their lusts. 'There is a use of marriage now, which God never thought of in the first institution of marriage; that it is a *remedy* against burning.'[49] These were words to make his audience double-check the reality of what they were hearing. Many of those assembled possessed treasured manuscripts of the work of 'Jack' Donne: sensuous, funny, open, defending the pleasures and hazards of the flesh. They had every reason to expect a measured, humorous blessing, freighted and no doubt pained, here and there, with Donne's experience. Instead they witnessed a renunciation of the life the couple had chosen. A wife, he instructed the bride, was not a lover

– she must be a mother and a 'helper' to her husband. And as for him, Donne warned, 'There is not a more uncomely, a poorer thing, then to love a Wife like a Mistresse.'[50]

As the friends and patrons listening from the pews knew well, he had loved his own wife this way, as the 'mistress' of the poetry he wrote for her, from the moment he married her in secret. His sense of carnality, though, had burnt out one Sunday in late summer two and a half years earlier, and now he was warning everyone from leading a life like the one he and Ann had shared.

18. Clay

No one could quite agree how the Archbishop of Canterbury, George Abbot, came to kill Lord Zouch's gamekeeper. Some said the arrow from the Archbishop's careless crossbow deflected unluckily on a branch, striking Peter Hawkins on the rebound. This became the favourite account: the tree was commemorated in local folklore for generations. But there was much debate about the missile's exact trajectory. Abbot was visiting Zouch's magnificent estate at Bramshill, near Reading, to consecrate the mansion's newly completed chapel. It was a full summer day near the end of July, and the host invited his guest of honour to join a hunting party in the parklands. He may have had his reservations when the old man asked to try out the crossbow. In Zouch's version of events, for some reason Hawkins got behind the deer Abbot was going for, and the animal moved at precisely the wrong moment. But others had less confidence in the accuracy of Abbot's aim. Some questioned his wisdom in the first place for 'meddling with so dangerous an engine in so great an Assembly'.[1]

There was never any question of Abbot intending to cause harm. 'An angel', King James was reported as saying, 'might have miscarried in this sort.'[2] Nonetheless, the fact remained that the patriarch of the established Church had killed another human being. Some senior clergymen refused to receive communion from the Archbishop. While voicing his support, even the King kept Abbot dangling. A keen sportsman himself, incidentally, James felt as a rule that 'it is a theeuish forme of hunting to shoote with gunnes and bowes'; though this feeling, expressed some years before, did not cloud his judgement.[3] Nevertheless, Abbot was suspended from his ecclesiastical duties pending a full inquiry into the incident, which was to be headed, ominously for him, by Bishop Lancelot Andrewes, who was no great friend of the Archbishop's. Late in August 1621, a month after the event, Donne met the Archbishop and was surprised to find him in good spirits. 'I see him retain his former cheerfulnesse,' he reported, in a long chatty letter to Goodyer, 'but I do not hear from Court, that he hath any ground for such a confidence, but that his case may need favour, and not have it.'[4]

Whenever a high-up cleric died – or, under exceptional circumstances, was frozen out of office like poor Abbot, who was never the same man after his accident – the vacancy put the rest of the Church's hierarchy, and all those aspiring to join it, on general alert. When the first gap was filled, others necessarily opened up behind it. The Court hummed with talk, gleeful and anxious, of who was in the running for the available mitre, and who would benefit from the successive shuffle of promotions. As a Chaplain Royal and Reader of Divinity at Lincoln's Inn, Donne was now a relatively well-established member of a vast social network with its own paupers and aristocrats, star candidates and contending political factions. Many, within the Church and about town, felt that his time had come for a leg up the ladder. Earlier in the year, it was rumoured that Donne would be made Dean of Salisbury Cathedral, following the death in March of John King, Bishop of London. Later, the grapevine had it that the King had changed his mind, and that Donne's next stop would be Gloucester. Donne struggled not to raise his hopes too high. The year before, when Court gossip had put odds on him rising to a deanery, it all came to nothing: 'poore Dr. Dun is cast behind and fallen from his hopes,' John Chamberlain had commented.[5]

As it happened, Archbishop Abbot's suspension was only temporary. He was reinstated and fully exonerated from any taint in November 1621 – the result, some thought, of a compromise by the investigators, in order to block Abbot's likely replacement, the newly ascendant John Williams. Better the devil they knew, the judges were supposed to have reasoned.[6] In any case, the main immediate effect of Abbot's mishap on Church politics was to delay the King's final decision on who would be the new Bishop of London, and who would be shifted upwards or sideways in the consequent ripples of new appointments. For Donne, this made for a long summer of sticky expectancy. Yet his letter to Goodyer dated 30 August shows that he had settled into calm, largely contented patterns of social and domestic routine. Most of his children, certainly his daughters, had by this time gone to live with relatives, in order to have the maternal care of their aunts. Donne himself was still living at the house in Drury Lane, spending most of the summer in town, with occasional visits to former in-laws and old friends; yet with an eye on his future career and social standing, he was also nurturing influential contacts at Chancery, meeting regularly, he said, with Sir Henry Hobart, Lord Chief Justice of the Common Pleas, and Sir Julius Caesar, victim of the most grandiose christening in the kingdom, Master of the Rolls. He was following the international news carefully, and summarized for Goodyer's benefit the latest reports of the Bohemian rebels' disastrous fortunes. He had company at home, meanwhile. His eldest daughter, Constance, had come to stay and was looking after him, acting as 'houskeeper, for a moneth; and so she is my servant below stairs, and my companion above'. She would, he explained, have signed the letter herself, and perhaps included a note to one of Goodyer's daughters, Lady Nethersole – the girls were good friends – but 'she is gone to bed two hours before I writ this'. He was glad of Constance's care and company: his health was not the best. He had to apologize for not copying and dispatching a sermon that one of Goodyer's patrons had requested – Donne's manuscripts were still in high demand – because a burst of his old neuritic spasms had curtailed his work. 'I have been travelled with a pain, in my right wrist, so like the Gout, as makes me unable to write' – at least for the solid 'eight hours' that transcribing one of his sermons would require. He appended this excuse with an apology for the afflicted scrawl of the letter he was writing. He was sorry, too, for not being able to see more of Goodyer.[7]

The summer before, a curious image of Donne emerged from another letter to his friend, a hurried note written on the road. Crawling along a 'back way' from Keyston, his rectory in Huntingdonshire, he had paused to eat at an inn, where 'through my broken casement at *Bedford*, I saw, for my best dish at dinner, your Coach.'[8] Seeing Goodyer's guests, however, he did not go out to greet him or make his presence known. Nor, on finding out where they were headed, to the Earl of Kent's estate at Wrest Park, did he feel able to follow and pay his respects. If our picture of Donne in 1620 is of an unusually diffident figure at a solitary meal, peering through a cracked window at an amiable company in the forecourt beyond, but flinching from approaching, then the Donne of a year later is a more reposed person, troubled by old aches and pains, but comfortable in his own home and social circle, talking of international affairs as personal concerns, namedropping casually, and waiting to see what his fortunes had in store.

Four years had passed since he was widowed. When spring came this year, he was able for the first time since Ann's death to talk about mortal love, marriage and women without grief or bitterness. He was asked in late May to speak at the society wedding of a friend of Lady Doncaster's, one Margaret Washington, which took place at his own local church of St Clement Danes, where Ann lay buried, and where he had given his first sermon after she died.[9] Standing in the same pulpit, he gave a fine, calm, open-hearted talk, terribly poignant no doubt for those who cared about him in the audience, who had witnessed his shattered efforts to discuss the same themes over the past few years: 'I have had the like occasion as this to speak before, in the presence of many honourable persons in this company,' he declared at the outset.[10] This time it was different, a big improvement on the Nethersoles' wedding in February the previous year. He still saw marriage as a 'remedy against burning', but the fire was not so infernal as it had seemed for a while. It must still be resisted, naturally – he would never quite lose his suspicions about sex – but the flames were facts of flesh again, life-signs. The 'mutuall help' partners should give one another was more genial.[11] He gave his views, too, on the marriage of priests, explaining what might have puzzled many of his listeners – his reasons for not remarrying.

. . . when men have consecrated themselves to the service of God in his Church, I would they would be content to try a little farther then they doe, whether they could abstain or no: But to dissolve mariage made after such a Vow or after Orders, is still to separate those whom God hath not separated.[12]

Marriage vows taken before entering the priesthood were not undone by ordination; but after it, the vow to God took precedence for the single or the widowed man. Donne spoke as a man of the world as well as the cloth, with advice more than admonition on jealousy, frustrated desire, respect. 'Where the Church is silent, let me be silent too,' he said, in raising the taboo subject of adultery, for example, which he nonetheless warned was 'a deadly wound' if not 'the death of mariage'.[13] Then, in moving on from his counsel for a married couple on earth, he described with genuine rapture the prospect of all souls in heaven, where he hoped to meet 'not some, but all this company'.[14] At that great wedding of everyone with God, he said, 'I shall see an end of faith, nothing to be beleeved that I doe not know; and an end of hope, nothing to be wisht that I doe not enjoy . . .'[15]

But there was still a world to negotiate, and pursuing a career in the Church could be a perilous business. A reputation could be lost in the flutter of a cassock if the wrong sentiment was voiced in a sermon, or voiced without enough flattery to smooth it over, and rivals were always ready to take advantage of misfortune. It was significant that the two most prominent churchmen who refused to receive the sacrament from George Abbot, after his unfortunate experience with the crossbow, were John Williams, Dean of Westminster, and William Laud, president of St John's College, Oxford. Williams was fiercely ambitious: he presently became the first cleric in many years to be elevated to the high post of Lord Keeper of the Seal – which Francis Bacon had lost after taking bribes. Laud, meanwhile, though ambitious too, belonged to a group that disliked Abbot on doctrinal and political grounds.

Death itself was no protection against defamation, as the ghost of Bishop John King discovered. Although known throughout his life as a vehement critic of Rome, soon after he died in 1621 the whisper went around that he had desperately converted to Catholicism in his last hours. The rumour precipitated a small official crisis: it could not be generally believed that one of the sternest Protestants in the land crumpled at the crucial moment if the Reformed Church was to retain its authority. King's son Henry, another successful cleric, gave a sermon at Paul's Cross to denounce the slur, crying out that 'Hee, whose conversion they now vrge, had been long an eye-sore to them, railed on by many of their Pamphleteers.'[16] The sermon, when it was published, even included a transcript of an interrogation in which the Roman Catholic priest who claimed to have given King his last rites retracted his story. But the tale continued to do the rounds for some years, in the form of a falsified 'confession' written as though by John King himself. Penned by a Papist called Musket, the fictitious King urged his brethren in the Protestant Church to abandon the perks of office, and follow his example: 'It is Wife, Children, Honours, Preferments, and the like (snares wherewith my selfe heretofore haue been shackled . . .) which withould the learnedest of you from open profession of the Catholike feyth. O madnes!'[17]

John King himself was at least beyond harm; no loss of income or status could touch him in the shades. But the living had to watch their prospects. An individual's progress in the Church lay at the mercy of the contending personalities and loyalties of patrons, both secular and clerical. The Church of England was a communion of interest groups with differing, often contradictory ideas of the Church's ideal nature. At about the time that Donne began to rise in the ranks of the clergy, the balance between these factions was at the very cusp of a slow, major change that would result, in the next two decades, in outright rupture. George Abbot, Archbishop of Canterbury and thus technically the most senior priest in the country, was an orthodox, committedly anti-Catholic Protestant, with Puritan leanings. John King, Bishop of London, was in some respects a similar figure, lambasting Roman Catholics from the pulpit yet, like Abbot, a pragmatist: both were content to leave private religious reservations to the individual conscience so long as a show of conformity was maintained by all those attending and conducting the Church's services. These robust yet flexible qualities made such men King James's ideal patriarchs. Personal shades of doctrinal interpretation were fascinating to James, who cultivated and encouraged learned preaching from his pulpits. Yet of paramount importance to him was the political act of showing obedience and commitment to the nation's established Church, with the monarch at its head.

The figurehead George Abbot provided was flanked by more extreme, opposing persuasions. On the one hand were 'godly' ministers, Puritans, who saw the Reformation as an incomplete historical project that needed to be taken further. The term 'Puritan' denoted a very wide range of religious peculiarities; yet, broadly speaking, puritanical or 'godly' worshippers (as they preferred to style themselves) were united by their belief in Calvin's theory that God had already decided who would be among his 'elect' in heaven, and indeed the 'reprobate' in hell. This was a doctrine that terrified Donne, especially in his Holy Sonnets. (He often opposed the idea of predestination, but he may have more than half-accepted it in the pit of his stomach.) Puritan beliefs were strongly reflected in the way a person behaved and worshipped. The things that most Christians tried doing some of the time – such as praying, fasting, avoiding casual sex, alcoholism and excessive eating – were things that Puritans claimed to do all of the time. They saw themselves as God's 'visible saints': they were devoted to personal involvement with his word, reading scripture for themselves and discussing it at enormous length in prayer meetings that could last for hours, especially on the Sabbath, which they kept stringently. The sermon, dealing as it did with a verse from the Bible, was for them the centrepiece of the service. Puritans also had strict opinions on the way their chapels should be set out and the way people should move within them. The decorations and images of Roman Catholic churches, candlesticks, crucifixes and (in particular) altars, were for Puritans idolatrous fixtures:

kneeling and bowing to such ornaments was the sign of a sheer heathen. They disliked the elaborate robes that the clergy were still strictly supposed to wear – the surplices, cloth-of-gold vestments and other accoutrements were for Puritans nothing less than 'rags of antichrist'.[18]

Puritanism also informed a distinct political attitude: the godly supported action against Rome wherever it tried extending its satanic influence. They were vehement supporters of the Protestant rebels in Bohemia, lamenting the King's failure to aid his son-in-law Frederick, and fierce opponents of the increasing tolerance towards Spain. For some years, it had been becoming clear that James was angling for the Spanish Infanta to marry his son and heir, Charles. In the King's view, this match was the way to peace in Europe; for Puritans it meant apocalypse. As long ago as 1603, soon after he came to the English throne, James had warned 'Puritans, and rash-heady preachers, that think it their honour to contend with kings, and perturb whole kingdoms' to know their limits.[19] But the godly saw the fate of the whole kingdom as being very much their proper concern. 'A Puritan (so nicknamed: but indeed the sound Protestant)', ran a satirical poem of the early 1620s, was really

> such another thing
> As says with all his heart, God save the King
> And all his issue: and to make this good,
> Will freely spend his money and his blood . . .[20]

The Puritans were the true patriots, they argued, and they had every right to contend with a King when he strayed from the path of the righteous, though they would back him to the hilt when he kept to it. Many were quite willing to die for what they believed. The Puritan commitment to the cause of true religion was graphically illustrated in 1622, when a force of godly English volunteers, fighting without the official sanction of King James, were wiped out defending Heidelberg against the Spanish-led Catholic League.

In contrast, on the other side, meanwhile, were clerics who

were more sympathetic to James's political difficulties, and who inclined towards the older ceremonies and decorations that the Reformed Church had never fully expelled, the very customs that Puritans branded as 'Popish'. Such men included Lancelot Andrewes and William Laud. Andrewes, Dean of the Chapel Royal and Bishop of Winchester, was one of the Court's greatest preachers, but he repeatedly attacked the prominence given to sermons at the expense of other parts of the service. In doing so, his main target was no one less than the King himself, who had a habit of only turning up at chapel when the preacher was about to speak.[21] Andrewes felt that other proprieties had gone into lamentable decline: he encouraged kneeling and bowing at key points in the service, and defended candles as mementos of the lights the early Christians had had to use in times of persecution, when they met 'in caves and grots underground'.[22] Andrewes supported too the use of a fixed altar, railed in to mark the zone around it as sanctified, instead of the movable 'Communion table' brought out in orthodox Protestant services to celebrate the Lord's Supper. He and his supporters tried to implement their ritualistic tastes in the chapels over which they had direct control.

Such measures were naturally seen as the height of decadence by Puritans; but from around spring 1619, when James fell seriously ill, recent research has suggested that such godly ministers began to lose the argument. When Andrewes visited the King on his sickbed, he took the chance to bewail 'the sad condition the Church was like to fall into, if God should take away his life', and convinced him to safeguard the liturgy that the Puritans were sure to scrap altogether given half a chance. The King agreed, and after his recovery took increasing care to shelter Prince Charles from the doctrine of the godly.[23] At this time, the aims of Andrewes, Laud and their 'high' Church followers also suited the drift of James's policy. These men were much more amenable to the prospect of a royal marriage with a Spanish bride, and the possible reconciliation of kingdoms and creeds that it betokened. But in both the short and the long term, alienating the Puritan faction only compromised the unity of the Church and indeed the realm itself. For almost twenty years, Puritans had formed a more or less accepted movement within the political and religious mainstream. Their 'sober Protestant values' had in fact reflected rather well on those in authority who may have lacked some of their zeal in practice but who nonetheless condoned their moral strictness in theory.[24] When, as the 1620s went on, Calvinistic Christians came to be seen as unorthodox and subversive, the royal and religious establishment put itself on a collision course with a very large cross-section of the populace.

Pinpointing John Donne's place amid these groups and values is no simple task, which is probably how he wanted it. He moderated his tone according to his audience. He also belonged to no self-contained set consisting exclusively of 'godly' or 'popish' worshippers. The lines between such sets weren't drawn, nor would they be for many years: they were merely implied, through the course of daily affairs, by the things different individuals said and did. His old patroness the Countess of Bedford was the centre of a more or less Puritanical Court circle, but with a strong alliance to George Abbot, the beleaguered Archbishop. While their former intimacy had lapsed many years before, Donne reported that he had still 'presented my service' to her and her party when she visited town in August 1621, and 'asked leave to have waited upon them at supper' (his messenger, as it happened, was too late, arriving just as the Countess was boarding her coach).[25] She was also to some extent still a patron of his writing: he had been invited to preach before her at her home, Harrington House, in January, and he had served up a suitably dour meditation. 'This world then is but an *Occasionall* world, a world to be us'd; and that but so, *as though we us'd it not*,' Donne had remarked then.[26] The practical necessities of 'using' the world obliged the Popish and the Puritan to interact; character and circumstance could even make them friends. Even Lady Bedford was in no position to freeze out those who were known as 'Church Papists' – lax Protestants who hid their Roman Catholic leanings by going through the motions of conformity. Queen Anne, the King's consort herself, was generally supposed to have been a Roman Catholic – and Lucy Bedford,

Puritan though she had become, had been the Queen's first lady-in-waiting and closest confidante.

Donne, like many others, enjoyed cordial relations with old associates whose sympathies covered the whole spectrum. His father-in-law, Sir George More, who had for some time begun to see him as a worthy relative, clearly had the tastes of a Puritan: standing up as ever to bore the living daylights out of his fellow MPs in the Parliament of 1621, he proposed a bill to ban the popish practices of dancing, May games, sports and general fun activities on the Sabbath (to no avail, this time). Yet another long-standing connection, however, one also connected with Donne's marriage in a very different role, openly attacked the Calvinistic beliefs that were part of the Puritans' basic creed. For Samuel Brooke, the college-mate who as a fledgling minister had married John and Ann Donne twenty years before, and who presently became Master of his old Cambridge college, Trinity, the doctrine of predestination was 'the root of all rebellions, disobedience and schisms'.[27] To Predestinarians and 'high' churchmen, people with opposing views about good Christian doctrine, Donne could still remain a friend, *and* be a sound Protestant minister.

He never expressed his own religious politics so forthrightly as Brooke or More – there is no quick way of captioning his views. But during his years as preacher at Lincoln's Inn, he manifested a politically much more valuable quality than partisanship. He had shown a readiness to abide by and to enforce the prevailing orthodoxy of the institution he represented. The Benchers of the Inns of Court had never tolerated Papists in their midst: offenders were required to convert and conform, or clear out. Many years before, Henry Donne provided an extreme example of a Roman Catholic afforded no protection by his Inn. Now Donne himself, in spite of his background, demonstrated that Papist students could not expect him to give them shelter. In November 1620, one Peter Clynton, because 'hee is a Popish recusant and will not conforme himself', was thrown out of the college. The following year another junior member, Anthony Hunt, was required to present before the Benchers 'a Certificate from Mr Doctor Donne of his Conformitie in Religion'. When he failed to do so, or when Donne found that he could not vouch for him, he was 'by order of this Counsell absolutelie expelled [from] the house'.[28]

Donne also showed himself willing to accept the majority rule when it came to sticking up for fellow members of his profession. In October 1621, the subordinate priest at Lincoln's Inn, the chaplain Edward May, got himself into trouble for criticizing the hierarchy. May published a sermon which attacked the Puritan sympathizers on the Inn Bench, who 'grow old in affected-Ignorance, learned mis-interpretation, zealous-malice, and in an holy contempt of all Sacred and spirituall things'. May, it turned out, was a 'high' churchman, who disapproved of bare Puritanical chapels and the suppression of old rituals. 'Sacred and spirituall things', for him, included the 'sacred *succession of Bishops and Presbyters*, sacred *orders*; sacred *offices*; sacred *ceremonies*'.[29] The text undermined the Puritans' idea of themselves as God's 'visible saints' on earth, and denounced the standard Protestant idea of the responsibility of the individual conscience, that 'Every man is a Priest to himselfe', as one of 'those Hereticall sounds'.[30] There was more than a whiff of Papism, too, in his praise for 'Bishops and Presbyters' as 'the *Makers* of Christ his body' – bringing the Real Presence of Jesus into the Church through transubstantiation.[31] This was Roman doctrine: for Protestants, the Communion was purely symbolic. The Benchers of Lincoln's Inn were not prepared to have such preaching associated with their 'learned society', as May anticipated in the preface to his sermon – well aware of those 'who have with much bitternesse (hauing not yet, I feare, tasted of the Spirit of goodnesse) cut me for it'.[32] Donne would in time, when it was required of him, uphold many of the practices May was defending; but for now, as Bald sums up, he 'must have at least acquiesced in May's dismissal and have been consulted by the Benchers, even if he did not take a more active part in securing it'.[33] He kept quiet, and trod safely.

At Lincoln's Inn he had proven himself a safe pair of hands, which was exactly what the King needed. To many, as Donne positioned himself in the best possible light for higher office, he may simply have appeared cynical, a religious pragmatist. 'Protestant', according to Puritan satirists, was for most a badge of convenience. The average minister at Court was merely out for whatever he could get.

> A Protestant is he that by degrees
> climbs every office, knows the proper fees
> they give and take, an entrance of the place,
> and at what rate again they vent that grace,
> knows in how many years a man may gather
> enough to make himself a reverend father . . .[34]

To unsympathetic eyes, Donne was one such Protestant who knew how to work the system. Many aristocrats, colleges and bishops had lucrative benefices within their gift, but the top appointments in the Church could only be won through royal favour. Or, in practice, through the grace of the man who by now virtually controlled access to the monarch and the Prince – King James's greatest favourite, the Marquis of Buckingham.

Early in August 1621, as courtiers and clerics alike assessed those likely to gain from the impending reshuffle, Donne was already looking past the prospect of disappointment this time around. He had been hoping to be made Dean of Salisbury, but that seemed unlikely because another vacancy had not opened up as expected. John Williams, savouring his promotion to Lord Keeper *and* Bishop of Lincoln, found that he could not dispense with his current position as Dean of Westminster. This meant that a series of jobs lower down the chain had not become available. Stomaching the letdown, Donne fixed everything on placing himself entirely at Buckingham's disposal.

Among his many other talents, Donne could be a masterful groveller. He assured Buckingham,

I ame so far from depending upon the assistance of any but your Lordship, as that I do not assist myselfe so far as with a wishe that my Lord Keeper would have left a hole for so poore a worme as I ame to have crept in at. All that I meane in usinge thys boldness, of puttinge myselfe into your Lordship's presence by this ragge of paper, ys to tell your Lordship that I ly in a corner, as a clodd of clay, attendinge what kinde of vessel yt shall please you to make of

Your Lordship's

humblest and thankfullest and devotedst servant,

J. Donne.[35]

He was Buckingham's, in short, a shapeless lump that the Marquis could mould however he wanted. All that 'so poore a worme' as Donne required was a hole somewhere to call his own. He was talking the kind of language that Buckingham liked to hear. Privately and no doubt unconsciously, however, this language was streaked with sacrilege. Donne had been interested in the image of himself as a clod of clay, awaiting form, for some time. In a sermon given in May, he had described himself as being 'not a Potters vessell of earth, but that earth of which the Potter might make a vessel if he would, and break it if he would'. On that occasion the potter was not the Marquis of Buckingham, but Christ, 'the bud and blossome, the fruit and off-spring of Jehovah, Jehovah himself'.[36]

Buckingham, in time created Duke, was once plain George Villiers, the second son of the second marriage of a Midland squire. Villiers was renowned for his fragile good looks and self-confident demeanour. He was planted by his sponsors among the King's entourage on a hunting trip to Northamptonshire in 1614, and James noticed him immediately.[37] He had, noted Henry Wotton, 'continually a very pleasant and vacant face . . . proceeding, no doubt, from a singular assurance in his temper'.[38] 'I saw everything in him full of delicacy and handsome features,' attested Simonds D'Ewes, on seeing him at a tournament; 'yea, his hands and face seemed to me, especially, effeminate and curious.'[39] The King, who had a weakness for such beautiful young men, found Villiers irresistible from the start. He expressed his fondness for him through unprecedented honours and confidence. This fascination, which he expected every other loyal follower to understand and share, was a mixture of doe-eyed crush, paternal care and the love of a guru for his favourite disciple. He warned his councillors not to say a word against Villiers, who by 1621 had been elevated to the peerage. 'I, James, am neither a god nor an angel, but a man like any other. Therefore I act like a man, and confess to loving those dear to me more than other men.' He then contradicted this by comparing himself to the Messiah. 'You may be sure I love the Earl of Buckingham more than anyone else here assembled . . . Jesus Christ did the same, and therefore I cannot be blamed. Christ had his John and I have my George.'[40]

Villiers was originally planted in Court by Lady Bedford and her set to divert the King from the previous ruling favourite, Somerset, who was soon enough engulfed in the scandal of the Overbury murder; but nobody could have predicted what power this girlish, inscrutable boy would attain. Within a few years he had established a virtual monopoly on patronage. The King accepted him as his own child, a surrogate for the dead Prince Henry, and built up a circuit of compulsory affection within the royal family for its new honorary member. Father and son nick-named each other cheekily in their private correspondence. King James was 'Dear Dad and Gossip', Buckingham was 'Steenie'. Prince Charles was encouraged to become best friends with Villiers, and did so, over time, thus ensuring that the favourite's existing influence would continue beyond the succession. James also needed his wife to love his Steenie. Keen to keep her husband's favour, she agreed. Their marriage succeeded through a peculiar emotional jury-rigging. King James was clearly fond of Anne – his health collapsed, into what appeared to be a mortal illness, after her death in 1619 – but he required her to show her love for him by tolerating his obsessions with younger men while keeping her distance. 'Hee had a very brave Queen that never crossed his designes,' wrote a grudging contemporary; yet 'he was ever best, when furthest from the Queen'.[41] When she died, she remained unburied for two months, apparently because James could not spare the funds for a state funeral.[42]

Labelling himself poor worm and clod of clay, Donne may have been suggesting little nicknames that Buckingham was welcome to call him by, too, if he would only help him to a promotion. Certainly, the only way to serious patronage in those days was to insinuate oneself into the climate of arch but obsequious intimacy that gripped the royal household under the spell of Steenie. Dad and Gossip's benevolence lay at the disposal of his beloved Buckingham. Some churchmen were indeed sufficiently insidious. John Williams, the new Lord Keeper, for example, was for some time thought to be interested in marrying Buckingham's mother; only, after his appointment, 'he did estrange himselfe from the company of the old Countesse, having much younger ware, who had keyes to his chamber.'[43]

For the time being Donne resigned himself to waiting, but his chance came sooner than he thought. When he wrote to Goodyer on 30 August, carelessly describing his social movements and giving updates on international developments, he already knew that the possibility of a break had been reopened. Four days earlier, the Bishop of Exeter had died, prompting another reshuffle, and this would prove to be Donne's moment. Valentine Carew, formerly a chaplain in Thomas Egerton's household, was promoted to the See of Exeter, and Donne was chosen to take his place as the Dean of St Paul's Cathedral. Carew was much less illustrious than his successor at St Paul's – 'He left behind him no published works, and he managed to quarrel with the Mayor and Corporation of Exeter almost as soon as he took up residence.'[44] Donne would make a happier first impression in his new posting. According to Walton, King James broke the good news in person. Donne was sent for and commanded to wait on James the following day.

When his Majesty was sate down, before he had eat any meat, he said after his pleasant manner, Dr. *Donne, I have invited you to Dinner; and, though you sit not down with me, yet I will carve to you of a dish that I know you love well; for knowing you love* London, *I do therefore make you Dean of*

Pauls; *and when I have dined, then do you take your beloved dish home to your study; say grace there to your self, and much good may it do you.*[45]

There may have been better ways of receiving this 'dish', since the King at table was not a pleasant sight. It was said that 'his tongue [was] too large for his mouth, which ever made him speake full in the mouth, and made him drink very uncomely, as if eating his drinke, which came out into the cup of each side his mouth.'[46] But James's slurping is unlikely to have spoilt such welcome tidings – if, that is, Donne had not already been told of his good fortune from another source. For others claimed the credit for the promotion. Bishop and Lord Keeper Williams later said that Donne's appointment to St Paul's was his doing. Like Donne and Carew, the new Bishop of Exeter, Williams had also served Egerton; and an early biographer claimed that it was the mutual connection to York House that clinched the bishopric and deanery. 'The Success was quickly decided, for these two prevailed by the Lord Keeper's Commendation against all Pretenders.' Williams regarded Donne as 'a Laureat Wit; neither was it possible that a vulgar soul would dwell in such promising features.' From this view, Donne's talents as a writer, his refined manners and his years as Egerton's secretary – qualities and time that for a long while had seemed largely wasted – served him in good stead in the end.[47]

But the surviving evidence suggests Donne owed his deanery mostly to another. In a letter dated 13 September, he again offered himself up for Buckingham to shape to whatever end he desired, indicating that his debt was all to him, the King's ruling favourite. He drew on the idea he developed years before, in his most sincere and cordial correspondence, of his letter transporting him almost bodily to the friend he wrote for.

I deliver this paper as my Image; and I assist the power of any Conjuror . . . that as he shall tear this paper, this picture of mine, so I may be torn in my fortune, and in my fame, if ever I have any corner in my heart, dispossessed of a zeal to your Lordships service . . . I protest to your Lordship, I know not what I want, since I cannot suspect, nor fear my self for ever doing, or leaving undone any thing by which I might forfeit that title, of being always

    Your Lordships, &c.

    J.D.

The ingenuity of former tributes is still there, but the charm has gone. Donne laid it on thick, to remove any room for doubt, in the process speaking somewhat inappropriately for a future Dean of the Church of England – invoking and assisting 'the power of any Conjuror' has a whiff of black magic to it. Donne also put his prayer and priesthood entirely at Buckingham's disposal, since 'as I am a Priest, made able to subsist, and appear in Gods service, by your Lordship, it is a sacrifice of myself to you.'[48]

Donne's expressions of indebtedness have raised the question of whether he paid Buckingham a bribe for his appointment. Buckingham's usual practice would strongly suggest that he levied a charge for the promotion – and there is no reason to suppose that he made an exception in this case. Donne himself was strongly critical of corruption in the Church: 'how shall I be believed to speak heartily against Ambition and Bribery in temporall and civil places,' he had asked his flock at Lincoln's Inn rhetorically, 'if one in the Congregation be able to jogge him that sits next him, and tell him, that man offered me money for spirituall preferment?'[49] It is a safe guess, nonetheless, that there were a few knowing nudges in the pews Donne addressed in the autumn of 1621. The question is not, perhaps, whether Donne paid Buckingham for his Deanery, but what form this payment took. When beneficed clergymen could not afford a single fee, Buckingham was reputed to take a regular cut from their income. But Donne, as we shall see, later recompensed his patron from the body of St Paul's itself.

For literary posterity, and the contemporary integrity of the Church, the appointment turned out to be the masterpiece of Jacobean patronage. For Donne personally, the post was almost beyond his dreams. King James was right, in Walton's version, in saying that Donne loved the city: by birth and instinct always a Londoner, his new job put him at the hub of the capital. But the publicity and prominence it also brought placed the incumbent at some political risk. To succeed as Dean – and progress further in the Church – Donne would have to keep the good graces of the lofty friends who had arranged his elevation.

On 22 November, he was formally elected by the Chapter of St Paul's, the assembly of priests (individually known as Canons) who were responsible for running the Cathedral. The Chapter followed the directions of a letter of royal command, issued a few days before. When the votes had been cast in the Chapter House, a tall-windowed, fourteenth-century hall, set amid cloisters on the Cathedral's north side, the new Dean was summoned and led, in full vestments, into the main body of the Cathedral by the Bishop of London and the Canons. The procession passed from the Episcopal palace into the north transept, the left arm of the cross-shaped citadel, and at the central crossing, where its limbs intersected and the main tower rose above the whole, turned left into the choir, where the clergy and singers had their seats and the principal services were conducted. For many years, to the disgust of London's Puritans, St Paul's had been a centre for the revival of old 'high' Church customs. The clergy bowed and kneeled eastwards at crucial moments of devotion, towards Jerusalem and the rising sun; and the Communion table, known to all as the high altar, had been restored to its former 'popish' position at the eastern end of the Cathedral.[50] This was the focal point to which Donne was now taken, as a *Te Deum* was sung, and where he then prostrated himself as the Bishop led prayers. The choir was vast. The path to the altar was narrowed and concentrated by pillared arcades along the sides, accentuating too the overwhelming height of the vaulted ceiling. At the far end, above and behind the altar, was an enormous rose window, installed three and a half centuries before. After a blessing, Donne raised himself and kissed the altar. He was then led back down the aisle to the west end of the choir, to take the seat that had been occupied by successive Deans since the Middle Ages.[51] When the service was completed, the company returned to the Chapter House, where an exchange of oaths took place. First Donne made the solemn promise 'to reside at the

Cathedral, to keep and cause to be kept its ancient laws and customs, and to preserve its possessions'. Then the Canons swore to obey their new Dean, who last of all made a similar oath of allegiance to the Bishop. With this he was sworn into a corporation, a society with its own customs and a tradition with strict expectations.[52]

He was now the senior priest, except for the Bishop himself, at the foremost church in the realm: St Paul's was in all but name the Cathedral of London, the capital's chief place of worship. Other cathedrals were above it in the Church of England's hierarchy – notably those of Canterbury and York – but no other church had greater involvement in the city's life, or greater popular influence beyond it. The edifice itself was London's outstanding landmark. This was not the domed neoclassical structure that Christopher Wren would build, more than fifty years later, after its predecessor was consumed in the Great Fire, but a medieval cathedral, or rather what remained of it, a vast and sprawling gothic hive. For Wren, surveying the wreckage in 1667, it was 'this great pile of Pauls'.[53] Yet many came to miss the gargantuan straggle of its 'old bold projections, and the venerable, time-worn, if dark and cumbersome, and ill harmonized, perhaps, but massy and imposing arches and buttresses'.[54] What the cupola of Wren's cathedral gave the city horizon in crisp uniformity, the old St Paul's made up for in flagrant unevenness. It was the result of no singular genius, but a composite giant that a community had pieced together over centuries. It had been restarted, continued, overlaid in various places after work gathered pace in the 1100s; scarred by fires, neglected, restored. Citizens of London had endowed chantry chapels, altars and shrines that had been desiccated by accident and reformation, and then replaced in time by successive monuments. Two features of St Paul's stood out, as on many cathedrals of its age – scale and detail. The looming complex was huge in all directions; its original steeple, destroyed by lightning in 1561, was over five hundred feet high. Laterally, by the popular estimate, the building was 'a myle long, or very neere'.[55] After recovering from the prospect's size – for example, as one crossed the river to the north bank, which the

Cathedral dominated – the next thing one realized was the sheer
multiple density of its design. The masonry of its crust and interior
was layered with intricate ridges, patterns, figures and emblems,
accumulated over hundreds of years.

It was a place that was used as much as sanctified, much to the
concern of the ecclesiastical powers. The Cathedral's great echoing
spaces, in the nave, choir and transepts, crumbled into a myriad of
apsidal chapels and crypts where prayer and worship often had to
make way for work and storage. Such nooks and crannies were
occupied by glaziers, builders, carpenters, schoolmasters. The charnel on the north side of the churchyard, 'wherein the Bones taken
out of sundry graves in that Cimeterie, were with great respect
and care, decently piled together', had given way to a bookseller
and stationer's shop.[56] This, and many of the other establishments
clustered nearby, would often be open for illegal business on a
Sunday, to take advantage of the crowds who assembled in thousands for the sermon at Paul's Cross. The Cathedral was exploited
for loitering as well as labour, and subjected to the continual drift
of tourists. The place stank with the living and the dead. The burial
grounds outside were overpacked; within, rubbish piled up in the
aisles, dunghills proved impossible to clear, and calls for civic-
mindedness went unheeded through successive generations.
Drunks would stumble in and collapse 'aboute the quire dores . . .
where they doe verie often tymes leave all that is within them very
lothsome to beholde'.[57] Reports would often reach the Cathedral
authorities of random mischief-makers, such as 'boys (saving your
Reverence) pissing upon stones in the Church . . . to slide as upon
ice'.[58] As an ecclesiastical sanctuary, the Cathedral was technically
immune, and isolated from civil authority – which might explain
the liberties people felt they could take with it. Part of Donne's
task and responsibility as Dean was policing the masses.

Supporting and enduring all this activity, the place was falling
apart. Besides mortal business, acts of God also proved hostile to
the integrity of the structure. The straight piercing spire, once the
pride of London, had burnt down in a thunderstorm some sixty
years earlier. The stump that remained, squat in proportion to the

rest of the building, was a sad reminder, for the old, of the original pinnacle. Its stonework discoloured by flame and chipped by human carelessness, its lead roofing the victim of countless dagger-made graffiti, the Cathedral was patched up sufficiently over the years to fend off utter dereliction, but would occasionally present a reminder of its need for comprehensive renovation, dropping a lump from its southern battlements in 1605, for example, killing an innocently profane carthorse at work in the precincts below.[59] The upkeep of the fabric was also, therefore, one of the more pressing points in Donne's brief. The latest initiative to restore the Cathedral properly had been struck up in 1616 by one Henry Farley, who wrote a poetic monologue in which he took on the voice of the maimed building itself, pleading for repair.[60] His motives, like those of most connected with St Paul's, were not wholly unworldly. Farley was an importer of stone, and looked to benefit from the reconstruction work he advocated. In any case, although the King got round to visiting St Paul's a few years after Farley's *Complaint* twinged consciences around the Court, no great progress had yet been made.

The inescapable, often jarring mixture of the secular with the sacred at St Paul's went well with a similar mixture – and mixed-upness – in Donne himself, however much he struggled with it. He was the ascetic divine, but also, still, the man about town: his skills as a courtier, as much as his preaching, had won him the deanery. 'Every man is a little world, sayes the *Philosopher*,' Donne said. 'Every man is a little *Church* too; and in every man, there are two sides, two armies: the flesh fights against the Spirit.'[61] The clash and combination between these corporeal and spiritual, civic and clerical elements came to a head in one region of the Cathedral in particular, the western half, beyond the more orderly and restric-ted sections of the choir and central crossing. The passage of the nave, and the aisle halfway along that cut across it, formed an intersection known as 'Paul's Walk'. This was the very heart of urban society, pumping out news – and social fiction – around the capital, the point where all the contending hypocrisies in the streetlife of Donne's first satire could be sampled. The Walk was

crowded throughout the day, and the din was relentless throughout the services conducted in the choir and the chapels branching
off from the thoroughfare. The general row, salacious news and
thievery of the Walk became commonplaces:

The noyse it is like that of Bees, a strange humming or buzze – mixt of
walking, tongues and feet: It is a kind of still roare or loud whisper. It is
the great Exchange of all discourse, and no businesse whatsoeuer but
is here stirring and afoot . . . The best signe of a Temple in it is, that it
is the Theeues Sanctuary, which robbe more safely in the Croud, then
a wildernesse . . . It is the other expence of the day, after Playes, Tauerne
and a Bawdy-House . . . It is the eares Brothell, and satisfies their lust,
and itch.

These words are by John Earle, another satirist who later turned
clergyman – eventually becoming Bishop of Salisbury – written in
the 1620s. They represent a prevailing idiom. Yet that overriding
itch of desire for gossip is an especially Donnean touch, reminiscent
of the language of the verse satires he composed thirty years earlier.
This was the space over which Donne the 'Laureat Wit' now
presided, and to a great extent he had taught the latest generation
of poetic sketch-writers how to depict it. The passage above is
taken from Earle's *Microcosmographie*, the title meaning 'picture of
a little world', and the Walk certainly gave one a kingdom in
bottled form. It was, as Earle put it, 'the Lands Epitome, or you
may call it the lesser Ile of Great Brittaine'. In a sense, Donne was
home.[62]
    He made little impact, as Dean, on the physical relapse and
social delinquency afflicting St Paul's, but made a good job of the
managerial responsibilities invested in him. From late in 1621 he
was in effect accountable for the stability of a very large civic
corporation, controlling property, great funds and employment.
He relished the status and estates that came with his office from
the moment he knew he had got it. 'Though I be not Dean of
Pauls yet,' he enthused to Goodyer, 'my Lord of *Warwick* hath gone
so low, as to command of me the office of being Master of my

game, in our wood about him in *Essex*.'[63] There he was, an exile
for so long, now answering suits from neighbouring Lords instead
of presenting them. An important episode from the following year
gives perhaps the clearest illustration of how he won and sustained
the confidence that brought this pleasurable sense of power and
inclusion.

By the summer of 1622 public discontent with King James's
policy of appeasement towards Spain was nearing its height. The
restrictions on Roman Catholics had been relaxed to an unprecedented level, a leniency that suited, among others at Court, Buckingham's mother, long suspected as a closet Papist, but which
provoked widespread dismay in other quarters. The crown faced
deep grumbling and outright condemnation from pulpits across
the land. To stifle such protests, on 4 August James issued his
'Directions to Preachers', forbidding any priest below the rank of
bishop or dean from preaching on 'the deep points of Predestination, Election, Reprobation, or of the universality, efficacy,
resistibility or irresistibility of God's grace'. That is, no low-level
ministers were now allowed to debate the key sticking point of
Protestant doctrine: whether or not God had already decided who
would burn in Hell, or whether there was a way out through
grace, faith or good works. An opinion on this matter invariably
determined which faction of the Church one followed: it was the
theological match to a keg of political dynamite. As a governmental
manoeuvre, however, the Directions were curiously miscalculated,
since the bishops and deans could also take outspoken stances on
these matters, and carried, more importantly, the necessary authority to influence the views of others. No one at all, meanwhile,
was to comment adversely on the 'Power, Prerogative, and Jurisdiction, Authority, or Duty of Sovereign Princes'.[64] Needless to
say, the Directions were not well received. In the autumn, it was
Donne who was chosen to lead the defence of the King's strategy
from the pulpit at Paul's Cross.

This was a tricky commission. James was not going to attend
the sermon in person, which meant Donne would not have the
support of the royal presence to back him up. On the one hand,

he needed to push the official line; on the other, he did not want bricks thrown at him by a turbulent public. His refuge, as so often, lay in circumspection. He chose a peculiarly obscure text as his theme for the sermon, using argumentative subtlety to avoid direct confrontation or outright servility. Many in the crowd that September day felt he made an awkward performance, giving 'no great satisfaction', as John Chamberlain commented, 'or as some say spake as yf himself were not so well satisfied'.[65] The Dean did succeed in making the point that only the most important of controversies were worth fighting about, those 'where men differ from God'. As he said many other times in many other ways, the greater obligation for all was to find a way to concord: 'Every man is bound to hearken to a peace, in differences, where men differ from men.'[66] The Calvinists in Donne's audience could immediately insist that the King, his Spanish friends and the 'Popish' climbers in the Church of England were indeed going against God; but such disagreements, Donne implied, were purely mortal affairs, spats between sects and nations, not digressions from the Almighty. He did his best to please everyone. There is a 'blessing reserved to *Peace-makers*', he declared, alluding to King James's motto, *Beati Pacifici*. He praised 'our Peace-maker' – the King – 'who hath . . . alwayes seriously and chargeably, and honourably endevoured' to bestow that blessing. Then, to appease the crowd, he went on, 'yet there is a *spirituall Warre*, in which, *Maledicti Pacifici*; Cursed bee they that goe about to make Peace, and to make all one, The warres betweene *Christ* and *Beliall* [the devil]'.[67] This was more palatable to the militant Protestants listening. But he then smudged over the issues they had in mind by saying that God's spiritual war was to be waged by his preachers, who accordingly had to stick together – hence the need for King James's Directions.[68]

The crowds in the smelly churchyard of Paul's were not impressed, but the sermon delighted the King, with its insistence that in the Directions 'his *Majesties* generall intention . . . is to put a difference between grave, and solid, from light and humerous [impulsive, whimsical] preaching.'[69] James, though not present, sent for a copy, and immediately ordered the work to be published.

He sent word of his approval through Donne's longstanding friend Lord Hay, Viscount Doncaster, newly promoted to Earl of Carlisle. The King, Hay wrote to Donne, found the sermon 'a piece of such perfection, as could admit neither addition nor diminution. He longs to see it in Print.' He also had a piece of advice: if Donne was to preface the sermon with a dedication, he hinted, 'in my opinion, it shall be fittest to my Lord of *Buckingham*'.[70] This support for the Marquis took some magnanimity from Hay. It was rumoured that a couple of years before Buckingham had been sleeping with Hay's wife, during his absence on diplomatic service.[71] But like Lord Hay, Viscount Doncaster, Earl of Carlisle, Donne understood. He knew the ropes.

19. The Spouse

The main service at St Paul's on Christmas morning, 1621, was at nine o'clock as usual.[1] First light had come only less than an hour before. People climbed through the shadow in the narrow lanes which fell south from the Cathedral down the steep slope to the Thames. The black mud at the bottom of these medieval gullies would barely thaw all day. Merchants and shopkeepers with their families, hurrying their apprentices, approached from Cheapside to the east. Lawyers and gentlemen scholars strolled in from the legal district to the west; a scattering of aristocrats from the big houses on the Strand rattled up in their carriages. St Paul's was London's church, and drew its congregation from throughout the city's environs: from beyond the old city walls, and from across the river, the districts of taverns, stews and theatres on the other shore.

It had been almost fifty years since the scientist Thomas Digges became the first writer in English to propagate Copernicus's theory of the cosmos, but most of the Londoners going to church were oblivious that they had been displaced from the centre of the universe, and were hurtling through space around a ball of fire. Such ideas 'cannot be understood by the common sort', a contemporary noted: it would be a long time before the Copernican view of things became an assumption.[2] But however the celestial bodies arranged themselves, it was impossible to think the sun could be a neutral, indifferent presence – not indifferent as a Greek god was indifferent, gazing stonily upon the plight of negligible mortals, but indifferent as only something inanimate, soulless, insentient could be, a mere object. Daybreak could not be conceived of as an event with no intentional bearing on human affairs, even at this time of year, when the day was little more than a streaky interlude. Donne, who had read Copernicus, still put Man at the centre of a great scheme. 'He is not a piece of the world, but the world it selfe; and next to the glory of God, the reason why there is a world.'[3] Without humanity, there would be no reason for a universe to exist – for there would be no one to glorify God or respond to the test the creator had set: to find a way back to him. In Donne's mind, the members of the crowd gathering in the draughty Cathedral that morning, a few days after the winter solstice, were not just pieces of a cosmic jigsaw: they each contained the whole puzzle within themselves.

The huge rose window at the east end of the Cathedral was still full of the pale early sun as the service began. After prayers, hymns and readings, Donne ascended the pulpit to speak; and for the hour that followed, began to show why over the next ten years he would become one of the country's most revered spiritual teachers. His theme was light. Light in its different forms: 'the light of things', giving brightness and warmth on earth; the sun and the moon in the heavens, the stars; and the light that was God, the light from which all light derived. Almost without having to think about it, the worshippers gathered in the choir of the Cathedral – and the Paul's Walkers milling about in the nave beyond – believed that Christmas commemorated the day when the maker of all things entered the world in human form, and that this was the light on which they all ultimately depended: 'from *him* flowes the *supernaturall light* of *faith* and *grace*'.[4] Donne also called up in his listeners' minds a light their minds all shared, a light of moral intellect.

Divers men may walke by the Sea side, and the same beames of the Sunne giving light to them all, one gathereth by the benefit of that light pebbles, or speckled shells, for curious vanitie, and another gathers precious Pearle, or medicinall Ambar, by the same light. So the common light of reason illumines us all; but one imployes this light upon the searching of impertinent vanities, another by a better use of the same light, finds out the Mysteries of Religion; and when he hath found them, loves them, not for the lights sake, but for the naturall and true worth of the thing it self.[5]

This light of reason came from God, Donne told them, and it should be used to know God better. It amounted to a little candle of spiritual potential in each of them, and by it they could survey all the points of faith, and could, if they chose, make out the flickering stable scene of the Christmas story, 'thy Saviour in a *Manger*, and in his *swathing clouts*, in his humiliation'.[6] This same light was refracted through many diverse media. It was a light of science, bringing about humanity's philosophical and technological advances, such as printing, and it was also a light of conscience, enabling any person to examine his or her character. Donne claimed that this was the most important illumination of all, making everyone, in theory, equal:

If after all this, thou canst turne this little light inward, and can thereby discerne where thy diseases, and thy wounds, and thy corruptions are . . . thou shalt never envy the lustre and glory of the great lights of worldly men, which are great by the infirmity of others, or by their own opinion . . .[7]

Some, though, he accepted, would corrupt the light, and use it for worldly advantage in the tactical games of politics, finance and sex. He spoke from experience of his own former life.

Others, by the benefit of this light have searched and found the secret corners of gaine, and profit, wheresoever they lie . . . They have found where was the easiest, and most accessible way, to sollicite the Chastitie of a woman, whether *Discourse*, *Musicke*, or *Presents*, and according to that discovery, they have pursued *hers*, and *their* own eternall destruction.[8]

Manuscript copies of his erotic *Songs and Sonets* and his elegies, tucked away in personal collections around the country, bore eloquent witness to his old powers of soliciting chastity. His past still bothered him. But whether the light was nurtured or stifled, he warned those before him to make no mistake where it came from. 'To end all, we have no *warmth* in *our selves* . . . we have *no light* in our selves,' Donne asserted.[9] The assembly broke up after a service of more than two hours. Those departing from the northern door, into the churchyard, past Paul's Cross, left with the shadow of the Cathedral stretching across their paths. Those leaving to the south met the weak sun filtering through slats in the December cloud above the river. Without the light from God, which could be taken for granted again now the sermon was over, the day for these people would have seemed immeasurably colder, and the earth a dim speck in the middle of nowhere particular.

The year that followed, as Donne established his new ministry, was dominated by political requirements. Spiritual instruction was the foremost way of directing public action; and the pattern of behaviour the King currently desired to control above all was the irrepressible culture of gossip and protest surrounding his policy towards Spain. James still wanted his son Charles to marry the Spanish Infanta, in the interests of European peace. With his son-in-law Frederick living in banishment in Holland, a conciliatory approach now seemed the only way to James of regaining the Palatine territories for his grandchildren. The Spanish, for their part, kept the negotiations grinding on for as long as possible, giving their Flemish-based forces plenty of time to annihilate the Bohemian rebellion and establish a strong Imperial control over Frederick's former demesnes. Simultaneously, they bargained for huge concessions for English Roman Catholics. The reaction of the general public in London and beyond, meanwhile, continued to be a mixture of agony and embarrassment: to most, their King had simply sold out. What James's courtiers and preachers tried selling as a strategy of wily conciliation seemed more like a shameful exhibition of spinelessness. Protest from the pulpit mounted. In April, a young academic clergyman in Oxford, John Knight, used a sermon to discuss 'whether subjects se defendendo in case of Religion might take up arms against their Sovereign?' The rhetorical question triggered a spate of further disputations on the same subject and earned young Knight, despite his hurried disavowal of any treasonous implication, two years in prison.[10] A succession of preachers met with similar reprimands. Many encountered direct protest from the King as they spoke in his presence. Donne's immediate superior, George Montaigne, Bishop of London, had to cut his words short and shuffle offstage when James began objecting in the middle of his Christmas Day sermon at Court in 1622.[11]

While he understood the cause for alarm, and to some extent shared it, Donne devoted himself to the King's cause. After months of struggling with the heedless tattlers of Paul's Walk, he condemned the popular appetite for inflammatory sermons. Speaking on Easter Monday at another of London's open-air preaching venues, the Cross outside the Hospital of St Mary (known as the 'Spittle'), he rebuked 'such itching Ears, as come to hear popular and seditious Calumnies and Scandals, and Reproaches, cast upon the present State and Government'. The public itself was to blame for entertaining such pernicious discourse in the first place. He also had little patience with the preachers who sneaked in their attacks on the King under the cover of godly utterances – 'For, a man may make a Sermon, a Satyr; he may make a Prayer, a Libel.'[12] The leading members of the audience comprised the city's foremost civic authorities. 'The Mayor, with his brethren the Aldermen,' John Stow recorded, dressed in their scarlet robes of office, made it their custom to hear a preacher at the Spittle on the holiday Monday, seated in a 'faire builded house in two stories in height'. A crowd of ordinary Londoners, meanwhile, surrounded the pulpit at the Cross itself, which was similar to the one at Paul's.[13] Donne's sermon at the Spittle in 1622 was by his modern editors' reckoning the longest that he ever gave, running to at least two and a half hours.[14] Towards the end, he acknowledged that his hoarsened voice might 'be so sunk, as that I may not be heard'.[15] The scale of the oration gave him space to range over many topics, voicing several of his recurrent preoccupations, and to meet a range of public commitments. He praised the sovereign fulsomely; and he warned the would-be statesmen of the street against speaking of things they knew nothing about. 'Leave the publick to him whose care the publick is,' he declared – meaning, of course, the King and his vetted councillors. At the same time, he would not allow any disgruntlement that ministers felt with government policy to be used as an excuse for shrugging off their civic responsibilities, taking on the 'darkness of a retir'd life, to avoid the mutual duties and offices of society'.[16] He saw his own task as a public duty.

At one moment in the sermon, Donne's historical perspective lengthened and opened, as he took in the larger political movements that had brought English Christians to the current point in time. He reflected on the preceding century of reformation that had made them all what they were, and defended the English Church it had created. Unlike the now war-ravaged nations on the Continent that had rejected the rule of Rome, England had not gone to Puritan extremes and destroyed its whole tradition of communal worship:

God shin'd upon this Island early; early in the plantation of the Gospel . . . and early in the Reformation of the Church: for we had not the model of any other Forreign Church for our pattern; we stript not the Church into a nakedness, nor into rags; we divested her not of her possessions, nor of her Ceremonies . . .[17]

The words are beautiful, and perhaps Donne's clearest justification of the English Reformation, but they required a wilful blinkeredness. They involved for one thing a straightforward denial of historical fact: as everyone knew, the old churches *had* been stripped bare in the sixteenth century. Decorated walls had been whitewashed, altars and monuments smashed, golden ornaments plundered and melted down, entire buildings demolished and the stone from them cannibalized. As Donne himself said in a late composition,

> So fell our *Monasteries*, in one instant growne
> Not to lesse houses, but, to heapes of stone . . .[18]

But Donne's point is that the Church itself remained intact, in an altered, improved form. Through to his last public poem, quoted above, written to mark the death of a Presbyterian Scots noble,

Donne continued to use the symbolic apparatus of his first faith in his writing: doing so, as John Carey has shown, was an inescapable habit of mind. But Donne himself did not regard this expressive mannerism as something that broke the rules, or feel that it made him deceitful. Rather, purging himself of such symbols, as the Protestants in Europe had, would have been an unacceptable act of psychological vandalism, a childishly destructive rejection of his own heritage. It would have left him unable to articulate some of his deepest spiritual concerns. Rather, the old language was still needed to speak in the present time.

A very personal poem composed around the time he became Dean of St Paul's, for a highly restricted readership, asks whether he had made the right choice in becoming a Protestant. He was brave enough to pose the question openly now he knew that he could answer it.

> Show me deare Christ, thy Spouse, so bright and clear.
> What! is it She, which on the other shore
> Goes richly painted? or which rob'd and tore
> Laments and mourns in Germany and here?[19]

Christ's 'spouse' here is his Church. Which, Donne is asking, was the true bride – the Roman Church, 'richly painted', or the long-suffering Protestant communion in England and Bohemia? 'Richly painted' should not necessarily be read as a pejorative phrase. Donne was on occasion much more permissive about women wearing make-up than many in his profession or of his age: 'Certainly the limits of adorning and beautifying the body are not so narrow, so strict,' he said, 'as by some sowre men they are sometimes conceived to be.'[20] 'Richly painted', then, may well just evoke a straight nostalgia for the decorative, sumptuous Church of Rome. Yet the poem's rhetorical question does seem to answer itself, in directing our sympathy to the Protestant victims of Imperial oppression in central Europe. Like others brought up as Roman Catholics, he clearly missed the old ways, with their form and reassuring regularity; yet like many others, as the 'Spittle' sermon makes clear, he tried convincing himself that they had not been reduced to 'rags' in the English Reformation. From the vantage of St Paul's, with its emphasis on 'high' ceremony, it was possible to believe that was true. True Catholicism lay with the Reformed rather than the Roman Church, because that was where most English people now practised Christianity. This idea is stated in a drastic form, verging on blasphemy, at the end of the Holy Sonnet quoted above. The spouse of Christ, Donne says, the Church,

> is most true, and pleasing to thee, then
> When she is embrac'd and open to most men.[21]

The more lovers she takes in, paradoxically, the truer she is to God. She could not exist, that is, as an abstraction: her strength lay in the combined energy of those she brought together, whether 'richly painted' or 'rob'd and tore'.

Unlike those of a Puritan persuasion, Donne's quarrel was with Rome's political influence more than its rituals. Certainly, in his Christmas Day sermon, he attacked the doctrine of transubstantiation – the Roman Catholic belief that in the Mass, the bread and wine truly become the body and blood of Jesus – and denounced what he called the Papist 'marts of miracles'. Yet at the same time he criticized the ultra-Protestant contempt for ceremony and sacrament as mere 'outward things'.[22] His real argument with the Papists was the threat they posed to the sovereignty of the realm, for no subject could acknowledge both the King and the Pope as supreme authority. So throughout 1622, as the climate of exasperation with James's apparent weakness towards Spain strengthened, while Donne continued to oppose any criticism of the King, he maintained a hard line against Roman Catholics, especially their clergy. The themes of *Pseudo-martyr* were still resonant in his writing: 'Those *Roman Priests* who have given their lives, those *Separatists* which have taken a voluntary banishment, are not competent witnesses for the glory of God,' he made plain: 'these *Missions* from the *Bishop of Rome* [the Pope] are unlawful . . . my neighbours setting his mark upon my sheep, doth not make my sheep his.'[23] In September, even as he defended King James's 'Directions to Preachers' – the measures that attempted to muzzle the dissenting clergy – he still had brutal words for the personal morality of Papist priests:

In the *Romane Church* the most disorderly men, are their men in *Orders*. I speake not of the viciousnesse of their life, I am no Judge of that, I know not that: but they are so out of all Order, that they are within Rule of no temporall Law . . . They may kill *Kings*, and yet can be no *Traytors;* they assigne their reason, *Because they are no Subjects.*[24]

Here was the crux of Donne's problems with Roman Catholicism: and it was the objection of a man trained as a civil lawyer as much as if not more than of a doctor of divinity. Since English Roman Catholics refused to recognize the legality of the monarch's position, and acknowledge themselves as his subjects, they refused to acknowledge any charge of treason. Catholicism was a bugbear for Donne because it challenged the order and authority of the state – and this was for him frankly a more important question than a disputation over clerical vestments. As the year progressed, English Papists had been granted more freedoms than they had enjoyed for many decades. Only four days before King James issued his Directions, the old penal laws against Roman Catholics – the same laws that had brought about the death of Donne's brother – were formally suspended: it was now possible for them to worship without fear of prosecution, imprisonment, or worse. Many in high places – including Buckingham's mother – took this opportunity to openly declare themselves as dissenters from the established Church; and as the Papists flaunted their new liberties, Donne, like many others concerned for the stability of the realm, was rattled.

The same principle of allegiance that made him condemn Catholic missionaries, nonetheless, also made him insist on obedience to the will of the King. Yet again he attacked the political gossips – with an unmistakable dig at the denizens of Paul's Walk:

'*They that walke up and downe*,' he raged, to the masses around the Cross on that early autumn day,

idle, discourcing Men, Men of no Calling, of no Profession, of no sense of other Mens miseries . . . Men that sucke the sweet of the Earth, and the sweat of other Men; Men that pay the State nothing in doing the offices of mutuall societie, and embracing particular vocations; Men that make themselves but pipes to receive and convay, and vent rumors, but spunges to sucke in, and power out foule water; Men that doe not spend time, but weare time, they trade not, they plough not, they preach not, they plead not, but walke, and walke upon the way . . .[25]

In short, Donne required everyone to see and support a common, 'mutuall' cause which they only undermined by vagrant whinge-ing against their ruler. In his next keynote sermon, given in November to commemorate the Gunpowder Plot, Donne took pains to reassure doubters of James's devotion to the Protestant cause, and exploited their memories of Queen Elizabeth: King James, Donne claimed, 'is in his heart, as farre from submitting us to that Idolatry, and superstition, which did heretofore oppresse us, as his immediate Predecessor, whose memory is justly precious to you, was.'[26] A vicious squall of November rain drove the congregation in from Paul's Cross to the sanctuary of the Cathedral, but critics were unlikely to have been dampened by Donne's defence of the King.[27] The allusion to Elizabeth only brought out the contrast with a more glorious age – a time when Donne himself, as many remembered, had joined in the buccaneering campaign against the Spanish in the raid on Cadiz. There was a general conviction that King James, who was rumoured to wear knife-proof underwear, was too lily-livered to act in England's best interests. When a few rowdy students at Lincoln's Inn let off a volley of small cannon one night that autumn, hearing the faint report of the explosion from across town, he leapt out of bed crying 'Treason! Treason!'[28]

Aside from coping with the political upheavals that had become his professional concern, Donne's personal circumstances were relatively peaceful. His colleagues and employers at Lincoln's Inn smoothed his departure with an affectionate and appreciative farewell. The Benchers' records show that they received with much gratitude his parting gift of a six-volume edition of the Bible; and, as 'fitting retribucion', they urged him to remain a member of their society. He was always welcome. They declared that 'Mr Doctor Donne shall continue his chamber in this house which he now hath'. Donne remained close to the life of the Inn for many years afterwards; he continued to preach there whenever he could until his successor, one John Preston, was appointed in May, and he was invited back to give the first sermon delivered in the lawyers' new chapel.[29]

By May 1622, Donne was signing his letters 'At my house at S: Pauls': this was the Deanery, 'a fayre old house', in John Stow's phrase, to the south of the cathedral – not far, in fact, from Bread Street, where Donne had been born.[30] According to Walton, as soon as Donne moved in, 'he employed work-men to repair and beautifie the Chapel.'[31] The house itself, having its own place of worship, was clearly a substantial residence, albeit one crowded in Donne's early days there with decorators and renovators. This was the first time Donne had moved house in ten years, since escaping his 'close prison' at Mitcham; and although it was only a shift across town, it was the first time that he had attempted straightening out a household by himself. His elder boy – and future editor – John, would leave in the autumn for a place at Christ Church in Oxford, from where his father hoped he would go on to enter the Church. John's younger brother George had probably been at Oxford since 1615. It is likely that Donne's surviving daughters – Constance, Lucy, Bridget and Margaret – were living with relatives: Donne mentioned that his eldest, Constance, was only visiting him in the summer of 1621.[32] All the same, he still had a family to take care of – two boys to send into the world and a clutch of girls to marry off. The problem of finding careers and husbands for his brood weighed heavily on him in the following years.

He was confident nonetheless that his daughters were good,

dutiful girls, who knew he wanted only the best for them and would have hated to see him miserable on their behalf: they 'cannot but see my desire to accommodate them in this world,' he said – that is, they could not miss his determination to get them safely hitched to financially secure young men. But they might well, he continued, have to make do with a life of chastity, fasting and prayer: 'so I think they will not murmure if heaven must be their Nunnery, and they associated to the B*lessed* virgins there.' One can imagine a wail of female protest going up if Donne ever muttered such words aloud at a family dinner. As it was, he was confiding his troubles, as he had done for years, to Henry Goodyer, who as a father with unmarried daughters himself knew just how he felt: 'I know they would be content to passe their lives in a Prison,' Donne went on, 'rather then I should macerate myself [waste away, steeped in corrosive liquid] for their sake.'[33] Perish the thought: although there was hope. With his daughter Constance – who was now nineteen – in mind, he was lining up 'an honourable person to give her one of his sons'. This man had a Church benefice worth £300 a year in his gift, which he intended to bestow on his son; the honourable person had also set aside the same amount as an annual inheritance for any children that the youth and his wife might have. A very attractive settlement beckoned. But unfortunately Donne's prospective son-in-law had plans of his own.

'Tell both your daughters a peece of a storie of my *Con.*,' he told Goodyer, 'which may accustome them to endure disappointments in this world.' The arrangements were all well in hand, the boy was earmarked for the priesthood, but

now the youth (who yet knowes nothing of his fathers intention nor mine) flies from his resolutions for that Calling, and importunes his Father to let him travell. The girl knows not her losse, for I never told her of it: but truly, it is a great disappointment to me.[34]

Donne's new mansion near St Paul's suggested an affluence that at first was illusory. Besides the Deanery and his other livings, he was soon presented with another parish, Blunham in Bedfordshire, by the Earl of Kent. But King James levied a heavy tax increase on his courtiers and clerics early in 1622, after Parliament refused to give him the funds his exchequer required; and this was one of the new expenses to which Donne's position now exposed him. He had magnanimously given up one source of supplementary income the previous year, resigning his living at Keyston, which the King gave him after he was ordained, on becoming Dean. He had begun restoration work on his new house, and been taxed heavily; yet when in 1622 his father-in-law, Sir George More, offered to pay him the first quarterly instalment of his dowry, Donne gently and honourably 'refused to receive it', closing More's outstretched hand with the words 'You have been kind to me and mine.' Now he knew what it meant to have daughters to find a good match for. More's fortunes were not what they once had been, as both men acknowledged, and Donne hoped that his own were still rising.[35] His position as Dean brought him a basic yearly income of more than £200, which in time would allow him to lead a moderately prosperous lifestyle, but it had to stretch a long way when he was starting out.[36] During his sermon at the Spittle, he expressed solidarity with his fellow professionals – the loyal ones, anyway – and gentle reproach at how little they were paid.

I may be bold to say, that this City hath the ablest preaching Clergy of any City in Christendom; must I be fain to say, that the Clergy of this City hath the poorest intertainment of any City that can come into comparison with it? it is so.[37]

At the end of the year, Donne complained that 'I had locked my self, sealed and secured my self against all possibilities of falling into new debts' – he had been balancing the books at last; but on becoming Dean, 'in good faith, this year hath thrown me 400[l] [£400 – a hefty sum] lower then when I entred this house.'[38] Goodyer as ever was the trusty recipient of Donne's grouches; though also, as ever, of his active and sensitive friendship. When Donne received an embarrassed note from Goodyer's son John, who had been arrested and thrown into prison as a debtor, he immediately sent funds (a matter of £3, John assured him) to procure his release. The following day, when another note arrived from the young man, promising that just a few pounds more would get him out of gaol, Donne took delicate steps to discover the true sum of the amount owed. He also took the advice of another acquaintance, John Selden, the brilliant and astonishingly prolific legal historian. Selden worked on the foundations of law, civil, ecclesiastical and divine, and was one of the unsung initiators of modern historical method in English letters. But he was not unaccustomed to the inside of a prison cell himself – he had been imprisoned for a while in 1621 for parliamentary services that were thought to have undermined royal authority.[39] All he could suggest for now was that he and Donne consult young Goodyer's father. In the meantime, Donne reassured Goodyer, he had dispatched a servant with some things for John 'to serve his present want'. Since then, he said, 'I heard no more of him, but I hear he is out.'[40] No more is heard of Donne's dealings with the young man: all we know of John Goodyer is that he died two years later.[41]

Neither Donne himself nor the elder Goodyer, a profligate spender, were strangers to this kind of predicament. So when he had been able to save some money, Donne slipped a hundred pounds to one whom Walton describes as 'an old Friend, whom he had known to live plentifully, and by a too liberal heart and carelessness, become decayed in his Estate'.[42] This was almost certainly Goodyer. They were both getting on in years, Donne told his old friend with indulgent gloom, and the crosses were harder to bear: 'In our declinations now, every accident is accompanied with heavy clouds of melancholy, and in our youth we never admitted any.' Goodyer, remembering the letters laced with dejection that Donne had been sending him since his late twenties, might have corrected him here – but, at least, Donne sighed, the trials of old age brought the cherishable wisdom of misery: 'yet truly, even this sadness that overtakes us, and this yeelding to the sadnesse, is not so vehement a poison (though it be no Physick neither) as those false waies, in which we fought our comforts in our looser daies.'[43] In his sermons, Donne comes across as a frighteningly austere moral authority; his letters soften that impression. Like everyone, he could sometimes just feel a bit sorry for himself.

Yet the authority was undeniable. Donne's wider reputation spread and rose during his first year at St Paul's. By the summer he had begun winning over some of those who were sceptical about his appointment. John Chamberlain, the faithful and assiduously gossipy correspondent of the diplomat Sir Dudley Carleton, had at first expressed some reservation about 'pleasant poeticall deanes', but realized in time that Donne was serious about his vocation.[44] At the same time, esteem for Donne's ministry only deepened among his loyal admirers. Lord Hay, on an embassy to France, sent Donne the present of a tun of claret, and warmly recalled the Dean's service as his chaplain on their trip to Bohemia a few years before. 'I must now live upon the crums of my German Devotions,' wrote Hay (a devotion is a personal prayer or religious observance), 'which, if I had carefullie gathered up, had been an eternall Feast.'[45]

In November 1622 Donne gave a sermon at a fundraising dinner held by the Company of the Virginia Plantation. He was warmly received. Many of his friends were members of the company, including Christopher Brooke and Sir John Danvers, the husband of Magdalen Danvers (formerly Herbert). In May Donne himself was made an honorary member of the executive board.[46] The colonial project had so far been something of a serial disaster, beset by organizational and supply problems, bickering among the leaders, famine, disease and skirmishes with native Americans: only recently, there had been a massacre of colonists that pricked a desire in London for genocidal revenge.[47] At the banquet, to which 'many of the nobilitie were invited but few came', Chamberlain reported that between three and four hundred men, admitted at three shillings a head, devoured twenty-one does between them.[48] Thirteen years before, Donne himself at a desperate point in his life had considered packing up and sailing for Virginia, and had applied for a post as secretary with the company. Now he told the sizeable assembly of sociable sorts, some of them his friends of many years, not to give up hope in the venture:

> though you see not your money, though you see not your men, though a *Flood*, a *Flood* of *bloud* have broken in upon them, be not discouraged. Great Creatures ly long in the wombe; *Lyons* are litterd perfit, but *Beare-whelpes* lick'd unto their shape; actions which Kings undertake, are cast in a mould; they have their perfection quickly; actions of private men, and private purses, require more hammering, and more filing to perfection.[49]

Donne could point to his own experience to support this principle of patience. It had taken years of battering and 'filing to perfection' for him to achieve his own current shape. He also had words of support for the colonial enterprise itself. 'A Land never inhabited, by any, or utterly derelicted and immemorially abandoned by the former Inhabitants, becomes theirs that wil possesse it.' There was still the question of what to do when there were in fact already people living there; but where there was space there was a right to occupy it. 'So is it,' Donne reasoned, 'if the inhabitants doe not in some measure fill the Land, so as the Land may bring foorth her increase for the use of men.'[50] The Company's days were numbered, as it turned out — a year and a half later it lost its royal charter, and went out of business — but Donne's sermon was much appreciated.

Eager to promote their cause in any way they could and grateful for his assistance, the council of directors urged that it be published. Donne made a show of reluctance — '*for the* Printing *of this sermon, I am not onely under your Invitation, but under your* Commandement' — but he was evidently proud to see his words in print. This was the second of his sermons to be put through the press: the first was the one on the 'Directions to Preachers' earlier in the year, 'a piece of such perfection' that the King had ordered it to be printed immediately. In a letter written in December, Donne intimated that he would not mind either if his Gunpowder Plot sermon were also brought out.[51] He had lost his old excruciating disdain for

printing his work. Once he had regarded publishing his poems as
an act of social suicide. But for some time now, he had been
starting to see the possibilities of print as something 'profitable
and usefull to the whole world . . . by which the learning of the
whole world is communicable to one another, and our minds and
our inventions, our wits and compositions may have trade and
commerce together.'[52]

The medium that transmitted a work, in Donne's mind, obviously had to suit the audience for which it was intended. His
poems had been private exercises, for a restricted few – although,
problematically, their circulation in manuscript was still expanding.
His sermons, however, were public statements, so it made sense
that they reached the widest possible readership. Donne now saw
himself as a public figure, whose reflections on contemporary
events could have influence beyond his immediate circle.

The political temperature was soon to increase dramatically. In
February 1623, Prince Charles and Buckingham slipped out of
England, wearing false beards and travelling under the aliases of
John and Tom Smith. They were bound for Spain, their plan to
bring about at last the long-discussed marriage to the Infanta. The
comic disguises and the implausibly banal assumed names lent a
scamp-like quality to their departure: all the pomp and deliberation
of the drawn-out talks between London and Madrid was completely undercut by what seemed like a boyish prank. Nonetheless,
the excursion immediately induced a national panic attack. There
were fears for the Prince's safety: with Charles in their clutches,
many were sure that the Spanish could dictate whatever terms they
pleased for the marriage treaty. There was also widespread despair
that an alliance with Spain now was all but a foregone conclusion.
On the following Sunday, by which time the news was known
everywhere, London's citizens flocked in even greater numbers
than usual to St Paul's for up-to-date information, either from the
pulpit or the unofficial bulletins circulating in Paul's Walk. The
preacher that day, however, had strict instructions 'only to pray
for the Princes prosperous journy and safe return', and to offer no
further reflection.[53] Donne himself made no mention of the affair

in the first sermon he gave after the Prince embarked, delivered to the Court at Whitehall, on the first Friday of Lent; though his comment may well lie in the text he chose, John 11:35, 'Jesus Wept'.[54]

In general, he was against the match, but he expressed his position on the crisis with some care. It was unwise to be too outspoken – as many were – by condemning the marriage outright, since the object of criticism in one sermon might well have to become the subject of obligatory praise in another not long afterwards; if, that is, anyone raging against the Infanta was given the chance of preaching another. So instead of blasting out rhetoric from the pulpit, Donne wrote guarded letters to two senior figures very close to the Prince. None, in fact, was closer than the recipient of the first, Buckingham. He dropped the prostrate style of his begging letters of a couple of years before. Donne was now firmly ensconced in St Paul's, and felt able to assume a supportive, almost avuncular attitude towards his young patron, directing his words from the comfort of his study.

Most Honoured Lord,

I can thus far make myselfe beleeve, that I ame where yor Lordship is, in Spaine, that in my poore Library, where indeede I ame, I can turne my Ey towards no shelfe, in any profession, from the Mistresse of my youth, Poetry, to the wyfe of mine age, Divinity, but that I meet more Autors of that nation [Spain], than of any other. Their autors in Divinity, though they do not show us the best way to heaven, yet they thinke they doe: And so, though they say not true, yet they doe not ly, because they speake their Conscience.

This qualified bit of commendation is manifestly reversible. Donne was warning Buckingham. They might not lie, 'because they speake their Conscience', but that was no reason to trust the Spanish: just because they sincerely believed their own lies did not mean they spoke the truth. To push the point home, he said the same was true of their conduct in everyday matters – almost dropping his reader a wink to make sure he had got the gist.

And since in charity, I beleeve so of them, for their Divinity, In Civility I beleeve it too, for Civill matters, that therein also they meane as they say: and by this tyme yor Lordship knowes what they say.[55]

The circumspection might seem excessive, but the letter involved a certain amount of political risk. Buckingham was widely perceived as the champion of the Spanish match at Court – and thus the prime deluder of the King. Privately, therefore, Donne evasively encouraged caution towards Spain, while on the surface appearing to embrace Spanish letters and conduct. In public, to avoid alienating himself from the pro-Hispanic faction that surrounded the King at Court, he deemed it sufficient to let it be known that he could read and speak Spanish himself.[56] An Englishman admitting this was enough to be taken as a sign of approval – a strategy that ran risks with the headstrong patriotic elements in his congregations, but trod a middle path nonetheless.

Many, however, were unafraid to show their true colours on the matter. Most likely to Donne's dismay, Henry Goodyer unwisely revealed himself as being wholly in favour of the match; and, indeed, of closer relations between England and Spain, and between the Reformed and Roman Churches. Goodyer penned a liberal poem commending the 'Admirable Prince' for taking what he saw as a step towards amity and unity. Rome and Geneva, he declared, were 'not directly opposite / As North and South Poles'. Here he borrowed and contradicted an image from his friend. In a letter to Sir Robert Ker, who had followed Charles and Buckingham to Spain, Donne pointed out that while east and west could meet when a map was pasted on to a globe, north and south could not. As in his letter to Buckingham, he was circuitously urging the courtier not to think that England (a northern country) and Spain (a southern one) could ever be brought together.[57] The map idea was one of his favourite and indeed most recognizable conceits, recurring in poems and sermons; but Goodyer turned its political meaning here upside down, most probably to Donne's alarm. Since the image had his stamp on it, people might have thought that Goodyer was merely relaying his friend's opinion.

In reality Donne was much more cautious. Goodyer's poem spoke of the need for reconciliation between faiths and nations, as Donne himself did on occasion – but these were unwise sentiments to voice at such a delicate moment. Many years before, Donne had agreed with Goodyer 'that in all Christian professions there is way to salvation'. This, he accepted, was a 'sound true opinion' but an unsafe one to express too openly – as he feared his friend sometimes did.[58] The matter should not be seen as being removed from the everyday consequences of these middling gentlemen's lives. As Donne knew well, such an indiscretion only narrowed the field of possible husbands for Goodyer's two remaining daughters. Many a patriotic Protestant squire was not going to let his son marry into a 'Popish' family – a hard-up one at that, as Goodyer's was, 'decayed in his Estate'.

When he felt he had a secure venue, away from the sectarian barricades, Donne could, however, express truly moderate thoughts on the nature of religion. And there was evidently a more permissive faction at the fringes of the Court that was willing to hear such thoughts. Addressing a private gathering convened by the Earl of Exeter, Donne felt able to suggest that there was a way to heaven for everyone – even non-Christians: 'by God's grace, there may be an infinite number of soules saved, more then those, of whose salvation, we discerne the *wayes* and the *meanes*. Let us embrace the way which God hath given us,' he advised his audience, 'which is, the knowledge of his Sonne, *Christ Jesus*.' Such a genuinely inclusive and universally compassionate idea was sheer poison to Calvinist Puritans who believed God had predestined a Protestant elect to share his paradise, and it was not one that Donne would have risked from the pulpits of St Paul's, Lincoln's Inn or Whitehall Palace. But he had a warning for those who saw themselves as chosen ones and all 'impure' believers as the chaff for the fire: 'such uncharitable Judges of all other men, that will afford no salvation to any but *themselves*, are in the greatest danger to be left out . . . nothing hinders our own salvation more, then to deny salvation, to all but ourselves.'[59]

20. Devotions

Prince Charles finally tired of his hosts' stalling tactics and left Spain as he arrived, a single man; albeit one who had been exposed, harmfully as many felt, to the direct influence of pernicious Roman Catholics. On his arrival back in London early in October 1623, he was engulfed in public jubilation. For the first time in many years an English royal had actually done something popular. Bells rang ceaselessly; 'reioycing noyses', cannon fire, drums and trumpets resounded through the city. Huge bonfires were lit and tended day and night, fireworks streaked the skies. After eight strenuously anxious months, the kingdom relaxed. London broke into almost hysterical, intoxicated merriment. Donne was close to the centre of the festivities. The roof of his Cathedral was one of the focal celebratory points on the horizon, decked out as it was with blazing torches to salute the Prince.[1]

Donne's year had been taken up with a steady series of public and private engagements. In May, he preached at the consecration of the new chapel at Lincoln's Inn, a sermon that was also presently published. Donne spent much of the summer, as he often did, visiting friends in nearby counties, including Lord Hay, now Earl of Carlisle, at the great manor the flamboyant diplomat was renting at Hansworth.[2] Yet he also took time in July to help out the wardens of St Dunstan's-in-the-West, a church on Fleet Street, not far from St Paul's. The wardens were pressing a legal claim against a colonial adventurer who was withholding funds that had been promised to the parish. An old parishioner called Nicholas Hare left £200 to the poor of St Dunstan's in his will and appointed one Captain John Harvey as his executor. Hare and Harvey were fellow travellers: both preferred life on the road and the open seas. When Hare died, Harvey put up a statue to his dead friend, but pocketed the remainder of the bequest for himself, and disappeared to Virginia, where he served for some time as governor. The church wardens tried taking him to court when he returned briefly a few years later, but by the time he came back for good, having been thrown out of office by the Virginians, there was little left of him to sue. The wardens appreciated Donne's efforts nonetheless – he no doubt used his connections with the Virginia Company as best he could – and it was soon understood that he would take over as vicar of St Dunstan's when the present incumbent died.[3] The parish, in the heart of the legal district, suited Donne entirely: he was ever the fellow and minister of London's gentlemen professionals. In October, he gave a sermon at the Law Sergeants' feast, joining a scramble through foul weather to splatter from the dining hall in the Temple to the Cathedral: 'In the forenoone they went dabling on foote and bareheaded,' Chamberlain reported, 'to Westminster in all the raine, and after dinner to Powles, where the Dean preacht . . . their feast (though otherwise plentifull and magnificent) was so disorderly performed, that yt was rather a confusion.'[4]

A couple of evenings before attending the lawyers' banquet at the Temple, Donne was joined for dinner at his Deanery by his brother-in-law, Sir Thomas Grymes, who with his wife had taken on much of the upbringing of Donne's daughters, and a retired actor, Edward Alleyn, who expressed an interest in marrying the eldest, Constance. Together the three men thrashed out a deal, diminishing by one quarter Donne's greatest domestic worry at this time. One of his four daughters was finally taken. Another year of quiet consolidation had almost passed.

'This minute I was well, and am ill, this minute,' he reflected, as he collapsed under '*earthquakes* in him selfe, sodaine shakings . . . *lightnings*, sodaine flashes . . . *thunders*, sodaine noyses . . . *Eclypses*, sodain offuscations, and darknings of his senses'.[5] The disease had been reported in London for over a month when it seized Donne at the end of November. By this time it was nearing epidemic proportions. 'Spotted' or relapsing fever hits the victim without warning, and induces a frightening schism between mind and body. The sufferer remains lucid but is left physically helpless, scorched and bewildered. Prostrate but wildly awake, Donne was able to register every advance the sickness made through a constitution which he felt at moments was being vaporized. 'Man, who is the noblest part of the Earth, melts so away, as if he were a statue, not of Earth, but of Snowe . . . but he feeles that a Fever doth not melt him like snow, but powr him out like lead, like yron, like brasse melted in a furnace: It doth not only melt him, but calcine him, reduce him to Atomes, and to ashes.'[6] He was forbidden to read, but seems to have insisted on having pen and paper to hand even as he struggled for life. He recorded his final impressions even as they burnt him up. He found his mind wandering far and near, concentrating deeply on himself, and his own condition, but also relating what he was going through to the rest of the species. The very fact of his infection reinforced this extrapolation, since he was exempt from nothing that could strike down another, or thousands of others. 'Man' became the recurring topic of the meditations he was roughing out. 'Woman', predictably, was subsumed or forgotten: female readers have been left to feel implied in or else excluded from Donne's sickbed words. Yet never before had he discovered such depths and recesses within his own being, and thus within all men.

It is too little to call Man a little World; Except God, Man is diminutive to nothing . . . If all the Veines in our bodies, were extended to Rivers, and all the Sinewes, to Vaines of Mines, and all the Muscles, that lye upon one another, to Hilles, and all the other pieces, to the proportion of those which correspond to them in the world, the Aire would be too little for this Orbe of Man to move in, the firmament would bee but enough for this Starre; for, as the whole world hath nothing, to which something in man doth not answere, so hath man many pieces, of which the whol world hath no representation.[7]

He recorded what the fever did to him, and what it made him think; and this took him far afield. One outcome of inquiry was the assertive humanism unfolded in the passage above; another was conjecture on the possibility of life on other worlds (a belief in which, he decided, came from a failure to see how 'singular' the concept of life was to *this* world). But he rarely lost sight of what was happening around him. He logged the great loneliness of the invalid, calling for help that was sometimes slow arriving: 'As *Sicknes* is the greatest misery, so the greatest misery of sicknes, is *solitude*; when the infectiousnes of the disease deters them who should assist, from coming; even the *Phisician* dares scarce come.' Since his thoughts were clear, he missed company. 'A long sicknesse will weary friends at last,' he thought ruefully, 'but a pestilential sicknes averts them from the beginning.'[8] He studied his doctor's expression keenly, contracting the worry he found in his face. 'I observe the *Phisician*, with the same diligence, as *hee* the *disease*; I see hee *feares*, and I feare with him: I overtake him, I overrun him in his feare.'[9] The doctor's anxiety may have been worsened by the fact that he was treating something of a celebrity, whose welfare now featured in the prayers of many around the city, and indeed in the highest places. King James sent his own physician to examine the patient, to the relief of Donne's, who had requested hours earlier 'to have others joyned with him'.[10] After a few days, the fever reached crisis point; the medical team resorted to the apparently time-honoured practice of applying dead pigeons to his feet 'to draw this *vapor* [of the disease] from the *Head*, and from doing any deadly harme there'.[11] They applied the traditional remedies, drawing out corrosive humours through the flesh by applying hot glasses, a process known as 'cupping'. Whether this helped or not is unclear; but the infection was at last being driven out into the open. Donne's skin broke into a rash: 'this sicknesse declares itself by *Spots*, to be a malignant, and pestilential disease', which at least helped the doctors know what they were dealing with. This had good and bad implications: 'if there be a *comfort* in the declaration, that therby the *Phisicians* see more cleerely what to doe, there may bee as much *discomfort* in this, That the malignity may bee so great, as that all that they can doe, shall doe *nothing*.'[12]

His thoughts spun on. He was unable to sleep. At night he sensed every sound, and every gradation in the light. The insomnia was endless, yet terminal:

oh, if I be entring now into *Eternitie*, where there shall bee no more distinction of *houres*, why is it al my businesse now *to tell Clocks*? why is none of the heavinesse of my *heart*, dispensed into mine *Eie-lids*, that they might fall as my heart doth? And why, since I have lost my delight in all objects, cannot I discontinue the facultie of seeing them, by closing mine *eies* in *sleepe*?[13]

By day, from his bedroom in the Deanery, he followed the varying acoustics of the city's business. In particular, however, he tuned into the messages that the peal of different bells relayed. Some merely gave the hour; some called people in for a service or prayers; some announced a wedding. One of these was the marriage of Constance Donne to Edward Alleyn on 3 December. Donne had requested that this should take place soon in case he died. Hearing the chimes, he felt connected to the event. He noticed how the ringing from different sources spanned across the city, even though it diminished, overlapping and allying separate parishes. The sound that inspired the greatest sense of community in him was the softest summons issuing from any bell: the tolling that signalled a death.

Here the *Bells* can scarse solemnize the funeral of any person, but that I knew him, or knew that he was my *Neighbour*: we dwelt in houses neere to one another before, but now hee is gone into that house, into which I must follow him.[14]

Not everyone would get married; not everyone, even, might go to church; but everyone would die. Of all the sounds in London, Donne felt, a funeral bell was the hardest to ignore. One couldn't help wondering who it was being buried, or help reflecting on the fact that someone who had breathed and lived was being covered in soil. Someone hearing the knell might even consider the fact they too would die, and that a bell would ring for them. The person who thought this, for Donne, was immediately 'united with God', by the mere intimation of the grave. 'The *Bell* doth toll for him that *thinkes* it doth.' It was a sound, too, that bonded everyone with everyone, and it provoked the great thought at the heart of Donne's life.

Who casts not up his *Eie* to the *Sunne* when it rises? but who takes off his *Eie* from a *Comet* when that breakes out? Who bends not his *eare* to any *bell*, which upon any occasion rings? but who can remove it from that *bell*, which is passing a *peece of himselfe* out of this *world*? No man is an *Iland*, intire of it selfe; every man is a peece of the *Continent*, a part of the *maine*; if a *Clod* bee washed away by the *Sea*, *Europe* is the lesse, as well as if a *Promontorie* were, as well as if a *Mannor* of thy *friends* or of *thine owne* were; any mans *death* diminishes *me*, because I am involved in *Mankinde*; And therefore never send to know for whom the *bell* tolls; It tolls for *thee*.[15]

All people, in Donne's mature opinion, are part of one sentient landmass. They are not equal, not all equally recognized – there are clods, and there are promontories – but whenever any portion of that continent disappears, no matter how infinitesimal it might seem, the whole is eroded, and a piece of each one of us goes with it. It is impossible to cut oneself off: there is no pure island-life, no life without relation to other lives. The thought behind this great paragraph is not original. The literature of the period is shot through with the idea of 'that general bond . . . wherewith man is bounde unto man, and the which without the taking away of humanity itselfe, cannot be broken'. Underlying it is the Christian concept of charity, though it also brings to mind the *Meditations* of Marcus Aurelius: 'We are all mere nuggets of incense on the one altar. Some burn down now, some later – there is no difference.'[16] Yet Donne opposes the notion of death as a single, momentous event at the end of our lives, an experience that is entirely our own affair. Involved in mankind, we die progressively, gradually, together, with every death under the sun, no matter whose.

The dilemma facing the doctors after Donne's rash appeared was when to try flushing the illness out of his system altogether. The great danger with his condition was the risk of the fever returning, a relapse that generally proved fatal. Yet in the medical orthodoxy of the time the patient's system had to be cleansed. Upon indications of 'digested matter', they finally felt it was safe to administer purgatives, inducing an exhausting ordeal of vomiting and defecation. After this Donne was judged to have survived the worst. In all, the heat of the illness may have endured for a week or ten days.[17] He was shattered. 'I cannot *rise* out of my bed, till the *Physitian enable* mee, nay I cannot tel, that I am able to rise, till *hee tell* me so.' He claimed to have lost all will of his own: 'I *doe* nothing, I *know* nothing of myselfe: how little, and how impotent a peece of the *world*, is any *Man* alone?' Yet when he tested his feet and tried walking to greet visitors to his bedchamber, he could not tell whether he or the world was more doddery and uncertain. 'I am *up*, and I seeme to *stand*, and I goe *round*.' A sick man stumbling across a room seemed to verify Copernicus: 'why may I not beleeve, that the *whole earth* moves in a *round motion*, though that seeme to mee to *stand*, when as I seeme to *stand* to my *Company*, and yet am carried, in a giddy, and *circular motion*, as I *stand*?'

Yet however helpless he felt, he had retained considerable autonomy. He had treated his condition with the sheaf of notes now lying at his bedside, and the more coherent sentences waiting in his mind. By January, he still faced months of recovery; there was still the danger that he would relapse. Yet by then, he had already written up the work he entitled *Devotions Upon Emergent Occasions*, his greatest single piece of prose and one of his most distinctive contributions to world literature. 'I have used this leisure, to put the meditations had in my sicknesse, into some such order, as may minister some holy delight,' he wrote, and since 'my Friends importun'd me to Print them, I importune my Friends to receive them Printed.'[18] The book consists of twenty-three sections, each containing a 'meditation', giving his thoughts and imaginative transformations of an event or stage in his illness, an 'expostulation' reacting to it, and a prayer making peace with it. Astonishingly, the volume was in final form perhaps only six weeks after Donne first fell ill.[19] It was dedicated to Prince Charles (after Donne had checked with Sir Robert Ker, a member of the Prince's household, whether this would be appropriate); yet *Devotions* is also flecked with gratitude for those who looked after Donne through his suffering. He describes his physician as 'my faithfull *friend*', and he thanked God for not allowing 'that my servants should so much as *neglect* mee, or be *wearie* of mee'.[20] For a moment he also remembered with fondness the tenderness of his parents – his mother was still alive, still living in London – who 'would not give mee over to a *Servants* correction'.[21] He was drained, yet renewed; merely waiting for his body to regain the strength his mind had never lost. He compared himself to a 'Prisoner discharged' who had not yet been able to leave the gaol.[22]

At this time he also wrote one of his finest yet also sparest poems, 'A Hymne to God the Father'. The hymn stands out for its calmness, asking God for pardon as so often before, yet ending by gently cancelling the terror of reprisal that marks his earlier verse prayers.

> Wilt thou forgive that sinne where I begunne,
> Which was my sin, though it were done before?
> Wilt thou forgive that sinne; through which I runne,
> And do run still: though still I do deplore?
> When thou hast done, thou hast not done,
> For, I have more.
>
> Wilt thou forgive that sinne which I have wonne
> Others to sinne? and, made my sinne their doore?
> Wilt thou forgive that sinne which I did shunne
> A yeare, or two: but wallowed in, a score?
> When thou hast done, thou hast not done,
> For I have more.
>
> I have a sinne of feare, that when I have spunne
> My last thred, I shall perish on the shore;
> But sweare by thy selfe, that at my death thy sonne
> Shall shine as he shines now, and heretofore;
> And, having done that, Thou hast done,
> I feare no more.

The peace achieved here is remarkable for Donne; the sad thing, perhaps, is that he felt it could only be reached by renouncing the past. The real sting of conscience comes in the second stanza, where he speaks of those he led astray, and thinks of himself as a door to others' damnation. Most moving of all, though, is the interplay between the puns on his own name, 'done', and on the maiden name of his wife Ann, 'more'. God can only have Donne when Donne no longer has More; and while fearing no more, Donne is not quite prepared to give her up. The hymn was one of his favourite compositions. According to Walton, 'he caus'd it to be set to a most grave and solemn Tune, and to be often sung to the *Organ* by the *Choristers* of St *Pauls* Church, in his own hearing.'[23]

By Easter, he was strong enough to preach again in the Cathedral.[24] He was also newly installed as the vicar of St Dunstan's-in-the-West, just opposite the Temple. The document granting the living to Donne concludes with the note 'And this is done by the order of the Lord Duke of Buckingham.'[25] Donne had picked up his career in the spring, it would seem, exactly where it was broken off the previous winter. Yet there was a new reconciled spirit in his preaching. 'The love of God begins in fear,' he told the urbane congregation of St Dunstan's in April, 'and the fear of God ends in love; and that love can never end, for God is love.'[26] This was an unfamiliar note. In his illness he had glimpsed what dying might really involve; he had been given a trial run at death, and found that he could cope. 'If man knew the *gaine of death*, the *ease of death*, he would solicite, he would provoke *death* to assist him, by any hand, which he might use . . . when these hourely *Bells* tell me of so many *funerals* of men like me, it presents, if not a *desire* that it may, yet a *comfort* whensoever mine shall come.'[27]

21. The Old Player

There were many vagabond years during Edward Alleyn's first decade on the stage, summers spent largely in bunking through the provinces, dodging the plague and offending the local authorities. Alleyn's first troupe, the Earl of Worcester's Men, had no permanent base of its own in the capital. The Puritan city fathers despised the theatre in any case: outbreaks of pestilence gave them the good excuse they needed to drive the players out into the country, since the press of people standing for hours through clamorous performances created ideal conditions for infection to spread. Unsurprisingly, Alleyn and his mates were rarely greeted with open arms in the areas they visited, for precisely the same reason. Sometimes they were even paid more if they agreed to forgo putting on their shows. One year in Norwich, they took the money and performed anyway; another in Leicester, on being refused permission to play, they took out drums and trumpets and jaunted through the town in defiance. They were cast as gypsy undesirables by the locals they worried, with their vans of tatty yet fabulous costumes, and their added presumption of acting like kings. And none more than Alleyn, on stage at least: he became the foremost tragedian of his time, pre-eminent especially in 'majestick' roles. He starred in the opening runs of Christopher Marlowe's bloodshot dramas – playing Tamburlaine, the commander who conquers the world and then takes on God in revenge for the death of his Queen, Zenocrate; and Faustus, the flawed scholar who sells his soul to the devil in return for useless knowledge.

He excelled at the part of the over-reacher, yet despite a commanding presence, in himself Alleyn was a contained, devout man whose life was centred and steadied by more than thirty years of matrimony. He had an actor's surfeit of energy for the world, but

was not a delicate, overcharged, highly strung type of thespian. He
and his bride were well matched. On a regional tour enforced by
another epidemic in 1593, he took the news with good humour
that his wife Joan, a sturdy-limbed woman, had been carted
through town in shame for some offence that has not been
recorded. She was staying in London with her family while he
travelled. 'My good sweett harte and loving mouse,' he wrote to
her, 'they say that you wear by my lorde maiors officer mad to rid
in a cart, you and all your felowes.' He urged her to run faster
next time around: 'you may thank your ij [2] suporters, your
stronge leges I mene, that . . . lett you fall in to the hands of such
Tarmagants.'[1] As letters informed him of neighbouring deaths to
the plague, however, the time apart from his loving mouse seems
to have made him reconsider his lifestyle. Unlike the playwright
who established him, Marlowe, stabbed through the eye in the
back room of a pub, Alleyn had no death wish.

There were other actors vying for his place at the top – Richard
Burbage, Shakespeare's leading man, and later Nathan Field. For
some time already, Alleyn had been looking for ways of moving
into the managerial side of the business, and over the next twenty
years he established stakes in a number of London theatres. His
greatest venture, along with his shrewd associate Philip Henslowe
– his wife's stepfather – was the construction of the Fortune theatre,
to challenge the dominance of the Globe, where Shakespeare's
company was based. He also took an interest in other public
entertainments, in particular the savage and immensely popular
spectator sport of bear-baiting. After a long frustrated suit at Court,
he and Henslowe were appointed Masters of the Bears in 1608,
and it was in this capacity, as much as for his booming renditions of
the great Marlovian roles, that he was remembered by Londoners.

As his affluence grew, Alleyn sought respectability to go with
it. A deeply religious man, he also cared sincerely about the suffering of the poor, the old and the sick. His father had been the head
warden of the Bedlam hospital, and the madhouse cries evidently
lived with him; he was a keen observer of deprivation around
London, and did what he could to alleviate it, collecting money

and tithes for the needy in his local Southwark. Much of his energy in the last twenty years of his life went into building a large charitable institution, Dulwich College, on land he had purchased in the south-east outskirts, where he and his loving mouse, who were unable to have children, moved into the old manor. The large brick college they built there eventually held a chapel, a school for disadvantaged boys and twelve almshouses for homeless people. The project strengthened further Alleyn's standing in popular esteem, though he never received the knighthood that many thought he deserved.[2]

He was not one, however, to be flattened by disappointment or loss. When his until then aptly named Fortune theatre burnt to the ground in 1621, he recorded the event with a neutral, one-line entry in his diary and proceeded to rebuild the theatre – taking more care, this time, to protect his liabilities. In the same spirit, it was only five months after the death of his first wife Joan in 1623 that he arranged to marry another, Constance Donne.

Donne's eldest daughter first caught Alleyn's eye in September the previous year, when accompanying her aunt and uncle, the Grymeses, his good friends, to dinner at Dulwich.[3] The following autumn, on 21 October, talking after dinner in the parlour of the Deanery at Paul's, he, Donne and Sir Thomas Grymes came to an agreement. The portion Donne was required to pay Alleyn to support Constance was £500, or more, if the money due from his 'prime lease' exceeded that amount. Alleyn offered in return to equal that sum on his death, and leave her a further £500. 'This gave not content,' he recalled, and Grymes urged him to increase his offer. Alleyn's record of the conversation shows that Donne was no pushover in his financial dealings: years of scrimping had toughened him. When Alleyn offered to pay two thousand marks (in the region of £1,300), 'This was accepted & security demanded.' After Alleyn's accounts and investments in property around the city had been explained in some detail, the deal was on the verge of being closed when Donne was 'called away by the coming of some ladies'. Grymes was left to conclude the business; and Alleyn, satisfied, rode to see Constance at her uncle's house in

Peckham, in the south of the city, where he 'told her what had past & more to show my Love to her of my own voluntary I told her before Sir Thomas I would make it [her jointure] up to £1500.' This interview suggests that Constance already knew about his intentions: the match was not being thrown at her out of the blue. The loving gesture of his final bid, he noted, was 'extraordinary accepted on' by all parties.[4]

The wedding arrangements were rushed by circumstances, with Donne apparently falling ill before a final prenuptial agreement could be tidily concluded. At the 'beginning of your sickness,' Alleyn reminded Donne later, 'you desired our marriage should be performed with as much speed as might be for as you said the world took large knowledge of it.' The marriage was indeed greeted with a mixture of incredulity and derision: 'The straungest match in mine opinion is that Allen the old player hath lately married a young daughter of the Deane of Paules,' wrote Chamberlain, who (rightly, as it turned out) expressed concern that this would diminish Alleyn's 'charity and devotion' towards his philanthropic projects.[5] It was an unusual family that was yoked together. Constance was twenty; her 'old player' was fifty-seven. His father-in-law, the Dean, was six years younger.

The marriage was one of unequal convenience. Alleyn, besides getting a young woman to share his bed and take care of him, bought his way into the hard-won propriety that Donne had made for himself. As for Constance, she was evidently a realist. She now at least had the security of being a married woman. If Alleyn predeceased her, she would be fairly well provided for and could attract another partner. But there are, in fact, faint signs that the couple were quite happy – certainly Alleyn, a warm, large-hearted husband, made every effort to make her comfortable, and described her in his will as 'my loving wife Constance'.[6] Donne's part of the bargain, meanwhile, is not so clearly ascertained. His quibbles over financial terms suggest unease with the match, which was evidently engineered by his brother-in-law, Grymes. There was no definite social inequality, and Alleyn's wealth certainly exceeded Donne's. Yet the old player brought something of disrepute to the Dean's assiduously cultivated clerical image. Actors and acting were treated as being never quite fit for respectable society. Although immensely popular, and widely praised for his works of charity, Alleyn brought a tang of the rough life, a whiff of the bearpit, into the sanctity of the Deanery parlour. He had fingers in all kinds of commercial pie. The taverns he leased on the Bankside, for example, which eventually formed part of Constance's marriage settlement, doubled up as notorious brothels.[7]

Donne had been desperate to get a daughter married off, and had succeeded. But in the months following his tentative recovery from spotted fever, his real opinion of Alleyn emerged in examples of trifling yet pointed coldness and meanness. He put a stop to little kindnesses he had offered his daughter. When the worst danger of his illness was over, 'the people all giving joy', Donne had promised to let Constance have 'her mother's childbed linen for a new year's gift', but he had found himself unable to part with it. Similarly, when she asked for 'a little nagg' of Donne's 'to use for her health to take the air' – which he had said many times was of no use to him – the horse was withheld. Her brother George, now a strapping lad with little interest in the bookish pursuits of his father and elder brother, had offered to take the mare over for her. She had 'very much joyed' in the prospect of riding around Dulwich. Yet, to Alleyn's disgust, 'to prevent her of the comfort [of having it] the nag was suddenly sent away to Oxenford' – for John Donne the younger, now well into his studies at Christ Church. There was more: Constance owned two diamond rings, both evidently given her by Donne, perhaps as an engagement gift. Abruptly, though, he asked Alleyn to tell her that he had actually promised one of these rings to someone else and thus needed it back, saying that he would give her in exchange the ring 'with 3 stones' that adorned his own hand. But he did not honour his word. (He had grown fond of trinkets; in his pocket he carried a little 'striking Clock'.[8]) Everyone had their foibles, yet such petty cruelties were incomprehensible to Alleyn. He was quite aware that the slights were aimed at him, by way of his wife. At one stage, he claimed, Donne had urged him to be 'as bold in your house as in my own', though when he needed a room for a period of work in town, and was 'willing to accept your former loving', Donne answered him 'with labour' – that is, squeezing out his reply – 'no.'

These twisted intellectuals perplexed Alleyn. He could not understand how Donne could clench and retract within himself his own previous openness. 'In plain terms give me leave to enquire what faults of mine hath caused so many unkind passages in you,' demanded Alleyn, who retaliated with crabby little barbs of his own. Constance's sister Lucy was staying with them in Dulwich, and though she 'was good company for my wife', Alleyn nonetheless pointed out that Donne was better able to pay for her keep than he was.

These were niggles, but the relationship was detonated into open hostility, predictably enough, by an argument over money. Both men harboured misapprehensions about the original marriage settlement. Donne expected an annual jointure for Constance of £200, which Alleyn denied he had ever agreed to pay. By early 1625, Alleyn's finances were becoming stretched and he found it hard to meet all his commitments. He had to rely on loans to tide him over, and was well satisfied when he got the mistaken impression that Donne had 'Lovingly' agreed to lend him £500. It can only be assumed that Donne thought he was talking about the five hundred he had agreed to pay as his daughter's dowry. When Alleyn turned up at his door to collect the loan – which he regarded as 'a common courtesy afforded to a friend', a 'Loan of unuseful money' (that is, spare cash) – Donne disclaimed ever offering it. A very public row erupted. Alleyn treated such snivelling evasion with hearty scorn. He only needed the money, he told Donne, in order to cover his expenses, which included the upkeep of Constance; but Donne, he said, evidently 'esteemed £500 before my honesty, your own reputation or your daughter's good.' This pricked Donne's sense of honour, and 'being inflamed', he spat back twice that 'it was false and a lie'.

Then it was Alleyn's turn to go into a huff of theatrical indignation. Having been slandered, called a liar to his face, twice in fact, all that prevented him from demanding satisfaction was Donne's priesthood. Such words, he stormed, were 'more fitting you 30 years ago when you might be questioned for them, than now, under so reverent a calling as you are.'

John Donne and Edward Alleyn were grandees of very different Elizabethan worlds. They had only been close 'this little time' – but Alleyn's allusion to the past of thirty years before claims a prior acquaintance. Donne's sphere of activity had been that of the college-educated, Inn of Court gentleman, shaking off his origins as an ironmonger's son. He wrote for other 'subtle-witted antic youths', 'wit-pyrats', decked out in their feathered capes, joined them on the aristocratic excursions against the Spanish, and hung around the Court his poetry claimed to despise.[9] As 'Master Secretary Donne', he had gravitated towards the centre of government.

Alleyn, by contrast, belonged to a grittier yet somewhat fresher environment. He was a navvy of the early theatre that relied on the patronage of nobles yet was run by workmen, and enjoyed by the riotous apprentices whom Donne and his kind frequently taunted. Shakespeare's 'rude mechanicals' in *A Midsummer Night's Dream*, the artisans who leave their shops to rehearse a comical tragedy in the woods beyond the city walls, are affectionate representations of the pioneers that Alleyn worked and travelled with. James Burbage, builder of the first purpose-built auditorium (with the explanatory name 'The Theatre'), was a joiner by trade; Francis Langley, who built the Swan, a goldsmith; Philip Henslowe, Alleyn's business partner, a dyer. While Alleyn toured the provinces, sleeping rough when he had to, only the metropolis was good enough for Donne, who poured scorn on the many failed lawyers turned playwrights who gave 'idiot actors meanes'.[10] Yet he knew the theatre. He was remembered as a great visitor of plays. After paying a penny or so extra, perhaps, to stand in the thatched gallery rather than amid the crowd below – which could be huge – in the open yard, he had evidently seen Alleyn's prisoner in *Tamburlaine*, King Bajazeth, brain himself on the bars of his cage rather than die at his captor's hand.[11] And Alleyn's cryptic remark suggests that he too knew who Donne was '30 years ago'. The hint of insider knowledge must have brought colour to Donne's cheeks. Their worlds had intersected before; both were known to call in the same places. He may not have read the stylish – 'facetiously Composed and scattered' – verses for which Donne was still remembered, nor known the women they were written about, but Alleyn knew of 'Jack' as well as 'Doctor' Donne.

Donne's 'reverend calling' now required him to repent for what he was then. 'Forgive me my sinnes, the sinnes of my youth, and my present sinnes . . . and the sinnes I cast upon my children, in an ill example; Actuall sinnes, sinnes which are manifest to all the world, as that now they are hid from mine own conscience, and mine own memory; Forgive me my crying sins, and my whispering sins, sins of uncharitable hate, and sinnes of unchaste love . . .'[12] For most of his judges in Paul's Walk, however, the past was nothing to get in a sweat about – so long as it was past. Prince Charles himself was evidently an admirer of Donne's poetry, a fact that gratified the Dean during a crisis of confidence two years later. Donne wrote little in verse now, and showed less: when he did, there were disapproving murmurs. When his last commissioned elegiac verses – written in March 1625 – were circulated in manuscript, Chamberlain remarked: 'Though they be reasonable wittie and well don yet I wish a man of his yeares and place to geve over versifieng.'[13]

At issue here is not the content of any particular poem so much as the fact that Donne had been and still was a poet. In an intriguing preface to the same poem, addressing his friend Sir Robert Ker, Donne himself said: 'you know my uttermost when it was best, and even then I did best when I had least truth for my subjects.'[14] In this snaky sentence, the sleek literary sophisticate of twenty or thirty years before re-emerges, to disavow any idea that poetic fiction needs to be true, and to defend his own works from the charge of distorting reality. Yet in the same sentence, the Dean of St Paul's also urges us – a little too defensively – not to read his old lyrics and satires too literally, too biographically: a lot of his works, he is saying, are exaggerations, tall stories, fantasies. This was precisely the idea, however, that many were uncomfortable with. They did not want their preachers to be men who, when 'versifieng', simply made things up. Being a priest was about telling the Truth.

'I must be branded either for a fool or a knave,' Alleyn raged, 'yet it seems it was your desire to drive me into that disgrace.' Donne was said to be 'by nature highly passionate, but more apt to reluct [struggle, resist] at the excesses of it' – that is, he was better at fighting his temper down than Alleyn was.[15] Certainly his adversary had been an adept bloodcurdler thirty years earlier.

> Go, villain, cast thee headlong from a rock,
> Or rip thy bowels, or rend out thy heart,
> T'appease my wrath; or else I'll torture thee,
> Searing thy hateful flesh with burning irons
> And drops of scalding lead, while all thy joints
> Be rack'd and beat asunder with the wheel . . .[16]

For the time being, however, Alleyn contented himself with slouching off resentfully and letting off steam, a few days later, in a passionate letter of protest. He swerved between paroxysm and appeal to fairness. He just felt cheated. In his heart, he wanted to be friends with Donne: 'before this violence broke forth you call'd me a plain man,' he remembered, and that still pleased him. Playing down his old talents as an actor, he insisted that 'I never could disguise in all my life & I am too old now to learn rhetoric of the curiousest school in Christendom, my heart and tongue must go together.' This was a dig at Donne's style. Rhetoric of the 'curiousest school' had always been his forte – it was partly his aptitude at making the farfetched seem tangible that made the language of his poetry and preaching stand out. Having vented his feelings, Alleyn ended by calling for peace: 'I hope you will pardon me in delivering my mind in plain terms. Your ever ready with my best love to your daughter & my best service to you.'

A few years later, Donne icily told a friend, 'when I lend the world a daughter in marriage, a son in a profession, the world does not alwaies pay me well again.'[17] As for the altercation itself, unfortunately, we only have Alleyn's version of events. Donne's reply, if he made one – if, in fact, he received Alleyn's letter at all, since it survives only in a frantic and incoherent draft, with many revisions and deletions – has not survived. But it should not be assumed from the episode that he was an ungenerous man. Like Alleyn, he was committed to charitable action: Walton reports that

he was inquisitive after the wants of Prisoners, and redeemed many from thence that lay for their Fees or small Debts; he was a continual Giver to poor Scholars, both of this and forraign Nations. Besides what he gave with his own hand, he usually sent a Servant, or a discreet and trusty Friend, to distribute his Charity to all the Prisons in *London* at all the Festival times of the year . . .[18]

He merely disliked the ageing impresario cadging more money than he had agreed to pay in a transaction that made him feel, in retrospect, distaste. Alleyn obviously expected Donne to be a man like himself and the other 'plain' dealers on the Bankside, ready to grant and ready to ask for a helping hand in little business affairs. Many times, he protested in his letter, he had asked Donne to smooth the way in 'matters of indifference [inconsequence] belonging to your place' – most probably in settling rents or making bids to lease properties owned by the Cathedral – 'but they were either put by to circumstances or flatly denied'. For Alleyn, these requests were common courtesies. For Donne, they were corruptions.

Running the Cathedral involved managing a very large financial concern; but while in general Donne's account-keeping 'gives one great respect for his care and efficiency', his use of resources was not always above question.[19] Little was done, during his years as Dean, to improve the decrepitude of St Paul's, though Bishop Montaigne did purchase a large quantity of Portland stone to be used on repairs. Yet Donne quietly allowed this to go missing, 'borrowed' by the Duke of Buckingham for the restoration of York House on the Strand – Donne's old home in the employ of Egerton – which he had made his main London residence: it served as a splendid warehouse for his staggering art collection, and, as with its previous tenants, put him next door to the centre of Court power at Whitehall. Buckingham made extensive modifications, and the one surviving remnant of the house, the water gate on the embankment, built in 1626, is made from a portion of this purloined stone. As John Carey puts it, 'perhaps Buckingham regarded this as a return for services rendered'.[20] Certainly if one looks for evidence of Donne paying up for his Deanery, then this is it.

Alleyn's letter puts the quarrel towards the end of the first quarter of 1625. As such, he may have been unlucky enough to make his approach for the loan precisely at a moment of great professional strain for Donne. On 27 March, King James died. He had been weakening for years, unsteady on his limbs and increasingly crippled by gout. With this, all courtiers went on tenterhooks over their future prospects. To some extent, however, such fears were misplaced, since the daily running of government remained in exactly the same hands regardless of the monarch's death. By now Buckingham was virtually the dictator of England, and his control over Prince Charles was even greater than it had been over his father. Despite the vast wealth, privilege and undeniable power he attained through James, his relationship to the King was always one of a subordinate, son, catamite; to Charles, he was all but an equal. James had never quite allowed his favourite a free rein with national policy.

As the old man faded, Buckingham's influence in this sphere strengthened. Since their return from Madrid, he and the Prince had been diligently shunting the country towards war with Spain and a royal match with France instead, alienating Parliament and the Privy Council. The Commons were understandably perplexed by the *volte face*, were reluctant to fund the huge war chest demanded of them, and could not see much difference between a Spanish Papist princess and a French one. Buckingham picked off his domestic opponents, former allies and rivals alike. It may have been the King who was Buckingham's foremost obstacle and most drastic victim. James only began his descent towards death after Buckingham's mother applied special plasters to his wrist, which were 'supposed to eat down into his stomach and cure his fever', but which, as his own physicians swore in protest, clearly brought on his end. It was immediately alleged by the Duke's enemies that he had poisoned his master, a charge that became an 'article of faith' after the Civil War; propaganda aside, there were, nonetheless, clearly grounds for suspicion.[21] This was someone to whom, if he asked you for your Portland stone, you gave it, and promptly at that.

Right to the end James never lost his affection for Steenie, although the Duke treated him haughtily in his final months. Regretting the distance between them, in the winter the King wrote to Buckingham

praying God that I may have a joyful and comfortable meeting with you, and that we may make at this Christenmas a new marriage, ever to be kept hereafter; for, God so love me, as I desire only to live in this world for your sake, and that I had rather live banished in any part of the earth with you, than live a sorrowful widow-life without you. And so God bless you, my sweet child and wife . . .[22]

The letter aches with insecurity. Buckingham had in effect already shouldered the rheumatoid old man for a younger 'wife', the malleable Prince. They were inseparable. It was symbolic that they slept together on the first night of Charles's reign.[23]

Donne's concern with larger political questions after the King's death were soon eclipsed by a more immediate worry: stage fright. On Saturday 2 April, he received the complimentary yet alarming command to preach before Charles the following day: this would be the first sermon the new King would hear since James died, after a week of strict mourning. It was scheduled for the 'after-noone', Donne informed his friend Ker, a senior member of the Prince's household, and would be delivered at Charles's residence, St James's Palace: 'into my mouth there must not enter the word after-dinner, because that day there enters no dinner into my mouth.'[24] Despite his nerves, he knew the order was an honour and a sign of approval; it also sent a tacit signal through the Court and clerical community. Charles was favouring a more or less 'high' churchman, a defender of ceremonies that some regarded as 'Popish', as opposed to a member of the Puritan faction that had earlier dominated his entourage at St James's Palace.[25] Donne was also, however, known as a consensus seeker. For him personally, the task was frightening on at least three accounts. Firstly, though the trust King James had placed on him was obviously an advantage, he could not be sure how to satisfy Charles, an even more ambiguous person than his father. Secondly, the venue was strange to him: he was a seasoned performer at the chapel of Whitehall, where the pulpit was frequently taken by preachers of quite different doctrinal persuasions, but St James's Palace across town was foreign territory. Thirdly, he had only a day to come up with potentially the most important hour-long address of his career.

His job was not made any easier by the conditions he had to work in. Giving a sermon at Court, the preacher could rarely see the person who was the focus of his efforts. In most chapels royal, the monarch sat in a second-storey private gallery at the back of the hall, looking down on the assembly, but hidden from view by a screen. A select number of courtiers might share this closet; at Hampton Court, King James and Queen Anne each had one of their own. Below, segregated according to sex or rank (or both), sat the followers of the Court. Pews were not conventionally positioned so that the congregation faced the pulpit, however. The rows of long stalls ran parallel to the walls on either side of the central aisle, obliging the preacher to speak to the crowd with their faces snubbing him at a right angle to his, and also project his words towards the invisible presence behind the latticed woodwork at the furthest extreme of the chamber.[26] All the time he was speaking, unable to tell how his words were being received, he might be interrupted by an angry royal voice, as many were.

The surrounding network of the palace itself was also intimidating. Donne needed somewhere to get ready – to put on his priestly vestments, pray, and take a last-minute look through his notes. At Whitehall, he had plenty of allies – not least the Earl of Carlisle – who could set aside a room for him; he may even have established a nook of his own in the complex. At St James's he was an outsider. His only patron there was Sir Robert Ker, who he realized might have 'businesse, or privatenesse, or company' of his own to deal with; yet he timidly asked if 'Towards the time of the service . . . I may hide my selfe in your outchamber,' or at the least some little 'closet'.[27] Sir Robert quickly assented, and invited Donne to dinner at midday, or later on if he preferred. Donne declined the offer nervously yet graciously, saying he would call at one o'clock. He planned to be as inconspicuous as possible: 'After the Sermon, I will steal into my Coach home, and pray that my good purposes may be well accepted, and my defects graciously pardoned.'[28]

The fact that he now had his own transport was a sure sign of the status he had achieved. Whether or not he felt satisfied – or safe – as his carriage took him back towards St Paul's that Sunday afternoon, he was soon enough informed that the King was pleased with what he had heard. There was usually no telling with Charles, a prim, temperamental character. Pale, dressed in a 'plain black cloth cloak to the ancle', he listened attentively.[29] The sermon itself was approved for publication.[30] Donne made a list for Charles's benefit of the 'foundations' of the Church, the State, and the Family, and warned him to beware of Roman Catholic influences. Later in the same month, in another high-profile sermon commemorating King James, Donne would take these points further by arguing that no ruler should try to outstrip the authority of the Church: 'an aptnesse to quarrell at the proceedings of the Church, and to be delivered from the obligations, and constitutions of the Church, is ever accompanied with an ambitious pride, that they might enjoy a licentious liberty.'[31] He felt confident enough to be modestly assertive towards the new monarch.

James's funeral was a massive spectacle, with nine thousand official mourners, an emphatic display of just how much the death of a King mattered. Yet there was a sense of compulsion about it all; James never captured the popular imagination as Queen Elizabeth had. Donne, who was sincerely fond of the King, and grateful for the favour he had shown, took his place with an attendant among the royal chaplains. Further back in the long, slow procession to Westminster Abbey, where James was buried, was Edward Alleyn, his presence required as Master of the Bears and Bulls.[32]

The weather that early spring was foul, 'windy and obstreporous', and the city's governors were preoccupied more with matters of survival than observing form. Since late March, around the time James died, the weekly death toll from the plague had been increasing steadily. Forty-five people died of it in the week of the funeral, which took place on 7 May. Attending must have been fatal for many. In times past, this level of infection had been sufficient for orders to be issued closing down the public theatres, banning street football and other informal urban gatherings. Those who could were already leaving the city.[33] In the populous parishes, with a dunghill at the front of each house, open sewers in the lanes and filthy rushes on the floors inside, the number of stricken homes kept creeping up. The spread of the disease disordered public business, although there was a show of trying to continue as normal. Buckingham travelled to France to finalize King Charles's marriage to the Princess Henrietta Maria, and managed to disgrace himself by attempting to seduce the French Queen.[34] Henrietta was brought to London in the middle of a torrential June, by which time the death rate had gone up to 165 a week. A distinctly edgy Parliament was convened. Its Members were eager to be out of town, but not in so much of a rush that they would grant the impossible sums that Charles and Buckingham demanded for the war on Spain.

Around this time, Donne was laid low by a respiratory illness that left him struggling 'to put out breath, almost to my last gasp'.[35] This must have been frightening for more than the symptoms themselves, since the plague had taken a pneumonic, as well as its more common lymphatic, form, which doctors had at first failed to recognize. Yet his lungs cleared; and as soon as he was well enough, he left the city, taking 'some few of my family', to stay with his friends Sir John and Lady Magdalen Danvers (formerly Magdalen Herbert) in Chelsea.[36] As the summer continued, the rain kept pouring down, the haymakers worked 'up to the ankles in water', and the rats spreading the pestilence thrived. The epidemic reached a scale unseen since the Black Death. By mid-August, it was killing over four thousand a week; the church-yard of St Paul's, where it was all but impossible in any case to dig a grave without disturbing the bones in another, was brimful. Blanketed corpses were thrown in lots of forty or fifty together into 'pest-pits', and quickly shovelled under. The scenes in the streets were wretched, as the rules of quarantine and segregation began to break down:

> Here, one man stagger'd by, with visage pale:
> There, lean'd another, grunting on a stall.
> A third, halfe dead, lay gasping for his grave;
> A fourth did out at window call, and rave;
> Yonn came the *Bearers*, sweating from the *Pit*,
> To fetch more bodies to replenish it.[37]

Many did all they could to escape, but the lesson of the time was that no one was an island: the plague would pursue you as far as you ran, until you dropped dead of exhaustion; and those who did try escaping the capital were not welcome where they called. Donne wrote of the lengths he had heard people enduring:

The Citizens fled away, as out of a house on fire, and stuffd theyr pokets with their best ware, and threw themselfs into the high-ways, and were not receyvd, so much as into barnes, and perishd so, some of them with more money about them, than would have bought the villadge where they dyed: A Justice of the Peace, into whose Examination it fell, told me, of one that dyed so, with £1400 about him . . .

Donne had made it as far as Chelsea, but as the disease overtook the village and the surrounding districts, it became obvious that he could go no further: 'the infection multiplyed so fast, as that it was no good Manners, to go to any other place, and so I have been in a secular monastery.'[38]

It was impossible to rest easy, but the Danvers' house and

grounds at Chelsea were spacious and quiet, with an exotic garden in an Italian style, and Donne was on excellent terms with his hosts. Sir John Danvers 'had in a fair body an harmonicall mind'.[39] He took pleasure in showing the points of antiquarian interest about his home, including the fireplace in his study and the 'two noble pyramids' adorning the front gate, which had been salvaged from the mansion of Donne's kinsman, Sir Thomas More.[40] Danvers was a great trader in anecdotes, one of the main conversational sources for the vivid biographical sketches written by his kinsman, John Aubrey, the author of *Brief Lives*. He would eventually be one of the parliamentary commissioners who signed King Charles's death warrant.

He was also a vague spendthrift who needed the care and direction of a strong woman. His wife Magdalen was the real head of the household. She was a friend from long ago for Donne, at one time possibly his lover. His stay, which lasted half a year, renewed their friendship. Now he was impressed by her '*holy cheerfulnesse*, and *Religious alacrity*'. She ran a devout household, insisting on visits to Church several times a week besides Sundays, hastening 'her *family*, and her *company* hither, with that cheerful provocation, *For God's sake let's go, For God's sake let's bee there at the Confession* [the prayer at the beginning of service].' Every Sunday, she would gather the whole family and guests to 'shut up the day, at night, with a generall, with a cheerful *singing of Psalmes*'. Yet there was more to Magdalen than a show of holiness. As the plague 'fell hotly' on Chelsea, she demonstrated a brave and active social goodness. Donne was full of admiration for her charity to the sick who crawled to her gate: 'When every [other] doore was shut up, and, lest *Death* should enter into the house, every house was made a *Sepulchre* of them that were in it', the afflicted who called on Magdalen were not turned away, but had 'releefe, and releefe *appliable to that very infection*, from this house'. She did not blanch, it seems, even at applying salve to bubonic sores.

She was in her late fifties. Donne was still struck by her mature, unforced attractiveness.

God gave her such a *comelinesse*, as, though shee were not *proud* of it, yet she was so content with it, as not to goe about to mend it, by any *Art*. And for her *Attire*, it was never *sumptuous*, never *sordid*; But always agreeable to her *quality*, and agreeable to her *company*; Such as shee might, and such, as others, such as shee was, did weare.[41]

For some time after Donne's first arrival, visitors could still come and go to the house. One who stayed on for some time was Magdalen's son, the poet George Herbert, who was then considering his future. Herbert, in his early thirties, had the build and complexion of a lifelong scholar, '*lean to an extremity*', but with a mild, cheerful, engaging manner.[42] He was contemplating entering the priesthood, and although Donne makes no mention of their talk, he was surely some help to the younger man finding his way. The reverse may even be true. Herbert's poetry is the unique record of someone finding sufficiency in life as a soul, and a soul, moreover, that could genuinely get on with God. The fear of punishment or annihilation is rarely far from Donne's religious verse. Herbert, by contrast, was a poet who could urge the Almighty to relax:

> Throw away thy rod,
> Throw away thy wrath:
> O my God,
> Take the gentle path.[43]

In time, Herbert would be content to live in secluded obscurity as a village priest. He was reconciled to all the things that Donne found temperamentally difficult. Yet Walton says they had 'such a Sympathy of inclinations, that they coveted and joyed to be in each others Company'.[44]

Back in London, by September public order was breaking down completely. Certain of waking up with the telltale sores on their bodies any day, people were gripped by a criminal fearlessness to seize and enjoy what they could while they were still alive. Nothing appals an authoritarian more than the mentality of those who have nothing to lose; yet Donne, though disgusted, nonetheless understood what motivated the spirit of suicidal hedonism that was loose in the city. Soon afterwards, he described those who said to themselves

We can but die, and we must die . . . *Let us eat and drink, and take our pleasure*, and make our profits, *for to morrow we shall die*, and so were cut off by the hand of God, some even in their robberies, in half-empty houses; and in their drunkenness in voluptuous and riotous houses; and in their lusts and wantonness in licentious houses; and so took in infection and death . . . Men whose lust carried them into the jaws of infection in lewd houses, and seeking one sore perished with another; men whose rapine and covetousness broke into houses, and seeking the Wardrobes of others, found their own winding sheet, in the infection of that house where they stole their own death . . .[45]

Donne himself, in the meantime, lodged at the manor house in Chelsea, was quietly preparing for posterity. Those able to get out of London, as he said, had 'stuffd theyr pokets with their best ware'. The prize possession he brought with him was his manuscript archive from over a decade now of preaching.

I have reviewd as many of my Sermons, as I had kept any notes of; and I have already written out a great many, and hope to do more. I ame already come to the number of 80: of which my sonne who, I hope will take the same profession, or some other in the world of middle understandinge, may hereafter make some use.[46]

His son John was dragging his feet over taking orders; but he would indeed make use of the sermons, though not in the way Donne expected.

As the autumn went on, the pestilence finally subsided. The city was devastated and starving. The people had forgone all kinds of public gathering for many months, but as the congregations began

regrouping in greater numbers again, there was criticism for 'run-
away' preachers who had abandoned their flocks – though they
were well used to churchmen with more than one living going off
during the summer to visit their other benefices.[47] Donne stayed
away until the end of the year, so long that a rumour got about
that he was dead. He wrote to Goodyer reassuring him that such
reports were at least slightly exaggerated: 'the report of my death,
hath thus much of truth in it, that though I be not dead, yet I am
buried.' He explained how when the infection reached Chelsea,
it had been impossible to go anywhere else. He had in fact done
the sensible and responsible thing of staying put – 'buried' – in a
region that was by no means safe: his 'manners' had prevented him
from seeking a surer refuge in one of the great country houses
where he had aristocratic friends. By way of catching up he offered
the snatches of news he had caught during his seclusion. Buckingham was trying to pawn the crown jewels in The Hague, to raise
money for the war effort; and of more personal interest to Goodyer,
Queen Henrietta had 'by way of recommendations to the Duke,
expressed her self royally in your behalf'. As ever, Donne sent
regards to his friend's still husbandless daughters.[48]

He was back in time to give his Christmas Day sermon at
St Paul's.[49] The people he addressed had been sequestered for
months, deprived of fresh food, watching friends and relatives die;
many, pressed into compulsory civic service, had had to enforce
segregation on their neighbours. The more lowly ones had inspected blighted homes and carried the dead. At Christmas, Donne
made no comment on what he saw. Yet speaking in the more
intimate setting of St Dunstan's a couple of weeks later, he gave
his listeners a chance to open their feelings about what they had
endured – and escaped – through a powerful account of the
collective ordeal. They were surrounded by the dead.

Every puff of wind within these walls, may blow the father into the sons
eyes, or the wife into her husbands, or his into hers, or both into their
childrens, or their childrens into both. Every grain of dust that flies here,
is a piece of a Christian . . .

Ending, though, he tried bringing them through their pain by urging them to see beyond the present in which they had been confined. Beyond a period shaped only by extermination, there was eternity:

Clocks and sun-dials were but a late invention upon earth; but the Sun it self, and the earth it self, was but a late invention in heaven. God had been an infinite, a super-infinite, an unimaginable space, millions of millions of unimaginable spaces in heaven, before the Creation. And our after-noon shall be as long as Gods forenoon; for, as God never saw beginning, so we shall never see end; but they whom we tread upon now, and we whom others shall tread upon hereafter, shall meet at once . . .[50]

For Donne, heaven meant continuing one's life indefinitely, regardless of days and times of day, and rejoining loved ones.

Nobody close to Donne was taken by the plague. Instead, his losses were held in a kind of suspended deficit as he threw himself into a year of heavy preaching and clerical business. The pro-fessional highlight came early, in February, when he was chosen as 'prolocutor' – the chairman – of the Convocation of senior churchmen. Convocation was an ecclesiastical parallel to Parlia-ment: it met at the same time, and was also split into two houses, one of bishops and one of deans. This was one more indication that Donne was intended for high things by his superiors, since the prolocutor was always appointed by the bishops. Part of his duties lay in keeping order, and he was also required to deliver a Latin oration to both houses. He accordingly set out to impress, with a dazzlingly convoluted composition in a high classical style that virtually none of his listeners, apart from the very best Latinists, could have understood: 'it is to be feared that Donne was showing off,' comments Bald.[51] In the public domain, doctrinal controversy was raging over an attack mounted by Richard Montagu on the Calvinists, but while the Puritans who dominated the Commons frequently sputtered over such writings, the assembled clergy tried avoiding the subject altogether. Convocation passed quietly enough under Donne's watch.

The trust and respect that was placed in him was built on
tremendous hard work. He set about all his duties with immense
care and commitment. According to Walton, he sustained his
youthful habits as an early riser – 'his bed was not able to detain
him beyond the hour of four in a morning' – and observed a
rigorous working schedule:

The latter part of his life may be said to be a continued study; for as he
usually preached once a week, if not oftner, so after his Sermon he never
gave his eyes rest, till he had chosen out a new Text [i.e. from scripture],
and that night cast his Sermon into a form, and his Text into divisions;
and the next day betook himself to consult the Fathers, and so commit
his meditations to his memory, which was excellent.[52]

Donne himself was critical of extempore evangelists who felt they
could speak spontaneously, as the spirit moved them. A sermon,
he felt, came from concentration and labour: 'he that will teach,
must have *learnt* before, many years before; And he that will preach
must have thought of it before, many days before.'[53] The annual
focus of his professional life, he once explained, was 'a necessitie
of Preaching twelve or fourteen solemn Sermons every year, to
great Auditories, at *Paules*, and to the Judges, and at Court';[54] and
there was no room for sloppiness – nor indeed, in the many other
less prominent sermons he gave during the year for patrons and
the parishioners in his various benefices.

Besides the dedication he put into his craft as minister and public
speaker, he was also assiduous in the civic duties his position
gradually brought him. In 1626 he was appointed a governor of
the Charterhouse – a charitable institute similar to the one that
Alleyn was setting up at Dulwich – and diligently attended board
meetings until his death five years later.[55] His great knowledge of
the law was also called upon during these years. Just as it had its
own counterpart to Parliament, so the Church also had its own
courts and legal administration, although the judiciary in some of
these courts generally consisted of a mixture of clerical and lay
members. Donne served as a judge in the Court of Delegates, set

up as a high court of ecclesiastical appeal, and the Court of High Commission, which investigated spiritual misdemeanours and malpractice within the Church. He had personal associations with the latter: more than twenty-five years before, it had helped him establish the legality of his marriage.[56]

Two of the most prominent cases he was involved with both fell in 1627. The first involved an ongoing religious vendetta. For the past few years, Puritans had been increasingly outraged by the provocative writings of Richard Montagu, a clergyman who followed the 'high' Church faction. Montagu was what was known as an Arminian (after the theologian Arminus, the leading critic of Calvin); that is, he opposed the Calvinist doctrine of predestination and the Puritan attitude to ornament and ceremony in church. In works such as the colourfully titled *A Gag for the New Gospel? No: A New Gag for an Old Goose*, brought out in 1624, and the still more incendiary *Apello caesarum* of 1626, Montagu argued that the Church of England was being mistakenly attacked for beliefs and practices that it did not in fact hold or advance: concentrating on the Thirty-Nine Articles that formed the Church's constitution, he said that Papists were criticizing Puritan ideas, not official ecclesiastical ones.[57] This naturally incited retaliation from the Puritan camp. One of the leading voices opposing Montagu was that of William Prynne, a member of Lincoln's Inn, who in October 1627 found himself in trouble for publishing *The Perpetuitie of a Regenerate Mans Estate*, a sustained attack on the new wave of 'Popish' custom that was swamping the Church. Whereas in James's reign a certain leniency to Puritan views and practices had been shown, to the new King they smacked of insubordination. The full formalities of the Church were now being more rigorously enforced. Charles protected Montagu by making him a royal chaplain – he would become Bishop of Chichester in the 1630s – and his chief disciplinarian, William Laud, Bishop of Bath and Wells, led an attempt to bring Prynne before the High Commission. This was thwarted, however, since anyone living within one of the Inns of Court was immune from being served with a summons. The bishops therefore tried prising Prynne from his sanctuary by asking the Benchers to present the summons on their behalf, and exploited Donne's connections with the Inn by getting him to sign their formal letter of request. But Prynne had been given enough time to wriggle free by challenging the ecclesiastical writ through the common law courts. The conflict was significant: the division between the state and the wider Puritan community was opening up.[58]

The other headline case involving Donne had little in truth to do with a religious matter. It was much more about vengeance in high society. Some years before, Viscount Purbeck, the Duke of Buckingham's mad brother John, had been deserted by his wife Frances. They were married in 1617, after Frances was kidnapped by her father and frogmarched to the wedding, and by 1622 were living apart. In 1625 she had a son with another man, Sir Robert Howard, and although Purbeck, on his more lucid days, gave every sign of still loving Frances – keeping vigil at her bedside while she suffered from a bout of smallpox – Buckingham himself was livid, and doggedly set out to destroy his sister-in-law. In 1625 both she and her lover Sir Robert were excommunicated; at which the couple went to live peacefully together in the country. This did not in any way satisfy the Duke. So two years later, when Frances and Sir Robert took the risk of visiting London, they were seized, and brought before the High Commission, where a panel of no fewer than nineteen lay and clerical worthies, including Donne, judged that the fallen woman should do an act of public penance. As current practice dictated, Frances was held to be the culprit of the adultery rather than Sir Robert, who as son of the Earl of Suffolk had powerful protection. The panel did not even consider making *him* parade in a white sheet in the Savoy Church, as they did Frances; a penalty she avoided through a daring escape.

She was staying in London with the Ambassador of Savoy at his house on the Strand, and when officers came for her on the day appointed for her penitential act, he distracted them with a decoy. While the men waited at the door, a pageboy was hurriedly dressed up in ladies' clothing and whisked into the Ambassador's carriage. Before anyone could react, the coach charged from the courtyard and along the Strand, presently pursued 'by a multitude of people, and those Officers', as though Frances herself were making a run for it; which sure enough, 'in that Hubbub', while the coast was clear, she did. Her baby boy, persecuted by the King's favourite Buckingham, grew up to be a committed Republican.[59]

Only one of the judges, Sir Charles Caesar, abstained from passing sentence on Frances; Donne went with the majority.[60] In general, nonetheless, he urged moderation in passing judgements: 'be not hasty in the execution of these Commissions; Come to an Inquisition upon another man, so as thou wouldst wish God to enquire into thee.'[61] He may have seen that it was an age in which the judge might some day end up as the accused.

He was living the life he had always wanted, absorbed in the 'mutual offices and duties of society', intellectually and spiritually engaged, and in demand. It was a life that he shared with no woman; but his later writings suggest no great libidinous ache or need of a spouse. This is not to say that the sermons lack sexual urgency. They strain on the page. To witness the gaunt, greying doctor preach was to share in an ecstasy. It was like nothing that Isaak Walton, a devout young linen merchant with a draper's shop on Fleet Street, had ever seen before: a living prophet,

preaching the Word so, as shewed his own heart was possest with those very thoughts and joys that he laboured to distill into others: A Preacher in earnest; weeping sometimes for his Auditory, sometimes with them: alwayes preaching to himself, like an Angel from a cloud, but in none . . .

This was a man gripped by *enthusiasmus*, literally a 'possession by the god', laying his heart bare. Yet Walton realized that Donne was also disrobing and opening the hearts of his listeners, his 'Auditory'; seducing them:

. . . carrying some, as St *Paul* was, to Heaven in holy raptures, and inticing others by a sacred Art and Courtship to amend their lives; here picturing a vice so as to make it ugly to those that practised it; and a vertue so as to make it be beloved even by those that lov'd it not; and all this with a most particular grace and an unexpressible addition of comeliness.[62]

Preaching involved 'Courtship', wooing an audience, making love to it. Yet it also required dramatic ability. Walton makes this clear by describing Donne's impersonations of vices and virtues, the stock characters of the early moralistic stage. A good preacher had to be a good actor – to have a refined technique as well as a reservoir of conviction. Donne was a charismatic evangelist, but also an accomplished 'old player', like his son-in-law. His technical mastery of the *art* of preaching comes out in other contemporary descriptions of his oratory. In June 1630 a diarist noted Donne's control of 'gestur and Rhetoriquall expression' in 'his powerfull kinde of preaching'.[63] Other sources speak of his control of both the auditory and visual experience of his listeners:

> What mysteries did from thy preaching flow,
> Who with thy words could charme thy audience,
> That at thy sermons, eare was all our sense;
> Yet have I seene thee in the pulpit stand,
> Where wee might take notes, from thy looke, and hand;
> And from thy speaking action beare away
> More Sermon, then some teachers use to say.[64]

His energies were absorbed in his work, and his ego satisfied by it. But his professional life had to sustain him through a string of bereavements that began just over a year after the plague subsided.

22. The Reprimand

The prelude to more heartfelt losses was one that cost Donne little grief. At the end of June 1626, he and Edward Alleyn at last concluded their marriage negotiations over Constance, two and a half years after the wedding. Alleyn agreed to settle on his wife the leases to his evocatively named Bankside brothels, the Unicorn and the Barge, Bell and Cock, providing Donne and Constance's uncles with legally binding assurances.[1] Then in July, Alleyn went to view some property in Yorkshire. The journey was long and tiring, and he was never the same afterwards. The old impresario died at the end of November, leaving his 'loving Constance' the healthy sum of £1,500 from the leases, plus an extra hundred in further testimony of his love.[2] One of Alleyn's Victorian biographers comments that his death 'adds one more proof to the many already existing, that life is generally much shortened, when a man, considerably past the prime and strength of his years, marries a comparatively young woman'.[3] He was sixty when he died, well looked after through his declining years, and Constance, a young widow of twenty-three, was well provided for.

Taking care of his daughters had long been Donne's greatest domestic worry. Grimly, early the following January, he was left with one less to worry about. Constance's younger sister Lucy, who seems to have been living with her, died quite suddenly.[4] She does not, at least, appear to have been staying with Donne, who in a letter of 4 January was completely oblivious to the fact that she was sick in any way. He wrote satirically to Ker of the trials of entertaining hordes of guests over the holidays, 'a solemn Christmas man' trying to 'sit out the siege of new faces every dinner . . . This day [again] I am in my bondage of entertaining.'[5]

Lucy was buried on 9 January.[6] There is no mention of her

death in any of Donne's surviving correspondence, yet in his Easter sermon that year, he asked the throngs in St Paul's to imagine what a father would give to have a dead child restored to life. 'Measure it but by the Joy, which we have, in recovering a sick child, from the hands, and jawes, and gates of death.' Weakly, he tried seeing heaven as a prospect that was even better for a young person than finding a career or making a prosperous match. 'If I had fixt a Son in Court, or married a daughter into a plentifull Fortune, I were satisfied for that son and that daughter. Shall I not be so, when the King of Heaven hath taken that son to himselfe, and married himselfe to that daughter, forever?'[7]

As the year continued, older members of Donne's circle now began slipping away. Perhaps the greatest blow was Goodyer's death, debt-ridden, on 18 March, a week before Donne preached at Easter. Again, he has left no response to this in the writings that have survived, and does not seem to have given a sermon in memory of his friend. The only person to whom Donne might have directly confided his feelings about Goodyer dying was Goodyer himself.

Late in May, the Countess of Bedford died; and early in June, Magdalen Danvers. Lady Bedford and Donne had been distant for some years, but his six months spent at Chelsea during the plague had renewed and deepened his friendship with Magdalen. Upsettingly, he was overwhelmed with work when she died, and fought to make time to pay his respects. '*Pre-obligations* and *Pre-contracts*, in the services of mine own Profession, which could not be excused,' Donne apologized, prevented him from preaching at her funeral; but he made amends by going to Chelsea to give a commemorative sermon in her honour at the beginning of July.[8] Among the many gathered was Isaak Walton, who had walked out to Chelsea especially to listen. At times, Donne wept as he spoke.[9] Magdalen had died serenely, though in their final meetings he noticed that 'some sicknesses . . . had opened her to an overflowing of *Melancholie*; not that she ever lay under that *water*, but yet, had sometimes, some high Tides of it'.[10]

Donne too had reason to sink into worry around the time he

gave his eulogy for Magdalen. He occasionally gave way to weariness: 'If there were any other way to be saved and to get to Heaven, then by being born into this life, I would not wish to have come into this world,' he admitted earlier in 1627.[11] While his son John was emulating his own more predominant early traits, living as a vague university man with no settled profession, his younger boy had chosen a life that Donne himself only sampled. George Donne was the brighter of the two brothers; like his father, he had gone up to Oxford while still very young. But he had decided to be a soldier, and although only twenty-two, he was already a captain, possibly through his father's connection to Buckingham.[12] In June, he was part of a madcap naval expedition that sailed against France under the Duke's command. Any anxiety Donne felt for his son was completely understandable: the Duke's military record was exceptionally abysmal. Two years before, a rickety fleet of ancient vessels had been sent to plunder the Spanish seaboard, in an attempt to recapture the Elizabethan glory days. Piteously ill-equipped, and led by admirals with barely any experience at sea, the force had wisely shied away from an attack on Cadiz, and struggled home with crews half-starved and riddled with sickness. While keeping a tight grip on his domestic supremacy, Buckingham had been seriously outmanoeuvred by foreign leaders. In the same year, 1625, he was duped into lending King Louis of France and his new chief minister, Cardinal Richelieu, the ships they needed to wipe out an uprising staged by their Protestant subjects, the Huguenots, along the French coast.

At this Buckingham's reputation at home had hit new depths. He now looked like an aider and abetter of international Papist aggression, and this was one of the crimes that Parliament remembered the following year when they unsuccessfully tried impeaching him. In the meantime, there was no prospect of French assistance against Spain or the Habsburg empire, the principal hope on which Charles's marriage to Henrietta had been founded in the first place. Exasperated, with no funds for the great martial schemes he envisaged, Buckingham hatched an elaborate plan to dislodge Richelieu, and thus redirect French policy, by agitating dissent in

France. This was to be ignited by English troops arriving to assist
the one Huguenot enclave that had not been overwhelmed by
force – the port of La Rochelle. Buckingham's forces, including
an eager George Donne, landed successfully on the island of Ré,
two miles off the coast, but were unprepared and completely
unequipped for the long siege it would take to capture the city.
After a sixteen-week standoff they were beaten back with heavy
losses. What remained of the fleet straggled back in November,
with George among the survivors – who for the most part were
furious with their general.

The ongoing disasters in foreign policy, and factions conniving
at home, made the atmosphere at Court distinctly edgy. A substantial but dissipated majority was keen to bring the Duke down, but
not organized or brave enough to find a way of doing it. The new
King, too, was a difficult character. While James had swerved
between foul-mouthed directness, weepiness and guileful reticence
in showing disfavour, his son Charles was consistently uptight,
standoffish and petulant. He accepted only Buckingham on anything like equal terms; apart from Steenie, he was alone with his
illusions and his unrealized insecurities at the centre of his own
illusionary universe.

In April 1627, as preparations for the French campaign got under
way, Donne fell foul of the King's twitchy temper. Charles liked
his poems and was often an appreciative listener to Donne's work:
'I hoped for the King's approbation heretofore in many of my
Sermons,' Donne comforted himself, 'and I have had it.' Yet in a
sermon given in the royal presence at Whitehall on 2 April, Donne
crossed one of the King's invisible lines of acceptability. Not long
after Donne had left the pulpit, disrobed and begun his usual
process of calming down, a note from his ally Sir Robert Ker
informed him that Charles was displeased with what he had heard.
A few hours later, Donne received word from William Laud, the
Bishop of Bath and Wells, 'commanding from the King a Copy of
my Sermon'. Donne was frightened and perplexed: he could not
think how he had offended Charles – 'I was never in any one
peece, so studious of his service,' he protested – and feared that he

was the victim of some slander or conspiracy: 'Freely to you I say,' he told Ker, 'I would I were a little more guilty: Onely mine innocency makes me afraid.'

Before writing up the sermon, he bolted to see Laud in person. Donne suspected that something he had said might have reminded someone of a controversial sermon given earlier in the year by Archbishop Abbot – the accidental crossbow-killer of a few years before. Abbot by this time was alienated and resentful. He was no extremist, but an orthodox Elizabethan Protestant who was furious at the Popish customs and rampant Arminianism that seemed to be taking over his Church. He had refused to license for publication a work of the 'high' churchman Richard Montagu, and a sermon by another of Laud's allies, Richard Sibthorpe, which argued that subjects must obey their King no matter how unjust his commands might be. Earlier in 1627 Abbot angered Charles by preaching in favour of Puritan views. This was a serious blow against the King's authority, given Abbot's position as Archbishop of Canterbury. Charles began bypassing Abbot, using Laud instead as the main agent of his religious policy. During his interview, Donne was most anxious to distance himself from Abbot's opinions, assuring Laud that he had 'never heard syllable' of the Archbishop's controversial sermon.[13] Laud, a dry, punctilious creature who enjoyed his authority and welcomed more, sent the Dean away to write out his sermon.

First thing the following day, Donne was back, to submit his manuscript in person, 'faithfully exscribed'. He then called morosely on Sir Robert Ker's chambers in St James's Palace, but found no one in: 'I was this morning at your door, somewhat early . . . yet after two or three modest knocks at the door, I went away.' He went away to fret alone. He was taking care, however, not to cast too lonely a figure, aware that once he was isolated he might be prey to the wolves of the Court. He had already been in contact with Lord Hay, the Earl of Carlisle, 'who assured me of a gracious acceptation of my putting my self in his protection', and now in writing he implored Ker to 'hearken' after the sermon and find out what the King thought of it: 'I am still upon my jealousie,' he explained, 'that the King brought thither some disaffection towards me, grounded upon some other demerit of mine, and took it not from the Sermon.' He claimed that he just could not see what the problem was:

I have cribated, and re-cribated, and post-cribated the Sermon, and must necessarily say, the King who hath let his eye fall upon some of my Poems, never saw, of mine, a hand, or an eye, or an affection, set down with so much study, and diligence, and labour of syllables . . .

And all this effort, he insisted, had gone into making two points – both entirely supportive of the King. He had encouraged 'obedience in the subject' and attacked the 'bed of whisperers' who were spreading gossip insulting the King and his favourites.[14] Such exhortations should have been wholly welcome to King Charles. The King faced great popular displeasure for trying to raise revenues by means of a forced loan from his subjects, thus bypassing the traditional tax-raising powers of a Parliament he could not control. Those who felt pained by Charles's disrespect for the English constitution and those who refused to pay were far from revolutionary by instinct. They included peers of the realm, including one of Donne's patrons, the Earl of Kent.

Donne's text in the offending sermon had been Mark 4:24, 'Take heed what you hear', and he had used it to urge 'take heed what you heare of *Kings*, take heed what you heare of *Priests*, take heed of hearkning to *seditious rumours*, which may violate the dignity of the State.'[15] At one point, Donne does seem to allude indiscreetly to the Roman Catholicism of Queen Henrietta, but despite a number of plausible theories it is hard to see what in the sermon could have caused such deep offence, or why indeed this particular sermon should have been singled out.[16] Yet the problem of course in urging people to take no heed of seditious rumours – such as 'the Kings inclining to *Popery*', as Walton put it – was that Donne necessarily stirred up exactly the slander he claimed he was trying to dispel. The fact also remains that the sermon Donne wrote up and submitted for Bishop Laud's scrutiny, which was eventually published, and which we can consult today, is not identical in every way to the one he gave from notes in Whitehall. Just one fleeting phrase, or a suspect tone of voice, would have been quite enough to upset a King who was ready to jump at shadows.

In any case, Donne knew better than to try bleating his innocence before Charles himself. When he was summoned on 4 April to hear his fate, he immediately got down on his knees before the King, and '*desired that he might not rise, till . . . he might have from his Majesty, some assurance that he stood clear and fair in his opinion.*'[17] Laud was present, and noted in his diary that the King loftily forgave Donne for 'certain slips' in his sermon. Charles had much warmer words for the Bishop, who had apparently perused the text and reported back: 'what he then most graciously said unto me,' Laud purred, 'I have wrote in my Heart with indelible Characters, and great thankfulnesse to God and the King.'[18]

Donne left admonished, but was soon forced into a closer working relationship with his censor. Laud was rising in power: firm with his subordinates, obsequious with his superiors, and with just the right fastidiousness when it came to form, ritual and vestments, he was exactly the minister Charles wanted running his Church. Yet the benefits at present of making Laud Archbishop of Canterbury were not worth the uproar that would result from disturbing the status quo and unseating George Abbot. So in 1628 Laud was made Bishop of London. The preceding incumbent, George Montaigne, protested vigorously at being put out to seed in the provinces. The idea at first was to make Montaigne Bishop of Durham; but when the Archbishopric of York, a much greater and more lucrative see, was vacated by the death of Tobie Mathew the elder, he craved this greater dignity 'with as much ambition, as he had earnestly endeavoured to decline the other'.[19] With Montaigne shifted, the way was clear for Laud, who on taking the helm at his new diocese immediately began enforcing 'high' Church rules on an unwilling populace.

Donne was required to act as disciplinarian. In doing so, he was not just obeying orders. The slovenly behaviour of his congregations in Paul's annoyed him greatly. Well before Laud became his direct superior, he complained about the way some people breezed into the service as if coming only for a chat: 'you come to God in his House, as though you came to keepe him company, to sit downe, and talke with him halfe an houre . . .' The rowdy gossiping and marketeering outside in Paul's Walk, meanwhile, had only got worse:

You meet below, and there make your bargaines, for biting, for devouring Usury, and then you come up hither for prayers, and so make God your Broker. You rob, and spoile, and eat his people as bread, by Extortion, and bribery, and deceitfull waights and measures, and deluding oaths in buying and selling, and then come hither, and so make God your Receiver, and his house a den of Thieves.[20]

After Laud became bishop, Donne continued to make occasional outbursts, urging his flock to observe the proprieties. They were supposed to kneel and bow at key moments of worship: 'God is your Father: aske blessing upon your knees; pray in that posture. God is your King: worship him with that worship, which is highest in our use, and estimation.'[21] On one occasion, he sent a man who refused to kneel down after being 'thrice admonished' to appear before the City magistrates – the culprit had shrugged off the orders of the vergers, and then 'in contempt did therevpon depart thence'.[22]

Yet the truth was that to many, often perfectly ardent Christians in the Cathedral, the up-and-down rituals of kneeling and standing were irrelevant to what they were there for. And to more serious Puritans, such customs were offensive distractions. Many also could have seen the political motive behind an important parallel that Donne's rhetoric developed. 'Doe but remember, with what reverence thou camest into thy Masters presence, when thou wast a servant, with what reverence thou camest to the Councell table, or to the Kings presence . . . such reverence, as thou gavest to them there, be content to afford to God here.'[23] The appropriate respect the dutiful subject showed the King was offered as a model of how one should worship God; but this was first and foremost a reminder of how the King should be honoured.

In the late 1620s Donne followed the official line not only on the conduct required in places of worship, but also on the physical arrangement of such places themselves. Laud and the 'high' Church faction wanted to have sumptuously decorated chapels and churches, decked out, in effect, like royal palaces, with permanent altars and crucifixes: ornaments that Puritans denounced as satanic toys. Out in the open at Paul's Cross in May 1627, Donne offered a defence of symbols and decorations. They were not the direct objects of worship – that would, he agreed, be idolatry – but they were needed for what they represented and what they transmitted. 'Rituall, and Ceremoniall things move not God, but they exalt that Devotion, and they conserve that Order, which does move him.' His personal wish, one that he had held for decades, that all Christians could be united, came out in his closing words. He asked for a Church in which differences of form might be tolerated through oneness of substance:

Blessed be that God, who, as he is without change or colour of change, hath kept us without change, or colour of change, in all our foundations; And he in his time bring our Adversaries to such a moderation as becomes them, who doe truly desire, that the Church may bee truly *Catholique, one flock, in one fold, under one Shepherd*, though *not all of one colour*, of one practise in all outward and disciplinarian points. *Amen*.[24]

The mere mention of the word '*Catholique*' was enough to ignite sectarian passions – destroying consensus even as he prayed for it. The Puritans were simply not having such claptrap from a thinly disguised Papist who was himself very far from being 'without change, or colour of change'. It is clear that very often they gave Donne a rough ride. 'They humm'd against him,' wrote one of his elegists. His critics complained that he gave 'As fine words [truly] as you would desire', but when it came to their actual meaning, he was a 'strong-lin'd man' – a hardliner, an authoritarian.[25] Another royalist pointedly exempted him from being counted among 'our Sonnes of Zeale', the Puritans.[26]

On the other hand, meanwhile, his efforts to keep order failed to satisfy the authorities. Paul's Walk was as untameable as ever; children were still playing, and Puritans and 'high' churchmen alike were intolerant of drunkards urinating against pillars inside the Cathedral. A report issued after his death criticized 'Mr Deane and the Canons' for failing 'to come into the bodie of the church some certayne tymes, and to requyre such as they fynde walkinge or talkinge there, eyther to come into the Quyre, there to heare divine service, or to depart the church'.[27] Sanctifying St Paul's may have been beyond Donne's strength and patience. In the 1630s, Bishop Laud took it upon himself to renovate and ornament the Cathedral, and tame its users – who resentfully came to see it as a citadel of popery. One scornful note tacked up in 1637 suggested Laud was renting the place from the devil.[28]

For almost sixty years, Donne had survived by altering. He had transformed himself from a closeted Catholic, as boy and youth, to a government secretary; from social outcast, after he married, to a pillar of the community, as a priest; from avant-garde poet, in his writing, to popular preacher. It would be interesting to know if he could have adapted again through the approaching decade of change. People who had been fixtures of his adult life continued to disappear. In February 1628 Christopher Brooke died. Brooke, who had met Donne at Lincoln's Inn – or quite possibly even before, at Cambridge – was his oldest companion. He stood as witness at Donne's clandestine marriage to Ann, and was in the neighbourhood to offer solace when she died. He left a painting, aptly depicting Apollo, the god of poetry, to his 'deere ancient and worthie friend doctor Dunn the Deane of Pawles'.[29] There were fewer and fewer of those who shared his past. Ever alert to all signs of decay – and unable to relay them without a certain morbid relish – Donne was aware too of his own advancing age. Looking at himself, he saw 'a dry cynder . . . a Spunge, a bottle of overflowing Rheumes . . . an aged childe, a gray-headed Infant, and but the ghost of mine own youth'.[30]

The world he knew was also vanishing. Later in 1628, a sea change occurred in British politics. Dismissing public criticism and the advice of his allies, Buckingham decided to try another assault on La Rochelle. In August he travelled from London to Portsmouth to inspect his navy, which was in the same ramshackle state it had been for years. He was greeted by riots of famished sailors demanding their pay. Buckingham ordered the militia to charge the crowd with swords drawn, and personally supervised the hanging of a man who had attacked him in his carriage. The next morning, Lieutenant John Felton infiltrated Buckingham's staff, made his way to the 'inward chamber' where the Duke was having breakfast, and stabbed him. Felton, 'by nature of a deep, melancholy, silent and gloomy constitution', who went to church at St Dunstan's-in-the-West, where Donne was vicar, had prayed long and hard for guidance as to whether his course of action was just or not. Eventually, he came to believe it was the only option. 'You have undone us all,' exclaimed one of the officers, as Buckingham tried holding himself upright against a table, blood slopping out of his mouth. 'No,' Felton snapped back, before being seized, 'I have made you all.'[31]

Late the following March, Donne was given two pieces of paper that were found in the yard at the front of his Deanery. One was a message for the Bishop of London, the other for a senior councillor. The first read,

Laud,
Look to thy self: be assured thy Life is sought. As thou art the Fountain of all Wickedness, Repent thee of thy monstrous Sins, before thou be taken out of the World. And assure thy self, neither God nor the World can endure such a vile Councellor to live . . .

The same evening, Donne handed in both death threats to the King. The Bishop was shaken. 'Lord,' he prayed – it must have been difficult to avoid the sense, sometimes, that he was speaking only to himself, *Laud* – 'I am a grievous Sinner; but, I beseech thee, deliver my Soul from them that hate me without a Cause.'[32]

At the beginning of the month, King Charles had dismissed the Commons and decided to govern without Parliament. During this last session before the onset of the Personal Rule, one Leighton, 'a fiery Puritan in Faction', who in time had his ears cropped, his nose slit and his forehead branded, published a book inciting his readers '*to kill all the Bishops,* and to smite them under the fifth Rib'.[33] It was becoming clear that such people were serious.

23. The Likeness

In his last years, when he brought his mother to live with him in the fine house at St Paul's, Donne fulfilled a promise made long before 'to do the office of a child'.[1] Her husband, Richard Rainsford, had died some years before. In her final widowhood, a Roman Catholic to the last, and by now well into her eighties, Elizabeth had become one of those figures whom dictators fear the most, a senior whose age and experience renders her immune to intimidation. She had seen all there was to be afraid of. Her memories stretched back to the violent height of the Reformation, the respite and revenge under Queen Mary, the earliest years of Elizabethan repression. A journal of her life would be a priceless document. We have only dim glimpses of her experiences: smuggling Jesuit priests into the Tower to confer with her imprisoned brother; bringing up her family in the old faith at the risk of losing all; losing a son, Henry, to the persecution, and choosing exile abroad rather than conformity at home. Taking up residence with Donne in the venerable affluence of the Deanery was something like reclaiming an inheritance. The house had been the home of Roman Catholic ministers for many, many years before the break with Rome. The huge old Cathedral itself was the same in which Catholic subjects had worshipped for centuries. Those with Elizabeth's conviction saw these edifices as their birthright.

The fact that she accepted his care suggests that she did not in the end resent her son for turning away from the creed she taught him. Donne's success may have struck her rather as a masterwork of infiltration; a way, in the end, of sneaking her in. How they got on together, though, is not clear. It seems that they were at least partially estranged for some years, as he struggled to establish himself as a conformist in his thirties and forties. In his one surviving letter to her, in which he tried to make amends for his 'negligences' towards her, Donne adopted the tone of a pious junior towards one who was fully conscious of her venerability. She had an intimidating tragic grandeur, the stranded votaress of a God who 'seemed to repent,' as Donne told her, 'that he allowed any part of your life any earthly happinesse'. Her experience of the 'calamities of this life' was offset only by 'continuall acquaintance with the visitations of the holy Ghost'.[2] As a young man, Donne had adopted as his motto the phrase '*Antes muerto que mudado*' – 'Sooner dead than changed'. But in the end, this was a more fitting epitaph for his mother. She had lost virtually everything except her principles, but had lived without compromise.

Donne set a more practical example for those who have to make the society they inherit work. He dealt intelligently with the formidable expectations pressed on him by his mother, adapting to his time instead of refusing to yield. It is important to avoid twentieth-century parallels in thinking about his political choices. Becoming a Protestant in the 1590s was not like joining the Nazi party in the 1930s: the Protestant regime Donne served was no more repressive towards dissidents than the Roman Catholic regime he would have worked for had the English Reformation been defeated. He did not choose between a threatened system supporting liberty and one imposing tyranny: such a choice did not exist. Instead he questioned whether the ideas for which Roman Catholics were persecuted were really worth dying for, and whether they might in fact be erroneous; and he found that parents and priests were wrongfully exhorting their children to harm themselves needlessly. We might invert his youthful motto, and say that Donne found it more sensible to change than be dead. Given his background, such pliancy indicates considerable strength of character. He broke with an incredibly powerful family pattern. Especially on his mother's side, the standard that all relatives had to live up to was set by Sir Thomas More, the saint who gave up his wealth, his power and eventually his head for his religious beliefs and personal integrity. For Donne More's actions were honourable in themselves, but not practical as a code of conduct for others to follow. One of the central realizations of Donne's life was that it was wrong and silly to will oneself towards martyrdom. To set oneself apart, to try being an island, was also a great mistake. It was impossible to resign from mankind or from the historical position of humanity. So Donne lived instead by continual metamorphosis, transforming himself to meet his circumstances. In the end, he put himself in a position to voice moderation.

Donne's life passed as it were in a deep valley, between the two great cataclysms that shaped early modern England. With regard to the second of these historical landmarks, the English Civil War and subsequent revolution, his position is genuinely ambivalent. There is no telling for sure which side he might have supported, Royalist or Cromwellian, mainly because the crisis that would compel his surviving contemporaries to make this choice was still some years away when he died. It is equally likely in fact that Donne would have abstained from taking sides altogether, sickened by schism. Yet with regard to the great upheaval that defined his background but preceded his birth by many decades, the English Reformation, his ambivalence can be over-emphasized. When it came to choosing between Roman Catholicism and Protestantism – or *English* Protestantism, as Donne would rather have called it – he made his decision and he stuck to it. He accepted, in a sense, that enough blood had been spilt already. He also discovered that the Reformed Church gave him ample room for the Catholic habits of mind and devotion his upbringing had instilled. Donne deserves recognition as the most thoughtful and qualified of the English Protestant apologists. His sermons condemning extremism – though often with a savage extremity of their own, whether Papist or Puritan, pro- or anti-Spanish, urging his listeners to see themselves all as fellow islanders, parts of one mainland – certainly made a contribution to peace and restraint in a period of such fierce sectarianism.

Among the congregation at St Paul's there were no doubt many who had known him, or known of him, from the beginning, and who remarked on how the womanizing satirist should end up as a Cathedral priest passing his twilight with his aged mother. But this also marked him out as what a good conventional Christian man was supposed to be. He was a dutiful son and a pragmatic father, by contemporary standards, making sound provision for both his mother and his children. Donne's life presents many discrepancies, certainly. It is startling to think of what time can do, when one compares Edward Alleyn's hard-bargaining father-in-law with an earlier Donne, the nervous romantic who married Ann More in secret. But all the way through, there are many likenesses between his different personae, essentials that he never gave away. He remained a witty, sociable person and a committed friend to all those he cared for. Another constant was a searingly moral nature. The often vicious social lampooning of pretence and double standards in his satires is not so far removed from the social and spiritual criticism he poured out later in his sermons. His intellect, too, was undiminished throughout. At all points Donne manifests an unshakeable commitment to a growth of mind, filtering his experiences through a massive intelligence that was unhappily conscious of its own complications.

Towards the end of his life, and never more so than in his final weeks, he sought to stabilize his public identity, to fashion the image that he wished to be remembered and defined by. Typically, this last icon would be forged in sensational style, with Donne preaching his own funeral sermon and posing for his last portrait as a living cadaver. Behind the self-conscious creation of a monument, however, his letters reveal him still looking for intimacy and support, describing the symptoms of his growing ailments and sharing worries about his family. We find him trying to plug the gap Goodyer left: resuming a close correspondence with his former room-mate George Garrard, and discovering comfort in a friendship he developed with an affluent yet harried mother of seven.

Mrs Ann Cokayne had married into a family with property that bordered on Sir Henry Goodyer's hard-pressed estate of Polesworth in Warwickshire. In 1616, not long after she gave birth to her youngest child, her husband Thomas had a crisis of commitment and left her, to pursue his lifelong dream of writing a Greek dictionary. He lived in London under the name Browne, but his

studies did not prevent him causing his wife further grief. He
wanted custody of the children, and drove her to the extreme of
hiding them with friends and relatives around the country. Donne
was well acquainted with 'the perverseness of the father', as he put
it.[3] He first met the family some time before he was ordained, and
had kept in touch with Mrs Cokayne over the following years.
The family's main home was an estate at Ashbourne in Derbyshire,
where it seems that Donne was a fairly frequent guest: a room in
the mansion, which became known as 'Dr Donne's Chamber',
was kept ready for his visits. Mrs Cokayne was described as 'an
honourable person', 'a royalist, of highest elevation, yet a woman
of sense', and was in early middle age as Donne neared the end of
his life.[4] Her character in the relationship can only be detected
from her reflection in Donne's letters – none of hers to him have
survived, sadly – and in these she comes across as a strong, deeply
maternal woman, who openly appreciated kindness and attention,
and was direct with her emotions.

The correspondence reveals a softer side to Donne that is hidden
in the force of the sermons, but was seemingly there all along. The
letters are a last reminder of why he had so many friends, and why
so many of them said he was a good friend to have. As a person,
he was at his best in showing and engaging warmth with wit. The
letters also show, one final time, how women found him charming.
Although a celibate for many years, he still took great pleasure in
female company: the letters to Mrs Cokayne trigger a memory of
the after-dinner chat with Edward Alleyn in the parlour of the
Deanery, when Donne was 'called away by the coming of some
ladies'. There was a 'love' between him and Mrs Cokayne, which
manifested itself, he said, in his prayers for her.

There were many different registers of prayer for Donne: it
could be the most solemn activity, or a courtesy a gentleman
extended to a lady friend who was taking the waters.

At this time, I knew not how to express that love . . . because not
knowing what seasons of weather are best for your use of the *Bath*, I
know not what weather to pray for. I determine my prayers therefore

in those Generalls, that God will give you whatsoever you would have, and multiplie it to you when you have it.[5]

He still responded generously and therapeutically to a friend's distress. Mrs Cokayne's younger son Thomas died about a year after Donne's daughter Lucy, in 1628. Offering support, Donne sent her a personal 'homily' containing a mixture of tender and brutal consolations. One beautiful paragraph has solace for any family trying to cope with a loss:

Our souls are trulie said to be in everie part of our bodies; but yet, if any part of the bodie be cut off, no part of the soul perishes, but is suckt in to that soul that remains, in that that remains of the body. When any limb or branch of the family is taken away, the virtue, the love, and (for the most part) the patrimonie and fortune of him that is gone, remaines with the family.

As so often with Donne, remarkably stark ideas – a maimed body, the money left by the dead – are used to convey a gentler, soulful one. Yet Donne also pushed much rougher cures for grief on Mrs Cokayne. He returned to the idea he developed in the Easter sermon following Lucy's death, that losing a child was just one more way of settling their future. 'We do but borrow Children of God, to lend them to the world,' he argued. 'But of all that I lend to, the Grave is my best pay-master. The Grave shall restore me my child.'[6] Grief, in the end, he felt, was something that had to be fought down: 'I know your easie apprehensions, and over-tendernesse in this kind' – losing a son, he accepted, was especially traumatic for her, given all she had been through for her family – yet these things had to be borne patiently and 'catechistically', as signs of God's will.[7] Even more than that, the death of a child was a positive cause for gladness:

We think it good husbandry to place our childrens portions [i.e. marital allowances] so, that in so many years it may multiply to so much: Shall we not be as glad to lay their bodies there, where onely they can be mellowed and ripened for glorification?[8]

Donne was aware that such a view might seem unfeeling – it is hard to savour putrefaction like ripe autumn fruit. It also cannot be said whether he truly believed it as much as he advocated; but he did see it as the only mental option left open to someone with so many of his own to mourn.

He too looked for sympathy from Mrs Cokayne, and found it. He became sick more frequently in the late 1620s, and he described his ailments to her:

I am come now, not onely to pay a Feavour every half year, as a Rent for my life; but I am called upon before the day, and they come sooner in the year than heretofore. This Feavour that I had now, I hoped, for divers daies, to have been but an exaltation of my damps and flashings, such as exercise me sometimes four or five daies, and passe away, without whining or complaint. But, I neglected this somewhat too long, which makes me . . . much weaker, than, perchance, otherwise I should have been.[9]

Except for a respiratory illness in June 1625, he had been reasonably strong since the fever in which he burnt out his most remarkable work, *Devotions Upon Emergent Occasions*, in 1623. A turning point seems to have come in August 1628, after a summer spent visiting his rural parishes in Kent and Bedfordshire. He came down with what was probably the first of the half-yearly fevers he describes above. It strengthened and persisted so much that he decided to return to London to consult his own physician, Dr Fox, who would tend him through his final sickness. Four miles from home, after a day 'and a piece' shivering and sweating in a jolting carriage, 'I was surprised with an accident in the Coach, which never befell me before.' He was shocked by 'a violent falling of the *Uvula*': the flap of flesh at the back of the palate, which normally dangles in front of the tonsils, had swollen and collapsed in his mouth. It was a part of the body he had paid little attention to before, and it 'therefore affected me much'. Back in London, he was diagnosed with a 'Squinancie', or quinsy, an acute form of tonsillitis. Dr Fox opened a vein in Donne's arm and bled him, to let the hostile humours causing the infection escape, and prescribed a further 'ten-daies starving'. After that, Donne wrote (a little feebly) to Mrs Cokayne, 'I am (blessed be God) returned to a convenient temper, and pulse, and appetite, and learn to eat.'[10] But his uvula remained collapsed and prevented him from speaking clearly.

In October, Sir Robert Ker wrote to Donne of his relief 'to fynde yow so much maister of those encumbrances which assail your invincible spirit through the mudd of your bodye'. Ker urged Donne to pay him a visit at his mansion at Kew, and instruct him 'how to be usefull to yow or my self, or any bodye els in this new spheare of courtship ue [we] are enterd by the Dukes death'.[11] A great power vacuum had opened up at Court following the assassination of Buckingham two months before, and Ker had yet to get his bearings: the King was still deep in shock. Back on the level of his own affairs, though Donne no doubt appreciated Ker's praise for his invincible spirit, he still needed his body, especially for his work the part of it that was currently most afflicted. After a short stay with Ker, he returned to London and in November began testing his voice again from the pulpit of St Dunstan's. His half-blocked throat was still not right: 'I should be sorry, if thys should make me a silenc'd Minister,' he told one of Buckingham's foremost henchmen, Lionel Cranfield, Earl of Middlesex. He could just about get through a sermon, but his uvula had still not regained its proper shape.[12]

Despite lapses in health, he kept up his official commitments through the following year. And his writing was still powerful. In a demanding and impressive series of sermons on texts from Genesis in the spring of 1629, he meditated on the origins of life. He was well able to imagine the time when 'all was surrounded with waters, all was embowelled, and enwombed in the waters'. He could envisage other worlds too. Speaking in staggered, telescopic sentences, reaching further and further into space, he was moved by the scale and detail of 'All that earth, and then, that heaven, which spreads so farre, as that subtile men have, with some appearance of probability, imagined, that in that heaven, in those manifold Sphears of the Planets, and the Starres, there are many earths, many worlds, as big as this, which we inhabit.'[13]

In worldly affairs, nonetheless, he kept his feet firmly rooted to the ground. In June 1629 Donne insisted that £100 he had lent his father-in-law be repaid promptly, before he left town for the summer. A late payment, he complained to More, 'wyll put me to so great a trouble as to make my poore wyll anew, and to substract from my other children their part of this £100.'[14] Walton reports that Donne had waived his quarterly payments of Ann's portion from Sir George More on becoming Dean, but there were limits to his largesse. The years of want at Mitcham had taught him to keep a close grip on his finances. Yet he still gave generously to charity: 'in these times of necessity and multitudes of poor,' he said in a letter, 'there is no possibility of saving to him that hath any tendernesse in him.'[15] The sermons in his final years often return to the subject of genuine poverty, and how the poor should be treated. He advised wealthy burghers not to worry that they would be punished for giving too much – the question 'How shall you know, whether he that askes be truly poore or no?' was not really theirs to ask. Whoever seemed needy should be helped in some way. However, like most people in his social class at the time (and since), he despised 'sturdy beggars', those who could work yet did not. He also said that giving money to a spendthrift who was unable or unwilling to use it properly, someone 'poore in his meanes' who deprived his children by spending all the family had on drink, was to be an 'oppressor of the poore ... *to give the childrens bread to dogs*'. Yet compassion should be the watchword, for spiritually selfish reasons if nothing else: 'Certainly, he that seares up himselfe, and makes himselfe insensible of the cries, and curses of the poor here in this world, does but prepare himselfe for the *howlings*, and *gnashings* of teeth, in the world to come.'[16] Involvement with mankind was paramount.

Closer to his own field, he told Mrs Cokayne that he supported a student at both Oxford and Cambridge: 'one Scholler in each Universitie sucks something, and must be weaned by me.' According to Walton, he was a 'continual giver to poor Scholars'.[17] Still, he drew the line at the aptly named Nathaniel Hazard, a cocky young clergyman whom Mrs Cokayne had employed as her children's tutor. Hazard came to see him in the hope of being helped to a benefice, or getting a trial as a preacher. Mrs Cokayne evidently trusted that Donne would be of assistance, but his position required him to be firm with requests for favours from friends. He also felt that employing Hazard, as yet wholly unproven, involved putting souls at risk. The young man, however, was completely oblivious to his own shortcomings, and bounced into Donne's study expectantly. During the conversation that followed Donne admitted that because he often fell sick, he frequently had to get a stand-in to take over at the pulpit; but he only ever considered a replacement who could preach as well as he could. He politely told Hazard, 'I do not know your faculties.'

He was not pleased by the reply he received. 'I will not make comparisons,' said Hazard, who thought highly of himself, 'but I do not doubt that I should give them satisfaction in that kind.'[18] This answer did not go down well. Donne's subsequent refusal to bestow a living on the youngster greatly upset Mrs Cokayne, who had adopted Hazard's cause with the same 'over-tendernesse' she devoted to her own sons. Donne was sharp with her:

Goes there no more to the giving of a Scholler a Church in *London*: but that he was a young Gentleman's School-master? You know the ticklishnesse of *London*-Pulpits, and how ill it would become me, to place a man in a *London*-Church that were not both a strong and sound man.

In her letter of protest to him, Mrs Cokayne had angrily accused Donne of intending to ruin her favourite. When he came to this, he shushed her gently, promising he would do what he could, while yielding no ground: 'You end in a phrase of indignation and displeasure, rare in you towards me, therefore it affects me greatly,' he told her; quite secure, nonetheless, in the thought they would make up immediately. 'The heat that produced that word I know is past . . . my most beloved Sister.'[19]

As for his own children, he had told her, 'I am well content to send one sonne to the Church, the other to the Warrs.'[20] John Donne the younger did eventually take orders, but his brother George embraced a life of adventure too heartily for Donne's peace of mind. He was his father's last great worry. After fighting the French, George was sent out to the West Indies as 'cheife commaunder' of the forces on the island of St Kitts. He got this posting almost certainly through the intercession of Donne's friend Lord Hay, the Earl of Carlisle, who was made Lord Proprietor of all the West Indian colonies in 1627.[21] A year or so in the Caribbean passed well, but in the autumn of 1629 the colony was attacked by a Spanish convoy en route to Brazil. George's men held off the Spaniards for as long as they could but were overwhelmed. The defeated colonists were then given the choice of defecting, or getting off the island. Most chose to leave, but five hostages were taken as security for the terms of surrender, and shipped back to Spain. George Donne was among these captives, as was a young relative of Carlisle's, Lieutenant George Hay. By March 1630 they were in prison in Cadiz.[22]

Donne had trouble getting his patrons to push for his son's release. Later that year, he even tried urging his old friend George Garrard to do what he could. Garrard was now working for Lord Percy, the Earl of Northumberland's son and Carlisle's brother-in-law, and although his ability to help was obviously limited, Donne was trying all available means. 'I besech you intreat my Lord *Percy* in my behalfe, that he will be pleased to name *George* to my L. *Carlile*, and to wonder, if not to inquire, where he is.' Strangely, Carlisle was blanking Donne's direct inquiries and appeals for help. Donne suspected that the Court's 'whisperers' had been at work.

The world is disposed to charge my Lords honour, and to charge my naturall affection with neglecting him [George], and, God knowes, I know not which way to turn towards him; nor upon any message of mine, when I send to kisse my Lords hands, doth my Lord make any kinde of mention of him.[23]

Donne feared he was being slandered with the charge of lacking 'naturall affection' as a father, by failing to do more for his son. The problem was that for some reason he did not know his main avenue of appeal, through the Earl of Carlisle, had been blocked. It was said at Court that Carlisle, meanwhile, was being apathetic in trying to recover the hostages – an opinion which the Earl may well have attributed to Donne himself, thus deepening the impasse. Garrard did his best, for what it was worth: 'I thanke you, for keeping our *George* in your memory,' said Donne, in his last surviving letter to him. Yet it took another four years before George was released. On his return, George wrote an account of his experience in which he declared that he owed his freedom to the diligence and loyalty of the Earl of Carlisle.[24] Donne never saw his son again; and because of the knot of misinformation between them, he seems to have been unaware that Lord Hay was still working on his family's behalf.

It was doubly frustrating for Donne that he was physically unable to reach Court in person, to clear the air with Carlisle and press his suit for action. When he wrote to Garrard, he was stranded in the country home of Constance's new husband, at Aldborough Hatch in Essex. Constance had married Samuel Harvey, a man about her age, in June. The match evidently satisfied Donne more than the last had, since after touring his country parishes, he went to visit the couple in August, bringing with him his mother and her servant. Shortly afterwards, he fell into one of his fevers, which 'hastened him into so visible a Consumption [a generally wasted state, rather than tuberculosis] that his beholders might say, as St. *Paul* of himself, *He dyes daily*.'[25] This seems to have been the strongest attack yet. His condition improved, but not enough for him to resume his duties, or even leave Aldborough Hatch. He was under no illusions about his long-term health. Answering Garrard's inquiries about his ailments, he affected toughness – 'it is not for my gravity, to write of feathers, and strawes,' he insisted.

Yet he admitted his decline by saying that he could accept life as an invalid so long as he could still work. All he asked for was the energy he would expend in performing his duties.

At this time, I humbly thank God, I am only not worse; for, I should as soon look for Roses at this time of the year, as look for increase of strength . . . if I can gather so much as will bear my charges, recover so much strength at *London*, as I will spend at *London*, I shall not be loth to be left in that state wherein I am now . . .[26]

This wish was not granted, however; for a week or so later he relapsed again: 'I was possessed with a Fever, so late in the year, that I am afraid I shall not recover confidence to come to *London* till the spring be a little advanced.'[27] He spent the winter getting over each burst of violent illness just enough to survive the next. In his final surviving letter to Garrard, written in December, he described how his 'frequent Fevers' lifted him to the gates of heaven, only to drop him back to 'the solitude and close imprisonment that they reduce me to after'. He apologized for the confusion and anxiety this brought his many well-wishers. He had had to arrange for a colleague to give the Christmas Day sermon at St Paul's – the only one he ever missed – and, as during the plague five years before, many people thought he was dead. He was touched by the tributes the false news evoked.

A man would almost be content to die (if there were no other benefit in death) to hear of so much sorrow, and so much testimony from good men, as I, (God be blessed for it) did upon the report of my death.[28]

With good humour, he advised his 'noblest sister', Mrs Cokayne: 'If you believed the report, and mourned for me, I pray let that that is done alreadie, serve at the time that it shall be true.'[29] Each bout of fever weakened him, meanwhile. Several times, it seems, he almost passed away, only to come back from the brink, enacting a scene he had imagined many years earlier:

> As virtuous men passe mildly away,
> And whisper to their soules, to goe,
> Whilst some of their sad friends doe say,
> The breath goes now, and some say, no.[30]

Donne's ministry had been a sustained exercise in training himself
to reach a point of reconciliation at which he could die in peace.
The condition of a dying man had also preoccupied him. He had
long foreseen 'what kinde of man I shall be at my end, upon my
death-bed, what trembling hands, and what lost legs, what deafe
eares, and what gummy eyes, I shall have then'.[31] But now the end
seemed in sight, he did not want to go out with a whimper. Lost
legs or no lost legs, 'it hath been my desire,' he told Garrard, 'that
I might die in the Pulpit; if not, that I may take my death in the
Pulpit; that is, die the sooner by occasion of my former labours.'[32]

He was impatient with his symptoms, eager to get back to
London. The account he gave Mrs Cokayne of his sufferings, in
fact, was much less melodramatic than the one he tendered to
Garrard: 'the hour of my death, and the day of my burial, were
related in the highest place of this Kingdom,' he told her, with
some satisfaction. Yet at this time, he claimed, he was feeling
relatively well, merely 'too weak at this time of the year to go
forth, especiallie to *London*, where the sicknesse is near my house,
and where I must necessarily open my self to more businesse, than
my present state will bear.' He felt it was unmanly to confide in
Garrard too much about his physical symptoms; but he was more
willing to write to Mrs Cokayne of the 'feathers, and strawes' that
ailed him. By January he had faded into 'a kind of half-life':[33]

I have never good temper, nor good pulse, nor good appetite, nor good
sleep. Yet I have so much leasure to recollect myself, as that I can thinke
I have been long thus, or often thus. I am not alive, because I have not
had enough upon me to kill me . . .

He joked that God was trying to remind him of past sins by
sending him all sorts of ailments that recalled different times of life:

'Therefore have I been more affected with Coughs in vehemence, more with deafenesse, more with toothach, more with the uvula, then heretofore.'[34] Like many terminally ill people, he often down-played the seriousness of his condition with banter, at some times more convincingly than at others. He got angry and depressed not so much with his particular ailments, but with how they wore on. He willed his condition to worsen rather than get better, to bring about some climax or decisive change, since he knew that any alleviation of his pains was only a maddening interlude before they came back. He felt robbed of a certain finality; he seemed to be dwindling, not dying:

My noble sister, I am afraid that Death will play with me so long, as he will forget to kill me, and suffer me to live in a languishing and uselesse age, A life, that is rather a forgetting that I am dead, then of living . . .[35]

It was this gradual extinction that he became determined to resist. First, though, he had to deal with the minutiae that he would leave behind. He knew that his existence on earth, like anyone's, would dissipate into a clutter of possessions, debits and credits. Before setting his mind entirely on higher things, he made an effort to settle his outstanding affairs by the end of 1630. On 13 December he made out his final will with his own hand, once again making use of his early training as a lawyer. The lengthy document shows that he died a wealthy man, with an estate worth between £3,000 and £4,000.[36] He remembered everyone. He left £500 for his mother, and expected that similar amounts would be available for each of his remaining children. He bequeathed a picture of Mary Magdalen, which he had received from Christopher Brooke and had hung in his bedroom, to George Garrard. Brooke's brother Samuel, 'my ancient frend', now Master of Trinity College, Cambridge, received a picture of the Virgin Mary and Joseph that hung in Donne's study. His watch went to his brother-in-law Sir Thomas Grymes. He left small sums, of five or ten pounds apiece, to the servants in his household. There was money for the poor of all the parishes he served, there were gifts for patrons such as the

Earls of Dorset and Kent, and remembrances too for people from long back in his past. Edward and Grace Dawson, his cousins and playmates from the Blue Boar in Oxford, where he was stowed as a boy-student almost fifty years earlier, were given twelve and six pounds apiece. Edward was now 'decayd', and Donne had been paying both him and his sister a little pension, it emerged, for some years. Some other artworks and collectables, including four large pictures of the 'fower greate Prophettes', hanging in the hall, and a sundial he had placed in the garden, he bequeathed to remain in the Deanery and its chapel.[37]

His last letters to Garrard also reveal his attempts to clear up a more mysterious matter with one of his aristocrat female friends, to whom he referred variously as 'the Lady of the Jewell' and the 'Diamond Lady'. She had borrowed some money from him, and left him in trust a precious stone worth much more than the amount he had lent her. It bothered him: 'I would be loath to leave any thing in my house, when I die, that were not absolutely mine own.' He asked Garrard to resolve the matter, directing him to instruct his manservant at the Deanery as he thought fit.[38] By the end of the autumn, the Diamond Lady's associates were close to settling up. As an afterthought, Donne suggested that they might pay him some interest: 'let them but be remembered how long it hath been in my hands, and then leave it to their discretion.' Surprisingly in an age that still saw usury as an unchristian practice, the principle was more important to him than the money itself – as he refused to accept any payment from the lady or her friends of anything worth more than four shillings. The jewel locked in his study at St Paul's house had agitated him: 'For the Diamond Lady, when time serves, I would fain be discharged of it.'[39]

While tying up such loose ends, he was working intently on a more enduring legacy. As in 1625, when the plague forced him into exile and redundancy, he spent the months stranded at Aldborough Hatch 'revising' and 'digesting' into longhand the remaining sermons he wished to preserve.[40] This would have been a heavy labour at any time: for a chronically sick man, suffering from the 'damps and flashes' of fever and migraine, producing such a manuscript of many hundreds of pages was a colossal task. Though some of the sermons were written out in full already – some had been printed, at least one had been called up for inspection by the King – this was not just a matter of copying material out. Most of the texts had to be re-expanded; some, no doubt, required some rethinking. 'I have better leasure to write, then you to read,' he told Garrard, as he wound up a letter; but while his final correspondence is frequently meditative, it lacks lateral vision. Currents of household news went unrecorded, nor did personal memories float to the surface. 'I should as soon look for Roses at this time of the year, as look for increase of strength,' he wrote sadly. Yet even if marvellous winter roses had really appeared, he might not have turned to look at them. He was at work on his ultimate bequest.

His aim was to get back to London to deliver his Lent sermon at Court – 'for as long as I live, and am not speechlesse, I would not decline that service.'[41] He travelled to London by coach 'some few days before his appointed day of preaching', which was to fall on Friday, 25 February. This gave him time to recuperate a little from the precarious journey, and mercifully he did not relapse into one of his fevers. His friends were shocked by the change in him – 'his sickness had left him but so much flesh as did only cover his bones' – but he dismissed their advice that he should not preach.[42] Judging from the text of the sermon he gave, which he wrote out in advance, there is no doubt he was sure that this would be his last. While concentrating on this climax to his work, however, he was not spared a final bereavement. Near the end of January, his mother died.[43] Early on in the text of the vehement address he gave the Court that Friday in February, it emerges that he was still deeply conscious of the bond to her. The maternal relationship, he went so far as to say, was one of continuous childbirth – the umbilical is never broken:

Wee have a winding sheete in our Mothers wombe, which grows with us from our conception, and we come into the world, wound up in that *winding sheet*, for wee come to *seeke a grave* . . . when the *wombe* hath discharg'd us, yet we are bound to it by *cordes* of flesh, by such a *string*, as that we cannot goe thence, nor stay there. We celebrate our owne funerals with cryes, even at our birth; as though our *threescore and ten years of life* were spent in our mothers labour, and our circle made up in the first point thereof. We begge one Baptism with another, a sacrament of tears; And we come into a world that lasts many ages, but wee last not.[44]

His appearance was as terrifying as his words. He had wizened during the long months of sickness: 'when to the amazement of some beholders he appeared in the Pulpit, many of them thought he presented himself not to preach mortification by a living voice: but, mortality by a decayed body and a dying face.' His 'preconceived meditations . . . were of dying', and his text was Psalm 68, verse 20: 'And unto God the Lord belong the issues from death' – 'Many that then saw his tears, and heard his faint and hollow voice, professing they thought the Text prophetically chosen, and that Dr Donne *had preach't his own Funeral Sermon.*'[45]

The sermon, published posthumously under the sensationalist title *Deaths Duell*, was not his best, but it was surely his most dramatic. The piece is a sustained barrage on life, treating everything – beginning, in the passage above, with the womb – as a presage of the end, a *memento mori*: 'all our *periods* and *transitions* in this life, are so many passages *from death to death.*'[46] The statement was especially true of the man who uttered it: the worn figure in the pulpit was the last of many John Donnes who had come and gone, as he reinvented himself. Yet however startled the listeners were by Donne's skeletal features, the sermon was relished in an age that kept death firmly in the foreground. The spectacles of mass slaughter and epidemic Donne had witnessed – in the burning harbour of Cadiz, or in the great plague of 1625 – and all the losses he had borne – his children, his wife taken early – would have been too unjust, too inexplicable to bear unless they could be taken as signs of a divine agency, a reaper taking in the quota God required. Death was treated as no arbitrary cataclysm or failure of technology, as today, but as a presence at the hearth, waiting for his moment. The idea was that by not pretending death wasn't there, one could better deal with it when it came. As the preface which Donne's commercially minded publisher Roger Michell attached to *Deaths Duell* expressed it, 'May wee make such use of this and other the like preparatives, That neither death, whensoever it may come, may seeme terrible; nor life tedious; how long so ever it shall last.'[47]

According to a friend who visited him the next day, Donne spent the night after the sermon thinking of dead friends, and preparing to join them. He had also been running his mind through the course of his life, and making sense of it in terms of his religious vocation.

I have liv'd to be useful and comfortable to my good Father-in-Law Sir *George Moore*, whose patience God hath been pleased to exercise with many temporal Crosses; I have maintained my own Mother, whom it hath pleased God after a plentiful fortune in her younger days, to bring to a great decay in her very old age. I have quietened the Consciences of many that have groaned under the burthen of a wounded spirit, whose prayers I hope are available for me: I cannot plead innocency of life, especially of my youth: But I am willing to be judged by a merciful God, *who is not willing to see what I have done amiss.*[48]

It is important to realize that these words are Walton's rather than Donne's. Notably, there is no mention of Donne's marriage, which Walton dismissed as 'the remarkable error of his life', or his lost children;[49] and it would be interesting to know whose the omission really was, the biographer's or the subject's. The two had grown close, teacher and avid disciple. A poignant memento of their friendship is a copy of Pope Gregory the Great's *De Cura Pastorale* (*Concerning Pastoral Care*), the front page of which bears both their signatures, Donne's 'failing powers being shewn by the shaky writing'.[50] There could hardly have been two different men. Plain, genial Walton, self-educated, placid to a fault, whose long, long life would be troubled by only one adventure, twenty years later, on a mission to rescue a royal jewel;[51] and Donne. In March 1631, however, both had their minds set on death for personal reasons, though from different angles. That same month Walton lost two little sons, six-week-old Thomas and three-year-old Isaak – he may have had his own reasons for not including or not remembering Donne's words about his own dead children.[52] For all its charm and fondness, there are certain regions and intensities of feeling the *Life* simply avoids.

Whether or not Donne wrapped up his life as neatly as Walton has him do in the passage above, the text is true to his impulse to settle questions and inconsistencies that had troubled him for years; or rather, to let them go, and relax. In one of his late sermons, given about two years before he died, he spoke of the need for the mind to aspire to a point of equilibrium.

It were a strange ambitious patience in any man, to be content to be racked every day, in hope to be an inch or two taller at last: so is it for me, to think to be a dram or two wiser, by hearkening to all jealousies, and doubts, and distractions, and perplexities, that arise in my Bosom, or in my Family; which is the rack and torture of the soul. A spirit of Contradiction may be of use in the greatest Counsels; because thereby matters may be brought into farther debatement. But a spirit of contradiction in mine own Bosome, to be able to conclude nothing, resolve nothing, determine nothing, not in my Religion, not in my Manners, but occasionally, and upon Emergencies; this is a sickly complexion of the soul, a dangerous impotencie, and a shrewd and ill-presaging *Crisis*.[53]

Much of Donne's work is a recording of precisely that 'rack and torture of the soul', a hearkening to all of those 'jealousies, and doubts, and distractions, and perplexities' he mentions here. Yet he left it to his admirers to agonize over the contradictions his life presented, and which he himself, if the spirit of Walton's text is to be believed, had learnt to live with.

The standard biographical thesis was not long in emerging. In 1633, when a collection of 'Elegies upon the Author' was included in the first edition of Donne's poems, many of the tributes saw the earlier, wilder and more uncertain part of his life as a preparation for the resolved and determined work of later years. His writing was made the index of the personal transformation. By a paradoxical alchemy, the art of the poet was transmuted into that of the preacher: 'he was a two-fold Priest', wrote Lucius Cary (later Viscount Falkland); 'in youth, / Apollo's; afterwards, the voice of Truth'.[54] Or in John Chudleigh's words,

> He kept his loves, but not his objects; wit
> He did not banish, but transplanted it,
> Taught it his place and use, and brought it home
> To Pietie, which it doth best become . . .[55]

Broadly speaking, this was the interpretation that Isaak Walton expanded into his *Life of John Donne*, the first version of which appeared in 1639. In Walton's handling of the story, the risky living of Donne's youth is safely contained and moralized by the exemplary behaviour that followed ordination. In the same way, the liberties of the earlier writing are reined in by the lessons of the sermons. Yet in some of the other elegies printed in the 1633 edition, the consequences and side effects of the transformation are not so straightforward. Thomas Browne, né Cokayne, wrote a poem questioning 'the *Promiscuous* printing of his Poems, the *Looser sort*, with the Religious'; and asking Donne's ghost, excruciatingly,

> How will they, with sharper eyes,
> The *Fore-skinne* of thy phansie circumcise?[56]

Donne's admirer and imitator Thomas Carew offered a more complex comment. For him, the idea of letting a poet with Donne's seductive force loose in the pulpit involved the release of something much more dangerous and exciting than Walton's biography would account for:

> The Pulpit may her plaine,
> And sober Christian precepts still retaine,
> Doctrines it may, and wholesome Uses frame,
> Grave Homilies, and Lectures, But the flame

> Of thy brave Soule, that shot such heat and light,
> As burnt our earth, and made our darknesse bright,
> Committed holy Rapes upon our Will,
> Did through the eye the melting heart distill;
> And the deepe knowledge of darke truths so teach,
> As sense might judge, what phansic could not reach . . .[57]

Where Walton found 'inexpressible comeliness' in Donne's ministry, Carew saw heat and light, burnt earth, holy rape and dark truths. This element was cause for concern more than celebration for other elegists. For Chudleigh, Donne was simply too good at describing the ways of wickedness – his exhortations became aids to temptation and Religion herself seemed almost sluttish:

> The first effects sprung in the giddy minde
> Of flashy youth, and thirst of woman-kinde . . .
> Tell me, had ever pleasure such a dresse,
> Have you knowne crimes so shap'd? or lovelinesse
> Such as his lips did cloth religion in?
> Had not reproofe a beauty passing sinne?[58]

These were lines by men for whom the different Donnes, the poet and the preacher, were fused together through the 1620s. They heard him preach in public, while reading and exchanging manuscript copies of his verse in private. In commonplace books of the later seventeenth century, the doctor of divinity became the protagonist of 'Jack' Donne's earlier adventures, as his poems – or, quite often, salacious lyrics wrongly attributed to him – took on unauthorized titles such as 'Dr Dunne to his mistress', 'Dr Dun to his Wife giving him the Lye', and 'Dr Dunne of his mrs rising (Ly stil my deare)'.[59]

Donne had firm views of his own concerning his posthumous image; yet he foresaw death and decomposition itself as a physical annulment of historical identity, a process that quite literally left prince indistinguishable from pauper.

In what wrinkle, in what furrow, in what bowel of the earth, ly all the graines of the ashes of a body burnt a thousand years since? In what corner, in what ventricle of the sea, lies all the jelly of a Body drowned in the *generall flood?* What cohærence, what sympathy, what dependence maintaines any relation, any correspondence, between that arm that was lost in Europe, and that legge that was lost in Afrique or Asia, scores of years between?[60]

Only the mind of God could follow the trickling of life's 'excrementall jelly' through the earth. Donne accepted and welcomed the idea of death as the great leveller – 'there is no meanes to distinguish Royall from Plebeian, nor Catholique from Hereticall dust'[61] – and he yearned, quite genuinely, for the relief it would bring from physical and emotional suffering. Yet the way he managed his own demise suggests he was very determined to resist the principle of oblivion on the surface of the earth, though he could do nothing about what happened to him beneath it. In his last weeks he went about fixing the profile he wished to leave with posterity.

Giving the Lent sermon exhausted him but did not bring his condition to the crisis that he thought it might. He did not 'die in the Pulpit', or take his death from preaching; nor, as Walton claims, were 'his spirits so spent, as indisposed him to business, or to talk'.[62] Instead, he tried returning to his old routine. The following day he was well enough to attend a governors' meeting at the Charterhouse. But this seems to have been his last public engagement.[63] After that, he was confined to his house. The Deanery became his 'prison' – as it would for many others, quite literally, twelve years later, when a Parliament hostile to the luxuries of churchmen ordered that the house be converted into a gaol. The sundial Donne left in the garden and the pictures of the four prophets in the main hall were among the spoils when the place was ransacked.

Donne's physician, Simeon Fox, the youngest son of the great Protestant chronicler of the Reformation, John Fox, still believed his patient had a chance of recovering – 'by Cordials, and drinking milk twenty days together'. Donne passionately rejected this treatment. He hated milk. Fox 'wearied him with solicitations' until he agreed to take it for ten days; after this length of time, he declared 'that he would not drink it ten days longer upon the best moral assurance of having twenty years added to his life'.[64] One suggestion of the doctor's that he did accept, however, was the idea that he might have a monument. Fox sensibly refrained from offering comments on what the statue should be like, but anonymously donated the funds for it to be made after Donne died. The question of the design occupied Donne's still plentiful creativity for the next couple of weeks. In mid-March, he ordered the props he required and got his servants to prepare the scene he had in mind. Following precise specifications, a carpenter made him a kind of wooden platform, with the front cut in the shape of a funeral urn, for Donne to stand upon, and provided him with a wooden board that was as tall as he was. With these things ready, an artist came to the house and the stage was set:

Several Charcole-fires being first made in his large Study, he brought with him into that place his winding-sheet in his hand, and, having put off all his cloaths, had this sheet put on him, and so tyed with knots at his head and feet, and his hands so placed, as dead bodies are usually fitted to be shrowded and put into their Coffin, or grave.

Donne stood upon the urn and had his portrait taken 'with so much of the sheet turned aside as might shew his lean, pale, and death-like face, which was purposely turned toward the East, from whence he expected the coming of his and our Saviour Jesus'.[65]

When he visited Donne the following week, Walton saw that the dying man was so pleased with the picture, which was drawn on the life-size wooden board, that he had had it installed at his bedside. His own death's head watched over him. The Monday after the sitting, Donne 'took his last leave of his beloved Study', no longer able to go far from bed. During the next few days, he summoned his friends and colleagues to take his official leave of them, not without giving them some parting advice in 'sentences useful for the regulation of their lives'. He had many final says, tuning each one to what he thought his listener best required. On Sunday, he instructed the servants in his household to complete any remaining business they might have with him in the next six days, for after the following Saturday he told them 'he would not mix his thoughts with any thing that concerned this world.'[66] There is surely no other poet who orchestrated his death so meticulously.

One of those in the habit of calling daily on Donne was his friend and colleague Bishop Henry King. Three days before his death, Donne handed over to King a huge clump of manuscripts, containing his sermons and his notes. When King and Walton, who was also present, examined the collection some time later, it was found to contain not only copy ready for the press, but also extensive commentary on between fourteen and fifteen hundred authors.[67] This phantom critique would undoubtedly give us a better idea of Donne's reading habits and working method. We might observe him thinking a text through, questioning, or just doodling. Yet the mere fact that it existed is enough to reinforce our sense of the range and rigour of his studies, and years of extraordinary intellectual exertion.

Six years earlier, writing up his sermons at Chelsea, Donne had said that he hoped they might be used by his son John, who by now had also taken orders, 'or some other in the world of middle understandinge'.[68] The comment is a pretty clear sign that he did not think all that highly of his son's faculties (or, admittedly, those of anyone who might have to 'use' the sermons instead of writing their own). Significantly, Donne on his deathbed chose to entrust them to a fellow senior professional rather than his son. However, while Donne the younger may not have had a great mind, he certainly did have a hard neck, and he was unafraid to stick it out if there was anything to be gained. He felt that his father's papers should be his to publish and profit from, and at some point in the next ten years succeeded in obtaining them. Bumblingly, neither King nor Walton were quite sure how they allowed such treasures out of their grasp. By the time 'honest Isaak' – as King called him – published his *Life* of Donne, the friends had given up arguing about it. 'How these were got out of my hands, you, who were the Messenger for them, and how lost both to me and your self, is not now seasonable to complain,' said King in a letter to Walton.[69] But although some material was lost, as R. C. Bald points out, without the young Donne's opportunism none at all of his father's sermons might have survived. King dawdled about publishing; and if he had still possessed them when parliamentary forces overran his Episcopal palace at Chichester in 1643, the whole set might have been lost forever.[70]

John Donne the younger was described as 'an atheistical buffoon, a banterer, a person of over free thoughts';[71] and he could turn nasty. After his father died, he spent a few years hanging around his old college, Christ Church in Oxford, living on a vague royal promise that he would be made a canon of the Cathedral there. One day in 1634, as he rode with another Christ Church man along St Aldate's, the long broad thoroughfare that leads past the college, his horse was startled by an eight-year-old boy who ran too close. Donne Jr immediately struck the lad several times about the head with the butt of his whip. A fortnight later the boy died, having complained of pains and fallen ill. No incriminating marks were found on the body, however, and Donne Jr escaped conviction; though he deemed it prudent to leave the country for Padua for some years, where he took a doctorate in law. Despite his disgrace, his great aim was still to be made a canon at Christ Church.

He spent much of the rest of his life railing and suing for what he felt were his dues. After successfully taking legal action against those who had published some of his father's work in the 1630s – including the *Poems* and *Juvenilia* – he was, he puffed, 'encouradged by most of the cheefe men in the Kingdome, to recollect and printe my Fathers Sermons, beeinge often told, how well I should deserue both from Kinge and People, by such an Act; for, by that meanes, I should not only preach to the present adge, but to their childrens children as longe as the Christian Religion should last'.[72] As a reward, King Charles again promised, he claimed, to install him at Christ Church. His edition of Donne's *LXXX Sermons*, containing the first version of Walton's *Life*, was published in 1640 and dedicated to the King. 'In this rumor of Warre I am bold to present to your sacred Majestie the fruits of peace, planted by the hand of your most Royal Father,' he wrote; but the rumour of war had made him look elsewhere for insurance.[73] Charles was in the thick of his troubles with the rebellious House of Commons, and on hearing that Donne Jr was, for all his unction, supporting both sides, 'deeply engadged in the service of the Parliament', he promptly cancelled his intention of making him a canon at Christ Church.[74]

Donne the younger went on to edit further volumes of his father's sermons, letters, poems and miscellaneous writings, including the tract on suicide, *Biathanatos*, which Donne himself had felt was unsuitable for publication. Although the years of the English republic were somewhat lean ones for him, he managed to survive into the Restoration as one of the shabby, contentious poetasters that hung around Bloomsbury and Covent Garden Market, a threadbare gentleman of letters drifting through the coffee houses. He was described unflatteringly by one of his peers.

> The Curre's as crank as any of you
> And frisks and fitchets up and down
> As you, to all the Clubbs of th' town.[75]

Yet he remained a clergyman, technically at least, and managed to pick up a few modest but comfortable benefices, which saw him through the winters. During Cromwell's Commonwealth he was obliged to sell many of his possessions – his books, his collection of birds – except for his doves – but did hang on to one extraordinary family heirloom. In his will, he bequeathed to a friend the head of his ancestor Sir Thomas More.[76] The head was rescued by More's daughter Margaret after his execution in 1535. She had wanted it to be buried in her arms, but these wishes appear to have been denied.[77] Unless the bequest is a mere bluff, or a joke on a family myth, the head was probably smuggled into the Deanery of St Paul's when Donne's mother came to stay. Hidden under a bed or in a cupboard somewhere, the Dean's Papist background was with him up to the very end.

In the epitaph he wrote for his wife's tombstone, Donne pledged to join his remains with hers, in their old parish church of St Clement Danes. This would be 'a new marriage', a wish that recalled his poem 'The Relique', with its image of two lovers curled together in the earth. It may be, however, that Donne meant his reunion with Ann to take place on the last day of time, after the resurrection. In any case, making his will thirteen years after she died, he decided not to lie beside her. He asked instead to be 'buryed in the moste private manner that maye be in that place of St Paules Church London'.[78]

This desire, as he realized, by asking for the most private entombment 'that maye be', was something of a contradiction in terms. St Paul's, to most Londoners a thoroughfare and job market, was not a private place. But Donne had accepted some years before that one should not expect seclusion in the grave. Even dead men cannot be islands. 'Death is not a banishing of you out of this world; but it is a visitation of your kindred that lie in the earth; neither are any nearer of kin to you, then the earth it selfe, and the wormes of the earth.'[79] He would be going from one public life to another, so it was apt that he lay close to the feet of the Paul's Walkers who had so exasperated him. His tomb was placed just inside the choir of the Cathedral, in the southern arcade.[80]

His bones are long lost, but his remarkable white marble statue, the only piece of sculpture to survive the Great Fire in decent condition, still stands on roughly the same spot in the present St Paul's. It was carved by Nicholas Stone, the same mason who made the memorial tablet for Donne's wife in St Clement Danes. The piece depicts Donne standing upright in his shroud, rising from his funeral urn, hands folded across his front. It is a scene from Judgement Day, an awakening soul expecting God's verdict: 'here, though set in dust,' reads the Latin inscription, 'he beholdeth Him Whose name is the Rising'.[81] With hands clasped inside the robe, and shoulders just a little hunched, knees bending slightly, it looks as though he feels the chill of the Cathedral stone, while waiting patiently. This was the final likeness he wished to leave with the world.

The face is peaceful, inclined downwards, eyes closed. '*It seems to breath faintly*,' remarked Sir Henry Wotton, Donne's old friend. '*Posterity shall look upon it as a kind of artificial Miracle.*'[82] Perhaps the most miraculous thing that strikes posterity about the figure, however, is its escape without blemish. By the time it was carted from the ruins of St Paul's, after old London was scorched clear in 1666, the statue had been through a lot. The battered gothic silo, the Cathedral of St Paul's, had been extensively repaired and decorated under the stewardship of Archbishop Laud, who made it the flagship of his royalist Church; and then picked clean by Puritan outrage at such idolatry. Parliamentary forces, garrisoned in the Cathedral at the end of the Civil War, had exercised their horses in the aisles and for years, during the English republic, the place had been little more than a giant barn. It is noteworthy, however, that while many statues were defaced and toppled, Donne's was not. In an age of long memories, this indicates that Donne was not definitively associated with the royalist camp, or, indeed, with any one faction. It was salvaged before the ruins of St Paul's were finally pulled down, and was left for many years among other oddments in the crypt of the new Cathedral.

In the intervening centuries, like his effigy, Donne's reputation was heaved around, neglected and recovered. For a long time he was thought of as too difficult, artificial, contriving ideas from unlikely conceits. However, by the next time the skies turned red above his statue, in the Blitz of 1940, his literary standing had enjoyed more than a century of steady restoration. One of the air-raid wardens scuttling around London, T. S. Eliot, was among the most recent who found Donne casting a shadow over his shoulder as he wrote. Eliot was the figurehead of a critical movement that reaffirmed Donne as one of the greatest of all English poets. Donne was seized on as being peculiarly modern, ahead of his age, because of his frankness with complexity, the way his writing exposed and explored the torsions of thought and emotion. Some of his contemporaries saw this too. But Donne was still one of them, just one more islander. His work is an extended dialogue with the world around him, friends, lovers, fellow-writers, patrons and parishioners. According to Walton, he was talking until the last minute of his life, on 31 March 1631. On falling silent, he arranged 'his hands and body into such a posture as required not the least alteration by those that came to shroud him'.[83]

Afterword

'In the great Ant-hill of the whole world, I am an Ant,' said Donne. 'In the great field of clay, of red earth, that man was made of, and mankind, I am a clod; I am a man, I have my part in the Humanity.'[1] For Donne, every individual is linked to every other on the planet. We are made of the same stuff, have the same basic faculties – grouped in what was then termed simply the soul – and all face the prospect of dying. The death of any person should make us pause, and reflect on our own mortality, since something of ourselves goes with them. In Donne's mind this involvement of everyone with everyone else was not a static connection, but something that altered even as it appeared to stay the same, like the teeming ants' nest, constantly frantic with collective industry, or the passive soil, ploughed, sown and harvested, or lying fallow in its season. Humans are inescapably historical: because we are all part of the world, we have no choice but to change with it, from year to year, and adapt to the circumstances it presents. Our state is one of continual flux:

I need not call in new Philosophy, that denies a settlednesse, an acquiescence in the very body of the Earth, but makes the Earth to move in that place, where we thought the Sunne had moved; I need not that helpe, that the Earth it selfe is in Motion, to prove this, That nothing upon Earth is permanent; The Assertion will stand of it selfe, till some man assigne me some instance, something that a man may relie upon, and find permanent.[2]

If the world stood still, Donne would have been spared the great trials of his life. He need never have worried about whether to join the Reformed Church or remain with the Roman Catholic one. He need never have carried out the painful metamorphosis from gentleman poet to patriarch. Since no man or woman is an island, but involved with humankind, and part of this forever mutable Creation, Donne felt obliged to keep reforming, accepting the pressures of the moment while fighting to preserve something essential about himself, something he could call his own soul.

The life and writings of John Donne provide us with an almost uniquely articulate commentary on the social, moral and intellectual dilemmas of his age. Yet he also remains a living guide to the problems raised by the 'new Philosophy' of more recent times. Far from all of those turning to his works in the last century have been historians or students of English. On the West Coast in the late 1930s, Jean Tatlock, a talented, fragile and politically passionate psychology student at Stanford University, introduced her lover, a professor of physics, to Donne's works. J. Robert Oppenheimer had been rather detached from the world until Tatlock took him in hand. She was a communist sympathizer, and their relationship was used against Oppenheimer when he became a target of the McCarthy inquiry in the 1950s. Before they finally split, having twice come close to marrying, Donne became a major part of their shared emotional archive.

Their political sensitivities, long strained in Tatlock, awoken by her in Oppenheimer, took the lovers along permanently separate paths. Horror and depression led Tatlock to take her life in 1944. As for Oppenheimer, reports that German scientists had split the atom led to his recruitment by the American military as head of the research unit that became known as the Manhattan Project. In July 1945, by which time European Fascism had been defeated, and along with it the real possibility of a Nazi atomic device, his work helped bring about the detonation of the world's first nuclear explosive at the valley of Jornada del Muerto – the 'way of death' – in an experiment he codenamed Trinity.

'I am become Death, the shatterer of worlds,' he famously exclaimed, as the bulbous cloud rose from the New Mexican desert. The line, as commentators quickly established, was from the *Bhagavad Gita*. Oppenheimer invested a number of his life's most notable deeds and statements with literary and scriptural resonance, and was not wholly averse to fuelling and participating in speculation about their meaning. Like Donne, he shaped his own personal iconology. Almost twenty years after the explosions, Oppenheimer was asked by the military director of the Manhattan Project, General Leslie Groves, why he had called the original test 'Trinity'. The fact that there had been three nuclear explosions in all was not a sufficient explanation. Oppenheimer's response was that he had been thinking of Donne. 'Why I chose the name is not clear, but I know what thoughts were in my mind. There is a poem of John Donne, written just before his death, which I know and love. From it a quotation: "As West and East / In all flatt Maps – and I am one – are one, / So death doth touch the Resurrection."' The line is from Donne's 'Hymne to God my God in my sicknesse'. By this time Oppenheimer had been largely ostracized from the defence establishment, after the McCarthy witch-hunt, and he may have been using the reference less to explain the meaning of 'Trinity' than to discredit the bi-polar division of the Cold War world he had helped create. East and West were illusions of a map; if one put the chart around a globe, those extremities merged together into one. As he admitted, 'That still does not make a Trinity, but in another, better known devotional poem Donne opens, "Batter my heart, three person'd God"'.[3] This invocation of the trinity was taken from Holy Sonnet XIV, where Donne begs to be beaten and eventually raped by God to be purged of his sin: 'o'erthrow mee, and bend / Your force, to break, blowe, burn and make me new'.

The God of this sonnet, to whom we can only turn to be battered for atrocities of conscience, may be the only realistic deity to have survived the snows of fallout in Japan. Oppenheimer's eye might also have caught a frightening passage in Donne's final and most anthologized sermon, *Deaths Duell*, which considers how all trace of individual life can vanish:

In that case where there were *bones* to be *seene*, something visible . . . it might be said, can this thing live? But in this death of *incineration*, and dispersion of dust, we see *nothing* that we call *that mans*; If we say, can this dust live? perchance it *cannot*, it may bee the meere *dust* of the *earth*, which never did live, never shall . . . It may be the dust of *another* man, that concernes not him of whom it is askt. This death of *incineration* and dispersion, is to naturall *reason*, the most *irrecoverable death* of all . . .[4]

Donne believed that there was more to death than 'naturall reason' could make out alone. Faith had to absorb and overwhelm the vision of irrevocable extinction that the world presented to the senses and the mind, and which Donne conveys so harrowingly here. Yet he could not diminish the power and reality of that vision. To one who had performed so many remarkable reformations and comebacks, it was only death that could not be 'undone'. A death changed all that remained by the vacancy it created. When the Dean of St Paul's passed away quietly in 1631, nobody was the same; and not because he was John Donne, a name in the literatures both of divinity and natural reason, but because he had lived. He was a man, he had his part in humanity. When a single life ended, Donne reasoned, let alone when countless numbers were reduced to nothing, something in him died as well, and in all those left behind. The bell at his funeral, as at any, tolled for everyone.

Notes

All references are recorded in the conventional manner in the following pages. Quotations from Donne's verse, however, are given by line number rather than by page in any particular edition. The editions of his poetry used as standard texts here are those by Sir Herbert Grierson (1912 and 1933), John Hayward (1929) and C. A. Patrides (1985). All other references are recorded in the usual way. The following abbreviated references occur throughout the notes:

A Collection of Letters	John Donne the younger, ed., *A Collection of Letters Made by Sr Tobie Mathews K^t* (1660)
Bald	R. C. Bald, *John Donne: A Life* (1970)
Devotions	Donne, *Devotions Upon Emergent Occasions*, ed. John Sparrow (1923)
Gosse	Sir Edmund Gosse, *The Life and Letters of John Donne*, 2 vols (1899)
Grierson (1912)	Sir Herbert Grierson, ed., *The Poems of John Donne*, 2 vols (1912)
Grierson (1933)	Sir Herbert Grierson, ed., *The Poems of John Donne* (1933)
Letters	Donne, *Letters to Severall Persons of Honour* (1651)
Sermons	*The Sermons of John Donne*, ed. George R. Potter and Evelyn M. Simpson, 10 vols (1953–62)
Simpson	Evelyn M. Simpson, *A Study of the Prose Works of John Donne* (1948)
Walton	Isaak Walton, *The Lives of John Donne, Sir Henry Wotton, Richard Hooker & Robert Sanderson* (1670, repr. 1927)

Introduction

1 John Stow, *Two London Chronicles*, ed. C. L. Kingsford (1910), p.6.

2 John Stow, *Survey of London*, ed. C. L. Kingsford, 2 vols (1908; repr. 1971), vol.1, p.347.

3 Stow, *Survey of London*, vol.1, p.347.

4 W. Milgate offers a survey and thorough collection of contemporary views in 'The Early References to John Donne', *Notes and Queries* 195 (1950), 229–31, 246–7, 290–2, and 198 (1953), 421–4.

5 Satyre III (79–84).

6 *Sermons*, vol.10, p.231.

7 Walton, pp.76–7.

8 'The Extasie' (18–20; 43–4).

9 *Devotions*, pp.394–5.

10 F. R. Leavis, 'The Line of Wit', in *Revaluation* (1936), p.11.

11 Aristotle, *Poetics* 8 [1451a15–20], trans. Stephen Halliwell (New Loeb edn, 1999), p.57.

12 *Sermons*, vol.4, p.107.

13 *Letters*, p.22.

14 For Donne's burial arrangements and his bequeathal of the artworks in his collection see the transcript of his will in Bald, pp.563–7.

1. The Den

1 Elegie IV: 'The Perfume' (13–25).

2 Elegie IV: 'The Perfume' (27–8).

3 Elegie IV: 'The Perfume' (45–6).

4 Elegie IV: 'The Perfume' (1–6).

5 Elegie IV: 'The Perfume' (47–9).

6 Satyre I (2).

7 Walton, *Lives*, p.67.

8 *Letters*, p.51.

9 'To Mr B.B.' (7–8).

10 *Pseudo-martyr*, B$_2$^{v}.

11 Walton, p.67.

12 Satyre I (1, 11–13).

13 *Sermons*, vol.2, no.13 [19 December 1619], p.275.

14 Antony à Wood, *Athenae Oxoniensis* (1813), ed. Philip Bliss, vol.1, p.480.

15 Richard Corbett, 'John Dawson, Butler at Christ-Church, 1622' (11–15), *Complete Poems*, ed. J. A. W. Bennett and H. R. Trevor-Roper, pp.72–3.

16 See H. E. Salter, *Survey of Oxford* (1960), vol.1, pp.227–8.

17 See Alan Davidson, 'An Oxford Family: A Footnote to the Life of John Donne', *Recusant History* 13 (1976), 299–300.

18 Her will (22 February 1562) is in the Prerogative Court of Canterbury, 33 Streat: see Bald, p.28.

19 Satyre IV (8–11).

20 J. H. Pollen, ed., *Miscellanea: Memoirs of Robert Persons, SJ* (1905), pp.71–3; text modernized.

21 Robert Southwell, *An Humble Supplication to Her Majesty*, ed. R. C. Bald (1953), p.34.

22 Dennis Flynn, *John Donne and the Ancient Catholic Nobility* (1995), p.27. Professor Flynn's book is the most comprehensive study yet of Donne's family background.

23 The will is dated 16 January; printed in Bald, pp.560–2.

24 'The Good Morrow' (1–4).

25 Flynn, *John Donne and the Ancient Catholic Nobility*, p.21.

26 Cresacre More, *The Life and Death of Sir Thomas More* (1631), p.389.

27 *The Epigrams of Sir John Harington*, ed. N. E. McClure (1926), p.135. See Baird W. Whitlock, 'Donne's University Years', *English Studies* 43 (1962), 1–20.

28 Flynn, *John Donne and the Ancient Catholic Nobility*, p.65.

29 Flynn, *John Donne and the Ancient Catholic Nobility*, p.103.

30 Sir Edmund Gosse, *Life and Letters of John Donne* (1899), vol.1, p.13.

31 J. H. Pollen, *Documents Relating to the English Martyrs*, Catholic Record Society, vol.5, 1908, p.60.

32 William Weston, *The Diary of an Elizabethan*, translated by Philip Caraman (1955), pp.10–11.

33 *Psuedo-martyr*, L₁ᵛ. See John Carey, *John Donne: Life, Mind and Art*, 2nd edn (1990), p.6.

34 *Psuedo-martyr*, B₂ᵛ.

35 Walton, p.23.

36 Walton, p.100.

37 Raphael Holinshed, *Chronicles* (1807 edn), vol.1, p.252.

38 *Letters*, p.51.

39 Antony à Wood, *Athenae Oxoniensis*, vol.1, p.480.

40 Elegie I: 'Jealosy' (32).

41 John Strype, *Annals of the Reformation* (1728), vol.3, p.420.

42 Southwell, *An Humble Supplication*, p.34.

43 *Sermons*, vol.6, no.13 [Easter Day, 1625], p.266. Aside from its humanitarian criticism, the passage still has sectarian overtones, and is an indication of how Donne's loyalties shifted: the mention of 'exquisite inquisitions' focuses the comment on the persecution of those on the Continent (in France and Spain especially) who dissented from the Roman Church – not the Catholic martyrs Donne may have sympathized with in very early youth.

44 Bald, pp.68–70; Walton, *Lives*, p.26.

45 Arthur W. Reed, *Early Tudor Drama* (1926), p.35.

46 Walton, p.26.

2. Henry

1 'A Sheaf of Miscellany Epigrams', in *Paradoxes, Problemees, Essayes, Characters, Written by Doctor Donne Dean of Pauls: to which is added a Book of Epigrams: Written in Latin by the same Author; translated into English by J: Maine, D.D.* (1652), p.101.

2 Flynn, *John Donne and the Ancient Catholic Nobility*, p.142. To make up their own minds on the question of whether Donne was a combatant in his early teens, readers and students should consult and weigh up Professor Flynn's chapter on 'Donne's Flight from the Persecution', pp.131–46, and Bald, pp.46–7.

3 *Paradoxes*, p.95.

4 *Devotions*, p.8.

5 Walton, p.24.

6 Holinshed, *Chronicles*, vol.1, p.252.

7 Bald, p.46.

8 Bald, p.46.

9 Strype, *Annals of the Reformation*, vol.3, p.51.

10 'To Mr B.B.' (2–6, 16) and 'To Mr S.B.' (4, 8, 11)

11 Bald, p.20.

12 John Carey's translation and correction of Walton's misrendering; *John Donne: Life, Mind and Art*, p.9.

13 Richard Baker, *Chronicles* (1643), part II, p.156.

14 Elegie XIX: 'To His Mistress Going to Bed' (1–12).

15 Elegie XIX: 'To His Mistress Going to Bed' (25–6).

16 Elegie XIX: 'To His Mistress Going to Bed' (31).

17 Walton, p.24.

18 *Letters*, p.110.

19 Simpson [letter no.8], p.312.

20 *Letters*, p.103.

21 Jasper Mayne, 'On Dr *Donnes* death' (19–22), in Grierson (1933), p.350.

22 Satyre II (7–8).

23 Philip Sidney, *The Defence of Poesy*, and George Puttenham, *The Art of English Poesy*, in *Sidney's 'The Defence of Poesy' and Selected Renaissance Criticism*, ed. Gavin Alexander (2004), pp.8 and 60.

24 Satyre II (13–14).

25 Satyre II (21–2).

26 Satyre IV (73).

27 'The Triple Foole' (1–16).

28 Elegie X: 'The Dreame' (1–6).

29 'Communitie' (22–3).

30 'Why Hath the Common Opinion Afforded Women Soules?', in John Donne, *Complete Poetry and Selected Prose*, ed. John Hayward (1929), pp.350–1. See *Sermons*, vol.9, introduction, pp.20–1; and no.8 [Easter Day, 1630], p.190.

31 'Loves Alchymie' (23–4).

32 Holy Sonnet XIII (10).

33 'The Indifferent' (1–7).

34 'A Defence of Womens Inconstancy', in Hayward, ed., *Complete Poetry and Selected Prose*, p.337.

35 Elegie VI (11).

36 'Farewell to Love' (20–3).

37 'Loves Usury' (13–16).

38 *Sermons*, vol.2, no.3 [spring or summer 1618], p.108; echoing St Augustine.

39 Michael Drayton, 'To Henry Reynolds, of Poets and Poesy' (1–8; 187–95), in Alexander, ed., *Sidney's 'The Defence of Poesy'*, pp.291–7.

40 Bald, p.199.

41 Thomas Freeman, *Rubbe, and a great Cast* (1614), part 2, no.84.

42 Richard Corbett, 'On Doctor *Donne*' (6), in Grierson (1933), p.342.

43 Satyre I (72, 55, 92).

44 From a list by Francis Davidson compiled around 1606: see Milgate, 'The Early References to John Donne', p.230. There is a shortage of manuscript copies of Donne's verse dating from his youth, unsurprisingly: much-thumbed documents were liable to early loss and destruction, and were unlikely to be kept before they became what Drayton sniffily calls 'wondrous relics'. It is towards the end of Donne's life, by which time his reputation had spread enormously, that one starts to see an increase in the number of carefully compiled and preserved copies of his work in manuscript collections. But obviously these texts were predated by others that have not survived. Despite the scarcity of such manuscripts, there is however indirect evidence that his poems and early prose pieces began to be circulated quite early on, a matter of some anxiety to Donne in his letters. For an introduction to Donne's early bibliography, from a wealth of scholarly research, see for example Deborah Aldrich Larson, 'Donne's Contemporary Reputation: Evidence from Some Commonplace Books and Manuscript Miscellanies', *John Donne Journal* 12 (1993), 115–30; Ernest W. Sullivan II, 'Who was Reading / Writing Donne Verse in the Seventeenth Century?', *John Donne Journal* 8 (1989), 1–16.

45 'To E. of D. with six holy Sonnets' (1–3).

46 *Letters*, p.51.

47 Walton, p.24.

48 Wilfrid R. Prest, *The Inns of Court Under Elizabeth I and the Early Stuarts 1590–1640* (1972), p.127. Prest's immaculately researched and lucidly written book remains the definitive study.

49 Quoted in Prest, *The Inns of Court*, p.123.

50 Quoted in Prest, *The Inns of Court*, p.92.

51 *Sermons*, vol.2, p.62.

52 Prest, *The Inns of Court*, p.91.

53 Prest, *The Inns of Court*, p.16.

54 Prest, *The Inns of Court*, p.154.

55 Paul Griffiths, *Youth and Authority: Formative Experiences in England 1560–1640* (1996), p.77.

56 W. Fletewood to Lord Burghley, 18 June 1584, in *Queen Elizabeth and Her Times: A Series of Original Letters*, ed. Thomas Wright, 2 vols (1838), vol.1, p.226.

57 Everard Gilpin, 'Satyra tertia', *Skialethia* (1598), C_8^v-D^r.

58 'The Sunne Rising' (6).

59 Flynn, *John Donne and the Ancient Catholic Nobility*, pp.74–6.

60 Prest, *The Inns of Court*, p.176.

61 *Queen Elizabeth and Her Times*, vol.1, p.467.

62 'To Mr E.G.' (8).

63 'To Mr R. W.' ('Kindly I envy') (9–10).

64 'To Mr R. W.' ('Kindly I envy') (5–6).

65 'To Mr R. W.' ('Kindly I envy') (7–8).

66 Fr John Morris, 'The Martyrdom of William Harrington', *The Month* XX (1874), 411–23, especially p.415.

67 Morris, 'Martyrdom of William Harrington,' p.417.

68 Transcript of 'The Will of Donne's Father', in Bald, p.560.

69 Morris, 'Martyrdom of William Harrington,' p.417.

70 Peter Ackroyd, *London* (2000), p.249.

71 *Tobie Mathew Collection*, p.323.

72 'To Mr E.G.' (8–13).

3. Cadiz

1 Baird W. Whitlock, 'The Family of John Donne, 1588–91', *Notes and Queries*, CCV (1960), 380–6, especially p.383.

2 Richard Baker, *Chronicles*, 1643, part II, p.156.

3 Shakespeare, *Henry VIII*, 5.3.60–1.

4 R. C. Bald, *Donne and the Drurys* (1959), pp.79–81.

5 Walton, p.24.

6 *Donne v. Danby*, Public Record Office C3/266/93; transcribed in Bald, pp.567–8.

7 Satyre II (63–4).

8 'To Mr I.L.' ('Of that short Roll of friends writ in my heart') (8–11)

9 Satyre IV (24).

10 Sir Walter Ralegh, *The Discoverie of the Large, Rich and Bewtiful Empyre of Guiana*, ed. Neil L. Whitehead (1997), p.161.

11 Ralegh, *The Discoverie*, pp.162–3.

12 Ralegh, *The Discoverie*, p.137.

13 Satyre IV (126); Satyre I (17–18).

14 Walton, p.26, claiming that Donne 'waited upon his Lordship'.

15 Shakespeare, *King John*, 2.1.68.

16 J. S. Corbett, *The Successors of Drake* (1900), p.19.

17 Walton, p.49.

18 Henry Wotton, *The Characters of Robert Devereux, Earl of Essex; and George Villiers, Duke of Buckingham*, ed. Sir Egerton Bridges (1814), p.19.

19 'Sir John Wingefield' (3).

20 Elegie V: 'His Picture' (5–20).

21 Corbett, *The Successors of Drake*, p.48.

22 Strype, *Annals of the Reformation*, vol.3, p.523.

23 Morris, 'The Martyrdom of William Harrington', p.419.

24 Strype, *Annals of the Reformation*, vol.3, p.562.

25 Satyre II (10).

26 John Stow, *Annales of England* (1631), pp.771–2.

27 Corbett, *The Successors of Drake*, p.48.

28 Corbett, *The Successors of Drake*, p.54.

29 Corbett, *The Successors of Drake*, pp.62–4.

30 Corbett, *The Successors of Drake*, p.97.

31 'Sir John Wingefield' (5).

32 Stow, *Annales of England*, p.775.

33 Stow, *Annales of England*, p.776.

4. The Islands

1 See the transcript of Donne's will in Bald, p.567.

2 'To Mr T.W.' (12)

3 'The Apparition' (6)

4 'The Apparition' (11–12)

5 See C. William Miller and Dan S. Norton, 'Donne's "The Apparition"', *Explicator* 4 (1946), 24.

6 'The Baite' (1, 3): the poem is a knowing yet affectionate variation
   on Christopher Marlowe's much-imitated 'The Passionate Shepherd
   to His Love'.

7 'The Baite' (17–20)

8 Elegie XIX: 'To His Mistress Going To Bed' (27–30)

9 'The Calme' (39–40)

10 Elegie XVIII: 'Loves Progress' (41–2)

11 Elegie XVIII: 'Loves Progress' (43–4)

12 Kenneth R. Andrews, *Elizabethan Privateering* (1964), pp.62–5.

13 Stow, *Annales of England*, p.783.

14 'The Storme' (19–21).

15 'The Storme' (9).

16 'The Storme' (27–8).

17 'The Storme' (45–8).

18 'The Storme' (41–4).

19 'The Storme' (70).

20 'The Storme' (57–8).

21 Sir Arthur Gorges, *A Larger Relation of the said Iland Voyage*, in *Purchas
   his Pilgrimes* (1905–7), vol.20, p.44.

22 'To Mr R.W.' ('If, as mine is, thy life a slumber be') (18–22)

23 Simpson [letter no.1], pp.303–4.

24 John Donne, *Biathanatos*, ed. Ernest W. Sullivan II (1984), p.62.

25 Henry Francis Whitfield, *Plymouth and Devonport* (1900), p.37.

26 'The Storme' (9); 'The Calme' (40)

27 Gorges, *A Larger Relation*, p.50.

28 Gorges, *A Larger Relation*, p.49.

29 Gorges, *A Larger Relation*, p.51.

30 Gorges, *A Larger Relation*, pp.54 6.

31 Gorges, *A Larger Relation*, p.61.

32 Gorges, *A Larger Relation*, p.65.

33 Freeman, *Rubbe, and a great Cast*, part 2, no.84.

34 'The Calme' (6–18); reference to 'Venices' at 38.

35 'The Calme' (35–7; 25–8).

36 'The Calme' (23–4).

37 'The Calme' (11–12).

38 'The Calme' (55–6).

39 Gorges, *A Larger Relation*, pp.65–6.

40 Elegie III: 'Change' (31–6)

41 Elegie XVII (1–2)

42 Gorges, *A Larger Relation*, pp.66–7.

43 Gorges, *A Larger Relation*, p.79.

44 Gorges, *A Larger Relation*, p.81.

45 Gorges, *A Larger Relation*, p.83.

46 Gorges, *A Larger Relation*, p.84.

47 *Sermons*, vol.1, no.4, p.229.

48 Gorges, *A Larger Relation*, p.90.

49 Gorges, *A Larger Relation*, p.112.

50 Elegie XX: 'Loves Warre' (21–4).

51 Elegie VIII: 'The Comparison' (3–6).

52 Corbett, *The Successors of Drake*, p.209.

5. Captain Donne

1 Corbett, *The Successors of Drake*, p.221.

2 Sir Edmund Chambers, 'John Donne, Diplomatist and Soldier', *Modern Language Review* V (1910), 492–3.

3 Bald, p.92.

4 Elegie XX: 'Loves Warre' (13–14).

5 Elegie XX: 'Loves Warre' (29–32).

6 Elegie XX: 'Loves Warre' (45–6).

7 'The Relique' (7–11).

8 'The Relique' (12–18).

9 'The Calme' (39).

10 'The Storme' (9): Donne pays tribute to England in a context where he also discusses the 'pre-eminence of friendship' – the inclination of friends to magnify one another's 'excellence', a subject he takes humorously but never cynically.

6. The Secretary

1 Stow, *Survey*, vol.2, p.102.

2 Everard Gilpin, 'Satyra tertia', *Skialethia* (1598), C_8^v–D^r. See R. E. Bennet, 'John Donne and Everard Gilpin', *Review of English Studies* 15 (1939), 66–72; P. J. Finkelpearl, 'Donne and Everard Gilpin: Additions, Corrections, and Conjectures', *Review of English Studies*, new series 14 (1963), 164–7. Also Bald, p.75.

3 John Lord Campbell, *Lives of the Lord Chancellors* (1856), vol.2, p.308.

4 Campbell, *Lives of the Lord Chancellors*, vol.2, p.313.

5 Louis A. Knafla, 'Mr Secretary Donne: The Years with Sir Thomas Egerton', in *John Donne's Professional Lives*, ed. David Colclough (2003), pp.37–72; especially p.46.

6 Knafla, 'Mr Secretary Donne: The Years with Sir Thomas Egerton', p.47.

7 *Sermons*, vol.6, p.266.

8 'Loves Exchange' (36–42).

9 Angel Day, *The English Secretary* (1599 edn), part 1, p.103.

10 Satyre II (58–60).

11 Satyre III (79–81).

12 Stow, *Survey*, vol.2, p.120.

13 Walton, p.29.

14 Walton, p.27.

15 *Letters*, pp.12–13.

16 Knafla, 'Mr Secretary Donne: The Years With Sir Thomas Egerton', p.44.

17 Stow, *Survey*, vol.2, p.115.

18 Walton, p.27. On the running of Chancery, the key work is W. J. Jones's masterful *The Elizabethan Court of Chancery* (1967); see also Louis Λ. Knaflar, *Law and Politics in Jacobean England: The Tracts of Lord Chancellor Ellesmere* (1977).

19 Antony Bacon, quoted in Francis Henry Egerton, *The Life of Thomas Egerton* (1828), p.166.

20 *The Letters of John Chamberlain*, ed. N. E. McClure, 2 vols (1939), vol.1, p.111.

21 Lord Campbell, *Lives of the Lord Chancellors*, vol.2, pp.318–19.

22 Lord Campbell, *Lives of the Lord Chancellors*, vol.2, p.321.

23 'To Sir Henry Wotton' (1–3).

24 'The Comparison' (47–8).

25 'The Anagram' (52–3).

26 Satyre IV (18–19). This was also the image Donne later chose to describe his own poetry: see 'To E. of D. with six holy Sonnets' (1–5): his highest pitch of jocular deprecation.

27 Satyre IV (45–6; 159–60).

28 'To Mr Rowland Woodward' ('Like one who in her third widowhood doth professe') (1–3).

29 *Sermons*, vol.2, no.11 [18 April 1619], p.244.

30 Verse letter from Sir William Cornwallis to John Donne, printed in Grierson (1912), vol.2, pp.171–2.

31 *Historical Manuscript Commission: Calendar of the Manuscripts of the Marquis of Salisbury* (1902), vol.9, part 8, p.386.

32 Walton, p.27.

33 Satyre V (28–30): the preceding paragraph paraphrases some of the first twenty-five lines of the poem. The other sixty or so continue in a similar vein.

34 *Manuscripts of the Marquis of Salisbury*, vol.9, part 8, p.318; Letter from Essex to Elizabeth, 26 August 1598.

35 Sir Thomas Egerton the elder to Sir George More, 6 March 1599, Lord Campbell, *Lives of the Lord Chancellors*, vol.2, p.332.

36 *Manuscripts of the Marquis of Salisbury*, vol.9, part 9, p.113.

7. Lost Words

1 *Calendar of State Papers, Ireland*, vol.205, p.38.

2 L. Pearsall Smith, *Life and Letters of Henry Wotton*, 2 vols (1907), vol.1, p.308.

3 'Henrico Wottoni, in Hibernia belligeranti' (1–3).

4 Simpson, [letter no.7], p. 311.

5 'To Sir Henry Wotton': 'Sir, more then kisses . . .' (1).

6 Simpson [letter no.8], p.312.

7 Simpson [letter no.6], p.310.

8 'To Sir Henry Wotton': 'Sir, more then kisses . . .' (47; 55–7). The poem was written a little later, after the disgrace of Essex, by which time Wotton had withdrawn from Court to keep his head low. Donne is kindly advising his friend to follow exactly the course that Wotton himself had decided upon.

9 Pearsall Smith, *Life and Letters of Henry Wotton*, vol.1, p.309.

10 Simpson [letter no.3], p.307.

11 *Letters*, p.63.

12 John McGurk, *The Elizabethan Conquest of Ireland* (1997), p.8.

13 Edmund Spenser, *The Faerie Queene*, Book 2, Canto 9, 13.3–4.

14 Pearsall Smith, *Life and Letters of Henry Wotton*, vol.1, p.310.

15 *Manuscripts of the Marquis of Salisbury*, vol.9, part 9, p.346.

16 *Manuscripts of the Marquis of Salisbury*, vol.9, part 9, p.349. R. C. Bald, as a matter of note, states that Egerton died on '23 August 1599' (p.104); this is probably a slip of the pen. In fact Egerton died a full month later, since the Lord Keeper received news of his son's condition throughout September. The younger Sir Thomas's funeral took place, as Bald notes, on 26 September.

17 Harleian MS 2129, fol.67; transcribed by Bald, pp.105–6.

18 *Manuscripts of the Marquis of Salisbury*, vol.9, part 9, p.393.

19 Rowland Whyte to Sir Robert Sidney, *Historical Manuscripts Commission: Report on the Manuscripts of De L'Isle and Dudley*, vol.2 (1934), pp.395–6.

20 *Manuscripts of the Marquis of Salisbury*, vol.9, part 9, p.361.

21 Walton, p.104.

22 Simpson [letter no.6], p.310.

23 Simpson [letter no.7], p.311.

24 Satyre IV (232).

25 Simpson [letter no.4], p.308.

26 Simpson [letter no.10], p.319. Donne had taken a purgative that confined him to close quarters: 'I am bound by making myself loose.'

27 Simpson [letter no.5], p.309.

28 Bald, p.108.

29 Simpson [letter no.11], p.316.

30 Printed in R. E. Bennett, 'Four Paradoxes by William Cornwallis the Younger', *Harvard Studies and Notes in Philology and Literature* 13 (1931), 219–40.

31 Simpson [letter no.12], p.317.

32 Simpson [letter no.11], p.316.

33 Rowland Whyte to Sir Robert Sidney, 24 and 26 January 1600; Arthur Collins (ed.), *Letters and Memorials of State* (1746), vol.2, p.164.

34 Rowland Whyte to Sir Robert Sidney, 16 February 1600; Collins, vol.2, p.166.

35 Rowland Whyte to Sir Philip Sidney, 9 February 1600; Collins, vol.2, p.166.

36 *Loseley Manuscripts*, ed. Alfred J. Kempe (1835), p.328.

37 Walton, p.26.

8. The Rebels

1 Edmund Spenser, dedication to 'The Teares of the Muses', in *The Shorter Poems*, ed. Richard A. MacCabe (1999), p.190.

2 Spenser, 'Colin Clouts Come Home Again' (464–571), *Shorter Poems*, p.360.

3 The Dowager Lady Russell to Sir Robert Cecil, September 1599; *Manuscripts of the Marquis of Salisbury*, vol.9, part 9, p.249.

4 *The Letters of John Chamberlain*, vol.1, p.111.

5 'Letter to the Countesse of Huntingdon' (23–70). It was J. Yoklavich, in 'Donne and the Countess of Huntingdon', *Philological Quarterly*

63 (1964), 283–8, who urged the view that the poem dated from just after Elizabeth's wedding.

6 *A Royalist's Notebook: The Commonplace Book of Sir John Oglander*, ed. Francis Bamford (1936), p.167.

7 Sir Nikolaus Pevsner et al., *Surrey*, 2nd edn (1972), p.355.

8 Simpson [letter no.11], p.316.

9 Campbell, *Lives of the Lord Chancellors*, vol.2, p.329.

10 *Manuscripts of the Marquis of Salisbury*, vol.9, part 11, p.30; John Barger to Lord Cobham, *c*.8 February.

11 *Manuscripts of the Marquis of Salisbury*, vol.9, part 11, p.29; Barger to Cobham.

12 *Manuscripts of the Marquis of Salisbury*, vol.9, part 11, pp.32–5.

13 John Barger to Lord Cobham, *c*.8 February 1601; *Manuscripts of the Marquis of Salisbury*, vol.9, part 11, p.30.

14 Donne's copy of the indictment is in Cambridge University Library, classmark Syn. 7. 60. 26; see Bald, p.113.

15 Francis Bacon, *Essays*, in *The Major Works*, ed. Brian Vickers (1996), p.396.

16 *Letters*, p.206.

17 Elegie VI (1–3).

18 *Manuscripts of the Marquis of Salisbury*, vol.9, part 11, pp.410, 545.

9. The Member

1 Oglander, *A Royalist's Notebook*, p.166.

2 Sir George More, *A Demonstration of God in His Workes: Agaynst all such as eyther in word or life deny there is a God* (1597), p.24.

3 Walton, p.26. For an elaborate, entertaining theory of what might have happened, see Ilona Bell, '"If it be a shee": The Riddle of Donne's "Curse"', in *John Donne's 'desire of more': The Subject of Ann More Donne in His Poetry*, ed. M. Thomas Hester (1996), pp.106–39.

4 J. E. Neale, *Elizabeth I and Her Parliaments*, vol.2 (1957), p.379.

5 Hayward Townshend, *An Exact Account of The Proceedings of the Four Last Parliaments of Elizabeth* (1680), p.217.

6 'A Valediction: of the Booke' (10–14).

7 Walton, p.31.

8 Pearsall Smith, *Life and Letters of Henry Wotton*, vol.1, p.306.

9 Walton, p.31.

10 M. Thomas Hester, ' "Faeminae Lectissimae": Reading Ann Donne', in *John Donne's 'desire of more'*, pp.18–34, especially pp.20–1.

11 Satyre V (28).

12 Neale, *Elizabeth I and Her Parliaments*, vol.2, p.391.

13 *Sermons*, vol.1, no.9 [19 April 1618], p.316.

14 Stanza VII ambiguously suggests that the final incarnation might have been 'the great soule which . . . / moves that hand, and tongue, and brow, / Which as the Moone the sea, moves us': see Dennis Flynn (who supports the argument that the poem is not 'incomplete', but a finished work presented as a fragment), 'Donne's *Ignatius His Conclave* and Other Libels on Robert Cecil', *John Donne Journal* 6 (1987), 163–83, especially p.164.

15 'Metempsycosis' (stanza V).

16 Townshend, *An Exact Account of The Proceedings of the Four Last Parliaments of Elizabeth*, p.222.

10. The Undoing

1 Bald, pp.128–9.

2 *A Choice Banquet of Witty Jests, Rare Fancies, and Pleasant Novels* (1665), p.72. See Ernest W. Sullivan II, 'Donne's Epithalamium for Anne' in *John Donne's 'desire of More'*, pp.35–8, especially p.37.

3 *Loseley Manuscripts*, p.328.

4 'The Expiration' (1–2).

5 Lawrence Stone, *The Crisis of the Aristocracy 1558–1641* (1965), p.596.

6 Walton, p.30.

7 Walton, p.60.

8 Elegie XVI (1).

9 'Loves Growth' (1–4; 26–8).

10 Diana O'Hara, 'The Language of Tokens and the Making of Marriage', *Rural History* 3 (1992), 1–40, especially p.10.

11 R. B. Outhwaite, *Clandestine Marriage in England 1500–1850* (1995), p.22.
12 Donne to Sir George More, 2 February 1602; *Loseley Manuscripts* pp.328–9.
13 Stone, *Crisis of the Aristocracy*, p.716.
14 John William Shirley, 'The Scientific Experiments of Sir Walter Raleigh, The Wizard Earl and the Three Magi in the Tower 1603–1617', *Ambix* IV (1949), 52–66, especially p.56.
15 Walton, p.28. Walton mistakenly reports that Sir George used his sister, 'Lady Elsemere', to press the case: Egerton's second wife had died two years previously.
16 Douglas Newton, *Catholic London* (1950), p.251.
17 Donne to Sir George More, 11 February 1602; *Loseley Manuscripts*, pp.330–2.
18 Donne to Sir Thomas Egerton, 12 February 1602; *Loseley Manuscripts*, pp.332–3.
19 Donne kept the portrait until the very end. The eventual Dean gave the picture, made 'very many years before I was in this profession', to Sir Robert Ker, to whose protection he also entrusted manuscript copies of his early writings. See the transcript of Donne's will in Bald, p.567.
20 Elegic XVIII (1–3).
21 Donne to Sir Thomas Egerton, 13 February 1602; *Loseley Manuscripts*, p.336.
22 Christopher Brooke to Sir Thomas Egerton, 25 February 1602; *Loseley Manuscripts*, pp.336–8.
23 Donne to Sir George More, March 1602; *Loseley Manuscripts*, pp.339–40.
24 Walton, p.30.
25 Walton, p.29.
26 Calendar of the Ellesmere Manuscripts (in the Huntingdon Library, San Marino), vol.1, no.213.
27 Walton, p.30.
28 Donne to Sir Thomas Egerton, 1 March 1602; *Loseley Manuscripts*, p.343.
29 'The Canonization' (28–36)

30 This was the Court of Audience in Canterbury. The only surviving copy of this document is in the Loseley manuscripts, preserved in the Folger Library; a sign that Sir George was shown the judgement in full, though he only accepted it grudgingly. See Bald, p.139 and note.

11. Sunrise

1 *The Diary of John Evelyn*, ed. E. S. de Beer (repr. 2004), vol.4, p.255; 24 August 1681.

2 'The Dreame' (6; 9–10).

3 More, *A Demonstration of God in His Workes*, p.24.

4 'The Sunne Rising' (1–4; 11–14).

5 *The Letters of John Chamberlain*, vol.1, pp.188–90; to Dudley Carleton, 30 March 1603.

6 *Sermons*, vol.1, no.3 [24 March 1617], p.217.

7 *Calendar of the Manuscripts of the Marquis of Salisbury*, vol.9, part 15 (1930), p.10; King James to Sir Robert Cecil, 27 March 1603.

8 *The Letters of John Chamberlain*, vol.1, pp.188–90; to Dudley Carleton, 30 March 1603.

9 *Manuscripts of the Marquis of Salisbury*, vol.9, part 15, p.302; King James to the Papal Nuncio, via Sir Thomas Parry, November 1603.

10 James's first speech to Parliament, in March 1604; *Constitutional Documents of the Reign of James I*, ed. J. R. Tanner (1930), p.24.

11 *Manuscripts of the Marquis of Salisbury*, vol.9, part 15, pp.27–8; Timothy Willis to Lord Cecil, 11 August 1603.

12 Bald, *Donne and the Drurys*, pp.81–3.

13 'The Sunne Rising' (5–10; 21–2).

14 *The Diary of John Evelyn*, vol.4, p.255.

15 Quoted in Allardyce Nicholl, *Stuart Masques and the Renaissance Stage* (1937), p.56.

16 'Communitie' (22).

17 Elegie III: 'Change' (35–6, 4).

18 'Womans Constancy' (1–2).

19 'Lovers Infinitenesse' (1–4; 33).

20 'The Good Morrow' (7–10).

21 'The Undertaking' (20).

22 'The Extasie' (2, 17).

23 'The Extasie' (74).

24 *The Life of Sir Tobie Mathew: Bacon's Alter Ego*, 'by his kinsman' Arnold Harris Mathew (1907), p.23.

25 *A Collection of Letters, made by Sr Tobie Mathews Kt* (1660), edited by Donne's son John, p.287; 17 November 1603.

26 Alan Bray, 'Homosexuality and Male Friendship', in *Queering the Renaissance*, ed. Jonathan Goldberg (1994), pp.40–61, especially p.42.

27 A letter from William Cornwallis to Donne presented with a gift, a paradoxical 'Encomium' in defence of Richard III; both are in the manuscript collection at Chatsworth. The letter is printed in Bald, p.118.

28 Quentin Skinner, *Reason and Rhetoric in the Philosophy of Hobbes* (1996), p.77.

29 *Letters* [to George Garrard, autumn 1631], p.286.

30 *A Collection of Letters*, pp.288–9; 12 March ?1604.

31 *A Collection of Letters*, p.290; 19 May 1604.

32 *A Collection of Letters*, p.294; 19 May 1604.

33 *Ignatius His Conclave* (1611), ed. T. S. Healy, SJ (1969), p.57. The idea of 'Britain' is, admittedly, recognized in a satirical context, but does not itself appear to be an object of satire. Donne was keen in *Ignatius* to win King James's approval.

34 *A Collection of Letters*, pp.291–4; 19 May 1604.

35 *Constitutional Documents*, p.26.

36 Walton, p.110.

37 Walton, p.112.

38 Ben Jonson, 'Conversations with William Drummond', in *Complete Poems*, ed. George Parfitt (1988), p.474.

39 Walton, p.113.

40 Wotton, *The State of Christendom: or, A Most Exact and Curious Discovery of Many Secret Passages, and Hidden Mysteries of the Times* (1657).

41 'To Sir *H.W.* at his going Ambassador to *Venice*' (1–14); Simpson, p.320.

42 See M. C. Deas, 'A Note on Rowland Woodward, the Friend of Donne', *Review of English Studies* 7 (1931), 454–7.

43 'To Sir *H.W.* at his going Ambassador to *Venice* (37–40).

44 *Calendar of State Papers (Domestic) 1603–10.*

45 'Song' (1–4).

46 Elegie XVI: 'On His Mistris' (1–41).

47 A. H. Mathew, *The Life of Tobie Mathew*, p.43; Tobie Mathew to Dudley Carleton, 16 March 1605.

48 Quoted in John Walter Stoye, *English Travellers Abroad 1604–1667* (1952), p.61; Carew to Lord Cecil, 23 January 1609.

49 Quoted in Bald, p.149.

50 *Letters*, p.124.

51 Donne's will, transcribed in Bald, pp.567, 563.

52 Walton, p.68.

53 Bald, p.151.

54 John Julius Norwich, *A History of Venice* (1982), p.511.

55 Thomas Coryat, *Coryat's Crudities* (1905), vol.1, pp.311–18, 401.

56 *A Collection of Letters*, pp.274–5. See Bald, pp.151–2.

57 *Sermons*, vol.9, p.197. See Bald, p.250.

58 W. A. B. Coolidge, *The Alps: In Nature and History* (1908), p.166.

59 Satyre III (79–81).

60 Elegie XVI (51–3).

61 *Letters*, p.43.

12. The Close Prison at Mitcham

1 Donne, *Ignatius His Conclave*, ed. T. S. Healy, SJ (1969), p.31.

2 *Psuedo-Martyr*, L_1^v.

3 *Letters*, p.101.

4 Bald, p.214.

5 Walton, p.31.

6 Walton, p.35.

7 *Letters*, p.204; 12 (9 October 1607).

8 Ben Jonson, epigrams to Sir Henry Goodyer, in *Complete Poems*, ed. George Parfitt (1975), pp.61–2.

9 *Letters*, pp.193–4.

10 *Letters*, p.160; spring/summer 1609.

11 *Letters*, pp.100–1; 1609.

12 *Letters*, p.11; 9 October 1607. Though addressed to Sir Thomas Lucy – the same who wearied the English ambassador in Paris with his determination to fight a duel – the letter seems to be addressed to Goodyer.

13 *Letters*, p.61; 1609.

14 *Letters*, pp.212–13.

15 *Letters*, p.137.

16 *Letters*, p.147.

17 'Upon a Horologue of the Clock at Sir George More's, at his Place of Loseley, 1603' in *Progresses of James I* (1828), vol.1, p.251.

18 *Letters*, pp.81–2; dated 13 June 1607.

19 Elegie VI (3)

20 Walton, p.30.

21 *Letters*, p.264.

22 'To *Sir Edward Herbert*, at *Julyers*' (1–2)

23 Walton, p.264.

24 Elegie IX: 'The Autumnall' (1–2, 45–6).

25 Walton, *Lives*, p.335.

26 'The Relique' (6, 17–18, 29–30).

27 Walton, p.336: the letter is dated 23 July 1607.

28 Walton, pp.265–6.

29 John Aubrey, *The Natural History of Wiltshire*, ed. John Britton (1847), p.93.

30 Elegie XV: 'The Expostulation' (1–2, 13–18).

31 Elegie XV: 'The Expostulation' (33–8).

32 Walton, p.84.

33 Elegie XV: 'The Expostulation' (53–66, 69–70).

34 Tobie Mathew, *A True Historical Relation of the Conversion of Sir Tobie Mathew to the Holy Catholic Faith*, ed. A. H. Mathew (1904), pp.60–1.

35 Mathew, *A True Historical Relation*, pp.85–6.

36 Tom Cain, 'Donne and the Prince D'Amor', *John Donne Journal* 14 (1995) 83–111.

37 Jonson, *Complete Poems*, p.66.

38 Nicholl, *Stuart Masques and the Renaissance Stage*, p.67.

39 *Letters*, p.204.

40 *Letters*, p.140.

41 Mathew, *A True Historical Relation*, pp.90–1.

42 *Letters*, pp.52–3.

43 *Letters*, p.143.

44 *Letters*, pp.137–8.

45 Christopher Burlinson and Andrew Zurcher, ' "Secretary to the Lord Grey Deputie here": Edmund Spenser's Irish Papers', *The Library* 6 (2005), 30–75. I'm very grateful to the authors for sharing this article with me ahead of publication.

46 *Letters*, pp.145–6.

47 *A Collection of Letters*, pp.330–1.

48 *Letters*, p.31.

49 *Letters*, p.57.

50 *Letters*, p.50.

51 *Letters*, pp.63–4.

52 *Letters*, p.71.

53 *Letters*, pp.20–1.

54 *Letters*, p.63.

55 *Letters*, pp.50–1.

13. Irregularities

1 *Letters*, p.59.

2 Richard Baddeley, *The Life of Dr Thomas Morton, Late Bishop of Duresme* (1669), pp.103–4.

3 Jonson, 'To John Donne' ('Donne, the delight of Phoebus, and each muse') *Complete Poems*, ed. Parfitt, p.41.

4 *Letters*, p.103.

5 *A Collection of Letters*, pp.330–1.

6 Bald, p.142.

7 Walton, p.26.

8 Walton, pp.32–5.

9 Baddeley, *The Life of Dr Thomas Morton*, p.140. Naylor's 'Further

Narrative', a thunderous tribute to Morton – 'Limned,' says Baddeley, 'by a curious Pencil' – appears in pp.113–89.

10 Baddeley, *Life of Dr Thomas Morton*, p.83.

11 Naylor, 'A Further Narrative'; *Life of Dr Thomas Morton*, p.153.

12 *A Complete Collection of State Trials*, ed. T. B. Howell (1816), vol.2, p.77.

13 Baddeley, *Life of Dr Thomas Morton*, p.100.

14 Naylor, 'A Further Narrative'; *Life of Dr Thomas Morton*, p.155.

15 *Collection of State Trials*, vol.2, p.79.

16 *Letters*, p.66.

17 Bald, p.208.

18 Baddeley, *Life of Dr Thomas Morton*, pp.87–9.

19 'To Mr Rowland Woodward' ('Like one who in her third widowhood doth professe') (16).

20 'To Sr Henry Goodyer' (1–4); the poem seems to belong to 1608 since it was written while Donne was still living at Mitcham, and in it he encourages Goodyer to travel overseas (21–4). Sure enough, Goodyer did take a long trip away in 1609 (see Bald, p.166), and whether or not he was heeding Donne's advice, Donne was unlikely to suggest a period abroad just after his friend had returned from one.

21 'The Annunciation and Passion' (25–30)

22 *Letters*, pp.116–17.

23 'To Lucy, Countess of Bedford, with Mr Donne's Satires' (6); *Complete Poems*, p.66.

24 'To the Countesse of Bedford' ('T'have written then, when you writ') (16).

25 'To the Countesse of Bedford' ('Madam, You have refin'd mee') (1, 19).

26 'To the Countesse of Bedford' ('Reason is our Soules left hand') (11–12).

27 *Letters*, p.64.

28 *Letters*, p.67.

29 *Letters*, pp.215–16.

30 Jonson, 'An Epigram on the Court Pucell', in *Complete Poems*, pp.195–6.

31 Jonson, 'Conversations with William Drummond', in *Complete Poems*, p.479.

32 Jonson, 'Stay, view this stone' (8–9), in *Complete Poems*, p.273.

33 Ben Jonson to George Garrard, quoted in B. N. de Luna, *Jonson's Romish Plot* (1967), pp.165–6.

34 *Letters*, p.39.

35 'Elegie on Mistris Bulstrode' (5–8).

36 *Letters*, p.32.

37 'The Litanie' (5–6, 22).

38 *Letters*, p.36.

39 *Letters*, pp.103–5.

40 'A Valediction: of the Book' (19–20)

41 *Letters*, p.107.

42 *Letters*, pp.226–7.

43 Robert Persons, *The Judgement of A Catholicke English-man, Living in Banishment For His Religion* (1608), p.2.

44 Persons, *Judgement of A Catholicke English-man*, p.17.

45 Bald, p.215.

46 *Letters*, pp.160–1.

47 *Pseudo-martyr*, 'A Preface to the Priestes, and Jesuits', B$_2$^{v}. Regular pagination begins only after the preface; for the sake of convenience, references to the main body of the text give page numbers rather than printers' signatures.

48 *The Kings Maiesties Speech to the Lords and Commons* (1609), A$_4$^{v}.

49 *Pseudo-martyr*, p.168.

50 *Pseudo-martyr*, p.172.

51 Gosse, *Life and Letters of John Donne*, vol.1, p.248.

52 *Pseudo-martyr*, 'Aduertisement to the Reader'.

53 Thomas Fitzherbert, *A Supplement to the Discussion of M.D. Barlowes Answere* (1613), p.107. See W. Milgate, 'The Early References to John Donne', *Notes and Queries* 195 (1950), 229–31, especially p.230.

54 *Letters*, p.284.

55 Bald, p.226.

56 *London Sessions Records, 1605–85*, ed. D. H. Bowler, *Publications of the Catholic Record Society* XXXIV (1934), pp.68, 73.

57 John Boys, Dean of Canterbury, *Works* (1629), p.277.

58 *Pseudo-martyr*, B$_2$^{r}.

59 Elegie XVII (2).

60 *Pseudo-martyr*, B$_3$^{v}.

61 *Pseudo-martyr*, B$_3$^{r}.

62 'To the Prince of Wales [1610]', in Donne, *Complete Poetry and Selected Prose*, by Hayward, p.463.

63 Walton, p.227.

64 *Thomas Coriate Traveller for the English wits: Greeting* (1616), p.37.

65 Coryat, *Traveller for the English wits*, p.45.

66 Thomas Fuller, *The History of the Worthies of England* (1662), 3D$_4$^{r}.

67 Jonson, 'Conversations with William Drummond' and 'To John Donne' in *Complete Poems*, pp.463, 41.

68 Epigramme 97 in *Scourge of Folly* (1611) in *The Complete Works of John Davies of Hereford*, ed. Alexander Grosart (private publication, 1878) vol.2, p.18. Grosart's pagination numbers each of Davies' books separately.

69 *The Mermaid and Mitre Taverns in Old London* (1928), pp.115–16. For more on the 'fraternity' and the 'convivium', see I. A. Shapiro, 'The "Mermaid Club"', *Modern Language Review*, XLV (1950), 6–17. A dog-Latin poem in celebration of the meeting is reprinted, along with a contemporary translation, in John Aubrey's *Brief Lives*, ed. A. Clark (1898), vol.2, pp.50–3, and John Hoskyns's *Life, Letters and Writings*, ed. Louise B. Osborn (1937), pp.196–9, 288–91.

70 'Upon Mr Thomas Coryats Crudities' (9–10).

71 Fuller, *Worthies of England*, 3D$_4$^{r}.

72 Fuller, *Worthies of England*, 3Q^v.

73 *Letters*, p.116.

74 John Earle, *Microcosmographie: A peece of the world discovered* (5th edn, 1629), D$_{10}$^{r}–12^r.

75 Holy Sonnet XII (5, 1–2).

76 *Letters*, p.263.

77 Holy Sonnet I (3–8).

14. The Apparition

1   *Ignatius His Conclave*, pp.5–7.

2   *Ignatius His Conclave*, p.81.

3   *Pseudo-martyr*, D$_1$^{r}.

4   *Letters*, p.102.

5   *Letters*, pp.100 (1609) and 29.

6   *Pseudo-martyr*, 3T^r.

7   Holy Sonnet XIII (9–10).

8   Holy Sonnet VI (5–6).

9   Holy Sonnet VII (3).

10 Edward Edwards, *Life of Ralegh*, vol.2, pp.152–3; Donne. 'On a Burnt Ship'.

11 Holy Sonnet IV (7).

12 Holy Sonnet X (1–4).

13 Holy Sonnet XI (1–2).

14 Holy Sonnet XIV (1–2, 12–14).

15 Holy Sonnet VIII (12–14).

16 *Letters*, p.28.

17 *Pseudo-martyr*, B$_3$^{r}.

18 Eamon Duffy, *The Stripping of the Altars: Traditional Religion in England 1400–1580* (1992), p.3.

19 *Devotions*, p.390.

20 Duffy, *Stripping of the Altars*, p.593.

21 *Pseudo-martyr*, D$_1$^{r}.

22 Holy Sonnet VIII (1–4).

23 *Letters*, p.101–2.

24 Freeman, *Rubbe, and a great Cast*, part 2, no.84; see also Milgate, 'The Early References to John Donne', pp.229–31, and Bald, p.283.

25 Letter in Latin to Goodyer, trans. John Sparrow, quoted by Helen Gardner in 'A Nocturnal Upon St Lucy's Day', in *Poetic Traditions of the Renaissance*, ed. Maynard Mack and George de Forest Lord (1982), pp.181–201.

26 Bald, *Donne and the Drurys* (1959), p.43.

27 Bald, *Donne and the Drurys*, p.37.

28 Joseph Hall, *The Shaking of the Olive-Tree* (1660), pp.13–14.

29 Bald, *Donne and the Drurys*, p.68.

30 'The First Anniversary: An Anatomy of the World' (286–301).

31 'The First Anniversary: An Anatomy of the World' (63).

32 Walton, *Lives*, p.39.

33 'A licence to travell graunted vnto *Sir* Roberte drury', printed in Bald, *Donne and the Drurys*.

34 *Letters*, p.94.

35 *Letters*, p.69.

36 *Letters*, p.137.

37 Oglander, *A Royalist's Notebook*, p.248.

38 'A Valediction: Forbidding Mourning' (24; 5–6)

39 *Letters*, p.94.

40 Bald, *Donne and the Drurys*, pp.95–6.

41 'The Second Anniversarie: Of the Progres of the Soule' (81–2; 165–6; 55–6).

42 *Letters*, p.95.

43 *Letters*, pp.264–5.

44 Gosse, *Life and Letters of Dr John Donne*, vol.1, p.289.

45 *Letters*, p.133.

46 *Letters*, p.30.

47 *Letters*, pp.130–1.

48 *Letters*, p.42.

49 *Letters*, p.124.

50 Jacques Vanuxem, 'Le Carousel de 1612 sur La Place Royale et Ses Devises', in Jean Jacquot, ed., *Les fêtes de la renaissance* (1956), pp.191–200.

51 *Letters*, pp.127–9.

52 *Letters*, pp.74–5.

53 Jonson, 'Conversations with William Drummond', in *Complete Poems*, p.462.

54 *Letters*, p.255.

55 'To the Countess of Bedford' ('Though I be dead') (11–13).

56 *Letters*, p.74.

57 Walton, pp.40–2.

58 Oglander, *A Royalist's Notebook*, p.168. I follow Bald's re-reading of 'St Johns' as 'Sr Johns' (see Bald, p.253).
59 *Letters*, pp.121–2.
60 *Letters*, p.252.
61 Oglander, *A Royalist's Notebook*, p.212.

15. A Valediction to the World

1   *Letters*, p.137.
2   'A Letter written by Sir H.G. and J.D. *alternis vicibus*.' (2, 4; 22, 24)
3   'Good Friday, 1613. Riding Westward' (9–10; 16–18; 39–42).
4   Bald worked out the co-ordinates of Donne's Good Friday journey from manuscript sources: 'In the same manuscript that contains the poem written by Donne and Goodyer together (which may thus have been compiled by someone with access to Goodyer's papers) the poem ['Good Friday'] is headed "Mr J. Dunn goeinge from Sir H.G. on good fryday sent him back this meditation, on the Waye".' Donne's visit in 1613 therefore lasted until 2 April, which was the date of Good Friday in that year. Another manuscript version of the poem describes it as composed while Donne was 'Riding to Sʳ Edward Harbert in Wales' (Bald, p.270).
5   John Aubrey, *Brief Lives and Other Selected Writings*, ed. Anthony Powell (1949), p.39.
6   *The Life of Edward, Lord Herbert of Cherbury, written by himself*, ed. J. M. Shuttleworth (1976), pp.61–5.
7   Jonson, 'Conversations', *Complete Poems*, p.464.
8   *Life of Edward, Lord Herbert*, pp.67–8.
9   *Life of Edward, Lord Herbert*, pp.15–16.
10 'A Valediction: Forbidding Mourning' (30–2).
11 *Letters*, p.179.
12 Bald, pp.263–6.
13 Oglander, *A Royalist's Notebook*, pp.193–8.
14 *A Collection of Letters, made by Sr Tobie Mathews Kᵗ*, pp.311, 318. Donne's first letter to Rochester is on p.321.
15 *Letters*, pp.180–1.

16 'Ecclogue. 1613. December 26' (1).
17 *Letters*, pp.280–1.
18 *Letters*, p.201.
19 *Letters*, pp.152–3.
20 *Letters*, p.168.
21 *Letters*, p.273.
22 Bald, p.279.
23 e.g. Satyre I (75–6), Satyre IV (26–7), 'The Sunne Rising' (5–6).
24 *Letters*, pp.170–1.
25 See David Colclough, *Freedom of Speech in Early Stuart England* (2005), pp.159–68 (Wotton's letter to Sir Edmund Bacon quoted and discussed on p.160).
26 *A Collection of Letters, made by Sr Tobie Mathews Kt*, p.312.
27 *A Collection of Letters, made by Sr Tobie Mathews Kt*, p.315.
28 Gosse, *Life and Letters of John Donne*, vol.2, pp.46–7.
29 *Calendar of the Ellesmere Manuscripts*, vol.1, no.213.
30 *Letters*, pp.172–3.
31 Walton, p.295.
32 *Letters*, p.104.
33 *Letters*, p.260.
34 'Good Friday, 1613. Riding Westward' (26–7).
35 Gosse, *Life and Letters of John Donne*, vol.2, p.48.
36 *Letters*, p.171.
37 *Essays in Divinity*, ed. Evelyn M. Simpson (1952), p.3.
38 *Essays*, p.41.
39 *Letters*, p.149.
40 *Letters*, pp.196–7.
41 *Letters*, p.195.
42 *Letters*, pp.218–19.
43 Bald, p.302.
44 Walton, p.23.
45 Donne, *Complete Poetry and Selected Prose*, ed. John Hayward, p.466.
46 'To Mr George Herbert, with my Seal, of the Anchor and Christ' (1–6): the Latin verses accompanied the seal which Donne left Herbert as a gift on his death (see Walton, pp.64–5).
47 Simpson, pp.333–4.

48 *Letters*, pp.288–9.

49 *The Letters of Sir John Chamberlain*, vol.1, pp.597–8.

50 *The Letters of Sir John Chamberlain*, vol.1, pp.588–9.

51 *The Letters of Sir John Chamberlain*, vol.1, p.591.

52 Walton, p.49.

53 Walton, p.48; *Sermons*, vol.1, pp.115–17.

54 *Letters*, p.296.

55 Bald, p.312.

56 Bald, p.313.

57 'To Mr *Tilman* after he had taken orders' (26–31)

58 Oglander, *A Royalist's Notebook*, p.166. For more on the Overbury affair, see Beatrice White, *Cast of Ravens: The Strange Case of Sir Thomas Overbury* (1965).

59 *Letters*, p.272. To Sir Robert Ker, asking him to stand as godfather to Margaret on 20 April 1615.

60 Walton, p.60.

61 *A Collection of Letters*, pp.323–6.

16. Stone

1 Stow, *Survey of London* (1720), vol.2, book 4, p.113. Other manuscript copies of the epitaph have survived, and W. Milgate and Ernest W. Sullivan II have pointed out that John Stow printed it in *The Remains or Remnants of Diverse Worthy Things*, added to the 1633 edition of the *Survey*. My rendering and discussion of the epitaph is greatly indebted to the transcription and translation from a Loseley Manuscript in the Folger Library (MS. L.b.541) given by M. Thomas Hester, in '*Fæminæ Lectissimæ*: Reading Anne Donne', in *John Donne's 'desire of more': The Subject of Anne More Donne in His Poetry* (1996), pp.17–36, pp.20–21. The Latin text is also printed in Bald, p.325.

2 Christopher Hill, *Economic Problems of the Church* (1956), p.227.

3 Walton, p.50.

4 Bald, p.317; also giving thorough details of the other documentation regarding Donne's first two benefices.

5 Bald, p.317.

6 V. Sackville-West, *Knole and the Sackvilles* (1922), pp.57–9. On Donne's relationship with the Countess of Dorset, see *Sermons*, vol.1, p.130n.

7 Chamberlain, *Letters*, vol.2 [29 March 1617], p.65.

8 *Sermons*, vol.2, no.8 [spring or summer, 1618], p.154.

9 Prest, *The Inns of Court Under Elizabeth I and the Early Tudors*, p.147.

10 Walton, p.53.

11 Bald, p.320.

12 *Sermons*, vol.2, Introduction, p.2.

13 *Sermons*, vol.1, no.3 [24 March 1617], p.209. This, in contrast with the thoughts voiced in *Biathanatos*, was Donne's public view of suicide.

14 Chamberlain, *Letters*, vol.2, p.67.

15 Chamberlain, *Letters*, vol.2, p.65.

16 *Sermons*, vol.1, no.3, p.221.

17 Lisa Jardine and Alan Stewart, *Hostage to Fortune: The Troubled Life of Sir Francis Bacon* (1998), p.395.

18 Letter to Buckingham, 8 May 1617, quoted in Jardine and Stewart, *Hostage to Fortune*, p.398.

19 *Sermons*, vol.2, no.1 [spring or summer, 1618], p.53.

20 *Sermons*, vol.2, no.10 [before 18 April 1619], p.227.

21 *Sermons*, vol.2, no.13 [19 December 1619], pp.276–7. My italics on 'understand'.

22 *Sermons*, vol.1, no.3, p.199.

23 For the evidence backing up Walton's assertion that Donne's 'first motion from his house was to preach, where his beloved wife lay buried' (Walton, p.52), see Bald, pp.327–8.

24 Walton, p.52.

25 Bald, pp.320–1.

26 John Newnham, *Newnams Nighcrowe: A Bird that breedeth many braules in many families and householdes. Wherein is remembred that kindely and prouident regard which Fathers ought to have towards their Sonnes* (1590), p.24.

27 Walton, p.51.

28 Mark 12:25.

29 *Sermons*, vol.1, no.4 [2 November 1617], p.231.

30 *Sermons*, vol.1, no.5 [14 December 1617], pp.237–8.

31 *Sermons*, vol.2, no.6 [spring or summer, 1618], p.147.

32 Holy Sonnet XVII (1–4).

33 Helen Gardner, ed., *Divine Poems* (1952), p.79.

34 '*hujus aurea*': Latin letter to Henry Goodyer (1611), printed in *Poems* (1633), p.369.

35 L'Oiseau's letter is printed in Bald, p.324.

36 See Adrian Wilson's essay, 'The Ceremony of Childbirth and its Interpretation', in *Women as Mothers in Pre-Industrial England*, ed. Valerie Fildes (1990), pp.68–107. *Women in Early Modern England 1550–1720*, by Sara Mendelson and Patricia Crawford (1998) is invaluable in showing what women went through.

37 Jane Sharp, *The Midwives Book* (1671), pp.171, 190–5.

38 *Letters*, p.137.

39 *Sermons*, vol.2, no.6 [spring or summer, 1618], p.155.

17. The Torn Ship

1 *Sermons*, vol.2, no.13 [19 December 1619], p.280.

2 *Sermons*, vol.1, no.6, [20 February 1618], p.260.

3 *Sermons*, vol.2, no.18 [3 March 1620], p.360.

4 *Devotions*, meditation 13.

5 *Sermons*, vol.1, no.2 [21 April 1616], pp.173–5.

6 *Sermons*, vol.1, no.2, p.177.

7 *Sermons*, vol.2, no.4, [spring or summer, 1618], p.122.

8 *Sermons*, vol.2, no.3 [spring or summer, 1618], p.112.

9 C. V. Wedgwood, *The Thirty Years' War* (1938), p.80.

10 *Letters and Other Documents Illustrating the Relations Between England and Germany at the Commencement of the Thirty Years' War*, edited by Samuel Rawson Gardiner, First Series, Camden Society, 40 (1865), p.16.

11 See Sir John Oglander's description of James as 'the most cowardly man that ever I knew'; *A Royalist's Notebook*, pp.193–8.

12 *A Collection of Letters*, p.330.

13 *Letters*, pp.171–2.

14 Chamberlain, *Letters*, vol.2, p.58.

15 *Sermons*, vol.4, no.6.

16 P.R.O., State Papers 106/4, no.44; indexed under 'Italy', dated '1614–1617'. Printed in Bald, Appendix D, pp.569–70.

17 *Letters* [March 1619], p.174.

18 Walton, p.54.

19 *Letters*, p.174.

20 *Letters*, p.22.

21 *Sermons*, vol.1, no.3 [24 March 1617], p.209.

22 *Sermons*, vol.2, no.11 [18 April 1619], p.248.

23 'A Hymne to Christ, at the Authors last going into Germany' (1–4).

24 *Sermons*, vol.2, no.15 [30 January 1620], p.316.

25 *Sermons*, vol.1, no.8 [19 April 1618], p.293.

26 *Sermons*, vol.1, no.7 [2 November 1617], p.223.

27 *Sermons*, vol.2, no.4 [spring or summer, 1618], p.125.

28 'A Hymne to Christ' (9–12).

29 *Letters*, p.223.

30 *Letters*, p.174.

31 *Sermons*, vol.2, no.9, p.197.

32 Bald, p.346.

33 *Letters and Other Documents*, First Series, p.30.

34 *Letters and Other Documents*, First Series, p.101.

35 *Letters and Other Documents*, First Series, p.130.

36 *Letters and Other Documents*, First Series, pp.131, 118.

37 Charles Richard Cammell, *The Great Duke of Buckingham* (1939), pp.88, 153.

38 *Letters and Other Documents*, First Series, p.133.

39 *Letters and Other Documents*, First Series, p.157. See Bald, p.363n, where a compelling case is made for identifying this prince as Ferdinand.

40 *Sermons*, vol.9, no.14, p.325.

41 *Sermons*, vol.2, no.12: 'Two Sermons, to the Prince and Princess *Palatine*, the Lady *Elizabeth* at *Heydelberg*, when I was commanded by the King to wait upon my L. of *Doncaster* in his Embassage to *Germany*' (p.250).

42 Egerton manuscript, quoted in Bald, p.359.

43 *A Collection of Letters*, pp.336–7.

44 *Letters and Other Documents*, First Series, pp.197, 201.

45 Wedgwood, *The Thirty Years War*, pp.104–5, 113–14.

46 *Letters and Other Documents*, Second Series, ed. S. R. Gardiner, Camden Society 48 (1868), p.10.

47 *Sermons*, vol.3, no.7 [undated, but probably in the winter of 1620, after the defeat of Frederick in November – see the introduction to this volume, p.10], pp.179, 183, 185. Commenting on the last passage, Evelyn Simpson notes that 'here *to hull* is to lie a-hull or drift to the wind with sails furled, and *to board* is to tack, to sail athwart the wind on alternate sides' (*Sermons*, vol.3, p.12n.).

48 *Sermons*, vol.2, no.17, p.341.

49 *Sermons*, vol.2, no.17, p.339.

50 *Sermons*, vol.2, no.17, p.341.

18. Clay

1 Paul A. Welsby, *George Abbot: The Unwanted Archbishop* (1962), pp.91–2.

2 Arthur Onslow, *The Life of George Abbot* (1777), p.31.

3 James I, *ΒΑΣΙΑΙΚΟΝ ΔΩΡΟΝ: or His Maiesties Instructions to His Dearest Sonne* (1603), p.121.

4 *Letters*, p.158.

5 Chamberlain, *Letters*, vol.2, pp.360, 382, 296.

6 James Orchard Halliwell, ed., *The Autobiography and Correspondence of Sir Simonds D'Ewes*, 2 vols, (1845), vol.1, p.200.

7 *Letters*, pp.154–9.

8 *Letters*, p.202. For the evidence supporting the dating of this letter, see Bald, p.367.

9 On the date and location of the marriage, see *Sermons*, vol.3, introduction, pp.19–20; on Donne's presumed connection to the Washington family through the Doncasters, see Chamberlain, *Letters*, vol.2, pp.379–80.

10 *Sermons*, vol.3, no.11 [30 May 1621], p.241.

11   *Sermons*, vol.3, no.11, p.244.

12   *Sermons*, vol.3, no.11, p.243.

13   *Sermons*, vol.3, no.11, p.249.

14   *Sermons*, vol.3, no.11, p.241.

15   *Sermons*, vol.3, no.11, pp.254–5.

16   Henry King, *A Sermon Preached at Pauls Cross: Vpon occasion of that false and scandalous Report (lately Printed) touching the supposed Apostasie of the right Reuerend Father in God, JOHN KING* (1621), p.53.

17   G. Musket, *The Bishop of London His Legacy* (1623), p.171.

18   John Spurr, *English Puritanism 1603–1689* (1998), p.30.

19   From James's treatise *Basilikon Doron* (1603), extracts from which on the topic of Puritans are printed in *Images of English Puritanism: A Collection of Contemporary Sources 1589–1646*, ed. Lawrence A. Sasek, pp.215–23 (p.218).

20   Thomas Scott, 'The Interpreter' (1622) in *Images of English Puritanism*, pp.95–108, p.98.

21   On James's habits and preferences as a worshipper, see Peter E. McCullough, 'James I and the apotheosis of court preaching' in *Sermons at Court: Politics and Religion in Elizabethan and Jacobean Preaching* (1998), pp.101–67; this is the most comprehensive book yet published on Church politics in the royal Court.

22   Nicholas Tyacke, 'Lancelot Andrewes and the Myth of Anglicanism', in *Conformity and Orthodoxy in the English Church c.1560–1660*, ed. Peter Lake and Michael Questier (2000), pp.5–33, especially p.27.

23   McCullough, *Sermons at Court*, p.204.

24   Spurr, *English Puritanism*, p.10; Spurr's general argument is also most convincing and I am much indebted to it here.

25   *Letters*, p.155.

26   *Sermons*, vol.3, no.8 [7 January 1621].

27   Spurr, *English Puritanism*, pp.83, 85.

28   Bald, p.368.

29   Edward May, *A Sermon of the Communion of Saints*, A_2^v–A_3^r.

30   May, *A Sermon of the Communion of Saints*, B_4^v.

31   May, *A Sermon of the Communion of Saints*, B_4^r.

32   May, *A Sermon of the Communion of Saints*, A_2^v.

33   Bald, p.370.

34 Scott, 'The Interpreter', in *Images of English Puritanism*, p.103.

35 The full letter is printed in Bald, pp.371–2.

36 *Sermons*, vol.3, no.11 [30 May 1621], p.250.

37 Jardine and Stewart, *Hostage to Fortune*, p.355.

38 Henry Wotton, *The Characters of Robert Devereux, Earl of Essex; and George Villiers, Duke of Buckingham*, ed. Sir Egerton Bridges (1814), p.18.

39 Halliwell, ed., *The Autobiography and Correspondence of Sir Simonds D'Ewes*, vol.1, pp.166–7.

40 Hugh Ross Williamson, *George Villiers, First Duke of Buckingham: Study for a Biography* (1940), p.68.

41 Anthony Weldon, *The Court and Character of King James* (1650), p.181.

42 Jardine and Stewart, *Hostage to Fortune*, p.429.

43 Weldon, *The Court and Character of King James*, pp.140–1.

44 Simpson, Introduction to *Sermons*, vol.3, p.56.

45 Walton, pp.54–5.

46 Weldon, *The Court and Character of King James*, p.178.

47 John Hacket, *Scrinia Reserata: A Memorial Offer'd to the Great Deservings of John Williams* (1693), p.63.

48 Letter printed in full in Bald, p.375.

49 *Sermons*, vol.2, no.7 [12 February 1619], p.173.

50 David J. Crankshaw, 'Community, City and Nation, 1540–1714' in *St Paul's: The Cathedral Church of London, 604–2004*, ed. Derek Keene et al. (2004), pp.45–70, especially p.54.

51 E. F. Carpenter, 'The Reformation: 1485–1660' in *A History of St Paul's Cathedral and The Men Associated With It*, ed. W. R. Matthews and W. M. Atkins (1957), pp.100–71, especially p.138.

52 Bald, p.381: Bald's source for the consecration ritual is William Sparrow Simpson, ed., *Registrum Statutorum et Consuetudinum Ecclesiae Cathedralis Sancti Pauli Londinensis* (1873), pp.14–15, 219–20.

53 Christopher Wren's Report to the Dean and Chapter on the ruins of Old St Paul's, transcribed in Matthews and Atkins, *A History of St Paul's Cathedral*, pp. 194–6, especially p.194.

54 Carpenter, 'The Reformation', p.159, quoting the nineteenth-century Dean of St Paul's, Henry Hart Milman.

55 Crankshaw, 'Community, City and Nation', p.54 (ballad, *c.*1605).

56 William Dugdale, *The History of St Paul's Cathedral in London From its Foundation Until these Times* (1658), p.126.

57 Crankshaw, 'Community, City and Nation', p.53.

58 Carpenter, 'The Reformation', p.150, quoting John Ramsay, a Lay Vicar of the sixteenth century.

59 Crankshaw, 'Community, City and Nation', p.57.

60 Henry Farley, *The Complaint of Pavles to all Christian Sovles* (1616).

61 *Sermons*, vol.4, no.7 [15 September 1622], p.194.

62 John Earle, *Microsographie, Or A Peece of the World Discovered*, 5th edn (1629), L_8^v–L_{10}^r.

63 *Letters*, p.227.

64 'Directions to Preachers', printed in Thomas Fuller, *Church History of Britain* (1655), book 10, pp.108–10.

65 Chamberlain, *Letters*, vol.2, p.451.

66 *Sermons*, vol.4, no.7 [15 September 1622], p.194.

67 *Sermons*, vol.4, no.7, pp.192–3.

68 *Sermons*, vol.4, no.7, p.195: 'Preaching then being *Gods Ordinance*, to beget Faith, to take away Preaching, were to disarme God, and to quench that spirit.' This could, out of context, be taken as a plea for freedom of speech – a protest against the suppressive 'Directions'. But Donne's larger point seems to be that preaching is disarmed when preachers disagree among themselves; that is, when they fail to say the things the King wants them to. Later (pp.206–7), Donne referred to the Church of England's 'Catechism' (as set out in the 'Thirty-nine Articles' of 1571) as though it were completely unambiguous, something it manifestly was not.

69 *Sermons*, vol.4, no.7, p.202.

70 *A Collection of Letters*, pp.303–4; also printed in full in Bald, p.435.

71 Roger Lockyer, *Buckingham: The Life and Political Career of George Villiers, First Duke of Buckingham (1592–1628)* (1981), p.60.

19. The Spouse

1 On the times of the services at St Paul's, see *Sermons*, vol.4, Introduction, p.2.

2 Thomas Digges, 'A Perfit Description of the cælestiall orbes according to the Pythagoreans, lately reuiued by Copernicus' in the revised edition he prepared of *A Prognostication of Right Good Effect* (London: T. Marsh, 1576), by his father, Leonard Digges, L_3^v–O_3^r. See Christopher Hill, *Intellectual Origins of the English Revolution Revisited* (1997), pp.19–22: Hill notes that Digges's work had gone through seven reprints by 1605 alone.

3 *Sermons*, vol.6, no.15 [8 May 1625], pp.297–8.

4 *Sermons*, vol.3, no.17 [Christmas Day, 1621], pp.371, 362.

5 *Sermons*, vol.3, no.17, p.359.

6 *Sermons*, vol.3, no.17, pp.360–1.

7 *Sermons*, vol.3, no.17, p.361.

8 *Sermons*, vol.3, no.17, p.360.

9 *Sermons*, vol.3, no.17, p.374.

10 Thomas Cogswell, *The Blessed Revolution: English politics and the coming of war, 1621–1624* (1989), p.31.

11 Chamberlain, *Letters*, vol.2, p.470.

12 *Sermons*, vol.4, no.3 [Easter Monday, 1622], p.91.

13 John Stow, *Survey of London*, vol.1, pp.167–8.

14 *Sermons*, vol.4, introduction, p.30.

15 *Sermons*, vol.4, no.3, p.127.

16 *Sermons*, vol.4, no.3, pp.108–9.

17 *Sermons*, vol.4, no.3, p.106.

18 'An hymne to the Saints, and to Marquesse Hamylton' (23–4)

19 Holy Sonnet XVIII (1–4).

20 *Sermons*, vol.5, no.15 [undated], p.302.

21 Holy Sonnet XVIII (13–14).

22 *Sermons*, vol.3, no.17, pp.371 and 368.

23 *Sermons*, vol.4, no.5 [Midsummer Day, 1622], pp.149, 157.

24 *Sermons*, vol.4, no.7 [15 September 1622]

25 *Sermons*, vol.4, no.7, p.190.

26 *Sermons*, vol.4, no.9 [5 November 1622], p.254.

27 See headnote to the sermon 'Intended for Paul's Cross, but by reason of the weather, preached in the church' (*Sermons*, vol.4, no.9, p.235).

28 Weldon, *The Secret Court and Character of King James*, pp.177–8; Cogswell, *The Blessed Revolution*, p.35.

29 Bald, p.383.

30 This, at least, is the traditional location given to the Deanery. According to William Dugdale, the first historian of St Paul's, the medieval house actually lay to the north of the Cathedral, 'standing within the precinct of the Church-yard, and being the mansion of Raph de Diceto, Dean of *Pauls* about the latter end of King Henry the Second's reign; [it] was, with the Chapell belonging thereto, by him granted to his successors in that office forever' (*The History of St Paul's Cathedral*, p.126).

31 Walton, p.55.

32 *Letters*, pp.158–9.

33 *Letters* [4 October 1622, 'almost at midnight'], p.136.

34 *Letters* [18 October 1622], pp.185–6.

35 Walton, p.54.

36 A survey of the value of benefices made in 1535 was not updated until 1831: assessing the two sets of data, Bald shows that the Dean's living in this period rose from £210 to £2695 (p.425).

37 *Sermons*, vol.4, no.3, p.113.

38 *Letters*, p.135.

39 For an account of John Selden's life and assessment of his work, see Daniel Sandler Berkowitz, *John Selden's Formative Years: Politics and Society in Early Seventeenth-Century England* (1988).

40 *Letters*, p.230.

41 Bald, p.495.

42 Walton, p.70.

43 *Letters*, p.135.

44 Chamberlain, *Letters*, vol.2, pp.408, 443.

45 *A Collection of Letters*, p.431.

46 Bald, p.436.

47 See Paul W. Harland, 'Donne and Virginia: The Ideology of Conquest', *John Donne Journal* 18 (1999), 127–52.

48 Chamberlain, *Letters*, vol.2, p.464.

49 *Sermons*, vol.4, no.10 [13 November 1622], p.271.

50 *Sermons*, vol.4, no.10, p.274.

51 Hayward, ed., *Complete Poetry and Selected Prose*, p.477.

52 *Sermons*, vol.3, no.17 [25 December 1621], p.359.

53 Chamberlain, *Letters*, vol.2, p.489.

54 *Sermons*, vol.4, no.13 [28 February 1622].

55 Hayward, ed., *Complete Poetry and Selected Prose*, pp.479–80; also in Bald, p.446.

56 *Sermons*, vol.4, no.14 [28 March], preached at St Paul's, p.347, where Donne mentions 'a vulgar [i.e. vernacular] Spanish Author [Geronimo Gracian], who writes the *Iosephina*, the life of *Ioseph*, the husband of the blessed Virgin Mary'. See the introduction to the volume, p.40.

57 *A Collection of Letters*, p.306.

58 *Letters*, p.100.

59 *Sermons*, vol.6, no.7 [13 June 1624], pp.161, 163. It would be inadvisable to imagine Donne addressing a sect of enlightened courtiers. By this time, when Prince Charles had turned his attentions from a Spanish to a French Catholic princess, Henrietta Maria, it may simply have been safer – and indeed more politically advisable – to utter such liberal opinions. French Catholics posed much less of a threat than Spanish ones – France was, indeed, a potential ally against the Holy Roman Empire.

20. Devotions

1 Cogswell, *The Blessed Revolution*, p.7.

2 *Letters*, p.84.

3 Bald, p.457; Baird W. Whitlock, 'Donne at St Dunstan's', *Times Literary Supplement*, 16 and 23 September 1955.

4 Chamberlain, *Letters*, vol.2, p.448.

5 *Devotions Upon Emergent Occasions*, ed. John Sparrow (1923), meditation 5, pp.1–2.

6 *Devotions*, meditation 2, p.6.

7   *Devotions*, meditation 4, p.16.

8   Meditation 5, pp.22–3.

9   Meditation 6, p.28.

10 Meditation 7, p.35. Meditation 8, p.42: '*The King sends his owne Phisician*'.

11 Meditation 12, p.70.

12 Meditation 13, p.74.

13 Meditation 15, p.88.

14 Meditation 16, p.92.

15 Meditation 17, pp.97–8.

16 John Stockwood, *A shorte learned and pithie treatize of the plague* (1580) [translating Cardinal Beza], $D_2{}^r$; Marcus Aurelius, *Meditations* 4.15.

17 On 6 December Chamberlain recorded that Donne was thought likely to survive, 'though he were in great danger' (*Letters*, vol.2, p.531).

18 *Letters*, p.249.

19 *Devotions* was entered into the Stationers' Register on 9 January: see Bald, p.451.

20 *Devotions*, expostulation 4, p.26; expostulation 21, p.131.

21 Meditation 1, p.8.

22 *Letters*, p.249, in which Donne also sounds out Sir Robert Ker about the aptness of dedicating *Devotions* to Charles.

23 Walton, p.62.

24 *Sermons*, vol.6, no.2.

25 Bald, p.456.

26 *Sermons*, vol.6, no.4 [25 April 1624], p.113.

27 *Devotions*, Meditation 16, p.93.

21. The Old Player

1   William Young, ed., *The History of Dulwich College*, 2 vols. (1889), vol.2, pp.8–9.

2   This sketch of Alleyn's life is based on S. P. Cerasano's biographical essay in *Edward Alleyn: Elizabethan Actor, Jacobean Gentleman*, ed. Aileen Reid and Robert Maniura (1994), pp.11–31; *Memoirs of Edward Alleyn*, ed. J. Payne Collier (1841); and Andrew Gurr, *The*

Shakespearean Stage 1574–1642, 3rd edn (1992) (see especially pp.90–5).

3 Young, ed., *History of Dulwich College*, vol.2, p.248.

4 The account of these early interviews and his later dealings with Donne are taken from Edward Alleyn's extraordinary letter to the Dean, written 'now allmost five quarters' since his marriage to Constance – i.e. sometime towards early spring 1625. The original, printed in Young's *History of Dulwich College*, vol.2, pp.36–8, was evidently scrawled in such a passion as to make it hard reading, orthographically and syntactically; so for the sake of fluency the text is modernized here.

5 Chamberlain, *Letters*, vol.2, p.534.

6 J. Payne Collier, *The Alleyn Papers* (1843), p.xxiii.

7 E. J. Burford, *Bawds and Lodgings: A History of the London Bankside Brothels c.100–1675* (1976), p.154. Many such brothels were, admittedly, as Burford demonstrates (his book was reprinted in 1993 as *The Bishop's Brothels*) the property of the Church.

8 Walton, p.68.

9 Satyre I (61).

10 Satyre II (13).

11 'The Calme' (33).

12 *Sermons*, vol.7, no.14 [11 February 1627], p.361.

13 Chamberlain, *Letters*, vol.2, p.613.

14 Letter to Sir Robert Ker, prefixed to 'An hymne to the Saints, and to Marquesse Hamylton'.

15 Walton, p.84.

16 *Tamburlaine*, part two, 3.5.121–6.

17 *A Collection of Letters* (Donne writing to Ann Cokayne), p.346.

18 Walton, p.70.

19 Bald, p.401.

20 Carey, *John Donne: Life, Mind and Art*, p.76. See also Bald, p.402.

21 Roger Lockyer, *Buckingham: The Life and Political Career of George Villiers* (1981), p.234. Lockyer argues for Buckingham's innocence, pointing to deep physical and emotional distress, and an enduring love for James. Williamson takes exactly the opposite view (see *George Villiers*, pp.170–4).

22 Again, the biographers quoting this letter draw very different con-
  clusions about the state of the King's relationship with Buckingham
  from it. For Lockyer, Buckingham reciprocated James's devotion
  (*Buckingham*, p.233); for Williamson, the correspondence only shows
  the extent of the King's emotional slavery.

23 Williamson, *George Villiers*, p.175.

24 *Letters*, p.314.

25 See Peter E. McCullough, *Sermons at Court* (1998), pp.183–209,
  discussing the chaplaincies of both Princes of Wales at St James's,
  Henry and Charles. The 'collegiate' Puritan atmosphere had nonetheless been infiltrated with the renovation of the palace chapels with
  a mind to receiving Charles's prospective bride, the Spanish Infanta
  (see McCullough, p.33).

26 McCullough, 'Architectural settings of court preaching', in *Sermons
  at Court*, pp.11–49, especially pp.14–16.

27 *Letters*, p.314.

28 *Letters*, p.311.

29 An eyewitness account is quoted by Bald, p.468.

30 *Sermons*, vol.6, no.12.

31 *Sermons*, vol.6, no.14 [26 April 1625], p.282.

32 Bald, p.469n.

33 F. P. Wilson, *The Plague in Shakespeare's London* (1927), pp.130–4.

34 Williamson, *George Villiers*, pp.178–9.

35 *A Collection of Letters*, p.307. On the dating of this letter, see Bald,
  p.471.

36 Letter to Sir Nicholas Carey, Bald, p.472.

37 Wilson, *The Plague in Shakespeare's London*, pp.136, 43, 148.

38 Hayward, ed., *Complete Poems and Selected Prose*, pp.486–7; a letter
  written to Sir Thomas Roe (as Bald argues [pp.473–4]), 25 November 1625.

39 Aubrey, *Natural History of Wiltshire*, p.93.

40 John Aubrey, *Brief Lives and other selected writings*, ed. Anthony Powell
  (1949), p.135.

41 *Sermons*, vol.8, no.2 [1 July 1627; commemorating Magdalen
  Danvers], pp.86, 90, 88.

42 Walton, p.285.

43 George Herbert, 'Discipline' (1–4)

44 Walton, p.64. Donne only mentions Herbert's presence in a letter to Goodyer late in the year: see *Letters*, p.476.

45 *Sermons*, vol.6, no.18 [15 January 1626], p.359.

46 Hayward, ed., *Complete Poems and Selected Prose*, p.489.

47 Wilson, *The Plague in Shakespeare's London*, p.155.

48 *Letters* [written 21 or 22 December 1625], pp.233–7.

49 *Sermons*, vol.6, no.17.

50 *Sermons*, vol.6, no.18, pp.362–4.

51 Bald, p.482: the speech itself, originally published in the 1650 edition of Donne's poems is reprinted by Bald in Appendix D, pp.573–5.

52 Walton, *Lives*, p.67. Donne himself confirmed that Saturday was his 'day of conversation and liberty' (*A Collection of Letters*, p.342).

53 *Sermons*, vol.6, no.4 [25 April 1624], p.104.

54 *A Collection of Letters*, p.354.

55 See Bald, p.424. Donne's only period of sustained absence from Charterhouse board meetings came in 1630, when the onset of his fatal illness stranded him outside London in Aldborough Hatch. For a close account of Donne's association with the Charterhouse and his conduct as a governor, see Robert C. Evans, 'John Donne, Governor of Charterhouse', *John Donne Journal* 8 (1989), 133–50.

56 Bald, pp.414–23, offers a thorough account of Donne's (often tedious) judicial duties. He also served as a Justice of the Peace for Bedford and Kent.

57 Spurr, *English Puritanism 1603–1689*, p.81.

58 Bald, p.419; E. W. Kirby, *William Prynne, a Study in Puritanism* (1931), pp.12–13.

59 Sir John Finet, *Finetti Philoxenis* (1656), pp.239–40; Bald, pp.420–2.

60 *The History of the Troubles and Tryal of William Laud* (1695), p.146.

61 *Sermons*, vol.7, no.18 [Whitsunday, 13 May 1627], p.443.

62 Walton, p.49. This is actually a description of Donne's first sermon at Whitehall, a performance that Walton himself could not have witnessed. As so often Walton has compressed a general comment about Donne's qualities and character into a particular event.

63 F. S. Boas, ed., *The Diary of Thomas Crosfield* (1935), p.43.

64 Jasper Mayne, 'On Dr *Donnes* death' (53–60), in Grierson (1933), p.353.

22. The Reprimand

1 A letter from Donne to Sir Nicholas Carey, printed in Gosse, *The Life and Letters of John Donne*, vol.2, p.233, confirms the arrangement. Gosse dates this wrongly; see Bald, p.485.

2 Collier, ed., *The Alleyn Papers*, p.xiii.

3 Collier, ed., *Memoirs of Edward Alleyn*, p.172.

4 Alleyn's letter of early 1625 mentions that Lucy was staying with them (Young, *History of Dulwich College*, vol.2, p.38); after his death she may have returned to live with her relatives the Grymeses.

5 *Letters*, pp.315–16.

6 Bald, p.491.

7 *Sermons*, vol.7, no.15 [Easter Day, 1627], p.375.

8 *Sermons*, vol.8, no.2, p.63.

9 Walton, p.267.

10 *Sermons*, vol.8, no.2, pp.86–7.

11 *Sermons*, vol.7, no.14 [probably 11 February 1627], p.359.

12 We know this, Bald reports, since after George's promotion to captain in 1626, one Ensign Otby petitioned the Duke of Buckingham for the now vacant commission of lieutenant in April 1626 (*Calendar of State Papers* [Domestic], *1625–1626*, vol.24, p.308): this also suggests that George's rank had lain in Buckingham's gift (Bald, p.552).

13 *Letters*, pp.305–6, Donne giving an account to Ker of his ordeal.

14 *Letters*, pp.307–10.

15 *Sermons*, vol.7, no.16 [1 April 1627], p.395.

16 See Bald, p.493.

17 Walton, p.57: Walton mistakenly puts the incident late in the reign of King James.

18 *The Troubles and Tryal of William Laud*, p.41.

19 Peter Heylin, *Cyprianus Anglicanus* (1667), p.175.

20 *Sermons*, vol.7, no.12 [January 1627], p.318.

21 *Sermons*, vol.9, no.1 [April 1629], p.60.

22 Bald, p.404.

23 *Sermons*, vol.9, no.5 [Christmas Day, probably 1629], pp.152–3.

24 *Sermons*, vol.7, no.17 [6 May 1627], p.430.

25 [Richard Busby?] 'In memory of Doctor *Donne*' (32–44), Grierson (1933), p.356.

26 Mayne, 'On *Dr Donnes* Death', in Grierson (1933), p.353.

27 W. Sparrow Simpson, ed., *Documents illustrating the History of St Paul's Cathedral*, Camden Society, new series, vol.24 (1880), p.131.

28 Crankshaw, 'Community, City and Nation, 1540–1714', p.60.

29 Brooke's will, quoted in Bald, p.501.

30 *Sermons*, vol.7, no.15 [Easter Day, 1627], p.390.

31 Sir Henry Wotton, *A Short View of the Life and Death of George Villiers, Duke of Buckingham* (1642), pp.22–6; Williamson, *George Villiers*, pp.224–9; Lockyer, *Buckingham*, pp.451–4.

32 *The Troubles and Tryal of . . . William Laud*, p.44.

33 *Cyprianus Anglicanus*, p.198.

23. The Likeness

1 *A Collection of Letters*, p.325. The evidence for Widow Rainsford moving in with her son comes from Walton, *Lives*, p.71, where he asserts that she died in Donne's house. This fact in itself is not quite accurate, as will be seen (and see Bald, p.524), yet the fact that she was staying with him is reliable. Walton by this time was a regular visitor at the Deanery. No precise date for her arrival can be determined; Walton seems to regard her as a fixture.

2 *A Collection of Letters*, p.325.

3 *A Collection of Letters* [1628/1629], pp.345–6.

4 Roy E. Schreiber, 'Thomas Cokayne', in *DNB*, vol.25, pp.1006–9, quoting Antony à Wood's *History and Topography of Ashburn*.

5 *A Collection of Letters* [December 1629], p.340.

6 *A Collection of Letters* [1628/1629], pp.345–6.

7 *A Collection of Letters*, pp.347–8.

8 *A Collection of Letters*, p.345.

9 *A Collection of Letters* [1628/9?], pp.349–50.

10 *A Collection of Letters*, pp.342–3.

11 Bald, pp.511–12.

12 Letter printed in *Sermons*, vol.8, pp.24–5.

13 *Sermons*, vol.9, no.3 [Whitsunday, 1629], p.99; *Sermons*, vol.8, no.1 [April 1629], p.47.

14 Letter, dated 22 June 1629, in Bald, p.514.

15 *Letters*, p.242.

16 *Sermons*, vol.8, no.12 [23 November 1628], pp.277–8.

17 *A Collection of Letters*, p.352; Walton, *Lives*, p.70.

18 *A Collection of Letters* [1629], p.354.

19 *A Collection of Letters*, pp.355–6.

20 *A Collection of Letters* [1628/1629], p.345.

21 Bald, p.519.

22 Bald, p.520.

23 *Letters* [November 1630], p.282.

24 George's account, 'Virginia Renewed', is in the British Museum, Harl. MS 7021, ff.289–318; see Bald, p.520.

25 Walton, p.60.

26 *Letters* [2 November 1630], pp.240–1.

27 *Letters* [autumn, 1630], p.286.

28 *Letters* [December 1630], pp.241–3.

29 *A Collection of Letters* [December 1630], p.338.

30 'A Valediction: Forbidding Mourning' (1–4)

31 *Sermons*, vol.4, no.6 [25 August 1622], p.171.

32 *Letters*, p.243.

33 Bald, p.522.

34 *Letters* [January 1631], pp.316–17. 'Uvula' is Bald's correction for 'vurbah' (p.522).

35 *A Collection of Letters* [1629?], p.351.

36 Bald, p.523.

37 Donne's will, printed in Bald, Appendix D, pp.563–7.

38 *Letters*, p.287.

39 *Letters*, p.282.

40 A heading to the sermon preached at The Hague in December 1619

states that the text was prepared 'in my sicknesse at Abrey-hatche in Essex, 1630' (*Sermons*, vol.2, no.13, p.269); many others must have been written up at the same time. See Bald, p.523.

41 *Letters*, p.244.

42 Walton, p.74.

43 Bald, p.524n, dispelling the claim by Gosse and Walton that Donne was survived by his mother: she was buried in Barking on 28 January.

44 *Sermons*, vol.10, no.11 [25 February 1631], p.233.

45 Walton, p.75.

46 *Sermons*, vol.10, no.11, p.231.

47 *Sermons*, vol.10, no.11, p.229.

48 Walton, p.76.

49 Walton, p.60.

50 Geoffrey Keynes, *A Bibliography of Dr John Donne*, 3rd edn (1958), pp.208–15.

51 Jessica Martin, 'Isaak Walton' in *DNB*, vol.57, pp.205–10, especially p.207.

52 Jessica Martin, 'Isaak Walton', p.206.

53 *Sermons*, vol.9, no.7 [12 February 1629], p.179.

54 Lucius Cary, 'An Elegie on Dr *Donne*' (7–8) in Grierson (1933), p.349.

55 John Chudleigh, 'On Dr *John Donne*, late *Deane of S*. Paules' (13–16), in Grierson (1933), p.364.

56 'To the deceased Author' (5–6), pp.340–1. So far as I know, this elegist has not previously been identified as Cokayne; but there was no other more eligible 'Tho. Browne'. The poem's eccentric bad taste certainly fits Cokayne's profile.

57 Thomas Carew, 'An Elegie upon the death of the Deane of Pauls, Dr John Donne' (11–20), pp.346–7.

58 Chudleigh, 'On Dr *John Donne*' (23–31), in Grierson (1933), p.364.

59 Aldrich Larson, 'Donne's Contemporary Reputation', p.124.

60 *Sermons*, vol.8, no.3 [19 November 1627], p.98. Gruesomely yet typically, these words were delivered at the wedding of the Earl of Bridgewater (John Egerton)'s daughter. They are emphatically inappropriate. It is worth wondering if the sermon is a long-delayed

bit of revenge against the greedy brother of Donne's friend and shipmate Thomas Egerton the younger.

61 *Sermons*, vol.9, no.2 [April 1629], p.69.

62 Walton, p.74.

63 Bald, pp.528, 424n; Evans, 'John Donne, Governor of Charterhouse', p.146.

64 Walton, p.77.

65 Walton, p.78.

66 Walton, p.80.

67 King's estimate was 'near Fifteen hundred'; Walton's was '1400' (*Lives*, pp.15, 67).

68 Hayward, ed., *Complete Poems and Selected Prose*, p.489.

69 Walton, p.15.

70 Bald, p.533.

71 Bald, p.552, quoting Antony à Wood in an appendix of documents on Donne the younger.

72 Bald, Appendix D, pp.575–7, 'Statement by John Donne the Younger', date and addressee unknown, transcribed from Folger Shakespeare Library MS V.b.201.

73 Donne, *LXXX Sermons Preached By That Learned and Reverend Divine Iohn Donne* (1640), A_3^r.

74 Bald, p.576.

75 *The Incomparable Poem Gondibert, Vindicated* (1655), A_2^v.

76 *Dr Donne's Last Will and Testament* (1662 Broadside).

77 Flynn, *John Donne and the Ancient Catholic Nobility*, p.21.

78 Donne's will, printed in Bald, p.563.

79 *Sermons*, vol.6, no.10 [30 January 1625], p.213; the phrase 'A quiet Grave' also occurs here.

80 See the floor-plan of the old St Paul's in William Dugdale's *History* of the Cathedral; an enhanced reproduction of this is given in Carol Davidson Gragoe, 'Fabric, Tombs and Precinct 1087–1540' in Derek Keene, ed., *St Paul's: The Cathedral Church of London 604–2004*, pp.127–42, especially p.128.

81 Translation by Francis Wrangham, printed in Gosse, *Life and Letters of John Donne*, vol.2, p.282, and Bald, p.535n. The original – com-

posed by Donne himself – reads 'Hic licet in occiduo cinere aspicit eum / Cujus nomen est Oriens'.
82 Walton, p.83.
83 Walton, p.82.

Afterword

1 Donne, sermon on Whitsunday, 1623, in *Complete Poems and Selected Prose*, ed. Hayward, p.616. For reasons that will become clear, I quote Donne's prose here from one of the standard compilations that made it available to non-specialist British and American readers in the twentieth century.

2 Donne, sermon preached on 12 December 1626; *Complete Poetry and Selected Prose*, p.671.

3 Taken from http://en.wikipedia.org/wiki/Trinity, which gives links to extensive biographical and bibliographical material and US state documents on Oppenheimer, Tatlock and the Manhattan Project.

4 *Complete Poetry and Selected Prose*, p.750.

Further Reading

To supplement the preceding notes, this section offers some general suggestions for those who wish to read more of Donne and his work, and on the historical contexts encountered in each section of this book.

Editions of Donne's Works

Biathanatos, ed. Michael Ruddick and M. Pabst Battin (1982)

Complete English Poems, ed. C. A. Patrides (1985)

Complete Poems and Selected Prose, ed. John Hayward (1929)

The Courtier's Library, ed. Evelyn M. Simpson, trans. Percy Simpson (1930)

Devotions upon Emergent Occasions, ed. John Sparrow (1923)

The Divine Poems, 2nd edn, ed. Dame Helen Gardner (1978)

The Elegies and The Songs and Sonnets, ed. Dame Helen Gardner (1965)

The Epithalamions, Anniversaries and Epicedes, ed. W. Milgate (1978)

Essays in Divinity, ed. Evelyn M. Simpson (1952)

Ignatius His Conclave, ed. T. S. Healy, SJ (1969)

Letters to Severall Persons of Honour, in facsimile, introduced by M. Thomas Hester (1977); a modern edition of Donne's collected letters has yet to be made.

Paradoxes and Problems, ed. Helen Peters (1980)

The Poems of John Donne, ed. Sir Herbert Grierson, 2 vols (1912)

Pseudo-martyr, ed. Anthony Raspa (1993)

The Satires, Epigrams and Verse Letters, ed. W. Milgate (1967)

The Sermons, ed. George R. Potter and Evelyn M. Simpson, 10 vols. (1953–62)

A Study of the Prose Works of John Donne, 2nd edn, ed. Evelyn M. Simpson (1948)

The Variorum Edition of the Poetry of John Donne, ed. Gary A. Stringer et al., 8 vols (1995–)

Biography

Bald, R. C., *John Donne: A Life* (1970)

— *Donne and the Drurys* (1959)

Carey, John, *John Donne: Life, Mind and Art*, 2nd edn (1990)

Clive, Lady Mary, *Jack and the Doctor* (1966)

Colclough, David, 'John Donne' in the new *Dictionary of National Biography* (2005)

— ed., *John Donne's Professional Lives* (2003)

Flynn, Dennis, *John Donne and the Ancient Catholic Nobility* (1995)

Gosse, Sir Edmund, *The Life and Letters of John Donne*, 2 vols. (1899)

Hester, Thomas M., *John Donne's Desire of More: The Subject of Ann More Donne in His Poetry* (1996)

Jessopp, Augustus, *John Donne, Sometime Dean of St Paul's* (1897)

Walton, Isaak, *The Lives of John Donne, Sir Henry Wotton, Richard Hooker & Robert Sanderson* (1670, repr. 1927)

Winney, James, *A Preface to Donne* (1970)

Other Works on Donne

Brown, Meg Lota, *John Donne and the Politics of Conscience in Early Modern England* (1995)

Coffin, Charles M., *John Donne and the New Philosophy* (1937)

Hughes, Richard E., *The Progress of the Soul: The Interior Career of John Donne* (1968)

Johnson, Jeffrey, *The Theology of John Donne* (1999)

Kermode, Frank, *Shakespeare, Spenser, Donne* (1971)

Leishmann, J. B., *The Monarch of Wit*, 5th edn (1962)

Marotti, Arthur F., *John Donne: Coterie Poet* (1986)

Sellin, Paul R., *So doth, so is religion: John Donne and diplomatic contexts in the Reformed Netherlands* (1988)

Shami, Jeanne, *John Donne and Conformity in Crisis in the Late Jacobean Pulpit* (2003)

Sherwood, Terry, *Fulfilling the Circle: A Study of John Donne's Thought* (1984)

Slights, Camille Wells, *The Casuistical Tradition in Shakespeare, Donne, Herbert and Milton* (1981)

Smith, A. J., ed., *John Donne: The Critical Heritage* (1975)

I   1572–1602

Alford, Stephen, *The Early Elizabethan Polity* (1998)

Andrewes, Kenneth R., *Elizabethan Privateering* (1964)

Bennett, H. S., *English Books and Readers 1558–1603* (1965)

— *English Books and Readers 1603–1640* (1970)

Bossy, John, *The Elizabethan Catholic Community 1570–1850* (1975)

Collinson, Patrick, *The Elizabethan Puritan Movement* (1967)

— *The Reformation* (2003)

— *The Religion of Protestants: The Church in English Society 1559–1625* (1982)

Curtis, Mark H., *Oxford and Cambridge in Transition, 1558–1642* (1959)

Duffy, Eamon, *The Stripping of the Altars: Traditional Religion in England 1400–1580* (1992)

Elton, G. R., *England under the Tudors*, 2nd edn (1974)

— *The Tudor Constitution: Documents and Commentary* (1960)

— *Star Chamber Stories* (1960)

Fox, Alastair, *Thomas More: History and Providence* (1982)

Graves, Michael, *Elizabethan Parliaments 1559–1601*, 2nd edn (1996)

Hartley, T. E., *Elizabeth's Parliaments: Queen, Lords and Commons 1559–1601* (1992)

James, Mervyn, *Society, Politics and Culture: Studies in Early Modern England* (1986)

Jones, W. J., *The Elizabethan Court of Chancery* (1967)

Loades, David, *The Tudor Court*, 2nd edn (1986)

MacCullough, Diarmaid, *Reformation: Europe's House Divided 1490–1700* (2003)

McGurk, John, *The Elizabethan Conquest of Ireland: The 1590s Crisis* (1997)

Mack, Peter, *Elizabethan Rhetoric: Theory and Practice* (2002)

Morgan, Hiram, *Tyrone's Rebellion* (1993)

Moss, Ann, *Printed Commonplace Books and the Structuring of Renaissance Thought* (1996)

Neale, Sir John, *The Elizabethan House of Commons* (1949)

— *Elizabeth I and Her Parliaments* (1953)

Outhwaite, R. B., *Clandestine Marriage in England 1500–1850* (1995)

Prest, Wilfrid R., *The Inns of Court under Elizabeth I and the Early Stuarts 1590–1640* (1972)

Simon, Joan, *Education and Society in Renaissance England* (1966)

Skinner, Quentin, *Visions of Politics, II: Renaissance Virtues* (2002)

Smith, Bruce R., *The Acoustic World of Early Modern England* (1999)

Starkey, David, *Elizabeth* (2000)

— *The Reign of Henry VIII: Personalities and Politics*, 2nd edn (1991)

Walsham, Alexandra, *Church Papists: Catholicism, Conformity and Confession: Polemic in Early Modern England* (1993)

Whiffen, Marcus, *An Introduction to Elizabethan and Jacobean Architecture* (1952)

II   1603–1616

Bellamy, Alastair, *The Politics of Court Scandal in Early Modern England* (2002)

Cathcart, Dwight, *Doubting Conscience* (1975)

Galloway, Bruce, *The Union of England and Scotland 1603–1608* (1986)

Hall, Marie Boas, *The Scientific Renaissance 1450–1630* (1962)

Kuhn, Thomas S., *The Copernican Revolution* (1957)

Mendelson, Sara, and Patricia Crawford, *Women in Early Modern England 1550–1720* (1998)

Orgel, Stephen, *The Illusion of Power: Political Theater in the English Renaissance* (1975)

Patterson, W. B., *King James VI and I and the Reunion of Christendom* (1997)

Peck, Linda Levy, *Court Patronage and Corruption in Early Stuart England* (1990)

Penrose, Boies, *Travel and Discovery in the Renaissance 1420–1620* (1952)

Rabb, Theodore, *Jacobean Gentleman: Sir Edwyn Sandys 1561–1629* (1998)

Sharpe, Kevin, *Sir Robert Cotton, 1586–1631: History and Politics in Early Modern England* (1979)

Smith, David L., *Stuart Parliaments 1603–1689* (1999)

Smuts, Malcolm, *Court Culture and the Origins of a Royalist Tradition: Early Stuart England* (1987)

Stone, Lawrence, *The Crisis of the Aristocracy 1558–1641* (1965)

Stoye, John Walter, *English Travellers Abroad 1604–1667* (1952)

Wiley, Margaret L., *The Subtle Knot* (1952)

— *Creative Sceptics* (1966)

III   1617–1631

Blench, J. W., *Preaching in England in the Late Fifteenth and Sixteenth Centuries: A Study of English Sermons 1450–c.1600* (1964)

Cogswell, Thomas, *The Blessed Revolution: English Politics and the Coming of War* (1987)

Dawes, Julian, *The Caroline Captivity of the Church: Charles I and the Remoulding of Anglicanism* (1992)

Doelman, James, *King James and the Religious Culture of England* (2000)

Goodchild, Peter, *J. Robert Oppenheimer: Shatterer of Worlds* (1980)

Hill, Christopher, *Economic Problems of the Church* (1956)

— *The Intellectual Origins of the English Revolution – Revisited* (1997)

Lake, Peter, and Michael Questier, *Conformity and Orthodoxy in the English Church c.1560–1660* (2000)

Maclure, Millar, *The Paul's Cross Sermons 1534–1642* (1958)

McCullough, Peter E., *Sermons at Court: Politics and Religion in Elizabethan and Jacobean Court Preaching* (1998)

Sharpe, Kevin, *Criticism and Compliment: The Politics of Literature in the England of Charles I* (1987)

Somerville, J. P., *Politics and Ideology in England 1603–1640* (1986)

Spurr, John, *English Puritanism 1603–1689* (1998)

Stanwood, Paul G., *Isaak Walton* (1998)

Trevor-Roper, Hugh, *Archbishop Laud*, 2nd edn (1962)

Tyacke, Nicholas, *Anti-Calvinists: The Rise of English Arminianism c.1590–1640* (1987)

White, Peter, *Predestination, Policy and Polemic: Conflict and Consensus in the English Church from the Reformation to the Civil War* (1992)

Wilson, F. P., *The Plague in Shakespeare's London* (1922)

Acknowledgements

Many people and organizations have prevented me from feeling like an island as I worked on this book. I should firstly acknowledge and thank the Jerwood Trust and the Royal Society of Literature for presenting me with one of their awards for non-fiction in 2004. The Jerwood scheme is designed to encourage writers engaged on their first book. It was an honour and a great material support to receive one of the prizes.

I would never have got the chance to write this biography had it not been for Toby Eady, literary agent and tremendous supporter both of writing and writers. I really hope the book goes some way to repaying his trust in believing I could do it. Warm thanks as well to everyone at Toby's office, especially his calm and considerate assistant, William Fisher. I was incredibly fortunate that Mary Mount at Viking agreed to edit the book. Her brilliant, sharp comments, questions and suggestions, all the way through the process, made writing an extremely enjoyable and exciting dialogue, rather than a solo effort.

I also owe thanks to the staff of Cambridge University Library, especially in the rare books and manuscripts sections; to the Earl of Ancram for permission to reproduce the Lothian portrait of Donne, and to Susan Eliot at Jedburgh House for her help with my inquiries about the picture. The index to the book was prepared by Janet Dudley.

Anyone working on Donne's life has the benefit of an extraordinarily rich tradition of scholarship, in which R. C. Bald's *John Donne: A Life* remains the cornerstone. At Cambridge I was lucky enough to meet David Colclough, who very kindly let me read his article on Donne ahead of publication in the new *Dictionary of National Biography*. This, a miracle of compression and clarification, along with the volume David edited on *John Donne's*

Professional Lives, has been with me ever since, and to my mind they mark the most important contribution to the field in recent years. David read virtually all of *John Donne: The Reformed Soul* for me, in one form or another. I have benefited enormously in our talks from his knowledge and encouragement; he has been unfailingly generous with both.

The influence of many mentors came through as the project developed. It was my A-level English teacher, Richard Lodge, who singled out for me the importance of the seventeenth section of Donne's *Devotions* many years ago. Alan Monger and David Dunton, who taught me history, gave me a lasting sense of how the past should be approached, and how to write about it. This is a welcome opportunity as well to thank and pay tribute to Nora Byrne, Richard Haighton and Eric Reader; to my former tutors at Oxford, John Fuller, Susan Hitch, David Norbrook and Frank Romany; and to my doctoral supervisor at Cambridge, Gavin Alexander. I have been very lucky in having such teachers.

I first discovered Donne when I was about fourteen, and I remember asking my father, 'Dad, what's a "hairy diadem"?' He looked up from his paper and said, 'You're too young to be reading poems like that.' Both he and Mum, along with my sister and brothers, read large lumps of the book in its early stages, and it meant such a lot when they gave it the thumbs up. The support and care of Denise and Robin Gallagher is another of the constants in my life that I could not have managed without. I would also like to thank Patricia Boulhosa, Christopher Burlinson, Adam Lauridsen and Aleš Novak for their companionship and solidarity. Above all to Katja and Lana, with all my love.

After I quietened my scruples about possibly bothering Donne's ghost, writing this book has been a great pleasure. But it would never have occurred to me to attempt such a thing, nor would it ever have been possible, without the friendship and guidance of Robert MacFarlane, who first suggested that I try. Talking with him over the years has helped me understand why I like books, and the things books keep for us. It's a real joy to be able to salute him here, my friend, and a very fine writer.

Index

Works by John Donne are indexed under their titles, as are anonymous publications. All other works are given under their authors.